Politico's Guide to
UK General Elections 1832–2001

GW00685749

To my wife, Julie,
and my daughters,
Emmeline and Eleanor

Politico's Guide to
UK General Elections
1832–2001

Peter Joyce

POLITICO'S

First published in Great Britain 2004 by
Politico's Publishing, an imprint of
Methuen Publishing Limited
215 Vauxhall Bridge Road
London SW1V 1EJ

A CIP catalogue record for this book is available from the British Library.

ISBN 1 84275 101 8

Printed and bound in Great Britain by Mackays of Chatham

Contents

Introduction

Elections are the key mechanism underpinning the conduct of politics. They provide citizens with the ability to exercise some choice over the personnel of government and the policies it pursues, and also enable governments to be retrospectively held accountable for the actions they have taken whilst in office. They are thus an indispensable link between the government and the governed.

Although there is a considerable volume of literature dealing with election statistics, there is no one volume which seeks to get behind the figures. There exist a number of accounts of individual elections (including the Nuffield election studies which deal with general elections since 1945) but some elections (especially those held in the nineteenth century) are without detailed coverage of this nature and information about them can only be obtained from literature which is not specifically concerned with election contests.

This book thus aims to fill a gap in the literature of UK elections by providing a brief account of all contests which have been held since 1832. This starting date has been chosen as the Reform Act of that year constituted a significant step in the development of liberal democratic politics in the UK. The book makes use of a wide range of secondary sources which have been combined with contemporary newspaper accounts of contests not currently discussed as discrete topics. To achieve this coverage, the work is organised under a number of headings.

The starting point for discussing each contest is the date it was held. Today general election contests are held on one day, but in the period 1832–1918 they took place over a number of weeks. This work cites the period during which contested elections took place, although some unopposed returns were declared before the commencement of the election proper.

Each election entry then lists the leaders of the main political parties. Party leadership was not, however, as clearly defined as in the contemporary period. In the early elections discussed in this book, the Conservative and Liberal parties frequently operated a dual leadership (with separate leaders in both Houses of Parliament) and between February 1849 and February 1852 the Conservative Party was governed by a triumvirate. The Labour Party acquired a formal leader (as distinct from a chair of the Parliamentary Party) only in 1922. This work has limited this list to the main parties contesting elections throughout the UK. However, a later section of this work discusses the performance of parties fielding candidates mainly in just one part of the UK (in particular in Scotland, Wales, Ireland/Northern Ireland).

A brief account is then given of the reason why each election took place. The main reasons for this include defeat in the House of Commons, a perception by an incumbent prime minister that prevailing political and economic circumstances are favourable to his or her re-election or the expiration of a government's term of office as laid by, initially, the 1715 Septennial Act and, latterly, by the 1911 Parliament Act. The account provided of elections will demonstrate, however, that in the nineteenth century especially the defeat of a government in the House of Commons did not automatically trigger an election but frequently led to the opposition assuming the reigns of government without recourse to the voters.

A more significant discussion is provided of the background to each contest. This includes (where appropriate) reference to any significant changes in electoral procedures and practices which took place during the lifetime of the previous Parliament. This section charts the progress of the development of the UK's system of representative democracy and included in the discussion are the key changes which have affected the right to vote, the distribution of parliamentary constituencies, the manner of voting, and the practices which govern the conduct of local contests and national campaigns.

Each entry provides an account of chief developments concerning the main political parties. This includes a discussion of the actions pursued by the governing party whilst in office and also of developments affecting the other parties whilst in opposition. Overall, this section provides a brief account of political history affecting the outcome of each general election.

A brief reference is also made to by-election contests. The requirements of the 1707 Succession to the Crown Act made these a common feature of political life since it required each new holder of leading ministerial posts to resubmit themselves to their electors at a by-election before taking office. The repeal of this legislation in 1926 had a significant impact on reducing the number of contests henceforth which were primarily caused by the death of an MP or his or her resignation or disqualification. The statistical information on which this section is based is derived from Rallings and Thrasher (2000), Craig (1987) and also from various editions of *The Times Guide to the House of Commons*.

The conduct of each election campaign is considered in detail and seeks to provide information concerning the key policies which were put forward by the main political parties during the course of the contest. In contemporary elections much of this information is to be found in the detailed election manifestos prepared by the parties. However, these were not produced for the early contests discussed in this work when information of this nature was provided from a number of sources which included the election addresses prepared by the party leader for their constituents. A particular problem arose when the party leader was a member of the House of Lords since a Sessional Order (dating from 1641) forbade peers to 'interfere' with elections to the other Chamber. Although this was widely ignored in the two 1910 contests (and finally abandoned in 1912) it was not religiously adhered to before that date. Both Lord Salisbury and Lord Rosebery, for example, played active roles in late-nineteenth-century general election contests.

The conduct of election campaigns since 1832 has been subject to major changes which are discussed in relation to the individual elections when they occurred. A major issue has been the way in which parties have presented their case to the electorate. Although some of the devices which have been utilised (particularly at constituency level), such as the issue of election addresses by candidates to their constituents, meetings and the canvassing of voters, remain in use, other developments (especially concerning the role of the media, in particular the press, radio, television and electronic forms of communication) have brought about important changes to the conduct of campaigns. Although party leaders (in particular Gladstone) played a significant role in some late nineteenth-century election campaigns, the involvement of television served to intensify the attention paid to the party leaders and thus 'presidentialise' election contests.

Each entry provides statistics concerning the result of the election in terms of the votes obtained by the main parties and the number of MPs they returned. These statistics are derived from Rallings and Thrasher (2000) and *The Times Guide to the House of Commons* for the 2001 election, although some minor changes have been made as to the way in which this information is presented. Each entry gives details of the vote obtained for each party (which adopts the adjustments made by Rallings and Thrasher (2000) to eliminate distortions caused by the existence of multi-member seats in elections held before 1950), the proportion of the total national vote which it obtained and the number of seats it won in the House of Commons. Statistics are also given (placed in square brackets) concerning the share of the vote obtained by national parties in Ireland/Northern Ireland, Scotland and Wales in each of these respective countries. The information provided in Rallings and Thrasher (2000) regarding the turnout figure for each election has also been adopted in this work. However, problems which include plural voting and the existence of constituencies returning more than one MP make this figure speculative, at best, for all nineteenth-century elections.

The more recent elections also provide information concerning the 'swing'. Factors such as changes in the franchise, the compilation of electoral registers, intra-party contests, and the very high number of candidates who were returned unopposed made it difficult to judge the movement of voters from one party to another at consecutive election contests held in the nineteenth and early twentieth century. An additional problem was that elections held in the nineteenth century were heavily influenced by local or regional factors, one consequence of this being the absence of any form of nation-wide swing: it was common for parties which lost an election to nevertheless win some seats which bucked the national trend (Hanham, 1959: 196–7). However, changes in the conduct of elections and the dominance of the two-party system made it possible to make generalisations concerning the movement of voters from one election to another in the more recent contests. There are two ways of calculating this – the 'total vote' swing developed by David Butler (which seeks to establish the relative changes in the position of the two major parties in comparison to the total vote cast) and the 'two-party' swing (formulated by Michael Steed) which is concerned only with changes affecting the two main parties irrespective of the performance of other political parties. The one used in this work is the Butler formula, applied to seats where the two major parties were in first and second place in consecutive elections, which has been derived from the Nuffield Studies since 1955.

Each entry considers the impact of the election on the respective political fortunes of each main party. Diverse issues such as the reason for defeat or victory, the nature of support won or lost are briefly considered. The outcome of the election in Scotland, Wales and Ireland / Northern Ireland is also discussed to enable peculiar factors affecting the politics of these three nations to be included in the account of the contest.

The consequence of each election is also briefly considered. In many cases this is straightforward – the leader of the party which wins the contest then goes on to form a government. There are, however, complications to this situation which arise in situations when no single party can claim outright victory or when one party secures a small overall majority in the House of Commons. This provides scope for inter-party discussions which in post-war Britain occurred in 1951 and February 1974.

Referencing has been deliberately kept to a minimum. The key works which have been cited or consulted in writing this work are contained in one list at the end of the book.

8 December 1832 – 15 January 1833

Party Leaders
The Duke of Wellington (Conservative)
Earl Grey (Whig)

Background to the Election
Electoral Procedures and Practices
The election was held on the basis of electoral reform provided by the 1832 Reform Act (which was officially entitled 'An Act to Amend the Representation of the People of Engand and Wales'). This measure imposed a uniform £10 household franchise in the boroughs and gave the vote to a wide range of persons residing in the counties, supplementing the 40 shilling free-holders with other categories which included £10 freeholders, £10 copyholders, tenants at a yearly rent of £50, and leaseholders for 60 years at a clear yearly value of £10. This added around 217,000 votes to an existing electorate of around 435,000. The Act also provided for redistribution whereby the borough representation fell from 465 seats to 399 and county representation increased from 188 to 253, thereby increasing the control of the landed aristocracy. Some attempt was made to address the over-representation of the agricultural south and the under-representation of London and the industrial North of England and Midlands by trans-ferring 64 seats from small English boroughs to larger ones that had previously lacked direct representation in Parliament. Pocket boroughs were reduced in number but did not entirely disappear. This legislation further reduced the duration of polling in individual constituencies from 15 days to two days and introduced the requirement that voters should be included in an official register of electors for which they were required to pay a fee.

Separate measures were passed for Scotland and Ireland. In Scotland, the archaic regulations which had previously restricted the electorate to around 4,500 were replaced by new voting qualifications. Although these were more restrictive than in England, the total elecorate increased to around 65,000 and the number of Scottish constituencies was increased from 45 to 53 through the transfer of eight English borough seats to Scottish burghs.

Political reform exerted a considerable influence on the subsequent conduct of British politics. A government needed to command the confidence of the House of Commons (rather than rely on the monarch's support) and this enhanced the importance of party organisation. Although it is important not to overstate the immediate extent of party cohesion in the House of Commons, the 1832 Reform Act paved the way for a new era of party politics and the demise of the truly independent MP.

Conservatives
The Tories were the dominant party in English politics between 1815 and 1830. Although divided between those who wished to resist any reform at all of the nation's major institutions of government (who were referred to as 'ultras') and those who were less afraid of it, party unity was preserved under the long premiership of Lord Liverpool (who served as Prime Minister from 1812

until 1827). However, Lord Liverpool's stroke in February 1827 disrupted this situation. The new Prime Minister, George Canning, was regarded by many Tories as holding views on Catholic emancipation and foreign policy which were too liberal, and a number of leading ultra-Tories (including the Duke of Wellington and the Earl of Eldon) resigned from the Cabinet and a coalition government including four Whig Cabinet members was formed. However, Canning's death in August 1827 brought the experiment in coalition to an end. The new Prime Minister, Viscount Goderich, encountered difficulties in constructing a government and solved the problem by himself resigning in January 1828. He was replaced by the Duke of Wellington under whom the Whigs refused to serve, although William Huskinson and some of the Canningites briefly took office until a Cabinet dispute over the redistribution of the seats of two boroughs (East Retford and Penryn) resulted in their resignations in May 1828.

This action had an unforeseen consequence when Wellington selected an Irish MP, Vesey Fitzgerald, to replace Huskinson as President of the Board of Trade. The 1707 Succession to the Crown Act required that an MP who accepted an important ministerial office should vacate his seat and contest a by-election. In the contest at County Clare in June 1828, Fitzgerald was roundly defeated by Daniel O'Connell who was the leader of the movement to secure Catholic emancipation (which he viewed as a necessary prerequisite of the repeal of the Act of Union with England). As a Catholic, O'Connell was unable to sit in the House of Commons but the government realised that continued opposition to Catholic emancipation would result in disorder in Ireland, especially if O'Connell's supporters contested a large number of Irish seats in the next general election. Accordingly, Catholic emancipation was granted in 1829 so that all Irish offices of state (with the exception of the Viceroy and Chancellor) were opened to Catholics. However, this Act was accompanied by punitive measures. The franchise qualification in Ireland was raised to £10 freeholders, O'Connell's organisation, the Catholic Association, was dissolved, and the lord-lieutenant was given powers to suppress any dangerous society. O'Connell was not allowed to take advantage of the 1829 measure and was forced to (successfully) seek re-election at Clare.

No sooner had this contentious issue been resolved, when parliamentary reform re-surfaced. The bloodless revolution in France in 1830 (in which Charles X was deposed in favour of Louis-Philippe) renewed interest in this issue, and it was an important issue in the general election of 1830 (which was caused by the death of George IV and the accession of his brother William IV). Organisations which included the London Radical Reform Association and the Birmingham Political Union agitated in favour of reform but the government was unyielding, Wellington declaring in November 1830 that the state of representation in Britain was perfect and needed no alteration. Such negative views on this issue might have brought the government down, but it took the opportunity of resigning on 16 November following a defeat on the Civil List. It was replaced by a Whig-dominated government led by Earl Grey but which included some liberal Conservatives (or Canningites), including the former Prime Minister, Viscount Goderich. Although heading a very aristocratic government, Grey made the acceptance of a Reform Bill a condition of forming a government and legislation was introduced into the House of Commons on 1 March 1830. This was opposed by the Tories.

A government defeat on the first Reform Bill on 20 April 1831 resulted in the dissolution of Parliament and a general election which secured the return of Grey's government. A second Reform Bill was brought forward in June which passed the House of Commons but was defeated in the House of Lords on 8 October 1831, the negative votes of the bishops being decisive. A third measure was reintroduced in the House of Commons in December 1831 but further problems in the House of Lords in connection with Lord Lyndhurst's motion to postpone consideration of the disfranchising clauses led Grey to ask the monarch to create around 50 peers to secure its passage. William IV's refusal to do this led Grey to resign on 9 May but Wellington's inability to form a Tory administration coupled with extra-parliamentary agitation in favour of reform resulted in Grey's return on 18 May on the understanding that the progress of the Reform Bill would no longer be hindered. This committed William IV to create new peers to get the Bill through the Lords, but this course of action was unnecessary as opponents in the Lords abandoned their opposition (and, indeed, their presence). The measure received its third reading in that House on 4 June 1832. Separate measures for Scotland and Ireland received the Royal Assent on 17 July and 7 August respectively.

Whigs

Earl Grey's Whig government had been in office since the resignation of the Duke of Wellington on 16 November 1830. However, although the Whigs had a large overall majority after 1831, they were not a cohesive party. The political crisis of 1830–1832 brought together a broad coalition. This was composed of the Whigs, radicals, nonconformists, and Irish repealers who had been able to make common cause through their support of political reforms embraced in the 1832 legislation. Although this coalition could have formed the basis of a new (Liberal) party, it was insufficiently cohesive to endure new challenges following the enactment of political reform in 1832.

The Whigs brought a tradition of aristocratic leadership to the reform movement. Their aim was to remove the worst abuses of the old electoral system (such as the rotten boroughs) and to extend the franchise to the 'sober, industrious, respectable "middling classes" thereby strengthening the existing institutional arrangements rather than seeking to undermine them' (Jenkins, 1994: 5). Their main aim was to preserve aristocratic government and they viewed the 1832 measure as a once-and-for-all adjustment of the system of parliamentary representation. This group was augmented by an influx of aristocrats who flocked to the Whig cause: around 100 of these stood in each election in 1831 and 1832 (Mandler, 1990: 72).

The second group in this coalition were the radicals whose strength increased in 1832 to a figure of around 150, with a 'hard core' of approximately 35 (Jenkins, 1994: 10). The relationship between the Whigs and radicals was buttressed by two-member constituencies which encouraged cooperation in order to defeat conservatism. The radicals were divided. Some (who included William Cobbett and Henry 'Orator' Hunt) drew their inspiration from the popular radicalism of the late eighteenth century and sought to extend the process of political reform (through measures which included household suffrage for parliamentary elections, the institution of the secret ballot and the repeal of the 1716 Septennial Act which required fresh parliamentary elections only every seven years). They further wished to eradicate aristocratic dominance over the institutions of government and endorsed universal elementary education. Other radicals (who included George Grote and John Roebuck) viewed themselves as heirs of the eighteenth-century 'age of reason' and were inspired by Jeremy Bentham. These 'philosophic radicals' sought to reform institutions in order to maximise the promotion of human happiness. They were, however, elitist in nature.

The third group which attached themselves to the Whig-led coalition was the nonconformists. Those attracted to nonconformity were likely to be 'craftsmen, tradesmen and artisans … men for whom religious dissent was an expression of social independence from traditional forms of social discipline' (Jenkins, 1994: 16). They had successfully campaigned to secure the repeal of the Test and Corporation Acts in 1828 (which theoretically excluded nonconformists from public office) and saw parliamentary reform as the prerequisite to further reforms. In particular, they favoured the abolition of slavery and the removal of other discriminations against nonconformists such as their exclusion from the ancient universities and the requirement that nonconformists should pay for the upkeep of the Anglican Church through the payment of the Church Rate.

The final group which comprised the Whig-led coalition was the Irish Repealers (who sought to repeal the 1801 Act of Union with Great Britain and re-establish a separate Parliament for Ireland). The repeal movement was headed by Daniel O'Connell and grew out of the activities of the Catholic Association, which had been founded in 1823 to agitate for the removal of discriminations against Roman Catholics. This resulted in the granting of Catholic emancipation in 1829.

Conduct of the Election

The election remained very much a local affair. The run-up to it was dominated by local registration issues, and with political reform no longer an issue, the election in many constituencies turned on parochial concerns. One example of this was in Westminster, where attempts by the ultra-radicals to secure pledges on an MP's future conduct were forcibly resisted by Sir John Hobhouse (who was nonetheless successfully elected). In some urban areas (in particular in Westminster and the surrounding metropolitan districts) the repeal of the House tax and window tax emerged as an election issue: those seeking repeal viewed these taxes as unfair as they mainly fell on the inhabitants of metropolitan areas, in particular upon the 'industrious and trading' classes.

Conservatives

The main national issue which was projected by the Tories throughout the election was the crisis in Britain's relations with Holland. The Treaty of the 24 Articles (which was formulated by the Conference of London and signed in November 1831) required both Belgium and Holland to surrender all places occupied by one of the these countries in the territory of the other. The Belgian government followed the obligations placed upon it by this Treaty, but the Dutch king refused to give up Antwerp (ostensibly on the grounds that this action would take place only after his country had ratified the Treaty). These actions prompted the British government to adopt coercive measures against Holland to enforce the Treaty. Britain sent ships to blockade the Dutch ports and a French army entered Belgium. Fighting occurred around Antwerp which threatened to escalate.

The Conservatives rallied to Holland's cause and during the election stated their desire to remain at peace with that country. They viewed France as Britain's enemy whereas Holland was an old ally. France (which had experienced a change of government in 1830 whereby Charles X was deposed by Louis-Philippe) was depicted as the aggressor, waging war in her own national interests. The Tories also believed that the prospect of increased British involvement in Holland would raise taxes and feared that war there could be the prelude to a more general European conflagration. However, fears of new French expansion in Belgium abated when her troops returned to France after the surrender of Antwerp on 23 December 1832. The Foreign Secretary, Viscount Palmerston, derived considerable credit from his handling of the situation which had both avoided war and kept the French out of Belgium.

Whigs

In so far as there was a Whig campaign, it sought to secure support on the basis of the achievements of Lord Grey's governments since 1830. A pamphlet entitled *The Whig Government* argued that Lord Grey's administrations had fulfilled the promises of 'peace, retrenchment and reform' on which it had originally entered office and particular attention was drawn to the government's economic policy. It was stated that savings had been made in naval expenditure and on the salaries of public officers and that in the past half-year there was an excess of income over spending of around £1.2 million (quoted in *The Times*, 9 November 1832). Although Tory opposition to the Reform Act was no longer an issue which Whigs could utilise (even if, as *The Times* argued on 17 November 1832, their stance was one of 'tardy acquiescence' in the 1832 measure's provisions), some Whig candidates did exploit the Tory defence of the unreformed system of local government in the towns and accused the Tories of abusing the power of landlords to secure support for their cause.

Result of the Election

Although the Whigs secured a victory of landslide proportions, the result of the election indicated that the 1832 Reform Act had no dramatic impact on the composition of the House of Commons. Five hundred members represented the landed interest and a large number of MPs were the sons of peers or baronets. A total number of 1,037 candidates contested the election, with 189 MPs being returned unopposed. The result was:*

Party	Votes	Vote %	MPs
Liberal	525,706	63.5%	408
Conservative	213,254	25.8%	147
Irish Repeal Party	31,773	3.8% [34.6%]	42
Irish Liberal	29,013	3.5% [33.3%]	33
Irish Conservative	28,030	3.4% [32.1%]	28
Total	827,776		658

*   In this and all subsequent elections, the figures in square brackets denote the share of the vote obtained by nationalist parties in their respective countries.

The turnout was 70.4 per cent.

The Parties

Although trailing the Whigs in terms of seats won in the House of Commons, the Conservatives emerged from the 1832 Reform Act as a relatively united party which also exercised control over the House of Lords. The Whigs secured support from areas which had benefited from the 1832 legislation and also polled well in the counties. The radicals increased the size of their representation: Cobbett was elected for Oldham, although Henry 'Orator' Hunt failed to recapture Preston which he had won in a by-election in December 1830 but lost in the 1831 general election.

Scotland, Wales and Ireland

The Whigs emerged as the dominant party in Scotland, securing 79 per cent of the vote and 43 of the 53 seats. In Wales, the strength of the two parties was relatively even, with the Whigs winning 18 seats to the Conservatives' 14. O'Connell's Repeal Party was the most successful in Ireland, winning 42 of the 103 seats. The Whigs won 33 and the Conservatives 28.

Consequence of the Election

Viscount Melbourne formed a Whig government.

5 January – 9 February 1835

Party Leaders
Sir Robert Peel (Conservative)
Viscount Melbourne (Whig)

Background to the Election
Timing of the Election
The election arose when William IV dismissed Viscount Melbourne, technically at his own suggestion. In November 1834, Lord Althorp (the Whig Chancellor of the Exchequer and leader in the House of Commons) succeeded to his father's title of Earl Spencer and, with it, acquired a seat in the House of Lords. Having made Althorp's support a condition of his taking office, Melbourne offered his resignation to the King, although he doubtless assumed that his suggestion to replace Althorp with Lord Russell would be acceptable. However, William IV was unhappy with Russell's stance regarding the appropriation for secular purposes of the surplus revenue of the Church of Ireland (an issue which is discussed below) and instead, therefore, accepted Melbourne's resignation. The Duke of Wellington headed an interim government (in which he also acted as Home Secretary, Foreign Secretary and Secretary for War and the Colonies) until Peel (who was in Rome at the time) returned home. Peel sought an immediate dissolution, one reason for his reluctance to face Parliament being the provisions of the 1707 Succession to the Crown Act which required those chosen as Cabinet ministers to resign their seats and face by-elections.

Conservatives
In opposition, the Conservative Party sought to adapt to the new political circumstances which were inaugurated with the enactment of the 1832 Reform Act by improving their organisation. The Carlton Club (established in 1832) aimed to provide a central focus for Conservative activities, and attempts were also made to construct organisation in the constituencies. The party leader, Peel, played little part in these developments but concentrated his energies in the House of Commons. In 1833 he summarised his approach to politics with the statement, 'I presume that the chief object of that party which is called Conservative ... will be to resist Radicalism, to prevent those further encroachments of democratic influence which will be attempted (probably successfully attempted) as the natural consequence of the triumph already achieved' (quoted in Woodward, 1962: 97–8). However, in contrast to the high Tories, his face was not entirely set against change and (as is discussed below) he developed these ideas more fully against the background of the 1835 general election.

Whigs
It was conceivable that the broad-based coalition led by the Whigs which secured the enactment of parliamentary reform would provide the basis for a new political party. However, the basis of agreement between these four key groups (which were identified in the 1832 entry) was fragile.

Whigs and 'democratic' radicals had nothing in common, and while all shades of anti-Conservative opinion had been able to unite in support of Catholic emancipation, there was little interest displayed by other members of the Whig-led coalition in remedying Irish grievances. The Whigs tended to view the Irish as a rebellious, backward people who were not suited to self-government (which prompted the Whig government to utilise coercive measures in Ireland), while nonconformists could not support a political movement which they perceived as driven by Popery. Many who were party to this coalition felt that Irish cultural identity was shaped by a force which they regarded as highly illiberal (the Catholic Church). There was thus a danger that the coalition which had succeeded in securing parliamentary reform would fall apart after it had been achieved.

In office after 1832, the Whigs possessed a substantial majority, but the government was not immune from defeat, such as that which occurred in connection with the malt tax in 1833. In office, a range of legislation was passed including the 1833 Factory Act and the 1834 Poor Law Amendment Act. Slavery was also abolished throughout the British Empire in 1833.

In 1834 (until 1840), the Whigs secured the support of O'Connell and his supporters who wished to repeal the Act of Union. Although repeal of the Act of Union was not conceded, this arrangement between the two parties ensured that some Irish grievances had to be addressed. Initial reform was provided by the 1832 Tithes Act which ammended three earlier Acts related to composition for tithe payment in Ireland, and the 1833 Irish Church Temporalities Act which streamlined the Church of Ireland and abolished the Church cess. These concessions were coupled with coercion if public order threatened to break down.

However, Irish policy threatened the stability of the government. In May–June 1834, Sir James Graham, Lord Stanley, the Earl of Ripon and the Duke of Richmond resigned from the Cabinet when Lord John Russell raised the question of the appropriation of surplus revenues of the Church of Ireland for secular purposes (such as education) in a debate in the House of Commons on the Irish Tithes Bill. This issue (which was underpinned by a power struggle within the Whigs between Russell and Stanley) kept the Whigs divided for many subsequent years. The Cabinet appointed a commission of inquiry into the position of the Irish Church in May 1834. Lord Grey retired in the summer of 1834 when he failed to secure the support of his leader of the House of Commons, Viscount Althorp, for an Irish Coercion Bill. William IV suggested he should be replaced by a coalition government, but there was no prospect of the Conservatives joining an administration of whose actions they thoroughly disapproved. Accordingly, the monarch turned to Viscount Melbourne whom he regarded as a conservative Whig. Melbourne formed his government in July 1834 but it fell later that year in circumstances which are discussed above.

In 1834 Graham resigned from the government and joined the Conservatives in 1835. This was due to his belief that the Whig government was increasingly moving in a radical direction.

By-elections

A total of 58 by-elections occurred in the lifetime of the 1832–35 Parliament, of which 35 were contested. In these, the Conservatives made a net gain of nine seats and the Whigs a net loss of nine.

Conduct of the Election

Conservatives

Following his acceptance of the office of Prime Minister on 26 November 1834, Peel published an address to his electors at Tamworth in preparation for the coming general election. Although not specifically written for an election, this statement is generally regarded as the first election manifesto. In this 'Tamworth manifesto' (which was quoted in *The Times* on 18 December 1834) he argued that he was never the defender of abuses or the enemy of judicious reform and referred to his record on the currency, on the consolidation and amendment of the criminal law and the revival of the system of trial by jury as proof that he did not acquiesce in acknowledged evils. He stated that the 1832 Reform Act (which he had initially condemned as the 'thin end of the democratic wedge') was 'the final and irrevocable settlement of a great constitutional question'. He asserted that the guiding principles for his future actions would be to act in the spirit of this measure which he defined as performing 'a careful review of institutions civil and ecclesiastical, undertaken in a friendly temper, combining with the firm maintenance of established rights the correction of proved abuses and the redress of real grievances'.

In terms of future policy, he pledged not to interfere with the progress of the current inquiry into the municipal corporations, and expressed support for Lord Althorp's resolution that, in future, pensions paid from the Civil List would be confined to persons with just claims as royal beneficiaries or who were entitled to consideration because of personal service to the Crown, of performance of public duties or of literary or scientific eminence. He referred to his support for relief to Dissenters in connection with marriage ceremonies and expressed support for the exemption of all classes from the payment of Church Rates. Additionally, although he was opposed to the blanket admission of Dissenters to the universities, he believed there was a case to modify entrance regulations to the medical and legal professions since the present system gave privileges to one class of citizens over another. He was firmly opposed to the alienation of Church property in any part of the United Kingdom from purposes that were strictly ecclesiastical but was willing to support the improved distribution of revenue of the Church in order to extend its influence and wished to see the tithe question settled on the basis of a commutation founded on a just principle.

He concluded that 'our object will be the maintenance of peace, the scrupulous and honest fulfilment ... of all existing engagements with foreign powers, the support of public credit, the enforcement of strict economy, and the just and impartial consideration of what is due to all interests, agricultural, manufacturing and commercial'.

He followed up the sentiments contained in this statement in a speech delivered at the Mansion House on 23 December 1834 when he stated that 'we require government to be administered for the sole purpose of promoting the true interests of this country, we require that there should be full and patient consideration of everything that can be fairly suspected as partaking of the character of abuse, and if, after patient consideration, the abuse be proved, we require that it should be corrected – first from hatred of the abuse, and secondly, from love and respect for those ancient institutions which abuse has the tendency to disfigure and impair'.

These statements were important steps in transforming the Tories to Conservatives, a party which would promote reform in order to preserve the key institutions of the state.

Whigs
During the campaign many Conservative candidates echoed the sentiments expressed by Peel in that they accepted the 1832 Reform Act but put themselves forward as defenders of the country's ancient institutions (which included the monarchy and the union of Church and state) against further changes whether these were motivated by despotic, aristocratic or democratic impulses.

This stance was used by Whig candidates to portray the Conservatives as opponents of reform. At a meeting of candidates standing in Tower Hamlets, Dr Lushington (who was subsequently elected) depicted Melbourne's ministry as a reforming one seeking to remedy abuses in the Church and state which the Tories wished to defend. He further spelled out future reforms he supported, including the secret ballot and triennial parliaments. His running mate in that contest (William Clay, who was also elected) asserted that the Conservatives had taken office under Peel not to promote reforms to the Church and state but to oppose them. Other Liberal candidates developed additional themes: Captain Pechell (who was elected for Brighton) declaring himself in favour of peace, the reform of all abuses in the Church and state, and retrenchment (which he defined as efficient and economical government).

The Whig campaign, however, suffered from a number of difficulties. The association of the Whigs with the radicals (or 'reformers' as they were sometimes called at this time) made it possible to identify the Whig-led coalition with extremism embracing policies such as universal suffrage, the secret ballot, annual Parliaments, the separation of Church and state and the abolition of the royal prerogative of creating peers. On 29 December 1834 *The Times* argued that a future Whig government would be forced to accommodate radicals with such views. The influence exerted by O'Connell on the Whig government further made it possible to question the Whig commitment to safeguarding the United Kingdom. There were also divisions within the ranks of the Whigs, Lord Stanley's address to his constituents in North Lancashire expressing his objection to the alienation of the property of the Irish Church (an issue on which he had resigned from the government in 1834).

Result of the Election
A total number of 945 candidates contested the election, with 275 MPs being returned unopposed. The result was:

Party	Votes	Vote %	MPs
Whig	315,002	51.6%	317
Conservative	235,907	38.6%	238
Irish Whig	34,866	5.7% [57.6%]	68
Irish Conservative	25,362	4.1% [42.4%]	35
Total	611,137		658

The turnout was 65.0 per cent.

The Parties
The Conservatives performed especially well in the English counties (where they won 73 of the 144 seats) and also made gains in boroughs, especially in older established urban centres such

as Bristol, York, Exeter, Newcastle and Hull (Jenkins, 1994: 23). Overall, the Whigs lost 56 seats in the United Kingdom compared with their performance in 1832. The party's worsened performance was especially apparent in England where 83 seats were lost.

Scotland, Wales and Ireland

The Conservatives made some gains in Scotland, but the Whigs remained the dominant party, securing 38 of the 53 seats and 62.8 per cent of the vote. In Wales the Conservatives overtook the Whigs as the largest party in Wales in terms of seats, winning 17 of the 32 constituencies to the 15 won by the Whigs. Two-party politics were restored to Ireland, the Whigs winning 68 of the 103 seats and the Conservatives the remaining 35.

Consequence of the Election

The Conservatives made substantial gains in the election, but were short of an overall majority. As the leader of the incumbent party, Peel insisted on testing opinion in the House of Commons. However, six defeats in as many weeks persuaded him to abandon what was obviously a lost cause and to resign, the final straw being defeat on Russell's motions to reaffirm the principle of lay appropriation of the surplus revenues of the Church of Ireland in April 1835 (an issue discussed in more detail in the 1841 entry). This also had the effect of asserting the supremacy of Russell over Stanley in the Whig Party since the circumstances surrounding the dismissal of Melbourne made many Whigs view this issue as related to the abuse of the royal prerogative. Accordingly, in April 1835 Viscount Melbourne formed his second Whig administration.

22 July – 18 August 1837

Party Leaders
Sir Robert Peel (Conservative)
Viscount Melbourne (Whig)

Background to the Election
Timing of the Election
The election was caused by the death of King William IV on 20 June 1837. He was replaced by Queen Victoria. It was customary that a change of monarch would be accompanied by a general election.

Electoral Procedures and Practices
Following the 1835 general election, the duration of the poll in a borough constituency was reduced to one day.

Conservatives
Initially Peel adopted a conciliatory attitude towards the Whig government. This was underpinned by Peel's belief that he lacked the strength and cohesion to form a stable government and had the effect of aiding the Whigs to resist the demands put forward by their more radical supporters. Conservative support was crucial in enabling the government to vote down proposals tabled by radical MPs in 1837 in favour of measures such as the secret ballot, the abolition of the property qualification for MPs, the repeal of the Septennial Act and the removal of bishops from the House of Lords.

Whigs
Three meetings occurred betweeen the Whig leaders and other potential opponents of a Conservative administration in February and March 1835. These were held at Lichfield House and included the Whigs, radicals and the leader of the Irish repealers, Daniel O'Connell. They resulted in the formation of Melbourne's second administration (1835–41) following the defeat of the Conservative government on the issue of the appropriation of the surplus revenues of the Church of Ireland for secular purposes. On 2 April 1835 the Committee of Supply approved (by 323 : 289 votes) Lord Russell's motion 'that this house do resolve itself into a committee of the whole house in order to consider the present state of the Church establishment in Ireland, with the view of applying any surplus of its revenue not required for the general purposes of the Church, to the general moral and religious instruction of His Majesty's subjects in Ireland without reference to their religious distinctions'. This matter was then considered by a committee of the whole House and was approved by 262 : 237 votes on 6 April. This defeat prompted Russell to move a further motion (in relation to the government's legislation in connection with tithes) 'that it is the opinion of this house that no measure upon the subject of tithes in Ireland can lead to a satisfactory and final adjustment except it embodies the

principle contained in the foregoing resolution'. This was passed on 7 April by 285 : 258 votes and resulted in Peel's immediate resignation.

The composition of Melbourne's new government was less radical than his previous government and excluded Lord 'Radical Jack' Durham and Lord Brougham. The coalition which was formed as a result of these meetings could be viewed as the basis of the formation of a new Liberal Party (Gash, 1979: 161), although (as with reform in 1832) the groups which were party to it had little in common other than opposition to the way in which the royal prerogative had been abused in the constitutional crisis of 1834–35 and the keenly felt desire to oust the chief beneficiary of the King's action, Peel.

O'Connell decided to give his support to the Whigs at the Lichfield House meetings, which meant that the Whig government devoted some attention to the concerns of Ireland (although O'Connell was not given a seat in the Cabinet). Reforms that were introduced included the introduction of the Poor Law into Ireland, the reform of the corporations and a consideration of the tithe question, although the inclusion of a provision to appropriate the Church of Ireland's surplus revenues for secular purposes ensured that the House of Lords voted down the latter measure which was thus not settled until after the election when in 1838 the Whig government abandoned the proposal for lay appropriation and instead instituted a rent charge of 75 per cent of the nominal value of the tithe in lieu of the tithe. Considerable improvements were also made in the administration of Ireland, especially due to the work of the Under Secretary, Thomas Drummond. His reforms in particular sought to give Catholics a fair share of jobs in public bodies such as the Irish Constabulary.

The Whig government also enacted important reforming measures which included the 1835 Municipal Corporations Act which sought to replace the existing system of urban administration in England and Wales which was based on undemocratic corporations with elected councils. This reform in particular provided nonconformists with the opportunity to take part in municipal affairs. Other measures pursued after 1835 also sought to appease nonconformist sentiment in England. These included legislation enacted in 1836 which included the abolition of the Established Church's monopoly of the registration of births, deaths and marriages and the granting of a Royal Charter to London University. The 1836 Tithe Commutation Act also sought to appease both nonconformist and agricultural interests. A Bill was also introduced in 1837 to abolish the legal requirement for nonconformists to pay the Church Rate, a measure that was identified by some nonconformists with the broader issue of disestablishment. However, dissent within the Whigs concerning this measure (which secured its second reading by only 5 votes) forced the government to abandon it.

Melbourne's chief problem in office was that his party lacked any coherent programme which could form the basis of his government. Instead, the government seemed controlled by the more militant elements which comprised the Liberal coalition, and the perception that the Reform Act had not led to the cessation of demand for further reform resulted in the Whigs losing the support of moderate MPs in the House of Commons who transformed their allegiance to the Conservative Party. Two Bills which sought to amend the operations of the 1832 Act (the Parliamentary Electors Bill and the Final Registration of Electors Bill) were brought forward by the government in 1837 but abandoned when the election was called due to lack of time to secure their progress.

By-elections

A total of 89 by-elections occurred in the 1835–37 Parliament, of which 47 were contested. The Conservatives made a net gain of seven seats and the Whigs a net loss of the same number. One notable government defeat occurred when Lord John Russell was appointed Home Secretary and thus forced to face a by-election in his constituency of North Devonshire. He was defeated on 7 May 1835 and forced to move to Stroud where a Liberal MP obligingly accepted the Chiltern Hundreds to enable Russell to re-enter Parliament and the Cabinet.

Conduct of the Election

Conservatives

Peel's main statement of Conservative policy was contained in a speech which he delivered on the occasion of the nomination of candidates for his constituency at Tamworth on 24 July 1837 (which was recorded in *The Times* on 25 July). In this speech he expressed opposition to the separation of Church and state or any attempt which might be made to subvert the ancient constitution and substitute a democracy in its place. In respect of the latter concern, he depicted himself as the defender of the 1832 Reform Act by stating he was against any attempts to reform this Act by measures which included the introduction of household suffrage, the secret ballot and triennial Parliaments, and asserting he would never consent 'to the gradual infusion of so much of the democratic principle as would ultimately convert the ancient monarchy into a republic'. He also stated his desire to maintain the privileges of the House of Lords.

Peel also made a vague reference to free trade when he stated his opposition to the 'false friends of agriculture' who argued that the exclusion of foreign products or an increased bounty on their own production was the means to achieve permanent prosperity for agriculture.

The close identification of the actions of the Whig government with O'Connell in Ireland and militant nonconformity in England enabled the Conservatives to campaign on the issue of 'the Church in danger' and to express their opposition to measures which they saw as advancing this objective such as the Church Rates Bill (which has been referred to above). Conservatives also campaigned against what they alleged was the extreme radicalism which they suggested aimed to control the actions of Melbourne's administration. Radicals were said to pose a threat both to the existence of Protestantism and to the character of the key political institutions of the state which Conservatives pledged themselves to defend. Conservative candidates (such as Lord Durham) expressed themselves as unambiguous defenders of the existing institutions of the country (which he defined as the Throne, the Lords, the Commons and the Established Church) and he rejected the annihilation of these institutions 'for the purposes of forming new ones on fanciful and untried principles'. In this respect, Peel asserted (in his speech on 24 July) that Conservative MPs had frequently come to the aid of the beleaguered Whigs to prevent radical measures (such as the introduction of the secret ballot or the removal of the bishops from the House of Lords) reaching the statute book. Conservatives also rejected the Liberal claim that the alliance with O'Connell had produced peace and tranquillity in Ireland, which was, alternatively, depicted as a country in which law and disorder was rife.

Additionally, the Poor Law as amended in 1834 was an important election issue. Conservatives viewed this measure as 'the starvation code' and a Conservative supporter at an election meeting in Tower Hamlets summed up the feelings of many Conservatives on this issue when he stated that 'if there is a greater curse in the Country, or single Act upon the statute book more vile and disgraceful than another, it is the Poor Law Bill'. Sir John Beckett (who was defeated at Leeds) argued that these laws should not be applied to manufacturing districts and he stated his opposition to sending the Poor Law Commissioners into Leeds, and Serjeant Adams (who unsuccessfully stood at Stroud against Russell) called for the amelioration of the Law's operations since 'a poor man should not be treated as a criminal'. Other Conservatives condemned the centralisation which underpinned the 1834 Act.

Whigs

The Whig campaign sought to defend actions undertaken by the government since its return in 1835. Concern regarding public misgivings about the 1834 Poor Law Amendment Act induced ministers to suspend its operations in manufacturing districts until January 1838. Some attempt was also made to defuse the Conservative criticisms of this measure. Sir George Strickland (who successfully fought West Riding for the Whigs) asserted that unpleasant aspects of the 1834 Act arose from amendments carried in the House of Lords tabled by Lord Wharncliffe. These included the bastardy clause. Thus while he defended the legislation he stated his wish to repeal the bastardy clause and asserted that the separation of a man and wife should occur only in the most urgent of cases. He also felt that the extension of the Act to Ireland would help to secure tranquillity. Radical MPs also campaigned in the election for political reforms which included the introduction of the secret ballot.

Result of the Election

A total number of 994 candidates contested the election, with 236 MPs being returned unopposed. The result was:

Party	Votes	Vote %	MPs
Whig	379,961	47.6%	271
Conservative	353,000	44.2%	284
Irish Whig	38,370	4.8% [58.5%]	73
Irish Conservative	26,694	3.4% [41.5%]	30
Total	798,025		658

The turnout was 63.6 per cent.

The Parties

The religious emphasis of the Conservative campaign secured them support from new quarters, including Methodists who did not advocate disestablishment of the Church of England and who were additionally uneasy concerning concessions made by the government to Catholic opinion in Ireland. The Party sustained the advance it had made in 1835 and increased its support in the counties (where it held 99 of the 144 seats), and the smaller boroughs (where it held 98 out of the 202 seats) (Jenkins, 1994: 28–9). The good relationship which the Whigs (and Melbourne in particular) were able to cultivate with Queen Victoria enabled the 'Royal

Card' to be played in the Whigs' favour. This aided the Party's performance, especially in the larger boroughs. However, the Whigs' majority was further eaten into (being reduced to around 30 seats) and the strength of the radicals was eroded at the election.

Scotland, Wales and Ireland

Although the Whigs remained the main party in Scotland in terms of seats, the Conservatives closed the gap by winning 20 of the 53 seats to the 33 won by the Whigs. The Conservatives increased their control of Welsh politics which they had secured in 1835 and won 19 of the 32 seats to the 13 won by the Whigs. In Ireland, the continuance of two-party politics provided the Whigs with a decisive lead over the Conservatives in terms of seats (73 : 30). O'Connell lost his seat at Kilkenny County to the Liberal candidate, Joseph Hume, by the margin of 57 votes to 50.

Consequence of the Election

Viscount Melbourne formed a Whig administration.

28 June – 17 July 1841

Party Leaders
Sir Robert Peel (Conservative)
Viscount Melbourne (Whig)

Background to the Election
Timing of the Election
The election was caused when Melbourne lost a vote of no confidence on 4 June 1841. It was moved by Sir Robert Peel and stated 'That Her Majesty's Ministers do not sufficiently possess the confidence of the House of Commons to enable them to carry through the House measures which they deem to be of essential importance to the public welfare, and that their continuance in office, under such circumstances, is at variance with the spirit of the constitution'. It was carried by 312 : 311, an opposition majority of one. The circumstances surrounding this episode are discussed in more detail below.

Electoral Procedures and Practices
The 1841 Bribery at Elections Act was passed in the dying days of the Whig administration. It was passed in an emasculated form by the House of Lords to provide for little more than giving direction to election committees on how to receive evidence and frame their reports in cases of alleged bribery.

Conservatives
Initially Peel continued to provide support to the government to resist radical proposals on a range of issues which included political reform, the abolition of Negro apprenticeship in the West Indies and the abolition of the Corn Laws. However, this goodwill was slowly eroded and in May 1839 the Conservatives adopted a critical stance in regard to the government's handling of an insurrection in Jamaica. In consequence, the government's majority slumped to five and the ministers resigned, only to resume office in the wake of the 'bedchamber crisis' which is discussed below. In a later speech delivered on the occasion of the nomination of candidates in his constituency of Tamworth, Peel emphasised that he had not sought to obstruct the course of government in Parliament by factious opposition and that on several occasions he had rescued the Whigs when he felt that they were pursuing a course of action which he felt was to the public good.

Whigs
Early in the new Parliament, Russell attempted to distance the Whigs from radical reform by declaring himself an opponent of any further extension of the franchise and also expressing opposition to the secret ballot and triennial Parliaments. This speech earned him the nickname of 'finality Jack' and the emergence of Chartism in 1838–39 encouraged Russell to make further pronouncements opposing political reform.

Melbourne's government had little in the way of a positive policy with which to hold the party together, and its standing was adversely affected by the bad harvest of 1838 which caused gold to be exported in order to purchase corn abroad. In early May 1839 the government carried a motion to suspend Jamaica's constitution by the narrow margin of five votes. This prompted Melbourne's resignation and the leader of the Conservative Party, Peel, took office. However, he was concerned that the Queen viewed the Whigs as her friends and the Conservatives as her enemies and accordingly wanted some form of gesture from the monarch. This took the form of suggesting that some of the ladies who held high office in her household and who were related to Whig ministers should resign. This became known as the 'bedchamber crisis'. The Queen took advice from Viscount Melbourne who promised her that his party would stand by her. She thus refused to make the changes required by Peel who promptly resigned.

Accordingly, Melbourne resumed office but his government continued to lack purpose, its future conduct being described as amounting to 'a state of paralysis' (Jenkins, 1994: 33). The government considered political reform (including the introduction of the secret ballot) but undertook no action. The repeal of the Corn Laws was an issue which might have provided his administration with political direction, but Melbourne was an implacable opponent of reform. Thus, the suggestion by Chancellor Baring, that the sliding scale of import duties on corn might be replaced by a modest fixed duty was not acted upon. After his return to office, Melbourne was troubled by the extra-parliamentary politics of Chartism. The government also experienced problems in foreign affairs, most notably in the heightening of tensions with America in connection with boundary disputes between America and Canada. The conflict between British merchants trading in opium and the Chinese government (which sought to repress the trade) erupted into the First Opium War which broke out in 1839 at the same time as the First Afghan War.

Economic policy was the key weakness of the government. The economic depression which commenced in 1837 deprived the government of revenue from import duties (hence the attempt to stimulate trade by measures put forward in the 1841 budget). Deficit budgets were introduced from 1839 and by 1841 this had grown to £6 million in 1841. The Whigs decided to address this in the 1841 budget by lowering the duty on imports of foreign timber and sugar. The Conservatives attacked what they regarded as the financial incompetence of the government but focused their attack on the proposal relating to sugar, arguing that the government's policy would increase the use of slave labour in Cuba and Brazil in order to meet the demands of the British market. In early 1841, four successive by-elections were lost and, in May 1841, the government lost a fiscal motion by 36 votes before succumbing to the vote of no confidence on 4 June 1841. On 10 June a further defeat occurred on a motion to compensate British subjects for the losses they had sustained through the seizure and confiscation of their ships by Denmark in 1807. However, Parliament was not prorogued until 22 June which led to accusations that the government was acting unconstitutionally by continuing in office and proceeding with contentious legislation (such as the 1841 Administration of Justice Act).

By-elections

A total of 105 by-elections occurred in the 1837–41 Parliament, of which 49 were contested. The Conservative Party made a net gain of 11 seats and the Liberals a net loss of the same number.

Conduct of the Election

At the outset of the contest, a Conservative victory was widely anticipated.

Conservatives

The Conservative Party entered the contest in good spirits. By-election defeats occurred in early 1841 culminating in April with the loss of the safe Whig seat of Nottingham. Peel again reiterated the philosophy of the Conservative Party, stating in a speech at Tamworth on 28 June that events which had occurred in France in 1830 (when he was first elected to Parliament) had suggested to him the importance of laying the foundations 'of a great Conservative Party, attached to the ancient fundamental institutions of the country, not disposed to resist such changes as the altered circumstances of society might require, but a party determined to maintain on their ancient foundations the institutions of Church and state'.

Opposition to the Whig Poor Law was an important issue at this contest and during the campaign the Conservative Party especially sought to exploit discontent to this legislation in Northern England. One of the unsuccessful Conservative candidates in Nottingham (Mr T. Charlton) argued for the reform of this legislation by stating it was not right to 'send the poor and destitute to bastilles, to pass the end of their days in misery and discomfort'. *The Times* newspaper aided this aspect of the Conservative campaign by mounting fierce attacks on Lord Russell, pointing out that, although his motion on 19 January 1841 to renew the legislation for a further period of 10 years had been dropped in May, Russell continued to declare his support for the legislation which, in the newspaper's view (which was expressed on 21 June 1841) provided a regime of 'half starvation, despotic tyranny, and want of all distinction between the deserving and undeserving poor'.

The other key policy which the Conservatives emphasised was opposition to the reform of the Corn Laws, where the Conservatives exploited unease in the countryside that the Whigs, if returned, would not merely revise this legislation but might actually abolish it. The censure motion in the House of Commons on 4 June prompted the government to drop its proposal to appoint a committee to study the Corn Laws but Conservative candidates frequently articulated their concerns regarding the Whigs' intentions on this subject. The Conservative candidates at Liverpool (Viscount Sandon and C. Cresswell) defended protection against alleged Whig desires to advance free trade, and Peel dealt fully with this issue in his speech at Tamworth on 28 June (which was quoted in *The Times* on 29 June). He asserted that he sympathised with the view that commerce should be free and that restrictions on commerce were wrong unless they were designed to offer protection to great existing interests. But he argued against the Whig proposal contained in the 1841 budget to amend the duty on the import of foreign sugar and then to allow the entry of foreign sugar into British markets on the grounds that he wished to keep sugar which had been produced by slave labour out of Britain. This pragmatic rather than principled objection to protection also informed his opposition to the proposal regarding corn which had been made by the Whigs (although not acted upon) which entailed substituting the sliding scale for a fixed duty. He argued that this proposal amounted to a policy which would provide an abundance of corn when British corn was plentiful (and thus was not needed) but that in times of scarcity it would be impossible to levy the duty. He rejected the view that a fixed duty would secure the reduction of the price of bread in time of hardship, and totally opposed the suggestion that the present depressed state of manufacturing and commerce in Britain had anything to do with the Corn Laws. Instead, he argued that explanations for the problems faced by manufacturing included over-expansion due to the actions of the joint stock banks and the disruption of trade with countries such as South America which were traditionally large importers of British manufactured goods. He thus rejected any proposal to make any 'radical, fundamental change' to the Corn Laws.

Opposition to the Poor Law and to the repeal of the Corn Laws facilitated a Chartist–Conservative alliance to be fashioned for this election. The Chartists were critical of both the Poor Law and the free trade ideas of the Anti Corn Law League. They believed that repeal was desired by the manufacturers in order to justify reducing working-class wages. In some constituencies (including Northampton and Bradford) Chartist and Conservative candidates ran in harness, and elsewhere Conservatives received the endorsement of local Chartist leaders. This alliance was, however, ephemeral. The Chartists viewed it as a means to defeat the Whigs who would subsequently be susceptible to making concessions in their direction.

Additionally, the Conservatives were aided by *The Times* newspaper which mounted a vigorous campaign in favour of a change of government. Numerous charges were levelled against the Whigs. They were accused of financial mismanagement and their record in government between 1831 and 1840 was unfavourably compared with the actions of Conservative governments between 1821 and 1830. On 22 June this newspaper argued that, whereas the Tories had reduced the annual interest on the national debt and left office with the Treasury in surplus, in 1841 the Party would inherit a deficit from the Whigs. Additionally, it was argued that Tory governments had lowered taxes far more than the Whigs had managed between 1831 and 1840. Some Conservative candidates adopted this theme, J. Masterman (who was elected for the City of London) referring in a speech delivered on 24 June to the Liberal Party's 'imprudent mismanagement of the financial department of the country' which resulted in a budget deficit.

The Times also acused the Whigs of abandoning the principles on which they were elected to office, by actions which included the extension of government patronage through the creation of numerous commissions (which included Poor Law, Railway and Factory Inspection Commissions), the suggestion (which was allegedly much influenced by O'Connell) of appropriating the surplus ecclesiastical revenues of the Church of Ireland for secular purposes, and the misuse of the royal prerogative which entailed bypassing Parliament and enforcing decisions (which included granting corporate powers to the City of London and appointing a Committee of the Privy Council to examine the issue of national education).

Whigs

Lord Russell stated at a meeting held in the London Tavern on 15 June 1841 that the key issue of the election 'was whether the country would affirm or reject the recent decision of the majority of the House of Commons'. The Whigs hoped that the proposals contained in their 1841 budget for tariff revision would aid their cause in the boroughs where voters would be especially susceptible to the appeal of cheaper bread and sugar. The Liberal candidates in Bath (Viscount Duncan and J. Roebuck) unambiguously called for the abolition of the Corn Laws and also appealed for the cancellation of the national debt. The Liberals also sought to adopt the scare tactic of arguing that the Conservatives would seek to encourage despotism abroad and maintain it at home. This charge brought a rebuke from *The Times* on 17 June which argued that despotism had been a facet of Whig rule evidenced by the emphasis they had placed on centralisation at the expense of the right of self-government and their use of the royal prerogative. The newspaper further accused them of corruption by seeking to spend money in order to buy seats at the election and concluded that the Whig-radical alliance constituted an unprincipled conspiracy which was designed to destroy the liberties of the people.

Result of the Election

A total of 916 candidates contested the election, with 337 MPs returned unopposed. The result was:

Party	Votes	Vote %	MPs
Conservative	286,650	48.3%	326
Liberal	256,774	43.3%	229
Irish Liberal	17,128	2.9% [35.1%]	42
Irish Conservative	19,664	3.3% [40.1%]	41
Irish Repeal Party	12,537	2.1% [24.8%]	20
Chartist	692	0.1%	0
Total	593,445		658

The turnout was 63.4 per cent.

The Parties

The election was held against the background of industrial depression and intense agitation by the Anti Corn Law League. Unease in the counties regarding future Whig policy on the Corn Laws resulted in the Conservatives securing a substantial victory in rural England. They won 124 of the 144 county constituencies in England. Whig strongholds such as the West Riding of Yorkshire (where the influence of Earl Fitzwilliam and the Earl of Scarborough had been dominant) fell to the Conservatives. However, the Conservatives also polled well in the smaller boroughs (containing below 1,000 voters), winning 111 of the 202 seats in this category and, overall, won 155 of the 323 English borough seats (Jenkins,1994: 34).

The Whigs attributed their defeat to the use of bribery by their Conservative opponents. In England, the Whigs performed best in the larger boroughs (with electorates in excess of 2,000 voters) where they made a net gain of two seats from the Conservatives compared to the previous election. They also secured victory in 34 of the 63 medium-sized boroughs (with electorates between 1,000 and 2,000 voters). A number of prominent Whig representatives were defeated, incuding Lords Morpeth, Milton, Howick, the Earl of Surrey and Sir Charles Cavendish. Lord Russell moved from Stroud to the City of London and although the Whigs lost two of the four seats in this constituency he managed to scrape home, a mere nine votes ahead of the Conservative candidate in fifth place. Palmerston was unsuccessful in securing election for Liverpool, but was re-elected at Tiverton. Agitation by the Anti Corn Law League resulted in the emergence of a new radical force in the Party which was especially associated with Richard Cobden (who was elected for Stockport) and John Bright.

Scotland, Wales and Ireland
There was a slight swing to the Conservatives in Scotland, where they won 22 of the 53 seats. However, the Whigs (with 31 seats) remained the dominant political force. The Conservatives remained as the dominant political party in Wales where they won 21 of the 32 seats.

In Ireland, O'Connell's relaunching of the campaign to repeal the Act of Union in 1841 was rebuffed by the voters and he won won only 20 of the 103 seats. O'Connell was defeated at the City of Dublin, although he was returned for Cork at the same election. There was a slight swing towards the Conservatives, who secured victory in 41 constituencies. This, and the re-emergence of the Repeal Party, reduced the Liberal representation from 73 seats in 1837 to 42 in 1841.

Consequence of the Election
Although the Whig government asserted its right to ascertain whether it possessed the confidence of Parliament, Sir Robert Peel possessed an overall majority in the House of Commons. As is discussed more fully in the 1847 entry, he used this to oust the Whigs when Parliament met in August 1841. He then formed a Conservative government.

28 July – 1 September 1847

Party Leaders
The Earl of Derby (Conservative)
Lord John Russell (Whig)

Background to the Election
Timing of the Election
The downfall of Peel in 1846 justified an election to enable the Whigs to strengthen their position in the face of Conservative disunity. Parliament was also approaching the end of its statutory lifespan.

Conservatives
The Whig government returned to the House of Commons to test its level of support. The Conservatives moved a lengthy amendment to the Queen's Speech, a key item of which was to 'humbly present to Her Majesty that we observe with great concern that the public expenditure has of late in each of several successive years exceeded the annual income, and that we are convinced of the necessity of adopting measures for the purpose of remedying so great an evil'. This was passed by the considerable margin of 360 : 269 votes and resulted in Melbourne's immediate resignation.

In office, Peel was faced with a number of difficulties abroad. Wars in China and India were inherited from the previous Whig administration. The First Opium War was settled by the Treaty of Nanking in 1842 (whereby Britain acquired Hong Kong), and the First Afghan War was successfully concluded in 1842. Colonial expansion (mainly driven by commercial considerations) also occurred under Peel's government, an important example of which was the annexation of Natal in 1842. However, the most serious foreign issues affecting Peel's government were tensions with France and America.

Attempts by the French government to regain its lost colonial empire resulted in clashes in the South Pacific, in particular following France's claim to establish a protectorate over Tahiti. British concerns were also raised by France's attempts to advance her interests in North Africa, especially Morocco (where Tangiers was bombarded in 1844), as these were viewed as threatening to Gibraltar and Britain's Mediterranean possessions. Fear of France resulted in Peel's government pursuing a policy of naval rearmament. Peel's government inherited tensions with America in connection with the American–Canadian boundary. The Maine–New Brunswick dispute was settled in August 1842, but Oregon then emerged as a key issue. The intention of American expansionists was encapsulated in the slogan 'fifty-four forty or fight', and for a time it seemed that war between Britain and America was likely to occur. However, the Oregon Treaty of June 1846 settled the dispute, by making the western boundary between Canada and America the forty-ninth parallel.

However, a more serious problem emerged closer to home in Ireland. Initially Ireland was tranquil. The Repealers had fared badly in the election and there seemed little reason for the government to intervene in Irish affairs. However, in 1843 agitation for repeal re-emerged against the background of the economic slump of the early 1840s. The need for an Irish Parliament was justified on the grounds that only this mechanism would effectively remedy key Irish grievances such as the tithe rent-charges, the system of poor relief and insecurity of land tenure which was the main disincentive to tenant farmers carrying out improvements. Huge meetings (sometimes attended by hundreds of thousands of people) were held, associated with O'Connell and the newly formed Young Ireland movement (which believed in the use of violence to secure repeal). O'Connell's language became more militant at these meetings and the government became alarmed by reports of intentions to establish an Irish 'counter-administration' involving the establishment of a Parliament and a judicial system. In response to these events the government resorted to a policy of coercion. The 1843 Arms Act sought to impose a tighter system of control over the traffic in Irish weapons, Irish magistrates deemed favourable to repeal were dismissed and additional numbers of troops were despatched to Ireland. A large meeting which O'Connell intended to address at Clontarf in October 1843 was banned by the government. Although O'Connell acquiesced in the ban, he was subsequently arrested, tried and convicted for treasonable conspiracy although this was ultimately overturned in the House of Lords. The lack of leadership of the repeal movement significantly tapped its vitality and it was further adversely affected by the onset of the famine in 1846. The Repeal Association finally collapsed in 1848.

The return of a relative period of tranquillity in 1844 prompted the government to adjust its policy and seek to conciliate Catholic opinion by pursuing a policy of 'reform in order to preserve'. The government actively promoted the appointment of Catholics to posts in Irish administration, and passed the 1844 Charitable Bequests and Donations Act which was designed to facilitate endowments to the Catholic Church, thereby placing the Catholic clergy on an improved financial footing. In 1845 (after much delay caused by Conservative opposition, which included the resignation of Gladstone as President of the Board of Trade in January 1845), the grant to the training college for Catholic priests at Maynooth was increased and made permanent (in the hope of detaching the Catholic clergy from supporting repeal). Legislation passed in the same year provided for the establishment of higher education colleges in the North, West and South of Ireland. Other attempts at reform were less successful. A commisssion was appointed in 1843 (under the chairmanship of Lord Devon) to consider the agrarian question. This body subsequently recommended in 1845 that Irish tenants should be given compensation in improvements related to fencing, drainage and building. However, opposition to this reform caused the resultant Compensation to Tenants (Ireland) Bill to be withdrawn and further action was halted by the onset of the Irish famine in 1846. Similarly attempts to broaden the franchise in Ireland were abandoned in 1844 due to opposition from Conservative MPs who felt that the government's proposal would advance democratic tendencies and also from Irish Liberals and Repealers who feared that the government's reform would extend the influence of the landlords.

Financial reform was given considerable attention by Peel's government. The 1844 Joint Stock Companies Registration and Regulation Act sought to protect the public more adequately against unscrupulous or unwise company directors. Peel sought a solution to bank crashes (which had become a serious problem after 1815) through the enactment of the 1844

Bank Charter Act. The problem was deemed to be that of the over-issuing currency by banks desirous of taking advantage of investment opportunities (such as the growth of railways in the 1840s) but which lacked adequate reserves to tide them over difficult periods. This Act limited the fiduciary note issue of the Bank of England to £14 million and insisted that coin or bullion should cover all notes issued above this sum. It also placed further restrictions on the issue of notes by other banks. The consequent restriction of credit was sometimes overcome by suspending the Act in subsequent years.

When Peel assumed office, the budget had not been balanced for five years. Following the abolition of income tax in 1816, most of the state's revenue at that time was derived from customs and excise duties. However, Peel wished to reduce these as customs duties ensured that some foodstuffs were beyond the income of poorer persons and also in order to boost trade by both reducing the costs of raw materials and aiding the exporters of British manufactured goods on the assumption that other countries would emulate Britain's free trade policies. In 1842 (and again in 1845) he personally introduced the budget (although Edward Goulburn was Chancellor) in which he cut duties on 769 items, mainly raw materials. To make good the loss of revenue he reintroduced an income tax, which was initially intended to be for a period of three years but was renewed in 1845. This movement in the direction of free trade was subsequently pursued in 1845 (when duties on 430 articles were abolished, the most important of which was that on raw cotton) and in 1846 when the duties on 605 articles were abolished and most of these that remained were cut. The government's measures succeeded in providing a budget surplus which amounted to £5 million when the 1845 budget was introduced. This enabled it to refund around £14 million of the national debt and cut the interest on around £250 million of stock, thereby reducing the annual debt charge by £1.5 million.

The prime concern of Peel's government was to mitigate 'the economic and social consequences of an industrialising nation' (Crosby, 1976: 138) and in particular to maintain social order which, in addition to events in Ireland which have been previously discussed, was threatened from working-class discontent in Britain. This was based on the economic depression which commenced in the late 1830s and reached its peak in 1842. Its main cause was overproduction of wool, cotton, iron and grain and it resulted in high unemployment and reduction in wages which aggravated other working-class grievances including poor housing, harsh conditions of work and urban environments in which disease was prevalent. Peel's government faced working-class agitation which included the Plug Plot of 1842 (which was caused by striking colliers objecting to wage reductions) and the Rebecca Riots of 1842 in the three counties of West Wales, where demonstrations and the destruction of property were based upon the complaints of nonconformist small farmers concerning high rents, arbitrary decisions meted out by the magistrates and the rates and tithes which had to be paid to the Anglican Church.

Working-class discontent was a concern of the the Young England Movement whose leading members were George Smythe, Lord John Manners and Benjamin Disraeli. This group emerged partly as a criticism of Peel's attempt to tighten party discipline through the Whip system, although its main concern was to preserve the status of the landed aristocracy. They believed that the exploitation of the working class by the manufacturers, aided by political radicalism, posed the threat of revolution and they sought to avoid this by creating a working class–landed alliance based on paternalism which highlighted the responsibilities of the wealthy rather than stressing the duties of the poor. However, the Young England Movement broke up in 1845 through divisions on Peel's grant to Maynooth.

Peel was aware of the potential of working-class grievances to create social unrest and public disorder. However, his background made him acutely aware of the need to avoid unnecessary government intervention in industrial and economic affairs since this might have a detrimental impact on the expansion of the economy which he viewed as a pre-eminent concern. Accordingly, he viewed cheap food derived from free trade as the key policy to placate the working class. However, mainly due to the influence exerted by Tory paternalists headed by Lord Ashley, his government did introduce some measures of social reform. The 1842 Mines Act abolished all female labour in the mines and that of boys below 10 years of age, and the 1844 Factory Act cut the working day for women employed in manufacturing industry to 12 hours. Ashley's attempt to reduce this to 10 hours was lost. In 1845 the labour of children in the calico printing industry below eight years of age was prohibited as was night labour for women and children.

Although opposition to the Poor Law had figured prominently in the Conservatives' campaign in 1841, they did little in office to alter the legislation, save enacting the 1844 Poor Law Amendment Act which enacted a new law of bastardy, defined more clearly the relations of pauper apprentices and their masters, sponsored district pauper schools and altered the voting procedure for guardians and their qualifications for office. Sporadic intervention in social affairs was accompanied by limited intervention in economic matters. Regulation of the railways was introduced in Gladstone's 1844 Railway Act which required railway companies deriving more that one-third of their income from passengers to run at least one train each day (the so-called 'parliamentary trains'), whose fare should be no more than one penny a mile. It was required to stop at every station and run at a speed of not less than 12 miles per hour.

Additionally, considerable extra-parliamentary pressure was exerted to repeal the Corn Laws. Bad harvests coupled with an industrial depression in the summer of 1836 revived this cause and the Anti Corn Law Association was set up that year. In 1838 the Manchester Anti Corn Law Association was established, and in March of the following year the Anti Corn Law League was formed. This was a nation-wide organisation which took advantage of cheap postage rates, the reduction of the newspaper duty and quicker means of transport to popularise its cause. The key figures in the Anti Corn Law League were Richard Cobden and John Bright. Cobden viewed repeal as part of a wider movement to bring about free trade, which he believed was the key to securing international peace. The League argued that the cost of importing foreign corn would be paid for by increased exports of textiles and other goods, and although this policy had an obvious appeal to the middle class, the League also attempted to sell it to the working class by arguing that repeal would bring about reduced food prices. Good harvests in 1842, 1843 and 1844 reduced the appeal of the Anti Corn Law League. Manufacturers were appeased by the reduction of the price of corn in this period which was abetted by Peel's alteration of the sliding scale of duties in 1842 (which varied inversely with the price of corn in the domestic market). Protectionists also fought back at this time, forming the Anti-League in 1843. One of their key arguments was that manufacturers wanted lower food prices to justify paying their workers reduced wages. The Chartists also felt that repeal could have a disadvantageous impact on the working class. They feared that the competition from foreign corn would drive agricultural labourers from the countryside to the towns where they would depress working-class wages.

The repeal of the Corn Laws was compatible with Peel's earlier free trade budgets, and in particular with his desire to provide cheap food to allay working-class discontent. He was, however, aware that there was considerable opposition within his party towards this principle, which would be considerably aggravated if applied to corn. In January 1842 the Duke of Buckingham resigned as Lord Privy Seal over Peel's free trade policies and in 1842 MPs representing agricultural constituencies (who believed that the budget was primarily directed at the manufacturing interests and contained little of benefit to them) put pressure on the government to raise the duties proposed in this budget for cattle and meat imports. In the resultant division in the House of Commons, 85 of Peel's supporters voted against the government. Conservative MPs were also uneasy about the 1843 Canadian Corn Act which proposed to admit Canadian corn at a nominal duty. This was justified on grounds of imperial preference rather than free trade in order to address these concerns.

Peel initially felt that sugar and corn should get special treatment, but Whig criticisms that the government's failure to cut sugar duties had a detrimental effect on the poor persuaded him to propose lowering the duties in the 1844 budget. An amendment by Philip Miles MP to increase the duty differential between foreign and colonial sugar (which was intended to aid the West Indies) marshalled protectionists and resulted in a government defeat which indicated the problems Peel would face if he sought to tamper with the Corn Laws. However, towards the end of 1845 news of the extensive failure of the Irish potato crop (on which a large proportion of the Irish population were dependent) coupled with a bad harvest in England provided him with a pretext for initiating this reform. Peel's concern was in part economic. The government would have to step in and take measures to avoid death through starvation in Ireland, and lowering the duties on corn might be cheaper. Initially he considered suspending the duties on corn by Order-in-Council which would then be made permanent. However, justifying suspension by the argument that this course of action was necessary to alleviate scarcity would make it difficult to reintroduce the duties subsequently since this would suggest that the government supported the general principle of ensuring scarcity. Accordingly, he proposed to retain the sliding scale but to lower the duties progressively so that they would disappear within around eight years, thus providing a repeal of the Corn Laws through the back door. However, opposition (especially from Viscount Stanley, the Secretary for War and the Colonies) and hesitancy within his Cabinet prompted him to resign on 5 December 1845.

The Whig position had previously been to abolish the sliding scale in favour of a fixed duty but on 22 November 1845 Russell publically announced his support for repeal in his Letter to the Electors of the City of London, and implied that this would be the Whig position in the next session of Parliament. Russell's actions were driven by political considerations. He could claim credit for driving Peel in this direction if he adopted this policy, and it also provided the Party with a policy to guide its actions in government. However, following Peel's resignation he became unsure whether he could get the necessary legislation through the House of Commons since he had not consulted members of his party regarding this course of action and he became aware that there was considerable opposition to it. Although he managed to secure Peel's support for a Whig measure which would advance the abolitionist cause, he then encountered problems in constructing a government. He insisted that both Palmerston and Grey would have to serve in any administration which he headed. Palmerston demanded the post of Foreign Secretary, but Grey would not accept office if Palmerston held this position. Divisions of this magnitude in what, in any case, would be a minority government, provided Russell with a pretext to abandon his attempt to form a ministry. Accordingly, Peel returned as Prime Minister 15 days after resigning the office. His reconstructed administration included Gladstone who filled the post previously occupied by Viscount Stanley.

Peel now proposed to scale down duties on imported corn and abolish them after February 1849. Additionally, duties on a wide range of imported foodstuffs were repealed and those on a large number of manufactured goods were either abolished or reduced. Some compensatory measures were proposed as a sop to the agriculturalists, including the reduction of seed duties, the free import of maize and buckwheat, the provision of state loans at low interest rates for the improvement of agricultural practices, and state funding of certain functions previously paid for by the localities.

The repeal of the Corn Laws was bitterly opposed within his party, particularly by the farming interest which viewed the Conservative victory in 1841 as an endorsement of the Corn Laws in the face of Whig proposals to liberalise them. They believed that Peel was selling them out by putting forward proposals which were more radical than those of the Whigs in 1841. The Anti-League sought to mobilise popular support against Peel and put considerable pressure on MPs representing rural constituencies to reject Peel's proposals. By-elections began to go against the government. Peel experienced considerable opposition to his proposals in Parliament, a situation which was aggravated by his failure to consult with rural MPs and explain his actions to them. Peel's parliamentary opponents managed to delay the legislation by six months. Disraeli and Lord George Bentinck bitterly attacked him and his policy in the House of Commons and some of Peel's supporters found themsleves rejected by the patrons of the 'pocket boroughs' which they represented in Parliament: one casualty was Gladstone who was thrown out of Newark by the Duke of Newcastle. Eventually on 25 June 1846 the Bill to reduce all duties on wheat, oats and barley received its third reading in the House of Commons.

The same night, the government was brought down on the Protection of Life Bill. This was designed to respond to disorders in Ireland by giving the Lord Lieutenant the power to proclaim a district as 'disturbed' and increase its police force as necessary. Curfews could be imposed and those guilty of instigating disorders could be transported. Opposition to this measure in the House of Commons, based on what the Duke of Wellington referred to as a 'blackguard combination' consisting of Irish liberals, Leaguers, Whigs and Protectionists, succeeded in defeating the government on the second reading of the Bill by 292 : 219 votes.

Peel decided against appealing to the country in a general election and resigned on 29 June 1846. His administration was replaced by a Whig government headed by Lord John Russell. The leadership of the Conservative Party was shared between the Earl of Derby in the House of Lords and Lord George Bentinck in the House of Commons.

Whigs

Disunity in the Whig-led coalition was evident following the 1841 election. In the House of Commons the Party was divided into Whigs and moderate radicals (who looked to Russell for leadership), the ultra-radicals (who followed Roebuck) and O'Connell's Irish supporters. There were many differences between these groups, including Russell's opposition to O'Connell's re-launched campaign to repeal the Act of Union (which as has been noted above became increasingly militant and outside his control during the lifetime of this Parliament). Outside Parliament, nonconformist opinion was disappointed by the failure of Melbourne's government to enact legislation in their favour (such as in connection with the Church Rates) and adopted a more militant form of campaigning to further these ends. In Scotland the support of Dissenters was threatened by overtures made by the Whigs towards the Free Church Presbyterians.

Following Melbourne's retirement in October 1842, Lord John Russell became the leader of the Whigs. The Whigs found life in opposition difficult, as they were constantly searching for issues on which to challenge the government yet rarely succeeding in finding one with which to mount a significant attack. However, following Peel's resignation in 1846, Russell became Prime Minister. His government was drawn primarily from the Whigs and included no Peelites, none of whom (despite Russell's overtures) were willing to serve under him.

In office the Whig government enacted an Act for the Administration of the Laws for the Relief of the Poor in England in 1847. The main purpose of this measure was to reconstitute the Poor Law Commission, although it also provided that persons who were married and over 60 years of age would not be compelled to live apart as a condition of receiving relief. Additionally, the 1847 Factory Act (which emanated from a Bill originally introduced by Lord Ashley in January 1846) limited the hours of employment for children and young persons to 10 hours a day (or 58 hours per week). The pupil teacher system (a reform which was proposed by a Committee of the Privy Council which dealt with educational matters) was established in 1846. This involved a measure of state aid for elementary education whereby teaching apprentices were paid from government funds. These pupil teachers would work for five years with a view to subsequently entering teacher training colleges to qualify as proper teachers. This measure was divisive to the Whig-led coalition since many nonconformists supported the voluntary principle and this issue also split the radicals. The government's Irish policy (which included extending the Poor Law to Ireland) was extremely limited in scope, underpinned by a belief that it was the role of landowners rather than of the state to provide for the starving peasantry.

By-elections
A total of 231 by-elections occurred in the 1841–47 Parliament, of which 62 were contested. The Conservatives made a net gain of two, the Liberals a net loss of eight, and others a net gain of six.

Conduct of the Election
Conservatives
Lord George Bentinck's election address to his constituents of King's Lynn (which *The Times* on 27 July 1847 dubbed 'The Protectionist Manifesto') continued the vitriolic attacks made on Peel in the debates on the repeal of the Corn Laws. He argued that the 'alleged' potato disease in Ireland in the autumn of 1845 and winter of 1846 had provided Peel with a fraudulent pretext for repealing the Corn Laws, and insisted that the Irish Commissariat's expenditure

evidenced that the provision of food in Ireland was abundant and cheap until June 1846 and thus there had been no need for Parliament to cheapen and augment the supply of food. He argued that Peel's actions on this issue had 'violated every political principle', had dishonestly broken the understanding on which he had been elected, and accused him of 'openly sporting with and disregarding and trampling under foot the rightful authority of the electors of the United Kingdom'. Peel stood accused of having 'lowered the national character and destroyed all confidence in public men'.

Bentinck stated the case for protection. He argued that manufacturing would suffer by a free trade policy which entailed exchanging their best and surest customers at home for the vague chance of new customers abroad and he thus expressed his support for reimposing revenue duties on foreign imports of agricultural and manufactured goods. He argued that the Navigation Laws which left the shipping interest as the last protected one would be the next to be repealed. He also argued the need to reconsider the nation's financial system, stating that the 1844 Bank Charter Act imposed 'mischievous and highly absurd' restrictions on extended credit which was needed to provide for financial prosperity. Other Conservative candidates (such as J. Masterman who was standing in the City of London) also supported the continuance of the Navigation Laws and expressed opposition to what were perceived as the restrictive regulations contained in the Bank Charter Act.

Bentinck also stated his opposition to the endowment of the Roman Catholic Church, although he supported the removal of disabilities affecting Catholics. The endowment of the Catholic Church was raised prominently by Conservative candidates during the campaign (such as Sir T. Ireland who stood in Bewdley and Stourport and Alderman J. Johnson who contested the City of London), thus enabling them to pose as defenders of the Protestant Establishment. Other issues raised during the campaign included the modification of the Poor Laws on grounds which included the extensive centralisation underpinning the legislation, the expense and the patronage it placed in the hands of the government.

Peelites

The policies on which the Peelites contested the election were contained in Peel's election address to his constituents at Tamworth (which was quoted in *The Times* on 17 July 1847). In this he referred to the government's achievements (which in foreign affairs included securing peace in India and improving relations with America). In order to distance himself from the Whigs he restated his opposition to the expropriation of the surplus ecclesiastical revenues of the established Church for secular purposes in any part of the UK, although he indicated support for the repeal of penal statutes relating to religion which were obselete and for the enactment of measures in Ireland which were brought forward 'in a spirit of justice and kindness towards our Roman Catholic fellow subjects in Ireland'. In the latter context he referred approvingly to the 1841 Charitable Donations and Bequests Act, the endowment of new colleges and the increased grant to Maynooth (where he was eager to point out that this was not intended to facilitate the endowment of the Catholic clergy).

In terms of financial and commercial policy, he argued that his government had inherited a budget deficit in excess of £2 million to which it had responded by introducing income tax and lowering duties. Financially these measures were stated to be successful in that they succeeded in transforming the budget deficit into a surplus of revenue over expenditure. He justified the actions he had pursued over the Corn Laws by arguing that events which had occurred in Ireland might subsequently be replicated and thus any temporary suspension would have to be repeated. However, he stated that it was not events in Ireland alone which had prompted him to repeal the Corn Laws. He believed that items of agricultural produce which had been affected by free trade policies previously pursued by his ministry (such as salted and fresh meat, oxen and cows) had not resulted in the extinction of agriculture and there was no reason to assume that the repeal of the Corn Laws would have this effect either since lower duties led to higher consumption. He pledged that his future course of action would be 'to support such measures as are calculated to remove any remaining restrictions on commerce, to abate duties that are levelled for the purposes of protection – to apportion equally the burdens of taxation – and to better the condition of those who labour for their subsistence'.

Further statements of his views were provided in his speech at the nomination of candidates for his Tamworth constituency on 28 July (which was quoted in *The Times* on 29 July). He expressed his support for the preservation of the prerogatives of the monarchy, stated that he wished to see the Church maintained in its legitimate influence, indicated that he wanted the House of Lords in possession of its just authority and expressed opposition to democratic change in the composition of the House of Commons. He argued that he had done no harm to the just interests of the Conservative Party and reiterated his view that the reduction of the duties on agricultural produce would increase consumption by the working class and thus enhance the prosperity of the agriculturalists. He insisted that the repeal of the Corn Laws did not entail sacrificing the landed interest to the commercial and monetary interests but involved rescuing the agricultural interests and conferring great benefits on it. He also stated in this speech that he did not seek to return to office.

Although the Peelites and Whigs agreed on free trade there were differences between the two parties. One of these concerned the Poor Law which (in common with protectionist Conservatives) Peelites wished to see reformed. G. Hudson (who stood as a Peelite Conservative in Lewes) argued the need for reform on the grounds that the existing law was 'unnecessarily cruel and severe, and not calculated to make a labourer an industrious or useful member of society, but a discontented man and a discontented subject' (quoted in *The Times*, 22 July 1847).

Whigs
Whig candidates were supportive of free trade. Baron Rothschild (who stood in the City of London) called for the removal of all unnecessary restrictions on commerce in order to improve prosperity, and G. Thompson (who contested Tower Hamlets) stated himself to be a free trader who was 'opposed to protection, monopoly and all restrictions on trade and commerce'. Some Liberal candidates also discussed political reform. Sir Charles Wood (who fought Halifax) said that while he was not in favour of the Charter he did not endorse the finality of the 1832 measure, and reforms such as the secret ballot, and shorter Parliaments found some support amongst Liberal candidates. Some Liberals (including J. Pattinson in the City of London) expressed their opposition to the endowment of the Catholic Church, although Lord Russell in a speech delivered in his City of London constituency on 20 July 1847 indicated that the Liberal Party had no intention of bringing any such measure before Parliament.

The Whigs also made education an issue in the election. On 20 July 1847 Lord Russell connected the expansion of education with increasing the liberties of the people but stated that he had no wish to interfere with the system of religious education provided in schools funded by public aid.

Result of the Election

A total number of 879 candidates contested the election, with 367 MPs being returned unopposed. The result was:

Party	Votes	Vote %	MPs
Conservative*	194,223	40.2%	285
Liberal	253,376	52.5%	267
Irish Conservative*	11,258	2.4% [34.0%]	40
Repeal Party (Ireland)	14,128	2.9% [43.6%]	36
Irish Liberal	5,935	1.3% [20.2%]	25
Others	3,509	0.7%	3
Total	482,429		656

* Including Peelites

The turnout was 53.4 per cent.

The 'others' were Fergus O'Connor (Nottingham, Chartist) and two Irish MPs, William Smith O'Brien (Limerick) and Anstey Chisholm (Youghal). These were variously categorised as 'Liberal' or 'Irish Confederate'.

The Parties

The provision of state funding to the pupil teacher system harmed Whig candidates in areas where there was strong support for the Voluntarist principle. Russell (one of whose problems was to convince voters that the City of London was an appropriate seat for a Minister of the Crown) required Peelite support to retain his seat but a junior minister, Benjamin Hawes, was defeated at Lambeth. A prominent radical, Roebuck, who supported this legislation was also defeated at Bath. Palmerston, however, fared better in Tiverton where his Chartist opponent, George Harney, failed to win a single vote. Around 100 of the Conservative MPs who were returned were free traders (or Peelite Conservatives).

Scotland, Wales and Ireland

In Scotland, Whig support in Parliament for the Maynooth grant resulted in the formation of an alliance between the United Presbyterians and the newly established Free Church which threatened to influence the outcome of contests in constituencies containing a large number of Free or Voluntary Church voters. Intra-party disputes affecting the Whigs occurred in Glasgow and Edinburgh which led to the defeat of one incumbent Whig MP in Glasgow and the defeat of the Paymaster General, T. B. Macaulay, in Edinburgh by both rival Whig candidates. Overall, the Whigs remained the dominant force in Scottish politics, marginally improving the position obtained in 1841 by winning 33 of the 53 seats, to the 20 won by the Conservatives.

There was little overall change in the position of the two parties in Wales where the Liberals won 12 of the 32 seats and the Conservatives 20. In Ireland the Repeal Party increased its representation to 36 seats, mainly at the expense of the Liberals who were reduced to 25 MPs. The Conservatives won 40 seats and independants secured victory in the remaining two.

Consequence of the Election
Lord Russell formed a Whig government.

6 July – 3 August 1852

Party Leaders
The Earl of Derby (Conservative)
Lord John Russell (Liberal)

Background to the Election
Timing of the Election
A minority Conservative government was formed in early 1852 under Lord Derby. He called an election in the hope that divisions in the Liberal Party would enable the Conservatives to improve their position.

Conservatives
The Conservatives emerged from the 1847 election in a divided state. Around 100 of their MPs (including most who had held ministerial office) were Peelites who would not associate with the remainder of the Party who were protectionists. Peel refused to organise his followers as a party, and the vitality of the protectionists was hindered by the absence of leadership in the House of Commons. Bentinck died in September 1848 but his claim to leadership had already been prejudiced when he offended his followers by voting in support of the reform of the oath each MP was required to swear 'on the true faith of a Christian'. This barred Jews from becoming MPs and emerged as an issue following the election of de Rothschild for the City of London in 1847. Following Bentinck's death, a triumvirate briefly led the Party in the House of Commons, but Benjamin Disraeli became accepted as the party's leader in that House. The inability of the Conservatives to form a government following Russell's defeat on a Private Members' motion to promote electoral reform in 1851 convinced him that to hold office it was necessary for the Party to abandon publicly the principle of protection.

Following the government's defeat in February 1852 (which is referred to below), Derby formed a Conservative government. Disraeli offered Palmerston the leadership of the House of Commons if he would join the new government, but Palmerston would not join a government which was not fully committed to free trade. This refusal limited Derby's choice of ministers. A very inexperienced ministerial team was formed, with Disraeli taking the post of Chancellor of the Exchequer. A late burst of legislation resulted in the Royal Assent being given by commission to 96 Bills on 30 June 1852.

Peelite Conservatives
Peel's one hundred or so supporters (who were variously referred to as 'Peelite' or 'Liberal-Conservatives') held the balance of power in the new Parliament and theoretically provided an alternative focus for the rallying of Liberal forces. However, Peel refused to give any leadership to them and thereby made a significant contribution to the suspended animation of the party system (Conacher, 1958: 431). However, he gave the Whigs general support when they sought to defend free trade against a revival of feeling in favour of protection against agricultural

imports when agricultural prices fell towards the end of the 1840s. In February 1850 the votes of Peel and 27 of his supporters were crucial in saving the Whig government from defeat on a protectionist motion put forward by Disraeli (which was lost by 273 : 252 votes). Peel also supported the Liberal repeal of the Navigation Laws in 1849 and was consulted by the government on financial matters, especially the 1847 commercial crisis, and on Irish affairs. He died on 2 July 1850, as the result of a freak riding accident.

Liberals

The early achievements of the government included the enactment of the 1848 Public Health Act which established a Board of Health. The designation 'Liberal' as opposed to 'Whig-Radical' was first used by *The Times* newspaper in 1846 as a description of the disparate groups which formed the Whig-led coalition whose origins predate 1832. Although the term 'Whig' was also used in connection with the party designation of Russell's government (Crosby, 1976: 157–8) the change of name (which was widely adopted by MPs who followed Russell in 1847) was significant. Following reform in 1832, the Whigs had become increasingly dependent on the support of urban and industrial Britain, and the name 'Liberal' implied a clear attempt to break with the past and identify with the beliefs and aspirations of these voters. Although opposition to agricultural protection and support for free trade were not exclusively identified with the Liberal Party after 1846 (since they were also endorsed by Peel's Conservative supporters) they would eventually become key Liberal policies. Free trade provided the Party with a semblance of unity, securing the acquiescence of Whig landowners and binding together radicals and nonconformists (whose support for free trade was based upon a mixture of economic self-interest and moral indignation against the power wielded by entrenched vested interests). The subsequent strength of the Liberal Party was founded on its ability to identify free trade with the optimism of Victorian England, based upon constant material progress, and the inexperience of the Conservatives in office which made it possible to associate them with incompetence, extravagence and corruption.

It is, however, important not to overstate the unity of the coalition led by Russell after 1846. Outside Parliament many nonconformists remained unhappy with any form of state aid to education (as had been introduced by the establishment of the pupil teacher system in 1846) and campaigned outside Parliament for the disestablishment of the Church of England. Although the Liberals benefited from the demise of the Repeal Party in Ireland (since most of its members affiliated themselves with the Liberals), they adopted a critical view of the government's Irish policy. In 1848 eight Irish Liberal MPs voted against the suspension of *habeas corpus* and the following year 24 rebelled. Russell lacked a reliable majority in the House of Commons throughout his period of government and the issue of electoral reform evidenced a division between Whigs and radicals in the late 1840s. In June 1848 Joseph Home's motion calling for household suffrage, the secret ballot, triennial Parliaments and equal electoral districts (termed the 'little Charter') was defeated by 351 : 84 votes in the House of Commons. Support for this motion occurred against the background of concern within the Party regarding government financial policy. A financial crisis occurred soon after the 1847 election which hindered the further pursuit of free trade measures as the government could not afford the loss of revenue derived from tariffs. This led it to renew income tax in 1848 and to consider increasing the rate of this tax, in part to finance a Militia Bill in response to the fear of a French invasion. Although radicals were divided as to whether electoral reform or financial reform underpinned by rigorous retrenchment in the budget for the army and navy to enable customs duties to be lowered should be regarded as the priority objective, this episode demonstrated the existence of a considerable level of unhappiness within the Whig-led coalition towards the policies of Russell's government and his leadership of it.

Russell's position as leader was threatened by the existence of the Peelites (who provided an alternative source of leadership to the Liberal coalition) and also from Viscount Palmertson. Palmerston was a former Tory who viewed himself as the heir to the principles of foreign policy associated with Canning. This entailed keeping Britain aloof from entanglements in Europe and using this freedom to promote Britain as the champion of liberty and freedom abroad (provided that this did not conflict with the nation's interests). In practice the objective of opposing forces of tyranny abroad could be translated into a crude form of xenophobia directed at smaller nations who had offended British sensibilities (as with the case of Don Pacifico in 1850 when gunboats were despatched to Greece to coerce them into paying for the damage to the property of a Portuguese merchant whose Britishness derived from having been born in Gibraltar). However, Palmerston's defence of his actions (*civis Britannus sum*), which imbued British citizens with rights formerly associated with those of the ancient Romans, was popular to many within Parliament associated with the Liberal coalition and also to public opinion in the country. Palmertson built on this by using the press to cultivate a good image of himself.

The problems which faced Russell prompted him to search for an issue which would cement the alliance back together again under his undisputed leadership. He believed that opposition to the Pope Pius IX's proposal to re-establish a diocesan structure for the Roman Catholic Church in England would provide such a unifying issue and would further serve to marginalise leading Peelite contenders for the leadership of a Liberal coalition (in particular Gladstone and Herbert, both of whom were High Churchmen tainted with the suspicion of being crypto-Catholics). In November 1850 he published his 'Durham Letter' to the Bishop of Durham in which he condemned this suggestion in uncompromising terms. Subsequently the government put forward an Ecclesiastical Titles Bill which forbade Catholic bishops to adopt English territorial titles. However, this ploy did not work since many radicals were unhappy with this display of religious intolerance towards Catholics and it infuriated his Irish supporters who viewed this as an infringement of religious liberty. A group of these, led by George Henry Moore, formed themselves into the 'Irish Brigade' (or, according to its enemies, 'the Pope's Brass Band'). Thirty-nine Irish Liberal MPs voted against the first reading of the Ecclesiastical Titles Bill and 48 opposed its second reading. Subsequently they consistently voted against the government on any issue where they felt there was a chance of defeating it and thus prevent the passage of this Bill.

Other divisions within the Party arose in connection with electoral reform. This culminated in the passing of a motion against the wishes of the government proposed by Peter Locke King in February 1851 to equalise the borough and country franchises. Russell's promise in the debate to bring forward an electoral reform bill the following year was unable to save the government.

Russell's defeat on this issue resulted in a hiatus in government which indicated the confused state of the political parties. Russell resigned, but Stanley was unable to form a Conservative administration. The Queen and Prince Albert favoured a Whig–Peelite government, but the Peelites refused to serve with the Whigs because of their objections to the Ecclesiastical Titles measure. Accordingly, Russell returned as Prime Minister because there was no other person who could be found to replace him (Woodward, 1962: 163).

On his return to office, improved economic circumstances permitted the government to lower the duties on timber, coffee, tobacco and paper, although income tax was renewed for a further period of one year (the Chancellor, Sir Charles Wood, proposing a three-year extension). An amended version of the Ecclesiastical Titles Bill was enacted and Russell also put forward an electoral reform measure. However, the key issue which subsequently emerged was Russell's sacking of Palmerston as Foreign Secretary in December 1851 when he somewhat prematurely voiced his approval of the *coup d'état* in France which led to the accession of Louis Napoleon Bonaparte. This event raised the spectre of a French invasion which Russell proposed to meet with the formation of local militias. He wished those appointed to be chosen by ballot with no ability for those chosen to employ substitutes to act on their behalf. Palmerston, however, wished the militia to be chosen on the basis of voluntary service without any recourse to the ballot unless sufficient men failed to come forward (which was unlikely to happen). On 20 February 1852 sufficient Conservative protectionists supported his proposal to defeat the government and thus provide Palmerston with his 'tit for tat' with Russell. His place was taken by a minority Conservative government headed by the Earl of Derby.

By-elections
A total of 172 by-elections occurred during the 1847–52 Parliament, of which 73 were contested. The Conservatives made a net gain of one seat, the Liberals a net gain of seven and others a net loss of eight.

Conduct of the Election
A Liberal victory looked likely at the outset of the contest. On 25 June 1852 *The Times* alluded to the outcome of the election being a foregone conclusion and later (on 5 July) argued that the contest was not a serious one. The election took place against the background of disorder which occurred in Stockport between Protestants and Catholics and witnessed attacks on Catholic churches and property. The mayor was required to summon troops in order to restore order.

Conservatives
The Times on 29 June 1852 pointed to a key problem facing the Conservative campaign which was that, although Derby's Cabinet veered heavily towards protection, they did not overtly advocate it since the policy lacked popular support. However, they had no alternative to offer in its place. Nonetheless, the National Committee for the Protection of Industry and Capital throughout the British Empire issued an address (which was published in *The Times* on 6 July 1852) which called for the return of candidates pledged to support Lord Derby's government. Some Conservatives openly advocated the case for providing protection for the agricultural industry. R. Christopher (who was elected for North Lincolnshire) argued that it was unfair that manufacturing benefited from protection whereas agriculture, he alleged, did not. He also blamed changes affecting protection for the agricultural industry as being responsible for the

decline in the rents which land was now able to attract. In his view, protection should be re-invigorated as it constituted a tax on the foreigner. W. Dunscombe (who was elected for East Retford and Bassetlaw) argued that abrogation of duties which formerly regulated the import of foreign corn had hit the agricultural interest hard and called on Parliament to mitigate and remove these injuries.

Many Conservative candidates attempted to whip up anti-Catholic hysteria in order to secure support. Support for the integrity of the Protestant Church and opposition to the Maynooth grant and alleged papal aggression were often cited to achieve this aim. R. Christopher expressed his opposition to any measure (including the 1829 Act concerned with Catholic emancipation) which was designed to benefit Catholics because, in his opinion, the Catholic religion was antagonistic to the Protestant institutions of the United Kingdom. He further expressed his disapproval of the influence which O'Connell had exerted on previous Liberal governments and of Russell's actions (when in office) of seeking to establish diplomatic ties with the Pope.

Some Conservative candidates also sought to praise the achievements of Lord Derby's government. R. Christopher referred to legal reforms affecting Chancery and Common Law, the grant of free institutions to some of Britain's colonies and the completion of treaties with a number of nations which were designed to aid the suppression of the slave trade.

Liberals

Free trade was the key election issue. Liberal unity was aided by the Conservative attitude towards protection for agriculture. The Liberals exploited concerns that a Conservative govern-ment would reintroduce the Corn Laws and this enabled Whigs, nonconformists and radicals to unite in support of free trade (which eclipsed the education issue which had cost the Whigs support in the previous election). Palmerston's speech at the nomination of candidates for his constituency of Tiverton on 7 July emphasised that this election would finally determine the issue of 'protection or no protection', although in his view this matter had been settled some time ago. He stated that protection entailed taxing the food of the many in the interests of the few and believed that Britain had not experienced the revolutions which occurred elsewhere in Europe in 1848 because the people were convinced that Parliament was capable of rising above sectional interest and acting in the public good. Other Liberals wished to develop free trade. Sir James Graham (who was elected for Carlisle) urged free trade to be extended to cover articles which incuded tobacco, soap and paper and Lord Stuart (who successfully contested Marylebone) called for the establishment of a universal system of free trade. His running mate in that contest, Sir Benjamin Hall, argued that a Tory free trader was 'a man who was a protec-tionist, but had not the moral courage or honesty of his convictions', and asserted that Lord Derby would impose a tax on food were the Conservatives returned to office. Some Liberal candidates argued in favour of the further repeal of the Navigation Laws in connection with coastal trade.

Religious issues also entered into the Liberal campaign, evidencing some divisions in the Liberal ranks. Palmerston's speech on 7 July expressed his opposition to revoking the Maynooth grant but T. Duncombe (who was elected for Finsbury) stated his disapproval of all religious grants and endowments made by the state, including Maynooth. G. Scorell (who was defeated at Southwark) contented himself by indicating his opposition to all future endowments for religious purposes.

Diverse views on political reform were made by Liberals during the election. Palmertson's speech on 7 July expressed support for 'a gradual steady improvement' of political institutions; he disapproved of 'rashly and hastily overturning those institutions under which the country had long flourished and prospered'. In particular, he stated his opposition to political reforms which included annual Parliaments and the secret ballot, arguing that 'I hold that the right of voting is a trust reposed in the elector for the public good … and I say that any trust reposed in a man for the public good ought to be performed in public'. Lord D. Stuart, however, declared his support for the secret ballot. G. Scorell, while rejecting both universal suffrage and annual Parliaments, stated his agreement to shorter Parliaments and proposed that all householders and lodgers who contributed to the relief of the poor should be enfranchised.

Some Liberal candidates also spoke of financial and taxation reform. Lord D. Stuart attacked the income tax and declared his support instead for the property tax. He also wished to see the reduction of taxes to the benefit of the middle and working classes. Sir J. Duke (who was elected for the City of London) alluded to the way in which income tax fell unfairly on the trading classes. G. Scorell, who also opposed the income tax and supported the property tax, stated his approval for an investigation into the introduction of a land tax.

Result of the Election

A total number of 953 candidates contested the election, with 255 MPs being returned unopposed. The result was:

Party	Votes	Vote %	MPs
Conservative*	249,809	33.6%	290
Liberal	360,387	48.4%	261
Irish Liberal**	70,495	9.5% [53.7%]	63
Irish Conservative*	61,672	8.3% [46.3%]	40
Other	1,541	0.2%	0
Total	743,904		654

* Including Peelites
** Including over 40 MPs associated with the Irish Brigade

The turnout was 57.9 per cent.

The Parties

The Conservatives marginally improved their position in England compared to 1847 in terms of seats won. Conservative willingness to exploit anti-Catholic sentiments was one factor which harmed the Peelites who, although continuing to hold the balance of power, were reduced to around 45 MPs. As in 1847, the Liberals trailed the Conservatives in both England and Wales in terms of seats won but remained the dominant party in Scotland.

Scotland, Wales and Ireland

The Maynooth grant remained a key issue in Scottish politics ensuring the continuance of the alliance of United Presbyterians and followers of the Free Church which posed a threat to Liberal candidates in burgh constituencies. Overall, however, the respective standing of the two parties was unchanged from the position in 1847: the Whigs won 33 of the 53 seats seats and the Conservatives 20. The position in Wales was, as in Scotland, unchanged from the previous general election. The Conservatives won 20 seats and the Liberals 12.

Irish politics were affected by O'Connell's death in Genoa in 1847 whilst on a pilgrimage to Rome, although the initiative in the repeal movement had already passed to the more militant Young Ireland movement, and especially William Smith O'Brien. As is referred to above, the 'Durham letter' resulted in the formation of the 'Irish Brigade'. This sought to establish grass roots support in the constituencies by organising the Catholic Defence Association of Great Britain and Ireland. In August 1851 the Brigade and the United Tenants' League entered into an alliance. It returned in excess of 40 MPs, which gave them and the Liberals a combined strength of 63 seats. The Conservatives won the remaining 40 seats.

Consequence of the Election

As is referred to in more detail in the 1857 entry, the Conservative government decided to test its support in the new House of Commons. It resigned following the defeat of its budget proposals.

26 March – 20 April 1857

Party Leaders
The Earl of Derby (Conservative)
Viscount Palmerston (Liberal)

Background to the Election
Timing of the Election
The election was brought about by the Liberal government's parliamentary defeat with regard to its policy in connection with China. Richard Cobden moved a resolution 'That this House has heard with concern of the conflicts which have occurred between British and Chinese authorities in the Canton River, and, without expressing an opinion as to the extent to which the government of China may have afforded this country cause of complaint respecting the non-fulfilment of the Treaty of 1842, this House considers that the papers which have been laid upon the table fail to establish satisfactorily grounds for the violent measures resorted to at Canton in the late affair of the Arrow.' The motion was passed by 263 : 247 votes on 3 March 1857 and the government sought an immediate dissolution of Parliament.

Electoral Procedures and Practices
The 1854 Corrupt Practices Act required an audit of accounts payable by candidates and defined a number of corrupt practices which included intimidation of voters. However, this measure did not end either direct or indirect bribery.

Conservatives
Following the 1852 election, the Conservative Party lacked an overall majority in the House of Commons. Its downfall was caused by Gladstone's attack on Disraeli's 1852 budget. This sought to compensate the landed interest for the abandonment of protection by cutting the malt tax and, additionally, the shipping interest was relieved of some financial burdens. The loss of revenue was made up by extending income tax to earned income of £100 per year and unearned income of £50 per year and by extending the house tax to cover houses of £10 rateable value. Whigs, radicals and also Peelites united to defeat this budget in December 1852 which led to the resignation of the government. Disraeli believed that the Conservatives needed to secure support from the urban voters, but, out of office, Derby provided the Party with poor leadership.

Liberals
Following the downfall of the Conservative government in December 1852, a coalition was formed under Lord Aberdeen. This was significant in that it brought the Peelites (who took the lion's share of Cabinet appointments) into the Whig-led coalition and constituted the basis of the Liberal Party (which at this stage, however, remained very much in an embryo state).

Gladstone's budgets constituted the main aspect of domestic policy pursued by the new government. He continued with Peel's free trade policy by reducing duties on most partially manufactured goods and foodstuffs and lowering duties on most manufactured goods. Although his inclination was to phase out income tax (the government in 1853 having laid down the principle of progressively reducing it until its projected abolition in 1860), the Crimean War forced Gladstone to raise it.

The main international issue facing Aberdeen's government was the war with Russia which commenced in 1854. Although this could be viewed as compatible with Palmerston's foreign policy (whereby Britain was coming to the aid of a weak Turkey which was being bullied by a despotic Russian Tsar who was bent on expansionism at the expense of the Ottoman Empire), news of the total mismanagement of the war caused the government to lose popularity. The Cabinet's refusal to appoint a committee of inquiry into allegations of mismanagement prompted Russell's resignation. On 29 January 1855 a censure motion on the government's inept handling of the military expedition to the Crimea (which was proposed by the Radical MP, Roebuck) easily passed the House of Commons by 305 : 148 votes.

The subsequent resignation of the government produced protracted negotiations to find a successor. The Queen sent for Derby. Disraeli again offered Palmerston the leadership of the House of Commons if he would join the new government, but his refusal prompted Derby to decline the chance of forming a Conservative administration. The Queen therefore turned to Russell, but he had insufficient support to assume office. Accordingly, Palmerston was sent for; although a member of the Aberdeen government, he had served as Home Secretary and was thus not directly implicated in the affairs which occurred in the Crimea. Initially he was able to keep the embryonic Liberal Party afloat but the thorny issue of a committee of inquiry into the management of the Crimean War torpedoed these fragile arrangements. Palmerston realised that the nation expected an investigation of this nature, and his insistence on establishing a committee led to the leading Peelites (Gladstone, Graham and Herbert) resigning since leading members of this group had held offices which were directly associated with the military arrangements of the Crimean War. This decision made it possible for Russell to rejoin the government which, devoid of leading Peelites, was distinctly Whig in character. However, revelations in July 1855 that Russell (who had served as British plenipotentiary at the Vienna Peace Conference) had been willing to grant an overly-generous peace settlement to Russia caused him to resign.

The government's main achievement was to end the Crimean War in 1856. Concessions secured by Britain by the Treaty of Paris (which included the exclusion of the Russian fleet from the Black Sea) could be depicted as triumphs. The extent to which Palmerston had consolidated his control over the diverse groups in the Liberal coalition was displayed in response to a Conservative censure motion regarding the surrender of the fortress of Kars in Armenia shortly before the war had ended. This was rebuffed by 303 : 176 votes with most members of the Liberal groups voting in support of Palmerston.

However, Palmerston's control of the Liberal coalition was not absolute. Opposition from Peelites, radicals, the 'Irish Brigade' (and also from Russell) frequently harried Palmerston's government and eventually (as has been stated above) brought it down with a motion condemning the government's reaction when a vessel, the *Arrow*, which flew the British flag, had British registration and was commanded by a British citizen, was attacked by the Chinese and its crew were taken away. Retaliation by British civil and naval personnel ultimately resulted in the bombardment of Canton by British naval forces in what became called the second war with China. This resulted in the resignation of this government in March 1857 and the dissolution of Parliament.

By-elections
A total of 218 by-elections occurred in the 1852–57 Parliament, of which 98 were contested. The Liberals made a net gain of 13, the Conservatives a net loss of 12 and others a net loss of one.

Conduct of the Election
Some contemporaries viewed the entire election as a contest revolving around Palmerston: Shaftesbury proclaimed that there was 'no measure, no principle, no cry ... simply were you, or were you not ... for Palmerston' and *The Times* declared on 23 March 1857 that the Liberals were putting forward a single name rather than a platform. Although factors other than Palmerston's personality were important to the outcome of the election (including the end of the Crimean War which enabled income tax to be reduced and improved prosperity in rural areas) it is clear that Palmerston occupied an important role.

Conservatives
The policies on which the Conservatives contested the election were outlined by Lord Derby in his speech on the second reading of the Income Tax Bill in the House of Lords on 16 March 1857, much of which consisted of negative attacks on the government.

He stated his belief that income tax was only justifiable in time of war and accused the government of breaking its pledge which was announced in 1853 to abolish this tax by 1860. He sought to equate Palmerston's foreign policy with high spending and argued that the level of government spending on warlike establishments was determined by its foreign policy and that Palmerston's perceived need to intervene militarily in the internal affairs of other countries in response to any petty quarrel, regardless of whether the interests of British subjects were affected, made it necessary to keep these establishments on a permanent war footing with consequential high costs.

In response to the emphasis that Palmerston placed on the government's China policy and the manner in which the government was brought down by a 'base and infamous coalition', he asserted that the Conservatives had intended to bring forward their own motion regarding China policy in the House of Commons but Cobden had beaten them to it, and the Party had no option other than to vote in accordance with their views on this subject. Derby pointed out that the Conservatives had not pursued a policy of opposition for opposition's sake in the House of Commons and on one occasion (concerning Locke King's motion to extend the franchise) had actually come to the government's rescue to save it from defeat. He accused the government of using the issue of China in order to provoke a quarrel from which it might politically benefit, by enabling it to dissolve on what might be seen as a favourable election issue.

Other issues which were raised by Lord Derby in this speech included Palmerston's ecclesiastical appointments (which he believed did not reflect all sections within the Church of England). Disraeli's election address to his constituents of Buckinghamshire (quoted in *The*

Times on 19 March 1857) accused Palmerston of being a Tory chief of a radical Cabinet, and 'with no domestic policy he is obliged to divert the attention of the people from the consideration of their own affairs to the distraction of foreign politics'. He argued that 'his external system is turbulent and aggressive that his rule at home may be tranquil and unassailed'. He also accused the government of incurring excessive expenditure which resulted in heavy taxation and the cessation of all social improvement.

Liberals

The main issues guiding the Liberal campaign were contained in Palmerston's election address to his constituents at Tiverton. He argued that the government's claim for re-election rested on its courage in taking office in the middle of the Crimean War which it then brought to a successful military conclusion and the procuring of a peace treaty which accomplished the war's main objectives. Peace enabled the 'war portion' of income tax to be removed at the beginning of the present session of Parliament. His address also pointed to other successful aspects of foreign policy, including improved relations with America.

His election address vigorously defended his actions in China which he placed at centre stage of his attempt to secure re-election. He argued that 'an insolent barbarian wielding authority in Canton had violated the British flag, broken the engagement of Treaties, offered rewards for the heads of British subjects in that part of China and planned their destruction by murder, assassination and poisons'. However, when British civil and naval personnel retaliated, 'a combination of political parties, not till this last session united' succeeded in passing a censure motion in the House of Commons. He condemned the actions of those who were party to this combination and suggested it implied that, in their view, the British government should have apologised and offered compensation to the Chinese. Thus, he regarded the issue which the election should determine as being whether British people 'would give their support to men who have thus endeavoured to make the humiliation and degradation of this country the stepping stone to power' (*The Times*, 24 March 1857).

In his address, he stated that the government's foreign policy was to secure peace abroad with honour and safety and to maintain national rights and security for fellow countrymen who resided in foreign lands. His statements of domestic policies were vague. He advocated 'a judicious and well-regulated economy, the progressive improvement of the welfare of the nation, the continued diffusion of education among the people and reforms which, from time to time, may be required by changes of circumstances and by the increasing growth of intelligence'.

Many of these issues were elaborated in his speech at Tiverton on 27 March 1857 accepting his unopposed re-election. He depicted himself as the defender of the 'honour, the dignity, the interests and the fair fame of England'. He rejected the accusation that he had pursued a 'turbulent and aggressive policy' towards China and instead accused the Conservatives of having pursued partisan politics over this issue. He again refused to be drawn into giving any specific pledges on domestic issues, but said that while he accepted the need for economy he would not prejudice the nation's security.

Result of the Election

A total of 860 candidates contested the election, with 328 returned unopposed. The result was:

Party	Votes	Vote %	MPs
Liberal	314,708	55.7%	306
Conservative*	157,974	27.9%	245
Irish Conservative*	35,258	6.2% [38.9%]	53
Irish Liberal	57,409	10.2% [61.1%]	50
Others	151	0.0%	0
Total	565,500		654

* Including Peelites

The turnout was 58.9 per cent.

The Parties

A significant aspect of the Liberal Party's performance was the gain of 23 seats in the English counties (as the result of which the Party held 52 of the 144 seats in this category). The Party's recovery in these constituencies was much aided by the prosperity enjoyed in agricultural areas, which offset the antagonism towards the Party for its part in the repeal of the Corn Laws. Additionally, the Liberals polled well in the smaller English boroughs (with below 1,000 electors) and held 120 of the 198 seats. Defeats were inflicted on leading radical critics of the government, including Cobden, Bright and Thomas Milner Gibson, and the Peelites were reduced to a rump of around 25 MPs (Jenkins,1994: 86). Lord Russell (who had initially been excluded by the London Registration from the list of names they put forward for nomination as candidates for the City of London constituency) was, however, able to secure re-election.

Scotland, Wales and Ireland

The alliance between the United Presbyterians and the Free Church disintegrated, mainly in connection with education: the United Presbyterians were voluntarists but the Free Church was willing to accept parochial schools being funded from the rates. This situation was to the advantage of the Liberals which secured domination over Scottish politics by winning 40 of the 53 seats. The Conservatives won the remaining 13. In Wales, the Liberal Party improved upon its performance in 1852 and won 15 of the 32 seats, but the Conservatives remained the major party with victories in 17 constituencies. In Ireland, two MPs associated with the 'Irish Brigade' (William Keogh and Jophn Sadleir) accepted office in Aberdeen's government. This organisation (and the Tenants' League) and was officially wound up in 1859 when most of its members returned to the Liberal Party. At the election the Liberals lost ground compared to 1852, and the Conservatives won a small majority (53) of the 103 seats with the Liberals winning the remaining 50.

Consequence of the Election

Lord Palmerston formed a Liberal government.

28 April – 20 May 1859

Party Leaders
The Earl of Derby (Conservative)
Viscount Palmerston (Liberal)

Background to the Election
Timing of the Election
The election occurred following a Conservative government defeat on 31 March 1859 on an electoral reform Bill. (This is discussed more fully below.)

Electoral Procedures and Practices
An Act to abolish the property qualification for MPs was passed in 1858.

Conservatives
The relative disinterest of Palmerston's government in domestic issues was not exploited by the Conservatives. Derby failed to provide any lead and many Conservatives distrusted Disraeli. However, the downfall of Palmerston's government resulted in the Conservatives taking office under Lord Derby. Gladstone was offered a ministerial post, but he declined.

Disraeli's main preoccupation in government was with the issue of franchise reform. He proposed that county and borough qualifications should be equalised. This would be coupled with special franchises to give the vote to the 'upper working class' and a limited measure of redistribution in favour of the larger unrepresented towns and highly populated county areas. However, while Gladstone was willing to give his support to this measure, the radicals were opposed to it as it failed to make any significant improvement on the extent of working-class enfranchisement. A measure to promote electoral reform by lowering the borough qualification was put to the House of Commons on 31 March 1859 but its proposals were so timid that all Liberals were able to 'unite in contemptuous rejection' of them (Jenkins, 1994: 88). A critical motion by Lord Russell which condemned what he regarded as the measure's worst features was carried by 39 and the government promptly resigned.

Liberals
In office, Palmerston concentrated on foreign affairs and domestic issues received far less attention. He did not initially attempt to further the development of the Liberal Party and neither did he give a lead on pressing policy issues. One of these was franchise reform. Although an opponent of the secret ballot, he was not opposed to a wider franchise embracing the most intelligent members of the working class. However, he did not seek to further this reform and failed to bring forward any proposals to achieve this end. Neither did he offer any lead on administrative reform, the importance of which had been highlighted by administrative deficiencies affecting the conduct of the war in the Crimea.

Foreign affairs proved to be the government's undoing. An attempt by the Italian revolutionary, Orsini, to assassinate Emperor Napoleon III in 1858 resulted in the government amending the law of conspiracy by introducing the Conspiracy to Murder Bill which covered the situation of foreign refugees plotting assassination attempts in Britain which were carried out abroad. However, this opened him to the accusation of pandering to the French and an alliance of Conservatives, Peelites, radicals, and Russell ensured the government's defeat on what opponents dubbed 'The French Colonels Bill' by 234 : 215 in 1858. Rather than ask for a vote of confidence (which he would probably have won), Palmerston resigned and was replaced in February 1858 by a Conservative government headed by Lord Derby. The subsequent conduct of the Liberals was adversely affected by the poor relationship between Palmerston and Russell and the disinclination of the radicals to accept Palmerston's leadership in particular because they disliked his views on electoral reform. These divisions enabled Derby's government to survive in office for around 15 months.

By-elections
Ninety by-elections occurred in the 1857–59 Parliament, of which 24 were contested. The Conservatives made a net gain of five seats, the Liberals a net loss of four and others a net loss of one.

Conduct of the Election

The election took place against the background of tension in Europe which was concerned with the issue of Italian independence. Emperor Napoleon III of France was supportive of freeing Italy from Austrian control, hoping that this would enable him to acquire Savoy and Nice for France. In July 1858 a secret treaty was concluded between the Emperor and Count Cavour (Piedmont's leading statesman), and it was widely believed in diplomatic circles that war between France and Austria was imminent in 1859. This eventually broke out in April 1859 and was ended in July by the Treaty of Villafranca.

Conservatives
The Conservatives mounted a weak campaign which was primarily centred on foreign affairs. In his speech delivered at the Mansion House on 25 April, Derby emphasised the delicate nature of the situation in Europe, perhaps in the hope that this would induce voters to support the status quo in government at such a delicate time. He informed his listeners of attempts which had been made by his government to mediate between the French and Austrian emperors (which entailed sending Lord Cowley to Vienna in February 1859). He stated that subsequently his government had supported the proposal of the Russian Emperor for a Congress of the Great European Powers to be held to consider the issues which were causing friction, but this came to grief when Austria refused to agree to Piedmont's participation and instead despatched an ultimatum to Piedmont to disarm within three days or face the prospect of an Austrian invasion. Although Derby sought to emphasise the efforts taken by his government to avert war in Europe, his government's stance was adversely affected by the widespread belief that it was favourably disposed towards Austria. This position became unpopular following that country's ultimatum to Piedmont which made war inevitable.

Very little was said by Conservatives about domestic reform, even though the issue of electoral reform had brought about the government's downfall. Some Conservatives viewed the ousting of Derby's administration as a cynical party manoeuvre.

Liberals

Liberals criticised the Conservative decision to hold an election in the midst of an international crisis. In his speech at the nomination of candidates for his constituency of Tiverton on 29 April, Palmerston pointed out that there was no need for an election since the negative vote which had been delivered by the House of Commons was a decision on that measure and should not have been treated as a vote of confidence. He pointed out that, when defeated on the Conspiracy to Murder Bill, he had resigned without asking for Parliament to be dissolved. He further argued that as Derby's government was a minority one, it had never enjoyed the confidence of the House in any case.

Liberals also discussed electoral reform. Palmerston, in his speech on 29 April, stated that Liberals objected to the measure brought forward by Derby's government on the grounds that he proposed to disqualify the county freeholders whose freeholds lay within the limits of a borough and for failing to lower the existing borough franchise which thus continued to exclude the experienced and intelligent members of the working class from the franchise. In answer to questions which were put to him he refused, however, to provide any precise details of a measure which he would propose but indicated his support for lowering both the borough and county franchises and for providing a limited redistribution of seats in favour of populous areas. A similar line was taken by other Liberal candidates. J. Montcrieff (who was elected for Edinburgh) argued that the measure of Derby's government was retrograde in that it was designed to increase the power of the landed aristocracy and diminish the influence possessed by the 'popular elements' by proposals which included disfranchising the 40 shilling freeholder in the counties and replacing it with a £10 occupancy qualification. However, while there was a reasonable amount of unanimity by Liberal candidates regarding the desirability of extending the franchise, many remained hesitant on other aspects of electoral reform which they favoured. Although radical Liberals at this election expressed their support for manhood suffrage, the secret ballot, equal electoral districts and annual Parliaments, others were less keen on measures of this nature. E. Cardwell (who was elected for the City of Oxford) expressed reservations about the introduction of a secret ballot and, instead, hoped that the enlargement of constituencies would enhance freedom and purity, thereby rendering this reform an unnecessary one.

Liberals could not avoid mentioning foreign affairs during the course of their campaign. The Party traditionally leaned towards supporting the cause of Italian independence. On 25 April, Palmerston made a speech in his constituency of Tiverton in which he articulated his hope that 'the liberties of Italy will be established on a good foundation' but urged that Britain should preserve a course of strict neutrality in the fighting which was then imminent, unless her own interests became threatened. Later, in a speech delivered on the occasion of the nomination of candidates on 29 April at Tiverton, he accepted that Derby's government had sought to maintain the peace, but criticised ministers for seeking to mediate between France and Austria when neither had accepted Britain performing such a role. He also attempted to capitalise on the widespread condemnation of Austria for its ultimatum to Piedmont by asserting that this action brought about a change of attitude towards Austria by Derby's government, which he attributed to its being misinformed on that country's intentions. Other Liberals echoed these sentiments. Sir De Lacy Evans (who was elected for Westminster) accused the government of having been too favourably disposed towards Austria and argued that its attempts at mediation had been 'vacillating and childish'.

Result of the Election

A total number of 860 candidates contested the election, with 379 MPs being returned unopposed. The result was:

Party	Votes	Vote %	MPs
Liberal	314,708	55.6%	306
Conservative*	157,974	27.9%	245
Irish Conservative*	35,258	6.3% [38.9%]	53
Irish Liberal	57,409	10.2% [61.1%]	50
Others	151	0.0%	0
Total	565,500		654

* Including Peelites

The turnout was 63.7 per cent.

The Parties

The election evidenced the support for the Liberal Party from the financial and commercial middle class which helped them dominate London politics where the Conservatives failed to win a single seat. The Conservative performance in England overall showed a marginal improvement on the results obtained in the 1857 general election. The Conservative campaign was joined by Sir Allan MacNab, the former prime minister of Canada who stood (unsuccessfully) in Brighton. He was, as *The Times* commented, 'a Tory candidate of an uncommon stamp'.

Scotland, Wales and Ireland

The Liberals remained the dominant party in Scottish politics, winning 40 of the 53 seats. The Conservatives won the remaining 13. The position in Wales was unchanged from the 1857 general election. The Conservatives won 17 of the 32 seats and the Liberals 15. In Ireland the parties emerged from the election on more or less equal footing. The Conservatives won 53 of the 103 seats and the Liberals 50.

Consequence of the Election

The Conservatives increased their representation by around 30 seats in the House of Commons, but lacked an overall majority. Disraeli sought to bolster the Conservatives' position by offering Palmerston office, which he refused. The outcome of the election encouraged the warring groups in the Liberal alliance to end their differences and a meeting was held in Willis's tea rooms on 6 June 1859. All groups were able to find common ground in support of the creation of an independent Italian state in Northern Italy, an issue on which the Conservatives had expressed no clear views during the election, and agreed to support a motion of no confidence in the Conservative government. This meeting is sometimes regarded as the date of the official formation of the Liberal Party. Disraeli was subsequently defeated on the Queen's Speech by 323 : 310 votes on 10–11 June 1859 (which is discussed more fully in the 1865 entry). The Queen then sent for Lord Granville, but his inability to compromise the competing claims of Palmerston and Russell for leadership in the House of Commons made it impossible for him to construct a government. Accordingly, Palmerston, at the age of 74, became Prime Minister again and the 67-year-old Russell (who was offered any ministry he wished) went to the Foreign Office.

10 July – 29 July 1865

Party Leaders
The Earl of Derby (Conservative)
Viscount Palmerston (Liberal)

Background to the Election
Timing of the Election
The election was a routine request to dissolve Parliament which was approaching the end of its statutory lifespan.

Conservatives
The Conservatives sought to remain in office following the 1859 election but were defeated on the Queen's Speech. The Marquis of Hartington moved an amendment which stated, 'We beg humbly to submit to your Majesty that it is essential for the satisfactory result of our deliberations, and for facilitating the discharge of your Majesty's functions, that your Majesty's government should possess the confidence of this House and of the country: and we deem it our duty respectfully to submit to your Majesty that such confidence is not reposed in the present advisers of your Majesty.' This was passed by 323 : 310 votes in the early hours of 11 June and resulted in the immediate resignation of Lord Derby's government.

The Conservative performance in opposition was weak. The Party faced two key problems after 1859. The first of these was to find a cause with which to challenge the Liberal government. Palmerston's moderation in the conduct of domestic policy made this difficult as he clearly posed no threat to the bedrock Conservative interests of the Church of England, the landed aristocracy or the Crown. Additionally, his foreign policy was generally popular with Conservative voters, although Derby attempted to challenge the government's Italian policy on the grounds that he believed that the issue of the temporal power of the Pope should figure in British policy. A second problem which the Party faced after 1859 was the dislike felt by some Conservative backbenchers towards Disraeli. This made it difficult for the Conservatives to muster their full strength when challenging the government in divisions in the House of Commons. Derby attempted to overcome these problems by focusing on divisions in the Liberal Party and offering support to Palmerston in these internal disputes, especially those with the radicals. However, this strategy failed to accomplish a split in the Liberal Party and was abandoned following the reconciliation of differences between Palmerston and Gladstone over the issue of paper duties in 1861.

Liberals
Palmerston's Liberal government which was formed following the resignation of the Conservative administration had a very aristocratic composition, containing three dukes, the brother of a fourth and five other peers or sons of peers. However, although its composition was sufficiently reflective of divisions within the Party to provide it with subsequent stability, signif-

icant divisions both within the government and the Party subsequently emerged. Initially Gladstone (who occupied the post of Chancellor of the Exchequer) and Palmerston clashed over military spending and fiscal policy, and Palmerston and Russell were in disagreement over electoral reform. Although these disputes became, to a large extent, resolved as the life of the government progressed, Palmerston's relationship with the radicals in his party was more problematic. Palmerston was placed under considerable pressure to prune government spending (James Stansfeld's motion to this effect in 1862 securing the support of 65 MPs) and to introduce a measure of electoral reform (which Palmerston was opposed to doing in the belief that there was no demand in the country for such a measure). Some of these issues are considered in more detail below.

Foreign affairs occupied much of the government's attention. France was seen as a key threat through actions which included the construction of the Suez Canal (which was viewed as a threat to India) and the acquisition of Nice and Savoy following a plebiscite held in 1860. The fear of a French invasion prompted the formation of the volunteer movement to strengthen the nation's home defence capabilities. However, tensions were much defused by the signing of an Anglo–French commercial Treaty (the Reciprocity Treaty) in 1860 which was negotiated by Richard Cobden. The government's preoccupation with the threat to national interests posed by France was in many ways an obsolescent attitude which tended to disregard the threat posed by a resurgent Prussia under the guidance of Bismarck. This was most obviously manifested in the Schleswig-Holstein dispute in 1863 in which the government's failure to cooperate with the French in response to Austrian and Prussian aggression towards Denmark (because they feared an extension of French territory along the Rhine) resulted in the defeat of the Danes and the loss of both Duchies in 1864. Although this was a humiliation for the government, a Conservative censure motion moved by Disraeli on 8–9 July 1864 was defeated when the House of Commons voted to amend it so that it expressed 'satisfaction … that at this conjuncture Her Majesty has been advised to abstain from armed interference in the war now going on between Denmark and the German powers'. This amendment was passed by 313 : 295 votes in the early hours of 9 July, although a censure motion was approved in the House of Lords regarding the government's conduct of this affair.

The government's financial policies were also influenced by the fear of France. Gladstone's 1860 budget included further measures of free trade. These were not controversial, but a separate proposal to abolish the excise duty on paper caused internal divisions within the government and a clash with the House of Lords. Palmerston was opposed to the measure as he viewed it as pandering to the wishes of the radicals for a cheap press and hindering national defence. Thus he did not offer support to Gladstone when the Lords rejected it. Gladstone responded by placing all financial provisions (including the abolition of the paper duty) in one budget measure in 1861 to stop the House of Lords interfering. This budget passed the House of Commons by 15 votes, and by way of compromise Palmerston was able to get the House to agree with his proposal for a programme of naval construction and the building of coastal ports.

The reduction of tensions between France and Britain aided the national finances and helped improve the relationship between Palmerston and Gladstone. Gladstone presided over a period of budget surpluses which enabled him to cut the rate of income tax and lower the tea duty in 1863. The following year he raised the limit of income tax exemption to £200 and cut the duty on sugar. In 1865 he again cut the rate of income tax and lowered the duty on tea still further. Gladstone's tariff cutting policies were successful in boosting government revenue and stimulating economic activity and his policies were attractive both to the business classes and to consumers. Against the background of increased prosperity, he established the Post Office Savings Bank in 1861 to stimulate working-class acceptance of the philosophy of self-help.

Although the personnel of the Parliamentary Liberal Party was heavily drawn from the aristocratic and landed classes, Palmerston's domestic and foreign policies were especially directed at securing support from the business community, in particular the urban financial and commercial middle classes. The government legislation enacted in 1862 (following from a measure passed in 1856) permitted the establishment of joint stock companies with limited liability for shareholders. Some aspects of Palmerston's foreign policy also appealed to this section of society by emphasising the government's willingness to defend the interests of British merchants.

Electoral reform became an increasingly important political issue. Russell's Bill to establish a £10 rating franchise in the counties and lower the borough franchise to £6 rental value was withdrawn on 11 June 1860. Russell's subsequent preoccupation with foreign affairs (and his elevation to the House of Lords as Earl Russell in 1861) ended his active interest in the subject. No further Bill was introduced and economic prosperity tended to divert interest from the topic. However, the issue remained an important issue on the radical agenda which became waged through extra-parliamentary organisations. In 1864 the Manchester-based National Reform Union was set up and, following the visit to Britain of a key leader in the fight for Italian independence, Giuseppe Garibaldi, and in 1864, the National Reform League was formed in 1865 to pursue the campaign for manhood suffrage. In Parliament, a Private Members' Bill to extend the borough franchise was given a second reading in the House of Commons in May 1864. On Palmerston's instructions, Gladstone (who had previously been an opponent of electoral reform) opposed this measure but, in the course of his speech, stated that the present nature of the franchise was not satisfactory and indicated his support for household suffrage.

On the eve of the election, the government suffered a defeat in the House of Commons on the issue of corruption in the appointment of public posts, with specific reference to the Leeds Bankruptcy Court where it was alleged that the Lord Chancellor's son had received a bribe from an applicant seeking promotion. A government motion to adjourn the debate on this topic was lost on 3 July by 177 : 163 votes which led to the resignation of the Lord Chancellor, Lord Westbury.

By-elections
A total of 221 by-elections occurred during the 1859–65 Parliament, of which 102 were contested. The Conservatives made a net gain of 12 seats and the Liberals a net loss of the same number.

Conduct of the Election
It was widely anticipated that the election would not bring about a change of government, and *The Economist* predicted an increased Liberal majority.

Conservatives

The Party's performance in opposition made it difficult for the Conservatives to say little that was constructive in connection with domestic affairs. Disraeli's election address to his constituents at Buckingham depicted the Church of England in a state of siege defended by the Conservative Party. Other Conservatives voiced their support for the key aspects of the Constitution which they defined as the Church, state, House of Lords and hereditary right. Like many Liberals, Conservative candidates felt that the country was not ready for a Reform Bill. Lord Stanley (who was elected for Lynn Regis) broadly agreed with this, arguing that any reform measure which was brought forward would have to be of a moderate character.

Some Conservatives were more vocal in their criticisms of Liberal foreign policy. Lord Ranelagh (who addressed electors in Middlesex) accused the government of sacrificing the honour of the nation in connection with their policy over Denmark and Poland (when the government had failed to place any pressure on Russia for the manner in which it had put down a revolt in Poland in 1863). However, this position was undermined by the unwillingness of Conservatives to declare openly they would have resorted to war to preserve what they regarded as British honour.

Liberals

Palmerston's election address to his constituents at Tiverton (which was quoted in *The Times* on 7 July 1865) emphasised Britain's prosperity, and the Party campaigned on what they regarded as their achievements in connection with economic affairs. It was argued that under the Liberal government taxes and duties had been reduced, material prosperity had been increased, and consumption had risen (which led to additional revenue derived from excise duties). A budget deficit had been transformed into a surplus, government expenditure and the national debt had also been reduced. The country's strong economic position had been sustained despite problems arising from the American Civil War, Ireland and China and the need to ensure that expenditure on the army and navy were maintained at a sufficient level to defend British interests. Some Liberal candidates specifically praised Gladstone's contribution to this happy state of economic affairs, and on 6 July 1865 *The Times* commented that 'with the single exception of Sir Robert Peel, no Finance Minister of modern times can be compared with Mr Gladstone in good fortune or in skill'. He also derived support from the Church for measures which included his introduction of the Post Office Savings Bank on the grounds that it was a counter-attraction to the public house and other forms of waste. In foreign affairs, the main appeal of the Party was that it had kept Britain at peace. E. Cardwell (who was elected for the City of Oxford) fully articulated this feeling in his speech delivered at the nomination of candidates on 11 July when he stated that 'peace has been preserved and ... the dignity, the honour, and the independence of the country have been maintained, and England now stands in as high a position as she ever occupied in the scale of nations'. Palmerston summed up the nature of the Liberal campaign in his speech at the nomination of candidates at Tiverton on 12 July when he stated that 'there cannot ... be found in the annals of the United Kingdom a period of six years during which the nation has enjoyed more advantages at home, more respect and honour abroad'.

However, there were some signs of discord in the Liberal ranks. Radicals put forward the demand for lowering the franchise and for the provision of equal electoral districts and the secret ballot. Bright (who was elected for Birmingham) expressed his unhappiness at the Party's attitude towards electoral reform and accused many MPs who had pledged themselves in 1859 to support this reform of subsequently abandoning this commitment. He accused the government of being 'treacherous to its professed principles'. On the other hand, Sir Charles Wood (who was elected at Ripon) asserted that the mood of the country did not support any extensive measure of political reform, although he expressed himself favourably disposed towards some degree of working-class enfranchisement and for the inclusion of persons who were not householders but who were nonetheless equipped to be granted the vote by virtue of their income, education and intelligence.

Result of the Election

A total of 922 candidates contested the election, with 303 MPs being elected unopposed. The result was:

Party	Votes	Vote %	MPs
Liberal	457,289	53.5%	311
Conservative	304,538	35.6%	244
Irish Liberal	51,532	6.0% [55.6%]	58
Irish Conservative	41,497	4.9% [44.4%]	45
Total	854,856		658

The turnout was 62.5 per cent.

The Parties

In 1860 the Liberal Registration Association was set up in an attempt to improve Liberal organisation in areas where the Party was weak. Liberal domination of London politics based on Palmerston's appeal to the financial and commercial middle class continued, with the Conservatives again failing to win a single seat. Gladstone was defeated at Oxford. The Party won the majority (49 out of 59 seats) of large English boroughs (with electorates in excess of 2,000 voters), and secured victory in 43 of the 63 boroughs with electorates between 1,000 and 2,000 voters and 104 of the 198 small English boroughs (with electorates of below 1,000 voters). It also won 52 of the 147 English county constituencies (Jenkins, 1994: 103). Palmerston's running mate in Tiverton (G. Denham) was edged out of Parliament by the narrow margin of three votes by a Liberal Conservative and Palmerston himself (facing opposition for the first time since 1847 when Harney polled no votes) was narrowly elected by 41 votes.

Scotland, Wales and Ireland

The Liberal Party slightly improved the position it obtained in Scotland in the 1859 election and won 42 of the 53 seats. The Conservatives won the remaining 11. In Wales, the Liberal Party slightly improved the position it obtained in the 1859 election and won 18 of the 32 seats. The Conservatives won the remaining 14. Palmerston's policy towards Ireland had been directed at Protestant opinion. He did not think it was possible to court Catholic support since they sought government intervention to restore the temporal power of the Pope which had been taken away in 1860 during the campaign for Italian independence. Palmerston was unwilling to commit the government to such a course of action. At the election, the Liberals secured victory in 58 of Ireland's 103 constituencies with the Conservatives winning the remaining 45.

Consequence of the Election

Palmerston was returned to office and formed a Liberal government.

16 November – 8 December 1868

Party Leaders
Benjamin Disraeli (Conservative)
William Ewart Gladstone (Liberal)

Background to the Election
Timing of the Election
The election was caused by Disraeli's replacement of Lord Derby as Prime Minister and leader of the Conservative Party in February 1868. He wished to obtain a mandate of his own from the electorate, although waited until the autumn of 1868 when the new electoral registers which embodied the provisions of the 1867 Reform Act were available.

Electoral Procedures and Practices
The election was based upon the extension of the franchise which was provided for in the 1867 Representation of the People Act (or the 'Second Reform Act', the contents of which are discussed in more detail below) which became law on 15 August 1867. Additionally, the first redistribution of seats since 1832 occurred in this legislation which involved 45 seats. Twenty-five of these were redistributed to the counties, 15 to the towns (mainly to new boroughs) and Birmingham, Leeds, Liverpool and Manchester were each given a third MP (although an amendment passed by the House of Lords gave electors only two votes in these three-member constituencies). However, the smaller boroughs remained over-represented. Separate measures which affected Scotland and Ireland were passed in 1868. In Scotland, the county occupation franchise was set at £14 but proposals to extend the borough franchise to rate-paying house-holders and lodgers were rejected by the House of Commons. Additional representation for Scotland was provided by disfranchising seven small English boroughs. In Ireland, £4 house-holders in the boroughs and £12 householders in the counties were enfranchised. However, the proposal to give Dublin the seat belonging to Portarlington was thrown out. A further measure, the 1868 Parliamentry Elections Act, removed the trial of election petitions from a committee of the House of Commons to the Courts.

Conservatives
The resignation of the Liberal government in June 1866 (an issue which is discussed more fully below) resulted in Lord Derby becoming Prime Minister for the third time, with Disraeli as Leader of the House of Commons. The government took office against the back-ground of the outbreak of the Austro-Prussian War and extra-parliamentary activity in support of the extension of the franchise. Its survival was much aided by divisions in the Liberal Party over the topic of electoral reform.

Trade union leaders had an added incentive to advocate the reform of the franchise in order to secure direct working-class representation in the House of Commons following the decision of magistrates in Bradford (which was supported on appeal in the High Court) in connection with a dispute involving the Boilermakers' Society. It was ruled that trade unions did not fall within the scope of the 1855 Friendly Societies Act and thus had no protection for their accumulated funds. It was further stated in the High Court that the Boilermakers were an association 'in restraint of trade'. Working-class concerns regarding electoral reform were added to by the 1866 economic crisis, and the government was finally pushed into action by a meeting organised by the Reform League which was scheduled to be held in Hyde Park on 23 July 1866. Although the government banned the event, a large crowd turned up and some of the railings around the park were knocked over. The fear of a popular uprising convinced the government of the need to reform the franchise.

Initially, the government proposed universal household suffrage based on two years' residence and the personal payment of rates in the boroughs and a reduction of the county franchise to a £15 rating limit. Gladstone attacked the Bill for not sufficiently broadening the franchise and in response Disraeli abandoned proposals relating to compound householders in favour of making all householders responsible for paying their rates. This extended the franchise to around 500,000 additional working-class voters and the franchise qualification for the counties was lowered to a £12 rating limit. In total the Act created around 938,000 new electors. The working class now formed a majority in most large towns, although most new voters in the counties were middle class.

In February 1868 Lord Derby resigned on grounds of ill health and was replaced as Party leader and Prime Minister by Benjamin Disraeli.

Liberal

Palmerston died on 18 October 1865 and was succeeded as Prime Minister by Lord Russell (who had now taken the title of Earl Russell and with it a seat in the House of Lords).

Russell's main domestic interest was in electoral reform, although this had not been an issue in the 1865 election. A Bill was brought forward to provide for a £7 annual rental qualification in the boroughs and a £14 occupancy qualification in the counties. Additionally, 49 seats were to be redistributed. The extension of the franchise to members of the working class was opposed by the Conservatives and also by a small group of Liberals who were termed the 'Adullamites'. These included Robert Lowe, Edward Horsman, Lord Elcho and Lord Grosvenor. A wrecking amendment to make rateable value rather than annual rent the basis of the franchise qualification in the boroughs was moved by the Adullamite, Lord Dunkellin, at the Committee Stage of the Franchise and Redistribution of Seats Bills and was approved by 315 : 304 votes in the early hours of 19 June. Over 40 Liberal MPs voted with the opposition. The government resigned the following week and was replaced by a Conservative administration led by Lord Derby.

Russell resigned as leader of the Liberal Party in December 1867 and was replaced as Party leader by Gladstone. In March 1868 he declared himself in favour of the disestablishment of the Church of Ireland and subsequently carried resolutions to this effect through the House of Commons. This had the effect of rallying the Liberal Party behind the moral cause of justice for Irish people and had obvious appeal to Catholic Irish MPs, nonconformists and radicals, while the Whigs were willing to give this proposal their support on pragmatic grounds. Thus in spite of the divisions which had been manifested over electoral reform, Gladstone was able to fight the 1868 election with a united party.

By-elections
A total of 141 by-elections occurred in the 1865–68 Parliament, of which 45 were contested. The Liberal Party made a net gain of three and the Conservatives a net loss of the same figure.

Conduct of the Election

The circumstances surrounding the passage of the 1867 Reform Act made it possible for both parties to claim credit for the measure and this situation tended to remove it as a front-line issue in the campaign. The main issue at the election was the disestablishment of the Irish Church.

Conservatives
Some of the policies raised in the Conservative campaign were put forward by Disraeli in his speech at the Guild Hall on 9 October. He referred to the achievements of his government, in particular in foreign affairs where it was asserted that the calmness displayed by the administration had contributed to the maintenance of peace in Europe. In a later speech, delivered at the nomination of candidates for his Buckinghamshire constituency on 20 November, he argued that, when he assumed office, Britain's relations with the European powers were 'not relations of confidence' and that Russell's mismanagement of British affairs in connection with Denmark, Germany, Russia and Poland had resulted in Britain being viewed with suspicion and distrust abroad. Britain's estrangement with Russia, Germany and France had been solved and, outside Europe, relations with America had been placed on an improved footing. He also justified increased expenditure on the army and navy by arguing that the military required the most up-to-date weapons which were available and also emphasised that Britain did not have conscription.

Disraeli's argument on 9 October that Conservative policy was to maintain the constitution of the country ensured that prominent attention was given by the Conservative campaign to the Liberal intention to disestablish and disendow the Church of Ireland. It was alleged that this course of action would alienate Irish Protestant opinion and result in increased religious animosity in the country. The Liberal proposal was also opposed on the 'democratic' grounds that this Church was supported financially by the Protestant landlords to the benefit of poorer persons.

Additionally, an attempt was made to utilise the Liberal intention to disestablish the Irish Church to argue that this set a dangerous precedent which could lead to the disestablishment of the Church of England. Colonel Corbett (who was elected for South Shropshire) pledged himself to resist any attempt to destroy the Protestant Church, and concerns such as these formed the basis of an appeal based on the cry of 'no Popery'. A Central Board which consisted of the Church Institution, the Ulster Protestant Defence Association, the Central Protestant Defence Association and the National Union was formed to defend the Irish Church and to mobilise Protestant feeling in the constituencies. However, outside Lancashire (where there existed historic anti-Irish sentiments), the anti-Popery campaign made little impact on the outcome of the campaign.

Disraeli also referred to other achievements of his government in his speech on 20 November. He argued that despite the collapse of credit and the consequent loss of revenue which had been experienced at the outset of his administration, his government had not raised taxes (save for a temporary increase in the income tax) and had now solved these problems. He argued that the 1867 Reform Act was of a Conservative character and to highlight divisions within the Liberal Party which had existed on this issue, he argued that the measure had not justified the alarm raised against it by some Liberals such as Robert Lowe. In this speech he also expressed his desire to extend the system of education and proposed the appointment of a Minister of Education. However, he stated that he was opposed to compulsory education. He argued that local taxation should be considered by a future Parliament, and while he accepted that reforms of this nature might increase public spending, he drew a distinction between an 'economical' as opposed to a 'cheap' government. A number of Conservative candidates in rural areas also expressed their wish to abolish the tax on malt and some sought to use the situation in which a Conservative government had existed in a House of Commons possessing a Liberal majority as proof of the disorganisation of the Liberal Party and its unfitness to govern.

Disraeli did not undertake a major speaking tour to advance the Conservative case. His election address to his constituents in Buckinghamshire constituted the Conservative manifesto, and he made only one public speech outside his constituency during the campaign.

Liberals

The general issues on which the Liberal Party contested the election constituted a broad agreement that Gladstone should be the next Liberal prime minister, that the Irish Church should be disestablished and disendowed, that there should be a reduction in public expenditure, that a national system of education should be introduced, that the army should be reformed, that the universities should be open to Dissenters, and that something should be done regarding liquor licensing (Hanham, 1959: 200). Some Liberal candidates emphasised Gladstone's fitness to become prime minister.

The key issue emphasised by Liberal candidates was the disestablishment and disendowment of the Church of Ireland. Liberals viewed this as a chief cause of discontent in Ireland and thus a solution to outbreaks of violence which occurred there. The Marquis of Hartington (who was defeated in North Lancashire) argued that this was 'a measure of civil justice to the Roman Catholics of Ireland' but explicitly denied that this policy had any implications for the Church of England. Gladstone also stated in a speech at Preston on 18 November that Liberals would not disestablish the Church of England, and later stated in his speech at the nomination of candidates at South West Lancashire on 22 November that, whereas in Ireland the Established Church 'is useless to the country and offensive to the people', the Church of England was supported by the majority of people in England.

Gladstone's election address and the speeches that he made (in particular in the constituency of South West Lancashire) also placed considerable emphasis on the need to reduce public spending and the importance of free trade. In the speech which he delivered at the nomination of candidates in South West Lancashire on 22 November he also referred to the record of the last Liberal government in reducing government spending.

The subject of the House of Lords was raised as an issue by some Liberal candidates. John Stuart Mill (who was defeated at Westminster) argued that the Conservatives had threatened to use this House to block the progress of future Liberal legislation, which he claimed was a novel attempt to determine who should govern the country. Mr W. Beaumont (who was elected for South Northumberland) referred to the addition of life peers to the membership of the House of Lords as a solution to this situation. Some Liberal candidates also expressed an interest in furthering electoral reform by measures which included the secret ballot.

Many Liberal candidates also urged the reduction of taxation and the revision of the system of local taxation. Some also called for the advancement of education.

Gladstone and Bright undertook major speaking tours to advance the Liberal cause.

Result of the Election

The 1867 Reform Act made no significant impact on the number of working-class MPs.

A total number of 1,039 candidates contested the election, with 212 MPs being returned unopposed. The result was:

Party	Votes	Vote %	MPs
Liberal	1,374,315	58.9%	321
Conservative	864,551	37.1%	234
Irish Liberal	54,461	2.3% [57.9%]	66
Irish Conservative	38,767	1.7% [41.9%]	37
Others	1,157	0.0%	0
Total	2,333,251		658

The turnout was 68.5 per cent.

The Parties

The Liberals emerged as the strongest party in the boroughs, in particular the larger ones and polled especially strongly in the Celtic Fringe where the Party's representation rose from 47 MPs who were elected in 1865 to 84 (Hanham, 1959: 216). The Party's campaign to disestablish the Irish Church won it obvious support from the Catholic vote but also succeeded in winning over many Wesleyans (who had previously inclined to the Conservative Party). Gladstone was defeated at South West Lancashire, but was elected for Greenwich, a seat which the Party Whips had kept open for him. Other notable defeats included that of Lord Hartington and Milner Gibson (which, as with Gladstone, occurred in Lancashire). An incoming member of the new Cabinet, H. A. Bruce, was also defeated at Merthyr Tydfil. Henry Labouchere and John Stuart Mill were beaten at Middlesex and Westminster respectively, and J. A. Roebuck lost at Sheffield.

The strength of the Conservatives remained in the county constituencies, although it made limited inroads in the business and suburban middle classes by capturing seats in Westminster and Middlesex. Significant advances were made in Lancashire and industrial Cheshire. Here they won 24 of the 36 borough constituencies and won all of Lancashire's eight county constituencies (Jenkins, 1994: 125). The most prominent defeats were experienced by the Attorney General, Sir John Karslake, the Solicitor General, Sir Richard Baggallay and the Lord-Advocate, Edward Stratheran Gordon.

Scotland, Wales and Ireland

Redistribution added five seats to Scotland. The Liberals swept the board, winning 51 of the 58 seats, with the Conservatives winning the remaining seven. One additional seat was allocated to Wales. The Liberals emerged as the dominant party, winning 23 of the 33 seats against 10 secured by the Conservative Party. The election in Ireland occurred against the background of heightened Fenian agitation. The Liberal Party improved upon its performance in 1865 and won 66 of the 103 seats, with the Conservative Party winning the remaining 37.

Consequence of the Election

Disraeli resigned before Parliament met, thus Gladstone formed a Liberal government.

30 January – 17 February 1874

Party Leaders
Benjamin Disraeli (Conservative)
William Ewart Gladstone (Liberal)

Background to the Election
Timing of the Election
Opposition from the Service ministers to Gladstone's 1874 budget (which is discussed more fully below) prompted him to hold an election on the proposals which it contained. It has also been suggested that the election (which was announced on 24 January 1874 before Parliament had reassembled) was timed to avoid Gladstone having to fight a by-election at Greenwich following his decision to take on the office of Chancellor of the Exchequer in August 1873. Greenwich was deemed a risky contest for Gladstone at that time, the other seat having been captured by a Conservative candidate in a by-election held in 1873. It was, however, an unexpected election, *The Times* on 30 January 1874 referring to 'the suddenness with which the dissolution burst upon the political world'.

Electoral Procedues and Practices
The 1872 Ballot Act introduced the secret ballot in order to guard the expanded electorate against bribery and intimidation. Although it was rejected by the House of Lords in 1871, it was enacted when reintroduced in 1872.

Conservatives
Conservative opposition to the policies of the Liberal government was especially directed at the Ballot Act and the Army Regulation Bill which suffered from obstruction tactics pursued by Conservative MPs in the House of Commons. Obstruction was a potent force available to the opposition as only two days a week were available to the government for its business. This forced the government to utilise the device of a Royal Warrant to force through the Army Regulation Bill's main provision, relating to the abolition of the purchase of commissions. Disraeli was relatively inactive in Parliament but used his time in opposition to modernise the Party. One facet of this was the formation of the National Union of Conservative and Unionist Associations. This had held its first meeting in 1867 and a particular aim of this organisation was to mobilise working-class voters in the boroughs behind the Conservative Party in the wake of the 1867 Reform Act. John Gorst played an important role in the development of Conservative organisation in this period. Major developments also occurred in Party policy whereby Disraeli opposed the 'Little England' posture of the Liberal government and advocated a stronger approach to foreign policy. He also committed the Party to undertaking measures of social reform based on the prosperity of the early 1870s.

Liberals

Gladstone's Cabinet reflected the diverse nature of the Liberal Party, and contained Whigs, radicals and a diverse group of reformers (or 'fads').

In 1868 Gladstone announced that his mission was to 'pacify Ireland' and Irish affairs received much attention in the early years of the government's life. The disestablishment of the Church of England in Ireland occupied much of the first session of Parliament. A number of the sections which comprised the Liberal Party found common cause with this reform which was implemented in 1869: nonconformists applauded it for obvious reasons, but the measure was also supported by Irish Whig landlords and those who were opposed to the maintenance of vested interests and who endorsed the principles of efficiency and economy in administration. Additionally, this measure implied that the favourite causes of other sections would receive favourable treatment in the government's legislative programme. This measure was followed by an Irish Land Bill which sought to address the grievances of Irish tenant farmers by providing them with compensation from their landlord for unfair eviction and the right to compensation for improvements.

In addition to Ireland, a series of reforms were promoted by the government which abolished a number of existing abuses and were guided by a desire to secure improved efficiency and professionalism in the operations of the state. These included the abolition of the compulsory payment of Church Rates in 1868 in England and Wales, the introduction of competitive examinations for entry into the civil service in 1870 and 1873, the 1871 Army Regulation Act (which reorganised the army and abolished the system whereby commissions could be purchased), the 1871 Abolition Act (which abolished the remaining religious tests for university entrance), and the 1872 Secret Ballot Act. Many of these reforms were uncontentious, but others created much greater opposition to the government, in particular from what has been referred to as the 'revolt of the nonconformists' (Jenkins, 1994: 134).

The first of these controversial measures was the 1870 Education Act which provided that school boards could be set up to provide additional elementary schools in areas where existing provision by voluntary agencies was inadequate. Although later history would view this measure as progressive in that it laid down the principle that schools should be available for children throughout the country, at the time the Act annoyed nonconformists because it failed to destroy the Anglican domination of elementary education. Further, it upset the Church of England by setting up a public system of education on a non-denominational basis which gave no special recognition to the position of the established Church. The National Education League was established in 1869 by discontented nonconformists who fielded candidates against Liberals in both by-elections and the general election.

A second controversial reform was the 1872 Licensing Act. Its forerunner was a Bill introduced in 1871 which sought to prevent any increase in the number of public houses and threatened the long-term security of publicans' licenses. Intense opposition from the licensing trade forced the government to introduce a watered-down measure in 1872 which regulated the granting only of new licenses and restricted the opening hours of public houses. The first measure had the effect of causing the brewing, distilling and publican interests to improve the level of their political organisation and to turn them against the Liberal Party (which they were previously inclined to support) and contributed towards the loss of Liberal seats at by-elections held at East Surrey and Plymouth in 1871. However, the second measure managed to annoy the Temperance Movement. The UK Alliance (which was dominated by nonconformists) adopted a hostile posture towards the government and stood candidates against official Liberal candidates in some by-elections (such as at Bath in 1873). Nonconformists were also unhappy that the policy of disestablishment which was applied to the Church of Ireland in 1869 was not extended to England, Wales or Scotland.

Other interests initially sympathetic to the Liberal government became disaffected by its subsequent actions. One of these was the trade unions. In 1867 a Royal Commission on Trade Unions was appointed and in 1871 the Trade Union Act gave legal status to trade unions (whose funds were thus protected). Also in 1871, the Criminal Law Amendment Act removed the threat of prosecution under the law of conspiracy for unions engaged in peaceful picketing. However, case law in 1872 involving the Gas Stokers restored the position as it was before the 1871 Act was enacted. What was perceived as inadequate policy towards the unions resulted in the formation of the Labour Representation League in 1869.

Finally, the support of Catholic Irish opinion was lost after 1868. The 1871 Irish Land Act was viewed as too moderate a measure by Catholic Irish opinion (which favoured the more radical demand of the three 'Fs' (fair rents, fixity of tenure and free sale) and the 1873 Irish Universities Bill (which proposed to set up a non-denominational Irish University to which Protestant and any Catholic institutions could affiliate) was similarly viewed as an unacceptable compromise which fell far short of the objective of a state-funded Catholic University. The government's position was severely undermined on 12 March 1873 when it was defeated by 287 : 284 on the second reading of the Irish University Bill. Forty-three Liberals, most of whom represented Irish constituencies, voted with the opposition. Gladstone resigned and, not wishing to subject his party to a general election at that time, suggested that Disraeli should form a minority government. However, Disraeli refused to do this and after a week's deliberation Gladstone resumed office. The main achievement of the reconstituted government was to pass the 1873 Judicature Act which established the High Court and Court of Appeal.

It was thus apparent that by 1873 the Liberal government was in a state of disintegration and its plight was mirrored in the country. The Conservative opposition made a net gain of 31 seats at by-elections between 1871 and 1874, and 10 of these occurred between May 1873 and the announcement of the dissolution in January 1874. The problems referred to above were aggravated by the opposition which some Liberal candidates at by-elections in borough constituencies faced from those campaigning for the abolition of the 1864, 1866 and 1869 Contagious Diseases Acts, and by administrative irregularities involving the Chancellor of the Exchequer, Robert Lowe, and the First Commissioner of Works and Buildings, A. S. Aryton, which led to their removal to other departments in 1873. This government reshuffle in August 1873 also brought William Harcourt into the government as a junior minister and the return of John Bright to the Cabinet in the post of Chancellor of the Duchy of Lancaster, with Gladstone taking on the office of Chancellor of the Exchequer. However, these changes were insufficient to salvage government fortunes, and by-elections continued to go against the Liberals.

In an attempt to reclaim the political initiative, Gladstone proposed some radical measures in his 1874 budget. Lowe had run into political difficulties with his plan for new taxes, including an increase in succession duties and a new tax on matches ,and had been forced to scrap his proposals in favour of a 2d rise in income tax. In 1874, Gladstone found himself with a healthy budget surplus and proposed to use this to abolish income tax and also the duty on sugar. The loss of revenue from these taxes required additional sources of funds which he proposed to raise through increasing the succession duties and duty on spirits, but a projected shortfall also required him to propose a £1 million reduction in military spending. Opposition from the Service ministers to this cut prompted Gladstone to dissolve Parliament unexpectedly and seek a popular mandate to introduce the changes proposed in his budget.

By-elections

A total of 176 by-elections occurred during the 1868–74 Parliament, of which 104 were contested. The Conservatives made a net gain of 25 seats, the Liberals a net loss of 33, and others a net gain of eight.

Conduct of the Election

The election occurred against the background of economic prosperity. The campaign was a quiet one with few speeches being made by the leaders of either major party. Although the election remained an essentially local affair, in which candidates fought their own contests with little central direction, a novel feature of the contest was the emergence of a genuine debate between Disraeli and Gladstone in connection with key concerns which were generated by the election and which also served to enhance the 'presidential' nature of the contest. Additionally, some attempt to transform constituency campaigns into a national one was made by the Whips' offices of both parties which, following the dissolution, became transformed into electoral organisations. These were able to find candidates for constituencies where local committees had failed to do so.

Conservatives

The Conservative campaign mounted a fierce attack on Gladstone and the actions of his government. Disraeli's election address (which was quoted in *The Times* on 26 January 1874) accused him of acting unconstitutionally both for hanging on to his Greenwich constituency without fighting a by-election and also for embarking on a war without communicating with Parliament or asking their approval to spend money on it. Particular attention was devoted to his financial policies. Conservatives argued that Gladstone's financial reforms (in particular the imposition of higher succession duties) would impose an unwarranted burden on the proper-tied classes and Disraeli argued that his proposals to abolish income tax and cut local taxation would lead inevitably to increasing other taxes. Disraeli also argued that while he wished to see the condition of people in the United Kingdom improved, this did not have to be achieved through legislation and he argued that the Liberal government should have devoted more attention to foreign affairs and less to domestic legislation in the previous five years.

A number of alleged shortcomings in foreign policies were condemned. Gladstone was attacked for presiding over a period of national weakness and imperial disintegration. The government's decision in 1872 to pay America $15.5 million (which had been awarded by an international tribunal meeting at Geneva) for the losses suffered to its shipping during the Civil War through the actions of the British-built ship, the *Alabama*, which had been supplied to the confederate navy, was put forward as an example of the former, and the attempts to make colonies such as New Zealand pay for their own defence as an illustration of the latter. Disraeli's election address drew particular attention to the government having relinquished the treaty which secured the freedom of the Straits of Malacca for British trade with China and Japan, and for entering into entanglements with states on the West Coast of Africa which had resulted in Britain being dragged into the Ashantee War. He stated that while the nation's honour required that this should be successfully completed, Parliament should investigate why Britain got involved in the first place since neither Parliament nor the country had approved it.

The Conservative campaign sought to portray the Party as the defender of key institutions of the state (the monarchy, the union of Church and state, property and the integrity of the Empire). The maintenance of religious education and the upholding of the honour of England abroad was often added to this list. Although Disraeli's election address conceded that Gladstone also endorsed these principles, it said that some of his supporters, 'attack the Monarchy ... impugn the independence of the House of Lords ... [and] there are those who would relieve Parliament altogether from any share in the government of one portion of the United Kingdom'. Other Liberals were accused of seeking to disestablish the Church of England and remove religion from the place it occupied in the system of national education. The actions of nonconformists pressure groups such as the Liberation Society and the National Education League made this cry of 'the Church in danger' seem plausible. Conservatives also sought to benefit from the activities of temperance organisations such as the UK Alliance by associating the cause of temperance with the Liberal Party and arguing that a Liberal government threatened the 'rights' of working men to their beer.

Disraeli also rejected the desirability of electoral reform which would equalise the county and borough franchise, and argued that Conservatives wished to see how the 1867 Reform Act and the introduction of the secret ballot operated before contemplating further reforms. He warned, however, that the equalisation of county and borough franchises would inevitably lead to the disfranchisement of many smaller boroughs. Other Conservatives alleged that the proposal to equalise the borough and county franchises constituted a departure from the time-honoured principle of differentiating between them.

During the campaign, Disraeli discussed some of the issues which were raised by his Liberal counterpart. He responded to references made in Gladstone's election address to the timing of the election by taunting him (in a speech delivered at Aylesbury on 31 January) for quitting office on the grounds that he only possessed a majority of 66 in the House of Commons. He further objected to the way in which Parliament had been summoned in December 1873 to meet on 5 February 1874 to despatch urgent business, only to be dissolved before it had been given the opportunity to do so. He further objected to Gladstone's references to the harm done to his government through its defeat on the Irish University Bill in 1873. He stated that this issue bothered Gladstone so much that when he returned to office he gave ministerial posts to two of the most vocal Liberal opponents of this measure, Dr Lyon Playfair and Sir William Harcourt.

Their cause was aided by improved local organisation (which was especially apparent in borough constituencies) and also at national level.

Liberals

Gladstone's election address to his constituents at Greenwhich (which was published in *The Times* on 24 January 1874) asserted that the Liberal case for re-election was in part justified by its record since taking office in 1868 and he especially welcomed the increase of wages in the agricultural districts. He drew attention to the government's record in financial affairs and boasted of achievements which included cutting expenditure on defence and reducing the national debt. He anticipated a large budget surplus in the current financial year which he proposed to utilise to provide aid to ratepayers in England and Wales (and possibly in Scotland and Ireland too), to repeal income tax (which he depicted as a war tax) and to provide relief to consumers by lowering the duties on articles of popular consumption. Liberal candidates accused the Conservatives of having failed to remove income tax because their government indulged in high spending. Additionally, Gladstone's election address expressed support for the equalisation of the county and borough franchises, proposed to consider amendments to the 1870 Education Act in the new Parliament and to allocate an increased role to local government and subordinate authorities in order to reduce the burden on Westminster. He also denied the charge levelled at the Party by some Conservatives that the Liberals had imperilled the institutions of the country.

His election address devoted much attention to the timing of the election, arguing that the government had been in a difficult position since March 1873 when what he described as a concurrent attack was mounted on the Irish University Bill by Disraeli and the Roman Catholic prelacy. This led to the government's defeat and its resignation. However, Disraeli declined to form a government and the Liberals were forced to return, albeit 'with an avowed reluctance'. However, the authority of the government had suffered from events in March 1873 and justified the holding of an election.

Other Liberals focused on foreign affairs. Robert Lowe's election address for his University of London constituency stated that the government had carried Britain successfully through the European crisis occasioned by the Franco–Prussian War without offending either of the two protagonists nor compromising British dignity or injuring Britain's allies. He asserted that a more 'energetic' government might have embroiled the country in these hostilities. He also drew attention to the settlement of the Alabama issue which he believed had served the cause of peace and enabled friendlier relationships to be restored with America. He argued that the Ashantee War had not been of the government's choosing but was caused by the aggression of the Ashantee King. Some Liberal candidates discussed the lessons learned by the government from the Franco–Prussian War, in particular, praising reforms such as the abolition of the ability to purchase commissions in the army. Ireland was also discussed by Liberal candidates, J. Walker (who was elected for Bedforshire) arguing that the 1870 Irish Land Act was 'a severe and stringent remedy … to an evil which had grown out of the ill-defined relations of landlord and tenant', and Gladstone in a speech delivered at New Cross on 2 February asserted that the policies of disestablishment and land reform had secured increased tranquillity in Ireland.

During the campaign, Gladstone sought to refute some of the charges which Disraeli levelled against him. In a major speech delivered at Greenwich on 28 January (which 6,000-7,000 people attended) Gladstone accused him of acting in a hypocritical manner regarding the Straits of Malacca issue. This event had occurred in 1871 and Disraeli had not raised the issue in

Parliament in either 1872 or 1873. Gladstone also alleged that there was no treaty regarding the freedom of these Straits for international trade and that the navigation of these waters had been placed in peril by a treaty concluded by the Dutch government which gave them almost sovereignty over the Kingdom of Siak. He triumphantly pointed out this had occurred in 1853 when there had been a Conservative government of which Disraeli had been a member.

In his Greenwich speech, Gladstone clarified his financial policy by stating that the abolition of income tax would be paid for by using the existing budget surplus, readjusting other taxes and through the use of economy in government. However, this statement produced further problems. Conservatives, who included Disraeli and Sir J. Parkington (who was elected for Droitwich), queried what exactly Gladstone meant by the phrase 'readjustment' of taxes, and stated that this implied that other taxes would rise to pay for the abolition of income tax. However, although the abolition of income tax was a key issue of the Liberal campaign it failed to capture public enthusiasm and dominate the campaign.

Result of the Election

A total number of 1,080 candidates contested the election, with 187 MPs being returned unopposed. The result was:

Party	Votes	Vote %	MPs
Conservative	1,000,006	40.6%	319
Liberal	1,241,381	50.3%	232
Irish Home Rule Party	90,234	3.7% [39.6%]	60
Irish Conservative	91,702	3.7% [40.8%]	31
Irish Liberal	39,778	1.6% [18.4%]	10
Others	2,936	0.1%	0
Total	2,466,037		652

The turnout was 66.4 per cent.

The Parties

Gladstone took the opinion that the Licensing Act was the undoing of the government and declared 'we were swept away in a torrent of gin and beer'. However, this explanation underestimated other issues which explained the Conservative victory. These included internal divisions within the Liberal Party, which resulted in 11 seats being lost as the result of Liberal candidates fighting each other and splitting the vote. In Nottingham, for example, the presence of four Liberals for this two-member constituency resulted in a split Liberal vote and the return of both Conservative candidates. Nonconformists were also disillusioned with the record of the Liberal government, in particular regarding education reform. Although this resulted in large numbers of nonconformists failing to vote in 1874, actions undertaken by Gladstone (such as Bright's return to the Cabinet in 1873) helped to stem this tide and a more significant feature of the Party's performance was its poor showing in borough constituencies in Southern England where moderate support was lost in large numbers to the advantage of the Conservatives. The activities undertaken by extremist pressure groups (or 'fads') which were associated with the Liberal Party was perhaps the most important explanation for the loss of moderate support. If a line was drawn to link the Severn and the Wash, the Liberal performance in boroughs north of this line (including Wales and Scotland) was significantly better than what was achieved below it. The Liberals were the dominant force in northern boroughs containing 2,000-5,000 voters and remained in firm control of northern boroughs with in excess of 5,000 voters (Jenkins, 1994: 145-6).

Two 'Lib–Lab' candidates associated with the Labour Representation League were elected (Alexander Macdonald for Stafford Borough and Thomas Burt for Morpeth). This organisation was formed after the passage of the 1867 Reform Act (in 1869) and sought to return working-class men to Parliament and secure the registration of working-class voters. Macdonald stood as a Liberal and succeeded in a constituency which had returned two Conservative MPs in 1869. Burt stood as a radical in a previously safe Liberal seat where he was given a straight fight against a Conservative candidate.

The Conservative victory owed much to their improved support in England which resulted in the net gain of over 67 seats compared to 1868. The strength of the Party especially rested in the English counties (where they won 143 of the 170 seats) and the smaller rural boroughs. The Party performed especially well in London (where it won 10 of the 22 seats, including three in Westminster which was the Party's best performance since 1841 when it had won two seats in that constituency), the Home Counties (evidencing the Party's attraction to suburban middle-class voters) and in boroughs in the South of England in general. They also sustained the advance made in the counties and boroughs in Lancashire in 1868 (Jenkins, 1994: 143).

Scotland, Wales and Ireland

The Liberals retained their dominant position in Scottish politics, winning 40 of the 58 seats with the Conservatives winning the remaining 18. However, in comparison with 1868, the Liberals lost ground to the Conservatives who made 11 net gains, polling especially well in the Scottish Lowland counties. The Liberal Party also retained its dominance over Welsh politics, winning 19 of the 33 seats to the 14 won by the Conservatives. This result was an improvement for the Conservatives of four seats on the result they had achieved in 1868.

Catholic discontent towards the government's Irish policy resulted in an important departure in Irish politics. Many Irish Liberal MPs threw in their lot with Isaac Butt's Home Rule League which was established in 1873. This won 60 seats of the 101 seats, and the Liberal Parliamentary representation in Ireland was reduced from 66 in 1868 to 10 in 1874. The Conservatives more or less held the position they had obtained in 1868 and won 31 seats. The number of uncontested seats fell from 67 in 1868 to 18 in 1874.

Consequence of the Election

Gladstone resigned before the new Parliament met and Disraeli formed a Conservative government.

30 March – 27 April 1880

Party Leaders
The Earl of Beaconsfield (Conservative)
The Earl of Granville (Liberal)

Background to the Election
Timing of the Election
The timing of the election was influenced by difficulties the government encountered with its Metropolitan Trust Water Bill (which is discussed below). There was a distinct possibility of the government being defeated in connection with its handling of this measure. The relatively good performance of Conservative candidates in three by-elections which were held in late 1879 and early 1880 (at Sheffield, Liverpool and Southwark) also influenced the government to call an election in early 1880. There was, however, some surprise when, on 8 March 1880, Beaconsfield announced the dissolution of Parliament for around two weeks later.

Electoral Procedures and Practices
The 1875 Parliamentary Elections (Returning Officers) Act amended the law regarding the expenses and charges which returning officers could make for parliamentary elections to provide that candidates were liable for the expenses reasonably incurred by these officials. The 1878 Parliamentary Elections (Metropolis) Act extended the hours of voting in London from the customary eight to 12, between 8am and 8pm. The 1880 Electoral Practices Act renewed the 1872 Ballot Act (which was due to expire) and also allowed candidates to provide free transport to polling stations in the boroughs (as was already the case in county constituencies). Opposition from Scottish and Irish MPs ensured that this later provision would not apply to either of these countries. A Bill to provide for a limited redistribution of seats was formulated but not proceeded with because of the timing of the general election.

Conservatives
In 1876 Disraeli assumed the title of the Earl of Beaconsfield and thus left the House of Commons.

The Conservative administration embarked upon a series of reforms some of which extended the existing scope of social reform to aid the circumstances of the working classes. These reforms included the 1874 Factory Act (which regulated the hours which women and children could work), the 1874 Licensing Act (which repealed some provisions contained in the earlier 1872 Act), the 1875 Public Health Act (which codified existing legislation and sought to extend policies pursued by progressive municipal authorities throughout the country), the 1875 Artisans Dwellings Act (which gave municipal authorities powers to acquire slum property and rebuild more modern housing), the 1875 Agricultural Holdings Act (which required a landlord to pay displaced tenants for agricultural improvements which they had carried out), the 1875 Conspiracy and Protection of Property Act (which gave unions the rights of peaceful picketing and legalised collective bargaining), the 1875 Employers and Workmen's Act (which made a breach of contract a civil offence whether committed by a workman or an employer), the 1875 Sale of Food and Drugs Act (which was the first comprehensive measure on the subject of food adulteration), the 1876 Education Act (which hesitantly introduced the principle of compulsory school attendance), and the 1878 Factory Act (which was designed to improve safety at work).

Attention was also paid in the early period to ecclesiastical legislation. The 1875 Public Worship Act was designed to curb the catholicising movement in the Anglican Church which was termed 'ritualism'.

It has been argued that this legislation was the logical consequence of Disraeli's franchise extension in 1867 and was the basis on which his commitment to 'Tory Democracy' was built. However, the scope and significance of these reforms were limited, and many of the new functions were allocated to local authorities in the form of discretionary powers which meant that they had to raise the resources from their own means if they decided to implement them. It was in this sense especially that these measures have been dismissed as 'not very exciting' (Lloyd, 1968: 7).

However, the Conservative government's interest in domestic policies was surpassed by the increasingly dominant role accorded to foreign policy. Disraeli's decision to purchase a large bloc of Suez Canal shares in 1875 owned by the Khedive (King) of Egypt gave Britain a short route to India as well as a keen interest in the subsequent internal affairs of Egypt. In 1876 the Royal Titles Bill made Queen Victoria Empress of India in an attempt to secure the loyalty of Indians to the Crown. The most difficult foreign policy issue facing the government, however, was the Eastern Question.

The stance of the government towards this issue was to support Turkey. Revolts by the Serbs in Herzegovina in 1875 (which spread throughout Bosnia) were put down by the Turks with a ferocity which prompted a number of European powers led by Austria-Hungary to draw up a programme for internal reform in Turkey which was embodied in the Berlin Memoranda. Disraeli refused to associate Britain with this document then news arrived in Britain of a further revolt in Bulgaria to which the Turks responded to with brutality which was carried out by the armed irregulars known as the Bashi-Bazouks. An estimated 12,000 Christians were killed. Disraeli was inclined to play down the the incident which he dismissed as 'coffee-house babble'. However, it would not go away. At first the issue generated extra-parliamentary opposition to the government which was fuelled by Gladstone's pamphlet *The Bulgarian Horrors and the Question of the East* (published on 6 September 1876). In this he identified himself with the outrage which many in Britain felt towards the Turkish atrocities and he called for the Turks to be expelled 'bag and baggage' from Bulgaria, the province 'they have desolated and profaned'. On 8 December 1876 a large public meeting at St James's Hall advocated that the government should throw its weight behind forcing Turkey to reform. Gladstone attended this meeting which marked his effective return to political activism. On 7 May 1877 he moved a resolution on the Eastern Question in the House of Commons which indicated disapproval of Turkish actions.

The issue was further complicated when Russia declared war on Turkey in the name of the oppressed Balkan peoples. This accentuated divisions in the Conservative Party whereby the anti-interventionists led by Lord Derby and the pro-Christians led by Lord Salisbury challenged the Prime Minister's pro-Turkish/anti-Russian stance. This opposition prevented Disraeli from intervening on Turkey's side but the outbreak of war between Russia and Turkey in 1877 witnessed the surrender of Plevna in 1877 and the occupation of Adrianople in early 1878. The threat posed by the Russian advance to Constantinople resulted in the despatch of the British Mediterranean Fleet through the Dardanelles. The imminence of war between Britain and Russia caused an outbreak of bellicose patriotism in Britain, summarised in a popular music hall song which gave birth to the new term, 'jingoism':

We don't want to fight, but by Jingo if we do
We've got the men, we've got the ships, we've got the money too
We've fought the Bear before, and while Britons shall be true,
The Russians shall not have Constantinople

Tensions between Russia and Britain subsided following the armistice of Adrianople in January 1878 but were soon resurrected by the terms of the Treaty of San Stefano which Russia imposed on Turkey as the price of peace. This treaty ceded Eastern Armenia to the Russians and gave them control over a very large state of Bulgaria, stretching from the Black Sea to the Aegean. This helped to unify the Conservatives behind an anti-Russian policy. Pressure by the British government forced the Russian government to back down and, by secret agreement, it agreed to relinquish some of the gains it had extracted from Turkey in the 1878 Treaty. Turkey's acceptance of these revisions (also secretly) meant that the British government could participate in the meeting of the Great European Powers at the Congress of Berlin in 1878 in the sure knowledge that it would emerge from the event with enhanced prestige. Lord Beaconsfield (the title taken by Disraeli when he entered the House of Lords) was able to present the treaties concluded at the Congress of Berlin as 'peace with honour' and they were approved by a large majority in the House of Commons. The Eastern Question had thus been concluded on terms which politically benefited the Conservative government.

In addition to the Eastern Question, other foreign policy issues emerged in the latter part of the Conservative government. The murder of the British envoy (Sir Louis Cavagnari) in Kabul, Afghanistan in 1879 prompted a British military response in which Kabul was occupied. The decision of the High Commisssioner of South Africa, Sir Bartle Frere, to launch a preventive war against the Zulus also resulted in a damaging blow to British prestige when a British column under the command of Lord Chelmsford was annihilated at Isandhlwana in 1879 by a Zulu army. In order to detract attention from this incident, public opinion was immediately directed to a successful British action at the Rorke's drift mission station when a tiny force of around 100 soldiers (most of whom were Welsh) successfully repulsed an attack by 4,500 Zulu warriors. A grateful government awarded 11 Victoria Crosses and nine Distinguished Conduct Medals to the defenders, although one expert, Garnet Wolseley, suggested that no awards were appropriate since the soldiers had no option other than to stand and fight: there was nowhere they could run to! The Zulus were eventually defeated at Ulundi in July 1879.

Although the government secured much prestige for its action which forced the Russians to back down from enforcing the Treaty of San Stefano on Turkey, other problems served to undermine its popularity. The economic boom had ended in 1873 (when the Liberals were in office) and economic conditions subsequently deteriorated. Wages fell and unemployment rose after 1874 and the industrial depression became acute by 1878. In addition, difficulties were experienced in agricultural areas. A succession of bad harvests occurred in 1873, 1875, 1876 and 1877. In 1879, a bad summer was accompanied by low wheat prices due to the impact of American grain on the domestic market. This situation led some Conservatives (most notably Lord Salisbury) to express interest in tariff protection. Income tax was also increased in 1876 and 1878. The government was also heavily criticised for its handling of the Metropolitan Trust Water Bill which was introduced into Parliament in March 1880. This proposed to unify the private water companies of London into a single municipal undertaking which would have a monopoly position. The rate of compensation was designed to give the shareholders the same income from government bonds as they had enjoyed from the water shares, which entailed a large capital gain. The price of water shares shot up and public opinion (including the Conservative press) condemned the Bill.

Liberals

Gladstone resigned the leadership of the Liberal Party in January 1875 and devoted himself to religious matters, writing a pamphlet which attacked the decrees of the Vatican Council on the subject of Papal Infallibility. He was replaced by Lord Granville, and Lord Hartington became the Party leader in the House of Commons. This arrangement marked the reversion of the Liberal Party to Whig control. However, there was considerable disunity in the Parliamentary Party, a problem accentuated by the different temperament of the two leaders (who were cousins) and the tendency of Gladstone to pursue an independent line on political issues such as financial affairs, the purchase of shares in the Suez Canal, the 1876 Royal Titles Bill and in particular on the Eastern Question (which is discussed in more detail below) where many Liberals felt his stance to be too pro-Russian. On occasions, Hartington dealt with disunity in his ranks by absenting himself from the House of Commons or by abstaining in votes which threatened to split the Party.

A key development affecting the operations of the Liberal Party was the formation in 1877 of the National Liberal Federation. This was the brainchild of Joseph Chamberlain who hoped to use this vehicle to mobilise the new electorate which had been enfranchised in 1867. He hoped that by providing the grass roots with a means to articulate their views to the Party leadership it would be possible to counter the control exerted over the Party by its Whiggish elements and thereby move it in a radical direction. The Federation's first conference (which was the forerunner of modern Party conferences) was held in Bingley Hall, Birmingham, on 31 May 1877 where an audience of 20,000 people was addressed by Gladstone (with Hartington refusing to attend).

The Eastern Question which arose in 1876 revealed important divisions in the Party. Nonconformists and High Churchmen empathised with the persecution experienced by the Bulgarian Christians, and nonconformist areas were at the forefront of the popular protest movement opposed to government inaction in bringing Turkey to heel. However, the Liberal leadership was more wary of uncompromising opposition to the government (in particular when the Russo–Turkish War broke out in 1877), viewing Beaconsfield's anti-Russian approach as both popular and constituting an attempt to wrest the Palmerstonian heritage of foreign policy away from the Liberals which Hartington was keen to preserve. In addition, the radical wing of the Party contained MPs such as Bright who were opposed to any form of intervention on this issue.

Gladstone's involvement in the Eastern Question in 1876 is briefly discussed above. However, once this crisis was over, he reverted to his position of semi-retirement. However, although the Conservatives could boast of success in their stance towards the Eastern Question, the fortunes of the Liberal Party began to improve. Economic depression enabled the Liberals to contrast the nation's current economic circumstances with the large budget surplus they had inherited from Gladstone in 1874. It was further possible to relate these to criticisms of Conservative foreign policy, by arguing that economic problems were accentuated by the government's unnecessary meddling in the affairs of distant countries. Opposition to Beaconsfield's imperialism helped to heal divisions which had arisen on the Eastern Question and Hartington's attack on the government's Afghanistan policy in December 1878 was favourably viewed by his left wing and helped consolidate his position as leader. Policies on which the Party would fight the next election began to emerge (in particular electoral reform in the counties, local government reform in the counties and London, and land reform affecting the laws of primogeniture and entail) and Hartington further sought to neuter the extremism of nonconformist pressure groups by urging them to work within the framework of the Liberal Party rather than engaging in militant forms of extra-parliamentary campaigning which alarmed moderate voters.

Against this background of improved Liberal circumstances, Gladstone resumed full-time political activism and in January 1879 accepted an invitation to fight the Conservative-held Scottish county constituency of Midlothian at the next general election. Towards the end of that year during the parliamentary recess he embarked upon a series of speeches in what is termed 'the first Midlothian campaign'. This entailed nine speeches delivered between 24 and 29 November in the constituency supplemented by a further 18 in a subsequent tour of the Scottish Lowlands. In this campaign he launched a scathing attack on what was termed 'Beaconsfieldism'. He focused on the government's foreign and colonial policy and accused Beaconsfield of pursuing actions which had lowered Britain's reputation in the eyes of the world, led to the massacre of tribal peoples in Afghanistan and South Africa, and resulted in a heavy burden of taxation being placed on the British people. It was asserted that the government's actions were not required in the national interest and had harmed Britain's reputation.

In contrast, Gladstone put forward his own principles which should guide British foreign and colonial policy: he argued that it was necessary to preserve the peace, to maintain cooperation between the great powers in the Concert of Europe, to avoid needless and entangling engagements, to acknowledge the rights of all nations and to pursue a foreign policy which was underpinned by the pursuit of freedom. Gladstone's actions sought to use foreign and colonial policy as the basis of a moral crusade which would take the initiative away from the Conservative Party which sought to revive the feeling of jingoism of 1877–78. It also served to detract from the foreign policies of his previous government which were viewed as a source of weakness.

The success of Gladstone's campaign was a considerable boost to Liberal morale which seemed confirmed by the results obtained by the 1879 municipal elections and led Gladstone to demand the dissolution of Parliament. However, Liberal defeats at by-elections held at Liverpool and Southwark in February 1880 suggested that the Liberal bubble may have burst and were one influence on Beaconsfield to hold an early election.

By-elections

A total of 193 by-elections occurred in the 1874–80 Parliament, of which 123 were contested. The Conservatives made a net loss of five and the Liberals a net gain of the same figure.

Conduct of the Election

The embryo state of centralised party organisation and the organisation of the media at that time made it hard for party leaders to inject entirely new issues into the campaign. The election was thus largely determined by issues which had received prominent airing before 1880, and new subjects (such as Beaconsfield's emphasis on Ireland) were unlikely to have much impact on the voters. The most prominent of these was foreign policy, in which the dominant theme of both parties was to cast a retrospective eye on events which occured between 1876 and 1878. The election was also important for the involvement of peers in a general election (which included Disraeli's open letter to the Duke of Marlborough and Lord Granville's speech on 20 March which was ostensibly to open the Liberal Club at Hanley). It also witnessed the use of a new election technique. Gladstone was the first major statesman to employ the technique of 'stumping' which he first utilised in his campaign in South West Lancashire in 1868 and which he further developed in the Midlothian campaign in 1879–80. This technique entailed directing a series of speeches at the whole country but making them within a relatively small geographic area to maximise their unity and sense of purpose. Each series had a central theme but was accompanied by a minor or secondary theme to set the speech off. Each speech was designed to cast new light on each of these themes so that the speeches in their entirety read like a course of lectures (Hanham, 1959: 202 and 204).

Conservatives

Beaconsfield broke with accepted practice that a peer should not issue an election address and set out the main themes of the Conservative campaign in an open letter to the Lord Lieutenant of Ireland, the Duke of Marlborough, which was published in *The Times* on 8 March 1880. The choice of recipient was deliberately designed to project Irish affairs as a key election issue in which the Conservatives could present themselves as defenders of the Union and attack the home rule sentiments of the Liberal Party who sought to pursue a 'policy of decomposition' which would procure the disintegration of the United Kingdom. The policy pursued by the Conservative government towards Ireland (which included the establishment of a system of public education) was referred to, and home rule was condemned as 'a destructive doctrine'. Beaconsfield's assertion in this letter (which was expressed against the background of food shortages in Ireland at that time) that home rule was 'a danger, in its ultimate results, scarcely less disastrous than pestilence and famine' ensured that England's Irish vote would be solidly cast against the Conservatives without any need for the Liberals to firmly commit themselves to any specific course of action and thereby run the risk of a split. The Irish Home Rule Confederation advised Irish voters in England to 'vote against Benjamin Disraeli as you should vote against the mortal enemy of your country and your race' (Lloyd, 1968: 20).

The Conservative achievements in foreign policy between 1876 and 1878 received prominent attention in their campaign, in part to detract from domestic problems, particularly the stagnation in trade (which the Conservatives felt was attributable to a worldwide phenomenon) and the agricultural depression. Attempts were also made to revive the jingoistic spirit of 1878 in the hope that this might secure support from Liberal voters. It was alleged that the policy pursued by the government in connection with the Eastern Question was based on the ideals of Lord Palmerston and it was claimed that they had succeeded in keeping Russia out of Constantinople without being forced to resort to war and had thereby enhanced Britain's international prestige.

Although little of any substance was put forward in relation to the Eastern Question in Beaconsfield's letter to the Duke of Marlborough, he did assert that the current European situation was critical and that the power of England and the peace of Europe would largely depend on the outcome of the election. He argued that the Conservatives had secured the peace not by pursuing a policy of non-intervention but by 'the presence, not to say the ascendancy, of England in the Councils of Europe'. Although this sentiment of a crisis on foreign affairs seemed to be contradicted by Northcote's address (which stated that that the period of anxiety was coming to an end and that the energies of the next Parliament could be focused on social and domestic improvements), other Conservatives campaigned on the theme of foreign affairs. The Home Secretary, R. Cross, delivered a speech at Warrington on 18 March in which he pointed out that the achievements of the Conservative government in connection with the Eastern Question had been to prevent Constantinople falling into Russia's hands and to keep the Dardanelles open. In a later speech at Tulbrook on 20 March he declared that 'I say honestly and fearlessly that what we did, the action which England took, was the only thing to save Europe from a Continental War, which would have cost the country millions of money and hundreds of thousands of lives'.

Social reform received relatively little attention in the Conservative campaign despite the achievements of the early years of the Conservative government in this field of activity. This was partly due to the limited impact which this legislation had on working people but also because the Conservative Party had no follow-up legislation in the pipeline. The main reason for this was that increased aid to the working class might entail higher taxes for the rich. Instead the Conservatives sought to attack their Liberal opponents, in particular by seeking to exploit divisions which they perceived existed within that Party in consequence of Gladstone's return to politics and the emergence of the National Liberal Federation as a vehicle to advance radical politics.

Liberals

The main themes of the Liberal campaign were laid down in addresses issued by Hartington and Gladstone. In these statements, both Liberals pledged to extend the county franchise and to improve the country's financial position. Hartington criticised the alleged incompetence of the Conservative administration, while Gladstone suggested that the election should be viewed as a state trial in which the government should be prosecuted for its past actions, in particular for the foreign and colonial policy it had pursued after 1876, with the nation acting as the jury.

Defeats experienced by the British in Afghanistan and Zululand invited electors to consider the wisdom of imperialism. However, the chief Liberal criticism of Conservative foreign policy was that it had been driven too much by expediency and too little by morality. Although by 1880 Liberals were willing to accept the Treaty of Berlin, they condemned the principles which underpinned it. A government which became embroiled in the dispute in order to safeguard the integrity of Turkey had ended up concluding two secret agreements which seemed to connive in Turkey's partition in Europe. The use of secret diplomacy with Turkey and Russia was also viewed as harmful to settling international affairs in the open at a Congress of Powers. W. Foster stated in a speech at Kendal on 20 March that the use of these methods resulted in 'the character of secret and unfair dealing' being stamped on British diplomacy. Liberals also attacked the Conservative government for having contemplated war in connection with the Eastern Question.

Liberals focused attention on the record of the Conservative government in financial and economic affairs. Conservative inexperience in government was stated to be a cause of waste. They criticised the budget deficit which had occurred after 1874 (and which by 1880 had risen to £8 million), comparing it unfavourably with the surplus achieved by the previous Liberal administration. The Conservatives were condemned for increasing taxation, raising spending, yet failing to reduce the size of the national debt. This was regarded as 'unsound finance' which had made the depression worse by causing business confidence to decline. They also subjected the Conservatives to an early dose of what was later called 'double whammy', criticising both the content of Conservative foreign policy after 1874 and the high spending which this policy necessitated.

Liberals were also critical of the Conservative response to the depression. Particular attention was paid in Liberal statements to the impact of depression on the countryside where, in addition to negative attacks on the Conservatives, promises were made regarding future Liberal policy. The advocacy of free trade and financial straightforwardness was accompanied by attacks on the power of the landlords. The operations of the Game Laws (whereby tenant farmers could not kill game on the land which they rented even though it damaged crops) were condemned, and Liberals proposed to tighten the provisions of the Conservatives' 1875 Agricultural Holdings Act to prevent landlords evading its provisions. Liberals also pointed out that the Conservatives had failed to implement their promise to abolish the malt tax, which had been made in 1874, and Hartington expressed his support for the use of the local option to determine the licensing question.

The Liberal campaign was dominated by Gladstone and Hartington. Chamberlain played little part in Liberal electioneering. The main features of the Liberal campaign were the speeches which Gladstone delivered on his train journey from King's Cross Station in London to his Midlothian constituency which commenced on 16 March. Speeches were delivered at King's Cross, Grantham, York, Newcastle, Berwick and Edinburgh. All the places where he stopped were subsequently won by the Liberal Party in the election, although during the campaign the Home Secretary, R. Cross, referred less kindly to this aspect of Gladstone's electioneering by arguing that he 'started from King's Cross, calling at every station and delaying the train by speeches'.

Gladstone succeeded in dominating not merely the Liberal campaign but also the tone of the election. Traditional Liberal themes of peace, retrenchment and reform were raised alongside an emphasis on morality. Gladstone effectively argued that the record of the Conservative government in both financial and foreign affairs was tainted with immorality.

Gladsone's significant contribution to the 1880 election campaign was (as had been the case in his first Midlothian campaign) his ability to draw out the moral aspects of political issues and use morality as a stick with which to condemn the record of the Conservative government. The focus on moral principles made it unnecessary for the Liberals to put forward specific pledges of their own which might split the Party but provided them with a yardstick with which to attack the actions of their opponents. Thus Gladstone drew attention to the plight of Afghan families who had been driven out into the snow following the government's response to the Afghan revolt: he advised Beaconsfield to 'remember the rights of the savage ... remember that the happiness of his humble house, remember that the sanctity of life in the hill villages of Afghanistan, among the winter snows, is as inviolable in the eye of Almighty God as can be your own'. He argued Britain had secured Cyprus in an underhand way. And in his speeches delivered en route to Midlothian he gave prominent attention to the Conservative reform of Probate Duties in the 1880 budget (which he depicted as a reform which benefited the rich but harmed the moderately well off).

Result of the Election

The 1880 election was characterised by the increased involvement of central party organs, the National Union of Conservative and Unionist Associations and the National Liberal Federation. Although these central bodies did not exercise control over local committees and associations, they played a limited role in electoral affairs and were engaged in some aspects of electioneering (for example, by disseminating political pamphlets). However, the conduct of individual constituency campaigns remained heavily determined by traditional electioneering practices. It has thus been argued that the 1880 election was the first fought on a national level and the last to be downgraded by the widespread use of corrupt practices (O'Leary, 1962: 158).

A total of 1,103 candidates contested the election. This figure was boosted by the reduced number of unopposed returns (109 in the United Kingdom compared to 187 in 1874), mainly the result of the Liberals contesting seats from which they had stood aside in the previous election. The result was:

Party	Votes	Vote %	MPs
Liberal*	1,780,171	53.0%	337
Conservative	1,326,744	39.5%	214
Irish Home Rule Party	95,535	2.8% [37.5%]	63
Irish Conservative	99,607	3.0% [39.8%]	23
Irish Liberal	56,252	1.7% [22.7%]	15
Others	1,107	0.0%	0
Total	3,359,416		652

* Includes three 'Lib–Lab' MPs associated with the Labour Representation League – Thomas Burt (Morpeth), Henry Burford (Stoke-upon-Trent) and Alexander macdonald (Stafford Borough).

The turnout was 72.2 per cent.

The Parties

Analyses of 52 constituencies fought by both main parties in 1868, 1874 and 1880 suggested that in 1874 there had been a 5 per cent swing to the Conservatives which was reversed in 1880 by a 5 per cent swing to the Liberals, thus restoring the parties to the same relative position as in 1868. However, this swing was not uniform so that in these sample constituencies the Conservatives emerged stronger in the smaller English and Irish boroughs than had been the case in 1868, whereas the Liberals were comparatively stronger in the larger English boroughs (Martin, 1874: 193–201, and Hanham, 1959: 193).

Liberal morale was boosted by the defection of Lord Derby (who had resigned as Foreign Secretary during the Eastern crisis) to the Liberals. However, the outcome of the election was in doubt at the outset, Conservative optimism being encouraged by the London press. The Liberals won a majority of seats in England and were overwhelming victors in Scotland and Wales. However, the Liberal performance in England was not consistent, the Party performing best in the Yorkshire/Lancashire and Midlands area (where it recorded one half of its total gains). York witnessed the election of two Liberal MPs for the first time since 1832. Twenty-eight net gains were recorded in the counties (in constituencies which included South East Lancashire, Norfolk, North Staffordshire, West Cumberland, Bedfordshire, East Derbyshire and South Warwickshire), although success was often achieved in county constituencies which were dependent on industry rather than agriculture. The relative lack of success in London and the surrounding area indicated that the Liberal Party was moving towards a position of being the 'Party of the Provinces'.

The main feature of the 1880 election was the increased size of the Liberal vote compared to 1874. This suggests that a number of those who deliberately abstained in 1874 decided to vote in 1880. Nonconformists were encouraged to vote by the actions of the Conservative government. The 1875 Endowed Schools Act was viewed as an attack on nonconformist interests and they were also unhappy concerning the rejection of legislation which would have remedied nonconformist grievances regarding burials. Other factors which helped the Liberal Party to obtain an increased vote were the heightened level of excitement aroused by the campaign, improved Liberal organisation at local level (which was especially important in marginal constituencies) (Hanham, 1959: 195–6), and nationally in consequence of the activities of the National Liberal Federation. The Party's performance was also improved by the absence of internal disputes (only one constituency, Tower Hamlets, witnessed rival Liberal candidates fighting each other).

It has been estimated that the Liberal victory was due to the appeal of Liberal foreign policy to political enthusiasts coupled with a more widespread vote against the Conservative government which was held responsible for the depression in trade. The Liberal focus on foreign and colonial affairs eclipsed other issues and by 1880 the Labour Representation League was integrated into the Liberal Party. However, although the Liberal Party secured a landslide victory measured in terms of seats in the House of Commons, the popular vote indicated that the election was a far closer run affair. Had 4,054 votes cast for the Liberals in the 72 seats in which a Conservative candidate was within 10 per cent of victory been instead cast for the Conservatives, they would have won every one (Lloyd, 1968: 136).

John Morley and Herbert Gladstone were both defeated (although Herbert Gladstone was soon elected for the Leeds seat which his father had vacated in preference to Midlothian).

The Conservatives tended to blame their defeat on economic factors, the government's identification with 'hard times'. Although the Liberal Party won the majority of seats in England, the Conservatives managed to hold the position they had achieved in 1874 in the Home Counties and to a lesser extent in London, and although the Liberals made significant gains in English county seats, the Conservatives also polled relatively well in rural areas. This was despite the poor record of the government towards agriculture which had prompted the formation of the Farmers' Alliance in 1879. However, although the Party continued to poll well in the smaller English boroughs, most of the gains in the larger English boroughs which had been made in 1874 were wiped out, and the advance of the Party in Lancashire was checked with the Liberals gaining eight borough and four county constituencies there (Jenkins, 1994: 166).

Scotland, Wales and Ireland
In Scotland, the agricultural depression resulted in a resurgence of anti-landlord feeling which cost the Conservatives the gains they had recorded in 1874. The Liberals registered gains in counties which included Peeblesshire and Berwickshire and emerged from the election winning 52 of Scotland's 58 seats to the six won by the Conservatives. The Liberals improved upon the position they had obtained in 1874 in Wales by winning 29 of the 33 seats. The Conservatives won the remaining four.

The election in Ireland was fought against the background of agricultural failure in 1879 and the formation of the Land League in the same year. This event prompted Parnell to visit America to raise funds for famine relief and he was out of the country when the dissolution of Parliament occurred. Although home rule was an important issue in Ireland during the election, his absence prevented it from becoming overwhelming and the the Home Rule Party (which consisted of Parnellites and moderate or Whig home rulers) did not sweep the board. In constituencies which included Dundalk and Athlone Liberals candidates defeated Home Rulers and overall, the strength of the Home Rule Party moderately increased to 63 MPs. Parnell was triply nominated and returned for three constituencies (Cork, County Mayo and County Meath).

The Liberals slightly improved on the position they had obtained in 1874 and won 15 seats and the Conservatives lost some ground compared to 1874 and won 23 seats. However, the attack mounted by the Liberal Party in Ulster was successfully repulsed by the Conservatives who displaced Liberal MPs in Carrickfergus, Newry and Coleraine.

Consequence of the Election
Gladstone was not the formal party leader during the election and the Liberal victory posed the dilemma of who would become prime minister. The Queen sent for the Marquis of Hartington (rather than the party leader, Lord Granville) on 22 April who explained to the monarch that Gladstone would not serve under him and that he would find it impossible to construct a Liberal ministry which did not contain him. The following day, the Queen received similar advice from a joint meeting of Hartington and Granville. Thus, with some reluctance on the Queen's part, the 71-year-old Gladstone was invited to form the new administration in which he also occupied the post of Chancellor of the Exchequer.

24 November – 18 December 1885

Party Leaders
The Marquis of Salisbury (Conservative)
William Ewart Gladstone (Liberal)

Background to the Election
Timing of the Election
Salisbury took office in June 1885 without a majority. His administration was thus in the nature of a 'caretaker government' which carried on the business of government until an election could be held.

Electoral Practices and Procedures
A number of significant changes were introduced after 1880 regarding the conduct of elections. The 1883 Corrupt and Illegal Practices Prevention Act sought to ensure that elections were contested through the use of fair means. Corrupt practice was defined as bribery, treating, intimidation, personation and making a false statement regarding election expenses. This offence was punishable by a one-year term of imprisonment and a £200 fine and the loss of the offender's political rights. Illegal practices were defined as spending in excess of the permitted maximum amount according to a scale of maximum spending which was stipulated in the Act (which differentiated, for example, between borough and county constituencies), paying for the conveyance of voters to the polls and the provision of party favours, and were punishable by a fine and the limited loss of the offender's political rights. A winning candidate would be unseated if he or his agent was held to be responsible for a corrupt or illegal practice. The 1884 Representation of the People Act (the 'third Reform Act') provided household franchise to the counties. It has been estimated that this meant that around 76 per cent of the male population could now vote (Searle, 1992: 49). The 1885 Redistribution Act sought to move towards constituencies of equal size in order to give substance to the ideal of 'one vote, one value'. This legislation adopted the formula of one MP for every 52,000 inhabitants and entailed 132 existing seats being available for redistribution. This measure tackled the over-representation of small borough seats in southern England, with Greater London being the main beneficiary. However, anomalies remained. A number of sparsely populated constituencies in the remote parts of the Celtic Fringe continued to exist, Ireland (which had experienced depopulation) was over-represented and a number of small-sized boroughs remained in the South West to the disadvantage of the Midlands and North Eastern England which were under-represented. This legislation also established the single-member constituency as the norm, although this was not universally established until the enactment of the 1948 and 1949 Representation of the People Acts. The Act also ended the 'minority' vote situation in three-member seats whereby electors were entitled only to two votes. The 1885 Registration Act assimilated the law concerning the registration of voters in the counties and boroughs.

Conservatives

Disraeli died in April 1881, and was replaced by a party leader in each of the two Houses of Parliament (the Marquis of Salisbury in the House of Lords and Sir Stafford Northcote in the House of Commons). These operated 'as a duumvirate with equal power' (McKenzie, 1963: 23).

This situation was not without its critics; Lord Randolph Churchill in particular sought to address it with proposals to 'democratise' the workings of the Party by transferring its executive control and financial affairs to the National Union of Conservative and Unionist Associations.

Together with Arthur Balfour, Sir Henry Drummond Wolff and John Gorst, Churchill was the leading light of the 'fourth party', one of whose chief targets in the House of Commons was their own leader, Northcote. The issue of leadership eventually resolved itself when the Queen summoned Lord Salisbury to become Prime Minister in June 1885 following the defeat of the Liberal government. Salisbury had enhanced his reputation in connection with the struggle with the Liberal Party over the 1884 Reform Act when the opposition from the House of Lords had forced Gladstone to agree a compromise with Salisbury which entailed the introduction of a redistribution measure.

The path leading to the downfall of the Liberal government had been paved by Lord Randolph Churchill who had entered into negotiations with the Irish Nationalists on the basis that a future Conservative government would discontinue the policy of coercion. Accordingly, the new Conservative government ended Lord Spencer's policy of firm government in Ireland and enacted Lord Ashbourne's Irish Land Purchase Act which gave a measure of state assistance for this purpose. The Party further toyed with the idea of home rule, although no action to implement it was taken in Salisbury's brief period of government. The other main achievement of this administration was military intervention in Upper Burma which was triggered by the decision of its King, Thibaw, to confiscate the property of the Bombay-Burma Company. The kingdom was formally annexed to the Crown on 1 January 1886.

Liberals

The factional nature of the Liberal Party was replicated in its parliamentary representation. Herbert Gladstone estimated that at the 1880 election around 70 Liberal MPs supported Chamberlain, another 70 Hartington and the remainder were broadly supportive of Gladstone (Lloyd, 1968: 35). However, Gladstone's Cabinet was very aristocratic in composition, most members being derived from the Whig aristocracy or landowning class. Differences between the Whigs and radicals (who were themselves divided in particular on imperial policy) frequently bedevilled the conduct of Gladstone's second ministry.

In comparison with Gladstone's first ministry, relatively little was accomplished in domestic policy after 1880. The main achievements of the government concerned measures of electoral reform which were pursued between 1883 and 1885, and in addition some legislation to the benefit of the 'fads' was enacted. The Farmers' Alliance was rewarded for the support it gave to the Party in rural constituencies in 1880 with the abolition of the malt tax in the 1880 Inland Revenue Act, and the enactment of the 1880 Ground Game Bill which gave tenant farmers exclusive powers concerning the killing of hares and rabbits on their holdings. Additionally, the 1882 Settled Land Act and the 1881 Conveyancing and Law of Property Act removed some of the worst anomalies affecting the operations of the land market. The 1880 Burials Law

Amendment Act appeased nonconformists by permitting non-Anglican services to be used at burials in Anglican cemeteries and minor extension of an employee's right to compensation for minor industrial accidents was a sop to labour. A further measure, the 1880 Elementary Education Act, made elementary education compulsory.

Unemployment continued to rise following the 1879 depression, and the early 1880s witnessed the growth in support for socialist ideas through the activities of bodies which included the Democratic Federation (formed in 1881) and the Fabian Society (established in 1884). The continuance of the agricultural depression also popularised the views of A. R. Wallace and Henry George concerning land reform. These developments prompted Chamberlain to attempt to seize the political initiative and move the party's domestic policies in a more radical direction. A series of articles published in the *Fortnightly Review* in 1885 provided the basis for the Radical Programme which was published in September of that year. Its timing was influenced by an agreement reached between Gladstone and the Conservative leader, Lord Salisbury, in November 1884 regarding franchise reform and redistribution which provided parliamentary time for domestic reform. The Radical Programme was fashioned by a small group of radicals associated with Chamberlain, and its contents included calls for public bodies (especially at local level) to be given enhanced powers to deal with problems such as slum housing, financed by graduated taxation.

A major explanation for the government's inability to pursue a vigorous programme of domestic reform was that its energies were required to deal with other issues after 1880. One of these was Ireland. Ireland had received little attention in the Liberals' election campaign, but the usage of 'new departure' tactics by Parnell and the Land League (which entailed exploiting agrarian grievances which were worsened by agrarian depression in order to gain support for the campaign for home rule) ensured that this issue would occupy a prominent place on the government's political agenda. This was accompanied by the use of tactics by Irish Nationalist MPs in the House of Commons to obstruct business. The approach adopted by the government towards Ireland swung between appeasement and coercion, reflecting the divergent views of the Whigs and radicals on this issue. The Whigs favoured coercion and feared that reform affecting issues such as land ownership might fuel the demand for similar measures to be enacted in England, whereas the radicals wished to address underlying grievances in Ireland for precisely the same reasons, and saw Irish Nationalist MPs as potential allies to the advancement of key radical policies in particular regarding the status of landed property.

The government's first response was a Compensation for Disturbance Bill which sought to stem the rising tide of evictions by penalising Irish landlords who evicted their tenants even if this action was due to non-payment of rent. This measure upset the Whigs and it was lost in the House of Lords. In 1881 the government adopted the twin approach of coercion and concession. An Arms Act was enacted to stop the spread of weapons and habeas corpus was suspended by the Coercion Act. A number of nationalist leaders (including Parnell) were subsequently detained without trial. This was accompanied by the 1881 Land Act which granted the 'three Fs' (fair rents settled by land courts, fixity of tenure for 15 years provided that the rent was paid and the free sale of an outgoing tenant's interest in the holding to the next tenant). The failure of the detention of Parnell to put an end to agrarian outrages in Ireland led the government to look for a further compromise which was provided in the 1882 'Kilmainham

Treaty'. The government agreed to introduce an Arrears Bill (whereby the state would pay off tenants' debts so that they could use the land courts set up by the 1881 Act) and in return Parnell promised to use his influence to end crime and disorder in Ireland. W. E. Forster resigned as Chief Secretary for Ireland, and his successor, Lord Frederick Cavendish, was murdered (along with the Under Secretary, T. H. Burke) in Phoenix Park. This led to further coercive legislation in the form of a Prevention of Crime Act which again exposed divisions in the government. In July 1882 an exasperated Gladstone lost his temper in the House of Commons and threatened to resign when a number of Whig backbenchers joined with the Conservatives to defeat an attempt by the government to tone down this measure.

Events abroad provided a further distraction from domestic affairs. The government had inherited foreign and imperial policies from the Conservatives which it was not inherently suited to handle. These issues also frequently evidenced splits in the Parliamentary Party which were broadly between those who wished to avoid all forms of foreign intervention (the 'Little Englanders') and those who were more imperially minded. These differences cut across other divisions in the Parliamentary Party, the radicals in particular being split on the approach which should be adopted towards foreign and colonial policy. Bright exemplified the desire for non-intervention abroad whereas Joseph Chamberlain and Sir Charles Dilke favoured a more aggressive form of imperialism.

Initially, the government achieved success in securing Britain's military withdrawal from Afghanistan in 1880 (mainly because the new Emir was willing to accept a virtual British protectorate over his country which thus safeguarded the route to India against hostile Russian intentions) but it was less fortunate in its dealings with South Africa, Egypt and the Sudan about which divisions were manifest within the Parliamentary Party. In 1877, the Transvaal had been annexed by Beaconsfield's government and initially Gladstone was inclined to pursue the previous government's intention of establishing a federal system for all of South Africa. However, the Boers wished to regain their independence and rebelled against British rule, inflicting a military defeat on the British at Majuba Hill in February 1881. The government was divided over whether it should seek military revenge or compromise. It determined on the latter course of action and conceded virtual independence to the Transvaal.

The overthrow of the Khedival regime by a nationalist revolt headed by Arabi Pasha forced Britain to intervene militarily in Egypt in 1882 (a decision which caused Bright to resign from the government), and the Dervish revolt in the Sudan led by the Mahdi (Messiah) led to further divisions in the Liberal Party as to whether Britain should evacuate its beleagured garrisons or intervene to reconquer the dependency. The situation was further complicated when General Gordon became cut off at Khartoum. The government hesitated before sending a large military force to relieve him but it arrived on 28 January 1885, two days after Khartoum had been stormed by the Mahdi's forces and Gordon was killed in the fighting. Gordon's death (and the subsequent evacuation of the Sudan) lost the Party support amongst the urban working classes who disbelieved that Gladstone was an adequate champion of British prestige abroad. This episode manifested further divisions within the Parliamentary Party. In Feburary 1885, 65 Liberal MPs voted for John Morley's motion which called for British evacuation of Egypt and the Sudan, but in a Conservative censure motion on the government's failure to take adequate steps to save Gordon, six Liberal MPs voted with the opposition and 36 abstained. The government survived this vote by the narrow margin of 14 votes. However, it resigned later that year following a defeat on 8 June 1885 on an item contained in its budget. An amendment moved by Michael Hicks Beach was carried by 264 : 252 votes with in excess of 70 Liberals failing to support the government. Lord Salisbury then formed a Conservative administration.

By-elections
A total of 193 by-elections occurred in the 1880–85 Parliament, of which 99 were contested. The Liberal Party made a net loss of 17 seats, the Conservatives a net gain of 14 and others a net gain of three. Three separate contests were held in Northampton. An atheist, Charles Bradlaugh, had been elected for this constituency in 1880. He insisted on making an affirmation of allegiance in place of the parliamentary oath but the House of Commons refused him permission to do this. He fought, and won, by-elections in April 1881, March 1882 and February 1884 but was unable to sit in Parliament until 1886 when a new Speaker refused to intervene (as had his predecessor) and prevent him taking the ordinary oath.

Conduct of the Election
The election was drawn out. Gladstone issued his election address in mid-Sepember and the contest lasted until December of that year. This gave ample opportunity for leading figures from each party to devote a considerable amount of time in electioneering.

Conservatives
The main statement of Conservative policy for the election was provided in speeches delivered by Lord Salisbury at South London, Newport and Brighton. The crisis in foreign affairs following the revolt in Bulgaria forced him to defend his government's policy towards the Eastern Question. At Newport on 7 October, he argued that his approach was to defend the Turkish Empire where it could genuinely and healthily be done but that, where its rule was proven to be inconsistent with the welfare of the population, to strive to foster strong self-sustaining nationalities. Other reforms were couched in vague language, some bearing a resemblance to those advanced by his Liberal couterpart. He argued that all persons should contribute towards the expenses of local government according to their ability, that the issue of Sunday closing of public houses should be determined by local authorities, and he expressed support for reducing the costs of land transfer, whilst rejecting any scheme whereby local government could purchase land compulsorily and let it out to smallholders.

Salisbury's Irish policy was underpinned by the necessity of preserving the integrity of the Empire and he also insisted that any reform to the system of local government in that country must take regard of the divisions in Irish society to avoid the majority in any locality acting in a tyrannical way towards the local minority. He also insisted, despite Gladstone's statement, that the Liberal Party intended to disestablish and disendow the Church of England. W. H. Smith's election address to his Strand constituency expressed opposition to the disestablishment or disendowment of any Church or institution which was identified with the best interests of the country, although he stated that he was prepared to consider proposals for their reform or improvement. Lord Salisbury, in his speech at South London on 4 November, stated that although Gladstone was arguing that the disestablishment of the Church of England was not an issue in that election, he had expressed similar sentiments in 1865 regarding the Church of Ireland which he then went on to disestablish. He argued that 'we have been misled by that language before but surely we shall never be taken in by it again'.

The erosion of Britain's pre-eminent position in world trade hit certain sectors of the British economy hard because of competition from nations such as America and Germany. A Royal Commission into the depression of trade and industry was set up by the Conservative government in 1885. A number of Conservative candidates responded to this development by calling for a policy of 'fair trade' (which entailed the use of retaliatory tariffs to protect British producers). This theme was developed by Lord Salisbury in his speech at South London on 4 November. In this speech he insisted that the Conservatives had no intention of restoring the Corn Laws or to provide for the 'dear loaf'. However, he emphasised his support for what he referred to as 'real free trade' whereby Britain would use the sanction of increasing duties as a lever to force other countries to lower theirs: he referred to this approach as 'an act of retaliation, and an act of fiscal war'.

Ireland was discussed in the Conservative campaign. The Liberal record in Ireland between 1880 and 1885 was criticised by some Conservatives. Concerning future policy, W. H. Smith's election address asserted that 'the unity and good government of Great Britain and Ireland, as one country linked together by every bond of interest and duty, should be the first aim of every MP'. M. Hicks-Beach echoed this sentiment in his speech at Bristol on 4 November and believed that Chamberlain's proposal for the establishment of National Councils in Ireland might result in a policy of home rule being secured through the 'back door'. He also referred to the Liberal government's inability to curb the level of disorder in that country.

The Conservative campaign also mounted attacks on Liberal foreign policy. In a speech given at Stretford on 6 November, Lord Randolph Churchill criticised the foreign policy of the Liberal administration for it alleged failure to defend British interests in India against the advance of Russia. He mocked the government for being 'courageous when they slaughtered helpless Egyptians' but then 'run away from sturdy Boers' or 'when they threatened and bullied the Sultan of Turkey and grovelled before Prince Bismarck'. He also attacked the Liberals' 'blind and selfish' neglect of colonial policy. He asserted that in domestic affairs there had been virtually no useful legislation and he accused the government of intensifying the trade depression. He also emphasised that the current level of Liberal disunity would ensure that a Liberal government would perform even worse in the future: 'If Mr Gladstone, with a united Party in 1880 was unable ... either to govern or to legislate or to economise your resources, how can you reasonably or sensibly expect that he will be able to do either of these functions now, when his party is torn by every conceivable division, and divided into at least half a dozen factions who are totally divided on all foreign and domestic issues.' M. Hicks-Beach developed this theme in a speech made at Gloucester on 18 November when he stated that 'Mr Gladstone endeavoured to fulfil the office of an elastic band to bind together the opposing factions of the Liberal bundle'.

Parnell instructed all Irishmen living in England to vote for the Conservative Party. A key explanation for this stance was a belief that Chamberlain's 'free schools' posed a threat to Catholic institutions.

Liberals

Chamberlain seized the early impetus in the Liberal campaign. The resignation of the government freed him from any constraints which the convention of collective ministerial responsibility would otherwise have imposed on him and he attempted to use this unexpected freedom to identify the Liberal Party with the radical measures contained in the Radical Programme. He selected three measures from this programme (free education, graduated taxation and the 'three acres and a cow' proposal whereby local authorities would be provided with compulsory powers to buy land and provide smallholdings or allotments). These collectively were referred to as the Unauthorised Programme and formed the basis of Chamberlain's campaign in the early part of the election. These ideas were put forward against the background of concern regarding poverty (which was evidenced in pamphlets such as that written by Andrew Mearns in 1883, *The Bitter Cry of Outcast London*), the rise of socialist societies (such as Henry Hyndman's Democatic Federation which was formed in 1881) and a severe business recession which resulted in considerable unemployment in 1885–86. Chamberlain wished to pursue social legislation in order to avoid the clash between capital and labour which revolutionary socialists desired. During the campaign, Chamberlain also developed other themes which included attacking (in a speech delivered at Birmingham on 9 November) the 'fair trade' policies which were gaining currency in the Conservative Party on the grounds that these would increase the cost of food since it would be impossible to provide protection to manufacturing industry but deny it to agriculture.

However, Chamberlain's approach to seize the initiative and identify the Liberal Party with radical proposals soon foundered. Moderates and Whigs were alarmed at his ideas (in particular with his rhetoric which seemed to threaten traditional forms of property ownership) and the Marquis of Hartington was vehemently opposed to them. Nonconformists were opposed to the introduction of free education unless it was accompanied by the disestablishment of the Church of England since they feared that Chamberlain's policy would result in the Church of England being provided with state money to run its schools. In addition, Chamberlain lacked the total support of radical opinion in the Party as some were opposed to further measures of state intervention (whether this was by the central or the local state) funded by graduated tax, and alternatively advocated self-help and voluntary effort as the mechanisms of social improvement. Vainly, Chamberlain sought to foist the unauthorised programme on the Party but he eventually backed down, downgrading them to 'open questions' which a future Liberal government might consider.

The dissension which Chamberlain caused within the Liberal Party in 1885 prompted Gladstone to announce his intention to remain as party leader in the hope of preserving party unity. He was, it has been asserted, seen by radicals 'as an ally against Whig inertia, while the Whigs saw his usefulness as a barrier against radical' 'extremism' (Searle, 1992: 22). His election address to his constituents at Midlothian (which was referred to as The Hawarden Manifesto and published in *The Times* on 19 September 1885) proposed far more modest domestic measures. The principal four items proposed were the reform of the procedures of the House of Commons (to deal with congestion and guard against obstruction), changes to the financing of local government (which would seek to rectify the balance of taxation between personal and real property, provide relief to ratepayers by making over for local purposes certain items of national taxation and give local government inducements to ensure economy), the reform of the system of voter registration and the reform of the land laws (which was designed to simplify land transfer and registration both during life and after death but which would uphold the principle of the freedom of bequest). Lord Hartington elaborated this latter policy in a speech delivered at Rossendale on 11 November when he stated that the future prosperity of the landed interest rested on a system which provided for the easier transfer of land so that estates could be transferred to persons with capital and enterprise. This would enable the prosperity of all, including agricultural workers, to be ensured through increased productivity based on the greater use of technology and the availability of money to finance improvements such as drainage.

Additionally, Gladstone put forward two vague proposals regarding the House of Lords (where he felt there was a case to consider its composition) and education (where he reserved his judgement as to whether a gratuitous system of elementary education should be established, although he asserted that as yet he did not feel that the role of the state in this matter had been shown to be an improvement on the role performed by religious or philanthropic bodies, and neither did he believe that the public wanted a universal system of secular education). He was similarly vague on future Liberal policy concerning Ireland. He believed that the country had reached an important epoch in its history and that it was now time to consider the nation's wants as well as its grievances. However, he argued that at present Ireland was greatly in arrears regarding local self-government in comparison to England, Wales or Scotland and believed that movement in this direction would prevent the break-up of the unity of the United Kingdom. He refused to give any precise details of his intentions, and in a speech at Calder on 17 November stated that he would give his utmost attention to the wishes expressed by the electors of Ireland but that at this stage he did not know what these wishes would be.

The issue of the disestablishment of the Church of England occupied a considerable degree of attention in the Liberal campaign. In his election address, Gladstone insisted that the separation of the Church of England from the state was not a 'practical question' until there had been a greater level of public discussion on this matter, and declared that any change in the status of the Church of England would require the general consent of the nation. However, Conservative insistence that the Liberals would carry out such a policy, coupled with the particular interest towards this issue in Scotland, forced Gladstone to clarify his Party's position on this topic. In a major speech delivered at Edinburgh on 12 November he pointed out that, while what was referred to as the 'Radical Programme' did advocate this course of action, the plan contained in this pronouncement would not be adopted even if people in England supported the objective of disestablishment. He reiterated that this issue should not figure in the election and stated that he would not regard a majority of Scottish MPs voting for Dr Cameron's motion on the disestablishment of the Church of Scotland as indicative of overall Scottish opinion. Other aspects of Chamberlain's programme were opposed, Lord Hartington expressing his opposition to the scheme for a graduated income tax in a speech at Nelson on 1 November.

Moderation was thus a key theme in Gladstone's campaign in 1885. In a speech delivered at Carlisle on 9 November, he summed up (in words which were reminiscent of Peel) his approach to politics as being 'we are Liberals because we desire to promote, along with the introduction of needful reforms, the warm attachment of the people to the existing laws and institutions of the country and will amend, or try to amend, everything which requires amendment, in order that we may more zealously preserve all that needs preservation'.

The Liberal campaign also sought to secure support based on the record of the 1880–85 Liberal government. Gladstone's manifesto praised the actions of his government in both domestic and foreign affairs, although he conceded that errors had been made in the Sudan. Lord Hartington developed this theme in a speech at Rossendale on 11 November in which he sought to answer accusations made by the Conservative Party that the Liberals had engaged in unnecessary wars and expenditure by asserting that in Egypt and on the Afghanistan border 'it is we who have preserved peace when it was difficult to maintain peace, who have maintained peace in spite of some provocation from without and some vituperation at home'.

The Liberal campaign also attacked the policies and stance adopted by the Conservative Party after 1880. Gladstone's election address condemned the obstructive attitude adopted by the Conservative Party in opposition, which was developed by Sir William Harcourt in a speech at Hackney on 13 November when he stated that the Conservatives after 1880 had used 'every legitimate and illegitimate method of obstructing every Liberal measure'. Lord Hartington (in his speech at Rossendale on 11 November) drew particular attention to the cooperation between Parnell and Conservatives in Parliament in opposing measures brought forward by the Liberal government on topics such as the administration of justice. This issue was developed by Lord Hartington who (along with Campbell-Bannerman) took the Liberal campaign to Ireland. In a speech at Belfast on 5 November, Hartington drew attention to the 'offensive alliance' between Parnell and the Conservative Party and argued that if the Conservatives were returned Parnell would be the virtual master of Parliament. He asserted that the only way to prevent this was to elect a Liberal government with a large majority which would defend the Union. In a second speech that day he expressed his opposition to any measure of self-government for Ireland which would amount to a total separation of Ireland from the remainder of the United Kingdom.

Gladstone played an active part in the Liberal campaign, deploying tactics similar to those used in 1880. On 9 November he left Hawarden for his constituency of Midlothian by train, making several speeches en route. He also delivered three subsequent major speeches to his constituents.

Result of the Election

A total number of 1,338 candidates contested the election, with only 43 MPs being returned unopposed. The result was:

Party	Votes	Vote %	MPs
Liberal	2,169,976	46.8%	319
Conservative	1,909,424	41.2%	233
Irish Home Rule Party	310,608	6.7% [67.8%]	86
Irish Conservative	111,503	2.4% [24.8%]	16
Others	106,702	2.3%	16
Irish Liberal	30,022	0.6% [6.8%]	0
Total	4,638,425		670

The turnout was 81.2 per cent.

The 'others' were W. Abraham (Rhondda, Labour), Sir R. Anstruther (St Andrews Burghs, Independent Liberal), J. Cameron (Wick Burghs, Independent Liberal-Crofter), Sir G. Campbell (Kirkaldy Burghs, Independent Liberal), Dr G. Clark (Caithness, Independent Liberal-Crofter), C. Conybeare (Camborne, Independent Liberal), J. Cowen (Newcastle-upon-Tyne, Independent Liberal), W. Fitzwilliam (Peterborough, Independent Liberal), G. Fraser-Mackintosh (Invernessshire, Independent Liberal-Crofter), G. Goschen (East Edinburgh, Independent Liberal), Sir G. Harrison (South Edinburgh, Independent Liberal), Dr R. Macdonald (Ross and Cromarty, Independent Liberal-Crofter), D. Macfarlane (Argyll, Independent Liberal-Crofter), S. Parker (Perth, Independent Liberal), Sir E. Watkin (Hythe, Independent Liberal), J. Wilson (Central Edinburgh, Independent Liberal).

The Parties

The redistribution of seats and the widespread adoption of single-member constituencies benefited the Conservatives considerably in 1885, and had been insisted upon by Lord Salisbury in November 1884 in return for his support for the government's electoral reform measures. Redistribution eliminated many of the smaller boroughs in Southern England in which the Liberals had traditionally fared well, and single member constituencies were frequently created in suburban areas, containing large numbers of the expanding group of white-collar workers in the tertiary sector (Jenkins, 1994: 200).

The Conservative Party recovered the ground it had lost in Lancashire in 1880 and performed well in the English boroughs. Although the growth of support in these areas was not entirely new (being a feature of electoral behaviour in the larger boroughs in 1874), in 1885 they secured for the Conservatives the first majority they had obtained in the English boroughs since 1832, winning 114 of the 226 seats (Jenkins, 1994: 193). The defection of middle- and working-class support from the Liberals gave the Conservatives their first ever victory in London where they won 36 seats. The Irish urban vote (alienated by the Liberal government's record on home rule and the handling of the issue of Catholic schools) also deserted to the Conservatives.

The Liberal Party suffered a severe setback in the English boroughs (the industrial region around Birmingham being the main urban area to buck this trend). The Party won 82 of these seats compared to the Conservatives' 80 (the remaining one being won by an Irish Nationalist MP who was elected for Liverpool, Scotland) (Jenkins, 1994: 223). This was due to a number of factors which included the impact of economic change such as the extension of factory-based production on occupational groups (such as those engaged in the woollen textile, hosiery and boot and shoe industries) which had traditionally been loyal to the Liberal Party. These groups had strong connections with nonconformity which was also becoming swamped in the expanding cities and towns in which the population was increasingly being concentrated (Jenkins, 1994: 199).

However, these setbacks were offset by the Liberal performance in the English counties where losses of industrial workers and the bourgeoisie were offset by the support given to the Liberal Party by the rural working class and other newly enfranchised groups such as miners, potters and weavers. The Liberal Party won 132 of these 231 seats and the Conservatives 99 (Jenkins, 1994: 232). The support obtained from these latter groups was especially significant in the 12 counties of Northern England where around one-half of Liberal gains in county seats were made (Jenkins, 1994: 200). A number of factors explain the Liberal performance in the counties. These include the impact of redistribution (which merged smaller Liberal-held boroughs in southern England into their adjacent counties which the Liberals were able to win), the problems of landowners being unable to exercise control over an expanded electorate, the dislike by rural workers of the Conservative policy of fair trade, and their attraction to aspects of the 'Unauthorised Programme', in particular the promise of 'three acres and a cow'. Additionally, outside England and Ireland the Liberal Party fared well.

Although the Labour Representation League was wound up in 1881, the 1884 Reform Act boosted the number of working-class candidates elected to the House of Commons. In total, 11 'Lib–Lab' MPs secured victory.

Scotland, Wales and Ireland

Redistribution resulted in an increase in Scottish seats from 58 to 70. The Liberals won 51 of these, the Conservatives eight and the independents 11. These latter were elected as independent Liberals, some registering their protest regarding Gladstone's refusal to endorse disestablishement and others protesting against the Liberal Party's failure to address grievances in the Highlands (some of whom were closely associated with the Highland Land League). Five MPs representing the Crofters' Party were elected. Wales gained one seat through redistribution. The position of the two major parties was unaltered from 1880: the Liberals won 29 seats, the Conservatives four and one was won by an independent Lib–Lab candidate. The 1884 Reform Act extended the franchise in Ireland on the same terms as in England which enhanced Parnell's grip on Irish politics. His Home Rule Party won 85 of Ireland's 103 seats (and one further supporter, T. P. O'Connor, was elected for the newly created constituency of Liverpool, Scotland). The Conservative Party won 16 seats and the Liberals were totally eliminated from the Irish political scene.

Consequence of the Election

Lord Salisbury formed a minority Conservative government. However, an amendment to the Queen's Speech (moved by the Liberal MP Jesse Collings on 26 January 1886) which condemned the government for its failure to bring forward legislation to improve the lot of agricultural labourers (which was popularly known as the 'three acres and a cow' policy) resulted in the government's defeat. It was replaced by an administration led by Gladstone who (metaphorically) rode into 10 Downing Street on Jesse Collings's cow.

1 July – 27 July 1886

Party Leaders
The Marquis of Salisbury (Unionist)
Wiliam Ewart Gladstone (Liberal)

Background to the Election
Gladstone's decision to pursue Irish home rule split the Liberals and led to the formation of the Liberal Unionists. The 1886 general election also witnessed the emergence of the concept of the mandate. This held that MPs should not vote for measures in Parliament which were not included in their election addresses.

Timing of the Election
Gladstone's defeat in the House of Commons on 8 June 1886 in connection with his Irish Home Rule Bill caused him to seek an immediate dissolution of Parliament. Although the Queen might have asked either Lord Hartington or Lord Salisbury to form a government, she acceded to Gladstone's request for an election.

Unionists
The Unionists remained in office to test the opinion of the House of Commons. However, on 26 January 1886 the Liberal MP Jesse Collings moved an amendment to the Address expressing regret that the Queen's Speech contained no measures to provide relief for the agricultural classes and in particular failed to grant facilities to agricultural labourers and others who lived in rural districts to obtain allotments and smallholdings on equitable terms in relation to rent and security of tenure. Parnell united with the Liberals to defeat the government by the margin of 329 : 250. Salisbury tendered his resignation on 29 January and Gladstone took office for the third time on 1 February 1886.

In opposition, Salisbury's path was cleared by Gladstone's decision to introduce a measure of home rule. He united his party behind outright opposition to this policy which was vigorously pursued by Lord Randolph Churchill who stirred up dissent in Ulster towards home rule. This opposition together with the reservation of many Liberals towards the wisdom of this course of action was sufficient to bring Gladstone's government to an end in June 1886.

Liberals
It was estimated that around 101, one-third of the Party's MPs, were radicals (Jenkins, 1994: 193). Many Liberals blamed Chamberlain for the setback experienced by the Party in the English boroughs in 1885.

Following the election, Gladstone turned his attention to Ireland. This topic had dominated the Cabinet deliberations of Gladstone's previous government in May and June 1885 when Chamberlain's proposal of a Central Board was discussed. However, Gladstone came to appreciate that this proposal was unacceptable to Parnell and, further, realised that his own attempt to undermine support for home rule through land reform had also failed. Gladstone's conversion to home rule was announced on 17 December 1885 when his son, Herbert, made a public pronouncement to this effect in what was termed the 'Hawarden Kite'. As Gladstone had said little about Ireland in the 1885 election campaign, Conservatives viewed this as a cynical ploy to obtain Parnell's support to oust Salisbury's minority government. Although there is evidence that Gladstone was moving towards this position before the election (but said little during the campaign as he realised it was a divisive issue for the Party), his overtures met with immediate success and, as is noted above, resulted in the ousting of the Unionist administration on 26 January 1886.

On 29 January *The Times* argued that the first issue facing the incoming government would not be Jesse Collings and the policy of 'three acres and a cow' but 'the demands of the Parnellites and the maintenance of order in Ireland'. Gladstone entered office on the understanding that his government would 'examine' home rule. However, a measure (the Government of Ireland Bill) was soon produced in April 1886. This provided for an elected Parliament in Dublin with full charge of all Irish domestic issues from which would be chosen an Irish executive. However, the Westminster Parliament would retain control of a number of key policy areas (such as foreign policy, defence and trade) and the Irish Parliament would make a financial contribution to the British Exchequer. There would, however, be no Irish MPs elected to the House of Commons. A second measure (the Land Purchase Bill) was also proposed whereby Irish landlords would be given the opportunity to sell their estates on the basis of the rents which would be derived over a period of 20 years. The bill for this would be funded by the Exchequer since it was deemed impossible for the Irish government to settle this question from its own resources.

The introduction of the home rule measure proved divisive. Although Gladstone may have viewed it as an attempt to provide coherence to the disparate nature of his Party (which would be invited to sacrifice sectional concerns to this one overriding issue on the grounds that no further progress could be made on domestic reform until this key issue was tackled), many Liberals were opposed to it. Gladstone obtained the backing of the National Liberal Federation for Home Rule in May 1886, but in the crucial vote in the House of Commons on 7 June 1886, he was defeated by 341 : 311 votes, with 93 of his own supporters voting against the government. The dissidents were a diverse group, and although MPs drawn from aristocratic and landed backgrounds constituted its largest component (hence the description of this fissure as 'the revolt of the Whigs' whose disaffection was especially marked in the House of Lords where the Liberals were subsequently reduced to a tiny group), other MPs (including Joseph Chamberlain and John Bright) had a background in business. Those who opposed Gladstone had little in common since the Whigs were among the most vocal opponents of Chamberlain's radical policies, in particular in connection with land reform and the financing of social reform through redistributive taxation.

Although Gladstone's opponents tended to share the belief that home rule would lend support to the disintegration of Empire on which they believed Britain's continued world status depended, their opposition to home rule was based on a more diverse range of considerations which included Gladstone having acted in an authoritarian manner and foisted the measure on his Party with no consultation regarding the implications of the measure were it enacted. Many of Gladstone's opponents felt that it would inevitably result in the total separation of Ireland. Whigs feared that this situation would result in the confiscation and redistribution of the land of the largest landowners while business interests feared that an independent Ireland would enact tariff barriers against British goods.

These Liberal dissidents became formally known as Liberal Unionists (as they wished to maintain the Union with Ireland) although Gladstone preferred to brand them the 'seceders'. They increasingly cooperated with the Conservative Party with whom they formally merged in 1912.

By-elections
A total of 38 by-elections occurred in the 1885–86 Parliament, of which 15 were contested. The Unionists made a net gain of two, the Liberals a net loss of one and others a net loss of the same figure.

Conduct of the Election
The election was inevitably dominated by the one issue of Irish home rule. The Liberal Party sought to justify the position it had adopted in bringing forward legislation and its opponents (consisting of Liberal Unionists and Conservatives) criticised the action taken by the government in this matter.

Conservatives
The Conservatives viewed Gladstone's sudden conversion to home rule as indicative that he had surrendered to Parnell and, by doing so, posed a threat to all the institutions that Conservatives were pledged to defend such as the unity of the United Kingdom, the maintenance of the Church of England, the House of Lords and the right of property ownership. The Conservative case was presented in a speech delivered by the Marquis of Salisbury at Hatfield Park on 12 June. He sought to depict Gladstone's home rule proposals as ideas which were concocted in secret and revolutionary in content in that they proposed the disintegration of the Empire. He particularly drew attention to the intention of the Government of Ireland Bill to set up an Irish executive and raised the spectre of this body being controlled by the National League with full powers over law enforcement and the disposition of military forces in Ireland. He regarded this situation as dangerous, both because of the hatred which he asserted was felt in Ireland towards Britain, and also because this proposal would place the minority Loyalists and the industrial, commercial and progressive forces of the country at the mercy of Parnell's National League. Salisbury elaborated on the plight of the Loyalist community in a later speech delivered at Leeds on 18 June when he asserted that self-government for Protestants entailed 'being governed by somebody who detests you. Londonderry, Belfast, the North of Ireland, and the Loyalists throughout Ireland are to be put by this Bill under the domination of a majority from whom they have been parted for generations, with whom, unhappily, they have many hereditary causes of quarrel, and from whom they are separated by the deep gulf of creed'.

Lord Randolph Churchill adopted a more scathing view of the Government of Ireland Bill. His address to the electors of South Paddington referred to 'this insane recurrence to heptarchical arrangements, this trafficking with treason, this exaltation of the disloyal, this abasement of the loyal, this desertion of our Protestant co-religionists, this monstrous mixture of imbecility, extravagence and political hysterics'.

Other Conservatives accused the Liberals of failing to address pressing domestic issues because of their preoccupation with Ireland. At the Hatfield Park meeting on 12 June, Lord John Manners argued that having ridden to power on Jesse Collings's cow, 'agricutural labourers may be reminded that the proposed boon to them has been postponed and lost sight of for the bringing forward of this wild scheme for the destruction of the legislative union between Ireland and England'.

Liberal Unionists

The main concerns of the Liberal Unionists were put forward in Joseph Chamberlain's election address to his constituents of West Birmingham (which was published in *The Times* on 12 June). Much attention was devoted to Gladstone having departed from the manifesto which he had published in 1885. He stated that, on that occasion, Gladstone had asked for a strong Liberal government to be returned which would not be reliant on the votes of Irish MPs to enable the Irish question to be tackled in Parliament in an independent manner without the need to pay regard to the Irish vote. He argued that Gladstone had also said that should a Liberal government be returned which was forced to depend on the votes of the Irish MPs for its survival the issue of Ireland would not be addressed. He insisted that the Liberals had not contested the 1885 election on the issue of establishing a separate Parliament for Ireland.

Chamberlain further argued that home rule detracted from domestic reform. He stated that in government Gladstone had laid aside the pledges which were made in 1885, in particular the promise to improve the lot of the agricultural labourer. This issue was developed in the address of Jesse Collings (who was standing as a Liberal Unionist in Birmingham's Bordesley constituency) to the agricultural labourers. He said that at the last election the Liberals had placed emphasis on the reform of the land laws and the reform of local government in the counties. He believed that progress on both of these issues would have been possible under Gladstone's Liberal government but they had been swept aside in order to concentrate on Irish home rule which had not been an issue addressed to the electorate in 1885. It was in this sense that the manifesto of the Lancashire Unionists (whose signatories included the Earl of Derby, Sir Thomas Brocklebank and A. H. Brown MP) asserted that 'we are not seceders from the Liberal Party but, on the contrary, we remain true to those principles which are at its very essence'.

Chamberlain's election address also attacked the content of the Government of Ireland measure. He believed that the existence of an Irish Parliament and Irish executive and the absence of Irish MPs at Westminster would inevitably lead to the total separation of Ireland from the rest of the United Kingdom and would lead to demands from Scotland and Wales for a greater degree of control over their own affairs. He echoed Lord Salisbury's concerns that Gladstone intended to desert the Loyalists and place them under the control of the National League which he believed was 'an act of ingratitude and cowardice unworthy of any nation'. He believed that this 'sell-out' would harm the prosperity of Ireland, result in disorder and civil strife and be expensive to the British taxpayer if Gladstone proceeded with his proposal to compensate the Irish landlords. Lord Hartington's election address to his Rossendale constituents (which was published in *The Times* on 17 June) developed the argument regarding civil unrest by asserting that Gladstone's policy was not an alternative to coercion since home rule would have to be imposed on Protestants by force.

Chamberlain did, however, seek to put forward a constructive policy to deal with Ireland. He felt that disorder and the need to utilise coercion were not inevitable consequences of the failure to legislate for home rule and could be avoided if outstanding Irish grievances were tackled. He supported amendments being made to improve the operations of the 1881 Land Act and also the extension of local control over Irish affairs through the medium of devolved powers being given to 'a complete system of popular local government'. One difficulty with this approach, however (as Earl Spencer pointed out to a Liberal audience at Chester on 16 June), was that this policy had no support within the Irish National Party.

Liberals

The nature of the contest was summarised by *The Times* on 8 June when it stated, 'Mr Gladstone sprang upon [the Liberal Party] a novel policy entirely at variance with the traditions of the Liberal Party, and diametrically opposed to the pledges by which a majority of Liberal candidates, including himself, won the suffrages of their constituents.' A later commentator observed, 'In 1886 Gladstone dissolved for the second election within six months, with his party rent by schism and with few of the prominent figures in the party sharing his suicidal enthusiams for home rule' (Blewett, 1972: 22).

The Liberal case was presented in a brief election address prepared by Gladstone for his Midlothian constituents (which was published in *The Times* on 14 June). In this he suggested that the actions of the Conservative government after the election had forced him to address Ireland. He stated that at that election a crisis had arrived in Irish affairs. The Conservative government had failed to bring forward constructive legislation to respond to the new situation. He believed that the support obtained by the Irish National Party was indicative of the sentiments of the Irish nation. Instead, the Conservatives proposed to resort to coercion and he stated that he had entered office pledged to find a method of governing Ireland other than through the use of force. He argued that the threat to social order posed by the failure of the government to address the sentiments expressed in Ireland in the 1885 election justified his incoming government setting all other issues aside, and he asserted that the issue before the country in 1886 was 'will you govern Ireland by coercion, or will you let her manage her own affairs?' He believed that the benefit of Liberal policy was that it would consolidate the unity of the Empire, add to its strength, result in a saving of public money, end the feuds in Ireland and lead to the development of resources there which were compatible with a free and orderly government. He also asserted that Liberal policy would remove from Britain what he described as the stigma attached to this country because of its treatment of Ireland which had been attacked by the entire civilised world, and would restore to Parliament its dignity and efficiency to transact the regular progress of the nation's affairs. He pointed out that while his opponents described themselves as 'unionists', 'the union which they refuse to modify is in its present shape a paper union obtained by force and fraud, and never sanctioned or accepted by the Irish nation.' As in 1880, Gladstone emphasised the moral dimension to home rule. In a speech at Edinburgh on 18 June which opened his campaign he appealed to the electorate 'with its strong sense of justice, and its sympathy with their fellow subjects in Ireland'.

Other Liberals endorsed the views put forward by Gladstone. Henry Campbell-Bannerman's election address insisted that the establishment of a domestic Parliament for Ireland would secure the friendship of the Irish people, consolidate the United Kingdom and help to develop the strength and integrity of the Empire. Attempts were also made to focus on divisions in Irish policy between the Conservatives and Liberal Unionists. Speaking at Bradford on 20 June, John Morley stated that while Salisbury seemed to be expressing support for Chamberlain's desire to extend local self-government to Ireland, this was qualified by the assertion that this would be done 'according to the conditions of time and opportunity'. Morley reminded voters that historically Salisbury was opposed to this course of action and warned that he would not go anywhere as far with this policy as was desired by the Liberal Unionists, if he proceeded with it at all.

During the campaign, Gladstone sought to respond to some of the detailed criticisms that had been levelled against both the Government of Ireland measure and the Land Purchase Bill. In a speech given at Edinburgh on 21 June he stated that both of these measures were 'for the moment, dead', and that the issue before the electorate was to approve the principle of giving local self-government to Ireland. He insisted, however, that no final decision had been taken as to how to give effect to this principle. In a speech delivered at Manchester on 25 June he sought to answer the Unionist charges that self government would lead to sectarian friction in Ireland and eventual separation from the United Kingdom. He stated that Europe was full of countries whose political differences had been mitigated or solved by granting local autonomy to separate portions of those countries. He cited examples which included Austria in connection with Hungary and Galicia, Norway with Sweden, Denmark with Iceland and Russia with Finland. He also stated that the granting of local autonomy by the British government to those who included the French speakers in Canada, the Dutch living in the Cape and to Tasmanians had not been followed by separation from the empire.

The Liberal case was aided by Parnell who gave a series of speeches at Portsmouth (on 26 June), Plymouth (27 June), Cardiff (28 June), Chester (29 June), Wrexham and Manchester (30 June). In these speeches he constantly asserted that he had entered into discussions with the Conservative Party prior to the 1885 election whereby Ireland would be provided with a statutory legislature. In particular he referred to discussions with Lord Carnarvon on the issue of a constitution for Ireland. One product of these discussions was alleged to have been the 1885 Land Purchase Bill. He argued, however, that following the election, the Conservatives had reneged on these agreements and that Lord Salisbury proposed to introduce coercion. Parnell endorsed Gladstone's argument that a measure providing home rule would not lead to the dismemberment of the United Kingdom and he also insisted that the government of Ireland contained adequate safeguards for Protestants, of whom he was one.

Gladstone secured the support of a number of key Liberal bodies for his stance on home rule. The National Liberal Federation of Scotland published its manifesto in support of him on 12 June. Hardly any mention was made to subjects other than Ireland during the campaign, although Morley did make a brief reference to the House of Lords obstructing measures put forward by the Liberal government in his speech at Bradford on 20 June.

As in the two previous elections, Gladstone's train journey from London to Midlothian (on 17 June) was punctuated by speeches which concentrated on Ireland.

Result of the Election

A total of 1,115 candidates contested the election, with 224 MPs being returned unopposed. The result was:

Party	Votes	Vote %	MPs
Conservative and Liberal Unionist	1,422,685	47.8%	376
Liberal*	1,351,671	45.4%	192
Irish National Party	97,905	3.3% [48.6%]	85
Irish Conservative and Liberal Unionist	98,201	3.3% [50.4%]	17
Irish Liberal	1,910	0.1% [1.0%]	0
Others	1,791	0.1%	0
Total	2,974,163		670

*Includes 10 'Lib–Lab' MPs

The turnout was 74.2 per cent.

The Parties

The outcome of the election confirmed the existence of a new alignment in British politics in which conservative elements of the urban bourgeoisie (including manufacturers and financiers) together with sections of the urban working class transferred their allegiances from the Liberal Party to the Conservatives. Changes in electoral behaviour had been evident since 1868 (which included the transfer of middle-class support to the Conservative Party in London and the Home Counties and the desertion of working-class support from the Liberals in Lancashire). However, the changes which were evident at particular elections before 1886 were not always immutable developments: in 1880 the Conservatives lost ground amongst Conservative working-class voters in Lancashire and the Liberal Party substantially improved its position in rural areas in 1885.

The changes which occurred in 1886 proved permanent and ensured that the Conservative Party would dominate national politics for much of the following 20 years. The durability of these changes, however, owed much to negative reasons rather than the emergence of popular enthusiasm for the Conservatives. Non-voting by Liberal supporters was a significant feature underpinning the Conservative electoral success in 1886, which arose from the 'failure of the Liberal leaders to arouse the Party workers and to rally the Liberal voters' (Blewett, 1972: 22). This problem continued in subsequent elections in the nineteenth century and led to the conclusion that the realignment of 1886 was 'a negative restructuring of political patterns' (Blewett, 1972: 23). The 1886 election inaugurated a new map of electoral politics in which Unionist strength was concentrated in a triangle, the apex of which was in Western Lancastria and the base of which ran from the River Exe in the south-west to Margate in the east. Additionally, the rural Ridings of Yorkshire was attached to the apex (Blewett, 1972: 16). The support for the Liberal Party was more scattered than that obtained by the Conservative Party and comprised the whole of Wales, Eastern Scotland and the industrial areas of the West Riding and Northumberland-Durham together with parts of the East Midlands (Blewett, 1972: 16; Jenkins, 1994: 224).

The Liberal Unionists operated an electoral pact with the Conservatives in 1886, and approximately 77 were elected. Liberal MPs who defected to the Liberal Unionists in general were able to secure larger transfers of support at the expense of the Liberal Party, which was the main explanation for the movement of support from the Liberals to the Unionists being subject to considerable variation in England and Scotland. Higher than average regional swings away from the Liberals were experienced in the West Midlands (all seven Liberal-held seats in Birmingham being lost), South Western England, East Anglia and Scotland. The Liberal Unionists emerged as a stong force in Western Scotland, the West Midlands, the South West of England, the Western Marches and some parts of East Anglia (Jenkins, 1994: 224).

The split in the Liberal Party had an especially damaging impact on Liberal organisation since many of the Party's wealthiest supporters deserted it. One consequence of this was an inability to find candidates which resulted in 116 Unionist MPs being returned unopposed (Jenkins, 1994: 224). The Party's performance was marked by an acceleration in defection of middle-class support to the Conservatives which had been apparent in previous contests. This was especially marked in Southern England and owed much to the issue of home rule which provided an opportunity to break with Gladstone 'in defence of unity, empire and the Protestant religion' (Blewett, 1972: 15). The Liberal Party was virtually obliterated in the Home Counties where it won only one of the 73 seats. However, this change in voting behaviour was much aided by the existence of Liberal Unionists who acted as a halfway house in the conversion to Conservatism. Additionally, the progress achieved in rural areas in 1885 was not sustained, one explanation for this being the disenchantment felt towards the Party by agricultural labourers because of the absence of reform benefiting them after the 1885 election. The Liberal vote held up better in working-class areas but it also lost support among the Catholic Irish vote where it had performed well in 1885. Gladstone was doubly nominated and returned unopposed both for Midlothian and for Leith Borough.

Scotland, Wales and Ireland

Home rule was an unpopular policy for many traditional Scottish Liberal supporters who feared that a Dublin Parliament would enact discriminatory measures against Ulster's Presbyterians. This resulted in Liberal Unionist gains at the Liberal Party's expense. The Liberal Party won 43 of Scotland's 70 seats and the Unionists the remaining 27. Seven Liberal candidates were associated with the Crofters' Party. In Wales, however, home rule for Ireland was compatible with the nationalist sentiments harboured by many Welsh people for their own country. Although the Unionists made minor gains (returning eight of Wales's 34 MPs), the Liberal Party continued to dominate Welsh politics and won 26 seats. However, some of the Liberal victories were secured by narrow margins: a transference of 890 votes from the Liberals to the Unionists would have given the latter an extra nine Welsh seats, and a transference of 140 votes would have given the Unionists an extra five seats. The situation in Ireland was virtually unchanged from that of the previous election. The Conservatives won 17 of the 101 seats and the Irish National Party secured victory in the remaining 84 (with one further MP, T. P. O'Connor being returned for Liverpool, Scotland). The Liberal Party disappeared from the political scene, and fielded only one candidate.

Consequence of the Election

Lord Salisbury formed a Unionist government.

4 July – 26 July 1892

Party Leaders
The Marquis of Salisbury (Unionist)
William Ewart Gladstone (Liberal)

Background to the Election
Timing of the Election
The election was a routine request for a dissolution as Parliament was approaching the end of its statutory lifespan.

Conservatives
The government faced an early difficulty in connection with the composition of the Cabinet. The budget which was drawn up by the new Chancellor of the Exchequer, Lord Randolph Churchill, proposed to lower income tax, the duty on tea and tobacco and set up a new system of local government grants. These proposals would be funded by a radical reform of the nation's finances which included raising death duties and house duties, lowering the Sinking Fund and making savings derived from the old system of local government grants and economies of around £1.3 million. He believed the economies could be found from the defence estimates, but this provoked opposition in particular from W. H. Smith, the Minister of War. Churchill insisted that either Salisbury forced Smith to back down or he would resign and Salisbury's refusal to coerce Smith led to Churchill's resignation. He was replaced by the Liberal Unionist, George Goschen. In January the Foreign Secretary, the Earl of Iddesleigh, was removed at the behest of Goschen (being replaced by Salisbury) and in March, Sir Michael Hicks-Beach, the Irish Chief Secretary, was forced to resign because of failing eyesight.

The government's domestic policy included the 1888 County Councils Act which entailed the extension of popular representation in local government, at the expense of control formerly wielded by the magistrates. The London area (excluding the City of London) was created a new county for the purposes of this legislation. In 1891 school fees for elementary schools were abolished. The 1891 Factory Act raised the minimum age for employing children in factories to 11, and imposed a maximum 12 hours of work for women, with 1 ½ hours for meals. The 1891 Tithes Act made tithes payable by the owner rather than the occupier of land and the 1892 Small Holdings Act provided for the provision of aid to agricultural labourers to acquire allotments.

The government was faced with industrial unrest, in particular from workers who objected to poor wages in the midst of general affluence. In 1889, the London dockers, led by Ben Tillett, struck to obtain a standard wage of 6d an hour. The strikers were assisted by Tom Mann and John Burns of the Amalgamated Society of Engineers, and eventually success was achieved. This, against the background of a trade boom, provided a stimulus to the growth of 'New Unionism' which witnessed the organisation of unskilled labour.

The government's initial policy towards Ireland was that of coercion in the form of the 1887 Crimes Act which entailed the loss of the right to trial by jury for those accused of offences against law and order. This was passed following an amendment to the procedure of the House of Commons in January 1887, whereby the closure could be carried on the bare majority on the motion of any member, provided that at least 200 MPs supported it, and the later introduction of the 'guillotine' resolution. This made a Bill's progress through its committee stage subject to a time restriction, upon the expiry of which clauses would be voted on without the possibility of amendment or discussion. A modest measure to aid tenants to buy their farms was also promoted, based upon the report of Lord Cowper's Commission. However, this approach did not secure tranquillity and the Land League adopted a form of direct action entitled the 'Plan of Campaign'. This involved tenants determining what they regarded as a fair rent and paying this into the campaign fund if their landlord would not accept it. Initially, the government's coercion policy failed to secure peace but its eventual success was aided by reforms which included measures such as the construction of light railways in Western Ireland and the enactment of a Land Purchase Act in 1891. Additionally, an abortive attempt was made to enact an Irish Local Government Bill in 1892.

Foreign policy was determined by Lord Salisbury who occupied the post of Foreign Secretary after 1887. The celebration of Queen Victoria's Jubilee in that year served to give prominence to the Empire, as all the self-governing colonies sent their prime ministers to London. The meeting of these representatives with the British government gave rise to subsequent colonial or imperial conferences.

In Europe, the main problem for peace arose as the consequence of the Bulgars overthrowing the 1878 Treaty of Berlin to create the new state of Bulgaria in 1885. Salisbury viewed Balkan nationalism as a more effective defence against Russian incursions in the Near East than propping up the ailing Turkish Empire and successfully prevented Russian intervention to uphold the former arrangements. Two 'Mediterranean Agreements' were concluded in 1887 by which Britain and Italy agreed to maintain the status quo in the Mediterranean, Adriatic, Agean and Black Seas. Italy pledged to support British interests in Egypt in return for which Britain agreed to protect Italy against France. Austria-Hungary subsequently joined this pact and a triple Mediterranean Treaty including Germany was signed in December 1887. The rival claims of Britain and Germany regarding East Africa were amicably settled by a convention of 1890 whereby Germany relinquished her ambitions to build an East African Empire. Agreements were also reached with France and Portugal in 1890 concerning the boundaries of most of the adjoining territories.

The 1890 Baring crisis (when the City firm of Barings almost collapsed because of over-speculation in South America) indicated the end of the economic boom of the late 1880s. By 1892, significant economic problems emerged which took the form of decreasing investment, reduced industrial activity, falling trade and rising unemployment. These were accompanied by a large fall in the price of wheat.

Liberal Unionists

Although Goschen became the first Liberal Unionist to take office in a Conservative government when he replaced Lord Randolph Churchill as Chancellor of the Exchequer in 1887, the downfall of Churchill prompted Chamberlain to consider the possibility of Liberal reunion. A series of meetings was subsequently held consisting of Chamberlain, Trevelyan, Harcourt,

Morley and Lord Herschell, and in April 1887 Chamberlain met with Gladstone. However, there was no positive outcome to these discussions (save that Trevelyan rejoined the Liberals).

There were several explanations for this, which included Gladstone's decision to remain as Liberal Party leader and his vehement criticisms of the support given by the Liberal Unionists to the Conservative government's policy of coercion in Ireland. Thus, reunion was no longer a realistic prospect by the end of the 1887 parliamentary session (Jenkins, 1994: 217). Liberal Unionist opposition to the Newcastle Programme (which is discussed below) was a further reason for this party's decision to cooperate more closely with the Conservatives.

Liberals

The schism in the Liberal Party which occurred in 1886 had important consequences for its future conduct. Desertions by the Whigs enhanced the reliance of the Party on the sectional concerns of its radical elements and the votes of nonconformists. Land reform emerged as a key issue on which the Party campaigned after 1890, an approach which was motivated by an attempt to recover support in agricultural constituencies where the Party had polled well in 1885. Radicals viewed land as inherently different from other forms of wealth since it was a natural monopoly: whereas capitalists did not acquire increased wealth by taking it from others, landowners could only acquire more land if the ownership by others was reduced. This view accordingly saw the landlord rather than the capitalist as the main enemy of the working class. However, although land reformers were agreed on policies which included land valuation and site value taxation, they disagreed on whether the ultimate objective was wider ownership of land or the total abolition of private ownership achieved by the policy of land nationalisation.

The annual conference of the National Liberal Federation in October 1891 approved the 'Newcastle Programme', indicating the dominant position which had been achieved by the radicals in the Party. This contained measures which included the taxation of land values and the reform of death duties but also included a number of more traditional sectional demands such as the disestablishment of the Church of Scotland and the Church of Wales, local government and temperance reform, amendments to the Employers' Liability Act, the reform of the House of Lords and free trade in land. The programme was dominated by the commitment to Irish home rule which radicals could support as it embodied an attack on feudalism and constituted an attempt by oppressed people to be free. The need to promote justice for Ireland could thus be seen as the pre-eminent issue which had first to be resolved since it was obstructing progress elsewhere on the political agenda.

By-elections

A total of 179 by-elections occurred during the 1886–92 Parliament, of which 102 were contested. The Unionists made a net loss of 20, the Liberals a net gain of 19 and others a net gain of one. Two of these contests involved the Chancellor of the Exchequer, George Goschen.

He had lost his seat of East Edinburgh at the general election but then, following the death of the incumbent Liberal MP, failed to win the marginal seat of Liverpool Exchange in a by-election held in January 1887 by the narrow margin of seven votes. One of the Liberal victories occurred in April 1892 at Carnarvon District, where David Lloyd George was elected by the narrow margin of 18 votes, recapturing a seat lost by the Liberals at the previous general election.

Conduct of the Election

Prominent attention was directed at Ireland, the poet Lord Tennyson articulating the views of many when he stated in *The Times* on 30 June, 'I love Mr Gladstone, but hate his present Irish policy.'

Conservatives

The opening shots of the Conservative campaign were fired by Lord Salisbury in a speech delivered at Hastings on 18 May. In this speech he attempted to divert attention away from Ireland and on to other issues of domestic policy. He believed it was necessary for labourers to possess sufficient resources for their maintenance and comfort and enough time to cultivate their moral and intellectual well-being. However, he believed that these aims should be achieved through the growth of the knowledge and wisdom of the community rather than by legislation, which he felt could not regulate the relations between capital and labour.

A considerable portion of this speech was devoted to free trade. He argued that other countries were adopting the policy of protection and that 'we live in an age of a war of tariffs'. However, Britain's commitment to free trade meant that the nation 'has deliberately stripped herself of the armour and the weapons by which the battle has to be fought'. He continued that 'if you intend, in this conflict of commercial treaties, to hold our own, you must be prepared, if need be, to inflict upon the nations which injure you the penalty which is in your hands, that of refusing them access to your markets'. However, he qualified his willingness to depart from free trade by stating that he did not endorse raising either the cost of food or the price of raw materials. Retaliatory protection should, instead, be directed at 'matters of luxurious consumption' such as wine, silk, spirits, gloves and lace.

Inevitably, Salisbury directed attention to Ireland. He condemned proposals made by Asquith to allow Irish MPs to continue to sit at Westminster following the grant of home rule on the grounds that 'it is offering to Ireland the maximum of independence and to England the minimum of relief'. He objected to the ability of Irish MPs to vote on matters pertaining to England whereas all Irish matters would be exclusively debated in the Dublin Parliament. He also referred to the position of Ulster, arguing that home rule would endanger and compromise the future lives of the Protestant community. He believed it was impossible to impose self-government on a community which was so deeply divided on the basis of traditions, religion and race.

Salisbury's policies were latterly detailed in an election address directed at 'the electors of the United Kingdom' (which was published in *The Times* on 28 June). In this he referred to the achievements of the Unionist government in areas which included local government reform, education, the relief of chronic suffering in Ireland, and the establishment of a system of sound finance. He stated his desire to proceed with legislation in the future directed at issues which included the relationship of capital and labour, the prevention of trade disputes, the protection of the lives and health of the industrial community, the reform of the Poor Law and the diminution of poverty. He also proposed the reform of the laws relating to the acquisition of land. He suggested that the election would determine whether issues such as these would dominate the attention of the next Parliament or whether it would concentrate on Irish home rule. He referred to Gladstone's proposals as 'this rash experiment, this dangerous novelty' and prophesied that civil war would probably arise from any attempt to impose such a policy on Ulster's Protestant community. A Unionist demonstration held in London on 22 June ensured that the people of England were aware of Ulster's objections to home rule.

Liberal Unionists

During the campaign, the Liberal Unionists sought to project themselves as genuine Liberals and emphasise that Ireland was the chief bone of contention between themselves and the Party led by Gladstone. Chamberlain's election address to his West Birmingham constituents (which was published in *The Times* on 22 June) emphasised his desire to maintain the Union of Britain and Ireland, and at a meeting of the Liberal Unionist Federation held at Westminster on 23 May the Duke of Argyll moved a resolution which condemned the Liberal Party's 'concealment' of its policy on Ireland. In his speech he emphasised that Ireland masked all other Liberal issues, in particular the support for individual liberty and freedom, and that Gladstone's proposals intended to sacrifice the liberties of those who lived in Ulster.

Additional issues were raised in the speech made by the Duke of Devonshire at Glasgow on 27 May. He referred to the successful record of the Unionist government in domestic and foreign affairs (an argument which was presented in detail in Chamberlain's election address) and in curbing disorder in Ireland, and argued that the election would determine four key issues – whether home rule would be introduced into the sphere of politics, the position of the Established Church in Scotland, whether temperance would be enforced by legislation, and if there would be legislative interference in the hours of labour. He argued that candidates should declare their views on these issues in advance of the election. He mocked Gladstone's party by asserting that Liberal candidates were free to vote on every issue in accordance with the views of their constituents, save on Ireland where they were obliged to vote as their leaders instructed them. He asserted that MPs should use their independent judgement and their conscience on this issue, and insisted that the House of Lords had the constitutional right to reject a measure on which the people had not been directly consulted.

Chamberlain devoted much attention to labour issues at a speech made at Smethwick on 9 June when he called for the establishment of arbitration courts to prevent strikes, and for the reform of employers' liability legislation. He also advocated improved financial support for the elderly and the introduction of old age pensions for those persons who were unable or unwilling to join a Friendly Society. The twin policies of Poor Law reform and land reform entailing the extension of the yeoman class throughout Britain as a solution to the problems faced by the agricultural labourer in times of 'sickness, calamity and old age' were advocated by A. Balfour in a speech at St James's Hall, Westminster, on 15 June. The outgoing Chancellor of the Exchequer, George Goschen, emphasised the government's financial record which included reducing income tax, lowering the duties on tea, tobacco and currants, diminishing the house duty at the lower end to aid the lower middle classes, providing Exchequer money to local authorities in order to reduce the rate burden and reducing the national debt.

Liberals

The Liberal campaign paid considerable attention to Ireland. At a speech delivered in Birmingham on 26 May, Lord Rosebery argued that it was not the Liberal Party but, rather, the

Conservative Party which was seeking to avoid discussing Ireland. He depicted the Irish Local Government Bill as the Conservative alternative to home rule and stated that this party was seeking to detract attention from home rule by devoting attention to other issues such as fair trade. Other Liberals criticised the stance adopted on home rule by the Unionist parties. Speaking at Braintree on 28 May, Sir William Harcourt rejected the spectre of Ulstermen dying in the 'last ditch', and accused the Liberal Unionists of seeking to stir up sectarian feeling. He also believed that the Irish Local Government Bill (which he depicted as the Unionist parties' alternative to home rule and which John Morley branded a 'mockery of a measure' in a speech at Exeter on 15 June) was dead in the water and he doubted whether, having laboured to achieve a second reading, the measure would be proceded with.

Gladstone's election address to his Midlothian constituents (which was published in *The Times* on 24 June) also devoted much attention to Ireland. He asserted that the Conservatives had failed this country with the exception of their 1887 Land Act, and that an Irish Parliament would enable the House of Commons to concentrate on the legislative requirements of the remainder of the United Kingdom. In response to goadings by Unionist politicians (and also from A. V. Dicey in a letter in *The Times* on 29 June, Gladstone argued (in a speech at Edinburgh on 30 June) that it was not necessary to provide precise details of his proposals for home rule since he viewed these as 'secondary difficulties' which could be resolved after the election had taken place. The Liberal campaign also addressed the constitutional issues raised by Conservatives in connection with home rule. On 28 May, Sir William Harcourt rejected the Duke of Devonshire's concept of a 'state mandate' which suggested that the House of Lords was entitled to throw out any measure whose precise details had not been placed before the nation in an election.

On 31 May, in a speech made in London, Gladstone argued that reforms which were contained in the Newcastle Programme could be proceeded with only when the 'tremendous impediment and obstacle' of Ireland had been removed. In a later speech at Chester on 26 June, Gladstone stated that home rule was required 'to clear the stage, and when the stage is cleared then let these subjects go forward. Parliament will then have had lifted from its shoulders a weight which now has crushed it almost to the ground'. However, this did not prevent issues other than Ireland being discussed in the Liberal campaign. At Braintree on 28 May, Sir William Harcourt responded to the Conservative advocacy of protection by alleging that this policy would impose a tax on food and articles of consumption in order to benefit particular classes and interests since the suggested taxes on luxury goods would fail to produce revenue. He condemned the principle of retaliation advocated by Lord Salisbury as an example of cutting off one's nose to spite the face, and further condemned this policy for failing to provide any aid to farmers or agricultural tenants.

Liberals also sought to respond to criticisms that the progress of domestic reform would be hindered by a preoccupation with home rule. On 28 May, Sir William Harcourt emphasised the Party's commitment to domestic policies which he repeated in his election address to his constituents at Derby (which was published in *The Times* on 25 June). These included land reform (in particular to tackle the issue of inheritance), temperance reform, the desire to tackle the unfair distribution of taxes between real and personal property, the reform of the law relating to voter registration, the need to address the relationship between capital and labour (in particular regarding the hours of labour in the mines and railway industries), the disestablishment of the Established Church in Wales and Scotland and the establishment of parish councils. As a first step to tackling the latter issue, he endorsed the proposal contained n the Newcastle Programme for the payment of MPs which would aid those who represented the interests of labour. On 31 May in a speech delivered in London, Gladstone gave prominent attention to the need to reform local government in London, and he endorsed electoral reform, viewing the suffrage as 'the instrument of all other reforms, and without it no effectual progress can be made towards them'. He also addressed the issue of the relations between capital and labour, although he was vague concerning precise proposals to aid the latter. Other Liberals gave greater prominence to this topic, and Sir Henry James devoted a significant part of his campaign to advocating the improvement of the conditions of labourers in the textile industry, and on 16 June an attempt was made by the London Trades Council to secure Gladstone's support for the introduction of an Eight Hours Bill.

Gladstone's election address drew attention to the alleged deficiencies of the Conservative government's policies concerning local government reform and smallholdings, and John Morley (at a speech delivered at Plymouth on 14 June) criticised Conservative policy on education by asserting that there was an insufficient element of local control in the free schools which they had created. In a speech at Exeter on 15 June, Morley further alleged that a future Conservative government would reimpose a tariff on manufactured goods which would invite retaliation by other countries and would not be of any help to agricultural areas. The Liberal Unionists were condemned as an appendage of the Conservative Party, and in a speech at Sutton on 9 June Lord Rosebery challenged Chamberlain's right to describe himself as a 'Liberal' and queried the 'Unionist' credentials of the late Conservative government.

Result of the Election

A total of 1,303 candidates contested the election, and 63 MPs were returned unopposed. The result was:

Party	Votes	Vote %	MPs
Conservative and Liberal Unionist	2,079,887	45.2%	292
Liberal*	2,083,692	45.3%	272
Irish Nationalist	311,509	6.8% [78.1%]	81
Irish Conservative and Liberal Unionist	79,263	1.7% [20.6%]	21
Others	39,641	0.9%	4
Irish Liberal	4,327	0.1% [1.1%]	0
Total	4,598,319		670

* Includes 10 'Lib–Lab' MPs

The turnout was 77.4 per cent.

The 'others' were J. Burns (Battersea, Independent Labour), J. K. Hardie (West Ham South, Independent Labour), Sir E. Watkin (Hythe, Independent Liberal), and J. Wilson (Middlesbrough, Independent Labour).

The Parties

The Liberal Party improved upon the position it had obtained in 1886 but won fewer seats than the Unionists and would require the cooperation of the Irish Nationalists in order to form a government. A number of gains were made in London (at West Ham North, West Ham South, Islington West, Lambeth North, Finsbury Central, Walworth, Bermondsey, Camberwell North, North Kensington, St George's-in-the-East, Limehouse and Bow and Bromley) and some further progress was made against the Liberal Unionists in constituencies which included Devonshire North West and Forfarshire. The Conservatives were the dominant force in the English counties, winning 130 of the 231 seats (Jenkins, 1994: 222). Approximately 45 Liberal Unionists were elected.

Scotland, Wales and Ireland

The Liberal Party remained the dominant force in Scottish politics and improved upon the position it secured in 1886 by winning 51 of the 70 seats. The Unionists won the remaining 19 seats. The victory obtained by the Liberal Unionist, Viscount Wolmer, in West Edinburgh was contentious and he was accused of winning by 'dirty tactics' which included stirring up religious bigotry, sectarian strife and class prejudice, and by trade boycotting. The Liberal Party also remained the dominant force in Welsh politics, and improved on the position obtained in 1886 by winning 31 of the 34 seats. The Unionists won the remaining three seats.

In Ireland, opposition to the imposition of home rule on the Protestant population was organised by a meeting of the Ulster Convention which took place in Belfast on 17 June. The scandal over Parnell's divorce case in connection with an affair with Kitty O'Shea resulted in his downfall. After this affair had been made public in 1890, his party was initially disposed to back his continuance as leader, but the Liberal leadership privately expressed their opinion that it would be impossible to continue working with the Nationalists if he remained in charge. This prompted the Irish National Party to debate the position at great length in December 1890 (in Committee Room Number 15 in the House of Commons) which led to a split between the Parnellites and seceders, who were led by McCarthy. The two sides began to fight against each other in subsequent elections and these divisions persisted even after Parnell had died in 1891. The Party was not reunited until 1900. At the election, Nationalists won 80 of the 101 seats (including nine 'Parnellites'). A further Nationalist, T. P. O'Connor was elected for Liverpool, Scotland. The Unionist parties won the remaining 21 seats.

Consequence of the Election

The Unionists chose to remain in office until Parliament met, when they were defeated by a no confidence motion moved by Asquith (which is referred to in greater detail in the 1895 entry).

13 July – 7 August 1895

Party Leaders
The Marquis of Salisbury (Unionist)
The Earl of Rosebery (Liberal)

Background to the Election

Timing of the Election
On 21 June 1895, a motion proposed by Mr St John Brodrick in the Committee of Supply which was considering the Army Estimates voted to reduce the salary of the Secretary for War, Sir Henry Campbell-Bannerman, for not having procured enough cordite (a smokeless propellant explosive) for the use of the army. This personal vote of censure was passed by 132 : 125 votes. Rosebery resigned and was replaced by Salisbury whose sole rationale for agreeing to take office was to dissolve Parliament.

Unionists
Salisbury's Unionist government did not resign following the 1892 election, but instead decided to test their support in the House of Commons. On 8 August 1892, Herbert Asquith moved an amendment to the Queen's Speech to insert, 'we feel it, however, to be our duty humbly to submit to your Majesty, that it is essential that your Majesty's government should posses the confidence of this House and the country, and respectfully to represent to your Majesty that such confidence is not reposed in the present advisers of your Majesty.' In the vote which took place on 11 August, the government was defeated by the margin of 350 : 310. Salisbury resigned and was replaced by Gladstone who formed his fourth government.

The main attack against the subsequent Liberal government was waged by the Conservative majority in the House of Lords which acted in a partisan way to thwart the passage of Liberal legislation. These clashes were the origins of the Liberals' 'filling the cup' strategy (which is discussed below). Following the resignation of the Liberal government in June 1895, Lord Salisbury formed his third government which included five Liberal Unionists.

Liberals
Following his resumption of office (in circumstances which are discussed above), Gladstone's energies were concentrated on the issue of Irish home rule. New legislation was introduced into the House of Commons in February 1893. It was similar to the 1886 measure save that the Irish MPs who attended the Westminster Parliament would only be permitted to vote on matters of Irish or imperial concern. This secured its second reading in the House of Commons on 21 April 1893 by 43 votes and its third reading on 1 September of that year by 34. However, on 8 September 1893 the House of Lords declined to give it a second reading by the massive vote of 419 : 41. Gladstone contemplated a dissolution but instead retired as Premier the

following year in March 1894. Rather than call an election on home rule, the Liberal Party alternatively adopted the 'filling the cup' tactic whereby it would proceed with a stream of legislation in the expectation that this would be vetoed by the House of Lords. It was anticipated that eventually this action would provoke a constitutional crisis on which an election could be called.

Following Gladstone's resignation, the Queen passed over the claims of Harcourt (who had been his lieutenant since 1886) and instead invited the the Foreign Secretary, the Earl of Rosebery, to form an administration. Rosebery was loosely associated with the Liberal Imperialists (who are discussed in more detail in the 1906 entry). He attempted to distance himself from Gladstone in his first speech in office when he declared that home rule for Ireland could only occur if England agreed to such a reform. His most notable successes, however, occurred outside Parliament. In 1894 his horse Ladas won the Derby and this was followed by a second victory the following year by Sir Visto.

The Liberal government subsequently encountered a number of political difficulties. Its 'filling the cup' strategy provoked internal disputes as to the order in which sectional demands should be put forward, and the desired clashes with the House of Lords were sometimes thwarted when the measure was defeated in the House of Commons. This was the fate of a local veto bill to restrict the sale of alcohol. Clashes with the House of Lords did arise in connection with the 1894 Local Government Act (which is usually referred to as the Parish Councils Bill). This was considerably amended by the Upper House which also killed off Asquith's Employers' Liability Bill when it inserted a contracting-out clause. Little was achieved in the direction of social reform, although the President of the Board of Trade, A. J. Mundella, established a Labour Department, and the 1893 Railway Servants (Hours of Labour Act) helped to improve the conditions of work of those employed in the railway industry although the measure was mainly promoted by the desire to benefit the travelling public. However, one positive achievement was Harcourt's 1894 budget which introduced graduated death duties on both real and personal property and reduced the liability of lower income earners to pay tax. Rosebery objected to these aspects of the budget which, although they could have presaged a progressive fiscal system in which wealth was redistributed from the rich in favour of the poor, were not subsequently followed up.

In addition to its disputes with the Lords, the Liberal Party failed to secure immediate improvements to the country's economic fortunes: unemployment continued to rise and wheat prices hit a new low in 1894. A Royal Commission was appointed in 1893 to investigate the problems of the agricultural industry; its recommendations included the partial derating of agricultural land. Although the nation's economic fortunes began to improve after 1894, it was too late to aid the fortunes of the Liberal Party whose 'most potent' cause of defeat in 1895 was, according to the Chancellor, Harcourt, the cry of 'bad trade'.

Foreign affairs occupied the government's attention. In late 1893 the government acquiesced in the actions of the British South Africa Company when it conquered Matabeleland, and in 1894 a British Protectorate was declared over Uganda following the collapse of the British East India Company. In 1893 tension between Britain and France in connection with the 'Mekong Crisis' was resolved to Britain's satisfaction by preventing France from annexing Siam. In 1894 a treaty with Japan was concluded to provide for the termination of British consular jurisdiction. However, there were internal divisions within the Liberal Party as to whether Britain should act unilaterally or work with the other European powers regarding atrocities carried out by Turkey against the Armenians in 1894.

Defence eventually brought about the downfall of the government. On 21 June 1895, the Minister of War, Sir Henry Campbell-Bannerman, was censured. This defeat was attributed by *The Times* on 22 June as being caused by 'slackness rather than disaffection' and only one Liberal MP (Sir Charles Dilke) voted with the opposition. It was quite possible that had the opposition followed this vote up with a no confidence motion, the government would have survived. However, the government's response was to consider whether to resign or dissolve Parliament. It adopted the former course of action and on 24 June Lord Salisbury formed his third government.

Independent Labour

The existence of poverty in the latter decades of the nineteenth century helped to develop support for the ideology of socialism. Although British socialism was inspired by a variety of impulses (which included the economic theories of David Ricardo, the ethical socialism derived from Robert Owen and the Christian Socialists, and the writings of Marx and Engels), all rejected a society in which inequalities in the distribution of economic wealth and political power resulted in the creation of social injustice. There was, however, no agreement concerning the manner in which reform should be brought about, nor regarding the nature of the fairer society which socialists desired to create. These differences led to the development of a number of socialist organisations in the late nineteenth century, which included the Social Democratic Federation, the Socialist League, the Fabian Society and the Scottish Labour Party. They differed on issues which included the desirability of cooperating with trade unions, the wisdom of working with the existing political parties, and whether socialism should be born from a working-class revolution or brought about through conventional political activity. Nonetheless, an attempt was made to create a single working-class political party with the establishment of the Independent Labour Party (ILP) in 1893.

The ILP attempted to reconcile the divisions in socialism between fundamentalism and reformism by advocating both the collective ownership of the means of production, distribution and exchange but at the same time giving prominence to a programme of reforms which were designed to benefit the working classes to be achieved within the existing capitalist framework. The leading figure in the ILP was Keir Hardie who advocated an alliance between trade unionists and socialists, but initially little progress was made in securing this because of the hostility of the trade unions.

By-elections

A total of 103 by-elections occurred in the 1892–95 Parliament, of which 53 were contested. The Unionists made a net gain of four and the Liberals a net loss of the same number.

Conduct of the Campaign
Unionists

The Conservatives and Liberal Unionists fought a united Unionist campaign. They sought to depict the Liberals as political cowards for not having the courage to call an election themselves following their defeat in June. This defeat was, however, handled delicately by the Unionists, Balfour insisting in a speech delivered at Manchester on 26 June that the vote in the Committee of Supply should not in any way be viewed as a personal attack on Campbell-Bannerman who was regarded highly in Unionist quarters. Other attacks mounted on the Liberals during the campaign included their record in office during which time, it was alleged, only two of the 24 items contained in the Newcastle Programme (the equalisation of death duties on real and personal property and the Parish Councils Act) had been translated into law.

The Unionist campaign also discussed the Liberal Party's position concerning the House of Lords. Speaking at North Lambeth on 6 July, Chamberlain asserted that the Liberals intended to abolish this body, and Balfour's election address (which was published in *The Times* on 8 July) argued that this party intended to destroy its 'constitutional position'. In a speech in the House of Lords on 6 July, Lord Salisbury pressed Rosebery to state what he meant by the term 'legislative preponderance' of the House of Lords, and stated that the Upper Chamber had done the nation a service by placing manacles on what he referred to as 'the Radical Party'.

Chamberlain sought to project social reform as a key election issue. In his election address to his West Birmingham constituents (which was published in *The Times* on 27 June), he argued that a Unionist government would 'lay aside the wild project of constitutional change and destructive legislation ... and ... devote their principal attention to the policy of constructive reform'. This view was articulated by Sir Michael Hicks-Beach in a speech at Bristol on 1 July when he stated that the aim of a Unionist government was to 'silence the cacklings of the radical faction' and to focus on social reform. He also insisted that a Unionist government would 'maintain in full efficiency the defensive resources of the Empire'. Chamberlain asserted that the Liberal Party could not embrace the social reform mantle. At North Lambeth on 6 July he stated 'as long as the Liberal Party ... is really a home rule Party, as long as is is bound hand and foot to the Irish Nationalists, so long they are powerless to deal with British legislation as you would wish them to do'. Other Unionist speakers explicitly attacked the Liberal Party's commitment to home rule, and argued that the Unionists sought to preserve the union between Great Britain and Ireland.

Other policies which were put forward included the provision of aid to the agricultural industry which was suffering from property depreciation.

Liberals

On 27 June, *The Times* published the manifesto of the National Liberal Federation (NFL). This drew attention to the achievements of the Liberal governments since 1892 which it cited as placing national defences on a sound and satisfactory footing, dealing sympathetically with India, governing Ireland without the need to resort to coercive legislation, reducing the extent of industrial conflict and extending local democracy through the mechanism of parish councils. In a speech delivered at the Royal Albert Hall on 5 July, Lord Rosebery also drew attention to the 1893 Railway Regulation Act (which regulated the hours of those employed on the railways), and the 1895 Factory and Workshop Act (which sought to improve working conditions in these places of work). The NLF manifesto alleged that progress with radical reform had suffered when the will of the House of Commons was thwarted by 'an irresponsible oligarchy' in the House of Lords which threw out measures such as home rule for Ireland and the Employers' Liability Bill. A future Liberal government was pledged to introduce home rule for Ireland, bring forward legislation to address employers' liability, secure the disestablishment of the Church of Wales and promote an Irish Land Act. Electoral reform based on the principle of 'one man, one vote' would be brought forward, localities would be empowered to determine the liquor trade, and unspecified reforms would be introduced for dwellers in towns and rural areas. The manifesto also stated that the constitutional issue of conflicts between the House of Commons and House of Lords would be resolved to ensure that in these circumstances the will of the elected House would prevail.

The views of the 'advanced radicals' were presented in the Manifesto of the National Reform Union (which was published in *The Times* on 2 July). This placed great emphasis on electoral reform (which entailed changes to the law relating to the registration of voters, the abolition of plural voting and the democratisation of Parliament by relieving candidates of the costs of election contests and paying MPs), changes in parliamentary procedure to prevent the wilful obstruction and delay of business, and the abolition of the legislative power of the House of Lords. It was argued these these reforms were the gateway to other radical demands which included home rule for Ireland, the disestablishment and disendowment of all state Churches, local option regarding the liquor trade, the reform of laws regarding the acquisition, tenure, transfer and sale of land (in order to enable farmers to enjoy fair rents, fixity of tenure and the freedom of sale and cultivation), and the discontinuance of all grants and pensions paid from public revenues save to those who had rendered conspicuous services to the community. This manifesto also called for the taxation of land values (including mine rents and mineral royalties), the extension of the financial principles put forward in Harcourt's 1894 budget, the economic administration of the revenue of the country, a relaxation of central control in the operation of the Poor Laws, fuller recognition of the claims of the sick and those experiencing temporary distress, and the practical admission of the claims of labour on issues which included hours of work, the right to combination, compensation for injuries and direct representation to Parliament. In foreign affairs, the manifesto argued for the acceptance of the principle of international arbitration, a recognition of the rights of weaker races, and closer union among the English-speaking peoples of the world.

The approach adopted by the National Reform Union to place emphasis on three aspects of policy won the broad approval of Lord Rosebery. In his speech to the 80 Club on 2 July, he warned his party against making the mistake it had made in 1892 by entering office with 'a mountain range of policy' derived from the Newcastle Programme. He refined the key election issues still further and argued that it should be fought on the one question of the power of the House of Lords which would thwart all Liberal reforms even when backed by a large majority in the House of Commons. He asserted that this was more important than either Irish home rule or the local option and stated, 'if you carry the annihilation of the House of Lords as regards its legislative preponderance, which keeps our Party in manacles, you will have gone not half, but three-quarters of the way to carrying your other reforms.'

However, not all Liberals agreed with Lord Rosebery's assessment of the situation. John Morley, speaking at Manchester on 4 July, insisted that home rule remained the pre-eminent question and that all other radical demands should be subordinate to it. He argued that 'it is our bounden duty … not to draw back, but to persevere, and to place this question of a better system of self-government for Ireland, for the third time formally, expressly, deliberately, before the electors in the very forefront of our programme'. He believed that this approach was the best one from which to place the reform of the House of Lords on to the political agenda. Although Rosebery endorsed home rule in his Royal Albert Hall speech on 5 July, he insisted that the House of Lords was the 'tap root of all political questions', and believed that the settlement of Ireland depended on the prior reform of the Upper Chamber.

Attacks on the Conservative Pary were made during the Liberal campaign. In his speech to the 80 Club at London on 2 July, Lord Rosebery replied to Unionist goadings concerning his decision to resign rather than dissolve Parliament by arguing that the Conservatives had no need to hold an election but had chosen to do so as they were afraid of providing the nation with evidence as to how they would administer its affairs.

Result of the Election

A total of 1,180 candidates contested the election, and 189 MPs were returned unopposed. The result was:

Party	Votes	Vote %	MPs
Conservative and Liberal Unionist	1,840,143	47.6%	392
Liberal	1,750,260	45.3%	176
Irish Nationalist	152,959	4.0% [66.9%]	82
Irish Conservative and Liberal Unionist	54,629	1.4% [26.0%]	19
Irish Liberal	15,006	0.4% [7.1%]	1
Independent Labour Party	44,325	1.1%	0
Others	8,960	0.2%	0
Total	3,866,282		670

The turnout was 78.4 per cent.

One candidate from an ethnic minority group (Sir Mancharjee Bhownaggree) was elected for North East Bethnal Green as a Conservative.

The Parties

The success enjoyed by the Unionists in London and the provincial English boroughs in the 1885 election was especially evident in 1895. This was built upon the continued defection of urban and suburban middle-class voters from the Liberals to the Unionists which was most pronounced in London and the Home Counties but less apparent in the North of England and South Wales. Additionally, the Unionists made noticeable inroads in working-class support in both London and Lancashire (Jenkins, 1994: 222–3). In London, the Unionists captured Bethnal Green North East, East Finsbury, Central Finsbury, South Hackney, North Kensington, Lambeth-Kennington, North Lambeth, Southwark-Bermondsey, three seats in Tower Hamlets (that of Bow and Poplar, Limehouse and St Georges-in-the-East), Shoreditch-Haggerston, West Ham North and West

Ham South. These victories attested to what *The Times* on 17 July argued to be 'the extraordinary demonstration ... of the strength of Unionist and Imperialist feeling in London' and went beyond merely recapturing ground which had been lost to the Liberals in 1892.

In total, the Conservatives won 100 of the 163 English borough seats to the Liberals' 41. Their Liberal Unionist allies won a further 21 and the Irish Nationalists won the remaining one seat. The Unionist strength was especially pronounced in the large cities: in London, Glasgow, Birmingham, Manchester, Liverpool, Leeds and Sheffield, they won 81 of the 98 available seats (Searle, 1992: 52). The Conservatives also dominated the English counties where they won 141 of the 231 seats to the Liberal Party's 63. The Liberal Unionists won the remaining 27 seats (Jenkins, 1994: 223). Unionist gains included North Bedfordshire, North Buckinghamshire, Cumberland–Egremont, Devonshire–Barnstaple, South Northamptonshire and Mid-Oxfordshire. The Unionists secured victories in the county constituencies of South Glamorganshire, Cheshire–Crewe, Lancashire–Gorton, Yorkshire–Shipley, Lincolnshire–Spalding, Somerset–Frome, Wiltshire–Westbury and Warwickshire–Rugby, none of which had previously returned a Unionist candidate.

Financial difficulties restricted the size of the Liberal front, and 132 Unionist MPs were returned unopposed. Gladstone did not stand and Harcourt's decision to base his campaign in Derby on the local option (whereby local authorities could restrict the issue of liquor licences) proved not to be a vote-winner and he lost his seat along with that of his Liberal running mate. A new constituency, West Monmouthshire, had to be hastily found for him to secure his return to Parliament in the general election. Other front bench Liberals who were defeated were John Morley, Arnold Morley, Shaw Lefevre, Sir John Hibbert, George Russell and Leveson-Gower.

All 28 ILP candidates (including Keir Hardie at West Ham South) were defeated, leaving labour interests to be represented by a handful of Lib–Lab MPs.

Scotland, Wales and Ireland

The balance between the Unionist and Liberal parties considerably narrowed both in terms of popular vote and seats in the House of Commons. In total the Liberals won 39 of Scotland's 70 seats and the Unionists the remaining 31. This trend commenced in 1886 and was influenced by a number of diverse trends. These included the opposition of Scottish Presbyterians to Irish home rule (as they were supportive of the concerns of their Ulster Protestant brethren), and opposition to the policy of Church disestablishment which became the official policy of the Scottish Liberal Party in 1892. Additionally, the Irish vote in Scotland (and also Wales and England) tended to be cast against the Liberals when they were unlikely to be in a position to deliver on home rule since their wish to maintain Catholic schools was at variance with the Liberal intentions to introduce undenominational and secular education. This latter situation helped to account for Liberal losses in Western Scotland (Searle, 1992: 32).

In Wales, the relative standing of the two main parties was similar to the position in 1892. The Liberals won 25 of Wales's 34 seats and the Unionists the remaining nine. In Ireland, the Anti-Parnellite manifesto (which was published in *The Times* on 11 July) called on electors to support only those candidates who endorsed Gladstone's Irish policy and urged the return to power of the Liberal Party as the party of home rule. The Nationalists remained split between the Parnellites (of whom approximately 12 were elected) and anti-Parnellites. The political situation was similar to that of 1892. The Nationalists won 81 of Ireland's 101 seats (with a further Nationalist, T. P. O'Connor, being elected for Liverpool, Scotland), and the Unionists 19. A lone Liberal, C. N. Hemphill, was elected for North Tyrone. This seat was gained from the Unionists and he was the first Liberal MP to be elected for an Irish constituency since 1880.

Consequence of the Election

Lord Salisbury formed a Unionist government.

1 – 24 October 1900

Party Leaders
The Marquis of Salisbury (Unionist)
Sir Henry Campbell-Bannerman (Liberal)
(The Labour Representation Committee did not have an acknowledged leader, although Keir Hardie was its senior political figure.)

Background to the Election
Timing of the Election
The election took place as the Unionist government felt that economic and military circumstances would be to their political advantage. Its timing during a lull in the South African War led to it being dubbed a 'khaki election', although the government argued that an election was needed to secure a mandate for a post-war settlement in South Africa.

Unionists
Following the 1895 election, a number of Liberal Unionists took office in Salisbury's government. Joseph Chamberlain became Colonial Secretary and Hartington (who had now acceded to the title of the Duke of Devonshire) became Lord President of the Council.

Chamberlain attempted to identify the Conservative Party with the cause of social reform. In April 1891 he had been the first major politician to declare himself in favour of a state-organised system of old age pensions and in 1896 the government appointed a Committee on Old Age Pensions which was chaired by Lord Rothschild. This committee examined a large number of schemes, disapproved of all of them and reported against this reform in 1898. Accordingly, Chamberlain instigated a select committee inquiry chaired by Henry Chaplin. Although it reported in favour of a scheme in 1899, the costs of the Boer War prevented any action being implemented at that time. However, it achieved greater success in connection with conditions of labour. It successfully promoted the 1897 Workmen's Compensation Act whereby an employee could obtain compensation for injury at work without having to prove negligence on the part of his employer. Other domestic reforms included the 1896 Agricultural Rates Act (which responded to the agricultural crisis by remitting one half of farmers' rates). In Ireland reforms included the 1898 Irish Local Government Act which gave Ireland elected county councils in line with reforms promoted to local government in England 10 years previously.

The relative dearth of domestic legislation (an Education Bill was abandoned in 1896) was due to the government's preoccupation with imperial concerns. Queen Victoria's Diamond Jubilee celebrations helped (as had similar Jubilee celebrations 10 years earlier) to popularise the Empire which assumed such a prominent role in Chamberlain's politics. Public opinion was supportive of the government's policies to further these interests even when they threatened to involve Britain in war. The decision of the government to gain security for Egypt and control the upper waters of the Nile entailed the conquest of the Sudan by Sir Herbert Kitchener. This objective conflicted with France's desire to secure the Upper Sudan for herself and in 1898

British and French soldiers faced each other at Fashoda. This incident was defused when the French expedition, led by Major Marchand, was withdrawn and it was consequently agreed to establish a joint British and Egyptian government over the Sudan.

South Africa proved to be a more complicated issue which eventually led Britain into a drawn-out and expensive war against the Boers. The 1881 Pretoria Convention settled the First Boer War by providing the Transvaal with self-government under the suzerainty of the British Crown.

However, in 1885 the British government annexed Bechuanaland which provided the only route by which Cape Colony could reach out to the north. This was soon followed by a further extension of British power in Matabeleland. This was accomplished by Cecil Rhodes and the British South Africa Company which conquered Matabeleland in 1896 and renamed the area Rhodesia. This meant that the Boers were hemmed in in the north by Rhodesia and the west by Bechuanaland.

In 1886 gold was discovered in the Transvaal. This resulted in a influx of new settlers, most of whom were British. These were termed *Uitlanders* and their presence was resented by the Boers who were treated as second-class citizens by them. This situation threatened Rhodes's expansionist plans in Southern Africa and he sought to solve this by organising an uprising in Johannesburg and an external raid into the Transvaal which was led by L. S. Jameson in 1895. This venture proved unsuccessful but strengthened the hand of the President of the Transvaal, Paul Kruger, while worsening relations between Britain and the Boers. War eventually broke out on the pretext of the British government supporting the claims of the *Uitlanders* for better treatment in the Transvaal Republic. Anticipating the arrival of British reinforcements, the Boers sent an ultimatum to Britain which demanded the removal of all forces from their frontiers. They declared war when this was rejected in 1899 and were joined by the Orange Free State, also a Boer Republic.

Initially the Boers enjoyed success against the British: Kimberley, Mafeking and Ladysmith were besieged and British armies were defeated at Magersfontein and at the Tugela River in five days of the 'Black Week' in December 1899. However, a change of command in which Lord Buller was replaced by Lord Roberts, with Lord Kitchener as his chief of staff, resulted in a change of fortunes the following year. The three besieged towns were relieved, Roberts occupied Johannesberg and Pretoria in June, and in August the last organised Boer army was defeated and Kruger fled. The two Boer Republics were annexed and it seemed the war was over.

However, it then entered into a guerrilla stage in which Boer commandos led by Botha de Wet, de la Rey and Smuts inflicted considerable casualties on the British forces between October 1900 and 1902.

The election was fought against the background of improved economic circumstances which had been artificially extended by the Boer War. Additionally, there were signs of economic revival in the countryside.

Liberals

Rosebery resigned as leader of the Party in 1896 on the grounds of seeking to ensure party unity. Lord Spencer became leader in the House of Lords with Sir William Harcourt continuing as Leader in the House of Commons (a post he held in Rosebery's government of 1894–95 and resumed in 1895 when a by-election at West Monmouthshire enabled him to return to Parliament following his defeat at Derby in the general election). However, internal disputes (especially with the Liberal Imperialists who are discussed in the 1906 entry) caused him to resign and in February 1899. Henry Campbell-Bannerman was elected to replace him.

The political ties between the Liberal Party and nonconformists were further enhanced by the creation of the National Council of Evangelical Free Churches in 1896. This aimed to unify the main dissenting churches and mobilise them for political purposes. Although this development entrenched the support given to the Liberals in areas where nonconformists were strong, it tended to ensure that the Liberal Party promoted nonconformist issues (such as Welsh disestablishment, local option, education and temperance reform) which lacked widespread popular appeal to the detriment of more popular issues such as social reform. It further tended to identify the Liberal Party with a style of politics which was akin to a moral crusade whose opposition to injustices was more suited to the conduct of an opposition party than to one seeking to exercise power (Searle, 1992: 42).

The main success enjoyed by the Liberals in opposition was to force the government to withdraw its Education Bill in 1896 which proposed to abolish the school boards established by the Liberals' 1870 Education Act.

By-elections
A total of 113 by-elections occurred in the 1895–1900 Parliament, of which 79 were contested. The Unionists made a net loss of 11, the Liberals a net gain of 10, and others a net gain of one.

Conduct of the Election
The level of popular support for Unionist South African policy and the disorganisation of the Liberals made a Unionist victory a foregone conclusion.

Unionists
The Unionists asserted that the election was taking place in time of national emergency. The manifesto of the Marquis of Salisbury viewed abstention as a major issue and sought to encourage voters to cast their ballots by arguing that if many refrained from voting it would cripple the ability of the winning party to carry out the policy decided upon by the nation. The need for a government with a strong parliamentary majority providing it with authority both at home and abroad was constantly reiterated throughout this brief statement. Foreign affairs and defence dominated this manifesto. It was argued that the next government would have to face a number of grave questions which included rebuilding the imperial power over the two South African Republics. Although colony status would eventually be bestowed on these two territories, it was argued that the timing of this step would depend on the disposition and conduct of the inhabitants whose submission was dependent on the strength of the British government. The recent troubles in South Africa were attributed to 'a shift of parliamentary opinion at a critical moment'. Lord Salisbury's statement called for an investigation and removal of the defects of Britain's military system in the light of scientific progress and the experience of other powers. Additionally, he referred to China, stating in vague terms his intention to maintain Britain's rights and join in the efforts of her allies to restore and secure tranquillity.

During the campaign, the Unionists denied that they were seeking to gain political advantage from holding an election at that time, and insisted that an election was needed to obtain a new mandate before embarking on the settlement of South Africa. Attacks were also made on the record of previous Liberal governments. In a speech delivered at Bradford on 22 September, the Duke of Devonshire criticised earlier Liberal actions such as home rule, the attack on the Established Church, temperance reform and other 'wild and impossible projects' which were contained in the Newcastle Programme. He emphasised the Party's disunity and the influence wielded by its radical element.

Liberals

The Liberal Party was critical of the government's decision to call an election at that time, arguing that in 1878 Lord Beaconsfield rejected such a course of action following the conclusion of the Berlin conference on the grounds that it would be viewed as a breach of constitutional practice. The manifesto of the National Liberal Federation accused the government of having displayed 'negligence, miscalculation and manifold misdoing' in connection with their policy towards South Africa, and referred to the 'shame, apprehension and distress' which fell upon the country by military reverses there which were removed 'not by the statesmanship and administration of the government, but by the genius of Lord Roberts and the bravery and endurance of officers and men'. The 'khaki election' was depicted as an attempt 'to prostitute the sacrifices of a whole people to the interests of one political party' and by refusing to introduce special legislation to put the new electoral register in force, the Conservatives were further accused of 'sharp practice unprecedented since the great Reform Bill', the effect of which was to disfranchise half a million electors. Liberals of all shades of opinion were urged to unite against 'such an obvious and discreditable electioneering trick'.

The Liberals sought to undermine the Unionist government's record in foreign affairs by arguing that in office 'their career has been marked by a continuous series of wars and rumours of war' and that in the crises and complications they had been called upon to deal with 'they have shown neither clear purpose nor resourceful diplomacy'. The alleged failures of the government included the slaughter of Armenian Christians, the humiliation of Greece, the outbreak of violence in India and the sacrifice of British interests in Siam, Tunis and Madagascar. The government's Far Eastern policy was especially criticised for having entered into a futile and unnecessary contest with Russia whose seizure of Port Arthur in 1898 led to Britain obtaining a lease of Wei-hai-Wei, which imposed a considerable burden on the nation's overtaxed military resources and was a source of naval weakness rather than strength.

The Liberal Party claimed that the emphasis placed by the Unionists on domestic policy at the previous election had given rise to 'a singularly bare and exiguous performance' in which the 'great social programme' had 'evaporated into air'. No progress had been made on the scheme for old age pensions or on the question of temperance reform, while the scheme of employers' liability was said to have resulted in a situation which was arbitrary and partial in its incidence and had proved the most litigious Act of modern times. By contrast, the Liberal manifesto referred to the need to solve the housing problems of urban and rural areas, to check the evils of intemperance, to secure religious equality, to extend the membership of

Parliament beyond the wealthy, and to broaden the franchise. Critical comment was also made regarding the ability of the House of Lords arbitrarily to overrule the House of Commons.

The Conservatives were also accused of having indulged in sectional favouritism and financial recklessness in the form of giving doles from the public Exchequer to those classes on whose support they relied. Examples of this were stated to be the payment of government money to agricultural landowners, clerical tithe payers and denominational schools which had resulted in the revenue derived from Harcourt's financial reforms being 'uselessly and mischievously dribbled away'. In consequence taxation was not reduced in time of peace and increasing income. The nation was thus urged to unite in condemnation of a government whose record had been to keep the Empire in a ferment, to squander resources and which had demonstrated neither the will nor the power to pursue or initiate a policy of progress and reform.

Attention was also devoted to future policy in South Africa following the annexation of the Orange Free State and the Transvaal to the Dominions of the Crown. It was argued that the task now facing the country was the reconciliation of a humbled but brave people to this new political situation and the manifesto asked whether it was likely that a government which so little understood the task before them at the beginning of the war would be able to cope with the more complicated problems which now needed addressing.

However, although some criticisms of Unionist South African policy were made (in particular that better diplomacy might have prevented the war), Liberals attempted to divert attention from this issue by arguing that war was not the only matter which electors should be considering. Sir William Harcourt's election address to his West Monmouth constituents accused the government of seeking to confine the election to the single issue of the war 'and to shut out, if possible, from the verdict of the electorate all other matters which concern the well-being of the country'. He argued that in the previous election the Unionists made a number of 'reckless promises' relating to matters which included improved working-class housing, shorters hours for shop workers, the eight-hour day in mining districts, the expansion of smallholdings, the provision of Poor Law and School Board rates from the Exchequer, and electoral registration reform. In office, however, nothing had been done to promote these measures. He also condemned the government's financial record on which social reform was dependent. He argued that they came to office with vast surpluses but had translated these into accumulated debt and increased taxes. Positive statements contained in Liberal speeches included the need to reduce public spending, the reform of the army, the need for popular control for public education financed from the rates, and Irish home rule (although most Liberals conceded that this was not an issue at that election).

Labour Representation Committee

The trade unions were initially opposed to throwing in their lot with an independent working-class political party inspired by socialist principles. Trade unions traditionally represented skilled workers and the Trades Union Congress endorsed the political tactic of 'Lib–Labism'. However, towards the end of the century, the stance of the unions and the TUC changed. Although the organisation of unskilled workers in the 1880s (in a development referred to as 'New Unionism') provided the basis for a reconsideration of working-class politics (since new union leaders were socialists, believing in working-class unity), this did not occur. The new unions represented only a small section of the unorganised working class and the depression killed off most of the new ventures. Of greater significance, therefore, was the change in attitude of the established trade unions towards independent working-class representation. Developments which included mechanisation, the adoption of increasingly hostile attitudes by employers towards craft unions (which was displayed by the formation of bodies such as the National Free Labour Association in 1893 and the Federation of Employers in 1894), the tendency of the courts to side with employers in mounting an offensive against workers (including the *Lyons v. Wilkins* judgements in 1896–9) and the failure of Salisbury's government to intervene in matters of this nature prompted 'traditional' unionists to cooperate with other sections of the working class (as was evidenced in the 1899 dockers' 'tanner' dispute).

These considerations prompted the TUC in 1899 formally to support the establishment of an independent working-class political party which would represent the interests of the unions in Parliament. In 1900, the Labour Representation Committee gave substance to this objective. It was an umbrella group representing the Independent Labour Party, the Fabian Society, some trade unions and – briefly – the Socialist Democratic Federation. Its philosophy was that of 'labourism': this emphasised working-class independence and self-reliance and stressed the importance of trade unions to an independent working-class political party whose role was that of advancing the 'bread and butter' needs of organised labour.

The manifesto of the Labour Representation Committee referred to a diverse range of domestic reforms which included the provision of adequate maintenance from national funds for the aged poor, the public provision of better houses for the people, the supply of useful work for the unemployed and the grant of adequate maintenance for children. The manifesto called for the nationalisation of land and railways, the relief of local rates by grants from the Exchequer, the introduction of graduated income tax and the introduction of a range of constitutional reforms which included shorter Parliaments, adult suffrage, registration reform, the payment of MPs and the abolition of the standing army which would be replaced by a citizen force. These policies were accompanied by other demands which included public control of the liquor traffic and the rejection of compulsory vaccination. Foreign affairs was dealt with briefly, with the demand for the granting of legislative independence to all parts of the Empire. It was argued that the object of these measures was 'to enable the people ultimately to obtain the Socialisation of the Means of Production, Distribution, and Exchange to be controlled by a Democratic State in the interests of the entire community, and the Complete Emancipation of Labour from the Domination of Capitalism and Landlordism, with the Establishment of Social and Economic Equality between the Sexes'.

Result of the Election

The position of the parties was virtually unchanged compared to 1895. A total number of 1,102 candidates contested the election with 243 MPs being returned unopposed. The result was:

Party	Votes	Vote %	MPs
Conservative and Liberal Unionist	1,722,344	48.9%	383
Liberal	1,569,454	44.5%	182
Irish Nationalist	91,055	2.6% [57.4%]	82
Irish Conservative and Liberal Unionist	45,614	1.3% [32.2%]	19
Labour Representation Committee	62,698	1.8%	2
Irish Liberal	2,869	0.1% [2.0%]	1
Others	29,448	0.8%	1
Total	**3,523,482**		**670**

The turnout was 75.1 per cent.

The 'other' was Sir J. Austin (Yorkshire, Osgoldcross, Independent Liberal). One candidate from an ethnic minority group (Sir Mancharjee Bhownaggree) was elected for North East Bethnal Green as a Conservative.

The Parties

The ability of the Unionists to appeal to working-class jingoistic impulses was one explanation for its increased support amongst this section of the electorate. This development commenced in 1886 but was especially evident in 1900. Eighty-five of the 98 seats in the largest cities of London, Glasgow, Birmingham, Manchester, Liverpool, Leeds and Sheffield were won by Unionist candidates (Searle, 1992: 52). The Party won 51 of the 59 seats in the county of London and 123 of the 155 seats in Southern England. Around 68 of the 402 Conservative MPs were Liberal Unionists. As in 1895, the Liberal Party found difficulty in getting candidates which resulted in 163 Conservative and Liberal Unionist MPs securing unopposed returns. The Party performed best in Northern England where it won 55 of the 153 seats and also fared relatively well in the Midlands where it won 27 of the 88 seats. The Labour Representation Committee secured two MPs and eight Lib–Lab candidates were also elected.

Scotland, Wales and Ireland

Changes in the balance between the Unionists and Liberals which commenced in 1886 reached their climax in 1900 when the Unionists secured more seats in Scotland than the Liberals (36 : 34). Their advance was especially marked in the urban and industrial areas of Scotland.

In Wales, the Liberal Party slightly improved its position compared to 1895 and won 27 of the 34 seats. The Conservatives won six and the Labour Representation Committee one. The situation in Ireland remained exactly as in 1895 – the Nationalists won 81 of the 101 seats (which was augmented by T. P. O'Connor being elected for Liverpool, Scotland), the Conservative and Liberal Unionists won 19 and the Liberals retained their one seat of North Tyrone.

Consequence of the Election

Lord Salisbury formed his third Unionist government.

13 January – 8 February 1906

Party Leaders
Arthur James Balfour (Unionist)
Henry Campbell-Bannerman (Liberal)
(There was no official leader of the Labour Representation Committee but Keir Hardie was the senior MP.)

Background to the Election
Timing of the Election
Internal disputes (which are discussed below) appeared in Balfour's government, in particular over the issue of tariff reform. However, Balfour sensed that the advantage these disputes gave to the Liberal Party could be offset by the divisions which existed within it. The Boer War had caused deep divisions within the Liberal Party and although a semblance of unity was restored when it was over, key MPs associated with the Liberal League were unhappy with Campbell-Bannerman's leadership and, in the autumn of 1905, Asquith, Grey and Haldane concluded the Relugas Agreement whereby none of them would accept office under Campbell-Bannerman unless he moved to the House of Lords and Asquith became Leader of the House of Commons and *de facto* leader of the Party. These problems were supplemented by a new dispute concerning the priority which should be attached to Irish home rule (which is referred to in more detail below). Balfour therefore perceived that the dissent within his own party might be masked if the Liberals were forced into accepting office, thereby bringing their divisions into the open and, in particular, forcing them to declare what they intended to do regarding Ireland. He anticipated either that Campbell-Bannerman would find the task of constructing an administration impossible or that, if he did succeed in forming a government, it would consist of second-tier Parliamentarians since none of the main Parliamentarians would serve. Thus, on 4 December 1905 he resigned the premiership, giving way to a Liberal administration headed by Campbell-Bannerman. Campbell-Bannerman was the first Prime Minister to be legally recognised following a warrant issued by Edward VII in 1905 which ended the situation whereby the post of prime minister was an informal one.

However, Balfour's ploy did not work as he had anticipated. Campbell-Bannerman found no difficulty in constructing an interim administration and his leading critics, including Asquith, Grey and Haldane, accepted his offer to serve in it. The extent to which the landed interest had deserted the Liberal Party was evidenced by the middle-class composition of the Cabinet. Additionally, the Labour Independent MP, John Burns, was appointed to the Local Government Board, the first former manual worker to become a Cabinet minister. The dissolution of Parliament took place on 16 December and was followed by an election held early in the new year.

Electoral Procedures and Practices
A Bill to secure redistribution was rejected in 1905 which meant that the election was contested on constituency boundaries established in 1885.

Unionists

The existing electoral system had been heavily to the advantage of the Unionists after 1885. The prevailing household, lodging and occupation franchises failed to make provision for multiple occupancy of property and excluded between 2 and 3 million adult males (Russell, 1973: 116–17). Registration procedures made it difficult for a person who had changed address to keep on the electoral register in consecutive years and was especially a problem for the working class and lower middle class who comprised the most mobile sections of the population. This bias against the working class was compounded by plural voting based on property ownership and the fancy franchises which gave around 600,000 persons more than one vote in the 1906 general election (Russell, 1973: 19). Finally, the distribution of seats (which had been unaltered since the 1885 legislation) favoured the Unionists since county constituencies and small boroughs were over-represented at the expense of larger boroughs. These were also the constituencies in which most plural voting was concentrated.

In 1902 Lord Salisbury was replaced as prime minister and leader of the Conservative Party by his nephew, Arthur J. Balfour. Balfour's administration enjoyed some successes in foreign policy, ending the Boer War at the peace of Vereeniging in 1902, concluding the Entente Cordiale with France in 1904 and entering into an agreement with Japan in 1905. The Committee of Imperial Defence, which was designed to coordinate the military defence of the Empire, was established as a formal body in 1903. Additionally, the government pursued the strategy of seeking to 'kill home rule through kindness'. In 1903 Wyndham's Irish Land Act provided state aid to enable all tenant farmers to purchase their farms. This measure enabled the purchasers to pay an annual redemption payment which was less than the normal rent in order to own their farms after a period of 68 years.

However, although Balfour had inherited a comfortable majority of around 130 from his uncle, his government subsequently got into severe difficulties. The loss of Bury in May 1902 inaugurated a bad run of by-election results for the government and between 1902 and 1905 the Liberal Party gained 20 seats in these contests. Defeats occurred in the House of Commons at the committee stage of the Irish Land Bill. Attempts to shore up the government by reshuffling the Cabinet in September–October 1903 failed to improve the government's position dramatically and by 1905 there was considerable speculation concerning when the government would finally collapse.

There were several reasons which accounted for this reversal of Unionist fortunes. The government was unpopular by 1900, but the Boer War transformed the contest into a 'khaki' election which served to mask its unpopularity. However, their ability to bask in the patriotism engendered by the war was soon undone following its conclusion in 1902. Almost as soon as the troops had returned home, the knives were out to blame the government for its mismanagement of the conflict, especially when ministerial and military incompetence was confirmed by the Report of the Elgin Commission in 1903.

A further problem concerned two contentious pieces of legislation affecting education and the brewing industry, both of which upset the sensibilities of nonconformist opinion. The 1902 Education Act abolished the school boards and handed their responsibilities to county and borough councils. Although this measure was responsible for establishing a system of state secondary education, it was subject to criticism for giving aid from the rates to Anglican and

Catholic schools. This was designed to enable these schools to raise their standards but was opposed by nonconformists on the grounds that ratepayers were subsidising church schools whose religious doctrines they opposed. In Wales, opposition to the Act coincided with an evangelical crusade led by Evan Roberts: Welsh local authoritites refused to implement the Act and Balfour had to introduce special legislation providing for direct control from Whitehall. This measure also created dissent within the government's ranks, in particular arousing hostility from the Liberal Unionists.

In 1904 the government passed a Licensing Act. Before this measure was passed, the licensing of public houses was in the hands of the local magistrates who were empowered to grant licences for one year and to refuse renewal on grounds which included the desire to reduce the facilities for the sale of drink in their area. The 1904 measure removed to Quarter Sessions the right to refuse a licence and also provided a fund to compensate dispossessed licencees. The temperance movement (which enjoyed strong support among nonconformists, radicals, trade unionists and socialists) was hostile to the measure which was viewed as being too lenient towards the brewing interests.

Both Acts served as a spur to nonconformists to turn out and vote against the Unionists in by-elections (and also in the 1906 general election). Thus, one pillar underpinning Unionist political supremacy after 1886 (abstention by Liberal voters) was removed. However, the mobilisation of Liberals to oppose the government was added to by disputes within the Unionist ranks which served as an inducement for some Unionist voters to transfer their allegiance to the Liberal Party.

Internal division was caused by the issue of tariff reform. Although a duty on corn had been imposed in the 1902 budget, its purpose was to raise money for the war rather than to introduce protection and it was repealed the following year. The 1903–04 recession prompted some Unionists to urge more vigorous action to tackle domestic economic and social problems.

In a speech at Birmingham on 15 May 1903, Joseph Chamberlain urged that the system of free trade should be abandoned and he attempted to convince the Cabinet of the need to abandon this policy. He wished to introduce a policy of tariffs which would tax all imports into Britain and thus protect native industries from unfair foreign competition. However, this was coupled with imperial preference whereby the food and manufactures from the colonies would be admitted at a lower rate of duty, thereby binding the Empire more closely together. He viewed tariff reform rather than collectivist policies as the means to deliver domestic reform since he anticipated that the revenues derived from tariffs could be used to raise money for both social reform and defence and help to lower the rate of unemployment.

Chamberlain's course of action was certain to split the Party for although his policy of fiscal reform enjoyed support in some areas (such as the West Midlands where light metal industries were located) it was strongly opposed elsewhere (including Lancashire which was heavily dependent on the cotton industry). Chamberlain also aroused the antagonism of the Party's diehard free traders and also its landed interest who saw his espousal of tariff reform as an attempt by himself and the Liberal Unionists to oust them from their positions of power within the Party and capture control of it both locally and nationally. A key political difficulty with his proposal was the suggestion of food taxes. Although Chamberlain felt that these would contribute to higher wages, more regular employment and could finance social reforms such as old age pensions, others in the Party felt that they would be electorally unpopular.

Accordingly, the issue of fiscal reform had an unsettling effect on the Unionists which inevitably had an adverse impact on its prospects at the next general election. Rival organisations were established within the Party to promote both sides of the argument. The Free Food League was established in July 1903 to oppose Chamberlain's proposals and in October 1903 he launched the Tariff Reform campaign and established the Imperial Tariff Commission and the Tariff Reform League to promote them. Additionally, the Free Trade Union (established in 1903) provided a non-party vehicle through which all supporters of free trade could cooperate. Some Unionist Free Traders (the most well-known of whom was Winston Churchill) defected to the Liberals and there were numerous examples of Unionist MPs seeking new constituencies for the 1906 election to ensure that their views on the subject of tariff reform corresponded to those of their local constituency associations. In Parliament the Liberal Party sought to expose divisions within the Unionists on this issue by bringing forward free trade resolutions.

Initially tariff reform helped to improve the fortunes of Unionist candidates in by-elections. However, the improvement of the country's economic fortunes (which were evident by 1905) undermined the case for tariff reform and by-election results again went against the government. Baldwin's main concern was to avoid a damaging split on this issue. Although the unity of the government was aided by the resignations of Chamberlain and three leading free traders (the Duke of Devonshire, Lord George Hamilton and C. T. Ritchie) in September 1903, the Party as a whole remained in disarray. On 14 November 1905, Chamberlain succeeded in getting the National Union of Conservative Associations to pass a resolution in favour of imperial preference and a general tariff (on the grounds that it would 'secure more employment and steadier wages for workers') against Balfour's wishes. The desire to prevent a party split on this issue was a major factor causing Balfour to resign as Prime Minister in December 1905.

The internal disputes experienced by the Unionists after 1900 were compounded by organisational weakness, especially in safe constituencies where inertia had set in. Problems were experienced in finding candidates, many of whom were last-minute adoptions.

Liberals

Significant ideological divisions existed within the Liberal Party towards the end of the nineteenth century. It was in this period that 'new Liberalism' and Liberal Imperialism which offered alternative views concerning the aim and direction of social reform emerged.

Social reform had not hitherto received priority attention within the Party. There were several reasons for this: they included the Gladstonian heritage (which asserted that money was best left to 'fructify' in the pockets of the taxpayer) and the dislike by middle-class Liberals associated with business of increased taxation and state interference in industrial freedom. Although the schism in 1886 witnessed a desertion of middle-class support from the Liberal Party, this was of a regional character, being most pronounced in London and the Home Counties but less obvious in Northern England and South Wales where businessmen continued to play a major role in Liberal politics (Searle, 1992: 57–9). Indeed, the negative reaction of many engaged in business to Chamberlain's proposals for tariff reform tended to strengthen the support of this group for the Liberal Party.

However, ambivalence towards social reform could not continue indefinitely, in particular because it was estimated that between 75 and 80 per cent of the electorate were working class, forming a majority between one half and two-thirds of the constituencies (Russell, 1973: 21). Many social investigators who studied the problem of urban poverty were supporters of the Liberal Party and, in addition, pressure for change was exerted by the working class. The Taff Vale judgement in 1901 (which ruled that employers could sue trade unions for damages arising from strike action) was a spur to the growth of trade union organisation amongst the working class and increased union affiliation to the LRC: between 1890 and 1914, the percentage of workers in trade unions rose from 8 to 27 per cent, and between 1902 and 1903, 127 trade unions affiliated to this body. The Liberal Party could not ignore the importance of this development which resulted in it displaying an interest in domestic social reform at the expense of its historic commitment to Irish home rule. There was, however, a considerable division in the Party concerning the aims and scope of social reform proposals.

New Liberalism was the main development to increase Liberal political support among the urban working class. This sought to effect a compromise between collectivism and the emphasis which Liberalism traditionally placed on individualism by redefining freedom in a more sophistical way (Searle, 1992: 66). New Liberalism emerged between 1880 and 1914 and sought to direct the Party's reforming energies to the economic, political and social circumstances of late-nineteenth and early-twentieth-century Britain, particularly the problems caused by industrialism and urbanisation.

The Manchester School had displayed a sceptical attitude towards state intervention and believed that if the obstacles to the free development of social and economic forces were removed by the abolition of monopolies, a harmony of interests would emerge naturally: social problems would, in time, solve themselves. This belief seemed anachronistic in late-nineteenth-century England and led some Liberals to redirect Gladstone's appeal to conscience towards social and economic questions and advocate state intervention to secure social justice. Thus, collectivism entered the agenda of Liberal political debates. This was reconciled with the traditional Liberal belief in individualism through the argument that state action to remove poverty and exploitation was a necessary preliminary to an individual's enjoyment of freedom. Although an ever-increasing role for the state might ultimately undermine individual liberty, at that time it was argued that poverty and its associated evils were unacceptable restrictions on personal liberty whose removal justified state intervention. Only then would it be possible to realise the traditional Liberal virtues of self-help and self-reliance. Unlike the Liberal imperialists, therefore, new Liberalism did seek to reconcile action by the state with traditional Liberal principles. These views were articulated in the universities: the traditional Liberal belief in freedom was redefined by philosophers who included T. H. Green, Leonard Hobhouse and D. G. Ritchie. But it also influenced some Liberal politicians (including Chamberlain, Dilke and Morley and, latterly, Lloyd George) and thus made some headway in party declarations of policy (principally the 1885 'Unauthorised (or Manchester) Programme' and the 1891 Newcastle Programme).

However, the influence of such ideas within the late-nineteenth-century Liberal Party was limited since radical measures of social and agrarian reform failed to command universal or consistent support. The political make-up of the Party (especially its middle-class head and working-class body) made it difficult for its leaders to pursue such a course of action consistently, and instead prompted a tendency to divert attention from these concerns by focusing the energies of the Party on broader domestic or foreign policy concerns. This was clearly demonstrated when Gladstone was returned to office in 1893. 'Bread and butter' issues of importance to the working class were subordinated to the issue of Irish home rule, and, following the Party's massive defeat in 1895, the concerns of the Celtic Fringe (which had remained loyal to Liberalism) dominated the Party's concerns.

New Liberalism, however, was not the only new direction within the Liberal Party in the late nineteenth and early twentieth century. Liberal imperialism provided a different solution to the Party's need to augment its support. This sought to rejuvenate the Party as a political vehicle whose concerns transcended class or sectional interests and which depicted itself as the guardian of the national interest. The Darwinian overtones of this new political departure advocated social reform at home in order to breed an imperial race which would seek the extension of Empire whose peoples would benefit through their association with an advanced power which would improve, raise and civilise them.

Liberal imperialism was a concept which was designed to unify and guide the conduct of the Party in many hitherto uncoordinated areas of policy. It entailed abandoning the primacy given to the issue of Irish home rule by Gladstone and sought to couple imperialism to measures (especially social reform) which were designed to improve 'national efficiency'. This approach arose in part as a response to criticisms of the Newcastle Programme which asserted that it constituted a catalogue of proposals rather than a policy. Additionally, the advocacy of social reform within the framework of developing the nation's economic efficiency undermined the 'socialistic' nature of domestic reform, thus broadening the scope of these policies which ceased to be purely working-class concerns. Indeed, the main appeal directed by the Liberal imperialists was to the 'centre ground' of politics which was primarily identified with the middle-class electorate whose desertion was regarded as a major source of the Party's electoral weakness in the latter decades of the nineteenth century. The advocacy of Liberal imperialism was especially identified with Asquith, Grey, Haldane and (more loosely) Lord Rosebery (who served as Prime Minister between 1892 and 1895). The Liberal League was formed in 1902 to establish this policy as a cardinal Liberal principle, seeking to convert the Liberal Party from within to the wisdom of its views.

Liberal imperialism was designed as a new political approach (a 'clean slate') for the Party, but its total lack of identity with anything which had occurred before lessened its appeal and opened its advocates to the charge of political opportunism and lack of principle. Liberal imperialism offered a complex approach to reconciling traditional Liberal sectional divisions, the subtlety of which restricted its support to an elite within the Party while working-class interest was minimal. The failure by Liberal imperialists to concentrate on organisation to mobilise support for their views weakened the appeal of their approach to the Party at large.

A key problem with Liberal imperialism was its willingness to abandon the traditional Liberal focus on the individual. State intervention became justified by the needs of the nation, even if this jeopardised the liberties of the individual. Imperial adventures potentially contradicted the historic Liberal support for struggles waged by small nations for freedom and, further, restricted the Liberal Party's ability to criticise Unionist imperialism which they had traditionally opposed. The Boer War clearly demonstrated this dilemma and evidenced a three-way split in the Party between the Liberal imperialists (who supported the war at the expense of voting against their own Party), the pro-Boers (whose leading figures were John Morley and David Lloyd George) and the remainder of the Party which, under Campbell-Bannerman, offered limited support for the war, called for a negotiated peace and latterly denounced the way it was being fought, in particular the 'methods of barbarism' which Campbell-Bannerman identified with Kitchener's use of concentration camps.

However, the raising of the issue of tariff reform by the Unionists provided the Liberals with the ability to mount a campaign in defence of free trade. This was viewed as the policy on which British greatness rested, and Liberals believed that interference with it would lead to inefficiency in British industries and result in increasing the cost of living to the particular detriment of the working class. Opposition to tariff reform and the defence of free trade thus muted divisions within the Party which have been outlined above and further reduced the importance of having to promote a programme of social reform at that time.

Liberal prospects were, however, almost undone in November 1905 when the issue of Irish home rule re-emerged. In a speech delivered at Stirling on 24 November 1905, Campbell-Bannerman enunciated a 'step-by-step' approach to home rule, whereby progress towards this goal would proceed by instalments. This might include the immediate enactment of administrative reform such as the granting of a general assembly elected by Irish people. This approach would remove the obstruction which home rule had exerted over the conduct of previous Liberal administrations and enable the new government to focus on other pressing domestic policies such as social reform. However, some Liberals viewed this as an unfettered commitment that the Party would introduce home rule and this feeling was articulated in a speech by Lord Rosebery on 25 November at Bodmin, which was given considerable prominence in the Conservative press. As has been argued above, the spectre of a disunited Liberal Party was a major influence on Balfour resigning the premiership. However, this failed to materialise, Asquith having put forward similar views concerning Ireland in a letter to his constituents on 1 March 1902.

Accordingly, the Liberal Party entered the 1906 election in good spirits. Organisation in the constituencies had markedly improved since 1900 and the placing of candidates was aided by the increased finances contributed to the Party by those who opposed tariff reform. The by-election results obtained by the Party since 1902 also augured well for the general election.

Labour Representation Committee
The Labour Representation Committee (LRC) was established in 1900 in the wake of the Taff Vale judgement. The social injustices arising from the unequal distribution of wealth and resources underpinned the momentum for independent working-class political action.

In the period following 1900, Liberals and the emerging Labour movement found much common ground. Increased support for collectivism within Liberal circles provided the potential for a policy of social reform which both parties could agree on. Both were hostile to the Taff Vale decision and the 1902 Education Act and each organisation contained critics of the Boer War. Additionally, the defence of free trade was an issue around which Liberals and Labour could find common ground. Accordingly, this raised the issue of electoral cooperation between the Liberal Party and the Labour movement which began to materialise in by-elections after 1900 and which was comfortable with existing Lib–Lab arrangements.

In addition to sharing certain common political objectives, both sides had vested interests in securing some form of arrangement. The LRC's status was that of a minor party operating within a first-past-the-post electoral system with limited funds and, consequently, an inability to field large numbers of candidates at general elections. It was unlikely to make much parliamentary headway without an accommodation with the Liberal Party, especially in an era in which not all adult males possessed the vote. It would, however, increase the proportion of working-class candidates elected to the House of Commons as it bypassed the traditional handicap faced by working-class candidates seeking to enter Parliament, which was the reluctance of local Liberal associations to adopt them. However, the Liberal Party also perceived advantages in an electoral arrangement with the LRC. This would maximise the size of an anti-Conservative front by enabling constituencies which the Liberal Party did not normally contest to be fought. An important consideration (since the Liberal Party would inevitably be fielding far more candidates than the LRC) was that working-class voters might be more inclined to support the Liberal Party in the absence of an LRC candidate if an agreement was concluded between the two organisations. It was also possible that Conservative working-class voters who would not consider voting Liberal might be tempted to vote for an LRC candidate. The existence of double-member constituencies made it relatively easy to secure local agreements and an electoral arrangement with the LRC would also cost the Liberal Party little if most of its candidatures were in Conservative-held constituencies.

Accordingly, in 1903 a non-aggression pact between the Liberal Party and the Labour Representation Committee was secretly drawn up between Herbert Gladstone and Ramsay MacDonald. Although this suggested that central influence would be brought to bear on local organisations to bring about such cooperation in the individual constituencies, it was essentially a constituency-level arrangement which relied on activists from both parties agreeing to implement it. It was, however, relatively successful, both by ensuring that the Liberal Party and the LRC fought each other in only a handful of constituencies and also helping to reduce the number of unopposed returns to 30 in England, Scotland and Wales, compared to 165 in 1900. There were other examples of cooperation between Labour and Liberal candidates during the election in constituencies which were covered by this pact. This arrangement did not, however, operate in Scotland and was strongly opposed by Liberal activists in North Eastern England and the West Riding of Yorkshire where Liberalism remained strong.

By-elections
A total number of 114 by-elections occurred in the 1900–06 Parliament, of which 81 were contested. The Unionists recorded a net loss of 25 seats, the Liberals a net gain of 16, Labour a net gain of three and others a net gain of six.

Conduct of the Election
Formal policy pronouncements were issued by the SDF, the LRC and the United Irish League. In other cases, political parties issued leaflets and other forms of policy statements which were used in the constituencies. During the campaign the Liberal Publication Department issued around 22 million leaflets and three million booklets and the Unionists issued around 2.5

million leaflets each day (Russell, 1973: 64). These were in addition to the election addresses which most candidates circulated to their constituents.

Election meetings were a major form of political activity and these were subject to a considerable amount of heckling and, in some cases, violence. The dissemination of political views was also aided by the growth of the mass circulation cheap press in the later nineteenth and early twentieth century and through the considerable involvement of pressure groups in the campaign. The motor car emerged as a major form of transport which enabled candidates to be more widely seen in their constituencies.

Unionists

Internal divisions mainly in connection with protection resulted in rival Unionist candidates fighting each other in 11 constituencies.

A. J. Balfour's election address gave prominence to the achievements of Conservative governments over the previous 10 years and asserted that future actions would be based upon the same principles as before, in order to promote peace among nations, secure closer union between different portions of the Empire and enact social legislation at home which was mindful of individual rights. Considerable criticism was levelled at the Liberal Party who were accused of having mounted both unscrupulous criticism of the actions of Unionists governments (as was stated to be the case with Chinese labour) and perverse criticism (as was evidenced in Campbell-Bannerman's attack on the humanity of the British army). Balfour sought to depict the Liberal leaders as revolutionaries whose anticipated future actions were said to include home rule, disestablishment, the destruction of voluntary schools and the spoilation of licence-holders. The one exception to this was free trade where the Liberals were said to adhere to the same fiscal creed as that embraced by the Party 60 years ago, regardless of changes such as the conditions of international trade and the relation of Britain to other industrial communities. By contrast, Unionists believed in adapting fiscal (and other) policies to the changing conditions of a changing world. Balfour pledged that the first task of a Unionist government would be to reform the fiscal system. In foreign affairs, Balfour questioned whether the Liberals could carry out a foreign policy which was 'pacific, honourable and consistent' by querying whether the Prime Minister was committed to a strong naval and military force and accusing the Liberals of being divided between 'Little Englanders' and 'Liberal imperialists'.

The most detailed statement of Unionist policy was the Conservative Central Office publication, *The Record*. The Unionist campaign was dominated by fiscal issues, and tariff reform was defended for both retaliatory and protective reasons (that is, it would both defend British industries from the impact of unfair foreign competition and would also benefit their development). However, while almost all Unionist candidates supported some measure of fiscal reform, most were vague on its precise details and relatively few candidates expressed explicit support for Chamberlain's programme, which was underlaid by a vision of imperial unity, envisaging a self-contained, self-supplying and federated Empire with the colonies acting as the granary of the Empire. During the campaign, Balfour was challenged to reveal his views concerning tariffs. The failure of most Unionist candidates to fully embrace the Chamberlain ideal made it hard to repudiate the Liberal allegation that protection would result in higher prices, in particular affecting food. This could have been countered by the argument that Chamberlain's policy of tariff reform would have made price rises irrelevant since they would have resulted in an improvement in working-class living standards. However, such an argument was not forcibly expressed, although many Conservative candidates did argue that tariff reform was a more effective solution to unemployment than the Liberal policy of the taxation of land values. A further attempt was made to sell this policy to the working class by arguing that free imports encouraged the use of sweated labour abroad.

Unionist candidates advocated the need to safeguard the 1902 Education Act and defended the 1904 Licensing Act as a preferable measure to those supported by Liberal fanatics who wished to replace public houses with temperance halls. Candidates made some reference to foreign and defence policy (in particular the creation of the Army Council and the Committee for Imperial Defence). Prominent attention was also devoted by candidates to the defence of the Union where it was alleged that the likely need of a Liberal government to rely on the votes of the Irish National Party at Westminster would cause them to revert to their policy of home rule for Ireland. This issue received considerable prominence in the early stages of the Unionist campaign, and was opposed for constituting the break-up of the Empire. It was also argued that this policy would result in impoverished Irish workers flocking to Britain to compete for jobs with native British people. The spectre of increased expenditure on the navy to guard Britain against any evil intent of an Irish government was also raised. The intensity of Unionist objections to home rule may, however, have helped to induce Nationalist opinion in Ireland to accept reform which fell short of this objective.

Balfour played a major role in the Unionist campaign. Bonar Law was regarded as one of the best platform speakers, but spent most of the contest in Glasgow.

Liberals

Divisions within the Party were largely masked in 1906, and there were only two examples of Liberal Party and Liberal League candidates fighting each other (in North Lambeth and South Hackney).

Campbell-Bannerman's election address concentrated much attention on the record of the previous Unionist government which he depicted 'as a well-nigh unbroken expanse of mismanagement; of legislation conducted for the benefit of privileged classes and powerful interests; of wars and adventures abroad hastily embarked upon and recklessly pursued'. In particular the government was criticised for the manner in which they had handled South Africa following the conclusion of the war so that the loss of prosperity and even ruin could only be avoided through the use of servile labour imported from China and for their alleged mismanagement of the economy. It was argued that when they entered office national finances were in good order with moderate taxation and the public debt being reduced. However, 10 years later expenditure and indebtedness had piled up, income tax was high, war taxes were continued in peacetime, and national credit was impaired. This had resulted in the restriction of enterprise and high levels of unemployment. In terms of domestic policy, it was argued that policies which had been pursued (such as the licensing question or the rating system) were motivated more by 'a desire to propitiate their powerful friends ... than to settle problems of national consequence with due regard to the needs, the sentiments, and the convictions of all concerned' and they were accused of abandoning, once in office, the programme of social reform which had figured prominently in the 1895 election campaign.

In terms of future actions, Campbell-Bannerman derided protection, which was promoted by the Conservative Party as being underpinned by the desire to promote class interests, and he argued that it would produce 'incalculable mischief to the nation and the Empire'. He defended free trade and argued that he did not believe that the experience of other countries suggested that by 'limiting our imports we shall increase our exports, that by raising prices, no matter by what kind of tariff expedients, we shall assist in equalising the conditions of international competition, or in enlarging the area of employment'. He also rejected the view that experience abroad suggested that the taxation of food was conducive to the welfare of the people. He thus rejected the view that because some individual industries were hampered and obstructed by foreign tariffs, it was right to sacrifice conditions which he believed were indispensable to the social welfare of British people and to Britain's industrial greatness and expansion. He branded protection as bad economy which was 'immoral and oppressive, based as it is, and must be, on the exploitation of the community in the interests of favoured trades and financial groups'. He also asserted that an Empire which was 'united' on the basis of food taxes would be an Empire with a disruptive force at its centre. In conclusion, he affirmed the time-honoured principles of Liberalism – 'the principles of peace, economy, self-government, and civil and religious liberty' – and pledged to resist the attack which the Unionists were mounting on free trade.

The main central statement of policy was contained in the publication *Ten Years of Tory Government*. In the campaign, Liberal candidates focused on free trade and the maintenance of sound finance and social reform. It was alleged that Britain's manufacturing supremacy was based on the cheap supply of food and raw materials, and Chamberlain was accused of seeking to turn back the clock and pursue a narrow system of protection which might aid a few specialist producers, but which would harm consumers and damage the economy. A popular Liberal campaign song urged the electorate to 'stamp, stamp, stamp upon protection' which was depicted as the underpinning of all key political issues, including foreign policy, economic policy and social reform. The price of food was a prominent election issue and Liberals sought to secure support for free trade by exploiting the consumer's interest in cheap food. A poster showed two loaves of bread of different sizes – the 'little loaf' of protection and the 'big loaf' of free trade, and one leaflet declared, 'if you want your loaf, you must shut up Jo.' It was also argued that tariffs imposed by Britain would produce counter-measures from other countries, and that key British industries, which included shipbuilding and heavy engineering, would be adversely affected. Liberals denied that imperial preference was the same as a system of free trade within the Empire and asserted that, instead, it entailed a complex system of bargaining which could involve Britain imposing duties against any colonies which refused to give her preference. Burns depicted Chamberlain's campaign in class terms and appealed to his electors in Battersea not to be 'misled by a fiscal pervert who has abandoned all he wisely knew, to advocate that which he … does not understand, in the interests of those who already possess too much, to the detriment of those who have too little' (Russell, 1973: 69).

A majority of Liberal candidates advocated social reform in their individual election addresses, although some candidates associated with the Liberal League argued that the basis of social reform was sound finance, which was the key priority. Specific reform measures included the introduction of old age pensions and the repeal of the 1902 Education Act and the 1904 Licensing Act. Working-class support was also wooed by the support given by many

Liberal candidates to the repeal of the Taff Vale judgement. Proposals to tackle unemployment tended to be vague. Liberals rejected protection as a remedy for unemployment but agreed that while free trade was the best vehicle to increase wealth, it was necessary to find ways to maximise the distribution and spread of wealth more widely. Policies to achieve this included the taxation of land values, and some Liberals also proposed the taxation of mineral wealth.

In foreign affairs, Liberals advocated the maintenance of peace through strength and understanding. It was argued that the South African War starkly differentiated between the Liberal reliance on arbitration in international affairs and Unionist irresponsibility. Many Liberals also advocated a range of constitutional reforms which included the abolition of plural voting and an end to the disqualification of those in receipt of poor relief. In Wales, the issue of the disestablishment of the Anglican Church was prominently advocated. Ireland was given relatively low priority in the Liberal campaign, although some candidates argued in favour of administrative reform.

Relatively little attention was devoted to the record of the Liberal government since 1905, although Burns was responsible for introducing new regulations to provide for the maintenance of dependants of able-bodied paupers in the workhouses and for out-relief of paupers who left workhouses in order to seek work. Considerable emphasis was devoted in the Liberal campaign to the Conservative record in government. In his speech at the Albert Hall on 21 December 1905, Campbell-Bannerman urged the nation to focus on past Unionist actions, which included militarism, extravagance and protection. During the campaign, electors were asked what had happened to the promise made by the Conservatives in 1895 that they would introduce old age pensions and whether, in 1900, this party had made any reference to its intentions to bring forward legislation concerned with education or licensing, or to introduce Chinese labour into South Africa. Following the Boer War, the Conservative government approved a measure to introduce 46,000 indentured Chinese coolies in South Africa to work in the Rand gold mines which added to the hostility towards the government. The labourers lived in compounds which they were forbidden to leave during their term of service, worked long hours for very low pay and were subject to corporal punishment. Conservatives justified this practice on economic grounds, but Liberals depicted them as being driven by the interests 'of an insatiable gang of cosmopolitan financiers', and the spectre of jobs being lost in Britain through the future import of Chinese slaves was raised by Lloyd George. Racial hostility (the 'Yellow Peril') was a major factor in ensuring that the issue of 'Chinese slavery' received considerable prominence during the campaign.

The main burden of the Liberal campaign was undertaken by Asquith and Herbert Gladstone while Lloyd George spear headed the Party's effort in Wales. Campbell-Bannerman (who was not a charismatic speaker) spent much of the election in Scotland although he enjoyed an unopposed return in his constituency of Stirling boroughs.

Labour Representation Committee
The manifesto of the Labour Representation Committee was written by Keir Hardie and Ramsay MacDonald. It was underpinned by reformism and emphasised the objective of social justice as opposed to socialism. It argued that social reform would be secured through the

election of more working men to Parliament – 'the House of Commons is supposed to be the people's House, and yet the people are not there'. Instead, 'landlords, employers, lawyers, brewers and financiers are there in force'. However, many of its policies were similar to those associated with the left wing of the Liberal Party. It forthrightly attacked privilege and monopoly, and argued that unemployment, slums and high rates were caused by the system of land ownership and spiralling and untaxed land values which were to the advantage of idle landowners. The South African War and the introduction of Chinese labour were also depicted as being in the interests of a privileged minority, the mine owners. Action against unemployment was urged (although numerous remedies were put forward by LRC candidates, including Keir Hardie's proposal to impose an additional half-penny on income tax to provide funds for poor relief), with protection being branded as a 'red herring' designed to obscure from the people the real cause of their poverty. Reforms to the Unionists' education and licensing laws and the Taff Vale decision were advocated. Constitutional reform to remove the anomolies and disabilities associated with the current electoral system were urged and a considerable number of candidates expressed support for free trade.

The Independent Labour Party issued its own election manifesto. This document condemned both the Unionists and Liberals for seeking to protect the interests of the rich and for keeping the working class divided. It was argued that this was achieved by appealing to religious prejudices, racial animosities, patriotism and pride and 'whilst you quarrel amongst yourselves, they quietly fill their pockets and empty yours'. Protection was opposed for having the effect of upholding domestic monopolies.

Result of the Election

A Liberal victory was seen as inevitable at the commencement of the campaign. A further feature of the result was the improved turnout compared to 1900, one explanation for which being that abstaining Liberal voters were fewer in number than in previous elections since 1886.

A total of 1,273 candidates contested the election, a marked feature of which was the low number of uncontested returns (which numbered 34 in Great Britain and 80 in Ireland). The result was:

Party	Votes	Vote %	MPs
Liberal	2,730,718	49.0%	398
Conservative and Liberal Unionist	2,353,089	42.2%	141
Irish Nationalist Party	35,031	0.7% [23.9%]	82
Labour Representation Committee	321,663	4.8%	29
Irish Conservative and Liberal Unionist	68,982	1.2% [32.7%]	15
Others	96,269	1.7%	4
Irish Liberal	20,339	0.4% [9.6%]	1
Total	5,626,091		670

The turnout was 83.2 per cent.

The 'others' were W. O'Brien, (Independent Nationalist, Cork City), T. H. Sloan (Independent Conservative, Belfast South), J. W. Taylor, (Independent Labour, Chester-le-Street) and J. Williams (Independent Labour, Gower).

The Parties

A significant swing away from the Unionists gave the Liberals a landslide victory. The swing was relatively uniform throughout Great Britain (being a little higher than average in urban and industrial areas and lower in rural ones). Ireland alone was exempt from the electoral movement to the Liberal Party. The scale of the Unionist defeat was emphasised on the first day of polling, when Balfour lost his seat of North East Manchester. Only three former Cabinet ministers (Austen Chamberlain, Akers-Douglas and Arnold-Foster) succeeded in retaining their seats and the Party performed badly throughout most of Britain (especially in areas in which it usually did well), the only crumb of comfort being found in the West Midlands where they won the majority of seats. The issue of protection was at the heart of the Unionist defeat. It had caused deep divisions within the Party, had an adverse effect on morale and led many supporters to switch their allegiance to the Liberals at the election. In particular, food taxation was an unpopular issue, especially among the poorly paid agricultural workers. The issue of Chinese labour also accounted for the Unionist performance. Although they viewed the use of the word 'slavery' as a deliberate misrepresentation by their opponents, they underestimated the extent to which the employment of cheap labour was viewed as an attack on the foundations of trade unionism.

The success of the Liberal Party was aided by a number of factors which included the support it obtained from nonconformist and Irish Catholic voters. The National Free Church Council (formed in 1899) provided nonconformism with organisation and its manifesto bore considerable similarities with Liberal and LRC policies. In particular, it opposed the Unionist policy of Chinese labour, and advocated social reform and changes to the Unionists' education and licensing legislation. The United Irish League also threw its weight behind the Liberal Party. This meant that the Liberal Party secured the support of around 600,000 nonconformist voters and around 200,000 Irish Catholic men of voting age. The latter were more geographically concentrated than the nonconformist vote and made a significant contribution to Liberal victories in cities in Lancashire, Yorkshire, Tyneside and the Clyde (Russell, 1973: 191–3). Additionally, Jewish opinion tended to side with the Party as Jewish refugees had been a target of the Unionist government's 1905 Aliens Act.

The Liberal victory was based upon increased levels of turnout by nonconformist supporters and the conversion of Unionist voters. The Party recovered most of the seats which had been lost in 1886, 1892 and 1900 in areas of traditional strength in Wales, Scotland, the West Riding of Yorkshire, Tyneside and the central counties of the Midlands. Additionally, it performed well in rural areas of Western, Eastern and Northern England and in London, urban areas of Lancashire and in the smaller boroughs of the South East. The Party advanced throughout England, Scotland and Wales and in general fared well in the counties as well as the boroughs. The scale of the Liberal success was aided by the effective distribution of the Party's vote, whereby votes were secured where they were needed to oust Unionists rather than piling up large majorities in safe seats.

Labour Representation Committee

Twenty-nine LRC candidates were elected, 24 of whom benefited from the Lib–Lab Pact whereby they faced only Unionist opposition or ran in harness with a Liberal candidate in a two-member seat. Most gains made by the LRC were in Conservative areas. It has been observed that the working-class vote was more solidly cast against the Unionists than at any other previous election (Russell, 1973: 200) and LRC candidates particularly benefited from this by securing a significantly higher swing from the Unionists than was achieved by Liberal candidates. Additionally, 23 Lib–Lab MPs were elected.

Scotland, Wales and Ireland

The Liberals were the largest party in Scotland, winning 58 of the 70 seats. The Unionists won 10 and Labour two. The Liberals won an overwhelming victory in Wales, winning 32 of the 34 seats. Labour and an independent Lib–Lab 'other' each won one seat and all Unionist candidates were defeated.

A significant feature of the election in Ireland was the unity of Nationalist opinion behind the United Irish League whose programme gave prominence to the goal of home rule. Only three contests between Nationalist candidates occurred in the South. New political movements also occurred which included the Independent Orangemen of Ireland associated with T. H. Sloan (which sought to unite Protestants and Catholics behind a programme of reform which included devolution) and T. W. Russell's attempt to mobilise small farmers in Ulster to make use of the 1903 Land Act at the expense of the large landowners. However, these made little headway and Irish politics remained dominated by the Nationalists, 73 of whose candidates were returned unopposed. This party won 81 seats in Ireland and one in England, (where T. P. O'Connor retained his seat at Liverpool, Scotland). Sloan won South Belfast as an Independent Conservative but all Russellites (save Russell himself at South Tyrone) were defeated.

Consequence of the Election

Campbell-Bannerman formed a Liberal government.

15 January – 10 February 1910

Party Leaders
Arthur Balfour (Unionist)
Herbert Asquith (Liberal)
Arthur Henderson (Labour – Chairman of the Parliamentary Labour Party)

Background to the Election
Timing of the Election
The election was precipitated by a constitutional crisis following the rejection by the House of Lords of Lloyd George's budget on 30 November 1909 (the details of which are discussed more fully below). However, the decision to hold the election in the new year was governed by a number of considerations. Both parties felt that it was in their interests to hold the election on the new register which would be current in January 1910, and for this reason, the government acquiesced in allowing the House of Lords to slow down its consideration of the budget, ostensibly to enable the large number of peers who wished to speak to be given the opportunity to participate in the debate. Unionists perceived that a long gap between the veto by the House of Lords and the commencement of polling would advantage them by enabling the intensity of feelings evoked by this issue to subside and permitting policies other than the rejection of the budget to figure in the election campaign.

Electoral Procedures and Practices
The election was held against the background of a constitutional crisis, when the House of Lords rejected the Liberal Party's budget in December 1909. During the seventeenth century it became undisputed that the House of Commons should exercise control over the nation's general financial provisions. However, the consolidation of all revenue measures in one Finance Bill was a relatively recent departure which, although developed towards the end of the eighteenth century, was not fully adopted until 1861. The election also witnessed the active involvement of a number of peers (who mainly campaigned for the Unionists). Theoretically, peers had been previously prohibited from participating in elections by a Sessional Order of the House of Commons, although in practice this restriction had been frequently ignored in the later years of the nineteenth century. The legality of this order was dubious and rendered ineffectual when the House of Commons Privileges Committee failed to treat the Duke of Norfolk's intervention by letter in the July 1909 High Peak by-election as a breach of this order.

Unionists
Following the 1906 election, the Parliamentary Party was briefly led by Joseph Chamberlain until Balfour returned to Parliament following his by-election victory for the City of London on 27 February 1906.

The main development affecting the Unionist Party after 1906 was its conversion to the policy of tariff reform. The Party emerged from the 1906 election divided on this subject, but tariff reformers made considerable progress subsequently in converting the Party to their viewpoint. Chamberlain's stroke in July 1906 made Balfour's conversion to the 'Whole Hoggers' cause (those who endorsed the full demands of Chamberlain's programme) important. He was aware of growing support for tariff reform within the Unionist Party and may also have felt that economic problems facing the country would help to popularise this course of action. Accordingly, in his speech to the National Union in November 1907 at Birmingham, he committed himself to supporting small and widespread duties, both preferential and protective. By 1908, the National Union was in the hands of those committed to tariff reform and in January 1909 Conservative Central Office stated that official support would be withheld from all candidates who did not unreservedly accept the fiscal policy laid down by Balfour in November 1907. This resulted in attempts (especially associated with extremist tariff reformers termed 'the confederacy') to purge Conservative free traders from the Party and by 1910 this element was virtually eliminated from the Unionist Party.

Lloyd George's 1909 budget aroused the anger of many of the interests which were associated with the Unionists. These included the well-organised licensed trade (which was hostile to the licensing proposals) and the financial and commercial interests of the City of London which were opposed to a wide range of the new taxation innovations. The landed interest were vehemently opposed to land valuation, which they viewed as potentially ruinous, and the tariff reformers were concerned that the budget undermined their case that the only way to pay for social reform was through fiscal reform. These interests (and especially the tariff reformers) helped to solidify Unionist opinion in favour of the House of Lords taking the constitutionally unprecedented step of rejecting the budget. Many Unionist peers believed that this step was necessary in order to uphold the power of the Upper Chamber (which would appear impotent if it could not resist the budget proposals concerned with land), and the Conservative Party organisation was also hopeful that the consequence of this step would be an early election which would give them the opportunity to wipe out the abnormal majority obtained by the Liberal Party in 1906. Even if the Unionists did not win this election outright, they figured it would force the Liberals to rely on the votes of the Irish National Party and inevitably project home rule back into the political spotlight to the Unionists' advantage.

There were other courses of action open to the House of Lords. The Lords could have amended the budget, thereby removing the land taxes to which they especially objected. However, this course of action might appear a partisan defence of selfish vested interests and it was necessary to identify rejection with a broader objective in order to sell the Unionist case to the general public. Thus, the entire budget was rejected on the constitutional justification that it was the legitimate purpose of the House of Lords to ensure that no new departure of major importance was embarked upon by a government unless it first consulted the electorate. Thus, the action of the House of Lords was depicted as a democratic defence of the rights of the people which were in danger of being usurped by the overbearing actions of the Cabinet and the House of Commons: however, some peers admitted to the partisan nature of their action, Lord Curzon arguing in the budget debate in the House of Lords that it was preferable to force a dissolution rather than have to endure 'two more years ... of insufficient attention to the defences of the country, two more years of socialist experiments, two more years of tampering with the Church'. On 30 November 1909 the budget was accordingly rejected by 350 : 75 votes.

Liberals

In office, the Liberal Party did not get off to a good start. The recovery of trade and unemployment which had commenced in 1904 came to an end in 1907, following which there was a downturn in the trade cycle and considerable increases in unemployment. Further difficulties arose against this adverse economic background and soon the government's political fortunes were suffering, evidenced by poor by-election results in 1908 and 1909. Several reasons account for the difficulties experienced by the government in this period.

The first problem concerned the government's relationship with the working class. The progressive credentials of the Liberal Party primarily depended on its ability to pursue social reform directed at working-class problems. However, the initial actions of the Liberal government displayed a concern to address the demands favoured by the various 'sections' of the Liberal Party. These included education and temperance reform whose appeal was primarily to traditional Liberal nonconformist supporters. However, attempts were made to appease the unions by enacting a range of measures which included the 1906 Trade Disputes Act (which overturned the Taff Vale judgement), the 1908 Mines Eight Hours Act, and the 1909 Trades Boards Act (which established wage fixing in some of the industries most affected by 'sweating'). Efforts were also made to court working-class support by introducing some measures of social reform. Asquith's actions as Chancellor (particularly in 1907) indicated an awareness of the potential of the budget as an instrument of social policy (such as the introduction of non-contributory old age pensions in the budget of 1908 which thus provided a modicum of security without the stigma of the old system of Poor Law relief) and domestic policy reflected a concern to provide for enhanced social justice. However, the appeal of many Liberal reforms to the working class was restricted.

One reason for this was that the traditional Liberal emphasis on individualism made it difficult for them to promote an active role for the state in advancing social reform. This was particularly obvious in connection with labour exchanges in 1909 which were introduced on a voluntary basis. Additionally, some social reforms reflected the views of the Liberal imperialists who exerted a considerable degree of influence on the composition and policies of the Liberal government. Thus, their goal of national efficiency, rather than the quest for social justice, guided some social reform legislation enacted in this period, as was apparent, for example, in Liberal support to a Labour measure to provide free school meals to needy children in 1906, and the 1909 Housing and Town Planning Act. A further reason for the government's limited appeal to the working class was that its policies in connection with unemployment were deemed to be inadequate.

A second problem concerned the relationship with the Irish Nationalist Party (INP). Very little legislation to benefit Ireland was secured in the government's early years and the 1909 Irish Land Bill produced a revolt from William O'Brien. Although the leaders of the INP were able to beat this off, it suggested that Irish support at Westminster could not be taken for granted.

The third problem affecting the government was the organised opposition which its policies attracted from vested interests. This was especially the case concerning the 1908 Licensing Bill to which the brewing industry mounted significant opposition.

The fourth problem faced by the government was the emergence of disputes with the House of Lords which sapped its vitality. The Upper Chamber embarked on a programme of sabotaging Liberal legislation by either vetoing it outright or drastically amending it. In 1906 they wrecked the Education and Plural Voting Bills, in 1907 they played havoc with land measures which were designed to aid the Celtic Fringe, and in 1908 they vetoed the Scottish Smallholders' Bill and forced the government to withdraw the Scottish Land Values Bill, following their amendments to the legislation. In November 1908 they refused to give the Licensing Bill a second reading. Although Campbell-Bannerman had proposed to limit the powers of the House of Lords in 1907, the government failed to act on this matter. The House of Lords was able to veto Liberal legislation with impunity since they were aware that it was unlikely that the government would consider any of them resignation issues (in particular when the Party's electoral fortunes did not look good). They were far more compliant concerning measures of social reform as they had no desire to antagonise the working classes who had flexed their political muscles in 1906. Accordingly, they passed the Trade Disputes Bill in 1906, accepted (albeit with some reservations) the introduction of old age pensions in 1908 and agreed to the eight hours' legislation for the coal miners in 1908.

A fifth problem facing the government was the issue of naval policy. The acceleration of Germany naval building led to demands that Britain should follow suit but this had a divisive impact on the Liberal Party whose existing Little England/Liberal imperialist divisions formed the basis of a Little Navy/Big Navy split. The essence of the division centred on whether the government should lay down four or six Dreadnought battleships. Asquith engineered a compromise whereby four would be laid down at once, but a further four might be laid down in the 1909–10 financial year if it appeared necessary and provided Parliament approved this course of action. To justify this approach, Liberal ministers had been forced to play up the threat posed by Germany's naval expansion but this rebounded against the government at the Croydon by-election in March 1909 where the Unionist candidate substantially increased his majority, campaigning on the slogan 'we want eight and we won't wait'.

A radical budget offered the hope of remedying many of the difficulties referred to above. This would restore the political initiative to the government and away from the House of Lords. The death of Campbell-Bannerman in 1908 resulted in Herbert Asquith becoming Prime Minister, and Lloyd George replaced him as Chancellor of the Exchequer. Lloyd George faced a situation in which there was an existing deficit coupled with increased spending on items such as the navy and old age pensions which required him to address a prospective budget deficit for 1909–10 of around £16 million. To cover this, his budget (which was delivered in a speech which lasted in excess of four hours) proposed the intro-duction of seven new taxes – a super tax of six pence on incomes of £5,000 and over; a tax on motor vehicles ranging from £2 2s to £40 according to horsepower; a duty of three pence per gallon on petrol; and four new land value taxes – a tax of 20 per cent on the unearned increment of land values, an annual duty of a half-penny in the pound on the capital value of underdeveloped land, a similar duty on ungotten minerals (which was amended in committee stage to a 5 per cent duty on the rental value of the rights to work minerals), and a 10 per cent reversion duty on any benefit accruing to a lessor at the termination of a lease. Additionally, the system of liquor licences was remodelled and an increased scale of duties was provided for. Death duties, succession duties and stamp duties were increased and the general rate of income tax was raised from one shilling to 1s 2d in the pound, but only for unearned incomes or for earned incomes in excess of £3,000 per annun. The duties on spirits were raised by one-third and those on tobacco by one-quarter.

Although Lloyd George's proposals were directed at the budget deficit, there were additional (and perhaps more important) reasons underpinning them. His budget enabled him to settle some outstanding scores with the House of Lords which had vetoed earlier land tax proposals but would find it difficult to resist them when contained in the Finance Bill. Gladstone had adopted a similar course of action when he incorporated his Paper Duties Bill (which the Lords vetoed in 1860) into his 1861 budget. His budget also enabled him to restore party morale. Land taxes were a popular proposal within the Party and nonconformist support would rally behind the government which had found a way to overcome the earlier rejection by the House of Lords of the Licensing Bill. The progressive nature of the taxation proposals would also be expected to find favour with the working-class electorate, especially if these would finance further measures of social reform. Some opposition was encountered within the Party, especially from its elderly upper-middle-class supporters, a group of whom (termed the 'troglodytes') mounted ineffective opposition in Parliament. However, most criticism came from outside the Party, characterised by Churchill as consisting of 'the woeful wail of the wealthy wastrel … the dismal dirge of the dilapidated duke'.

Lloyd George's budget made a showdown between the Liberal Party and the Unionist-dominated House of Lords inevitable. This could have been associated with the broader issue of 'social economics' which would have concentrated attention on how social reform should be financed. This would have placed the Liberal Party's policy of financing social reform through direct taxation, which fell disproportionately on the rich, within the social democratic context of the function of the state as the mechanism to secure wealth redistribution. However, Liberals were concerned about the impact which a Unionist accusation that such a policy was 'socialistic' might make on what remained of their middle-class support. Accordingly, reform was put forward primarily in the guise of a constitutional issue, albeit one which could be identified with progressive politics and which was presented in a populist guise of 'the peers against the people'. This strategy was made clear in a speech which Lloyd George delivered at Limehouse on 30 July 1909 when he mounted a direct attack on the key interests which had attacked his budget – landlords, financiers and the dukes. He followed this up with a subsequent speech at Newcastle in October 1909 when he asked 'who ordained that a few should have the land of Britain as a perquisite? Who made ten thousand people owners of the soil, and the rest of us trespassers in the land of our birth? Who is it who is responsible for the scheme of things whereby one man is engaged through life in grinding labour … and another man who does not toil receives … more than his poor neighbour receives in a whole year of toil?'

Following the rejection by the House of Lords of the budget on 30 November, the government tabled a resolution in the House of Commons, 'That the action of the House of Lords in refusing to pass into law the financial provision made by this House for the service of the year is a breach of the Constitution and an usurpation of the rights of the Commons.' This was debated on 2 December and, in his speech in support of it, Asquith rejected the argument that it was the role of the House of Lords to protect the people from their elected representatives and instead insisted that the Lords had vetoed the budget simply because they hated its contents. The government also considered what course of action it should adopt to ensure that revenue continued to be raised until a new budget was presented following the election campaign. They considered the possibility of introducing a temporary measure to legitimise the collection of income tax and tea duties but ultimately decided to utilise extra-legal means to collect taxes.

Labour

Early in the new Parliament, the Labour Representation Committee adopted the title of 'Labour Party' and, to emphasise its distance from the Liberal government, it sat on the opposition benches. In 1908 Keir Hardie was replaced as chairman of the Parliamentary Labour Party by Arthur Henderson and, also in 1908, the Miners' Federation of Great Britain affiliated to the Party. Following the dissolution of the House of Commons in January 1910, 13 MPs representing the mining interest who had sat as Lib–Labbers in the 1906 Parliament formally severed their links with the Liberal Party.

However, Labour did not benefit from the troubles which faced the Liberal government. Initially, it could boast some legislative successes in connection with the provision of free school meals to needy children in 1906, and in securing substantial changes to the 1906 Trade Disputes Bill and the 1907 Workmen's Compensation Act. Henceforth, however, the Liberal Party tended to exert more influence over the content of social reform measures, leaving Labour with little choice other than to support measures even if they were not entirely happy with the content of them. Additionally, Labour made little progress in by-elections. Jarrow was gained in July 1907 and in the same month Victor Grayson (standing as an independent Socialist) gained Colne Valley. But thereafter, Labour began to poll less well, and in 1907 and 1908 it was clear that the main beneficiary of popular disenchantment with the Liberals was the Conservative Party.

By-elections

A total of 100 hundred by-elections took place in the 1906–10 Parliament, of which 68 were contested. The Liberals made a net loss of 16 seats, the Unionists a net gain of 12 seats and Labour a net gain of three.

Conduct of the Election

Parliament was prorogued on 3 December and the subsequent election campaign lasted for eight weeks. It was characterised by considerable bitterness and violence (much directed against the Unionists) especially in the latter weeks. Initially, the Liberals seemed to be doing well, but this situation altered in the new year as the focus of public attention shifted from the reform of the House of Lords to the issue of the Unionists' choosing, tariff reform. The Liberal Party acquiesced in this departure, in part as they perceived that the policy would prove unpopular and also because the economic climate was favourable. Towards the end of 1909, unemployment fell and trade was buoyant and these factors might serve to undermine the Unionist claims that fiscal reform was required in order to counter the slump and that Lloyd George's budget had depressed economic activity.

Unionists

A. J. Balfour's election address devoted prominent attention to Lloyd George's budget, viewing the election as having been caused by the resolution of the House of Lords that the country should be consulted on these proposals. He was careful in this document to avoid any reference to the House of Lords rejecting the budget and, instead, preferred to insist that they were merely making it possible for the electorate to express their opinions on it. In this vein, he argued that at this election it was the rights of the people rather than the privileges of the House of Lords which was threatened. He asserted that this action by the House of Lords was justified because Lloyd George's proposals entailed subjecting property to exceptional taxation. He depicted these as 'the first instalment of a socialist budget' which treated property 'not according to its amount, but according to its origin'. He further alleged that the attack on the House of Lords was the 'culmination of a long-drawn conspiracy' by a government which wished to destroy the constitution by emasculating the powers of the second Chamber and creating what was in effect a single Chamber legislature.

The main aim of the Unionist campaign was to ensure that the election was fought on issues other than the House of Lords. Accordingly, they attempted to make tariff reform the key election issue and as this issue became increasingly projected in the new year Unionist political fortunes began to improve. Balfour's election address referred to tariff reform as the first 'plank' of the Unionist programme. It was projected as an alternative to the 'socialism' of Lloyd George's budget, and it was alleged that this policy would both solve unemployment and also unify the Empire. Joseph Chamberlain's election address argued that it was time to abandon Cobdenism and introduce colonial preference and this theme was replicated in a large number of election addresses issued by other Unionist candidates. Unionist speakers increasingly directed their attention to this issue and this subject was given prominent attention in the election addresses of individual Unionist candidates. On 12 January, Balfour delivered a speech at York in which he made specific pledges to impose import duties across a wide range of goods, to introduce a tax on foreign wheat and to institute a protective tariff to prevent the British market being unduly trespassed upon by rival producers. On the eve of the poll, Balfour and Chamberlain issued a joint pledge on tariff reform and the cost of living. Other isssues which were referred to included aid to the small cultivator (alleging that Liberal scepticism towards private ownership of land had prevented any help to be forthcoming).

The Unionist campaign also benefited from the re-emergence of a naval scare. In a series of articles in the *Daily Mail* in December 1909, Robert Blatchford alleged that Germany was preparing to destroy the British Empire and the Cabinet were accused of failing to mount an appropriate response. A large number of Unionist candidates adopted this theme, including Balfour, who in a speech at Hanley on 4 January 1910 accused the Liberal Party of squandering Britain's naval supremacy, an issue which he depicted as important since, he argued, a struggle between Britain and Germany was inevitable at some time in the future.

Balfour was ill at the commencement of the Unionist campaign, so their argument was presented by a number of leading peers, including Curzon, Milner, Cawdor and, latterly, Lansdowne.

Liberals

One major issue was settled in advance of the opening of the campaign. Under pressure from Redmond (who threatened to tell his English supporters to vote against Liberal candidates, a course of action which might prove costly in Lancashire and Scotland), the Liberals committed themselves to home rule.

The main concern of the Liberal Party's campaign was to focus on the constitutional issue in which the non-representative House of Lords had assumed the power to control taxation. The actions of the House of Lords was the prominent theme of Asquith's speech at the Albert Hall in London on 10 December which opened the Liberal campaign. In an attempt to create a broad-based anti-Unionist coalition, he depicted the House of Lords as the barrier to progress across a wide range of issues which included educational reform (desired by nonconformists), the extension of the franchise (a radical demand), the disestablishment of the Church of Wales (a popular issue in Wales), land and leasehold reform (of particular concern in Scotland), social reform (sought by the working class) and Irish home rule. Asquith asserted that the House of Lords' veto would block progress on all of these issues. Lloyd George's speech at the Queen's Hall on 16 December echoed these sentiments when he accused the Lords of blocking key nonconformist issues such as education and licensing reform.

However, although Liberal candidates emphasised the constitutional question in their individual election addresses, Liberal policy concerning the House of Lords was surrounded by a considerable degree of vagueness. In his Albert Hall speech, Asquith referred to legislation which would prevent the Lords meddling with national finance in the future and he promised to end that Chamber's absolute veto. His election address asserted this to be 'the first and most urgent step to be taken'. However, it was not clear what would replace it. Asquith further insisted that the Liberal Party would require guarantees to prevent the future indiscriminate destruction of their legislation as a condition to agreeing to take office again. Although the general public assumed that he was referring to the creation of new peers to destroy the House of Lords' inbuilt Unionist majority, this was not explicitly stated. The subsequent revelation that unless the Liberals were returned with a large majority the King would expect a second general election to be held before he agreed to such a course of action (Blewett, 1972: 94) ensured that further references to 'guarantees' before assuming office were dropped from Liberal electioneering.

In addition to the House of Lords, other issues were raised during the Liberal campaign. The Party responded to the Unionist bait on tariff reform. Some attempt was made to tar this issue with the unpopularity of the House of Lords, a Liberal poster declaring that 'Tariff Reform Means Happier Dukes'. The assertion that the action of the House of Lords was motivated by a desire to save tariff reform from the 'mortal blow' that Lloyd George's budget would inflict upon it was articulated in Mr H. H. Asquith's election address. He argued that Lloyd George's budget sought to provide money for defence and social improvements at home 'by an equitable distribution of the burdens among the different classes and interests in the community'. This approach was 'within the limits of free trade finance', and realising that it would be the death warrant of tariff reform its supporters engineered the rejection of the budget by the House of Lords. It was also argued that the solution for unemployment was not tariff reform but, rather, the approach embodied in the 1909 budget which sought to impose reform on those whose wealth was based on land ownership. Liberal speakers sought to pin down the Unionists on the precise details of their policy of tariff reform. An attempt was also made to depict the Unionists as accomplices in the decision by the Law Lords in the 1909 Osborne judgement (which ruled that compulsory trade union levies for political purposes was illegal) and a scare tactic was deployed which alleged that the Unionists would substitute a contributory old age pension scheme in place of the Liberal non-contributory scheme.

The Liberal campaign was forcibly projected by Asquith, Lloyd George and Churchill. One difficulty which was encountered was that the heavy burden of electioneering exerted a physical toll on these leading Liberals.

Labour

The Labour manifesto 1910 made no specific reference to socialism and emphasised the constitutional issue. It was argued that the election had been forced upon the country by the House of Lords rejecting the budget and 'the great question you are to decide is whether the peers or the people are to rule this country'. Strong support was given to the proposals in Lloyd George's budget to tax the unearned increment on land and it was unambiguously stated that 'The Lords must go'. Labour argued that in Parliament the Labour Party had succeeded in accomplishing a number of reforms which included the restoration of the rights of trade unions, drastic housing reform and the introduction of old age pensions. Further domestic issues which required tackling included the right to work, the breaking-up of the Poor Law, the extension of old age pensions and the abolition of restrictions on the franchise, including the sex bar. Constitutional and social reform were discussed prominently in the election addresses of individual Labour candidates. The general themes projected in Labour's campaign were similar to policies associated with the radical Liberals.

Result of the Election

The outcome of the election was uncertain. The central organs of both main parties were optimistic regarding their chances of success and a series of six forecasts of the result which was published in the *Observer* on the Sunday before the first polls occurred gave predictions which ranged from an overall Unionist majority of 90 to an anti-Unionist majority of 200 (Blewett, 1972: 131). This uncertainty helped to boost turnout which on the first day of polling averaged 88.9 per cent.

A total of 1,315 candidates contested the election. There were very few unopposed returns, all seats in Scotland and Wales being fought and excluding the university seats, only six in England were uncontested. The O'Brienite revolt contributed to 38 contests taking place in Ireland. The result was:

Party	Votes	Vote %	MPs
Liberal*	2,845,818	42.7%	273
Conservative and Liberal Unionist	3,035,425	45.5%	253
Irish Nationalist**	126,647	1.9% [54.1%]	82
Labour	505,657	7.6%	40
Irish Conservative and Liberal Unionist	68,982	1.0% [32.7%]	19
Others	64,532	1.0%	2
Irish Liberal	20,339	0.3% [9.6%]	1
Total	6,667,400		670

*   Including six Lib–Lab MPs
**   The votes and seats for the Irish Nationalist Party includes the 11 Independents.

The turnout was 86.8 per cent. The overall swing to the Unionists was 4.3 per cent.
The 'others' were A. Corbett (Glasgow-Tradeston, Independent Liberal) and S. Storey (Sunderland, Independent Conservative).

The Parties

The national swing was subject to considerable variation both regionally and also between urban and rural areas (Blewett, 1972: 400). The Unionists polled well in borough constituencies in the West Midlands and in the South and South West outside London. They also polled well in county constituencies and their success in reducing the gap between themselves and the Liberals was mainly derived from their performance in the South where the swing to the Unionists tended to be much above the national average. The main reason for the improvement of the Unionist position compared to 1906 was that a large number of their supporters who had abstained in that election turned out to vote for the Party on this occasion. Leading Unionists who were defeated included the Liberal Unionist Whip, Sir George Doughty, at Darlington.

The Liberal Party performed well in boroughs to the north of a line drawn on the map of England which ran from Grimsby to Chester. However, their overall performance south of that line was much weaker. Outside Wales and Scotland, the Liberals also performed badly in county constituencies, especially so in the Home Counties, East Anglia, the Midlands and the West Country. Contemporary commentators drew attention to the emergence of a North–South divide based upon the emergence of two nations – the urban, industrial, working-class England and the rural, suburban, middle-class England (Blewett, 1972: 400).

The cooperation between the Liberal and Labour parties which operated for the 1906 election was continued in 1910. However, whereas the size of the Liberal majority obtained in 1906 made this arrangement irrelevant to the outcome of the election, the anticipated closeness of the result in 1910 made it potentially more significant. Labour concentrated its 78 candidates in industrial conurbations and in the coalfields. The majority of these seats (51 in total) were in constituencies where a Labour or miners' candidate had won or achieved second place in 1906. Liberal candidates stood down in all but three of these contests but more readily intervened in 23 of the 27 constituencies which the Labour Party had either not fought before or in which it had trailed behind the Liberals in 1906. There was a significant degree of cooperation between the Labour and Liberal parties, in particular in the 11 two-member borough seats where representation was shared by both parties. Thirty Labour MPs were retuned in straight fights, 10 were elected in double-member seats in harness with a Liberal candidate but no victories were secured in any of the 27 seats in which three-cornered contests took place.

Scotland, Wales and Ireland

In Scotland, the Liberal Party reverted to the position of political supremacy which it had enjoyed prior to 1886. Two regions which had subsequently become marginally Unionist (Southern Scotland and the Clyde Valley) returned to the Liberal fold. Overall, the Liberals won 58 of Scotland's 70 seats, the Unionists nine, Labour two and the Independent Liberals one. The Liberal Party also performed well in Wales and won 27 of the 34 seats. Labour was the second party, winning five seats and the Unionists won the remaining two.

The O'Brienite revolt (which was partly based on personality but also on his belief that in order to avoid partition it was essential for Nationalists and Loyalists to enter into dialogue) meant that Nationalist candidates fought each other in 18 constituencies and the election witnessed considerable violence between thethese two factions. In total, Nationalist candidates won 81 of the 101 seats, the Unionists 19 and the Liberals one.

Consequence of the Election

The Liberal Party lost its overall majority and relied for its majority henceforth on the votes of the Irish National Party. The perception that the Lords would block Irish home rule as it had done in 1893 induced this party to acquiesce in constitutional reform, the quid pro quo of which was the immediate introduction of Irish home rule. This measure, introduced in 1912 following the second 1910 general election, and the attendant problems arising from Ulster's resistance to it, dominated the domestic political agenda henceforth, thus ensuring that working-class needs were not catered for.

2 December – 19 December 1910

Party Leaders
Arthur Balfour (Unionist)
Herbert Asquith (Liberal)
George Barnes (Labour – Chairman of the Parliamentary Labour Party)

Background to the Election
Timing of the Election
The outcome of the first 1910 election led to immediate speculation that a second would be held that year. However, the death of Edward VII on 6 May 1910 complicated the political situation, in particular as Asquith felt it would not be appropriate to insist that the new monarch should agreed to contingent guarantees (that is, the promise to create peers) in order to ensure the passage of legislation to reform the House of Lords in the new Parliament. Accordingly, a compromise was sought in which a constitutional conference was held between the leading members of the two main parties (but excluding Labour and the Irish Nationalists) to see whether a compromise regarding the future of the House of Lords could be fashioned. However, no agreement proved possible and the conference broke down on 10 November. This made an election inevitable and it followed soon after, one factor inducing ministers to go to the country quickly being the Liberal Party's good performance at the Walthamstow by-election on 1 November (where a small swing to the Liberals occurred). The final barrier to an election was the issue of contingent guarantees to which George V agreed (albeit reluctantly and under considerable pressure from his adviser, Lord Knollys) on 16 November. This entailed an under-taking to create peers provided that the Liberals obtained an 'adequate' majority. On 18 November, Asquith announced that the dissolution would take place on 28 November with the first polls to be held a few days later on 3 December.

Unionists
The Unionists believed that the Liberal Party's dependence on the votes of the Irish Nationalist MPs meant that they could claim no mandate to introduce major constitutional reforms. They also believed that the election result would strengthen the hand of the King in refusing to create more peers to get legislation of this nature through the House of Lords. However, the Party emerged from the first 1910 election in a divided state which made the rewriting of policy for a second contest a difficult proposition.

A key problem concerned the prominence which should be given in future to tariff reform. Those who favoured Chamberlain's approach (the 'Whole Hoggers') believed that the Unionists' failure to win the first 1910 contest derived from their failure to make fiscal reform the key issue and, instead, had become sidetracked into dealing with the budget and reform of the House of Lords. For this reason, many out-and-out tariff reformers were sympathetic to the reform of the House of Lords, believing that this course of action would sideline constitutional reform and enable them to focus unambiguously on tariff reform in a future general election contest. Many

Unionists of this opinion also felt that it was possible to construct a deal with the Irish Nationalists whom they regarded as favourable towards protection, provided the Party adopted some version of home rule. These views were divisive. The Unionists embraced a wide range of opinions regarding the future of the House of Lords (including the diehards who were opposed to any reform whatsover) and the leadership in particular had no desire to enter into any deals with the Irish Nationalists. Of greater significance was the fiscal reform issue itself. Many Unionists viewed this as the issue which cost them victory in the first 1910 contest. They regarded the issue of food taxes as especially problematic and were also aware that the improving economic climate (measured in terms of increasing levels of employment, production and overseas trade) removed an important justification for introducing a radical policy of this nature.

The consequence of these internal divisions was that the Unionists failed to make any major policy changes and fought the second 1910 election largely on the policies on which they were defeated in the first one. The only major change was to remove the proposal to impose duty on colonial wheat.

Liberals

The main issues facing the Liberal Party after the election were to pass a budget and to announce their proposals regarding the reform of the House of Lords. The order in which these matters were tackled was important, since a combination of radical MPs, together with Labour and Irish Nationalist representatives wished the constitutional grievance to be settled before they would agree to the granting of supply. This forced the government to firm up its hitherto vague intentions to reform the House of Lords with proposals of a more concrete nature which were embodied in the Parliament Bill. These proposals entailed preventing the Upper Chamber rejecting or amending a money bill, and to limit its powers whereby it could only delay Bills rather than veto them absolutely. This restriction enabled a Bill which had been passed in three successive sessions by the House of Commons to become law provided that two years had elapsed between the Bill's introduction and its final approval by the House of Commons. It was also proposed to limit the lifetime of Parliament to five years. Although these proposals were modest in their scope, it was hoped that radical opinion would be satisfied by reference being made in the preamble to the Bill to future reform 'hereafter' without giving any details concerning the precise content of what was proposed.

In the wake of proposals regarding the reform of the House of Lords being put forward, the budget which Lloyd George had originally brought forward in 1909 passed the House of Commons on 27 April, was accepted by the House of Lords the following day and received the Royal Assent on 29 April. Ministers were subsequently accused of buying the votes of the Irish Nationalist MPs by betraying the Constitution, and in the second 1910 election Unionists depicted the Liberals as the puppets of the Irish Nationalists.

Labour

Following the first 1910 election, Henderson was replaced by Barnes as chairman of the Parliamentary Labour Party. Labour's key interest in the Parliament which met in February 1910 was the repeal of the Osborne judgement. The Liberal government was not willing to acquiesce to this demand, but as a compromise proposed the payment of MPs and official election expenses. On the eve of the election, a further concession to Labour was made, whereby trade unions were permitted to provide funds for political purposes, but individual trade unionists were able to contract out of this arrangement.

By-elections

A total of 21 by-elections occurred during the lifetime of the Parliament elected in January 1910, of which 10 were contested. These contests evidenced a very small movement of public opinion following the general election – in five there were swings to the Unionists, in four swings against the Unionists and in one the Liberal Party held off the challenge of Labour in a straight fight. The three main parties emerged from these contests with no net gains or losses.

Conduct of the Election

Unionists

Unlike in the first 1910 election, the Unionists gave greater prominence to constitutional issues. In his Nottingham speech, Balfour gave his support to Lord Rosebery's resolutions of March 1910 which proposed to reform the composition of the House of Lords. However, these did not constitute a challenge to the substance of the programme contained in the Parliament Bill, and to do this a series of Unionist-inspired proposals (known as the Lansdowne resolutions) were debated by the House of Lords on 23 and 24 November. These proposed to institute a joint sitting to settle disputes between the two Houses arising over ordinary Bills, the use of a referendum to settle disputes when they arose on 'a matter of great gravity which had not been adequately submitted to the judgement of the people', and the formation of a joint committee presided over by the Speaker to determine whether a Bill was a Money Bill or not. If this were done, the Lords would forego their right to reject or amend Money Bills which were of a purely financial character. Although Unionist candidates failed to give detailed justifications of these resolutions (which would have been difficult given their vague nature), they seized upon the referendum suggestion which was given prominent attention in the Unionist campaign. Its main merits were that it would not tamper with Unionist domination of the Upper Chamber and could be used as a device to thwart the policies of non-Unionist governments. The referendum might further be a way to solve the issue of tariff reform which had proved to be a divisive issue in the Conservative Party.

The issue of tariff reform posed a major problem for the cohesion of the Unionist campaign. This matter was raised at the outset when Balfour opened the Party's campaign with a speech at Nottingham on 17 November. Here he accepted the principle of food taxes and claimed that tariff reform would have only a marginal impact on the cost of living. However, as the campaign progressed there was much pressure from within the Party to modify the commitment to food taxes in the belief that this would cost the Party the election which in turn would endanger the House of Lords and threaten the Union. The main difficulty with advocating a policy of industrial protection whilst abandoning (at least for the immediate future) the commitment to agricultural protection was the fear that this course of action might be regarded as a sell-out of the agricultural industry which would cost the Party dearly in county constituencies in the South of England.

A compromise position (and one that was favoured by the free food section of the Party) was that the whole issue of tariff reform should be submitted to a referendum. This would have the advantage of preserving party unity over what was a highly divisive issue and was also likely to regain support for the Party in the pivotal region of Lancashire where tariff reform was viewed unfavourably by Conservative working-class opinion. Accordingly, on 29 November, before an audience of around 10,000 people, Balfour formally announced that he had no objection to submitting the principles of tariff reform to a referendum. He further challenged the Liberals to submit the issue of Irish home rule to the same test.

This commitment smacked of desperation by a party which felt that the prospects of victory were fast slipping away. It did not, however, end the controversy either within or outside the Party. Those who favoured the full Chamberlain programme of tariff reform (the 'Whole Hoggers') were concerned that Balfour's motive was to ensure that fiscal reform ceased to be an election issue. However, his insistence that it retained its pre-eminent position in Unionist policy begged the question as to what would be subject to a referendum – the principle of a protective tariff or a budget prepared on tariff reform principles introduced by a newly elected Unionist government as one of its first actions. In a speech at Dartford on 12 December, Balfour implied the latter course of action but the public remained confused by what Asquith depicted as 'a bewildering series of twists, gyrations and somersaults' on fiscal reform. Balfour's suggestion that each voter would only have one vote in this referendum caused further consternation in the Party as it seemed to undermine its defence of plural voting.

The Unionist campaign also embraced a number of negative sentiments. A. J. Balfour's election address complained about the timing of the election, arguing that it would ruin Christmas trade and (by virtue of being held on the old electoral register) would disenfranchise a significant number of voters. He further queried the need for the election as the government had suffered no defeat in either House. There was also an attempt to villify Redmond in the hope that the Liberals would suffer as the result of guilt by association. Unionists alleged that he had dictated the timing of the election in order to destroy the House of Lords so that his goal of Irish home rule could be realised. His visit to America to raise funds for his party led the Unionists to abandon their description of him as the 'Irish Dictator' and instead to dub him the 'Dollar Dictator'. The Labour Party was attacked in similar vein, and the Liberals – whom Balfour labelled as the 'party of revolution' – were depicted as the stooges of their socialist and nationalist allies who were aware 'that their darling projects are not in harmony with the considered will of the people' so that they pressed for the abolition of the House of Lords which Balfour stated was the only constitutional safeguard which, at critical moments, ensured that the will of the people would prevail. He also sought to force Asquith to provide details of the vague Liberal commitment to home rule and, in particular, to declare his intentions for Ulster.

The Unionists did not pledge to seek to remove the land taxes introduced in Lloyd George's budget but, instead, proposed further relief for agricultural land and building trade. It was also proposed to allocate revenue from urban land taxes to the municipalities.

Balfour dominated the Unionist campaign. Fewer peers were utilised in their campaign than in the first 1910 election.

Liberals

H. Asquith's election address argued that the election concerned only one issue, on which hung the future of democratic government. This was: 'Are the people, through their freely chosen representatives, to have control, not only over finance and adminisative policy, but over the making of their laws? Or are we to continue the one-sided system under which a Tory majority, however small in size and casual in creation, has a free run of the Statute Book, while from Liberal legislation, however clear may be the message of the polls, the forms of the Constitution persistently withhold a fair and even chance?'

The Liberal campaign was initially distracted by issues which included suffragette agitation and the riots in Tonypandy. However, in his speech which opened the Liberal campaign, delivered at the National Liberal Club on 19 November, Asquith mocked Unionist interest in reforming the House of Lords as deathbed repentance: 'the parricidal pickaxes are already at work, and constitutional jerry-builders are hurrying from every quarter with new plans'. In his election address, he asserted that these were designed to perpetuate the existence of a second Chamber which was mainly Conservative in character. Lloyd George went further, mounting a direct attack on the peers themselves at a speech in Mile End on 21 November. He asserted that there were descended from 'French filibusters', church-plunderers and the ennobled 'indiscretions of Kings' and he likened the aristocracy to cheese – 'the older it is, the higher it becomes'. In subsequent speeches delivered in Wales and Scotland, Lloyd George attempted to invoke pro-nationalist and anti-landlord sentiments against the peers. The attention given by the Unionists to the Lansdowne resolutions ensured that Liberals would devote considerable attention to the constitutional issue. Their response to these reform proposals was that they entailed superficial modernisation which, far from limiting Conservative power, might actually serve to enhance it since the referendum proposal would circumvent the need for the monarch to create peers in order to break a deadlock between the two Houses.

However, the Unionist focus on the referendum device forced the Liberals to respond to it directly. They argued that it would thwart representative government and was partisan in nature. Lord Crewe sought to emphasise the latter accusation by introducing a resolution in the House of Lords which challenged the Unionists to submit the issue of tariff reform to a referendum. This demand was avidly taken up by Liberal speakers who hoped the suggestion would expose the referendum as a device the Unionists wished to adopt, not for all issues of constitutional importance, but only for those which would offer them partisan advantage. However, when Balfour adopted this position in his Albert Hall speech on 12 December, Liberals branded this conversion (or, as they depicted it, a retreat) as opportunistic and pointedly asked what would happen if a Unionist government placed a budget proposing to introduce protection to a referendum and lost. Would it resign or stay in office and have another try the following year?

The Liberal campaign was dominated by Asquith. Churchill undertook a major speaking tour and Lloyd George campaigned energetically in the Celtic Fringe.

Labour

The Labour manifesto unambiguously asserted that the 'Lords must go' but also called for the reversal of the Osborne judgement and supported the payment of MPs. It argued the need for 'a strong and independent party of labour sitting in the House of Commons' in order that issues such as the right to work, sickness insurance, land reform, adult suffrage, Poor Law reform, factory inspection and medical inspection of schoolchildren could be appropriately addressed. As in the first 1910 manifesto, no specific reference was made to socialism.

Result of the Election

The second 1910 election campaign was a short and relatively quiet affair which was dominated by the constitutional issue. Unionist as well as Liberal candidates gave this issue the spotlight in their individual election addresses.

A total of 1,191 candidates contested the second 1910 election. One hundred and one seats in Great Britain (and a further 62 in Ireland) were uncontested, reflecting a inclination by both major parties to conserve resources by not contesting the strongholds of their rivals. This reduced commitment by all main parties was the main explanation for the reduced turnout compared to the first 1910 election. The result was:

Party	Votes	Vote %	MPs
Liberal*	2,274,866	43.4%	271
Conservative and Liberal Unionist	2,363,761	45.2%	254
Irish Nationalists**	131,720	2.5% [60.3%]	84
Labour	371,802	7.1%	42
Irish Conservative and Liberal Unionist	56,408	1.1% [28.6%]	17
Irish Liberal	19,003	0.4% [9.6%]	1
Others	17,678	0.3%	1
Total	5,235,238		670

*   Icluding six Lib–Lab MPs
**   The votes and seats obtained for the Irish Nationalists includes 10 Independents.

The turnout was 81.6 per cent.

The 'other' was F. Bennett-Gouldney (Canterbury, Independent Conservative).

The Parties

London and its suburban fringe was the key battleground for both parties since the Liberal Party was defending 30 marginal seats in this area and the Unionists 12.

The second 1910 election evidenced hardly any overall swing in public opinion from the result obtained in the first election. Both major parties were able to pick up a small number of marginal seats from their rival without markedly affecting the balance between them. In total 56 seats changed hands, giving the Unionists a net loss of one seat in the United Kingdom compared to their performance in the first 1910 election. The regional variations in swing were less pronounced than had been the case in the first 1910 election which had a marginal effect in modifying the spectre of the North–South divide in England.

Unionists directed their attention at moderate opinion. Their campaign concentrated on the 22 seats it lost to the Liberals in the first 1910 election and on the 30–40 where Liberal MPs had been returned with slim majorities. They devoted particular attention to Lancashire, believing that the cause of tariff reform would be lost if they were unable to convince voters in a region where there was a tradition of working-class conservatism. This was emphasised by the decision of Bonar Law (the 'Whole Hogger' leader) to quit his seat at Dulwich in order to fight North West Manchester which had been won by the Liberals in the first 1910 election. However, although the Unionists did improve their performance throughout Lancashire, (especially in Liverpool and the surrounding areas) Sir George Kemp was able to hold off Bonar Law's challenge in North West Manchester. 'Whole Hogger' opinion was that the referendum pledge had been costly to the Party and had lost them considerable support among working-class voters who favoured tariff reform. Unionist leaders, however, emphasised the decay in organisation as a key factor in the Party's defeat.

The key feature of the election for the Liberal Party was its performance in London. Although there was an overall swing to the Unionists, the Liberal Party was able to secure votes in those constituencies where they mattered most. Accordingly they lost only two seats (North Islington and West St Pancras) but offset them with gains in five (Peckham, Bow and Bromley, Stepney, Woolwich and West Southwark). The cooperation between the Liberal and Labour parties which operated in the 1906 and first 1910 elections was continued for the second 1910 contest. In order to conserve financial resources, Labour reduced the size of its electoral commitment compared to the first 1910 election. Its 56 candidates stood in consituencies in which victory had been achieved in the previous election or where factors such as organisation or local success made victory likely.

The relationship between the Liberal and Labour parties was generally good and there were some notable examples of goodwill: in Bow and Bromley the Liberal candidate stood aside to let George Lansbury (who had secured second place in January 1910) have a straight fight against the Unionist (in which he was successful).There was, however, some ill will in the South Wales coalfields arising from the aftermath of the Tonypandy riots. Three of Labour's 42 MPs were returned unopposed, 26 were returned in straight fights, 11 in two-member boroughs in harness with a Liberal candidate, and two were elected in straight fights with a Liberal candidate. None of the eight Labour candidates involved in three-cornered fights was successful.

Scotland, Wales and Ireland

Hardly any swing occurred in Scotland. The Unionists gained one seat (St Andrews) as did the Liberals (who won Kirkcudbright). As in the first 1910 general election, the Liberals won 58 seats and the Conservatives nine. Labour won the remaining three. There was also hardly any swing in Wales. The Liberals lost Cardiff and Montgomery District but gained Radnorshire. Overall, the Liberals won 26 of Wales's 34 seats, Labour five and the Conservatives three.

The Irish National Party was able to contained the threat of the O'Brienites. South Mayo (which had been won in the previous election but was not contested in the second 1910 election) and North Louth were lost by this faction who also failed in their bid to capture West Mayo but they gained the two seats of Cork City and Cork South. The Irish Nationalist Party gained two seats (South Dublin and Mid-Tyrone) from the Unionists and (including the 10 Independents) the Nationalist parties won 83 of the 101 seats, the Unionists 17 and the Liberals one.

Consequence of the Election
Asquith formed a new Liberal government.

14 December 1918

Party Leaders
David Lloyd George (Coalition Liberal)
Andrew Bonar Law (Coalition Conservative)
Herbert Asquith (Liberal)
William Adamson (Chairman of the Parliamentary Labour Party)

Background to the Election
Electoral Procedures and Practices
The 1911 Parliament Act reduced the life of Parliament from seven years to five and ended the absolute veto over legislation possessed by the House of Lords. Henceforth, the Upper Chamber was given the power to delay legislation which had passed the House of Commons for two years and lost its ability to interfere with Money Bills.

The 1918 Representation of the People Act greatly enlarged the electorate by giving the vote to women when they had reached the age of 30. This legislation further abolished the property qualification for voting and in total increased the electorate from approximately 7.7 million (December 1910) to 21.3 million. This was not solely to the benefit of the working class since the dominant household voting qualification in the boroughs and counties (following electoral reform in 1867 and 1884) excluded younger, single men of all social classes (Tanner, 1997: 114–5). The 1918 Act also legislated for general elections to be held on one day rather than over the course of several weeks, ended the system whereby the charges of returning officers had to be paid by candidates, and instituted a requirement that candidates were required to lodge a deposit of £150 when nominated which was forfeited if they failed to poll one-eighth of the votes cast. Candidates were allowed free postage for their election address. The Act also provided for the redistribution of constituency boundaries, the first which had taken place since 1885, and provided for the use of the single transferable to elect MPs to university constituencies returning more than one member. Additionally, polling in the constituency of Orkney and Shetland was permitted to take place over two consecutive days (a provision which was repealed in 1926).

Conservatives
A major concern of the Unionists in opposition was the attitude which it should adopt towards the 1911 Parliament Bill. The Unionist leader, Balfour, was not immediately aware of the King's promise to secure the passage of the legislation by the creation of sufficient peers to overcome the resistance of the House of Lords. When he became aware of this in July 1911, he advocated that the measure should be allowed to pass but the Shadow Cabinet was deeply divided with a number of members (known as the 'diehards') wishing to fight the Bill to the bitter end regardless of the consequences of pursuing this course of action. Although a minority, the diehards refused to accept Balfour's advice and mounted a vigorous campaign to reject the Parliament Bill which in the House of Lords was conducted by a group of diehard Tory peers (the 'ditchers') led by Lord Halsbury and Lord Willoughby de Broke. They believed

that Asquith would not utilise the sanction of creating peers to secure the Bill's enactment. Other Unionists (including the leadership) wished to 'hedge'. In August 1911 the ditchers lost by 17 votes and the Parliament Bill became law. Balfour was considerably distressed by the way in which the Unionist stance on this measure had undermined his authority as leader, and in November 1911 he resigned, citing poor health as the explanation for his action. He was replaced by Andrew Bonar Law (in preference to the leading contenders, Austen Chamberlain and Walter Long). He was faced with an initial problem concerning the decision of the National Union annual conference in 1912 to retain the duty on foreign wheat (subject to some conditions) in the Party programme, a subject on which the Party was deeply divided.

The Conservatives and Liberal Unionists formally merged in 1912. In opposition, Bonar Law pursued an aggressive stance towards the Liberal government. This was most evident in the attitude adopted by the Conservatives towards Irish home rule. Bonar Law sided with Protestant opinion which wished to secure Ulster's exclusion from the Home Rule Bill which was initially introduced in 1912 and would become law in 1914 when the two-year veto of the House of Lords could be overridden. The opposition of the Conservative Party to this measure found sympathy within the military establishment (which was evidenced by the Curragh 'Mutiny' in 1914) and convinced the government of the need to pursue a compromise solution which involved partition. However, the outbreak of the First World War temporarily halted further consideration of this issue. The Conservative Party was forced into the position of offering its support to the Liberal government but was not included in office until May 1915 when Bonar Law and seven other Conservatives joined the government.

Liberal

Following the second 1910 general election, the Liberal Party enacted important measures of social reform. These included the 1911 National Insurance Act (which made insurance against poor health and unemployment compulsory in a selected number of industries), the 1912 Miners' Minimum Wage Act, and the 1913 Trade Union Act. In conjunction with the introduction of payment of MPs in 1911, the latter legislation was designed to reverse the 1909 Osborne judgement which ruled that it was illegal for a union to use its funds to support candidates for Parliament. This legislation legalised expenditure for political purposes provided it was approved by a special ballot of the members and also enabled any member to decline to contribute for this purpose by the process of 'contracting out'. The Anglican Church in Wales was disestablished in 1914. Additionally, the government enacted a major piece of constitutional reform in the 1911 Parliament Act. This Act took away from the House of Lords its power to amend or reject Money Bills, and provided that if any Bill was passed by the House of Commons in three successive sessions of Parliament (subject to a minimum period of two years) and was three times rejected by the House of Lords, it should nevertheless become law.

Legislation to provide for home rule for Ireland was introduced in 1912. This was vetoed by the House of Lords in this and the subsequent two sessions but under the procedures laid down in the 1911 legislation became law in 1914. However, the imminence of the First World War resulted in the 1914 Home Rule Act being accompanied by the Suspensory Act whereby home rule would not be proceeded with until international tensions had been resolved.

However, the years leading to the First World War saw the Party embroiled in a number of problems. This period witnessed intense industrial unrest which perhaps suggested that the scope of the government's social reform programme was insufficiently progressive to remedy working-class grievances and, additionally, many workers were unhappy about having money deducted from their wages to finance the new National Insurance Act. Trade union membership dramatically increased from 2.6 million in 1910 to 4.1 million in 1914, and this development was considerably to the Labour's benefit so that by 1914 trade unionism was 'firmly identified with the Labour Party' (Laybourn, 1988: 21–2). This association was aided by the revision of the 1909 Osborne judgement (in the 1913 Trade Union Act) and also by the payment of MPs in 1911.

Developments affecting trade union activities and organisation resulted in major industrial disputes which compelled the state to intervene. In 1912, 1,233,016 workers were involved in 857 strikes in which a total of 38,142,101 working days were lost (Dangerfield, 1980: 307). The formation in 1913 of the 'triple alliance' of dockers, railway and transport workers implied that these problems would escalate in the future. The nature and extent of industrial unrest was compatible with syndicalism whereby class consciousness would translate into class conflict, culminating in a revolutionary general strike which would abolish capitalism. The Liberal Party's advocacy of an identity of interest between employer and employee, and its rejection of class conflict in favour of the goal of social harmony made it appear anachronistic in this new era of working-class assertiveness. In particular, the Party's traditional belief in laissez faire had to be sacrificed in order for the state to intervene actively in these disputes to uphold the national interest. A major conciliating role was played by George Askwith, a civil servant at the Board of Trade.

In addition to industrial militancy, challenges to bedrock Liberal values emerged from other quarters. These included the suffragette campaign and the home rule dispute in Ireland which also forced the Party to depart from its traditional principles. The Liberal tradition of voluntarism and dislike of compulsion was challenged by the response to the militant suffragette campaign which included the forced feeding of female prisoners. The support historically accorded to small nations in their fight for freedom seemed to have been abandoned in Liberal policy towards Ireland, where the government had been faced with the unusual prospect of armed resistance to its proposals which were abetted by Conservative connivance, and the apparent disinclination of the army (evidenced at the Curragh mutiny in 1914) to take positive action to deal with the problem. In particular, all of the issues which have been identified above (in addition to the protracted dispute with the House of Lords which had triggered the two general elections in 1910) undermined the Liberal value of 'reasonableness' in a political age seemingly dominated by conflict and unwillingness to compromise.

A further problem was that the domination of the political agenda by issues not of the government's choosing prevented the Liberal Party from more actively pursuing reform which benefited the working class. The suffragette campaign, in particular, made it virtually impossible to put forward a measure to increase working-class enfranchisement (which may have benefited the Party at that time) since it would have had to address the issue of female enfranchisement. Although many Liberals were in favour of such a measure the Party was not officially committed to it and its introduction would have been divisive since the demands put forward by the Women's Social and Political Union entailed enfranchising women on a limited basis, thereby enhancing the existing social exclusivity of the electorate.

The ad hoc pragmatic responses delivered by the government to the problems outlined above were compatible with the image of a 'punch-drunk' party which progressed from one crisis to the next unguided by any ideology concerning the nature of the society it wished to create. These difficulties and the government's response might imply that the Liberal Party was a spent force which would inevitably be swept aside by its new rival on the progressive side of politics, the Labour Party, especially when further electoral reform gave this party the ability to poll its full potential vote amongst the working class. However, this view is not necessarily an accurate one. The tendency of trade unions to affiliate to the Labour Party in the early years of the twentieth century, yet to continue to support Liberal candidates in elections, is one example of the continued appeal of the Liberals to the working-class electorate. Syndicalist ideals had a limited attraction to a working class which was far from united at that time, and there are reasons for assuming that the scale and nature of the problems which beset the Party especially after 1910 were untypical and did not reflect any deep-rooted malaise in the Party or its standing with the electorate. It has been observed that 'very few prime ministers in history have been afflicted with so many plagues in so short a space of time' (Dangerfield, 1980: 334), and there were signs that political recovery was under way before war broke out in 1914. Although the Party lost 14 seats to opposition candidates in by-elections between 1911 and 1914, the Liberal Party's performance in by-elections showed signs of improvement by 1912, and it has been suggested that, were a general election held in 1915, the ability of the Liberal government to win it was an open question (Clarke, 1981: 389).

The 1914–18 War inflicted a further range of damaging blows to the Party. This event can be used as further evidence of the inability of the Liberal Party to cope with changed conditions of the early twentieth century but might alternatively suggest that the decline of the Party in the early decades of the twentieth century was attributable less to its inherent shortcomings as a vehicle of progressive opinion but, rather, to a series of errors and misfortunes which would otherwise have been avoided. In particular, the war 'placed Lloyd George in a position to displace Asquith' whose seizing of 'this opportunity for his advancement' (Wilson, 1968: 47) had a disruptive effect on party harmony.

The events leading up to the outbreak of war posed the Party deep ideological problems. It seemed that in an age of aggressive nationalism and power politics driven by imperialism, the Cobdenite principles of peace, arbitration, non-intervention and disarmament were out of place. Although in the long term this dilemma could be solved through the force of intellectual authority and international cooperation (the concept of a League of Nations finding support among both Liberal opponents and supporters of war as it progressed), for the immediate future the main alternatives with which the Party was presented were either to compromise with or abandon its principles (which ran the risk of alienating traditional supporters through the adoption of 'war socialism'), or to enter into apparent self-deception as to the true character of international relations (which was effectively the stance adopted by the pacifist radicals).

Radicals were particularly divided concerning the stance to adopt towards war. The belief that war was an inhuman, irrational act which would additionally impede the likelihood of further measures of social and political reform made them initially urge neutrality in the Belgian crisis, but splits in their ranks occurred as subsequent events unfolded. Some radicals supported the view that war with Germany could be justified on democratic grounds (viewing it as an attack on Prussian 'Junkerdom' which was perceived as anti-working class and reactionary) and for moral reasons. The defence of Belgium could be depicted as an honourable cause which was compatible with the Gladstonian doctrine of international morality and the earlier support accorded by the Party to the struggle of the Boers for freedom in South Africa. Other radicals, however, continued to oppose war following its outbreak by endorsing pacifism. The Union of Democratic Control (formed in 1914 in protest at the speech delivered by Sir Edward Grey on 3 August in support of war with Germany) was opposed to secret diplomacy and supported democratic control of foreign policy.

The initial conduct of the war was heavily influenced by the traditional Liberal principles of individual liberty and an aversion to the state performing an active role in industrial or economic affairs. This explained the Party's unwillingness to introduce conscription, its failure to finance the war adequately at the outset and the absence of industrial organisation (which contributed to the shell shortage on the Western Front in 1915). However, state intervention in labour practices to speed up production (which included the acceptance by most major unions of dilution of labour under the Treasury Agreement of March 1915), McKenna's war budget of 1915 (which introduced duties on imported luxury goods) and the establishment of a Ministry of Munitions in the same year suggested an abandonment of these time-honoured principles in order for the government to get to grips with the entirely novel demands made upon the state by total warfare. However, any credit which the government might have derived from these innovations was offset by the emergence of a political crisis which took the form of a clash between Asquith and Lloyd George.

The source of the differences between these two leading Liberals rested with the politics of the Party in the late nineteenth century (which is discussed in more detail in the 1906 entry). Asquith was associated with the Liberal imperialist wing of the Party led by Lord Rosebery, whereas Lloyd George was identified with the radical wing then led by Sir William Harcourt and with whom Henry Campbell-Bannerman was also associated. The war gave Lloyd George an opportunity to wrest the premiership from Asquith which would not have arisen in normal circumstances. He achieved this goal by supporting the case for a coalition government as an alternative to holding a general election during the war. In return for Conservative involvement in this arrangement, the Conservative Parliamentary Party supported Lloyd George as Prime Minister.

This 'coup' took place in two stages. The first was the establishment of a coalition government under Asquith in 1915 following Lord Fisher's resignation over the Dardanelles operation and revelations concerning the shell shortage on the Western Front. The belief that these shortcomings would be exploited by opponents to his government prompted Asquith to accept these changed political arrangements. In the reshuffling of responsibilities, Lloyd George became Minister of Munitions. This event caused dissension within the Liberal Party, many of whose members were unhapy concerning the way in which the coalition government was brought into being and the subsequent treatment of Liberal ministers. Haldane was dismissed and others, such as Samuel, lost their Cabinet positions.

The second stage of this coup was the enforced resignation of Asquith in 1916 following Lloyd George's proposal that the direction of the war should be entrusted to a War Committee composed of Lloyd George, Bonar Law, Lord Curzon and Arthur Henderson and of which the Prime Minister would not be a member. Perhaps not unsurprisingly, Asquith felt unable to accede to this suggestion, believing it to be inconsistent with his responsibility as Prime Minister. The resignation of Lloyd George and the Unionist members of the government in response to his rejection of this proposal left Asquith with little option other than to resign himself. His replacement by Lloyd George split the Liberal Party.

Liberal ministers agreed with Asquith's refusal of the course of action proposed by Lloyd George and further opposed the King's suggestion that Asquith should serve in an administration headed by Bonar Law on the grounds that Lloyd George would be its ostensible head. Additionally, Liberals desired Asquith to remain distanced from such a government in order to provide an alternative government which they felt the country's interests required. Thus the loyalty that many Liberals felt towards Asquith, coupled with disapproval of the way in which Lloyd George had secured power, formed the basis of deep-rooted divisions within the Party. Lloyd George's attempt to restore party unity by the conciliatory gesture of asking Samuel to remain at the Home Office was unsuccessful and the the Liberal Party effectively had two leaders. The problems inherent in this division of power were compounded by Asquith's failure to provide the leadership which his supporters desired of him. He refused to give guidance to leading Liberals as to whether they should take office in Lloyd George's new government and failed to provide a source of alternative inspiration on the grounds that party should not come before national unity during a war. Only in 1918 (in the Maurice debate) did Asquith lead his group of Liberals in opposition to the government. Lloyd George's resounding victory, however, seemed to emphasise his position of political asscendancy. Future opportunities open to Asquith to rally progressive opinion (for example, on the issue of indemnities) were ignored.

Differences amongst nonconformists over involvement in the war caused disunity and served to kill them off as a political force (Wilson, 1968: 26–7). This served to enhance the role played by social class as a determinant of voting behaviour. Both of these developments pre-dated 1914 but were accelerated by the First World War.

Labour

The chairmanship of the Parliamentary Labour Party was held by George Barnes (1910–11), Ramsay MacDonald (1911–14), Arthur Henderson (1914–17) and William Adamson (after 1917). The main internal political development of this period was the adoption by the Labour Conference of a new constitution in February 1918. This replaced the old objective of the Party (which was 'to organise and maintain in Parliament and the country a political labour party') with a new goal which was unambiguously socialist – 'to secure for the producers by hand or by brain the full fruits of their industry, and the most equitable distribution thereof that may be possible, upon the common basis of the common ownership of the means of production, and the best obtainable system of popular administration and control of each industry or service'. A further Party Conference held in June 1918 led to the adoption of a detailed policy statement entitled Labour and the New Social Order which committed the Party to evolutionary socialism.

Initially, the relationship between the Liberal and Labour parties deteriorated. Although Labour benefited from the decision in 1911 to pay MPs a salary and the reversal of the Osborne judgement in the 1913 Trade Union Act, the Party was encouraged to pursue a course of independence from the Liberals because of factors which included the growth of trade union affiliated membership after 1910. However, the breakdown of the Liberal–Labour pact in by-elections in 1912 and 1913 did not benefit Labour but, rather, tended to aid the Conservative Party. Both parties were united behind the desire to eliminate plural voting and the emphasis which the Conservatives placed on Ulster and opposition to home rule (as opposed to measures of social reform). These served as an inducement to continued cooperation between the two progressive parties after 1912.

As with the Liberals, the outbreak of war caused some reservations within Labour's ranks. MacDonald spoke against entry into the war in the debate in the House of Commons on 3 August 1914, but appreciated that his view was a minority one within the Party, following Germany's violation of Belgian independence. He resigned the following day and was replaced by Henderson. The formation of the War Emergency Workers' National Committee in 1914 (which was designed to protect working-class living standards against the economic distress and social dislocation which might be caused by the war) provided a continued focus of activity for Labour opinion during the conflict.

The Labour Party participated in the electoral truce and supported the war effort and participated in both Asquith's and Lloyd George's coalition governments, thereby providing the Party with experience in holding office. Henderson was a member of the War Cabinet, but resigned in August 1917 following the War Cabinet's refusal to allow him to participate in a conference of socialists to be held in Stockholm to discuss the future of Russia following the overthrow of the Tsar. His place was taken by George Barnes.

By-elections
A total of 247 by-elections occurred in the 1910–18 Parliament, of which 115 were contested. The Conservatives recorded a net gain of 13 seats, the Liberals a net loss of 10, Labour a net loss of five and others a net gain of two. The outbreak of war led to a party truce which entailed the suspension of by-election contests.

Conduct of the Election
The Coalition
Lloyd George's position as Prime Minister was dependent on the support of the Conservative Party. He sought to reduce this weakness by offering Asquith the post of Lord Chancellor in his government and thereby reunify the Liberal Party. However, this objective was thwarted when the former Prime Minister rejected the offer. This reinforced Lloyd George's need to retain the support of the Conservative Party if he were to remain in office. The Conservatives were willing to back Lloyd George's continuance as Prime Minister in the belief they would benefit through association with the successful war leader. In return for this support, Lloyd George issued letters of endorsement (which were termed 'coupons') to candidates who supported his retention of office. Most 'coupons' were awarded to Conservative candidates, many of whom were standing in traditional Liberal constituencies.

A joint programme of the two parties in the Coalition government was put forward in the manifesto of Mr Lloyd Geroge and Mr Bonar Law. This referred to the victory which had been secured in Europe and argued that the unity of the nation should be continued in order to tackle the 'many anxious problems which the war has bequeathed to us'. However, it was argued that before these problems could be tackled, a new Parliament should be elected, possessed with the authority to make peace in Europe and deal with the period following the cessation of hostilities. An election was needed both because the present Parliament had gone beyond its appointed term of office and also to enable large numbers of new voters (including women) to express their views.

The manifesto argued that the Coalition government sought to further the general good rather than to devise policy in the interests of any class or section of the nation. The first task was stated to be the conclusion of a just and lasting peace and to establish the foundations of a new Europe so that further wars would be averted. Support was expressed for the formation of a League of Nations. It was stated that the government would seek to assist those members of the armed forces who wished to undertake special industrial training to equip them for a return to civilian life, and that plans had already been prepared to make it the duty of public authorities, and if necessary the state, to acquire land cottages, allotments or smallholdings for the use of men who had served in the war. The manifesto also referred to the experience of the war, demonstrating that land needed to be more effectively cultivated to provide food and other agricultural products. Support was expressed for the promotion of scientific farming and for the improvement of the conditions of those living in rural areas.

The manifesto stated that the government's principal concern was 'the condition of the great mass of the people who live by manual toil'. Accordingly, it was asserted that one of the first tasks of the government was to tackle the housing of the people 'on broad and comprehensive lines'. Additionally, expanded education, improved material conditions and the prevention of degrading standards of employment would be promoted. Fiscal policy was not discussed in detail, although reference was made to the need to reduce the national debt without inflicting injury on industry and credit and it was argued that fresh taxes would not be imposed on food and raw materials needed for industry. Preference would be given to the colonies on existing duties and any new ones which were subsequently imposed. The need to preserve and maintain the nation's key industries was emphasised; this included measures to provide them with security against unfair competition through the dumping of goods produced abroad which were then sold below the actual cost of production. It was also stated that active measures would be taken to secure employment for the workers and that industry would be freed from government control as soon as possible.

The manifesto also made a vague commitment to reforming the House of Lords to make it more representative, to provide for the development of responsible government in India by gradual stages, and to explore all practical paths towards the settlement of the Irish question on the basis of self-government. However, the complete separation of Ireland from the United Kingdom or the imposition of home rule on the six counties of Ulster without the consent of those who lived there was specifically ruled out.

Other authorative statements of Coalition policy were issued during the election. On 6 December 1918, Lloyd George issued a statement of Coalition government policy. This expressed the nation's gratitude to those who had fought in the armed services during the war and insisted that the first item of government policy was to discharge the nation's debt of honour to its soldiers and sailors. He argued that these persons should be restored to the employment in which they were engaged before the war and also that provision should be made for ex-servicemen to be provided with smallholdings, cottages or allotments. He expressed support for profit-sharing in industry, for the improvement of housing (which was to be achieved by a combination of effort from central government, local government and private enterprise), for better wages and conditions of work, for the reorganisation of the provision of health services across the country, and for the development of transportation and electricity. This, and other of Lloyd George's campaign speeches, also placed emphasis on the need to increase production as the basis of domestic reform. In his later publication of a six-point statement of Coalition government policy (which was quoted in *The Times* on 11 December), referred to the need to rehabilitate those broken by war and the desire to create a happier country for all. The continance of conscription was also raised during the campaign, and in a speech at Bristol on 11 December, Lloyd George rejected the suggestion that he wished to retain it, although he insisted that the terms of peace would dictate the nature of the nation's future defence needs.

The treatment to be accorded to Germany was prominently raised in the Coalition campaign. In a second speech delivered at Newcastle-upon-Tyne on 29 November, Lloyd George advocated a just peace, but insisted that Germany should pay for the costs of the war up to the limit of her capacity to do so. He further insisted, however, that Germany ought not be allowed to pay any indemnities by dumping cheap goods across Europe. He also made clear his view that the Kaiser should be made personally responsible for the less savoury aspects of the way in which Germany prosecuted the war, citing submarine warfare and the cruel treatment of British prisoners of war. He concluded, 'I do not want when the war is over to pursue any policy of vengeance, but we have got so to act that men in future who feel tempted to follow the example of the rulers who plunged the world into this war will know what is waiting them at the end of it.' The attitude to be adopted towards Germany tended to harden as the campaign progressed. Lloyd George's statement of policy issued on 6 December argued that the Kaiser should be prosecuted by an International Court, since it was a crime to have embarked upon war, and his six-point statement of policy advocated the trial of the Kaiser, the punishment of all those who had committed atrocities during the war, and the need for the fullest indemnities to be exacted from Germany. The Coalition's First Lord of the Admiralty, Sir E. Geddes, was less temperate with his sentiments. In a speech delivered at Cambridge on 9 December, he stated, 'Germany is going to pay restitution, reparation, and indemnity, and I have personally no doubt we will get everything out of her that you can squeeze out of a lemon, and a bit more.' He proposed that 'not only all the gold that Germany has got, but all the silver and jewels she has got should be handed over'.

Other issues were raised during the Coalition campaign. In his speech at Newcastle-upon-Tyne on 29 November, Lloyd George referred to the record of the Coalition government. He cited the introduction of a minimum wage for agricultural labourers, the compulsory cultivation of land, the imposition of restrictions on raising rents, the 1918 Education Act, the placing of shipping under government control, the reduction of rates for carrying goods and the control which the government had exerted over the mines. He argued that these were all 'progressive measures' which were in total accord with Liberal principles. He further held out the hope of domestic reform when he stated that the task of reconstructing the country entailed 'the lifting away of wretchedness, of hopelessness'.

The Coalition campaign devoted some attention to the timing of the election. Speaking at Glasgow on 25 November, Bonar Law argued that Parliament had far exceeded its allotted lifespan, and that it was important for the new electors to be able to have their say concerning the nation's affairs. He also believed that the delegates to the Peace Conference should attend, having first obtained a new mandate to ensure that they truly represented national opinion. His speech also sought to justify the use of the 'coupon' with the argument that the election was not based on the usual contest between the parties but that, instead, electors were being asked to endorse candidates who supported the continuance of the present Coalition government.

Liberals

The use by Lloyd George of 'coupons' solidified divisions within the Liberal Party between those willing to support Lloyd George and his Conservative-dominated administration (the coalitionists) and those (who were termed the 'wee frees' and led by Herbert Asquith) who were opposed to a continuance of this government.

Liberal policies were contained in Mr H. H. Asquith's election address. In this he referred to his own record both as MP and Prime Minister and asserted that 'throughout the war, whether in or out of office, I have supported every measure for its efficient prosecution'. In foreign affairs he supported the establishment of the League of Nations, the inter-imperial development of common resources in men and material and the early redemption of pledges which had been given to India. He also called for self-government in Ireland to be transformed into a reality.

Domestic policy emphasised the importance of not tampering with the essentials of free trade and stressed the need to remove the temporary restraints which had been imposed during the war upon personal liberty and the free expression of opinion. He emphasised the nation's duty to those who had enabled the victory to be won and stated that they had the first claim on the priorities of reconstruction. He argued that they should be given reinstatement, protection against want and unemployment and training and equipment to enable them to secure fresh careers. He indicated his willingness to support any programme put forward by any party which was designed to secure for every British citizen a standard of existence which made life worth living and which opened the road to attaining life's best and highest possibilities.

The Liberal campaign attacked the timing of the election. In a speech given at Edinburgh on 3 December, Asquith asked what kind of mandate could the government obtain from 'a hurried and rushed election, and rushed appeal to an inchoate and truncated electorate'. In a later speech at the Royal Albert Hall in London on 10 December, he asserted that 'it is, in my judgement, an unnecessary election, it is a precipitated election, it is a mutilated election'. In particular he argued that service voters were disenfranchised. Asquith also defended his personal conduct, arguing at Edinburgh on 3 December that he had loyally supported the government for the past two years and stating that he felt he could do greater service to the nation by supporting the government from outside rather than within.

Asquith's domestic policies entailed what he referred to (in a speech at Hull on 5 December) as a 'national minimum', by which he meant that, as far as was possible, the law should promote equality of opportunity. He also tended to adopt a less aggressive posture towards Germany as the campaign developed. In his speech at Rochdale on 7 December he stressed the importance of treating the enemy justly, and speaking at the Royal Albert Hall on 10 December, he stated that it was necessary to find a place for old enemies as well as friends in post-war Europe, and called for what he termed a 'clean peace'. He expressed opposition to any peace which was effectively the continuance of war. He stated, for example, that an aggressive economic boycott was simply war under another name.

The split within the ranks of the Liberal Party which occurred during the First World War opened the possibility of cooperation between Asquith's Liberals and the Labour Party. Henderson's withdrawal from the coalition government, his firm opposition to Bolshevism and advocacy of reformism made the alliance of these political forces feasible. In 1918, the journal *Nation* called for an Asquith-Grey-Lansdowne-Henderson government, and discussions between the Labour Party and Asquithian Liberals took place, with the Liberal Chief Whip, John Gulland, meeting Arthur Henderson in November 1918. Henderson suggested that the prospects of a khaki election might induce Labour to seek accommodation with the Asquithian Liberals and he discussed the idea of the merger of the two parties resulting in a new democratic party containing Liberals and Labour. However, Asquith's negative sentiments to such a proposal prevented Henderson from furthering the idea at that time and neither was it possible to construct any agreement between these two parties on either candidates or policy which might have offset the appeal of Lloyd George and his Conservative allies.

Labour

Labour policies for the election were contained in its manifesto, *Labour's Call to the People*. These were designed to 'build a new world … by constitutional means'. The manifesto emphasised the role which workers both at home and in the armed services had played in securing victory and insisted that the fruits of victory should not be wasted in the interests of riches or reaction. The Party's domestic policies expressed support for land nationalisation, for the building of at least one million new houses at the state's expense to be let at fair rents. Labour also endorsed the enactment of a comprehensive Public Health Act based on prevention rather than cure, and for what was described as 'real public education, free and open to all'. The Party committed itself to resist any attempts which might be made to impose burdens on the poor by indirect taxation and expressed itself in favour of free trade. It was also proposed that those who had profited from the war would be liable to a special tax on capital and that a heavily graduated income tax would be introduced. The Party demanded the immediate nationalisation and democratic control of vital public services which included the mines, railways, shipping, armaments and electric power and stated that trade unionism should be accorded the fullest recognition and utmost extension in both private and public sectors. Labour proposed to recognise the right to work and to improve working conditions through measures which included a national minimum wage, placing a legal limitation on the hours of work and drastically amending the Acts dealing with factory conditions, safety and workmen's compensation. The Party also called for the repeal of all wartime measures which imposed limitations on civil and industrial liberty. A specific appeal was also addressed to women with policies which included equal pay in industry and complete adult suffrage.

Labour's foreign policy expressed support for a peace based on international cooperation and explicitly opposed secret diplomacy. The Party called for the immediate withdrawal of all Allied forces from Russia, freedom for Ireland and India, and recognition of the right of self-determination for all subject peoples within the British Commonwealth.

During the campaign, Labour spokesmen justified the role its MPs would play in the new Parliament. At Derby on 4 December, J. Thomas argued that they would not be 'manacled or handicapped, but free to fight for the best interests of the people they represented'. Prominence was given to the need for a programme of national reconstruction, and for the fair treatment of the German people. In a speech at Glasgow on 10 December, G. Barnes argued that while he favoured a tough peace, he was not against the German working men and stated that Britain should conduct itself in the tradition becoming a great people. He supported the principle of reparations, but felt they should not be set at an amount which would never be paid.

Result of the Election

The Coalition government secured a landslide victory, securing 473 seats (332 being couponed Conservatives, 127 couponed Liberals and 14 couponed Independents (including nine from the National Democratic Party). Only 68 candidates who received the Lloyd George coupon were unsuccessful (Cook, 1975: 6). Additionally, the government could count on the support of some uncouponed Conservatives and Ulster Unionists. They were opposed by 57 Labour MPs and 36 Independent ('wee free') Liberals. There were additionally 18 other MPs who often voted against the government. Sinn Fein would have formed the largest single opposition party, but none of its 73 members took their seats. A total number of 1,623 candidates contested the election, of which 107 MPs were returned unopposed. The result was:

Party	Votes	Vote %	MPs
*Coalition Supporters**			
Conservative	3,472,738	32.2%	332
Liberal	1,396,590	12.9%	127
National Democratic Party	156,834	1.5%	9
Labour	53,962	0.5%	4
Others	9,274	0.1%	1
(Total	5,089,398	47.2%	473)
*Opposition **			
Sinn Fein	497,107	4.6% [47.0%]	73
Labour	2,245,777	20.8%	57
Liberal	1,388,784	12.9%	36
Conservative	382,241	3.5%	27
Irish Conservative	289,213	2.7% [28.4%]	23
Others	656,101	6.1%	11
Irish National Party	238,197	2.2% [22.0%]	7
(Total	5,697,420	52.8%	234)
Total	**10,786,818**		**707**

*   This term is defined as those who received the official 'coupon'.

** This term includes all those who did not receive an official 'coupon', although some of those who were elected did, nonetheless, support the government in the House of Commons.

The turnout was 57.2 per cent.

The Coalition 'other' was H. King (Norfolk North, Conservative Independent). The opposition 'others' were R.
Barker (Yorkshire, Sowerby, Independent), N. Billing (Hertford, Independent), H. Bottomley (Hackney South,
Independent), J. Jones (Silvertown, National Socialist Party), F. Rose (Aberdeen North, Independent Labour), Sir O.
Thomas, (Anglesey, Independent Labour), J. Wedgewood (Newcastle-under-Lyme, Independent Liberal), Sir R. Woods
(Dublin University, Independent Conservative), A. Waterson (Kettering, Cooperative Party), H. Croft
(Bournemouth, National Party) and Sir R. Cooper (Walsall, National Party). Countess Constance Markievicz
became the first woman to be elected (as the Sinn Fein MP for Dublin St Patrick's). As a Sinn Fein Member, she did
not take her seat.

The Parties

The Coalition polled strongly in London, the South East, the Midlands and in Scotland. Its opponents performed relatively strongly in Northern England and in Wales. The outcome of the election was disastrous for the independent Liberals. Only 20 candidates managed to defeat a couponed Coalition candidate and its leadership was defeated. Losses included Asquith, Sir John Simon, Walter Runciman, Reginald McKenna, Herbert Samuel and John Gulland. The remnants of the Party were briefly led by Sir Donald Maclean until Asquith returned to Parliament at the Paisley by-election in Feburary 1920.

Labour greatly increased its number of candidates which rose from 56 in December 1910 to 361. This increase only brought about a modest increase in the size of the Parliamentary Party, in part because respectable polls were obtained in seats which the Party did not win. It failed to make significant headway in the largest cities (including London) and performed best in Northern England and also in the Midlands (where the decline of Lib–Labism aided the Party's progress). However, its 57 MPs (49 of whom were sponsored by trade unions) and total national vote of around 2.25 million meant that Labour eclipsed the Liberals as the main parliamentary opposition to the Coalition government. Its ability to act in this capacity was, however, hindered by the loss of its leading Parliamentarians which included Ramsay MacDonald, Philip Snowden and Arthur Henderson.

Scotland, Wales and Ireland

Coalition candidates secured victory in 51 of Scotland's 71 seats with Liberal and Conservative participants being more or less evenly balanced, winning 25 and 28 seats respectively. The remainder of the seats were distributed among Coalition Labour (one), Conservative (two), Liberal (eight), Labour (six) and Independent Labour (one). In Wales, supporters and opponents of the Coalition were relatively evenly divided winning 19 and 16 seats of the 35 seats respectively. Coalition Liberals secured 17 of the Coalition forces' 19 victories with the Coalition Conservatives and National Democratic Party each winning one seat each. The seats won in opposition to the Coalition government were shared between Labour (nine), Independent Labour (one), Conservatives (three) and Liberals (three).

In Ireland, the willingness of the Liberal government to proceed with legislation to provide for home rule seemed to justify the constitutional approach of the Irish National Party to the attainment of this objective. However, the vigorous objections of Protestant Ulster to this legislation (which was evidenced by the Solemn League and Covenant in 1912 and the formation in 1913 of the Ulster Volunteer Force to resist by force any attempt to impose this legislation on Ulster) forced the government to consider a compromise whereby Ulster would be outside the scope of this legislation and retain its links with the United Kingdom. Fears by Nationalists that the government would renege on its commitment to home rule resulted in the the 1916 Easter Rising which was designed to seize independence by force (in the form of a stand-up fight with the British army). Initially this was not popular in Ireland but the policy of reprisals associated with General Maxwell in the wake of this event together with a realisation that Britain would almost certainly introduce some form of partition after the war was over resulted in a new departure in Irish politics.

In 1900 the organisation, Cumann na Gaedheal (which was the origins of a new political Party, Sinn Fein) was formed in 1908 whose guiding light was Arthur Griffith. Its policy was to contest election to the Westminster Parliament but then to refuse to take up the seats won and, instead, to use the mandate obtained by the Party to establish an Irish Parliament, the Dail Eirann. After 1917 Sinn Fein began to challenge the Irish National Party in by-elections, and pursued this policy at the general election, winning 73 of Ireland's 101 seats. The Conservatives won 23 and the Irish National Party was swept aside and reduced to six MPs (to which was added T. P. O'Connor's victory in Liverpool, Scotland.) During the election, a number of leading unionists in Southern Ireland published a statement which opposed any future partition of Ireland.

Consequence of the Election
Lloyd George formed a Coalition government.

15 November 1922

Party Leaders
Andrew Bonar Law (Conservative)
Herbert Asquith (Liberal)
John R. Clynes (Labour – Chairman of the Parliamentary Labour Party)

Background to the Election
The economic boom which followed the First World War ended by 1920 and towards the end of that year high unemployment occurred, reaching the figure of 2,171,288 persons (or 17.8 per cent of the insured workforce) (Thorpe, 1991: 2).

Timing of the Election
The election was caused when Lloyd George resigned in response to the decision of the Conservative MPs taken at the Carlton Club to fight the next election as an independent party. (This is discussed below.) However, this decision (and the timing of the election) was considerably influenced by the Chanak crisis (which is discussed in greater detail below).

Electoral Procedures and Practices
The number of MPs elected to the House of Commons was reduced to 615 following the conclusion of the Treaty of 1921 which gave Southern Ireland dominion status within the British Commonwealth but left six Northern counties remaining part of the United Kingdom. Southern Ireland was formally called the Irish Free State in 1922. The 1922 Irish Free State (Agreement) Act provided that no further writs would be issued for constituencies in Ireland other than the 12 in Northern Ireland.

Conservatives
Bonar Law resigned the leadership of the Party in March 1921 on grounds of ill health. His successor was Austen Chamberlain who was unanimously elected by Conservative MPs on 21 March 1921. The party which Chamberlain inherited was divided on two key issues. The first of these was Ireland. Following the 1918 election, an Irish Parliament, the Dail Eirann had been set up and in 1919 a new organisation, the Irish Republican Army, waged a guerrilla war against the British forces, in particular the Royal Irish Constabulary. Initially, this war enjoyed considerable success but in 1920 the government despatched aid to the hard-pressed police force in the form of the Auxilliaries and the Black and Tans. Acts of violence flowed freely on both sides, culminating in the murders of British intelligence agents on 21 November 1921 and reprisals which involved firing into a crowd watching a football match at Croke Park, Dublin, and the deaths of three persons who had been arrested in connection with the murder of the British intelligence agents, ostensibly for trying to escape. Events on this day indicated both to the IRA and to Lloyd George that no side would win this war and discussions were entered into to bring about the cessation of violence. However, a significant diehard element in the

Conservative Party saw no need to enter into discussions with Sinn Fein and instead favoured sending more troops to Ireland in order to secure a complete military victory against the IRA. Chamberlain, however, favoured negotiations and was one of the brokers of the treaty which was concluded in December 1921. Opposition to this policy was articulated at the conference of the National Union in Liverpool in November 1921. At this meeting, Chamberlain's position was skilfully and forcefully defended by Alderman Archibald Salvidge and his views carried the day.

The second issue which divided the Party was the attitude which should be adopted towards the Coalition. Many in the Party observed that the prestige of the Coalition government was waning as was measured by indicators such as by-election defeats. This opinion feared that the Conservatives would suffer through guilt by association which would be to Labour's long-term advantage. Chamberlain, however, wished to continue the Party's involvement in the Coalition and fight the next election within this political umbrella. He believed that the Conservatives alone would not secure outright victory and that Labour would benefit most if the Coalition was terminated before the next election was held. He also had a further motive for wishing to continue this political arrangement, which was to secure the merger of most Conservatives and Coalition Liberals in one 'constitutional and progressive Party' (initially under Lloyd George's leadership) which in his view would be more suited to resist the advance of Labour.

The trigger for Chamberlain to advance the proposal for continued cooperation with Lloyd George was provided by Turkish incursions in Asia Minor, contrary to the spirit of the 1920 Treaty of Sevres. Under the leadership of Kemal Pasha, the Turks advanced into this area. France and Italy accepted the new situation, making peace with Turkey in 1921. However, the Greeks were determined to hang on to Smyrna and Lloyd George was disposed to support them. In August 1922 the Greeks were defeated at Smyrna and the Turks advanced towards the neutral zone, where the outpost of Chanak was held by a small British garrison. War with Turkey seemed a distinct possibility, and military aid was sought from the Dominions. The tense situation, however, was resolved without fighting. Britain did not issue an official ultimatum to the Turks to withdraw and neither did they attack the British forces. Both countries then signed the Pact of Mudania in October 1922 by which they agreed to respect the neutral zone until peace had been concluded. Although there is no evidence that war with Turkey would have been a popular cause, this episode prompted Lloyd George and his supporters to use the mood of excitement in the country to their advantage and fight an immediate election as a Coalition.

At a meeting of senior Coalition ministers held at Chequers on 17 September 1922, Chamberlain called for an immediate general election in which the Conservative Party would fight within a Lloyd George-led coalition. He had some support within his party for this course of action, including Unionist Cabinet ministers (who – with the exception of Baldwin – were party to a Cabinet decision on 10 October 1922 to fight the next election as a coalition led by Lloyd George) and grass roots Conservatives in Scotland and the industrial areas of the North and Midlands. However, there was considerable opposition to Chamberlain's views, which was mobilised by leading figures who included the Marquis of Salisbury (and latterly Bonar Law). Although Chamberlain was willing to make some minor concessions to his opponents (for example, by suggesting that each party in the Coalition would issue its own manifesto in the coming election), he failed to placate those who opposed him which included MPs, some junior ministers and many rank-and-file Conservatives in the constituencies. In order to avoid a fractious debate at the National Union, he offered instead to convene a meeting of all Conservative MPs. This was held at the Carlton Club on 22 October 1922.

Chamberlain restated the case for maintaining cooperation both during and after the election at this meeting, although he agreed that Conservatives could stand under their own party banner in the contest. However, the argument that the Conservative Party would not win an outright victory in a future election was undermined by the result of the Newport by-election in which an anti-Coalition Conservative won the seat against Labour and Liberal opposition. Eventually, a motion put by Capt. Prettyman MP declaring that the Conservative Party, although willing to cooperate with Coalition Liberals, should fight the next election as an independent party with its own leader and its own programme was put to the vote and carried by 187 : 87 votes. The Coalition government immediately resigned as did Chamberlain as leader of the Conservative Party and he was replaced by Bonar Law. It was concluded that 'Austen Chamberlain tried to lead a party in a direction in which the great majority of its members both inside and outside Parliament did not want to go. They therefore rejected his leadership and his authority collapsed' (McKenzie, 1963: 109).

The main action undertaken by the new Conservative government was to determine that war disablement pensions, widows' pensions and dependants' pensions would not be reduced despite the decrease in the cost of living. Instead they were to be standardised for a further period of three years.

Independent Liberals

The Liberal Party was handicapped by a number of factors after 1918. Its first difficulty was the reduced ability of local elites (particularly landowners) to dominate political behaviour. These developments arose from factors that included urbanisation and geographic mobility which had an adverse impact on established communities. Although these changes pre-dated the First World War, they assumed significant dimensions after 1918. The second problem faced by the Party after 1918 was the adverse impact which the war had on religious belief. The ability displayed by former Liberal leaders such as Gladstone to base their political appeal on Christian values became impossible in an era dominated by the emergence of secular forces. This had a detrimental effect on the ability of religion to underpin political loyalty. Although the Conservative Party stood to suffer from the reduced hold exerted by the Church of England after 1918, the Liberal Party was severely hampered in its attempts to sustain itself as a political party contending for power following the decline of nonconformity which was perceived to be the Party's 'backbone' (Clarke, 1981: 56).

One consequence of the decline of religious belief was that social class henceforth became an increasingly influential factor in determining political loyalty. This suggested a new framework within which British politics would be conducted, in which the Conservatives would put forward the interests of capital and property and Labour would advance the needs of the working class. The Liberal Party, which had deliberately eschewed appeals to class loyalty, would thus find it difficult to adjust to the new world of class-based politics. This new situation was underpinned by the boost given to trade unionism during the war and by electoral reform in

1918 which enabled the Labour Party to poll its full potential vote. While it was possible that the Liberal Party might offset the impact of social class on its political fortunes by actively pursuing the approach hesitantly embarked upon after 1906 and promoting progressive, collectivist policies designed to remedy the problems of the working class, its post-war preoccupation with internal feuds prevented the Party from vigorously pursuing such a course of action. This (coupled with Lloyd George's failure to deliver a 'land fit for heroes') rather than the emergence of social class per se resulted in progressive opinion transferring its support to the Labour Party. This was greatest in areas in which employment was dominated by trade unionism (especially in mining areas) and in the newly constructed urban developments of the 1920s where class overcame the traditional hold exerted over the working class by Liberal radicalism.

A third problem faced by the Party was the decline of its organisation in the constituencies which made it difficult for it to fight elections effectively and, in particular, to retain seats once they had been won: between 1918 and 1929 the Liberals won around 281 seats on different occasions but managed to secure victory in only 22 seats on all five occasions (Cook, 1975: 174). An important aspect of Liberal weakness was the decline of the Liberal Party as an important force in municipal politics. Although this decline pre-dated 1918, it became especially marked in the period between 1919 and 1929 and has been attributed to its lack of distinctive municipal policy once nonconformist issues (particularly education) declined in importance (Cook, 1975: 79). It became hard to distinguish between Liberals and Conservatives at municipal level, and there were many examples of both parties cooperating to fight the Labour Party whose rise closely mirrored the Liberal Party's downfall. There were some areas where the Liberal Party remained strong (such as Huddersfield, Oxford and the London Metropolitan Borough of Bethnal Green) but these were exceptions.

Asquith resumed the leadership of the Party when he was returned for Paisley at a by-election in February 1920. In general, however, the Party lagged behind Labour in these contests gaining 24.8 per cent of the vote in all contests held after 1918 to Labour's 35.1 per cent (Cook 1975: 10). The Party retained its strength only in rural, noncomformist areas. A particular problem was the collapse of Liberal organisation which meant that the Party was often unable to field a candidate at a by-election. Asquith's return to Parliament presaged a more aggressive stance being taken against the Coalition Liberals. Animosity between the two wings of the Party was apparent at the general meeting of the National Liberal Federation held at Leamington in May 1920 when a number of Coalition Liberals were subjected to boisterous behaviour. This antagonism was one factor which led to the creation of separate Coalition Liberal organisation at local level.

Coalition Liberals

Lloyd George's behaviour after 1918 is subject to various interpretations. One of these suggests that he viewed socialism as the key threat and sought to create a centre party, based upon a permanent fusion of the partners to his Coalition government. He had actively advocated this course of action in 1910, but it foundered on the unwillingness of Conservatives to endorse Irish home rule (Semmel, 1960: 240–4). Lloyd George resurrected this idea after 1918, and a Coalition Committee was established in 1919 to advance this objective. Its purpose was to prevent class conflict and socialism by mobilising the political centre under one roof and leaving the political extremes marginalised and politically impotent. However, while the Conservative

Party leadership became willing to sanction such an objective (Cook, 1975: 13), the majority of Coalition Liberals were opposed to it. The aggressive attitude adopted by the Independent Liberals after 1920 towards them prompted them to organise nationally (with the formation of a National Liberal Council in 1922) and in the constituencies. However, despite aid from the Lloyd George fund, little was achieved. Lacking significant grass roots support, the Coalition Liberals were thus 'a party of chiefs without Indians' (Cook, 1975: 14).

Labour

In 1921 John Clynes became chairman of the Parliamentary Party in place of William Adamson. The Party made significant progress in by-elections after 1918, gaining 14 seats and losing only one (East Woolwich). Most of these gains occurred in working-class constituencies at the expense of the Coalition although increased support was also secured in suburban and middle-class areas. Significant advances were also secured in local government in London and in the boroughs.

However, the position of the Parliamentary Party within the Labour movement was challenged by the use of extra-parliamentary tactics after 1918. Following the war the Labour movement benefited from full employment (which was partly caused by removing women from the jobs they had occupied during the war) and an inflationary boom which was underpinned by a high level of public spending. In consequence, trade union membership continued to increase and the strength of organised labour enabled it to flex its muscles in connection with industrial issues (which is discussed more fully in connection with the mining industry in the 1924 entry) and also concerning more general political affairs (which included the decision by London dockers in 1920 to 'black' war materials to Poland for use in their war against Russia). Success in this venture prompted some advocates of direct action to suggest that this tactic should be used to force Lloyd George to call a general election.

The conditions which were favourable to the use of extra-parliamentary politics to further the causes of the Labour movement were undone by an economic downturn in the latter months of 1920. Tax rises, interest rate increases and reductions in public spending had a particularly damaging effect on exports, and unemployment began to rise steadily, reaching the figure of around 2.1 million in May 1921. Industrial disputes in the mining and engineering industries resulted in defeats for the workers. These developments tended to boost support for the use of conventional political methods to advance Labour interests. Considerable attention was devoted to central and constituency organisation, although progress in rural areas was slow, especially following the decline of agricultural trade unionism in the early 1920s. However, the Party made political headway by exploiting domestic issues such as housing (where it urged the development of public sector provision) and unemployment, and criticising the policy adopted by the government towards Ireland, the terms imposed upon Germany at Versailles and the massacre which occurred at Amritsar in India in 1919.

By-elections

A total of 108 by elections were held in the 1918–22 Parliament, of which 78 were contested. The Conservative Party made a net loss of 10 seats, the Liberals a net loss of six, Labour a net gain of 13 and others a net gain of three. In some contests in 1919 the coupon was used. The by-election at Plymouth–Sutton on 15 November 1919 secured the election of the first woman to take her seat (Lady Nancy Astor, Conservative). The first female Liberal MP was Mrs Margaret Wintringham, who was elected for Louth in a by-election held on 22 September 1921.

Conduct of the Election
Conservatives

Conservative policies were set out in Mr Bonar Law's election address. In this he referred to the emergence of a sudden crisis which justified an appeal to the nation and argued that the main need at that time was for tranquillity and stability, both at home and abroad. He stated the need to return as soon as possible to the procedures which existed before the war and, to secure this, he proposed changes to the machinery of central government whereby the role of the Foreign Office on matters which included the machinery of the League of Nations would be transferred from the Cabinet Secretariat to the Foreign Office. It was argued that the re-establishment of peace was the chief foreign interest of Britain and this would be achieved through international cooperation with Britain's allies both in Europe and the United States and also through the League of Nations.

It was argued that, if returned to power, the government's first task would be to ratify the Irish Treaty, emphasising the desire to cooperate with the Irish government alongside the pledge to safeguard the Parliament and government of Northern Ireland. The desire to promote the orderly development of India under the constitution granted by the 1919 Act was also referred to. The main issue of domestic policy was the promise to introduce emergency measures to deal with unemployment, although it was emphasised that the revival of trade and industry was the key to economic recovery, which the Conservatives would promote by reducing government expenditure in order to provide relief for taxpayers and by seeking to develop trade within the Empire to replace the markets lost in Europe as the consequence of war. Unspecified proposals were also put forward to aid the agricultural industry.

During the election, Bonar Law promised he would not introduce any general tariff until a second general election had been held specifically on this issue. He also defended the break-up of the Coalition government against the charges made by Lloyd George. In a speech at Drury Lane, London, on 2 November, he insisted that the Coalition government was only intended to last for the lifetime of one Parliament and that Lloyd George had no right to claim, on the basis of his achievements in war, that he should be Prime Minister for life.

Independent Liberals

The issues on which the Liberal Party fought the election were contained in their *Manifesto to the Nation*. This unambiguously condemned the record of the Lloyd George Coalition government both at home and abroad, and stated that this political arrangement resulted in 'the abandonment of principle and the substitution of autocratic for parliamentary government'.

The Party placed the state of the economy at the forefront of their policies and called for 'drastic economy' in public expenditure. Emphasis was also placed on free trade. It was argued that the Coalition government's departure from this principle was responsible for hampering Britain's industrial recovery and the manifesto called for the return to unqualified free trade and the immediate repeal of the Safeguarding of Industries Act and similar protective measures.

This government was also criticised for its use of 'undisciplined force' in Ireland and for undertaking 'disastrous and costly adventures' in Russia and Mesopotamia.

The policies which were promoted in the manifesto included peace and disarmament made secure through the League of Nations, the prompt revision of reparations and inter-Allied debts, and security for workers against unemployment. The Party advocated the defence of essential social services such as education, housing and public health, the institution of political and legal equality for women, the introduction of the taxation and rating of land values and the introduction of proportional representation. It was emphasised that the Liberal Party existed to promote the well-being of the community as a whole rather than that of any particular section or class and it sought to distance itself from Labour by arguing that Liberalism repudiated the doctrine of warfare against private enterprise.

Coalition Liberals

Following the collapse of the Coalition government, Lloyd George declared, 'I am a free man. The burden is off my shoulders. My sword is in my hand.' He immediately embarked on a speaking tour visiting Bedford, Wellingborough, Kettering, Leicester, Nottingham, Sheffield and Leeds on 21 October. At Sheffield he declared that 'the National Unity which won the war has been deliberately and wantonly smashed by the Carlton Club. It was done merely in the hope of snatching a party advantage'. In his speech at Leeds, he dwelt at length on the achievements of the Coalition government. His programme for the election was formally set out in a speech which he delivered at the Hotel Victoria in London on 25 October. He alleged that the Coalition had been destroyed at a time when its successes were becoming more evident. He stated that the nation's finances were being successfully handled, credit was being restored, trade was increasing and unemployment was declining. He described the downfall of the Coalition as 'a rash act. It was a reckless act. It was 'an act ... instigated and perpetrated by ... men without experience, and without any particular ability'. His policies for foreign affairs included supporting the League of Nations (which he wanted all countries in Europe to join), and he urged a renewal of the pact with Russia. In connection with reparations, he expressed the view that 'you should not attempt to impose on Germany any payment beyond her capacity, and what is within her capacity, she should pay it'. He accepted that there would be a case for reducing the reparations demanded of her, provided that this reducation was not entirely at Britain's expense.

Lloyd George's domestic policy emphasised the need to improve trade and increase employment. He rejected the use of what he described as the 'unhealthy stimulants' of tariffs and inflation to create trade but did endorse the use of state credit to achieve this objective.

During the campaign, the Coalition Liberals were concerned about the attitude which the Independent Liberals and Conservatives would adopt towards them. In his speech in London on 25 October Lloyd George attacked the decision of the Independent Liberals to run candidates against around 30 sitting Coalition Liberal MPs, and in an attempt to prevent the Conservative Party opposing sitting Coalition Liberal MPs, Lloyd George threatened to reciprocate and insert his own candidates to challenge sitting Conservative MPs. This threat did not, however, materialise, and the Coalition Liberals fielded the comparatively low number of 151 candidates. Varying attempts were made at local level to define the relationships between these three parties. Some Coalition Liberal associations effectively attached themselves to the

Conservative Party while others sought a reconciliation with the Independent Liberals which was achieved most notably in Manchester. For these reasons, the Coalition Liberal campaign was mainly directed against the Labour Party, who were depicted as extremists. In a speech delivered at Pembroke Dock on 9 November during his election tour of Wales, Lloyd George argued it would be a 'fatal error' for a country which depended on foreign trade to 'throw over the fabric of our trade and destroy the motive power which had driven trade' for the programme of the Labour Party. He believed this would set in motion an economic crash from which the nation would never recover. The proposal to introduce a capital levy was especially singled out for criticism. He asserted that this would harm trade and business and create a large volume of unemployment.

Labour

Labour's policies were put forward in its manifesto, *Labour's Call to the People*, which was depicted as a bulwark against violent upheaval and class war. The manifesto argued that the purpose of the Conservative government was to carry out a policy of 'naked reaction' and instead put forward proposals for a policy of international peace and national reconstruction.

It was argued that a revision of the peace treaties was the first step to peace and that Germany's reparations should be brought within her capacity to pay. Support was expressed for the League of Nations as the forum where the ultimate goal of disarmament could be obtained. Labour demanded the acceptance of the new constitution of the Irish Free State and supported every move to make Ireland united, prosperous and contented.

A prime objective of the Labour Party was to secure a more equitable distribution of the nation's wealth by constitutional means. Its economic policy proposed to lift from trade and industry the burden of the national debt by creating a War Debt Redemption Fund which would be funded by a special graduated levy on 'fortunes' which exceeded £5,000. This was viewed as a mechanism to secure restitution from those who had made huge fortunes out of the war. Taxation reforms were proposed which would distribute the burden according to the principle of ability to pay. Increased death duties on large estates and super tax on large incomes were proposed, with exemption from income tax for incomes below £250 per year and reduced income tax for incomes below £500 per year. The taxation of land values was also advocated, and it was proposed to reduce the rate burden in the severely depressed districts by a revision of the grants-in-aid given to local government. Opposition was expressed to indirect taxation. The Party stood for the untaxed breakfast table and wished to free trade and industry from customs and excise duties and from stamp duties.

Domestic policy emphasised the objective of tackling unemployment by opening trade with foreign countries, by the national organisation of production, and through a large programme of public works. Improved conditions in agricultural areas were called for (including the restoration of the Agricultural Wages Board to enforce an adequate national wage standard), and it was proposed to establish Councils of Agriculture to promote improvements in the use of land, the development of cooperative methods and the fostering of rural industries.

The manifesto expressed the need to change the social and economic system which conferred unfair privileges on the few and undeserved hardship on the many. Labour's policy included the nationalisation of the mines and railways and an improved Workmen's Compensation Act. The manifesto called for a national scheme of housing to end homelessness and replace the slums, improved provision for old age pensioners, and the complete replacement of the Poor Law. Political reforms included opposition to the restoration of the veto of the House of Lords, and the removal of disabilities affecting women as citizens, voters and workers.

The Party's campaign was jeopardised on the eve of the election when it suffered heavy losses in the municipal elections. The Conservatives were the main beneficiary of this setback for Labour.

Result of the Election

The election was contested by 1,441 candidates (a figure boosted by 414 Labour candidates and 334 Independent Liberals), and 57 MPs were returned unopposed. The result was:

Party	Votes	Vote %	MPs
Conservative	5,394,326	37.5%	334
Labour	4,237,349	29.4%	142
Liberal	2,668,143	18.5%	62
National Liberal	1,471,317	10.2%	53
Others	410,556	2.9%	11
Ulster Unionist	107,972	0.8% [55.8%]	10
Irish Nationalist	102,667	0.7% [36.3%]	3
Total	14,392,330		615

The turnout was 73.0 per cent.

The 'others' were J. Newbold (Motherwell, Communist Party), H. Becker, (Richmond, Independent Conservative), J. Butler, (Cambridge University, Independent Liberal), J. Erskine (Westminster St George's, Independent Conservative), G. Hall Caine (Eastern Dorset, Independent Conservative), A. Hopkinson (Mossley, Independent), G. Jarrett (Dartford, Constitutional), O. Mosley (Harrow, Independent), G. Roberts (Norwich, Independent), E. Scrymgeour (Dundee, Scottish Prohibion Party), S. Thomas (Anglesey, Independent Labour). Two women MPs were elected. One ethnic minority candidate was returned, S. Saklatvalo, (Battersea South, Labour).

The Parties

The electoral system translated the 37.5 per cent of the total poll obtained by the Conservative Party into a comfortable majority in the House of Commons. The Party won considerable support from middle-class voters and polled well in London, the South East, West Lancashire and the agricultural areas of North Yorkshire and the South and West Midlands. There were few significant Conservative losses of whom the most important were the Minister of Agriculture, Sir Arthur Griffith-Boscowen, at Taunton and Major J. W. Hills, the Financial Secretary to the Treasury, at Durham. The Labour Party performed well, making a net gain of 85 seats. It thus consolidated its position as the main opposition party. Its support was greatest in mining areas (where 39 seats were gained), Glasgow and the Clyde, parts of London, Tyneside and Sheffield. However, it performed less well in agricultural areas (especially in the

South Midlands) and in the textile areas of East Lancashire and West Yorkshire. Four of its MPs were sponsored by the Cooperative Party and 86 by trade unions.

The election had significant implications for the future of the Liberal Party. Although the Coalition Liberals led by Lloyd George were organisationally weak in most parts of Britain, they were strong in North Wales. One hundred and fifty-four Coalition Liberal candidates contested the election (121 without Conservative opposition) but the result they obtained was poor. In 1918, the Coalition Liberals won 127 seats. A net loss of 74 seats was made in 1922 (21 of which were not defended) and only three seats were gained. Prominent defeats included Winston Churchill at Dundee, Guest, Kellaway, Edwin Montagu and Hamar Greenwood. The Coalition Liberal performance was especially poor in industrial areas. The disinclination of Scottish Conservatives to oppose Coalition Liberals (as they felt the Coalition should have been continued) failed to help them in Scottish industrial seats.

The outcome of the election emphasised Asquith's pre-eminence over Lloyd George. However, although the showing of the Independent Liberals improved, it revealed trends which were likely to prove harmful to the Party in the long run. Sixty-two seats were won, although 14 held in 1918 were lost, nine of them to Labour. The Party performed best in rural areas (some of which had no tradition of supporting the Liberal Party) often in straight fights with Conservative candidates. Here the Liberal vote was mainly in the nature of a protest against the failure of the Coalition government to offer effective responses to the rural depression. The Party gained only one seat from Labour and largely failed to win back its former strength in urban and industrial working-class areas where the decline in party organisation was profound. In particular it performed badly in mining areas.

Scotland, Wales and Northern Ireland
Labour was the largest party in Scotland, winning 29 of the 71 seats. The Liberal Party won 15, the Conservatives 13 and the National Liberals 12. The remaining seats were divided between the Commmunist Party and the Scottish Prohibition Party, each of whom won one. Labour was the largest party in Wales, winning 18 of the 35 seats. The National Liberals won eight, the Conservatives six and the Liberal Party two. The remaining seat of Anglesey was won by an Independent Labour candidate. In Northern Ireland, the Ulster Unionist Party won 10 of the 12 seats and Nationalists won the other two seats. T. P. O'Connor retained his seat of Liverpool, Scotland as an Irish Nationalist.

Consequence of the Election
Bonar Law formed a Conservative government.

6 December 1923

Party Leaders
Stanley Baldwin (Conservative)
Ramsay MacDonald (Labour)
Herbert Asquith (Liberal)

Background to the Election
Timing of the Election
The election was a 'snap' election called by the Prime Minister, Stanley Baldwin, on the issue of free trade. The decision to hold an election on this one issue honoured a commitment given by Bonar Law during the 1922 contest.

Conservatives
The Conservative government was required to face a number of key problems with a ministerial team which lacked experience. The issue of war debts and German reparations were pre-eminent concerns which divided France and Britain and led to the French occupation of the Ruhr Valley in 1923. In the Near East, Turkish resurgence under Mustapha Kemal resulted in the abandonment of the provisions of the Treaty of Versailles regarding that region and the negotiation of the 1923 Treaty of Lausanne which required Greece to give up territories she had gained in 1919. Domestic policy was affected by issues which included the housing shortage and the agricultural depression. Its decision to decontrol rents in 1923 (coupled with the 1923 Rent Restrictions (Notices of Increase) Act which obliged landlords to maintain their property in a habitable state) and its failure to advance any meaningful solutions to the problems of rural areas cost the government electoral support. There were divisions within the Party, and a bloc of Conservative MPs (numbering between 25 and 30) supported Austen Chamberlain. Disunity made the government's overall majority more fragile than should have been the case, and in April 1923 it was embarrassingly defeated on a motion regarding the employment of ex-servicemen. A number of by-elections were lost after 1922 both to Labour (which gained a particularly spectacular victory at Mitcham in March 1923) and to the Liberal Party. The pressure of office told on Bonar Law's health and forced his resignation. He was succeeded by Stanley Baldwin in May 1923.

Under Baldwin, the government's position initially began to improve. Party disunity was ameliorated when some Chamberlainites agreed to enter his government, and the problems with which the government had to cope tended to lessen in urgency. The Party began to perform better in by-elections and much effort was expended on improving Conservative organisation at local level in preparation for the next general election. Although public opinion in 1923 tended to feel that the Party hierarchy had forced Baldwin into an election (a perception which tended to suggest he was not in control of the Party), the decision to do so was his. Baldwin perceived that protection was a solution to the problem of unemployment. He may also have felt that a campaign centred on this issue would help to restore the unity of his party since free trade had the potential of driving a permanent wedge between Coalition Conservatives and Coalition Liberals.

Labour

Following the election, J. R. Clynes was replaced by Ramsay MacDonald who assumed the new position of leader of the Labour Party. The change in leadership resulted in an improvement in the effectiveness of the Party in Parliament whose leaders became less involved in internal party affairs or trade union matters. The make-up of the Parliamentary Party had become more middle class as the consequence of the 1922 election and this helped Labour to shed its image as a mere appendage of the trade unions, and to depict itself as a party bidding for support from across the nation.

Considerable effort was devoted to building up Labour local organisation after 1922. The Party performed well in by-elections, which tended to suggest that Labour was able to hold on to the votes it had captured from the Liberal Party and to further consolidate its position in industrial areas at the Liberals' expense. The Morpeth by-election on 21 June 1923 was an important indicator in this respect: the decision of the Conservatives not to field a candidate failed to enable the Liberals to recapture this constituency which was dominated by the mining industry.

Labour sought to assert itself as the main progressive party by depicting the Liberals as being bankrupt of principles.

Liberals

Reunification was the most significant development affecting the Liberal Party. Calls were made from both sections of the Liberal Party for reunion following the 1922 general election, prompted by factors which included the perception that conflicting Liberal candidatures had an adverse effect on the Party's political standing, especially in relation to Labour. However, there was no immediate progress made in attaining this objective, in part as Asquith was less keen on such a development than Lloyd George and his Coalitionist Liberal supporters whose cohesion and morale were adversely affected by the uncertainty of their political position. Lloyd George expressed his willingness to serve under Asquith's leadership and openly argued for reunion in a speech at Edinburgh in February 1922, but Asquith's position on this matter was to insist that a prerequisite to reunion was the constant cooperation of all Liberal MPs in the division lobbies at Westminster. However, he vetoed a proposal to establish a Consultative Parliamentary Committee (consisting of himself, Lloyd George, Simon and Mond) to discuss policy to be pursued in the House of Commons and plan concerted action. This issue was considered at the Buxton meeting of the National Liberal Federation in 1923. Although it declared its satisfaction with the growing desire for reunion, it rejected an amendment to translate these sentiments into actions which would advance this objective. However, greater progress was made both at local level and also in Parliament. In March 1923, 73 Members of Parliament signed a motion in support of this development and 92 Liberals voted together on a joint amendment on the address in reply to the King's Speech in 1923.

However, the event which precipitated reunion came from an unlikely source. Baldwin's 'snap' election on the issue of protection made it possible for the two wings of the Liberal Party to unite in defence of the traditional Liberal principle of free trade. In response to Baldwin's decision, Lloyd George declared himself to be firmly in favour of free trade which opened the door for discussions to take place between the two Liberal leaders. This led to the formation of a Liberal Campaign Committee which organised a united Liberal Party election campaign. The issues which the Party emphasised were unemployment, the extended use of national credit, the full operation of the Trade Facilities Act, the development of imperial resources, the government's handling of the Ruhr question, and reparations.

In particular the campaign centred on the issue of free trade. The Party offered an orthodox defence of free trade, arguing that protection would force food prices to rise. This argument may have influenced the women's vote. As in 1906, the Liberal position was aided by Conservative deficiencies which enabled the Party to embark upon a campaign which was essentially negative. It was observed that 'the Liberal Party entered the election of 1923 on the most favourable of all issues, with the Conservatives confused, divided and unenthusiastic, with a policy of protection only half thought out, with the press hostile or only lukewarm and with public opinion believing that Baldwin was not master in his own house' (Cook, 1975: 123–4). Its defence of the status quo in opposition to the Baldwin's attempt to inaugurate radical reform enabled the Liberals to present an essentially conservative stance to the electorate.

There was very little in the Liberal campaign to reassert the Party's radical credentials. Liberals who were contesting Labour-held seats frequently devoted much attention to attacking socialism, while in rural areas, the main thrust of the Liberal argument was to attack the Conservatives' newly proposed agricultural subsidy (which they regarded as ill-considered and unworkable) without putting forward any detailed policies of their own (the manifesto making some vague references to the improvement of credit facilities, cooperative marketing and the provision of better housing for agricultural labourers). There were few positive proposals put forward by the Party during the campaign which might have enabled it to re-establish itself as a force able to compete with Labour for the working-class vote. The Party failed to offer a radical approach to combat unemployment, enabling Conservatives to suggest that its attitude towards this issue was one of 'wait and see'. Lloyd George made some vague references in his speeches to the objective of introducing further measures of social reform, and the remodelling of the National Insurance Act was also discussed during the campaign.

By-elections
A total of 16 by-elections occurred in the 1922–23 Parliament, all of which were contested. The Conservatives made a net loss of three, the Liberals a net gain of two, Labour a net gain of two and others a net loss of one.

Conduct of the Election
Conservatives
A statement of Conservative policies was contained in Mr Stanley Baldwin's election address. This identified unemployment and under-employment as a major problem which was in part blamed on the political and economic disorganisation of Europe as a consequence of war which had been accompanied by higher tariffs throughout the world. All of these factors had contributed to a reduction in Britain's foreign trade, and factors such as the occupation of the

Ruhr added to the nation's difficulties. Additionally, British industry was said to be suffering from high levels of cheap imported goods as the consequence of depreciated European currencies. This was said to be 'essentially unfair and is paralysing enterprise and initiative' in Britain, and the problem was said to require 'drastic measures'. However, before embarking on a fundamental change in Britain's fiscal system, the Conservatives wished, in accordance with the pledge given by Bonar Law during the 1922 contest, to seek a mandate from the electorate for this change.

The Conservative proposal was to impose duties on imported manufactured goods in order to assist employment in British industry. It was argued that the introduction of these duties was designed to raise revenue which was not derived from local or national taxation, to provide special assistance to industries which were suffering from foreign competition, and to use them as a lever to negotiate for a reduction of foreign tariffs in order to benefit Britain's export trade. Additionally, they would help fund the reduction of duties on tea and sugar which fell heavily on working-class households. The duties which were suggested would be adjusted to give substantial preference to countries in the British Empire. The Party stated that under no circumstances would duties be imposed on wheat, flour, oats, meat, cheese, butter or eggs, and the policy which was proposed was depicted as one which would, when normal circumstances returned, enable Britain to work to secure a greater measure of real free trade both within the Empire and with foreign countries. Although it was accepted that these proposed duties entailed placing limitations on the fullest extension of imperial preference, it was argued that the concessions which would be made were of real benefit to the Dominions and, further, that part of the revenue derived from tariffs would be devoted to schemes of economic development in the Empire, including cotton growing.

Direct aid (the revenue for which was also to be derived from the tariff) was also promised to the agricultural industry in the form of a bounty of £1 an acre on all holdings of arable land in excess of one acre. This was designed to maintain employment on the land and keep up the wages of agricultural labourers (since this bounty would be denied to employers who paid below 30 shillings a week to these workers).

Protection was seen as the long-term solution to unemployment, However, for the short term, measures which were designed to increase employment would continue to be taken by the government, local authorities and private enterprise. Shipbuilding was singled out as an industry facing acute problems, which the Party proposed to tackle by an accelerated programme of light cruiser construction. The solution to unemployment was depicted as the key to every other social reform, although it was argued that the various schemes which provided insurance against old age, ill-health and unemployment required reorganisation in order to promote 'thrift and independence'.

The decision to hold an election on the issue of protection caused deep divisions in the Party. Many Parliamentarians (both in government and on the backbenches) were opposed to a 'snap' election on this issue (which included many who endorsed the policy of protection), trade organisations were opposed to a contest so close to Christmas and the Conservative press was also hostile. During the campaign, Conservative disunity over the timing of the election was aggravated by the hostile view which many Conservatives had towards protection. Conservative candidates often depicted themselves as suppporters of free trade. The Conservative campaign also suffered from Baldwin's neglect at the outset to give precise details of what he proposed, which left individual candidates free to put forward their own views concerning this. Towards the end of the campaign the Conservatives directed their attack on the Labour Party and its socialist principles. Some Conservative candidates used 'red scares' which sought to identify the Party with communism.

Labour

The Labour manifesto, *Labour's Appeal to the Nation*, argued that the election on the issue of tariffs was largely an attempt by the Conservatives to mask their failure to handle the issue of unemployment. The government's programme of winter work was branded as inadequate and the manifesto argued that tariffs offered no solution to unemployment and carried with them additional problems since 'they foster a spirit of profiteering, materialism and selfishness, poison the life of nations, lead to corruption in politics, promote trusts and monopolies, and impoverish the people. They perpetuate inequalities in the distribution of the world's wealth won by the labour of hands and brain'.

The Labour Party's programme to deal with unemployment embraced the immediate adoption of national schemes of productive work, which included the establishment of a national system of electrical power supply, the development of road, rail and canal transport, and the improvement of national resources by land drainage, reclamation, afforestation, town planning and housing schemes. Adequate maintenance for those who could not obtain work was proposed, and it was stated that full educational training with maintenance should be provided to young people in order to reduce the flow of young workers on to the labour market.

Other issues of domestic policy included the provision of equality of opportunity in education, the improvement of support for aged people, widowed mothers and sick and disabled citizens and the insistence that ex-servicemen and their dependants were given fair play with regard to pensions. Labour stated its intention to abolish the slums, build an adequate supply of homes and to resist decontrol until the housing shortage was reduced. Equal political and legal rights between men and women (including the principle of equal pay for equal work) were advocated. Special measures to restore prosperity to agriculture and give agricultural workers a living wage were put forward, which included establishing machinery for regulating wages and providing state insurance facilities for farmers and smallholders. Labour intended to restore to the people their lost rights in the land by policies which included re-equipping the Land Valuation Department and facilitiating the acquisition of land for public use.

Labour's economic policies gave prominence to the need to take steps to reduce the war debt and proposed a graduated war debt redemption levy to achieve this which would be imposed on all fortunes in excess of £5,000. This measure, together with reduced expenditure on armaments and increased income derived from the taxation of land values, would enable money to be provided for social services and secure the reduction of income tax, the abolition of food duties, the entertainment tax, and the corporation profits tax. The Party pledged to apply the principle of public ownership and control to the mines, railways, electrical power stations and to develop municipal services.

Labour's foreign policy emphasised the development of international cooperation through an enlarged League of Nations, the use of conciliation and judicial arbitration to settle international disputes and the convening of an International Conference to deal with the revision of the Versailles Treaty, especially concerning reparations and debts. The resumption of economic and diplomatic relations with Russia was also called for. These policies were compatible with disarmament which was described as 'the only security' for nations.

Liberals

The Liberal Party's manifesto, *A Call to the Nation*, accused the Conservative Party of stampeding the country into a general election on the basis of their allegation that tariffs were a cure for unemployment. The Liberal Party asserted that the basis of Britain's economic recovery was the restoration of world trade and the foreign policy pursued by the government was condemned for having hindered progress in this direction. The Liberals alleged that the government's failure immediately to condemn the occupation of the Ruhr and to participate in an impartial examination of Germany's capacity to pay war reparations had contributed to insecurity in Europe, which had an adverse impact on trade and credit. The acceptance by the government of the Treaty of Lausanne was criticised for having virtually ended all trade with Turkey. The government was thus branded as having failed 'to make one single effective effort to assert our rights, to restore our trade, or to bring back peace and order to a distracted world'. The Liberal Party asserted that the economic restoration of Europe was essential to reviving British industries and securing peace. To achieve this, the Party wished to settle the issue of reparations promptly, to cooperate with America to bring peace to the world, to reopen full relations with Russia, and to cooperate fully with the League of Nations as the mechanism to end national enmities.

The manifesto branded Conservative policies to deal with unemployment as totally inadequate and it was asserted that trade restrictions would not cure this problem but threatened to aggravate it, since high prices and scarcity would lower the standard of living, reduce the purchasing power of the country and thereby curtail production. The manifesto specifically addressed women electors by arguing that protection would raise the prices of household necessities and alleged that import duties would harm the agricultural industry by raising the cost of what the famer bought. Baldwin was further accused of vagueness regarding his proposals. The Party also argued that the remedies put forward by the Labour Party to address this problem (socialism and the capital levy) would also prove disastrous since it would destroy enterprise and frighten away capital.

The Liberal Party's proposals to counter unemployment included public expenditure on enterprises which would permanently improve and develop this country and the Empire (such as afforestation, land reclamation and drainage, and railway building in the Dominions and India). The Party proposed to remodel the Insurance Acts to provide reasonable subsistence to a man and his family without aid from Poor Law Relief and promised to take steps to promote the cooperation of employers and the employed through an approach based upon a partnership between capital and labour, security of livelihood for the workers and placing public advantage before private profit. Other aspects of Liberal social policy included removing the thrift qualification attached to the receipt of old age pensions, providing an adequate supply of housing (with rents being decontrolled until the present shortage was relieved), and allowing localities to determine the facilities for alcohol consumption. The reduction of public spending in areas which were unproductive or destructive was advocated, although the manifesto insisted there should be no false economies made in education. The manifesto referred to the need to make reforms in local government and rating, and called for the introduction of site value rating. Political, legal and economic equality between men and women was called for.

The manifesto advocated that special consideration should be given to British agriculture through policies which included giving the farmer credit facilities and the provision of government assistance for the introduction of large-scale cooperative marketing. Land purchase schemes to enable cultivators to become the owners of land on reasonable terms was called for and it was proposed to raise the standard of living of agricultural workers and improve rural facilities, especially housing.

Result of the Election

A total of 1,446 candidates contested the election, and 50 MPs were returned unopposed. The result was:

Party	Votes	Vote %	MPs
Conservative	5,397,380	37.1%	248
Labour	4,439,780	30.5%	191
Liberal	4,301,481	29.6%	158
Ulster Unionist	117,161	0.8% [49.4%]	10
Others	193,900	1.3%	5
Irish Nationalist	97,993	0.7% [27.3%]	3
Total	14,547,695		615

The turnout was 71.1 per cent.

The five Independents were G. Davies (University of Wales, Christian Pacifist), A. Hopkinson (Lancashire, Mossley, Independent), Rhys Hopkin Morris (Cardiganshire, Independent Liberal), O. Mosley (Harrow, Independent) and E. Scrymgeour (Dundee, Scottish Prohibition Party). Eight women MPs were elected.

The Parties

The reduced turnout in England, Scotland and Wales perhaps indicated that many Conservative supporters (especially those who supported free trade) chose to abstain rather than transfer their political allegiance. Several patterns of voting behaviour were apparent in the contest. In constituencies where meaningful comparisons can be made between the 1922 and 1923 contests, the swing from the Conservative Party to Liberals or Labour was greatest in middle-class constituencies but lower in agricultural constituencies. However, the ability of the Liberals to gain support at Labour's expense in rural areas did result in a number of Liberal gains in such seats.

The Conservative Party performed especially badly in Lancashire (where many Conservatives supported free trade) and in London, but their support held up in the chemical and heavy engineering towns in North West England (such as Wigan, Workington and St Helens) and in the West Midlands generally. The Labour Party continued to advance in urban, industrial constituencies at the expense of both Liberal and Conservative parties. It did very well in the big cities, especially in the greater London area where it doubled the number of its MPs. Two rural seats (South Norfolk and Maldon) were won from the Conservatives where the local Liberal associations failed to field candidates and actively supported Labour. Six of its MPs were sponsored by the Cooperative Party and 102 by trade unions.

Reunion did not totally restore the unity of the Liberal Party. Acrimony between the two wings remained evident (especially in Scotland), and in two constituencies (Cardiganshire and Camborne) candidates from both wings of the Party fought against each other. However, reunion did help improve the Party's morale and, aided considerably by finance provided from Lloyd George's fund, the reunited party fielded 457 candidates. Nonetheless, the Party faced difficulties in obtaining candidates in Labour-held industrial seats. The free trade issue tended to limit the extent of cooperation between the Conservative and Liberal parties at local level, although some anti-Labour pacts were concluded in Labour-held seats in industrial and mining areas and in some large cities. Liberal–Labour pacts at local level largely died out in the boroughs (Birkenhead and Preston being the exceptions), although some were concluded in rural areas.

The Liberal Party emerged from the election with 158 seats, polling around the same total number of votes as Labour. The Liberals were the second largest party in English county constituencies, the second largest party in Welsh and Scottish boroughs and the largest party in Welsh counties. The Party was also the alternative to the Conservatives in non-industrial England and a rival to Labour in industrial areas such as the North East or Yorkshire (Cook, 1975: 179).

However, the outcome of this election verified the altered position of the Liberal Party in the political spectrum. As in 1922, most of its gains were at the expense of the Conservative Party, and occurred primarily in rural constituencies and in middle-class, suburban areas. The rural nature of the Party was reflected in its representing 43 of the 86 most rural constituencies in Great Britain (Cook, 1975: 159). The Party performed especially well in the South West (where it registered 12 gains), and in the South Midlands, Northern Home Counties, Lincolnshire and East Anglia. It lost ground to Labour in urban and industrial areas, performing especially badly in the industrial Midlands and losing seats in London, Bristol and Norwich. However, the Party succeeded in retaining working-class support in the North East and in some Lancashire and Yorkshire textile towns. This might imply that voters now viewed the Liberal Party on the right of the political spectrum, competing with the Conservatives for the right-of-centre vote. However, while this election confirmed the Liberal Party's inability to regain support in working-class urban and industrial areas which had been previously lost to the Labour Party, it did succeed in winning back the rural working-class vote previously lost to Labour, especially in nonconformist areas and where trade union organisation was weak (Cook, 1975: 166). The outcome of the election affirmed the dominance of Asquith over Lloyd George within the Parliamentary Liberal Party.

Scotland, Wales and Northern Ireland

Labour was the largest party in Scotland, winning 34 of the 71 seats. The Liberals won 22 and the Conservatives 14. The remaining seat was won by the Scottish Prohibition Party. Labour was the largest party in Wales, winning 19 of the 35 seats. The Liberals won 11 and the

Conservatives four. The remaining seat was won by an Independent Liberal. In Northern Ireland, the Ulster Unionists won 10 of the 12 seats and the Nationalists won the remaining two. T. P. O'Connor retained his seat of Liverpool, Scotland as an Irish Nationalist.

Consequence of the Election

The 1923 general election produced a situation of political stalemate. The Conservatives remained the largest party with 248 MPs, Labour returned 191 and the Liberals 158. Baldwin chose not to resign and returned to the House of Commons to test the political water.

The Liberal Party was in a dilemma and considered various courses of action (including first turning out the Conservative government and then ousting a Labour one in the expectation of then being asked to form a Liberal administration) but eventually decided to turn out the Conservative government and then adopt a non-committal attitude towards an incoming Labour government.

There were also concerns within Labour ranks about the desirability of assuming office in a minority position, but MacDonald felt it was important for the Party to seize the opportunity in order to prove its competence to govern. On 21 January 1924, Labour's amendment to the debate on the Address on 21 January resulted in a defeat for the Conservatives by 328 votes to 256. One hundred and thirty-eight Liberals voted for the Labour amendment, 10 voted against and 10 abstained. Baldwin resigned the following day and Ramsay MacDonald was invited to form a Labour administration.

Thus, for the immediate future, a minority Labour government would be supported by Liberal votes. No prior negotiations had taken place between the two parties (perhaps seeking to get Labour to pledge electoral reform in return for Liberal support): it is doubtful, however, whether Labour would have entered into agreements of this nature since their stance towards the Liberals had been hostile during the election campaign and the Liberal Party was in a weak bargaining position since its choices were either to support the Labour government or to force a fresh election for which they were financially and organisationally ill-prepared.

29 October 1924

Party Leaders
Stanley Baldwin (Conservative)
Ramsay MacDonald (Labour)
Herbert Asquith (Liberal)

Background to the Election
Timing of the Election
The government's precarious parliamentary position meant that an election could not be indefinitely postponed. Its situation was made even harder by MacDonald's refusal to countenance any form of cooperation with the Liberal Party. Consequently, the government lacked control over the parliamentary timetable and had no automatic majority for government business. The election was finally caused by a parliamentary defeat in connection with the Campbell case. On 5 August 1924 the offices of the *Workers' Weekly* were raided, following its publication of an article which the Director of Public Prosecution referred to the Attorney General in the belief that it could be read as an attempt to seduce soldiers from performing their duty. The editor, Campbell, was arrested but on 13 August the government abandoned the prosecution, accepting the argument that the article constituted a comment on the state's use of the military to repress industrial disputes. The decision to terminate the prosecution caused the Conservatives to take the offensive in Parliament and to ask why this action had been taken and, in particular, whether MacDonald had agreed to the withdrawal of the prosecution. On 30 September, MacDonald stated that he had not been consulted regarding either the institution or the withdrawal of the prosecution and had only read of the matter in the press. This reply, which was dubbed 'neither skilful nor true' (Cook, 1975: 274) prompted the Conservatives to table a motion to censure the government for its handling of the Campbell case. The Liberal Party then joined in the attack and tabled its own amendment to the Conservative motion calling for the establishment of a Select Committee into the matter. The government determined that they would ask for a dissolution if either of these motions were carried. At the end of the debate on 8 October, Baldwin withdrew his amendment in preference to the Liberal one and the government was defeated by 364 : 199 votes.

Conservatives
The scale of the 1923 defeat had an initial adverse impact on Conservative morale and there was much dissent expressed within the Party regarding the way in which Baldwin had foisted his tariff reform proposals on the Party without adequate prior consultation. However, this dissent did not have an adverse long-term impact on Baldwin's authority within the party and he was able to consolidate his position and initiate steps to restore its political strength. On 2 February 1924, he announced in a speech delivered at the Hotel Cecil that the proposal for a general tariff on which the Conservatives had fought the last election would be dropped from Party policy and that, instead, social reform would be focused upon. In May and June 1924

Baldwin delivered a series of 10 speeches in which he outlined his ideas concerning Tory democracy. The constructive nature of this appeal was added to by attacks on Labour's record in office, in particular regarding unemployment. Baldwin also sought to restore party unity by including former Coalitionists (including Austen Chamberlain) in his team. By the autumn of 1924 the Party was willing to pursue a more aggressive line in Parliament and to force a general election.

Labour

The Labour Party had not anticipated being in a position to form a government as the consequence of the 1923 general election, but MacDonald had gladly seized the opportunity in order to prove that Labour could govern. This consideration, coupled with his government's minority status, dictated that the Party would pursue a moderate (rather than a socialist or radical) programme.

The most important aspect of domestic policy was the 1924 Housing Act, introduced by John Wheatley, which was the basis of the subsequent expansion of housing construction. The capital levy was not proceeded with and no attempt was made to nationalise either the coal mines or the railways. Some minor reforms were introduced in connection with unemployment insurance (whose weekly benefits were increased and the scheme was extended to juveniles) and Snowden's budget of April 1924 was underpinned by Liberal and free trade ideals. The duties on sugar, tea, cocoa, coffee and chicory were lowered as was the entertainment tax and the McKenna duties were abolished. The government also showed itself willing to confront the trade unions in disputes affecting the docks and London tram drivers in 1924. Additionally, the Prime Minister (who also served as Labour's Foreign Secretary) derived credit from his attempts to reconcile Germany and France which resulted in the London conference in 1924 at which Franco-German acceptance of the Dawes Plan regarding repatriation was secured. In both domestic policy and foreign affairs, Labour's stance of moderation was one which many Liberals could support both in Parliament and in the country.

The performance of the Party in government was not, however, totally to the liking of all of its supporters and opposition was expressed especially by Independent Labour Party MPs who alternatively desired a full-bloodied socialist programme. Many Labour MPs were also unhappy concerning the government's approach towards unemployment. The minority status of the government also resulted in 10 defeats in the House of Commons during 1924, although only one (on the Rent Restriction Bill on 7 April 1924) concerned a major issue.

Foreign affairs almost proved to be Labour's undoing. One of MacDonald's first actions as Prime Minister was to recognise formally the Soviet government. He sought to develop this diplomatic initiative by negotiating a trade agreement with Russia and negotiations were commenced in April 1924. However, the repudiation by the Soviet government of pre-revolutionary debts to British bondholders proved a thorny issue since the Russians demanded a loan as part of any commercial treaty to settle the payment of these debts. Eventually an agreement was signed between the British and Soviet representatives in August 1924. This provided for a commercial treaty and for a wider general treaty which proposed further negotiations between the bondholders and the Soviet government. The successful conclusion of these negotiations would result in a third treaty being signed, after which the British government would guarantee a loan. However, the Conservative Party insisted that there should be a delay between the signing of the agreement and its ratification by the government and during that time political oposition was marshalled. The attitude adopted by the Liberals was crucial as they could secure Labour's defeat. MacDonald refused to enter into any sort of arrangement with the Liberals to avoid this but the Liberals had little to gain from precipitating an election underpinned by anti-Russian sentiments which might benefit the Conservatives. However, the Liberal Party's difficulties were solved by Labour's defeat on the Campbell case (which is referred to above).

Liberals

The Liberal Party had performed unexpectedly well in 1923 and this prompted some measure of organisational reform at local level. However, progress was impeded by financial problems, in particular the very weak position of the central organisation which Lloyd George was reluctant to cure by the use of his fund, believing instead that the federations should be self-supporting. One consequence of this situation was the inability of local associations to adopt candidates.

There were three key problems facing the Liberal Party after 1923. The first of these was weak leadership. Inadequate leadership in Parliament made the Party appear as 'a pathetic, disorganised and leaderless group' (Cook, 1975: 249) and resulted in divisions appearing in the ranks of the Parliamentary Party on a very wide range of issues.

The second problem after 1923 was the Party's failure to a develop radical policy in areas which included economic and industrial policy and social reform with which it might outflank Labour whose record in government was dominated by a stance of moderation. The Liberal Party had sold itself easily at the 1923 election by opposing Conservative protectionism. However, to survive in the subsequent political world it needed to develop new policy. Asquith's age and the hostility which his closest colleagues held towards Lloyd George impeded party unity. Lloyd George did seek to initiate radical ideas by embarking upon inquiries into the coal and electricity industries and into the system of land tenure. He sought to popularise these reforms by launching a nation-wide 'Great Liberal Campaign' in 1924. However, his assertiveness aroused the concern of Asquith's supporters. Devoid of firm leadership and constructive policy, the Party merely drifted along. Its weakness was displayed by poor performances in by-elections after 1923, which evidenced the decline of the Liberals and the rise of Labour in areas of traditional Liberal strength such as Carmarthen and Oxford. Desertion from the Party occurred both from radicals who wished to pursue reform aggressively (and believed Labour was the best vehicle to achieve this) and also from those who believed that the key political objective was to fight socialism (and became attracted to the Conservatives).

Liberal Party difficulties were compounded by a third problem which was Labour's attitude towards it. In Parliament, Labour adopted a hostile attitude towards Liberals, who were subjected to 'constant abuse, vituperation and enmity' (Cook, 1975: 234). This was replicated at constituency level where improvements in Labour organisation made it possible for them to adopt candidates to challenge sitting Liberal MPs (making no discernment between radical and right-wing Liberals) and to stand candidates in rural and residential areas in which previously only the Liberals had been in a position to challenge the Conservative Party. This situation was caused by factors which included the refusal of Labour's fundamentalists to contemplate any arrangement with the Liberal Party and the apparent desire of Ramsay MacDonald to secure the total annihilation of the Liberals, thereby guaranteeing Labour's position as the main progressive force in British politics. Although Lloyd George wished to adopt a more assertive position towards the Labour administration, particularly its handling of unemployment, Asquith was less inclined to embark on this course of action. He indicated this early in the Parliament when he backed away from opposing the removal of the Order banning the Poplar Board of Guardians from exceeding the prescribed scale of outdoor relief. In a humiliating climbdown he supported the government's closure motion in order to prevent his own motion regarding Poplar being voted on. This indicated that the Liberal Party was extremely reticent about using its ultimate sanction of voting against the government and thereby forcing a general election.

The problems encountered by the Liberal Party after 1923 had an adverse impact on party morale. However, it is possible that these difficulties could have been ameliorated (or at least masked) by a measure of electoral reform. Although much Labour support had been secured for the Alternative Vote Bill in March 1923, in office they refused to provide parliamentary facilities for the Representation of the People Act (1918) Amendment Bill which sought to provide for the alternative vote in single-member seats and proportional representation in multi-member constituencies. The Bill was thus defeated at its second reading stage on 2 May. The failure of this measure further dented Liberal morale and meant that the Party would face the forthcoming general election without electoral reform.

By-elections

Ten by-elections occured in the 1923–24 Parliament of which nine were contested. The Conservatives made a net gain of one seat and the Liberals a net loss of one.

Conduct of the Election

The 1924 campaign witnessed the first use of party political broadcasts on the radio.

Conservatives

The Conservative Party entered the election as a united party which, unlike 1923, was widely supported by the Conservative press: only the titles owned by Lord Beaverbrook (who favoured Conservative–Liberal cooperation) had reservations about some aspects of the Conservative campaign. Its manifesto, which was contained in Mr Stanley Baldwin's election address, devoted much attention to attacking Labour. It was criticised for choosing to hold an election 'not on any great issue of principle … but on the plea that it was incompatible with their dignity to tolerate any inquiry into their conduct in connection with the withdrawal of the Campbell prosecution'. It argued that the timing of the election was also influenced by the government's treaty with the Soviets (which was allegedly foisted on the government by the same group of extremists who had secured the withdrawal of the Campbell prosecution). Baldwin argued that, based on its previous record, the Russian government was unlikely to repay the loan which was an important element of these negotiations. He also accused Labour of timing the election to mask their total failure to deal with unemployment which was stated to be as bad, if not worse, than it had been when Labour entered office. This situation was partly ascribed to Labour's abolition of the McKenna duties and Part Two of the Safeguarding of Industries Act

The Conservatives put forward constructive alternatives to Labour in areas that included unemployment, housing, education and national insurance provision. Although it was argued that a general tariff was not part of the Conservatives' programme, the Party pledged to use the Safeguarding of Industries Act or analogous measures to protect employment and the standard of living of persons in any efficient industry which was imperilled by unfair foreign competition. It argued that the best hope of industrial recovery rested with the development of the resources and trade of the British Empire. Accordingly, the policy of encouraging mutual trade in the Empire by measures of imperial preference would be pursued. Housing was asserted to be the next gravest problem behind unemployment and reference was made to the beneficial effects of the 1923 Housing Act. It was stated that a Unionist government would also utilise new materials and new methods of construction to speed up the house building programme. The improvement of slum dwellings would be undertaken as soon as the shortage of accommodation had been sufficiently eased. Education reform included objectives such as the reduction of the size of classes, the improvement or replacement of insanitary schools and the development of Central Schools and other forms of education above the elementary stage. Reforms to old age and widows' pensions were put forward.

Considerable attention was devoted to Conservative policy for rural areas where it was hoped to make good the reverses suffered by the Party in 1923. The manifesto pledged a Conservative government to continue providing relief for agricultural ratepayers, to develop the sugar beet industry and rural industries generally, and to extend credit for efficient cooperative enterprises. Explicit opposition to land nationalisation and the taxation of land values was expressed. It was also proposed to appoint a Royal Commission to investigate the cost of foodstuffs.

The Conservative Party also emphasised foreign policy. Their approach entailed strengthening and developing imperial unity, maintaining friendly relations with Britain's allies, re-establishing a settled state of affairs in Europe and cooperating with America. It was argued that supporting and strengthening the League of Nations should be viewed as 'a cardinal principle' of British foreign policy.

Baldwin's election address concluded with an appeal for 'strong and stable government, based on an independent majority in Parliament'. He asserted that 'the experiment of a minority government has proved a short-lived failure'. The Conservative campaign was centred on Baldwin whose speeches advocated the improvement of social conditions in addition to arguing the importance of stable government. He focused on Labour's failure to combat unemployment successfully and also criticised them for their negotiations with the Soviet government. This theme was developed at constituency level into what has been described as a 'rabid and emotional anti-communist campaign' (Cook, 1975: 300) which sought to identify the Labour Party with communism. MacDonald (whose pacifist stance in the First World War was frequently referred to by Conservative candidates) was depicted as a stooge of the Communist Party and it was argued that another Labour government would destroy established British moral values, especially religion and family life. This 'Red Scare' culminated in the publication on 25 October 1924 by the *Daily Mail* of a letter allegedly signed by G. E. Zinoviev (President of the Soviet Praesidium) and Arthur McManus (of the British Communist Party) which contained a number of subversive instructions for the British Communist Party and which made the Labour Party appear as, at worst, their accomplices or, at best, their stooges.

The main problem from Labour's perspective was the manner of their response to this letter. MacDonald (who suspected it was a forgery) delayed reacting to it immediately and instead asked the Foreign Office to obtain proof of its authenticity. The Foreign Office then prepared a draft letter of protest for MacDonald which he rewrote but did not sign on 24 October and thus it was not sent. Only when the *Daily Mail* threatened to publish a second copy of the Zinoviev letter which they had received did the Foreign Office publish the protest, but without first referring the revised draft to the Prime Minister. MacDonald, for his part, did not break his silence on the matter until 27 October in a speech at Cardiff and, in the interim period, Labour leaders left without guidance concerning how to react to the issue came up with a wide variety of responses. In his Cardiff speech, MacDonald claimed that he had reacted with commendable speed on this issue but asserted he had expected his civil servants to return his rewritten draft of the protest along with their proof of the letter's authenticity. This suggested that MacDonald was attempting to foist the blame on the civil service for prematurely publishing the government's protest before the authenticity of the letter had been proved but was also asserting that the government had acted decisively on the issue. The Conservative press rose to the defence of the civil service and the government's handling of the matter was criticised both by Conservative and Liberal leaders.

Labour

Labour morale was high at the commencement of the contest. Improved organisation enabled the Party to increase the number of candidates it was able to field, which now included rural areas previously beyond the capacity of the Party to fight. Labour policies were contained in its manifesto, *Labour's Appeal to the People*.

This blamed the government's defeat in the House of Commons on a partisan combination of Liberals and Conservatives and placed the restoration of peace among the nations of the world and the restoration of industry and commerce as the main needs of the country. It argued that the foreign policy of the Labour government had achieved much in attaining the former objective, and cited the improvement of Britain's relations with France, and the honouring of both the spirit and the letter of the treaty with the Irish Free State. The manifesto insisted on the need to include Russia within measures to secure world peace and argued that the treaties with Russia then awaiting ratification were designed to achieve this and also create new markets for the British manufacturing industry. The manifesto also praised the domestic record of the Labour government in areas which included house building and financial affairs (where it was argued that taxes on food had been considerably reduced and reforms to old age pensions had been instituted). It was argued that positive progress had been made in attaining the objective of giving every child equality of opportunity in education by measures which included reducing the size of classes and increasing the number of qualified teachers. Labour's policy for the countryside had included the provision of loans to farmers to further cooperative enterprises, and the supply of aid to help develop the sugar beet industry. A vast increase of cottages in rural areas at low rents had also been secured. The Labour government had addressed unemployment by stimulating useful enterprises, providing approved schemes of work and making improvements in the operation of the Unemployment Insurance Acts.

The mainfesto drew attention to future proposals which the Party would act upon if reelected to office. These included the reorganisation of the mining industry on the basis of national ownership, the continuance and amendment of the Rent Restriction Acts, drastic reform of the Poor Law, and the taxation of land values. It was proposed to establish a national electricity-generating scheme, to undertake a systematic reorganisation of the whole system of national transport under public control, to appoint a Royal Commission to consider the licensing laws, to introduce bulk importing of foodstuffs and household necessities as a means to prevent profiteering and to establish reasonable and stable prices and to improve working conditions through measures which included reforming the Workmen's Compensation Acts and limiting excessive hours of labour in occupations which included the distributive trades.

The Labour campaign was heavily centred on MacDonald who undertook two speaking tours. His deliberate wooing of the progressive vote led him to seek to identify the Liberal Party with the Conservatives. MacDonald's early speeches echoed the manifesto's claim that the negative attitude adopted by the Conservative and Liberal parties had hindered the progress of the Labour government and he spoke of a Liberal–Conservative intrigue which had been designed to topple him from power. Early in the campaign, MacDonald also justified his actions in connection with the Campbell case and the Russian treaties, but this line of argument tended to highlight issues being raised by the Conservatives whose 'Red Scare' tactics increasingly forced Labour on the back foot.

Liberals

Unlike Labour, Liberal morale was not good at the commencement of the election campaign. Finance was a major problem which made it difficult for headquarters to provide aid to the constituency parties. Although Lloyd George made a belated contribution of £50,000 to central funds (and donated a further sum to be used in Wales) this was not a sufficient incentive either to induce candidates to come forward or to encourage local associations to adopt them. A malaise descended upon the Party in 1924 and even constituencies where the Liberals had performed extremely well in 1923 (such as Penrith and Cockermouth, Waterloo, Kinross and West Perthshire, Windsor, Wallasey and Moray and Nairn) went uncontested. A number of agreements were entered into with the Conservative Party, especially where these already existed for municipal elections. Some of these in 1924 were of a regional nature (including South Wales, the industrial area of Lancashire and around 25 constituencies in the Glasgow–Paisley and West of Scotland area). In addition to these pacts, 12 candidates (six who were former Liberals and six others who still remained on the list of officially approved Liberal candidates) stood as Constitutionalists in an attempt to secure Conservative support. These pacts reinforced Labour arguments related to the similarities between the Conservative and Liberal parties. By contrast, only one formal anti-Conservative pact (in Preston) remained.

Liberal policies were contained in *The Liberal Manifesto*. This blamed the timing of the election on the refusal of the Labour government to face an impartial inquiry regarding the Campbell case and for seeking to evade parliamentary scrutiny of their proposed loan to Russia. The manifesto sought to depict the Liberal Party as a progressive alternative to Labour which stood opposed to both 'unthinking resistance to change' and 'unbalanced experiments and impracticable schemes which will destroy the whole social and economic system upon which the prosperity of the country has been built'. It insisted that while Liberal MPs had resisted crude schemes of nationalisation proposed by Labour, they had assisted its attempts to promote sound social reform where Labour's progress was stated to have been 'halting, ineffective and unimaginative'. Labour was accused of instigating a new naval race in the construction of new cruisers but had failed to carry out their 1923 manifesto pledge to cure unemployment, which was now stated to be more serious than when the government had entered office. Their housing policies had failed to take effective measures to train young apprentices in the building industry or to increase the number of building craftsmen so that fewer houses were now being built than when Labour came to power.

The manifesto argued that the neglect of agriculture required changes in the system of land tenure and the liberation of agricultural labourers from poverty and lack of opportunity. It gave considerable attention to the issue of land, and advocated policies to tax land values, to reform the leasehold system, to allow occupiers of dwellings to purchase them at a fair price, and to give local authorities wider powers to acquire land. The building of new industrial towns was presented as a radical cure for slums. A 10-year programme of educational advance (which included reducing the size of classes in elementary schools and making additional provision for pupils over 14 years of age) was put forward. The manifesto proposed a further extension and complete coordination of the National Insurance Acts entailing the introduction of a comprehensive policy of contributory insurance, and the elimination of the thrift disqualification for the receipt of old age pensions. It proposed to secure industrial peace by ensuring the cooperation of all engaged in it and the fair distribution of profits amongst them. The Party's policy for coal and power was for the state to acquire all mineral rights and then give assistance and direction to construct super power stations. The Party advocated electoral reform to ensure that parties secured parliamentary representation in accordance with their electoral strength and proclaimed its unshakeable commitment to free trade.

The Liberal document somewhat unrealistically (since the Party was able to field only 340 candidates) stated the Party's aim to be the return of a Liberal government which would pursue the path of 'Peace, Social Reform and National Development'. Asquith's need to devote much of his energy in defending his constituency of Paisley meant that he played a less prominent part in the Liberal campaign compared to Baldwin or MacDonald. This situation created a vacuum for other leading Liberals to perform an active role, but their desires to promote their own hobby horses (Mond and anti-socialism, Lloyd George and land, coal and power, and Simon and free trade) helped to present the Liberals as a disunited Party. At constituency level, some Liberal candidates preferred to refight 1923, emphasising free trade and arguing that the Conservatives would tax food (a policy which Baldwin had specifically ruled out).

Result of the Election

A total of 1,428 candidates contested the election, and 32 MPs were elected unopposed. The result was:

Party	Votes	Vote %	MPs
Conservative	7,403,245	44.5%	400
Labour	5,489,087	33.0%	151
Liberal	2,928,737	17.6%	40
Ulster Unionist	451,278	2.7% [83.8%]	12
Others	321,475	1.9%	12
Sinn Fein	46,457	0.3% [9.9%]	0
Total	16,640,279		615

The turnout was 77.0 per cent.

Four women MPs were elected. One ethnic minority MP was elected, S. Saklatvalo (Battersea South, Communist). The 'others' elected were W. Churchill (Epping), Sir H. Greenwood (Walthamstow East), A. H. Moreing (Camborne), J. Edwards (Accrington), A. England (Heywood and Radcliffe), Sir T. Robinson, (Stretford) and J. Ward (Stoke). All of these seven MPs were returned as Constitutionalists, although the latter four were also included on the official list of Liberal candidates. The remaining 'others' were S. Saklatvalo (Battersea South, Communist), T. P. O'Connor (Liverpool, Scotland, Irish Nationalist), Dr E. Graham-Little (London University, Independent), A. Hopkinson (Mossley, Independent) and E. Scrymgeour (Dundee, Scottish Prohibition Party).

The Parties

The swing to the Conservatives was not uniform and was affected by factors such as the collapse of the Liberal vote. This tended to benefit the Conservatives in some areas (especially where anti-socialist pacts underpinned two-party cooperation) but advantaged Labour in other places (especially where there existed a nonconformist working class radical vote) (Cook, 1975: 324, 327). Leading members of the Labour Party felt that the Zinoviev letter was responsible for securing their defeat. Labour gained 16 seats from the Liberals and six from the Conservatives. These victories occurred in industrial constituencies (13 of which were in Yorkshire, the North East and in Scotland). Overall, 62 seats were lost, although the Party managed to raise its vote compared to the previous general election in 52 of these constituencies. Labour losses were greatest amongst middle-class voters and the Party performed especially badly in London suburbs and in Scotland. Five Labour MPs were sponsored by the Cooperative Party and 88 by trade unions.

Outside Northern Ireland, the Conservative Party gained 152 seats overall, 105 of which were at the Liberal Party's expense. Fifty-five gains were also secured from Labour, especially in industrial constituencies in Northern England where the Party had performed badly in 1923. Although it has been argued that extent of the Conservative victory was exaggerated by factors which included the fall in the number of unopposed returns and the inflated nature of the Unionist vote in Ulster caused by Sinn Fein contesting eight seats and Independents a further two (Cook, 1975: 319–20), the Party won a significant victory measured in terms of seats in the new Parliament.

A key problem which the Liberals encountered in 1924 was that the Party had little to say on the key issues which emerged during the course of the campaign (relations with Russia, the need for stable government and the record of the Labour government especially in connection with unemployment and housing) (Cook, 1975: 301). The party fielded 339 candidates (failing to contest136 seats which had been fought in 1923), and its vote declined from 4.3 million to 2.9 million. Overall, the Party lost 127 seats (mainly to the Conservative Party) and gained nine (eight of which were won from Labour with the help of anti-socialist pacts concluded with the Conservative Party). It successfully defended only 34 of the 158 constituencies it had won in 1923. Excluding the four Liberal candidates who stood as Constitutionalists, the Party's parliamentary representation was reduced to 40 in a House of Commons in which the Conservative Party possessed a large overall majority.

The Liberal Party lost heavily to the Conservatives in rural constituencies and was all but obliterated in the boroughs, succeeding in returning only six MPs in the 11 largest towns in England and Scotland. The Liberal performance was impeded by the intervention of the Labour Party in a number of marginal, Liberal-held constituencies. In addition to Asquith who lost Paisley in a straight fight with Labour by in excess of 2,000 votes, many leading Liberals were defeated. These included: Macnamara, Seely, Pringle, Lambert, Leif Jones, Geoffrey Howard, Isaac Foot, Spiers, Vivian Phillips, Walter Rea, Mackenzie Wood, Gwilym Lloyd George, Maxwell Thornton and A. J. Bonwick.

Scotland, Wales and Northern Ireland

The Conservative Party edged ahead of Labour as the largest party in Scotland, winning 36 of the 71 seats to Labour's 26. The Liberal Party won eight and the Scottish Prohibition Party one. Labour remained the largest party in Wales winning 16 of the 35 seats. The Liberal Party won 10 seats and the Conservatives improved their 1923 position by winning nine. In Northern Ireland, Ulster Unionists won all 12 seats. Sinn Fein contested eight constituencies (and Independents a further two). The reduced number of MPs returned unopposed compared to 1923 (two rather than eight) and had the effect of considerably raising the Ulster Unionist poll.

Consequence of the Election

Stanley Baldwin formed a Conservative government. However, the election had important consequences for the other main parties. Labour had confirmed its position as the only viable alternative government to the Conservatives as the election indicated that the Liberal Party could no longer claim to offer this option.

30 May 1929

Party Leaders
Stanley Baldwin (Conservative)
Ramsay MacDonald (Labour)
David Lloyd George (Liberal)

Background to the Election
Electoral Procedures and Practices
The 1926 Re-election of Ministers Act (1919) Amendment Act removed the need for newly appointed ministers of the Crown to seek re-election on accepting office. The 1928 Representation of the People (Equal Franchise) Act gave women aged 21 the right to vote. The enfranchisement of what was termed the 'flapper vote' provided political equality between men and women.

Conservatives
Party unity was aided by the inclusion of a number of prominent Coalitionists (Austen Chamberlain, Churchill, Lord Balfour and Lord Birkenhead) in Baldwin's Cabinet. The government enjoyed success in government with the conclusion of the Locarno treaties in 1925 regarding reparations which implied a new era of international cooperation. Economic policy included reducing spending and returning to the gold standard (at the pre-war parity) in 1925, the immediate effect of which was to increase drastically the price of British exports. Derating measures were introduced in 1929 to reduce the burden on agriculture and industry whereby farms were totally exempted from rates and manufacturing industry was partially exempted with the loss to local government revenue being made up by the Treasury. Other measures of domestic policy included the 1925 Pensions Act (which enabled contributors to the National Health Insurance Scheme to draw old age pensions at the age of 65), and the 1926 Electricity Act (which set up the national 'grid').

The government's response to the 1926 general strike (which is dicussed in more detail below) was to enact the 1927 Trades Disputes and Trade Union Act which outlawed general (or sympathetic) strikes, forbade trade unionism among civil servants and replaced 'contracting out' of the trade union political levy with 'contracting in'. However, severe economic difficulties remained, in particular a high level of unemployment which was above one million and stood in contrast to prosperity in America. A major difficulty with government policy was that the return to the gold standard had the effect of reducing exports. However, many Conservatives felt that enhanced British prosperity required protection but, although the restoration of the McKenna duties on the import of luxury goods aided some industries (such as motor car manufacture), Baldwin was loath to introduce the policy more widely and instead adopted a policy of caution which was encapsulated in his election slogan 'Safety First'.

Labour
Following the 1924 election, support grew in the Labour movement to utilise extra-parliamen-

tary methods to improve the conditions of the working class, which in part arose from the inability of the 1923–4 Labour government to improve substantially working-class conditions. These sentiments culminated in the general strike of 1926. The background of this event was conditions in the mining industry. During the First World War the mines had been taken under national direction and once the war had ended it was necessary to determine what to do with them. The Sankey Commission proposed nationalisation, but Lloyd George objected and the mines were eventually handed back to their private owners in 1921. This was followed by a wage cut and a lock-out.

The post-war economic depression especially hit the mining industry and following the end of the French occupation of the Ruhr coalfields in 1925, a fall in demand for British coal prompted the mine owners to press for wage reductions and an increase in the hours worked. The miners responded with the attitude of 'not a minute on the day, not a penny off the pay'. By 1925 the mines were losing around £1 million per month. The government responded by paying a temporary subsidy to the industry mainly to support wages (which amounted to around £23 million over a period of nine months) and appointed a Royal Commission (which was chaired by Sir Herbert Samuel). Samuel reported in 1926 and urged reorganisation (but not nationalisation), an end to the subsidy, a wage cut and the nationalisation of royalties. However, his proposals were accepted by neither side. The end of the subsidy prompted the mine owners to demand wage cuts and the miners' refusal to accept them led to a lock-out which started on 30 April 1926. This led the miners to turn to the general council of the Trade Union Congress.

The breakdown of the triple alliance (of miners, railway workers and transport workers) had left a vacuum in the labour movement which the general council of the TUC attempted to fill by securing authority to handle industrial disputes. This action arose from mixed motives which included a desire to protect the miners (and prevent another humilation of the kind which had occurred in 1921) and also to prevent strikes in particular industries by threatening sympathetic action as a sanction to secure compromise and/or government intervention. Thus in 1926 the general council intervened in the hope of fashioning a compromise acceptable to miners, mine owners and the government in the form of reorganisation and a pay cut. However, the government called the general council's bluff on a general strike which forced them to embark upon this action although their principal aim, having called it, was to end it at almost any cost. For this reason, the general strike lasted only a handful of days (3–12 May), whereas the miners soldiered on unaided for a period of seven months before being forced to return to work for lower wages and longer hours.

The government viewed the general strike as a constitutional issue in which the trade union movement was posing a threat to the ability of the government to rule. This attitude was fuelled by the move to the left in the TUC general council in 1924 in which a number of moderates were replaced by left-wingers who believed that industrial action rather than parliamentary politics was the only way to secure social justice for the working class. Accordingly, the government decided to face the unions head-on. The subsidy paid prior to Samuel's report enabled the government to stockpile essential supplies and a volunteer organisation – the Organisation for the Maintenance of Supplies – was established to perform strike-breaking duties. The police adopted an aggressive stance towards strikers during the general strike and both this and the prolonged miners' dispute were effectively countered by the state. Subsequently, the trade unions reverted to the control of moderates and adopted the stance of seeking an accommodation rather than a confrontation with capitalism, endorsing a corporatist stance which was evidenced by entering into discussions with employers' organisations in 1927 and 1928. In the Labour movement as a whole, support increased for parliamentary politics whose leaders had adopted a sceptical attitude towards the events of 1926.

A statement of Labour policies was published in the 1928 programme, *Labour and the Nation*. This put forward a wide range of policies to which Labour was committed but failed to provide a blueprint of the key issues which would be dealt with by a Labour government. Its hallmark was moderation, seeking to convince uncommitted, middle-of-the-road voters that they had nothing to fear from a Labour government. The ILP, however, attempted to put forward a more radical programme which called for the inauguration of a new period of class struggle. Labour was aided by the unpopularity of the Conservative government and, following its gain at Stockport in September 1925, it won a number of by-elections.

Liberals

The 1924 election affected the balance of power within the Parliamentary Party since over half of those elected in 1924 were former Coalition Liberal MPs or candidates. This enabled Lloyd George to become chairman of the Liberal MPs in December 1924 although Asquith (who had lost his seat but took a peerage in 1925 as the Earl of Oxford and Asquith) officially remained party leader. The rivalry between these two former Liberal prime ministers and their supporters was unabated. A group of nine Liberal MPs refused to accept Lloyd George and organised itself as a 'Radical Group' under Runciman. Asquith and Lloyd George then publicly disagreed during the 1926 general strike when Asquith supported the government's handling of the dispute, whereas Lloyd George favoured negotiation. However, a stroke forced Asquith to resign the Party leadership in October of that year and this position was assumed by Lloyd George who set about consolidating his control over all organs of the Party. However, his authority was adversely affected by the distrust and dislike which many in the Party felt towards him and which was replicated by public opinion. In addition to the dislike of Asquith's supporters towards Lloyd George, radical Liberals were also antagonistic towards him, the coercive policy pursued by his administration during the Irish War of Independence (which included the use of the 'Black and Tans') effectively disqualifying him in their eyes as a leader of progressive opinion. Accordingly, his renewed association with the Liberal Party drove many of them into the ranks of Labour. Herbert Samuel became Chairman of the Liberal Party Organisation in 1927 in an attempt to provide a bridge between Lloyd George and the Asquithian Liberals but this failed to produce total unity as was widened by the formation of the Asquithian organisation, the Liberal Council, in 1927.

Attempts were made after 1924 to improve Liberal organisation, in particular its finances which influenced the Party's ability to field candidates. A 'Million Fund' was launched in January 1925 which sought to raise money from ordinary Liberal supporters but this failed to make any significant improvement to Liberal finance. Liberal opponents of Lloyd George were particularly hostile to his insistence of retaining control over his personal political fund rather than handing it over to the Party organisation. The control over this fund (which in 1929 amounted to £765,000, producing an annual income after tax of over £30,000 a year), provided Lloyd George with the power to threaten to deprive the Party of finance as and when it suited him and created an image of a party which, in the words of the *Daily News* on 1 January 1929, could only exist on 'crumbs spoonfed from some rich man's table'.

Considerable and significant developments took place after 1926 in connection with the development of policy. Lloyd George and Herbert Samuel exerted much influence over this aspect of party affairs, seeking to take up the challenge of social and economic reform which the Party had embraced after 1906. This course of action aimed to rectify the situation faced by the Party following the 1923 general election when it had no distinctive policies on issues such as unemployment, the agricultural depression and social reform which could form the basis of a distinctive Liberal appeal to the electorate and which would justify radicals remaining in the Party. Influential thinkers (including Keynes, Layton and Rowntree) provided advice to the Party which produced significant contributions to major political problems. These included the report on coal and power in 1924, and the report on land and the nation in 1925. The latter, popularly known as the 'green book', proposed a range of reforms directed at the rural working class which could have formed the basis for progressive politics in the counties. Perhaps the most notable achievement, however, was the *Liberal Yellow Book, Britain's Industrial Future*, published in 1928, which sought to secure social justice through state involvement in the management of capitalism. Although this entailed state intervention, it provided an alternative to Labour's policies of large-scale nationalisation and central economic planning.

There were some signs that improvements in organisation and developments in policy associated with Samuel and Lloyd George were succeeding in improving the political fortunes of the Party. A number of seats were gained in by-elections. With the exception of Southwark North (which was gained from Labour in March 1927), these comprised Conservative defeats in rural, agricultural areas.

By-elections

A total of 63 by-elections occurred in the 1924–29 Parliament, of which 61 were contested. The Conservatives made a net loss of 16 seats, the Liberals a net gain of four, and Labour a net gain of 12.

Conduct of the Election

Conservatives

The Conservative election manifesto was contained in Mr Stanley Baldwin's election address. Trade and employment policies received considerable emphasis in this document. It renewed the promise made in 1924 that a Conservative government would not introduce the protective taxation of food and would not put forward a general tariff. However, the continuance of policies introduced after 1924 to provide for 'safeguarding' (which entailed providing protection to industries which were demonstrably suffering from unfair foreign competition) was endorsed in this document on the grounds that employment had been improved both in the safeguarded industries and those which relied on them for orders. An impartial tribunal would adjudicate on further requests made by manufacturing industries to be protected by safeguarding.

Other measures to aid British industry and help to stimulate exports included giving relief to productive industry from three-quarters of its rates burden, and reducing railway freight charges and dock dues. It was argued that railway modernisation had been aided by the remission of railway passenger duty in the budget, and road building and improvement had been (and would continue to be) financed by the state. The government also boasted of its progress in reorganising the generation and supply of electricity through the mechanism of the Central Electricity Generating Board (which was established in 1927). Measures designed to restore industrial prosperity were supplemented by innovations such as Training Centres which were designed to enable the unemployed to find work. It was asserted that the government had succeeded in reducing unemployment, despite the setback to trade in consequence of the 1926 general strike.

Other policies concerned with industry included the 1927 Trade Disputes Act which was designed to protect trade unions against the misuse of the strike weapon 'for political and revolutionary ends' and the trade unionist 'against intimidation and coercion in the free exercise of his industrial and political rights'. Much attention was directed at agricultural policy which was designed to relieve burdens, find markets, provide credit facilities and develop education and research. Opposition was expressed to the nationalisation of the land which was advanced by Socialists and Liberals.

The importance of social reform was emphasised in Baldwin's address. It was argued that the government had fulfilled its 1924 election promise regarding the provision of pensions to widows, orphans and old people, and had built 930,000 houses during its term of office which provided accommodation for around four million people. Plans were in place to improve the present procedure for slum clearance and attention had been paid to the welfare of mothers and children by extending the provision of facilities such as ante-natal clinics and infant welfare centres. A comprehensive system of education to enable people to pursue a connected course of study from childhood to manhood was proposed, utilising the cooperation of all types of schools and every type of educational effort.

The election address drew attention to the success of government policy in reducing the cost of living which had been achieved by policies which included lowering income tax, increasing the earned income allowance and the rates of children's allowances for income tax purposes, abolishing the duty on tea and rearranging the duty on sugar. These measures were supplemented by the return to the gold standard which had made a significant contribution to lowering the cost of living. It was argued that since 1924 wage rates had risen slightly while the cost of living had fallen by 10 per cent. The Conservative government had thus enhanced material prosperity. It was argued that proposals of the Socialist Party to increase direct taxation and of the Liberals to drain the nation's credit threatened to halt the improvements which had been made in the resources and spending power of the individual home.

The Conservative Party stated that the 1926 Imperial Conference had laid down the principles for the future development of the British Commonwealth and argued that imperial preference was the chief form of cooperation between these countries. It was also proposed to establish a Colonial Development Fund to assist colonial governments to finance approved projects of development. It was stated that the promotion of peace and disarmament had been the main objective of Conservative foreign policy. Security, on which peace depended, had been advanced by Germany entering the League of Nations and the Kellogg Pact whose signatories renounced war as an instrument of policy. The improvement of the international situation held out the prospect of an early advance towards disarmament.

Baldwin asked for the Conservative Party to be returned with an independent majority, stating that the alternatives were 'a socialist government with, or without, Liberal support, or a state of political chaos and uncertainty through the existence of three parties, none of which has a clear majority over the other two. Either of these contingencies would be disastrous to the welfare of industry and to the welfare of the nation as a whole'.

The Party faced a number of problems during the campaign which included the hostility of the Beaverbrook and Rothermere press.

Labour

The Party's election manifesto, *Labour's Appeal to the Nation*, was based on the 1928 policy statement, *Labour and the Nation*. This condemned the Conservative government's failure to deal effectively with unemployment and argued that Conservative policies to improve trade and solve unemployment consisted of 'safeguarding', which was argued to be responsible for unemployment, low wages, poverty and high costs of living. Labour gave an unqualified pledge that a Labour government would deal 'immediately and practically' with this issue. Its programme to achieve this consisted of stimulating national development and trade prosperity through measures which included housing and slum clearance, the reorganisation of railways and transport and electrification. Emphasis was placed on restoring prosperity to the depressed industries, increasing the purchasing power of the working classes, developing markets overseas (especially in India and the Crown colonies), and using export credits and trade facilities guarantees to stimulate the export trades of iron and steel, engineering and textile manufactures.

Measures to alleviate distress for the unemployed would be introduced pending their return to work, and the school leaving age would be raised to 15 to relieve congestion in the labour market and to provide young persons with improved education and vocational training.

Other domestic policies contained in the manifesto included the nationalisation of the mines and minerals, building houses for rent and dealing drastically with slum clearance. Taxes on food and other necessaries would be abolished, with the shortfall of revenue being made up by death duties on large estates and by graduating income tax and surtax with the aim of relieving the smaller taxpayers. A comprehensive coordination and extension of all existing pension schemes would be undertaken, and workers' conditions would be improved through measures which included enacting a Factories Bill and amending the Workmen's Compensation Acts and Trade Union Law. Labour's policy for land and agriculture was to transfer land to public control.

In foreign affairs, the manifesto stated that international peace was one of the key election issues and accused the Conservative government of obstructing the work of the League of Nations and the International Labour Office. Labour pledged to accept the general Act of Arbitration, Conciliation and Judicial Settlement approved by the League.

The government was accused of provoking the industrial unrest which led to the general strike and of rewarding its friends by remitting taxation while workless men and women had been thrown on to the Poor Law. It was argued that indirect taxation had increased under the Conservative government. A considerable part of the manifesto was devoted to responding to Conservative scare tactics which, it was asserted, cost Labour victory at the previous election. It was argued that the Labour Party 'is neither Bolshevik nor communist. It is opposed to force, revolution and confiscation as means of establishing the New Social Order'. The manifesto insisted that a Labour government was the only alternative to the present Conservative one since the Liberals could be no more than a small minority in the new Parliament.

Liberals

The Liberal party sought to reverse its political fortunes at the 1929 general election by fielding 500 candidates with the intention of securing the return of a Liberal government. The key items of Liberal policy were specified in Mr Lloyd George's election address. This stated his belief that the Conservatives would be defeated at the election and asserted that the issue was whether the nation would entrust its destinies to the Liberal Party or the Socialist Party. The experience and statesmanlike qualities of the Liberal leadership were contrasted with the inexperience of the Socialist Party which, additionally, was committed to policies which would be 'disastrous to trade, commerce and industry of the land'.

Lloyd George asserted that peace was the most important issue before the country. He affirmed his support for the League of Nations and the Kellogg Pact and argued that, by contrast, the Conservative government was spending £112 million a year on armaments but only £100,000 a year on the League of Nations. He emphasised the importance of arms reduction in line with the suggestion of President Hoover.

It was argued that unemployment was the main domestic issue facing the country. Lloyd George insisted that freer trade for all nations was the only road to national, imperial and international prosperity. He stated that Conservative policy for dealing with this issue was to persevere with the policy that had been pursued since 1924 and which by 1929 had left one million Britons out of work. He dismissed Labour's policy as 'if they are returned to power they will appoint another committee'. Liberal policy was developed in greater detail in the pamphlets *We Can Conquer Unemployment* and *A Liberal Call to the Nation*. These proposals were based on Keynesian economics and derived from ideas which were initially enunciated in the 1928 *Yellow Book*. It was argued that the many separate problems that faced the nation today (such as problems of trade, of employment, of overcrowding, and of restricted opportunities) could be dealt with only by an organised plan of reconstruction, opening the road to a more ample prosperity which all the people would share. It was intended to cut unemployment by introducing an emergency programme of public works, financed by borrowing on schemes of national utility and development such as electricity, telephones, housing, roads and railways. It was implied, without being fully articulated, that such actions would free 'frozen savings' for investment purposes, thereby triggering industrial activity. In his election address, Lloyd George stated that the essence of Liberal proposals was to break down barriers to international trade, encourage harmonious relations between employers and employees, seek greater efficiency in industry and restore the Trade Facilities Act.

In addition to the conquest of unemployment and the restoration of prosperity to British industries, the Liberal campaign emphasised other issues which included the reduction of unproductive expenditure, temperance reform, the completion of proper housing for the people and slum clearance, the revitalisation of agriculture, leasehold reform, the expansion of education, imperial unity, and the devolution of government.

Result of the Election

A total number of 1,730 candidates contested the election, with seven MPs being returned unopposed. The result was:

Party	Votes	Vote %	MPs
Labour	8,370,417	37.0%	287
Conservative	8,301,568	36.7%	250
Liberal	5,208,635	23.0%	59
Ulster Unionist	354,657	1.6% [68.0%]	10
Others	288,818	1.2%	6
Irish Nationalist	24,177	0.1% [6.6%]	3
Irish Liberal	100,103	0.4% [16.8%]	0
Total	*22,648,375*		*615*

The turnout was 76.3 per cent.

The 'others' were Dr E. Graham-Little (London University, Independent), N. McLean (Glasgow Govan, Independent Labour), Sir R. Newman (Exeter, Independent), Miss E. Rathbone, (Combined English Universities, Independent), Sir T. Robinson (Stretford, Independent), E. Scrymgeour (Dundee, Scottish Prohibition Party). Fourteen women MPs were elected.

The Parties

Labour made significant gains at the Conservatives' expense in London and also improved its position in South East England. It made considerable gains at the expense of the Conservatives in Northern England and overtook the Conservatives as the dominant party in the Midlands (which included winning six of Birmingham's 12 seats). Although Labour's progress in East Anglia was halted by a Liberal resurgence, overall Liberal intervention aided Labour to win a number of seats on minority votes. Nine of Labour's MPs were sponsored by the Cooperative Party and 115 by trade unions.

The radical programme put forward by the Liberal Party failed to produce more than a minor revival, in which 59 Liberal MPs were returned with 23.4 per cent of the popular vote. Twenty-eight of these seats were held on narrow majorities with a margin of less than 5 per cent over the candidate in second place, which in most cases (20) was a candidate of the Conservative Party for whom 1929 was a bad year. The Liberal Party gained 38 seats and emerged from the election strong in the Celtic Fringe (winning 13 seats in Scotland, nine in Wales, five in Cornwall and one seat in each of the Scottish and Welsh universities). In county areas it performed best in rural rather than in middle-class seats and won 34 of the 150 most agricultural seats in the United Kingdom. However, Labour's appeal to rural working-class voters impeded the Liberal Party's progress in these areas. Overall, the Party lost 19 seats, 17 of which were won by Labour. This resulted indicated the inability of the Liberal Party to recapture the working-class vote in industrial areas (further ground being lost to Labour in the North East, Yorkshire, Lancashire and London's East End).

Scotland, Wales and Northern Ireland

Labour overtook the Conservatives to become the largest party in Scotland, winning 36 of the 71 seats. The Conservatives won 20, the Liberals 13, and Independent Labour and the Scottish Prohibition Party each won one seat. Labour increased its domination of Welsh politics by winning 25 of the 35 seats. The Liberals won nine and the Conservatives one.

In Northern Ireland, the Unionists won 10 of the 12 seats and the Nationalists two. A further seat was won for the Irish Nationalists by T. P. O'Connor who retained his seat of Liverpool, Scotland. The Liberal Party's campaign in Northern Ireland secured them in excess of 16 per cent of the total poll but failed to provide them with any MPs.

Consequence of the Election

Labour was the largest single party in the new House of Commons (with 287 seats to the Conservatives' and Ulster Unionists' 260) but, as in 1923, lacked an overall majority. Additionally, including the votes obtained by the Ulster Unionists, the Conservative Party obtained a higher national poll and a large number (in excess of 120) of Labour MPs held their seats on minority votes. However, Baldwin chose not to test his position in the new Parliament and immediately resigned, thus not requiring the Liberals to 'put Labour in' as had been the case in 1924. The election also confirmed the permanency of the Liberal Party's third party status.

27 October 1931

Party Leaders

Stanley Baldwin (Conservative)*
David Lloyd George (Liberal)*
Arthur Henderson (Labour)
(*The Conservative and Liberal parties fought the election as members of the National government under the leadership of Ramsay MacDonald.)

Background to the Election

Timing of the Election
As is discussed in more detail below, in August 1931 a flight from sterling forced the government to consider reducing public spending in order to restore confidence and balance the budget. No agreement could be fashioned within the Labour government concerning a package of spending cuts and in consequence the government resigned. MacDonald agreed to remain as head of a National government which comprised a few Labour Members together with the Conservative and Liberal parties. It was initially intended that this new government would remain in office in order to carry through an emergency budget and enact legislation to deal with the economic crisis and, having achieved that, a fresh general election fought on the basis of party politics would be held.

Conservatives
The defeat experienced in 1929 surprised many Conservatives and there were initial moves against Baldwin's leadership. However, these came to nothing, in part as there was no clear alternative to replace him and also as much of the opposition to him was led by Lords Beaverbrook and Rothermere who were respectively 'disliked' and 'hated' within Conservative circles (Thorpe, 1991: 38). The Loyalist Duff Cooper's victory at the Westminster St George's by-election in March 1931 against a candidate sponsored by these two press barons significantly reinforced Baldwin's position.

Key developments in policy occurred after 1929. Protection was more vigorously advocated within Conservative circles and at the 1929 Party Conference the leadership accepted a vaguely worded resolution in favour of Empire trade and development. Beaverbrook actively promoted protection to the extent of running candidates against official Conservatives in by-elections and Baldwin's eventual willingness to formally adopt this policy, in the form of protection of manufacturing industry, imperial preference and the use of measures such as duties and quotas on imports of foreign foodstuffs to protect the agricultural industry, secured Party unity. Baldwin had long been in favour of protection but moved hesitantly towards endorsing it after 1929 since (as had been shown in 1923) public support for free trade remained strong and this policy also had the potential to split the Party (and alienate free trade Liberals such as Sir John Simon whose support Conservatives wished to court). However, the economic slump served to popularise protection and also to minimise the level of internal dissent. Churchill, a leading free trader, chose the issue of Conservative policy towards India rather than free trade as his pretext for resigning from the Shadow Cabinet.

Conservative dissent towards protection was also minimised by a second policy development which was to emphasise the need to cut public spending. This implied halting the expansion of social services until the nation was in a better position to pay for them. There were several arguments in favour of this course of action which included the belief that tax rises had a stifling effect on enterprise and directly contributed to increased unemployment. An emphasis on retrenchment was also politically astute since the Labour government and the Labour Party were divided on this matter (especially the issue of unemployment insurance) and it was appealing to Liberal opinion. Thus while protection remained a key topic in Conservative speeches, as the election approached it was relegated into second place behind the call to reduce public spending.

After 1929 the political fortunes of the Conservative Party began to improve markedly. This was measured by progress in organisation in the constituencies and the performance of the Party in by-elections in which, after February 1930, the Party demonstrated advances at Labour's expense. Some divisions occurred (especially regarding India where the official line of seeking to liberalise British rule and move towards Dominion status as was advocated by the Viceroy, Lord Eward Irwin, was rejected by diehard opinion led by Churchill) but they had no major impact on the vitality of the Party. The key problem was how to secure Labour's defeat and bring about a general election. The assiduous wooing of Sir John Simon (who was unhappy with the Liberal policy of keeping Labour in office) was attempted but he moved slowly to break with the Liberals and when he finally resigned the Liberal whip in June 1931 he brought with him only two other MPs. A pact with Lloyd George was also contemplated (in which he would be offered electoral reform by a future Conservative government as the price for ousting Labour) but this too came to nothing. These failures to secure Labour's defeat ultimately led Conservatives to contemplate the formation of a National government as the route to power.

Labour

The government achieved some early successes, especially in the area of foreign affairs (which included Egypt and the reparations issue). In October 1929, MacDonald visited America where he became the first British Prime Minister to address Congress. Progress was also made in organising a world disarmament conference. In domestic policy, some liberalisation of the administration of unemployment benefit and pensions occurred and some success was achieved in the clearance of slum houses.

However, the key issue facing the government was economic policy and especially unemployment which the 1929 election manifesto had specifically pledged to cut. In the summer of 1929 the number of unemployed rose to 1.2 million. However, the October 1929 Wall Street crash and the subsequent Great Depression in America significantly worsened the situation: 1.5 million became unemployed by the spring of 1930 and this figure rose to two million in June and 2.7 million in December. Some small falls were recorded during the early months of 1931 but by July of that year the figure again stood in excess of 2.7 million.

MacDonald's initial response was to appoint a team under J. H. Thomas (consisting of Lansbury, Mosley and Thomas Johnston) to formulate policy. However, this failed to secure any improvement in the situation. Thomas proposed a limited scheme of public works and colonial development but his suggestion for the rationalisation of industry threatened to make matters worse rather than better. Other members of this team produced alternative ideas which were contained in the 'Mosley Memorandum' which was sent directly to MacDonald in January 1930. This memorandum proposed economic expansion through public works, the development of imperial self-sufficiency removing the need for imports, and the reduction of the size of the labour market through the provision of increased pensions and the raising of the school leaving age. This programme would be implemented by a small executive modelled on Lloyd George's War Cabinet. This was rejected by the Prime Minister and resulted in Mosley resigning from the government in May 1930 when he complained of the lethargy affecting the Cabinet. His ideas did, however, win considerable support at the Labour Conference later that year and his popularity was demonstrated by his election to the NEC at the expense of Thomas. A ministerial reshuffle saw Thomas moved to the Dominions Office and MacDonald took personal control of unemployment policy, but no radical initiatives to deal with the problem were forthcoming. This inaction, or a policy of 'drift and wait for better times', perhaps reflected the views of MacDonald and Snowden that unemployment was more acceptable than a crisis of confidence leading to the collapse of Sterling which would have devastating consequences for a nation which imported much of its food (Thorpe, 1991: 12).

The government's inability to offer any constructive policy to combat unemployment gravely affected party unity. The Independent Labour Party was especially disenchanted with Labour's record on this issue and at its 1930 Conference a resolution was passed to instruct its MPs to give priority to ILP policy over government policy. A key difficulty was the impact which the economic crisis posed for reformist socialist ideology. The nature of the economic crisis challenged the vitality of the beliefs of those whose approach was based on capitalism producing profits which could be redistributed to the poorer and weaker members of society.

The Labour government experienced problems other than economic and ideological ones. The Cabinet was acrimonious, MacDonald having poor relations with both Snowden and Henderson. Relations with the trade unions also became strained. Too little was done to address issues of concern to the unions, and only in the 1930–31 session of Parliament was an attempt made to repeal the 1927 Trade Disputes and Trade Unions (when reform was sabotaged by Liberal amendments). The appointment of a Royal Commission on Unemployment Insurance in December 1930 aroused particular union criticism since its brief was to consider economies whereas Labour's policy was to improve benefits and extend the insurance scheme to all workers. This episode led the TUC general secretary, Walter Citrine, to protest directly to MacDonald. The government's attempts to raise the school leaving age to 15 also resulted in dissent and had to be abandoned. Many working-class people were opposed to a measure which would have a detrimental impact on their family economies and the Catholic Church viewed it as an attempt to impose secular education.

The difficulties which the government encountered after 1929 affected party morale and this had a particularly adverse impact on constituency organisation. Support for the Party began to fall away: Labour performed badly in by-elections, commencing with Sheffield Brightside in February 1930 and in the November 1930 municipal elections.

The Sterling Crisis and the Formation of the National Government
The problem of unemployment was then aggravated by a further economic problem in the form of a Sterling crisis whose roots lay in the European financial crisis which led to the collapse of a leading Austrian bank in May 1931 and the subsequent freezing of British assets held in Austria and Germany. Foreign assets held in London began to be withdrawn, which led the Bank of England to raise the bank rate by 1 per cent on 23 July to counter the drain on gold. Short-term remedies were sought in borrowing from the Federal Reserve Bank in New York and the Bank of France and increasing the fiduciary issue, but longer-term measures were suggested in the May Report on National Expenditure which predicted a large budget deficit and proposed to balance it by measures which included introducing major economies in national insurance expenditure (including a 20 per cent cut in unemployment benefit), reducing salaries throughout the public sector and introducing new taxes. Although the Chancellor, Snowden, accepted the general drift of the report, viewing the maintenance of free trade and the gold standard as key priorities, many in the Labour movement were opposed to economies, especially those which affected the unemployed.

MacDonald appreciated that he would have difficulties in getting proposals emanating from the May Report through Parliament and thus consulted leading representatives of the Conservative and Liberal parties. Urgent action was required, however, since the scale of the budget deficit was undermining confidence in Sterling. Between 4 and 11 August, the Bank of England spent £21 million to support Sterling. Both opposition parties favoured cutting spending as the means to balance the budget and the issue was considered by the Cabinet Economic Committee which met several times in August against the background of a higher budget deficit than had been predicted by the May Report. Spending cuts of £56 million were eventually approved by the Cabinet on 19 August, but these were deemed insufficient by Snowden andunacceptable to the TUC. Subsequently, it became clear that the scale of these cuts were viewed as insufficient by the opposition leaders and by the bankers, all of whom believed that more drastic action was required in order to restore prevent a flight from sterling. Further Cabinet meetings were held on 22 August but it was agreed to defer any decision on an additional £20 million package of cuts until the New York bankers J. P. Morgan and Co had been sounded out as to whether they would be willing to give the government either a long-term loan or short-term credit. MacDonald was also by now warning the opposition leaders that resignations from his government were likely if further economies had to be made and was also advising King George V that he might have to resign. In response, the monarch met with the opposition leaders, whose acceptance of the undesirability of holding a general election in the middle of an economic crisis led them to express support in principle for backing MacDonald either as leader of a Labour government or as Prime Minister of a newly constituted National administration.

On 23 August, MacDonald put economies to his Cabinet which included a 10 per cent cut in the rate of unemployment benefit. Nine members refused to accept this proposal, and it was clear that the Labour government could not continue in office. MacDonald thus tendered his resignation to the King, but George V urged him to reconsider and informed him he would secure backing from the opposition parties. A further meeting on 24 August, consisting of George V, MacDonald, Baldwin and Samuel, resulted in the formation of a National government whose one specific purpose was to save Sterling by implementing measures to balance the budget. Only four members of the Labour Cabinet (Snowden, Thomas, Sankey and Lord Amulree) followed MacDonald's lead.

The National government secured a majority of 60 in the House of Commons on 9 September. The government's main action was to bring forward a National Economy Bill which provided for spending cuts of £56 million together with a 10 per cent cut in national insurance benefit. Additionally, on 10 September Snowden's budget proposed to raise taxes by more than £80 million. However, these measures failed to stave off a further run on Sterling in September. Confidence in the pound was adversely affected by factors that included the possibility that an early election would return a Labour government which would reverse all the cuts introduced by the National government. The Invergordon 'Mutiny' added to the general sense of unease. Withdrawals became so heavy between 16 and 19 September that MacDonald, Baldwin and Samuel were forced to suspend the gold standard. Legislation to do this (the Gold Standard (Amendment) Act) was passed on 21 September and the bank rate was also increased from 4.5 per cent to 6 per cent. The consequence of leaving the gold standard was that the pound lost around one-third of its value and this was likely to increase the cost of living. This, in conjunction with higher taxes and benefit cuts, would inevitably create unpopularity for the government, even though MacDonald announced that no cut would exceed 10 per cent. Although leaving the gold standard was a symbolic defeat for the government, Sterling did not subsequently crash.

The National government had been formed through the action of political elites and had no mandate from the electors. Pressure by the press and political opinion (especially within the Conservative Party) to hold a general election as soon as measures to counter the economic crisis had been put in place were made almost as soon as the government was formed, but the continuance of the emergency which brought the National government into being justified the maintenance of inter-party cooperation on a longer-term basis. Baldwin favoured an early election so that a mandate could be obtained for the introduction of tariffs to remedy the adverse balance of trade but he was willing to remain a member of a National administration under MacDonald. Although the Liberal Party favoured remaining in a National government, they were deeply divided as to the desirability of holding an early election. The recuperating Lloyd George (and Samuel too) feared that an election at that time would renew the flight from sterling and would also be used to sanction the abandonment of free trade. As part of a National administration, Liberals would not be in a position to argue the case against protection, in particular the tax on food which was likely to be highly unpopular. This might benefit Labour who could make out such a case. However, others, who took their lead from Sir John Simon, supported an early election, partly because they were concerned that a delayed election might be held against the background of a further deterioration in economic circumstances, such as high unemployment, which would benefit the Labour Party.

The Conservative Party attempted to heighten divisions within the Liberal Party on this issue by their insistence in Cabinet on 28 and 29 September that, in placing an appeal before the electors at a general election, the National government should be able to use any measures, including tariff reform, to solve the nation's economic difficulties. This insistence might be expected to force the Samuelites from office who could then be replaced by the Simonites.

Samuel did contemplate whether an alternative political arrangement (in the form of a Liberal–Labour administration under MacDonald) could be organised, but eventually (to the surprise of Conservatives) he was willing to accept a formula agreed in Cabinet on 5 October, whereby the National government would ask electors for a free hand to deal with the economic crisis but would make only vague references to import controls. Each of the three party leaders would have the right to place their specific views on economic policy and measures to redress the balance of trade in their own manifestos.

Samuel's decision about remaining in the National government and fighting the next election on this basis were influenced by several factors. Contesting the next election within the framework of a National government would enable his party to benefit from anti-Labour pacts in the constituencies. He would subsequently be in the position of being able to attack tariffs from within the government rather than from the political margins outside it. He may also have calculated that public opinion would not have endorsed the Party leaving a government which had been formed only a few weeks previously in order to rescue the country from its financial difficulties, and was aware that quitting the government would have split the Party which would have performed badly in consequence. Additionally, the electorate may not have placed similar prominence to the issue of free trade as did Liberals such as Samuel and Lloyd George, viewing economic problems including the adverse balance of trade and the possible collapse of the currency as more important matters.

Liberals

The result of the 1929 election opened the possibility of Lloyd George being in a bargaining position in which electoral reform could be demanded as the price for Liberal support for a government formed from either of the two major parties. Although electoral reform had not previously assumed a major position in Liberal policy, the Party's relative failure in that election prompted some Liberals to view it as a key issue. One justification for this was that in this election more than two candidates stood in 461 constituencies and only 173 of these secured 50 per cent or more of the vote. However, Baldwin's decision to resign before meeting Parliament ensured that a Labour government under MacDonald would be formed. Lloyd George was thus left with the option of supporting it or risking a further general election in which it was most likely that the Party's position would deteriorate.

Accordingly, Lloyd George determined to support the Labour government in the hope of securing concessions from them, in particular regarding electoral reform. Labour was not traditionally sympathetic to electoral reform, believing that electors would find the system confusing, that the size of multi-member constituencies would be too large and that it would be difficult to devise a satisfactory method to cater for casual vacancies which were currently dealt with through by-elections. Negative sentiments of this nature help to explain the Liberal Party's inability to secure a measure of electoral reform from the 1923 Labour government.

Lack of progress in securing this objective led Lloyd George to flex his political muscle and oppose the second reading of the Coal Mines Bill in December 1929. He then voted against the government in amendments which were tabled during the Bill's subsequent committee stage. However, this decision resulted in splits in the Parliamentary Party which witnessed Liberal MPs voting in different division lobbies. This situation led Lloyd George to consider resigning but his position was strengthened when a meeting of the Parliamentary Party gave an overwhelming vote of confidence to his leadership on 21 February 1930. This prompted Lloyd George to end further opposition to the coal mines legislation and encouraged him to seek a closer relationship with the Labour government. This course of action was aided by the government's announcement on 18 March that it would introduce legislation on electoral reform if it remained in office, which gave the Liberal Party a vested interest in ensuring Labour's survival. Ultimately, Labour introduced an electoral reform measure in 1931 which proposed the introduction of the alternative vote. This passed the House of Commons but had not passed through the House of Lords when the administration fell that year.

However, the close relationships between the Liberal Party and the Labour government resulted in further divisions in the ranks of the Parliamentary Liberal Party. A number of Liberals believed that the Liberal Party stood to gain very little by offering support to the Labour government, whereas an alliance with the Conservative Party might produce more tangible and long-term benefits, particularly inclusion in government which Labour would not offer the Liberals. Sir John Simon marshalled the case for Liberal backing of a Conservative government. Divisions within the Liberal Party over their attitude to a Labour government soon became evident on issues which included the Land Tax and the reversal of the Trade Disputes Act. These divisions culminated in a major schism in the ranks of the Parliamentary Party in March 1931. The decision of a number of Liberal MPs to defy their whip and vote against the government on the Electoral Reform Bill on 16 March 1931 in order to distance themselves from Labour prompted the immediate resignation of the Chief Whip, Sir Archibald Sinclair (although he subsequently agreed to resume this position). A meeting of the Parliamentary Party later took place, at which Lloyd George's leadership was again on the line. At this meeting a resolution was passed which sought to preserve party unity. This affirmed the independence of the Party, enunciated Liberal policy and agreed to support 'this or any government' to put it into effect. It was passed by 33 votes to 17. A further challenge to Lloyd George was mounted at the meeting of the National Liberal Federation in May 1931 but was overwhelmingly defeated. This resulted in a permanent breach in the ranks of the Parliamentary Party in which leading opponents to the tactic of cooperating with the Labour government, John Simon, Sir Robert Hutchison and Ernest Brown, resigned the Liberal whip in June 1931.

In addition to problems underpinned by Liberal support for the Labour government, other difficulties affecting the Party's position occured after 1929. The further development of radical policy enunciated in the 1929 election manifesto was halted after 1929 when, in addition to the quest for electoral reform, the Party adopted a more negative stance in which it reverted to its historic roots, and advocated retrenchment and free trade. Atrophism went beyond policy and affected other aspects of the Party's political activities. The reduced availability of money from the Lloyd George Fund had an adverse effect on central and local organisation, and particularly the selection of candidates. The Party fought around half of the contested by-elections after 1929 and was unlikely to improve on this position in a future general election.

However, the difficulties encountered by the Party after 1929 were temporarily masked when MacDonald's government broke up in August 1931. This led not to a general election but to the formation of the National government under Ramsay MacDonald which was designed to prevent the collapse of Sterling. The Conservative and Liberal parties joined the new administration, with a number of leading Liberals including Samuel, and Sinclair (but not Lloyd George who was ill at the time) taking ministerial office.

By-elections

A total of 36 by-elections occurred during the 1929–31 Parliament, of which 33 were contested. The Conservative Party made a net gain of three seats, Labour a net loss of two and the Liberals a net loss of one.

Conduct of the Election

Victory by the National government was viewed as inevitable at the outset of the campaign.

The time-honoured practice of holding public meetings was used by all parties to get their case across to the electorate. Some of these witnessed violence, an extreme example of which was a riot in Birmingham on 17 October in which 15,000 persons prevented Sir Oswald Mosley from speaking. Additionally, the media was used to project the parties' political messages.

Newspaper circulation considerably increased amongst the working class in the inter-war years. In 1931 the National government was aided (and Labour believed that their cause was substantially harmed) by the support given to it by all national daily newspapers in England, Wales and Scotland with the exception of the *Daily Herald* and by all Sunday papers save the *Reynolds Illustrated News* which supported Labour. The major provincial titles, with the exception of the *Manchester Guardian*, also backed the National government. Additionally, the *Daily Worker* supported the Communist Party. Other sources of information came from party political broadcasts on the radio (six broadcasts being given by supporters of the National government and four by those opposed to it), and by newsreels shown in the cinemas (although politics was only one subject among many covered by the five companies concerned with this medium, one of which chose to totally ignore the election campaign). BBC news bulletins also provided objective information related to the election.

Supporters of the National Government

The key objectives of the National government were to balance the budget, restore confidence in Sterling and remedy the trade deficit. Policies which included the need for exerting strict controls over public spending were put forward during the campaign to achieve these objectives. Each party which participated in the National government issued its own election manifesto. These were, however, linked to a statement entitled, *An Appeal to the Nation by the Rt Hon. J. Ramsay MacDonald, Prime Minister*, the key feature of which was to ask for a free hand (or a 'doctor's mandate') to cope with the crisis then facing the nation. This meant that no options were eliminated in advance and this course of action was justified on the grounds that, 'As it is impossible to foresee in the changing circumstances of today what may arise, no one can set out a programme of detail on which specific pledges can be given. The government must therefore be free to consider every proposal likely to help such as tariffs, expansion of exports, and contraction of imports, commercial treaties and mutual economic arrangements with the dominions.'

There was no formal attempt (as had been the case in 1918 with the use of 'coupons') to ensure that only one candidate who supported the National government was fielded in each constituency. MacDonald favoured an arrangement whereby the incumbent party in a constituency would be given a free run in the election and this was largely achieved, with candidates from parties associated with the National government standing against each other in only 88 constituencies (Thorpe, 1991: 177). However, Conservative withdrawals in favour of Liberal candidates were heavily biased towards the Simonites (35 : 19) (Stannage, 1980: 22) and particular sources of Samuelite Liberal discontent were Conservative challenges to five Liberal ministers. In total, 11 Samuelite Liberals (compared to only three Simonites) faced Conservative opposition, including Samuel himself (a situation which Baldwin admitted was not 'quite what I should call playing the game') (Thorpe, 1991: 168).

Liberals
As has been observed above, the Liberal Party entered the 1931 general election as a disunited Party whose official leader, Lloyd George, was recuperating from surgery. The Simonites were moving closer towards constructing permanent ties with the Conservatives and Lloyd George was implacably opposed to holding an election and angry with Samuel for the concessions he had made. Lloyd George and his supporters were quick to point out the dangers of too close an alliance with the Conservative Party under the banner of a National government which might prove to be permanent. Lloyd George was concerned that the Liberal manifesto, *Liberal Address to the Nation*, contained criticisms of the Labour Party (in particular its proposals to restore recent economies) but none of the Conservatives. He thus refused to give the manifesto his endorsement, nor would he fund the Liberal campaign with the exception of those candidates who were unequivocal in their support of free trade (which was limited to his 'family' group of four and Frank Owen and Edgar Wallace, since the Party's official line was to campaign for the 'free hand'). Lloyd George effectively ran his own campaign in 1931 in which he emphasised the virtues of free trade (arguing that the Conservatives and their 'malarial swamp' of protection were the main danger facing the nation), and urged electors to vote Labour in the absence of a Liberal candidate.

The manifesto stated the Party's objections to holding an election at that juncture in the nation's affairs but argued that it was a duty to cooperate in securing a strong and stable government composed of people from all parties. However, reference was also made to the need for an independent Liberal Party which would exert effective influence on the government and in the coming Parliament. This perhaps suggested a view that Liberal participation in the National government would be of limited duration (Thorpe, 1991: 158).

The manifesto emphasised that the prime concern was to avoid inflation and resultant financial disaster which was alleged would be the consequence of a Labour victory. The longer-term requirement of restoring the balance of trade was forcibly advocated through measures which included the production of more food, reduction of imports, and the increase of exports. It attacked existing tariffs for being responsible for the existing level of depression and unemployment and pointed out that high tariffs had failed to save either America or Germany from heavier unemployment than that in Britain which had adhered to a policy of free trade. The traditional free trade attack on food taxes was articulated and it was concluded that Britain's abandonment of free trade would aggravate the divisions between nations. International action to stabilise currency and deal with war debts and reparations was called for and the document also emphasised the importance of the forthcoming world disarmament conference, the League of Nations and the Indian round table conference.

The Liberal manifesto implied that the Conservative Party was reactionary. The Liberal campaign did go somewhat further than in its criticisms of this party by arguing that an election at that time was unnecessary, asserting that tariffs were unnecessary, and declaring opposition to the imposition of any food taxes. Individual candidates frequently expressed support for free trade in their election manifestos.

Opposition to Lloyd George's decision to support the Labour government was mounted by Sir John Simon, and ultimately resulted in the establishment of the Liberal National Group in 1931. Although the Liberal Nationals did not issue their own election address, Simon's election address to his constituents in Spen Valley, entitled 'A National Call to Liberals: Sir John Simon on the Need for National Unity', served as a statement of policy for this segment of Liberal opinion. In this document he argued that the election of the TUC-dominated Labour Party would be a national disaster and advocated 'some application of tariffs'. Simon further envisaged that the government's work would take 'some years' to carry out. During the contest, relations between the Samuelites and Simonites became strained, and Simon's speech at Cleckheaton on 12 October 1931 was one occasion during the 1931 campaign when the leaders of these two wings of the Liberal Party (Simon and Samuel) attacked each other,

Conservatives

The Conservative Party entered the contest as a united party under Baldwin. Their election manifesto, *The Nation's Duty: Mr Stanley Baldwin's General Election Message*, gave prominence to the need to balance the budget and placed considerable emphasis on remedying the trade deficit. Although reference was made to securing international action to solve some of Britain's problems, it was argued that a 'carefully designed and adjusted tariff' was the quickest and most effective way of protecting the British home market and promoting the reduction of existing tariffs against British goods. It was further argued that agriculture should be aided by the prohibition of dumping and by other measures which included prohibitions, quotas or duties. The manifesto also argued that imperial economic unity should be secured when the imperial conference resumed at Ottawa. Baldwin (who was uncontested in his constituency of Bewdley) was able to devote much of the campaign to touring the country, and the Conservative case was also presented through the novel mechanism of cinema vans.

National Labour

Labour supporters of MacDonald began to organise themselves at local level in order not to be considered as a mere appendage of Conservative Central Office. The need to establish an independent organisation was also caused by MacDonald's expulsion from the Labour Party on 28 September.

Labour

Although the National government was widely viewed in Labour circles as a Conservative administration in disguise, its formation under MacDonald posed the Party with a number of dilemmas. MacDonald retained some support among reformist opinion and it remained possible that Labour could belatedly join the government, a course of action which would stave off an early general election. It was also hoped that a delayed election would help Labour, since their deficiency in government between 1929 and 1931 would be fading from the minds of the electors and they would be in a position to blame both Conservatives and Liberals for the cuts introduced by the National government. Considerations of this nature contributed to delaying the formal expulsion of MacDonald and his supporters from the Labour Party until 28 September. However, it was most unlikely that Conservative supporters of the National government would agree to a delayed election as they wanted an immediate appeal to be made to the country in order to secure a mandate for protection.

A joint meeting of the TUC general council, Labour's NEC and the executive of the Parliamentary Labour Party took place on 26 August at which it was agreed to oppose the new government. This action was approved by a meeting of the Parliamentary Labour Party on 28 August and was confirmed by the overwhelming vote of Labour MPs who opposed a vote of confidence in the new government on 8 September 1931. The 26 August meeting applauded the actions of the nine former ministers who had opposed MacDonald and a committee was formed to draft a manifesto. This document branded the government as a stooge of the financiers who sought to reverse recent advances in social policy and (in contradiction to the stance which had been formerly adopted by the ex-ministers) all cuts were condemned. Measures such as the mobilisation of foreign investments, the temporary suspension of the sinking fund, the taxation of fixed interest-bearing securities and of other unearned income and measures to reduce the burden of war debts were advocated as responses to the economic crisis. However, this statement failed to provide the basis of a unified policy on which the Party could fight the forthcoming election and it was subsequently subject to much revision.

Labour faced numerous difficulties following the formation of the National government. The new Labour leader, Arthur Henderson (who was also the Party's secretary and treasurer), failed to provide dynamic leadership in Parliament, and in particular failed to go for the jugular when the government (which was formed in order to preserve the gold standard) was forced to abandon it. Instead he meekly offered the government cooperation to pass the relevant legislation (although 112 Labour MPs subsequently ignored his advice and voted against the Second Reading of the Gold Standard (Amendment) Bill). Insufficient attention was devoted to policy development, which resulted in a tendency to blame the failures of the 1929–1931 Labour governments on MacDonald and Snowden and to attribute its fall to the actions of the bankers. Divisions also arose regarding ideology and the direction which Labour should take in the future and these led to 'socialism' rather than reformism being more widely advocated in Labour circles. These were supplemented by wrangles at the October 1931 Scarborough Conference on the Standing Orders of the Parliamentary Labour Party which were directed at the Independent Labour Party. Subsequently, the NEC determined that a Labour candidate had to sign an undertaking to abide by these standing orders. Failure to do so would enable a Divisional Labour Party to run a candidate against him or her. Financial and organisational difficulties also harmed the Party's electoral prospects.

On 25 September, Henderson put forward an important statement of policy. He criticised the government for pursuing measures which he believed would increase unemployment and he attacked the Conservatives for insisting on an early general election in order to advance their own political ends. He asserted that Labour was committed to a balanced budget and he put forward a range of short-term measures to address the economic crisis such as the mobilisaiton of foreign securities, public control of banking and machinery to prevent profiteering following devaluation. Tariffs were condemned for the effect they would have on the cost of living and promoting industrial inefficiency. Longer-term measures included public control of the main industries as public corporations or cooperatives, marketing schemes for agriculture and international action to reduce tariff barriers, encourage economic cooperation, restore the basis of world credit and restore peace.

On 28 September, the NEC approved resolutions which (when approved by the Scarborough Conference in October) would form the basis of the Party's election manifesto. These included Conference reaffirming its conviction 'that socialism provides the real solution to the evils resulting from unregulated competition on the one hand and the domination of vested interests on the other and presses for the extension of publicly owned industries and services conducted solely in the interests of the people'. Labour's manifesto, *Labour's Call to Action: The Nation's Opportunity*, attacked the National government for having failed to deliver its prime objective, preserving the gold standard, and argued against giving a blank cheque to an administration which, although masquerading as an instrument of national unity, was acutely divided and certain to fall apart in the near future. The manifesto sought to defend the record of the 1929–1931 Labour government, especially in the field of foreign affairs, and argued that further progress had been thwarted because of its minority position and obstruction by the House of Lords. A further document issued during the campaign, *Two Years of Labour Rule*, continued this theme. In positive terms, the manifesto proposed that banking and credit should be nationalised, a national investment board be established, prices stablised and an international conference should be convened to deal with monetary problems and cancel war debts and reparations. Free trade was endorsed by arguments which included tariffs benefiting private interests at the expense of the community, artificially increasing the cost of living and damaging international relations. During the campaign, Labour candidates argued that the 'free hand' was an underhand device to secure the adoption of protectionism. As an alternative to tariffs, Labour proposed to nationalise the power, transport and iron and steel industries, impose price regulation and set up import and export boards to regulate international trade. In his election broadcast delivered on behalf of the National government on 17 October 1931, Lord Snowden drew a distinction between 'sane and evolutionary socialism' and 'a revolutionary policy' as was set out in Labour's 1931 election manifesto. He argued that this was 'not socialism. It is Bolshevism run mad'.

Labour experienced a number of difficulties during the campaign. The conduct of the former Labour ministers was subject to intense criticism for agreeing to spending cuts and then deserting MacDonald. A number of criticisms were levelled at Labour's policies during the campaign. Their pledge to restore cuts lacked credibility as they did not say how they could do this and still manage to balance the budget especially as policies which might aid the attainment of this objective (such as protection) were also ruled out. Their defence of free trade failed to take into account shifts in public opinion towards protection because of factors which included the depression. Their proposals to nationalise the banks (including the Bank of England) were vague and were put forward at least in part as a response to the view that the bankers had been responsible for bringing down the Labour government. Snowden argued that these proposals would mean that the City's business would be transferred to Transport House in the event of a

Labour victory, and one Conservative candidate equated Labour's desire to control the banks with the motives which inspired burglars (Thorpe, 1991: 225). Labour's focus on their record in office between 1929 and 1931 made it possible for their opponents to refer to their inadequate response to unemployment in that period and to point to improvements which had taken place under the National government arising from factors which included devaluation making British exports more competitive.

However, Labour felt that much of the campaign mounted against it was unfair. They believed that they were the subject of much hysteria during the contest, constituting attempts to impair their electoral prospects by unfair and dishonest means. Revelations that the 1929–1931 government had borrowed from the Post Office Savings Bank to augment the unemployment insurance fund led to accusations that they had endangered the deposits. Allegations that the return of a Labour government would lead to starvation were also made by supporters of the National government. These were based on the country's heavy reliance on food imports, and it was argued that a Labour victory would cause depreciation of the currency and make it impossible to buy essential imports. The *Daily Mail* said that a Labour government would lead to national ruination, hyperinflation and be the cause of people starving to death. Snowden's 'Bolshevism run mad' accusation against Labour was taken up by the *Daily Mirror* (which backed the National government) by publishing pictures of starving children in Russia's Volga region. Sensationalism of this nature was not, however, confined to the National government. On polling day, the *Daily Herald* made claims that MacDonald favoured a fascist style of government, arguing that a vote for the National government was a vote against democracy and political freedom and indicated support for 'the pinchbeck Fascism of a bunch of pinchbeck Mussolinis'.

Henderson spent much of the election in his own constituency. Leading trade unionists, including Citrine and Cramp, undertook much of the national campaigning, although this tended to reinforce the arguments of the Conservative press that Labour was a party controlled by the TUC.

Result of the Election

A total of 1,292 candidates contested the election and 67 MPs were returned unopposed. Straight fights occurred in 409 constituencies. The result was:

Party	Votes	Vote %	MPs
National Government Supporters			
Conservative	11,756,359	54.3%	460
National Liberal (Simonites)	809,302	3.7%	35
Liberal (Samuelites)	1,372,595	6.5%	32
National Labour	341,370	1.5%	13
Ulster Unionist	149,566	0.7% [56.1%]	10
Others	100,193	0.5%	4
(Total	14,529,385	67.2%	554)

Opponents to the National Government

Labour	6,324,737	29.2%	46
Independent Labour*	324,893	1.5%	6
Independent Liberal (Lloyd Georgeites)	103,528	0.5%	4
Others	227,773	1.0%	3
Irish Nationalist	123,053	0.6% [38.9%]	2
Scottish National Party	20,954	0.0% [1.0%]	0
Plaid Cymru	2,050	0.0% [0.1%]	0
(Total	7,126,988	32.8 %	61)
Total	**21,656,373**		**615**

* Independent Labour primarily consisted of official candidates of the Independent Labour Party. *The turnout was 76.4 per cent.*

The four Lloyd George Liberals were David Lloyd George (Carmarthen), Megan Lloyd George (Anglesey), Gwilym Lloyd George (Pembroke) and Goronwy Owen (Caernarvonshire). The 'others' who supported the National Government were I. Horobin (Southwark Central, National), G. Campbell (Burnley, National/National Liberal), W. Craven-Ellis (Southampton, National) and W. Allen (Burslem, National/National Liberal). The 'others' who opposed the National Government were Sir E. Graham-Little (London University, National Independent), A. Hopkinson (Mossley, National Independent) and Miss E. Rathbone (Combined English Universities, Independent). Fifteen women MPs were elected.

The Parties

The National government won a landslide victory, winning 554 seats. The Conservative Party formed the largest group in the National government, winning 470 seats (including the 10 won by the Ulster Unionists). The reduction in the size of the 1929 Liberal vote (including the 236 seats which the Party did not contest in 1931) was mainly to the benefit of the Conservative Party. The Samuelite Liberals fielded only 111 candidates, a situation which derived more from inertia in the constituencies than from lack of money. Nine seats were lost to the Conservatives although 16 were gained (14 from Labour), resulting in a Parliamentary Party of 32 MPs (excluding the four won by Lloyd George's 'family group' which sat on the opposition benches in the new Parliament). The Party performed worst in mining and middle-class seats and best in working-class and agricultural constituencies and areas suffering from high unemployment (Thorpe: 1991: 266). Thirty-five Simonite Liberals were returned in 1931. Following the election the monopoly enjoyed by the Samuelites over ministerial posts allocated to the Liberals was ended and a number of positions were allocated to members of this group, including Simon (who became Foreign Secrteary) and Runciman (who was President of the Board of Trade). National Labour fielded 41 candidates. All sitting MPs were re-elected.

The Labour Party fielded 491 candidates. This number was augmented by 24 members of the ILP who were refused endorsement for failing to sign the pledge to obey the PLP's standing orders and one further candidate who was refused nomination on the grounds that the local party at Glasgow Hillhead lacked the finance or organisation to warrant the adoption of a candidate. One hundred and thirty-one Labour candidates were sponsored by trade unions, of whom 32 were elected. An additional MP was sponsored by the Cooperative Party. The Party failed to gain any seats (including any of the 236 which the Liberal Party had contested in 1929 but failed to field a candidate in 1931) and was reduced to a rump of 46 MPs, most of whom were trade union sponsored. A further six members of the ILP were also elected. A large number of leading Labour politicians were defeated and only three ministers in the 1929–31 government (Lansbury, Attlee and Cripps) survived. Losses included the leader Arthur Henderson at Burnley, Herbert Morrison at South Hackney, and Addison at Swindon.

A large number of Labour safe seats were lost, including Bermondsey, Rotherhithe and Sheffield Attercliffe. Clynes lost Manchester Platting (a seat he had represented since 1906) partly due to the hostility of the Catholic Church to the educational reforms which had been put forward in Trevelyan's Bill. The decline in Labour's support was most prominent in middle-class and agricultural seats and in areas of low unemployment although it also fared badly in areas which had experienced high unemployment. It performed better in working-class and mining areas. It has been argued that the ability of members of the working class to vote for the National government served to stunt the development of class-based politics which had been a feature of the 1929 general election even in areas where working-class Conservatism had a long historical pedigree (Stannage, 1980: 245). The fall in Labour's support was especially notable in London, the West Midlands, West Lancastria and Scotland but held up better in North Eastern England and the East Midlands.

Scotland, Wales and Northern Ireland
Labour performed badly in Scotland, winning only seven of the 71 seats. Supporters of the National government won 64, of which the Conservatives (with 48 seats) were the largest party. The National Liberals won eight seats, the Samuelite Liberals seven and National Labour one. Labour performed better in Wales, winning 16 of the 35 seats. The four won by the Lloyd George Liberals gave opponents of the National government a majority of seats in that country. Supporters of the National government won 15 seats (the Conservatives winning six, the Samuelites and National Liberals four each and National Labour one). In Northern Ireland, the Ulster Unionists won 10 seats and the Nationalists two.

Consequence of the Election
Ramsay MacDonald formed a new National government.

14 November 1935

Party Leaders
Stanley Baldwin (National)
Clement Attlee (Labour)
Herbert Samuel (Liberal)

Background to the Election
The National government could claim some successes after 1931. The budget was balanced in 1932 and outside the depressed areas of Wales and the North East industry began to recover and unemployment began to fall after 1932. The cuts imposed in 1931 were restored in 1934 and 1935. After 1933, the cost of living began to fall and wages in most industries (with the notable exception of coal) began to improve in 1934 and 1935. Agricultural reform was provided for and the government could also point to the construction of one million new houses since 1931. Abroad a significant measure of constitutional reform was provided for India in the 1935 India Act. The political extremes of communism and fascism failed to emulate the growth in support which was evident in many European countries.

Timing of the Election
The perception that the National government was formed primarily to handle the immediate economic crisis facing the country in 1931, following which there would be a return to normal party politics, raises the question as to why the contest was delayed until 1935. There are several explanations for this, which include Baldwin's lack of desire to force an election and MacDonald's realisation that one would not be in his interests since his likely election defeat in his Seaham constituency would consign him to political oblivion. Thus, the government continued in office, although rumours of an impending election circulated during the early months of 1935 (triggered by poor by-election results) and in May and June (when it was assumed that the celebrations of the King's Jubilee in May would create a feeling of goodwill throughout the nation which the government could tap into). The government declined this option, however, partly as it felt it important to secure the passage of the India Bill before dissolving Parliament.

A number of factors explained an election in late 1935. By that time the mandate of the National government which had been secured in 1931 was old and justified a new appeal to the country, in particular because in June 1935 MacDonald had been replaced by Baldwin. The nation's economic fortunes showed signs of improvement, evidenced by indicators which included trade and employment figures (the August figures showing that unemployment was below two million for the first time since 1930). This improvement enabled the April 1935 budget to provide a measure of tax relief. An election late in 1935 would also permit the government to avoid having to announce a new set of unemployment regulations which when attempted previously had caused considerable unpopularity and a subsequent climbdown. Divisions within the Conservative Party were largely healed when the India Act was eventually passed in 1935, whereas Labour seemed disunited on both policy and leadership. Additionally, a new electoral register would be current by mid-October 1935. Finally, Baldwin was aware of likely international tension arising from Italy's invasion of Abysinnia. The National government pursued the policy of collective security against Italy through the League of Nations. Baldwin believed that the decision to apply economic sanctions against Italy would provide only a brief lull in international tension and was keen to hold the election before the situation deteriorated.

Conservatives

Prior to 1931, Baldwin's position was not secure, but the election of 150 new Conservative MPs who regarded themselves as beholden to him for their victories made his position henceforth unassailable. The key issue to be faced by the Party after 1931 was its attitude towards remaining within the umbrella of a National government or withdrawing and contesting the next election as an independent party.

Those who wished to fight the next election independently could point to the strains within the Party caused by the need to comply with National government policy rather than to develop their own distinct approach towards political issues. This tension became especially acute in relation to its India Policy where the government line was opposed by Winston Churchill and the India Defence League which argued that Baldwin and the Conservative ministers had surrendered to Socialist and Liberal elements in the National government. It could also be argued that by the middle of 1933 key objectives sought by the National government (in particular fending off the financial crisis) had been achieved. Many Conservatives felt that the lack of local organisation by their partners in the National government meant that they had to carry the lion's share of work in by-elections even when the candidate was not a Conservative. Finally, by-election reverses which occurred in October and November 1934 gave credence to the view that long-term association with the National government could be harmful to the Conservative cause.

However, there were contrary views to this course of action. Some Conservatives were concerned that MacDonald had sufficient support among progressive opinion to pose a significant threat to Conservative chances at a future general election. A return to traditional party warfare would also drastically reduce the number of straight fights which might result in split voting to the detriment of the Conservative Party. Additionally, new political developments (especially the rise of fascism in Europe and the threat this posed for world peace) could be used to justify the continuance of a National government. By late 1933 Baldwin thus began to assert that a National government was still required to defend constitutional democracy in Britain and to secure peace in the world, and by late 1934 was overtly advocating contesting the next election under the umbrella of a National government. Some elements of Conservative opinion wished to go further than merely supporting a National government by making these arrangements permanent. On 13 June 1934 100 Conservative MPs signed a declaration in *The Times* in support of the creation of a National Party.

Although the leadership wished to continue as part of a National government, it could not ignore the views of those Conservatives who wished to pursue an independent course of political activity, and who began to run their own candidates against Conservsative supporters of the National government in by-elections. In one of these contests (at Liverpool Wavertree in February 1935) the resultant split vote secured a Labour victory. A compromise lay in the reconstruction of this government to give Conservatives a greater degree of power and to redefine its key purposes. The poor health of MacDonald facilited this change: in July 1935 he resigned and was succeeded as Prime Minister by Baldwin. Other changes included the replacement of Sir John Simon by Sir Samuel Hoare as Foreign Secretary.

Labour

Henderson (who had lost his seat) remained party leader with George Lansbury assuming the position of leader of the Parliamentary Labour Party. However, on Henderson's resignation Lansbury became the official leader of the Party in October 1932. Following the 1931 election, a report by Henderson to the NEC attributed Labour's failure to a number of circumstances. These included a perception by voters that, whereas MacDonald and Snowden had placed the national interest above party concerns, the Labour Party had run away from the financial crisis. The lack of funds (which meant the Party contested fewer seats than in 1929), the difficulty in getting candidates given the 'snap' nature of the contest, the hostility of the press towards Labour, the post office savings slander and the belief that Labour had failed to aid the unemployed were also cited to explain Labour's showing.

Following the election defeat, a number of views were expressed concerning the future direction of the Labour movement. The ILP believed that it was time to abandon reformism for ever and to endorse a socialist programme which could be put forward when what they viewed to be the inevitable collapse of capitalism under the National government occurred. This resulted in the ILP leaving the Labour Party in 1932, although many of its members disagreed with this decision and formed the Socialist League which was allowed to affiliate to the Labour Party.

These arguments associated with the left of the Party were countered by a vigorous attempt to secure TUC control over the affairs of the Labour Party and push it in a right-wing political direction. At a meeting between the NEC and representatives of the TUC general council which was held on 10 November 1931, Citrine pointed to the lack of contact between the 1929–1931 Labour government and the general council. To redress this, it was agreed to reinvigorate the National Joint Council which Citrine viewed as a mechanism to assert TUC control over the actions of the NEC and the Parliamentary Labour Party. This objective was not totally realised, however, and the Parliamentary Labour Party moved more to the left.

This left versus right debate in the Party was manifested at the 1932 Party Conference at which left-wing sentiments were forcibly expressed. An NEC resolution to nationalise the Bank of England was amended to extend the principle of public ownership and control to the joint stock banks. NEC resolutions to nationalise the transport and electricity industries were referred back because there were no provisions for worker representation on the new boards. Additionally, a resolution proposed by Charles Trevelyan was carried which instructed a future Labour government and the Parliamentary Labour Party to agree that on assuming office in the future the Party would put forward 'definite socialist legislation' and would stand or fall in the House of Commons on these principles.

The rise of fascism in Europe (in particular Hitler's accession to power in early 1933) posed additional problems regarding the stance which should be adopted to this development. Calls were made by the Communist Party, the ILP and the Socialist League for Labour participation in a united front against fascism. Initially the TUC and the NEC sought to head off such demands through the publication of their own policy document, *Democracy versus Dictatorship*, which denounced dictatorships of left- as well as right-wing political orientation and argued that the best defence against this development was to strengthen the Labour Party. However, the international situation continued to create internal divisions within the Party which were most apparent in its defence and foreign policy statements. In September 1933, the NEC resolved to embark upon the preparation of policy proposals for the next election. These were contained in a statement entitled *Victory for Socialism*. However, statements committing the Party to pursue international disarmament and affirming its belief in the League of Nations were amended by the Hastings Conference (mainly at the instigation of the Socialist League) to pledge the Party to take no part in war and to resist it by all means available, including a general strike. Subsequently, attempts were made to reverse this decision and reaffirm the Party's support for the League of Nations and the obligations which this entailed. These views (supported by the NEC and the TUC) were embodied in a policy statement entitled *For Socialism and Peace* which was overwhelmingly approved by the 1934 Southport Conference.

However, as the Party moved towards an acceptance of the stance that collective security might involve the use of force against fascist aggression, the position of its leader, Lansbury, became more difficult. As a Christian pacifist, he could not endorse any use of force, and at the 1934 Conference he stated he was prepared to resign if his views were regarded as an obstacle to the Party's progress. His situation subsequently became even less tenable when the 1935 TUC Conference called on all governments which subscribed to the League of Nations to take all measures provided by the Covenant to oppose Italy's attack on Abyssinia. By the time the Labour Party Conference met at the end of that month, Italy had invaded Ethiopia. On behalf of the NEC, Hugh Dalton proposed a resolution which called upon all governments represented at the Council and Assembly of the League of Nations to use all measures provided by the Covenant to prevent Italy's 'unjust and rapacious attack' on the territory of a fellow League member and to support any action consistent with the principles and statutes of the League to restrain the Italian government and uphold the authority of the League in enforcing peace.

Lansbury addressed the Conference and, in asserting his pacifist views, offered to resign at the next meeting of the Parliamentary Labour Party. Although he was received sympathetically by the Conference, his views were roundly condemned in a vitriolic speech delivered by Ernest Bevin in which he stated that Lansbury was placing the NEC and the Labour movement in 'an absolutely wrong position' by 'taking' (some versions of the speech substitute this word for 'trailing' or 'hawking') his conscience round from body to body and asking to be told what he ought to do with it. He criticised Lansbury for allowing himself to be the spokesman for a policy with which he was in total disagreement and accused him of betraying the movement. The motion was passed by in excess of a million votes for the motion to only 102,000 against. Lansbury submitted his resignation to the Parliamentary Party and although they asked him to reconsider his mind was made up. He was replaced by Clement Attlee but only for the remainder of the parliamentary session which thus implied his leadership was of a stop-gap nature.

Labour fortunes showed signs of improving during the 1931–35 Parliament. By-election successes were secured in late 1933 and Labour won the London County Council elections the following year. The decision by the National government to introduce the means test enabled

Labour to advocate its repeal and provide it with a popular policy with which to challenge the National government. In 1935 it successfully led an attack on the government's new unemployment regulations which sought to reduce the scale of payments. However, Labour's appeal was adversely affected by its proposals to nationalise the banks and public scepticism towards its stance of relying on the League of Nations to provide security in the face of Hitler's aggressive actions in Europe.

Liberals

Following the 1931 general election, David Lloyd George relinquished the leadership which was taken over by Herbert Samuel. Subsequently, the Liberal Party became riven by internal dissent. Three major divisions became apparent.

The Independent (Samuelite) Liberals

Following the election, the major problem for the Samuelites was the issue of tariffs. Within two months of the election, three tariff measures had been passed and a significant difficulty arose in early 1932 when a Cabinet Committee was appointed to consider the balance of trade in isolation from the more general issue of industrial recovery. This was chaired by Neville Chamberlain and was designed to secure approval for the introduction of protection. Following its recommendation in January 1932 to introduce a general tariff immediately (whose provisions were subsequently included in the Import Duties Act which came into force on 1 March 1932), Samuel, Sinclair, Sir Donald MacLean and Lord Snowden offered MacDonald their resignations. However, in private conversation with the Prime Minister they managed to fashion a compromise whereby they would remain in government but the principle of collective ministerial responsibility would be suspended, thus giving them full liberty to speak and vote against the measures which they opposed but continuing to support the government on all other issues, thereby enabling the unity of the National government to be preserved. The 'agreement to differ policy' was viewed as a purely provisional arrangement, only justified by the scale of the economic crisis facing the country.

The agreements which were reached at the Ottawa Imperial Economic Conference proved to be the downfall of this fragile arrangement. This conference pledged the British government to continue the preference scheme for a range of imports from the Dominions, in return for which British exports to the the Dominions would receive preferential treatment through the mechanism of increasing tariffs against foreign goods. The Samuelites believed that the benefit to be expected from the agreements in reducing the volume of unemployment in the United Kingdom was likely to be very small, whereas the principle of restricting and taxing foreign supplies of food and raw materials would become firmly established. They believed that it illustrated the manner in which the the National government had been used by the Conservative Party to secure the enactment of its tariff policies. They argued that, at the forthcoming World Economic Conference, Britain needed to be free to enter into any arrangements in order to expand trade with foreign countries since they constituted the largest proportion of British commerce. But Ottawa tied the hands of the government. Accordingly, they wished these agreements to be suspended until the World Economic Conference had met.

Liberals perceived the Ottawa agreements as an attack on their fundamental principles and they were not prepared to support them in Parliament. They needed to assert themselves in the face of this attack on their principles to avoid those who disapproved of their apparent subservience to the Conservative Party turning to Labour. There was considerable pressure in the constituencies in favour of the resignation of the Samuelites. While it was conceivable that the threat of resignation could force MacDonald to yield to the Liberal pressures, Liberals believed that this was unlikely to happen because MacDonald was now viewed as subservient to the Conservatives. Nonetheless, there were problems associated with resignation. It could not be assumed that the Ottawa agreements or the general principle of free trade would rally public opinion behind the Liberal Party who might be additionally blamed for putting party objectives before the cause of national unity in a period of acute national tension. It was also bound to have the effect of splitting the Liberal Party, perhaps irrevocably. It was anticipated that Simon and Runciman would remain in office supported by a sizeable proportion of the Parliamentary Party.

The decision to resign was decided upon in early September 1932, but its announcement was delayed until 28 September in order for the Ottawa papers to be considered by the Samuelite group of ministers and for a Cabinet meeting to be held at which the resignations could be put. In this interim period, MacDonald pleaded with Samuel to reconsider the situation but Samuel's response was that the Liberals would remain in government if the Conservatives were willing, for the first time, to make a gesture and put the national interest before their political concerns. He thus suggested that the government should announce it would suspend the operation of the Ottawa agreements until the World Economic Conference met later that year when it would review the situation. MacDonald had stated his belief that that this step was not possible which made the resignation of the 11 Liberal ministers (and Lord Snowden) inevitable.

However, the resignation of the Samuelites in 1932 did not terminate the support which they gave to the National government. They decided at a meeting held on 8 September 1932 not to join with Labour and go into opposition, but to retain their seats on the government side of the House. But this course of action created tensions within the Liberal Party and in particular between the rank-and-file activists and the Parliamentary Party. A particular difficulty related to by-elections, since the stance adopted by the Parliamentary Party towards the National government prevented it from endorsing Liberal candidates to oppose National government candidates in these contests. A second problem associated with the decision not to enter into opposition was that the continued association of the Samuelites with the Conservative-dominated National government served to drive progressive opinion towards the Labour Party as the only opposition party.

However, the transition of the Samuelites into an opposition party pursuing an independent course of political action presented a number of difficulties. First, the Party was in a weak organisational and financial position to operate as an independent political party. Without Lloyd George's financial support the Party was impoverished. This weak financial position presented the immediate problem in connection with fighting by-elections and would also present difficulties in connection with the financing of future general election campaigns. A further issue was the need for the Party to project a philosophy and policies which would justify political independence. The most obviously distinct Liberal position related to free trade, but there was doubt expressed within the Party as to whether this could serve as a rallying point for the electorate in an era of intensified economic nationalism. In 1933, the Samuelites commenced on the task of producing a comprehensive statement of Liberal policy by the end of that year.

Increasingly, therefore, the Samuelites moved towards a position of opposition to the government and adopted an increasingly critical attitude towards it. They opposed measures which included the Agricultural Marketing Bill and the Rent Restrictions Bill and, in July 1933, Samuel delivered a scathing attack on the government's trade policy which culminated in the Party voting against the Board of Trade Estimates. This suggested that it was only a matter of time before the Party became a party of opposition. The issue was finally resolved through pressure exerted by the rank-and-file activists. In May 1933 the NLF Conference at Scarborough urged the Parliamentary Party to move into a formal position of opposition and these views were repeated in a motion passed at the autumn meeting of the General Council of the Scottish Liberal Federation at Ayr in October 1933. The leadership acquiesced and on 13 November 1933, 29 of Samuel's parliamentary group moved to the opposition benches following a broadcast by Samuel in which he attacked the general record of the government following Ottawa.

However, the Party faced considerable problems following this decision. Its performance in by-elections was poor and the Party lacked a distinct policy which it could put to the electors. It also had major problems concerned with constituency organisation and finance. These problems had an adverse effect on morale and the period witnessed further defections to the Labour Party. One solution to this was a reconciliation with Lloyd George who retained a considerable degree of support within the Party. However, this failed to occur.

National Liberals

Simon refused to attend a meeting with Samuel following the 1931 election to discuss the future of the Party, which suggested that the Liberal Nationals had effectively divorced themselves from the Samuelite Liberals. The decision of Liberal ministers to resign from office in 1932 following the government's decision to introduce agreements reached at the Ottawa Imperial Economic Conference widened the gulf between Liberal Nationals and the Samuelites since the Simonites wished to remain in office.

Liberal Nationals endorsed the view that rigid adherence to the principle of free trade in the early 1930s was unwise when other nations were imposing quotas. A further motive for the cooperation of Liberal Nationals with the Conservative Party after the 1931 general election was that it gave such Liberals influence over the conduct of political affairs. The Liberal Nationals were, however, at this stage keen to secure their long-term political future as an independent party. Financially, they were in good shape, but they lacked organisation in the constituencies. Accordingly, they sought assurances from Baldwin that Liberal National MPs who proved themselves to be good allies of the Conservative Party by supporting the Ottawa Bill through its stages in the House of Commons would not be contested by Conservative candidates at the next election. The positive response of Baldwin to this suggestion helped to make divisions within the Liberal Party permanent. Separate organisation in the form of the

Liberal National Council (1932) and Area Committees (1933) served to formalise divisions within the Liberal Party and paved the way for what effectively amounted to a realignment of right-wing Liberals with the Conservative Party.

Lloyd George

Lloyd George and his 'family group' operated independently after 1931. The Samuelites' refusal to move into outright opposition after leaving the government infuriated Lloyd George and although discussions with the Samuelites subsequently occurred after they 'crossed the floor' in November 1933, these failed to produce permanent reconciliation. In 1934 he put forward his New Deal proposals which sought to unite all those opposed to the actions undertaken by the National government over a wide range of issues and to secure the election of progressive MPs at the next general election. To promote this objective he funded the Council of Action for Peace and Reconstruction. This was essentially a nonconformist pressure group which promoted a Keynesian approach to economic recovery and reducing unemployment. This provided Lloyd George with an organisation under his personal control which could underpin his attempt to reappear as a major actor on the political stage. However, an alternative possibility was that the policies identified with the Council for Peace and Reconstruction could have formed the basis of a new political alignment in which the parties of opposition came together under a progressive banner led by Lloyd George. He retained considerable influence in the Liberal constituency associations and the National Liberal Federation, and during the period between the Liberal ministers leaving the government and the move into opposition, Liberal leaders were aware of the possibility of Lloyd George acting as a rallying point for disaffected rank-and-file activists. Additionally, Lloyd George's claim after 1931 to belong to no party hypothetically enhanced his ability to court Labour's rank and file. A policy which included control of the banks, turning transport and the mines into public utilities or nationalised concerns, free trade, disarmament and a radical agricultural policy could provide the basis on which Lloyd George could unite the opposition.

By-elections

Sixty-two by-elections occurred in the 1931–35 Parliament, of which 50 were contested. The Conservatives made a net loss of nine seats, the Liberal Party a net loss of one and Labour made a net gain of 10.

Conduct of the Election

In March 1933, a National Coordinating Committee was established whose task included preparing publicity for the National government and its policies. The government felt it needed to devote energy into this aspect of its work since the press tended to be more critical of its actions after 1931. As the election approached, this was replaced by the National Publicity Bureau whose work was performed by mechanisms which included cinema vans touring the country, a method with which the Labour Party could not compete on equal terms. In addition to this method of disseminating propaganda, electors were provided with political commentary from the newspapers (the circulation of which grew considerably during the 1930s) (Stannage, 1980: 175), the radio (the ownership of which increased after 1931 to include many members of the working class) (Stannage, 1980: 178) and cinema newsreels (which became more influential after 1932 when 'voices' were added to the pictures and became an important source of information for the working class who were particularly identified with cinema attendance) (Stannage, 1980: 175). These sources supplemented election meetings which tended to be less well attended because of the growing diversity of the media. The tendency of the broadcasting media to let government themes (especially the extent of social and economic recovery after 1931) set the agenda after 1931 gave it an advantage over its opponents.

National Government

Politicians supporting the National government defended the holding of the election at that time by arguing that while there was no immediate prospect of danger in Europe this would alter in the future. The manifesto of the National government, *A Call to the Nation: The Joint Manifesto of the Leaders of the National Government*, was prepared by a Cabinet committee and was signed by MacDonald, Baldwin and Sir John Simon. It gave prominence to the League of Nations as the keystone of British foreign policy and pledged to take no unilateral action in connection with the dispute between Abyssinia and Italy but stated that the government would pursue any course of collective action determined by the League. It was stated that government defence policy was underpinned by the objectives of ensuring the safety of the country and Empire and being able to fulfil Britain's obligations towards the League. However, it was bluntly admitted that the actual condition of Britain's defence forces was not satisfactory and the gaps which had appeared in the last decade would have to be remedied over the next few years.

Rearmament was vocally advocated by Conservatives such as Winston Churchill during the contest. Snowden (who was officially an Independent but was allocated one of the Liberal Party's election broadcasts) argued that Baldwin was seeking a mandate to rearm and particular attention was drawn to the state of the navy. Some Conservatives argued implicitly or explicitly that it needed to be upgraded in order to defend Britain in the future, and Conservatives further asserted that rearmament would create jobs, especially in the depressed areas. However, Baldwin's promise (in a speech delivered to the Peace Society on 31 October) that there would be 'no great armaments' helped to draw some of the sting from criticisms voiced by the opposition parties on this issue.

The manifesto placed emphasis on the improvement to the nation's fortunes which had taken place since 1931. Particular attention was drawn to government policy of protecting the home market and creating a regime of cheap money for facilitating enterprise and industrial expansion which had succeeded in reducing the level of unemployment. Additionally, credit or other state resources had funded schemes such as the building of the *Queen Mary* and improvements to London Transport which had also helped reduce unemployment. The unification of mining royalties and setting up a Royal Commission into the industry were put forward as proposals to aid the depressed areas whose plight was primarily attributed to the contraction of the coal mining industry. The manifesto asserted that the key issue was the need to preserve the stability and confidence which this government had built up in a period of special difficulty and anxiety. During the campaign, Baldwin spoke of the improvement in international trade and economic recovery at home and argued that the position of the working class had improved since 1931 under the National government. Similarly, MacDonald's election broadcast on 5

November referred to signs of improvement in the depressed areas. The appeal to the working class was coupled with arguments that the Labour Party was no longer led by members of the working class, but by a clique of socialist intellectuals whose views were as un-British as communism or fascism.

In connection with social welfare, the manifesto highlighted the contribution made by the government's cheap money policy which had resulted in the 'phenomenal growth' of the building industry and the erection of one million new houses since 1931. Many of these, it was argued, were houses for letting which had facilitated a programme of slum clearance. Although the manifesto argued that the introduction of a substantial programme of social reforms had been given second place to the need to restore national finances, proposals to increase the child allowance and raise the school leaving age to 15 were introduced into Parliament on the eve of the election. The reform of the system of unemployment assistance was promised, but no details were given of what would inevitably prove to be a contentious issue. A means test would be introduced but the precise details of the scheme were not discussed.

Considerable attention was devoted to the Labour Party in the National government's campaign where it was presented as a party unfit to govern. This accusation was presented in stark contrast to Baldwin's slogan of 'You May Safely Trust Me'. Conservatives argued that Labour was pledged to enact a series of 'revolutionary measures' which would result in a 'collapse of confidence' causing severe upheavals in economic and social life. It was also argued that Britain's influence in world affairs would not be maintained under a Labour government whose key statesmen had deserted it, which was divided on the important aspects of foreign policy and led by a relatively unknown person lacking authority in the Party. The appeal in the Communist Party's manifesto for the return of a Labour government also helped National government spokesmen to identify the Labour Party with communism during the campaign, and towards the end of the campaign, Lord Hailsham raised the spectre of a Moscow-dominated Labour government. Proposals put forward by Labour were dismissed either as vague or (as was the case with their proposed pensions reform) financially unsound.

Labour

Labour spokesmen especially queried the need for an election at that time, arguing that the nation supported the principle of collective security through the League of Nations and the imposition of sanctions against Italy. They also suggested that Baldwin sought to benefit from the sense of national unity created by the Abysinnia crisis, which would further enable the National government to divert attention from its inability to solve the problem of unemployment. Labour also believed that the government would use the election as a mandate to introduce rearmament.

The Labour manifesto, *The Labour Party's Call to Power*, was based upon the 1934 policy statement. It alleged that the National government had been returned to power in 1931 following a campaign of 'fraud, misrepresentation and panic' and was now seeking to hold a 'snap election' in the middle of an international crisis in order to exploit the situation to its own political advantage. Much of Labour's campaign consisted of negative attacks on the National government. Economic improvements were attributed to developments affecting the world economy rather than National government policy, and the government was criticised for inventing the means test, failing to deal adequately with unemployment, reducing education facilities, neglecting the social services and handing over housing to be administered on the basis of private profit.

Considerable attention was devoted in the manifesto to alleged National government failings in foreign policy. It was criticised for doing nothing to check Japanese aggression in the Far East, thereby undermining the collective peace system and for failing to warn Mussolini unequivocally that Britain would join with other nations to uphold the authority of the League if Italy broke the peace in Africa. It criticised the government for helping to restart the arms race whilst paying lip service to the League and asserted it was a 'danger to the peace of the world and to the security of this country'. The slogan 'a vote for the Tories is a vote for war' was utilised during the campaign. Although Labour pledged to maintain Britain's defence forces as was necessary and consistent with membership of the League, it made clear its view that the best defence was collective security against any aggressor and the agreed reduction of national armaments everywhere rather than huge competitive national armaments.

Criticisms were also voiced in the manifesto concerning National government domestic policy. They were accused of handing over housing to private profit and of actively discouraging the development of the social services. During the campaign it was asserted that limited reforms (such as raising the school leaving age) had been cynically proposed on the eve of the election. Labour promised to develop vigorously the health services (especially to tackle the issue of maternal mortality), to increase the value of the old age pension and to introduce a comprehensive programme of industrial legislation to secure reasonable hours and conditions of employment for all workers. The Party pledged to nationalise banking and the coal, transport, electricity, iron and steel and cotton industries, and also proposed the public ownership of land so that the community should profit by its value and proper use. It proposed to initiate far-reaching schemes of national development to reabsorb idle workers into productive employment and to tackle the problems of the distressed areas by a vigorous policy of national plannning. At a much more local level, Morrison promised an audience at Dartford that a Labour government would build a tunnel there under the River Thames. Labour's domestic policies were presented as *Labour's Programme of Socialist Reconstruction* and unashamedly asserted that the aim of the Party was to seek a majority in Parliament to promote socialism at home.

During the campaign, Labour spokesmen also replied to Conservative criticisms. They viewed the claim that the return of a Labour government would result in a financial crisis as a scare tactic.

Liberals

Criticisms articulated by Labour which suggested the election was unnecessary at that time and that the decision to hold it was underpinned by partisan considerations were also made by Liberals. The *Manchester Guardian* likened it to a 'khaki election'. The Party election statement, *The Liberal Manifesto*, asserted that an election should not be held when the ability of the League of Nations to penalise aggression was in the balance. However, Liberal defence policy was similar to that of the Conservative Party, advocating that national defences should be kept efficient and large enough for the needs of the time but asserting that a 'colossal, panic expenditure in arms is not the road to peace'. The manifesto attributed unemployment to the 'disastrous reduction in the volume of world trade' and asserted that the solution to the problem was to eliminate tariffs, subsidies and quotas. It was further proposed to employ idle capital and idle labour on a number of urgently needed enterprises. Reference was also made in the manifesto to the 1934 policy document, *The Liberal Way*, which contained proposals relating to agricultural reform and the reform of the social services.

Lloyd George

Lloyd George's activities in the election were primarily confined to generating support for his Council of Action. Candidates of the other parties were invited to complete a questionnaire on the basis of which electors who were sympathetic to the Council would be advised how to vote. In his election broadcast on 6 November, Samuel urged electors to vote Liberal or for a candidate who supported the aims of the Council of Action. Lloyd George's efforts were mainly designed to secure personal control over the nonconformist vote. However, its task was undermined when on 8 November the leader of the Free Church, Dr Scott Lidgett, urged his followers to vote for the National government and against the Socialists, arguing that the government was progressing towards the objectives of the Council of Action.

Accordingly, Lloyd George failed in his attempt to rally progressive opinion behind the Council for Action and give him the political influence which he sought. The Council formally approved 362 candidates, of whom 67 were elected. It was thus concluded that 'the Council proved largely irrelevant, securing nonconformist support – itself of questionable worth – for candidates who, for the most part, would have had it anyway. And all at a cost of £400,000 from Lloyd George's funds alone' (Koss, 1975: 214).

Result of the Election

The victory of the National government seemed likely as polling day neared and even the *Daily Herald* failed to predict a Labour victory. There were two main factors to explain this – the appearance of economic prosperity at home and the adoption of a limited rearmament programme which was viewed by electors as a more realistic response to deteriorating international circumstances than Labour's appeal for peace. The Conservatives performed well in the municipal elections held on 1 November, and the following day, a cut of 40,000 in the numbers of unemployed in October compared to the previous month gave substance to National government claims that Britain was on the road to economic recovery. The expenditure of £100 million on road building was also announced on 2 November which indicated a government willingness to finance expenditure on public works in order to reduce unemployment. Thus by the time Baldwin asked (in a speech delivered at Newcastle-upon-Tyne on 12 November) for a mandate for the National government to keep the nation safe from war and to restore its prosperity, the outcome of the election was a foregone conclusion and the bookmakers Ladbrokes were taking bets on the size of the National government's majority.

A total of 1,348 candidates contested the election. The result was:

Party	Votes	Vote %	MPs
Supporters of the National Government			
Conservative	10,203,460	46.4%	377
National Liberal	866,354	3.9%	33
Ulster Unionist	292,840	1.3% [64.9%]	10
National Labour	339,811	1.5%	8
National	53,189	0.2%	1
(Total	11,755,654	53.3%	429)
Opponents of the National Government			
Labour	8,325,491	37.9%	154
Liberal	1,443,093	6.6%	21
Others	142,861	0.7%	5
Independent Labour Party	139,577	0.6%	4
Irish Nationalist	101,494	0.5% [22.5%]	2
Scottish National Party	29,517	0.1% [1.1%]	0
Plaid Cymru	2,534	0.0% [0.3%]	0
Republican (Northern Ireland)	56,833	0.3% [12.6%]	0
(Total	10,241,400	46.7%	186)
Total	**21,997,054**		**615**

The turnout was 71.1 per cent.
The 'others' were Willie Gallagher (West Fife, Communist), Sir E. Graham-Little (London University National Independent), A. P. Herbert (Oxford University, Independent), A. Hopkinson (Mossley, National Independent) and Miss E. F. Rathbone (Combined English Universities, Independent). Nine women MPs were elected.

The Parties

The swing against the National government to Labour was relatively even across the country, although was higher in London, Liverpool, Nottingham and North Eastern Scotland and less in the West Midlands, Birmingham and Edinburgh. Fifty-seven Conservative MPs retired in 1935 (compared to only two Labour MPs). The National government targeted seats in the North of England and the Midlands and did especially well at the expense of the Liberal Party. Prominent losses included MacDonald (National Labour) at Seaham.

Labour's cause was hindered by the financial weakness of both Transport House and the Divisional Labour parties. The Cooperative Party sponsored 20 candidates and the trade unions 128 (nine and 79 respectively being elected). Overall, the Party gained over 100 seats, most from the Conservatives. However, although it fared particularly well when contesting Liberal National or National Labour as opposed to Conservative candidates, it failed to recapture all of the ground which had been lost to the National government in 1931. Low morale and financial weakness had an adverse impact on Liberal candidatures, enabling the Party to contest only 161 constituencies. Overall, the Party performed badly and most of its leading parliamentary spokesmen were defeated. Losses included the leader, Samuel, at Darwen.

Scotland, Wales and Northern Ireland
Overall the National government performed well in most of Scotland, winning 43 of the 71 seats. The Conservatives won 35 seats, the National Liberals seven and National Labour one. Opponents of the National government won 28 seats (Labour 20, Independent Labour Party four, Liberal three and Communist one). Although the swing to Labour was lower than the national average in Wales, as in 1931, the majority of the 35 seats were won by opponents of the National governent. Labour won 18 and the Liberals six. Suporters of the National government won 11 (Conservatives six, National Party one, National Liberals three and National Labour one). The political situation in Northern Ireland remained unchanged from 1931, with the Ulster Unionists winning 10 of the 12 seats and the Nationalists the remaining two.

Consequence of the Election
Stanley Baldwin formed a National government.

5 July 1945

Party Leaders
Winston Churchill (Conservative)
Clement Attlee (Labour)
Sir Archibald Sinclair (Liberal)

Background to the Election
Timing of the Election
The election was caused by the decision of the Prime Minister, Winston Churchill, to resign from office on 23 May 1945, thus bringing to an end the Coalition government which had governed the United Kingdom since May 1940. He had suggested to Attlee, Sinclair and the leader of the Liberal National Party (Ernest Brown) that they should either remain in the Coalition government and postpone the general election until the war with Japan was over or hold an immediate election in July. The leaders of the Labour and Liberal parties rejected Churchill's proposal regarding the war with Japan but wanted an election to be held in the autumn when a new electoral register could be prepared and service voters would be better enabled to become acquainted with the key political issues. Churchill refused this course of action and Parliament was dissolved on 15 June. In taking this decision, he was accused of seeking to advantage the Conservative Party who might benefit from a 'snap election', basing its appeal on his prestige as the successful war leader.

Following his resignation, Churchill was reappointed Prime Minister to head a 'caretaker government' mainly composed of Conservatives and National Liberals.

Electoral Procedures and Practices
Parliament should have ended in November 1940, but the difficulties which holding an election in wartime would have entailed resulted in its life being prolonged until 1945. This was effected by the passage of Prolongation Bills which were presented to Parliament each year by the Home Secretary.

On 26 September 1939 the Chief Whips of the Conservative, Labour and Liberal parties concluded an electoral truce. They agreed not to nominate candidates at by-elections against the candidate of the party which held the seat when the vacancy occurred. This truce held until the dissolution of Parliament in 1945, although it did not prevent independents and candidates from newly formed political parties (including Common Wealth) from standing in these contests.

All votes were counted on 25 July, although the casting of votes took place in two stages. The bulk of the United Kingdom voted on 5 July but nine constituencies in Northern England and 13 in Scotland were permitted to poll on 12 July, in order to accommodate the annual holidays (or 'wakes') which occurred in these areas. In one further English constituency (Nelson and Colne) voting took place on 5, 12 and 19 July to accommodate the staged holidays of this nature which occurred there.

Conservatives

Following the 1935 general election, much of the government's attention was devoted to the India Act which became law in 1935. This legislation introduced parliamentary government, with the Viceroy controlling foreign affairs and finance. It was also proposed to institute a federal system of government for India including both the provinces of British India and the states controlled by Indians. The major domestic issues facing Baldwin's government were the abdication crisis and severe public disorder occasioned by the activities of the British Union of Fascists and its opponents, which resulted in the enactment of the 1936 Public Order Act. Following Edward VIII's abdication and the coronation of his successor, George VI, in 1936, Baldwin retired from politics in 1937 and was replaced by Neville Chamberlain.

The Conservative governments were preoccupied with foreign affairs. In 1938 an agreement was reached with Eire which ended the trade war between herself and Britain and a payment of £10 million was made to wipe out the loans which had been provided to provide for land purchase following independence. The issue of partition, however, remained unaddressed. The major concern, however, was in connection with the rise of fascism in Europe. Before the election a number of events had occurred which posed a severe threat to world peace. These included the accession to power of Mussolini in Italy in 1925 and Hitler in Germany in 1933, the weakening of the authority of the League of Nations by events which included the Japanese seizure of Manchuria in 1931, and the failure of the World Disarmament Conference in 1932–33, which was irrevocably undermined when Germany walked out in 1933 following the refusal of her demand for equality of armed strength with other nations. However, fascism became increasingly aggressive after 1935.

In 1935 Italy launched an unprovoked attacked on Abyssinia against which the League of Nations proved to be totally ineffective. Overly weak sanctions failed to halt the Italian attack which resulted in total victory in 1936. In 1936, Hitler sent troops into the demilitarised Rhineland, thereby overturning key clauses of the 1919 Versailles Treaty and both fascist countries supplied military aid to the fascists engaged in fighting the republican forces in Spain in the 1936–39 Spanish Civil War. The British government took no meaningful action to oppose these acts of aggression, as British policy after 1935 sought to cultivate the support of Italy as a potential ally against Germany. However, public opinion and the parliamentary opposition favoured a tougher line. In 1935, the Foreign Secretary, Sir Samuel Hoare, was forced to resign when his agreement with his French counterpart, P. Laval, to halt the war in Abyssinia by dividing that country to Italy's advantage was leaked. He was replaced by Anthony Eden, who was effectively sidelined because Chamberlain feared that his opposition to Italian aggression in both Abyssinia and Spain would offend Mussolini.

Germany subsequently emerged as the key threat to European peace. In March 1938 Austria was incorporated into the 'Third Reich' and Czechoslavakia was threatened with invasion. This might have proved the trigger for a European war since France had an alliance with that country. In an attempt to avert this, Chamberlain met face to face with Hitler at Munich in September 1938 and emerged clutching a piece of paper which he claimed had secured 'peace in our time'. The policy of appeasement was at the expense of Czechoslavakia which was required to surrender her border regions to Germany. Munich secured a temporary respite in tensions in Europe, but in March 1939 Czechoslavakia was invaded in breach of the Munich agreement. Poland was now in imminent danger, which became even more apparent when a Russo–German Pact was announced in August 1939. On 1 September, Poland was invaded, in response to which Britain declared war on 3 September.

The Chamberlain government fell following Germany's conquest of Norway (and, en route, Denmark). Britain's inability to prevent the overrun of Norway resulted in a two-day debate in the House of Commons which commenced on 7 May. Although the campaign was not an unmitigated disaster for Britain (since the German navy suffered considerable losses in the fighting) the legacy of appeasement weighed heavily around Chamberlain's neck who was accused of failing to equip the country with adequate armed forces and air power.

Early in this debate Morrison intimated that Labour intended to divide the House on this issue. At the conclusion of proceedings, the government motion to adjourn the House was carried by 281 : 200 votes. Over 40 Conservatives voted with the opposition and around 60 abstained. Chamberlain recognised the need to strengthen his government by bringing in the opposition parties. The Labour leaders, however, would join only if there were a new prime minister. On 10 May, Winston Churchill formed a Coalition government in which he also served as Minister of Defence. As is referred to above, this government served until 23 May 1945.

The Conservative Party initially undertook little active political work after war had been declared and did not hold a Party Conference until 1943. Organisation in the constituencies was especially adversely affected. The Party fared badly in by-elections in seats they had won in 1935, losing a number to Independents. This suggested that at the general election the record of the Party in the inter-war years (in particular their slowness in recognising the dangers of Nazism, their policy of appeasement and their inability to offer a successful remedy to unem-ployment and other domestic policy issues such as housing) would stand against them and that only Churchill's prestige as the successsful war leader could offset this disadvantage.

Labour

The rise of fascism in Europe resulted in two separate calls for joint action by the parties of the left during the 1930s which were to exert some influence over the conduct of Labour politics in that period. The first of these was the united front (which was initiated by the Communist Party of Great Britain, seeking an alliance of all socialists). In 1937 it published the *Unity* manifesto which called for common action by all sections of the working class to oppose fascism, Britain's National government (which was depicted as the agent of both fascism and imperialism), all restrictions placed on civil and trade union liberties and the militarisation of Britain. Although some of Labour's left wing displayed an interest in supporting joint action of this nature, the official stance of the Labour Party was to oppose any form of cooperation with the Communist Party. The second of these ventures was the popular front which sought the unity of all who opposed fascism (including the Liberal Party and Conservatives opposed to appeasement). Action along these lines was initially instigated following Italy's invasion of Abyssinia but a more determined campaign was launched in response to the deteriorating military position of the Popular Front government in Spain which was denied any form of military aid from Britain or France whereas its opponents, led by General Franco, were lavishly aided by both Germany and Italy. In 1938 a National Emergency Conference on Spain was organised which served as a spur to the formation of a popular front in Britain to aid Spain and also to remove Chamberlain. Members of both the Labour and Liberal parties were involved in this venture which resulted in both parties subsequently withdrawing their candidates at by-elections to give electors the opportunity to vote for a progressive candidate. One of these, Vernon Bartlett, secured a victory at Bridgwater in 1938.

Officially, however, the Labour Party remained sceptical of the merits of involvement in a popular front. This issue was debated at the 1936 Party Conference, when an amendment to a motion in favour of the united front urged the Party to consider seriously the formation of a 'national progressive front'. The 1938 National Emergency Conference prompted Labour to publish its response to the formation of a popular front. However, the NEC document, *Labour and the Popular Front*, opposed this development for reasons which included the belief that a popular front would not lead to the fall of the National government or an early election, nor would it necessarily be more electorally successful than the Labour Party acting independently, since Liberal voters could not automatically be relied upon to vote Labour in the absence of a candidate of their own party. The document argued that the best way to defeat Chamberlain and his government was through a Labour victory at the polls.

However, further pressure was exerted on the Party by Sir Stafford Cripps. In October 1938 he organised a conference which passed a resolution in favour of the formation of a people's government which would be led by the Labour Party but based upon the broad agreement of all progressive forces in the country. He subsequently circulated a memorandum to all Divisional Labour parties concerning this objective. These activities resulted in Cripps being expelled from the Labour Party in January 1939 and in March other prominent popular front supporters (including Aneurin Bevan and Sir Charles Trevelyan) were similarly thrown out. Cripps subsequently launched a petition which was designed to exert pressure on the Party's 1939 Conference. This highlighted a world which was threatened by war and fascism and put forward six areas on which progressive opinion could be rallied (the defence of democracy, planning for plenty, guaranteeing the security of Britain, protecting the people's interests, defending the people and building for peace and justice). In a speech which he gave at Birmingham on 10 February 1939, Cripps stated that the aims of the petition were to intensify opposition to the National government, to reinvigorate the Labour Party and to convince the Labour leadership that there was considerable rank-and-file support for inter-party cooperation. However, the 1939 Conference affirmed the views of the NEC on the popular front and also its decision to expel Cripps. Subsequently, Cripps terminated his campaign and sought readmission to the Party.

The subject of a popular front was again raised towards the end of the war. The 1944 Labour Conference considered (in connection with its discussion of the Conference Arrangement Committee's report) the wisdom of securing 'a coalition of the left for the purpose of bringing about socialism', and the following year an attempt was made to refer back a section of the report of the Conference Arrangements Committee because the Conference agenda contained no specific resolution concerning the conclusion of arrangements with other progressive parties at the forthcoming general election. This motion was defeated on a card vote by the narrow majority of 1,314,000 to 1,219,000.

Labour participated in Churchill's Coalition government. Attlee and Arthur Greenwood were initial members of the War Cabinet and in February 1942 Attlee assumed the additional post of Deputy Prime Minister and his replacement, Sir Stafford Cripps, became a member of the War Cabinet. Greenwood left the government in February 1942 and the Home Secretary, Herbert Morrison, became a member of the War Cabinet in October of that year when Cripps left the government. During the war, the Labour Party clearly distinguished between an electoral and a political truce, and while they subscribed to the former they conducted political activity in preparation for the resumption of partisan political life when the war was over. Annual conferences were held each year.

Liberals

The Liberal Party responded to rising tensions in Europe in the late 1930s by calling for the creation of a Ministry of Supply to organise the nation's defences. The Party was also caught up in the debate concerning the popular front (which is discussed above). Joint action with the Labour Party could be justified on grounds which included the similar views held on foreign policy. Both endorsed support for the League of Nations and for the principle of collective security in response to Italy's invasion of Abyssinia and Liberals (including Gilbert Murray and Wilfrid Roberts MP) addressed the National Emergency Conference on Spain in 1938. A key difficulty faced by Liberal involvement in a popular front was that it was driven by a socialist ideology and Liberals could not condone the destruction of private enterprise and the suppression of liberty which they associated with this course of action. Liberals were also sceptical that Labour or Liberal voters would automatically transfer their allegiances to a popular front candidate (especially when this candidate was associated with socialism). Prompted by perceptions of an imminent Liberal revival, the 1937 Assembly reiterated the importance of independent Liberal action at by-elections.

However, the policy of appeasement helped to modify Liberal attitudes towards a popular front. The 1938 Assembly further considered the possibility of cooperating with other parties to further its own foreign policy objectives, and in October of that year the Liberal Party Executive Committee expressed itself ready to cooperate with men and women of all parties. A draft manifesto which provided guidelines for inter-party cooperation on international and defence questions was debated by the Party's Executive Committee and constituted an attempt to appeal to progressive voters over the heads of the leadership of the Labour and Conservative parties. A further debate in the Liberal Party Council in March 1939 sought to seize the initiative in candidate selection for the next general election by stating that the Liberals would contest only those seats which it held or where it secured second place in 1929, 1931 and 1935 and that elsewhere it would be willing to endorse a progressive or a Labour candidate.

There were, however, reservations within Liberal circles to the principle of inter-party cooperation envisaged by the popular front. They believed that Conservatives who were unhappy with their party's stance on key political issues (especially concerning foreign policy) were more likely to desert to the Liberals than to either a socialist Labour Party or an organisation driven by this ideology. Cooperation with Labour was also impeded by the negative views of this party held by many Liberal activists (especially in Northern England) who viewed it (rather than the Conservatives) as the principal enemy and also by the reluctance of Liberal associations and Liberal candidates to stand aside in order to give Labour a straight fight against the Conservatives. The Party further felt that, whereas it had given a number of Labour candidates active support in by-elections held after 1935, this had not been reciprocated by Labour. However, its desire to remain on good terms with the Labour leadership was one reason for the Liberal Party failing to endorse officially the Cripps petition, although individual Liberals were left free to determine their own course of action on this matter.

The Liberal Party participated in Churchill's Coalition government. The Liberal leader, Sir Archibald Sinclair, held the post of Secretary of State for Air (although he was not a member of the War Cabinet).

By-elections

A total of 219 by-elections occurred in the 1935–45 Parliament, of which 150 were contested. The Conservatives made a net loss of 28, Labour a net gain of 12 and others a net gain of 16.

By-elections which took place after 1935 all used the old electoral register save the contest in Chelmsford in April 1945 for which a new register had been prepared.

Conduct of the Election

A novel aspect of the 1945 election campaign (which became a feature of subsequent contests) was the use of the radio broadcast as a key means of communicating with the electorate. In 1945 this was at the expense of public meetings in the constituencies which were less well attended. The mood of the electorate in 1945 has been described as 'sober' with domestic issues (most notably housing and also employment, pensions, social insurance and food) being uppermost in their minds.

Conservatives

The Conservative campaign was built around Winston Churchill, the election manifesto being entitled, *Mr Churchill's Declaration of Policy to the Electors.* Individual candidates carried Churchill's endorsement and electors were requested to give him the opportunity to form a further government (which, regardless of its composition, Conservative propaganda insisted would be 'national') in order to complete the tasks initiated by the Coalition government in both domestic and foreign affairs. The main domestic policies contained in this declaration were based on a 'Four-Year' Plan which Churchill had announced in 1943 and which had subsequently spawned the 1944 Education Act and a number of White Papers concerned with post-war reconstruction. In 1945 Churchill expressed his desire to fulfil all obligations to servicemen which included the maintenance of a high and steady level of employment, the provision of homes (which was stated to be 'the greatest domestic task'), and the creation of a comprehensive health service. Churchill's declaration also spoke of the need to encourage efficiency in industrial processes but expressed opposition to state ownership and control of industry, and stated the Party's intention to remove controls as quickly as the need for them disappeared.

Foreign affairs were emphasised in the Conservative campaign in which it was argued the experience of Churchill and Eden was essential in order to implement key objectives which included continuing the alliance of the three major powers in which Churchill had played a major role during the war, the formation of an international organisation to preserve the peace, the successful conclusion of the war against Japan and dealing with a range of problems which would surface in post-war Europe. A poster thus enjoined the electorate to 'help him finish the job: vote National'.

Much of the Conservative campaign was of a negative character. Churchill made use of scare tactics which were designed to frighten electors from voting for the Labour Party. In his first election broadcast he alleged that freedom was incompatible with socialist policy and that a socialist administration would require a tough police or 'some form of Gestapo', a claim so improbable that even leading Liberal politicians jumped to Labour's defence. The attempt to denigrate the Labour Party subsequently shifted to focusing on the power structure of the Labour Party and alleging that the Party's National Executive Committee would exert control over the actions of a Labour government which would entail replacing Britain's parliamentary system of government by the dictatorship of the NEC. This issue initially arose when the chairman of the NEC, Professor Laski, sought to limit the capacity under which Attlee could accompany Churchill at a meeting of the 'big three' powers at Potsdam and the subject of the alleged power of an outside body over the Labour leadership became a major theme of Churchill's attack on the Labour Party.

Labour

The Labour Party (whose policy was contained in the manifesto, *Let Us Face the Future*) emphasised domestic policy during the campaign, seeking to rebuild Britain especially in order to repay those whose efforts had secured the victory against Germany. Labour's programme was presented by a team of leaders and did not focus on Attlee. Although there was a considerable degree of agreement in the domestic policies put forward by the main parties (including support for the Beveridge scheme of national insurance and the development of a national health service, a commitment to guaranteeing full employment, and an acceptance of the need to implement a major programme of house building), Labour argued that the Conservative record in office in the inter-war years when they had failed to provide a 'land fit for heroes' indicated that they could not be trusted to deliver on their promises. The explanations offered for this were that in the inter-war years the Conservatives were dominated by economically powerful 'hard-faced men' whose responsibility was to themselves rather than the nation. It was argued that the contemporary Conservative Party's concern with 'sound finance' would prevent high spending on social projects, and that this Party was a 'party of privilege' dominated by vested interests which would prevent the drastic actions proposed by Labour to secure domestic reform from being pursued.

In particular it was stated that Labour would rein in private enterprise (in contrast to the Conservatives who, they argued, would enhance its autonomy) within the context of national planning. A number of key industries (namely coal, gas and electricity undertakings, inland transport, iron and steel) would be nationalised under a Labour government, although the reasons for this were 'technical' rather than political, being designed to enhance economic efficiency in the national interest and thereby provide the basis for inaugurating a more equal society. For similar reasons, public supervision over monopolies and cartels was proposed. The manifesto stated the Party's ultimate commitment to land nationalisation but proposed that as a first step the state and local authorities should be given wider and speedier powers to acquire land for public purposes whenever the state interest demanded it. During the campaign, the Conservative Party attacked nationalisation on political grounds, although this argument could be justifiably made only in connection with proposed nationalisation of the Bank of England.

Labour said less than the Conservatives on foreign policy, although they did suggest that they, rather than the Conservatives, were in the best position to maintain good relations with the Soviet Union. Although the manifesto asserted that 'the Labour Party is a socialist party ... Its ultimate purpose at home is the establishment of the Socialist Commonwealth of Great Britain', Labour's appeal in 1945 was directed at 'all men and women of progressive outlook, and who believe in constructive change'. The deliberate toning down of the socialist aspects of their programme was aimed to court this electorate and especially to secure middle-class support for the Party.

The manifesto insisted that those who had served in the armed services, the merchant navy, home guard and civil defence 'deserve and must be assured a happier future than faced by so many of them after the last war. Labour regards their welfare as sacred'. The Party benefited from the 'Vote for Him' campaign which was mounted by the *Daily Mirror*. This derived from the paper's criticism that the rushed nature of the election was unfair to those in the services and attempted to ensure that their concerns about post-war domestic issues were taken adequate notice of by those who were able to vote.

Liberals

Liberal policy was contained in the programme, *The Twenty Point Manifesto of the Liberal Party*. This emphasised the need to repay the debt owed by the nation to its warriors through the pursuance of policies which included the Beveridge schemes for social security and full employment, the application to house building of the same drive as was used to produce aircraft and munitions during the war (including the utilisation of comprehensive measures of Town and Country Planning), and the improvement of health services and education. Traditional Liberal policies of free trade, site value taxation and profit-sharing in industry were also proposed.

The Liberal campaign was based on the assumption that the Conservative Party was unpopular but that there was no widespread desire to replace them with a socialist administration. Accordingly, Liberals attacked the Conservative record in the inter-war years (citing their failure to respond to the economic slump of the 1930s, their policy of appeasing fascists and their overall resistance to any form of progressive change) and in particular sought to distance Churchill from the party he now led by arguing that during that period he was a most vocal critic of Conservative governments and that his most loyal supporters were the Liberals led by Sinclair. Relatively little atention was devoted by the Party to attacking Labour, although doubt was cast on its progressive credentials by arguing that its role was mainly to serve the interests of the trade unions. It was further suggested that political and economic liberty would be placed in peril by that party's emphasis on state involvement in people's everyday lives. By contrast the Liberal manifesto emphasised the Party's commitment to safeguarding and enlarging civil liberties.

Liberal policy was based upon radical liberalism which was willing to embrace a wide degree of state involvement in order to tackle the 'five giants' of want, ignorance, idleness, squalor and disease and to secure the goal of 'full employment in a free society'. In particular, the Party emphasised the objective of social freedom, putting forward a policy based on the Beveridge report. Beveridge (who was elected as a Liberal MP in 1944 and chaired the Party's General

Election Committee) suggested that the policies of the Conservative and Labour parties would not abolish poverty and want, and he was especially critical of their approach towards social insurance, family allowances and old age pensions. The Party's policy on monopolies was to advocate government action to curb them and to use the policy of nationalisation where this was impossible. The manifesto proposed public control of the railways, the reorganisation of electric power as a public utility and the transformation of the coal-mining industry into a public service.

The Liberal campaign was directed at progressive voters. They especially courted younger electors whom, they assumed, had not cultivated an established pattern of voting behaviour and who were more numerous than was usual because of the deferment of a general election in wartime. The image which was portrayed was that of a party with no sectional axe to grind.

Result of the Election

There had been no redistribution of seats since 1918 and one was overdue in 1945. However, in order not to further complicate the election, a number of overly large constituencies were divided, thereby adding 25 MPs to the total elected in 1935 (which thus became 640). A considerable proportion of the electorate (2.8 million of a total of 33 million) were overseas, serving either in the armed forces or as merchant seamen. These were allowed to vote either by proxy or by having a ballot paper sent to them. Around 1.8 million of these voters appointed proxies.

A total of 1,683 candidates (the largest figure since 1929) contested the election, with three MPs being returned unopposed. Eleven boroughs in England and one in Scotland returned two members as did three counties in Northern Ireland and three of the university seats. Additionally, the Combined Scottish Universities returned three MPs. The result was:

Party	Votes	Vote %	MPs
Labour	11,967,746	47.7%	393
Conservative*	9,579,560	38.2%	202
Others	708,319	2.8%	23
Liberal	2,252,430	9.0%	12
Ulster Unionist	392,450	1.6% [53.7%]	8
Nationalist (Ulster)	148,078	0.6% [18.8%]	2
Scottish National Party	30,595	0.1% [1.3%]	0
Plaid Cymru	16,017	0.0% [1. %]	0
Total	25,095,195		640

*This figure includes the votes obtained by those candidates describing themselves as National (two of whom were elected) and Liberal National (11 elected).

The turnout was 73.3 per cent. The swing from the Conservative Party to Labour was 12.2 per cent.

The 'others' were J. McGovern (Glasgow – Shettleston, Independent Labour Party), J. Maxton (Glasgow – Bridgeton, Independent Labour Party), Rev. C. Stephen (Glasgow – Camlachie, Independent Labour Party), E. Millington

(Chelmsford, Common Wealth), Vernon Bartlett (Bridgwater, Independent Progressive), J. Beattie (Belfast West, Independent Labour), W. J. Brown (Rugby, Independent), W. Gallacher (Communist, West Fife), W. D. Kendall (Grantham, Independent), D. L. Lipson, (Cheltenham, National Independent), Rev. D. J. Little, (Down, Independent Conservative), Sir M. Macdonald, (Invernessshire, Independent Liberal), J. H. Mackie, (Galloway, Independent Conservative), J. MacLeod, (Ross and Cromarty, Independent Liberal), P. Piratin, (Stepney Mile End, Communist), D. N. Pritt, (Hammersmith North, Independent Labour), Sir J. Boyd Orr (Combined Scottish Universities, Independent), Sir E. G. G. Graham-Little (London University, National Independent), H. W. Harris (Cambridge University, Independent), A. P. Herbert, (Oxford University, Independent), K. M. Lindsay (Combined English Universities, Independent), E. F. Rathbone (Combined English Universities, Independent), Sir J. A. Salter (Oxford University, Independent). Twenty-four women MPs were elected.

The Parties

The national swing was subject to regional variation. The swing to Labour was slightly below average in Lancashire (where it was 10 per cent) but higher (20 per cent) in the West Midlands. The Conservative Party polled badly in London and in industrial areas in general. It did better in non-industrial areas including some middle-class towns (such as Blackpool, Southport and Brighton) as well as the rural county constituencies in general. Labour fielded its highest-ever number of candidates, 603. The party made a net gain of 239 seats compared with 1935, 79 of which were in constituencies which had never previously returned a Labour MP. Twenty-three Labour MPs were sponsored by the Cooperative Party and 121 by trade unions.

An attempt to secure a reunion of the Liberal Party before the election foundered on the issue of contesting the election as an independent party (which the Sinclair-led party insisted upon but which the Liberal Nationals would not contemplate), and in the 1945 election little difference could be discerned between the Liberal Nationals and the Conservative Party. The Liberal Party fielded only 306 candiates in the election and suffered from placing unclear electoral objectives before the electorate. The formation of a Liberal government was an unrealisable objective, but the Party gave no clear indication of what alternative role it sought to fulfil in the newly elected Parliament. The size of its parliamentary representation shrank to 12 MPs, only two of whom were elected in three-cornered contests. All leading Liberals (including Sinclair, Beveridge and the Chief Whip, Sir Percy Harris) were defeated and the Party lost its last remnants of urban representation in the House of Commons. Sixty-four Liberal candidates lost their deposits.

Other parties on the left of the political spectrum included the Communist Party, the Independent Labour Party (whose campaign was centred in Glasgow) and the Common Wealth Party. The latter had been formed during the war and advocated common ownership.

Scotland, Wales and Northern Ireland

In Scotland, the swing from the Conservative Party to Labour was 7 per cent overall, although there were some pronounced local variations (being 2.5 per cent in Glasgow and 8.5 per cent in the Lowlands). Overall, Labour won 37 of Scotland's 71 seats, the Conservative and National Liberals 27, the ILP three, the Communist Party one and Independents three. The swing from Conservatives to Labour was only 6.5 per cent in Wales, a situation partly accounted for by the support obtained by the Liberal Party which won six of the 35 seats. Labour was the largest party (winning 25 seats), and the Conservatives and National Liberals won the remaining four.

The Ulster Unionist Party retained its dominant position in Northern Irish politics (winning eight of the 12 seats), although it lost two seats to Irish Nationalist candidates in Fermanagh and Tyrone. Independent Labour and Conservative candidates won the remaining two seats.

Consequence of the Election
Clement Attlee formed a Labour Government.

23 February 1950

Party Leaders
Winston Churchill (Conservative)
Clement Attlee (Labour)
Clement Davies (Liberal)

Background to the Election

Timing of the Election

The size of the majority which Labour obtained in 1945 meant that the Party was in a position to hold the subsequent election at a date of its own choosing. However, advance preparations by the parties helped to develop a sense of election fever and this was further fuelled by devaluation on 18 September 1949 which was a significant feature of the campaign waged against the government in the future election contest. Pressure on the government to call an election was added to by the media and by some within the Labour Party whose advocacy of an election was based on fears that the economic situation might deteriorate further and harm Labour's prospects of securing re-election if the date was much delayed. The perception that uncertainty regarding the date of the election was harming trade and industry prompted Attlee on 12 October 1949 to announce his decision not to hold an election in 1949. However, pressure for an election in early 1950 was added to when a compromise was fashioned in November 1949 between the two Houses of Parliament concerning the Iron and Steel Bill and the legislation to revise the powers of the House of Lords. The completion of Labour's legislative programme also justified a new appeal to the electorate. However, its timing meant that the election register was considerably out of date.

Electoral Procedures and Practices

Significant changes to electoral practices were provided for in the 1948 Representation of the People Act, whose provisions were largely incorporated into the 1949 Representation of the People Act. Boundary commissions were set up in 1944 and their eventual recommendations were embodied in the First Schedule of the 1948 Representation of the People Act. This constituted the first redistribution since 1918. Extensive changes were made to constituency boundaries with only 80 being totally unaffected. It was estimated that this cost Labour around 25 seats, although this was slightly offset through a government amendment which provided 17 extra seats for large towns (Nicholas, 1951: 4-5). Future changes in constituency boundaries were provided for in the 1949 House of Commons (Redistribution of Seats) Act, whereby reports from boundary commissions for England, Scotland and Wales were required to be submitted at intervals of not less than three or more than seven years.

Additionally, the 1948 Representation of the People Act abolished the two remaining forms of plural voting. The university constituencies (which had returned 12 MPs in 1945) were abolished, which affected in excess of 220,000 voters. The separate representation of the universities at Westminster commenced in 1603 when James I granted Oxford and Cambridge universities the right each to send two MPs to the House of Commons. This legislation also abolished the business vote (affecting around 70,000 voters) and provided for the universal use of single-member constituencies. The 1948 legislation also made provisions for several categories of voters to vote by post or proxy (an entitlement which had only applied to service voters in 1945). It was estimated that the Conservative Party was the main beneficiary of this reform, securing them around 10 seats in 1950 (Nicholas, 1951: 9). The legislation further placed an obligation on returning officers to issue polling cards to electors (a function which had previously been discharged by the parties), forbade the hire of vehicles to take persons to the polls, encouraged local authorities to provide a sufficient number of polling stations and placed lower limitations on election expenditure. A further measure, the 1949 Electoral Registers Act, provided for persons coming of voting age between November and June of each year to be included in the electoral register, marked by the symbol 'Y'.

Labour also enacted the 1949 Parliament Act. This legislation arose against the background of difficulties in the House of Lords regarding the legislation to nationalise the iron and steel industry. This measure reduced the delaying powers of the House of Lords from two years to one year. Henceforth, any Bill which was vetoed by the Lords would automatically become law when reintroduced in the House of Commons in the following session.

Conservatives

The Labour government's schemes to improve the provision of social services were derived from schemes which were prepared during the Coalition government's period of office and were thus relatively uncontroversial, although the Conservatives exploited Labour's problems in connection with the opposition of medical professionals to the administrative structure for the National Health Service. Greater controversy between the two main parties was aroused by Labour's nationalisation proposals. The Conservative Party was ideologically opposed to nationalisation regardless of what reasons were put forward to justify the application of this policy to particular industries on the grounds that the concentration of the major industries in the hands of the government posed a threat to economic liberty and, ultimately, to political freedom. They also believed that nationalisation would subordinate industrial policy to political pressure which might result in inefficiency whereas radical restructuring was required to address the real problems faced by industry. Conservative opposition to the Transport Bill was thus based on the view that rather than seeking to improve the services, the measure had been brought forward in order to prevent road hauliers from competing with the newly nationalised railways. Conservatives also feared that a state monopoly would stifle economic progress. Their opposition to nationalisation reached a climax when proposals to nationalise the iron and steel industry were brought forward. This resulted in a clash between the government and the Conservative-dominated House of Lords. Eventually, a compromise was reached, whereby the Act was passed in 1949 but the Minister of Supply was not authorised to appoint members to the Iron and Steel Corporation before 1 October 1950 and the vesting date was deferred until 1 January 1951.

Between 1945 and 1950 the Conservative Party undertook a detailed examination of party organisation and policy. Organisational reform was masterminded by the party chairman, Lord Woolton, and was particularly directed at improving the vitality of the constituency parties.

R. A. Butler was especially prominent in the development of policy which sought to respond positively to Labour's interventions in both economic and social spheres, whilst emphasising the Party's commitment to private enterprise and individual freedom. An important aspect of this policy reformulation was the publication of the Industrial Charter in 1947, whose recommendations included joint consultation and co-partnership as aspects of a proposed workers' charter. The Party adopted a pragmatic attitude towards much of Labour's nationalisation programme, many perceiving that it was unsound government for one party to spend much of its time in office merely undoing the work of its predecessor and also that it would be difficult to find private business interests that would be prepared to take over the nationalised concerns which might be renationalised if a Labour government subsequently entered office.

A considerable effort was also devoted after 1945 to enhance the degree of Liberal–Conservative cooperation. In May 1947 the chairmen of the Conservative and National Liberal parties (Lords Woolton and Teviot) concluded an agreement which sought the establishment of joint constituency associations on the grounds that there was no longer any substantial differences separating Liberalism from Conservatism to justify the continued existence of separate Conservative and National Liberal organisations. However, the Liberal Party's objections centred on the sudden creation of new local organisations where there was no (or hardly any) prior involvement of National Liberals which would justify the name 'Liberal' being included in the organisation's title. For their part, the Conservatives argued that the 'Independent' Liberals led by Davies could make no exclusive claim to be the sole heirs of the Liberal tradition or to have the sole right to use the 'Liberal' name. During the election campaign, Churchill offered one of his party's broadcasts to Lady Violet Bonham Carter (who was not being employed in this capacity by Davies's Liberals) to emphasise the Conservative claim that many 'Independent' Liberals shared the Conservative view that the most important task for Liberals at that time was to defeat socialism. The Liberal criticisms of Conservative actions were further undermined by the Party's willingness to accept straight fights against Labour candidates when these were offered by Conservative associations who withdrew their candidates.

Labour

Labour's domestic programme entailed a considerable amount of nationalisation. In 1946 the government nationalised the Bank of England, the coal industry and the civil aviation. In 1947 the railways, electricity and road haulage were placed under public ownership and in 1948 gas was nationalised. These were placed under the day-to-day control of public corporations which operated at 'arm's length' from government. Labour also created a welfare state which gave the poorest members of society a considerable measure of economic security. The 1946 National Health Service Act created a health service to enable all persons to receive free medical treatment. Reforms were also made to state pensions, unemployment and sickness benefits. The 1946 National Insurance Act increased the scale of unemployment and sickness benefits and extended the period for which they would be paid. Labour thus introduced a 'cradle to the grave' protection against ill health and economic insecurity. Further domestic reform included attempts (in particular by the 1949 Housing Act) to stimulate house building, although initially many of the new constructions took the form of temporary ('prefab') buildings. In 1947 the school-leaving age was raised to 15. These reforms were financed by taxation policies which fell more heavily on the richer members of society, thus providing for a limited measure of wealth redistribution. The Labour government also enacted reforms desired by the trade unions. In 1946, the 1927 Trades Disputes Act was repealed, thereby restoring to the unions the legal powers they possessed before the general strike of 1926. The political levy was also restored, although individual union members were able to contract out of paying it. The government also pursued reforms to electoral procedures and practices and enacted the 1949 Parliament Act (all of which have been referred to above).

The inherent divisions between fundamentalist socialism and social democracy were temporarily masked after Labour's election victory in 1945 since the reforms embarked upon after 1945 secured a wide measure of support within the Labour Party. Reformist opinion was placated by the ability to justify nationalisation on technical grounds, by the considerable reluctance to interfere in the operations of the private sector of the economy, and the absence of any fundamental challenge to the opinion that a socialist society could be brought about by dynamic private enterprise. Nonetheless, there were signs that the accommodation between the left and right wings of the Party was fragile. Those on the left of the Party sought increased nationalisation, while others associated with the centre and right of the Party sought to consolidate the government's achievements before embarking on further measures of state control. Although the government departed from its reliance on technical reasons to justify nationalisation when it proposed to nationalise the iron and steel industry in 1949 (thereby causing concern to reformist opinion), the left wing of the Party grew increasingly restless as the government's period in office progressed. Intra-party conflict was occasioned over issues which included the government's decision to continue with military conscription and also emerged in connection with a telegram sent by a number of left-wing MPs to Signor Nenni (who sought the fusion of Socialist and Communist parties) on the eve of the Italian elections in April 1948.

The performance of the Labour administration was considerably influenced by economic difficulties. The war had imposed an immense strain on Britain's economy, and Attlee's government was heavily reliant on American aid in order to finance domestic reform. However, American loans were provided with stern conditions attached to them in the form of interest charges and also the requirement that by 1947 Sterling would become a fully convertible currency. However, putting the pound on full convertibility with the dollar on 15 July 1947 instigated a run on Sterling. A balance of payments crisis occasioned by the increased American price of American imports (aggravated by a fuel crisis and a high level of unemployment in early 1947 which led to a loss of production affecting exports) caused foreign gold and currency reserves to be withdrawn from Britain. Emergency measures which included the reduction of food imports and a cut in the basic petrol ration were taken but this failed to stem the run on the Pound. On 20 August 1947 the government suspended convertibility and introduced further cuts in items such as the meat ration and the suspension of foreign travel for pleasure purposes.

In November 1947, the Chancellor of the Exchequer (Hugh Dalton) resigned following an inadvertent leakage of the contents of his budget and was replaced by Sir Stafford Cripps who pursued the policy of austerity with enhanced intensity. This entailed measures such as reducing imports and expanding exports through a system of licensing and the continuance of rationing (which included food and, until 1949, clothes). Controls were also exerted over prices and incomes (the latter in the form of a wage freeze). Taxes and duties were raised in the 1948 budget, and further increases (coupled with a reduction in excise duties) were made in the 1949 budget. Although these measures (coupled with the provision of Marshall Aid in 1948) had some success in securing improvements to the nation's economic fortunes, they failed to remedy them completely and further problems were encountered as capital began to flow from the country at a considerable rate. By the summer of 1949 a renewed balance of payments crisis occurred which was countered by further cuts in dollar imports. This problem, coupled with a minor recession in America and renewed speculation against the Pound, prompted devaluation on 18 September 1949. Convertibility and then devaluation had a detrimental impact on the government's ability to deliver domestic reform and, following devaluation, attempts were made to rein in government spending by introducing limited cuts in current spending and capital investment programmes.

The government's record in foreign affairs included British participation in the Western Union Alliance, the Council of Europe, and the North Atlantic Treaty Organisation which was established in 1949 to provide collective security for its members whereby an attack against any one of them would be treated as an attack against all. British rule in India was ended in 1947, and independence was granted to both Ceylon and Burma in 1948.

Liberals

The pledge by Sinclair's victorious opponent to submit to a by-election as soon as the war with Japan had ended prompted many Liberals to assume that Sinclair's absence from Parliament would be a temporary one. Clement Davies assumed the chairmanship of the Liberal MPs, although the failure of any by-election to materialise in Caithness and Sutherland led him to become the accepted leader of the Party.

In the period after 1945, much emphasis was devoted to improving Liberal organisation and finances. In 1945 a Reconstruction Committee was appointed and its 1946 report, *Coats Off For The Future!*, provided detailed proposals to achieve this aim. The 1949 Party Conference endorsed the principle of contesting the next general election on the basis of a broad front, although the Party's performance in by-elections (which saw a Liberal candidate achieve just 1 per cent of the poll in Camlachie in January 1948) did not augur well for the coming election. Speaking in Manchester in February 1948, Davies declared, 'If you want to take up politics and office, don't join the Liberals. I have nothing to offer. I am weak in organisation and penniless.' A particular difficulty faced by the Party after 1945 was the use made by the Conservative Party of the Liberal name which Liberals perceived as deceitful.

By-elections

There were 52 by-elections in the 1945–50 Parliament. The Labour Party held 35 seats, the Conservatives held 11 and gained three (two from Independents in university constituencies and one from the ILP), the ILP held one seat, the Ulster Unionists held one seat and gained another (from the Independent Ulster Unionists). One further vacancy (Hemsworth in 1946) was uncontested.

Conduct of the Election

The rationing of newsprint meant that election broadcasts were a key aspect of the campaign. Five were allotted to the Conservative and Labour parties, three to the Liberals and one to any party fielding 50 or more candidates (a provision which gave the Communist Party a broadcast). All broadcasts were radio transmissions and ceased four days before the poll. There were no television broadcasts, although some of the radio broadcasts were available in a television soundtrack at the end of the night's programmes. Apart from the election broadcasts, the BBC gave the campaign no coverage, and removed almost every reference to party politics from its programmes. It was as if the election 'had been occurring on another planet' (Nicholas, 1951: 126).

The campaigns of the three major parties were subject to a considerable degree of central organisation. The agenda of the election was very heavily influenced by the party manifestoes. There were two exceptions to this. The first was Churchill's suggestion (in a speech delivered at Devonport) that the basic ration of petrol for cars and motorcycles should be raised. Labour condemned this proposal on the grounds that it would result in fewer dollars being available to spend on food and raw materials and the *Daily Mirror* depicted it as a 'petrol bribe'. However, their opposition was somewhat undermined by Gaitskell alluding to this course of action, which further implied that Labour practised austerity for austerity's sake rather than out of necessity. The Conservative press also viewed this policy as evidence of Labour's partisanship against motorists. A second departure from the text of the party manifestoes was Churchill's suggestion in a speech delivered at Edinburgh on 14 February (which was developed in a later speech in Manchester and in his election broadcast) that the atomic bomb was not a satisfactory guarantee of world peace and that high-level talks between America, the Soviet Union and the United Kingdom should be initiated in an attempt to end the Cold War. This was dismissed as 'soap box diplomacy' by Morrison.

Labour

The proposals of the Labour Party for the 1950 general election were developed in 1949. In February, a meeting of Labour ministers and members of the NEC to consider a policy statement took place in the Isle of Wight; this formed the basis of a publication, *Labour Believes in Britain*, which was considered by the June 1949 Party Conference. An alternative manifesto entitled *Keeping Left* was also published in 1950 whose proposals included tighter controls, cuts in defence expenditure, a capital levy and 'socialist wage fixing'. However, it made little impact on the subsequent campaign.

The Labour Party's policies were contained in its manifesto, *Let Us Win Through Together*. Its campaign emphasised Labour's record in government. The manifesto lauded the nation's achievements since 1945 (which included high employment, social security and the relative infrequency of industrial disputes) which, it alleged, was based upon vigorous, sensible leadership. Full employment and the social services received prominent attention in Labour's election broadcasts. The manifesto stated that the maintenance of full employment was the Party's 'supreme aim'. To achieve this, special measures were proposed for areas of special need and private enterprise would be freed from the stranglehold of restrictive monopolies. The government proposed to address the exploitation of the public by monopolies and in this context pledged to transfer beet sugar manufacture, sugar refining and the cement industry to public ownership. Additionally, public ownership of sections of the chemical industry would be considered in order to safeguard national interests and water supply would become a wholly public responsibility in order to improve the amenities of the countryside. However, earlier proposals to nationalise industrial assurance were watered down to a scheme for mutualisation (which would only apply to proprietary companies which would become owned by policy-holders). Favourable reference was made to the government's record in combating inflation, and it was proposed to bring down excessive prices by policies which included the establishment of more wholesale and retail markets under municipal or other public ownership, the development of cold storage through public ownership and the extension of buying by public bodies in order that the housewife could be supplied with goods at reasonable prices.

The manifesto also praised the government's achievements in providing for social security and establishing a national health service, the latter benefiting all sections of the community including the middle class and professional families. Labour promised to build upon the foundations which they had laid and the manifesto compared Labour's achievements in these areas with the dole queues and means test associated with Conservative governments in the inter-war years and it also referred to Conservative opposition to Labour's social reforms. The manifesto thus concluded that the Conservatives could not be trusted to safeguard the welfare of the sick, the poor and the old, and voters were asked to vote Labour to ensure that the bleak years of poverty and unemployment which were associated with Conservative inter-war years governments would not return. A large number of Labour candidates' election addresses focused on the hardships of the 1930s, which were epitomised by events which included the Jarrow marchers. More explicit references to Conservatives favouring a higher level of unemployment and suggestions that the return of a Conservative government might lead to war were made in 'whispering campaigns' associated with the Labour Party. Towards the end of the campaign, Labour speeches warned the electorate to be on their guard against some form of Conservative 'stunt' but this failed to materialise.

In the area of foreign affairs, the manifesto attacked the pre-war policies of Conservative governments, arguing that collective security could have prevented the 1939–45 conflict. Labour pledged to work for peace, remaining ready to cooperate with Russia and advocating closer association between countries that subscribed to the Charter of the United Nations and the strengthening of ties between the Commonwealth, the Atlantic Community and Western Europe. The Party promised to create the economic and social basis for the democratic self-government of the colonies.

Attlee undertook an extensive speaking tour to put Labour's case across. He epitomised the reasonableness of Labour in office. The Party's appeal was especially directed at progressive, middle-class opinion and a party political broadcast delivered in January by the author J. B. Priestley sought to reassure middle-class Labour supporters who were troubled by the restric-tions associated with Labour's period in office by referring to the achievements that had taken place in that period.

A major aspect of the campaign against Labour was associated with industries threatened with nationalisation. Two of these in particular (industrial assurance and the sugar industry) mounted a vigorous campaign opposing this course of action which was waged by methods which included Tate and Lyle's 'Mr Cube' who appeared on every packet of sugar. Labour viewed this as an unacceptable attempt by big business to interfere in politics, but the indus-tries concerned believed their campaign constituted the exercise of their rights of self-defence and free speech. No attempt was made to test whether the expenditure by these industries was legal under the provisions of section 63 of the 1949 Representation of the People Act (since it implicitly aided the Conservative Party) but the calling of the election significantly limited the campaign although Mr Cube continued to appear and Lord Lyle launched an anti-nationalisation petition in January 1950. Although the Conservative Party saw no difference in the aid given to their cause by the anti-nationalisation campaign and the money received by Labour from the trade unions, they officially remained aloof from it and called for its cessation once Parliament had been dissolved to enable them to spearhead the opposition to nationalisation during the election campaign.

Conservatives

In 1949 the Conservative Party prepared a draft statement of policy which was entitled *The Right Road for Britain*. This accepted many of the policies pursued by Labour since 1945 (including the commitment to full employment, the welfare state and the temporary continuance of controls including food rationing) and was dubbed 'Tory socialism'. However, it was relatively sparse in providing precise details of policy (in particular regarding the economic crisis) and was attacked by Labour for promising both enhanced social security benefits and reduced levels of public spending.

Conservative policies were contained in its manifesto, *This is the Road*, which was broadly similar to the 1949 document. This emphasised the need for Britain's economic independence to be restored and her citizens to be granted their full personal freedom and power of initiative. Peace was stated to be the Party's supreme purpose which required a partnership of the Commonwealth, Empire, Western Europe and the Atlantic powers.

Much attention was devoted to attacking the record of the Labour government by concentrating on what they perceived to be mismanagement, folly and extravagance. Policies such as nationalisation, rationing, shortages and taxation were cited as examples of these failures. It was argued that Labour had squandered national resources, discouraged or suppressed individual effort and injured national unity. In their campaign, the Conservatives put forward an alternative version of the inter-war years to that projected in Labour accounts, and argued that the Labour government had eroded key national values and intended to create a socialist state which owned everything, employed everybody and smothered enterprise and initiative in bureaucracy and red tape. Churchill's election broadcast emphasised this argument by referring to the product of Labour government being a broken and disspirited people. The Conservatives aimed to reinvigorate the nation by restoring these traditional values, the manifesto stating that the Party's purpose was 'to denationalise wherever possible, to decentralise as much as possible, to encourage and reward personal responsibility, to give enterprise and adventure their heads'. A Conservative government would bring the people of Britain together once again, acting as the servants of the people, not their master.

Labour's economic policy was especially attacked in the Conservative manifesto. It was stated that, under Labour rule, the value of the Pound had declined to 16s 4d and full employment had only been achieved as the consequence of American aid. It was alleged that devaluation had not solved the economic crisis facing the country and that things would get worse rather than better. Reducing the role of the state figured prominently in Conservative policy which included the promotion of larger and more efficient production at lower prices, the reduction of public spending and reduced taxes, commencing with the reduction of purchase tax on necessities and semi-necessities. Direct government purchasing of food would stop and the present system of food subsidies be ended with compensatory measures for those most adversely affected (such as larger family allowances, pensions and other social benefits). Nationalisation would cease. The Iron and Steel Act would be repealed before it could come into force and the nationalisation of buses and tramways would be halted. The operations of the National Coal Board would be decentralised and British Railways would be reorganised into a number of regional railway systems. Conservatives were pledged to reduce controls to a minimum, end the bulk purchase of commodities by the state and abolish the direction of labour. Proposals to apply a workers' charter to provide employees with security, incentive and status would be discussed with unions and employers.

Conservative social security policy was designed to provide a solid base below which no person should fall and above which each should be encouraged to rise to the utmost of his or her ability. Those who wished to create more security for themselves and their families through their own efforts would be encouraged to do so. Conservatives pledged to maintain and improve the National Health Service. The Party was committed to a property-owning democracy and the house building record of the Labour government was condemned for its inadequacy whereby 30,000 fewer houses were being built each year than at the height of the economic crisis in 1931. Housing emerged at the key issue discussed in the election addresses of individual Conservative candidates.

Conservative proposals for constitutional reform included the establishment of a Minister of State for Scotland with Cabinet rank, the proposal to convene an all-party conference to discuss the reform of the House of Lords, and a pledge to restore the university constituencies. In the areas of foreign affairs, the Party expressed its allegiance to the ideals contained in the Charter of the United Nations. Conscription would be continued until the challenge to the United Nations' authority had ended.

The Conservative Party argued that the timing of the election was dictated by Labour's desire to have the contest before the effects of devaluation and the budget were felt. Churchill played a less prominent part in the national campaign than he had in 1945, which involved a greater number of leading Conservatives. His reduced prominence was especially notable in the election addresses of Conservative candidates: in 1945 virtually all carried a letter of endorsement from Churchill, whereas in 1950 only a small minority (estimated at one-eighth of the total) did so, while one-half failed to refer to him at all (Nicholas, 1951: 215). As with Labour, their appeal was especially directed at the middle-class vote. An appeal to the discontented lower middle class was the theme of an election broadcast delivered by Dr Charles Hill. In this broadcast he disputed Labour's version of the misery of the inter-war years and equated socialist planning with a protection racket. Appeals for support from Liberal sympathisers were an important feature of the Conservative campaign (Dr Hill, for example, argued that support for Liberal candidates was a wasted vote and one which could aid the Socialists to attain victory). Conservative candidates made wide use of a leaflet, *A Word to Liberals*, to secure Liberal support. Distractions during the campaign included exchanges between Churchill and the junior Labour minister, Ness Edwards, regarding Churchill's actions in 1910 in sending troops to Tonypandy when he was Home Secretary and exchanges with the *Manchester Guardian* in connection with remarks he made at his adoption speech at Woodford when he accused Labour of frittering away American aid by permitting the import of 'indulgencies' (including food and fruits) which were not indispensable to national recovery. These exchanges were developed by Churchill in a speech at Manchester on 20 February into an attack on the haughty, almost autocratic, bearing of the the newspaper's editor.

Liberals

The Liberal manifesto, *No Easy Way*, affirmed the Party's intention to offer the electorate the opportunity of returning a Liberal government. It emphasised its ability to unite the nation in contrast to the Conservative and Labour parties which were allegedly locked in a class struggle.

The manifesto affirmed the Party's commitment to the maintenance of full employment in a free society and to support the social services. Prominent attention was devoted to the economic crisis facing the country. It was argued that enormous savings in government expenditure were proposed in order to avoid economic disaster following the end of Marshall Aid in 1952 with lower taxes being deferred until increased production resulted in enhanced exports. Savings would be achieved by cutting food subsidies (with increased social security benefits for those most adversely affected), and ending all controls not required to ensure fair shares or avoid scarcity. Co-partnership and profit-sharing would be introduced into major units of industry in order to reconcile the interests of workers and employers, and it was proposed that there should be no more nationalisation of industry for a period of five years, until the results of nationalisation to date had been digested. The nationalisation of the iron and steel industries would be repealed, road transport would be freed, and the control of nationalised industries would be decentralised. The Party's historic commitment to free trade (to be achieved by the reduction of tariffs by stages until all were abolished) was affirmed.

It was proposed to establish a Land Bank to provide cheap capital and credit for agricultural and horticultural development, and to appoint one minister with overall responsibility for coordinating a housing drive. It was asserted that social security could only be established when its benefits were related to the cost of living but pledges were made to extend the family allowance to the first child, to upgrade living conditions for the elderly and to improve the administration of the National Health Service. The school leaving age would not be raised to 16 until accommodation and teachers could be found. Constitutional reform included the introduction of proportional representation through the single transferable vote for election to the House of Commons, the reform of the composition of the House of Lords by eliminating heredity as a qualification for membership and the establishment of Parliaments for Scotland and Wales.

In the area of foreign affairs, peace was stated to be the first need. The Party pledged itself to work to speed up the process of creating an international order under the rule of law and desired quicker action to develop the Council of Europe. The Party was opposed to peacetime conscription. The Liberal manifesto tended to focus on the present and future state of the nation, although the Party's election broadcasts did refer to the Conservative record in the inter-war years.

Result of the Election

Two sets of opinion polls, the British Institute of Public Opinion (the 'Gallup' poll) and the *Daily Express* Poll of Public Opinion, indicated that the Conservative Party was comfortably in the lead until November 1949, when its popularity began to diminish. Towards the end of January and beginning of February 1950, both polls indicated that the race was neck and neck. However, the election got off to a slow start, constituting a lull in hostilies reminiscent of the 1939 'phoney war'.

A total of 1,868 candidates contested the election. This figure surpassed the previous record of 1,730 which had been established in 1929 and included 475 Liberal and 100 Communist candidates. There were 112 straight fights (compared to 274 in 1945) and in only two constituencies was a candidate returned uncontested (both in Northern Ireland). The result was:

Party	Votes	Vote %	MPs
Labour	13,266,176	46.1%	315
Conservative	12,140,070	42.2%	288*
Ulster Unionist	352,334	1.3% [62.8%]	10
Liberal	2,621,487	9.1%	9
Irish Nationalist (Ulster)	65,211	0.2% [11.6%]	2
Others	298,558	1.0%	1
Scottish National Party	9,708	0.0% [0.4%]	0
Plaid Cymru	17,580	0.1% [1.2%]	0
Total	28,771,124		625

*This figure includes support obtained by National Liberal and Conservative candidates.

The turnout was 83.9 per cent and in only 27 seats did this figure fall below 75 per cent. The swing from Labour to the Conservatives was 2.9 per cent.

The 'other' was J. MacLeod, Independent Liberal, Ross and Cromarty. The number of women MPs elected was 21.

The Parties

The election was tightly contested. Seven MPs were returned with majorities below 100 votes, and 45 had majorities of below 1,000 votes (*Times Guide*, 1950: 26).

The national swing was subject to a number of significant variations: in London suburbs, Essex, the Hampshire ports and North Lancashire it was approximately double this figure, whereas it was less in the Severn area, Western England, East Anglia, the North East Midlands, Lincolnshire, Wales and the Fife/Stirling/West Lothian area of Scotland (Nicholas, 1951: 320). One feature of the result was that the 'cube law' (which stated that if the votes for the major parties was in the ratio of A:B, the seats each obtained in the House of Commons would be in the ration of $A^3:B^3$) failed to operate as precisely as had been the case in the three previous general elections, denying Labour around 18 seats which were instead won by the Conservative Party. One reason for this was the impact of redistribution which led Labour to pile up large majorities in safe seats whereas the Conservative vote was more effectively spread. If the Labour vote is scaled down by around 500,000 to take this wastage into account, the cube law formula fits the results of the 1950 election (*Times Guide*, 1955: 252–3).

The high level of voter participation was attributed to the dominance which election manifetoes exerted over the parties' campaigns which meant that a relatively small number of issues were given widespread consideration (Nicholas, 1951: 115). Another was the growing pressure of the activities of government on the individual (Nicholas, 1951: 296).

The Labour Party viewed their campaign as having been successful. It had obtained the highest total of votes polled by any party in UK electoral politics, saved all its deposits and had lost a number of seats by a small number of votes. These failures were often attributed to intervention by the Liberal or Communist parties. The Party lost considerable headway in the dormitory areas of big towns, especially London, indicating a movement away from the Party by middle- and lower-middle-class electors, professionals and office workers. By contrast, it polled well in industrial and working-class areas which had experienced high unemployment in the 1930s.

One hundred and forty Labour candidates were sponsored by trade unions (of whom 110 were elected) and a further 36 were Labour and Cooperative Party candidates (of whom 18 were successful). One Labour minister, Lewis Silkin, was unable to find a new constituency after his seat was abolished by redistribution. Labour losses included one Cabinet minister (A. Creech Jones, Secretary of State for the Colonies), five junior ministers and the Solicitor-General, Sir Frank Soskice.

A number of former Conservative MPs who had not sat in the 1945–1950 Parliament were elected in 1950. These included Duncan Sandys, Henry Brooke and Geoffrey Lloyd. The Party's main strength continued to be in the counties. The Liberal Party's offer to the electorate of the chance to return a Liberal government was rebuffed. Only nine MPs were returned and 319 of the 475 Liberal candidates lost their deposits. The average poll obtained by a Liberal candidate was 11.4 per cent, and the Party obtained 25 per cent or more of the vote in only 24 constituencies. The Party's lack of success in securing the election of candidates to the House of Commons was hampered by the very even spread of Liberal support nationally, although seven of their nine MPs represented constituencies in the Celtic Fringe. The Party's former leader, Sir Archibald Sinclair, failed to regain his former constituency of Caithness and Sutherland and the former Chief Whip, Sir Percy Harris, was also unsuccessful at Bethnal Green. The current Chief Whip, Frank Byers, also narrowly lost his North Dorset constituency by 97 votes. The Party blamed the electoral system for failing to give them a Parliamentary Party which reflected their national share of the vote.

Five Labour Independents (sitting MPs who were expelled from the Party because of their views on foreign policy) – Pritt, Platts-Mills, Hutchinson, Solley and Zilliacus – were all defeated, and W. J. Brown ('Billy Brown of Rugby town' according to his campaign slogan) also lost his seat at Rugby which he had represented since 1942.

Scotland, Wales and Northern Ireland

Labour was the dominant party in Scotland, winning 37 of the 71 seats, to the 31 secured by the Conservative and National Liberal parties. The Liberals won two seats and the remaining one was won by an Independent Liberal who, in the new Parliament, joined the Liberal Unionist Group of MPs. In Wales, Labour won 27 of the 36 seats, the Liberals five and the Conservative and National Liberal parties won the remaining four seats. The Ulster Unionist Party won 10 of Northern Ireland's 12 seats and Nationalist candidates won the remaining two.

Consequence of the Election

Clement Attlee formed a second Labour government. However, the 'fuzzy' nature of his mandate was reflected in the omission of fresh nationalisation proposals in the 1950 King's Speech.

25 October 1951

Party Leaders
Winston Churchill (Conservative)
Clement Attlee (Labour)
Clement Davies (Liberal)

Background to the Election

Timing of the Election

The small size of the majority obtained by Labour in 1950 (six) led to widespread speculation that a new election would not be long delayed. Attlee's decision to call an election (which was announced in a news bulletin on 19 September, the first time this forum had been used for such a purpose) was based on two key considerations. The first of these was the perception that adverse economic circumstances which emerged in 1951 might get worse and thus weaken Labour's chances of re-election. The threat of a coal shortage (which in the winter of 1950–51 was solved by American imports) was one tangible indicator which might cost votes. The second was the problems faced by Labour in avoiding defeats in the House of Commons which made it difficult to put forward any programme of substance. Although the government was defeated only on seven minor issues in the 1950–51 Parliament, parliamentary procedures could be exploited by an opposition which was determined to make the life of the government difficult.

Electoral Procedures and Practices

The 1949 Electoral Registers Act was first used in the 1951 contest. Under this legislation, persons whose 21st birthday occurred after the date on which the register was compiled (but within three months of it coming into force) were entitled to be entered on the register with a 'Y' against their name. This meant that 400,000 young persons who would previously have been disenfranchised were entitled to vote in 1951. Additionally, the period in which persons could apply for a postal vote was extended, which added in excess of 150,000 of these votes in 1951 compared to 1950. A small number of boundary changes affected 25 constituencies.

Labour's campaign was, as in 1950, affected by campaigns mounted by industry. On 19 October 1951, several newspapers carried an advertisement by the Tronoh-Malayan Tin Group of Companies which attacked Labour policy in general and their proposals for dividend limitation in particular. This resulted in a legal challenge which was resolved in 1952 when it was ruled that general political advertisements were not illegal under section 63 of the 1949 Representation of the People Act, provided they did not seek to promote the election of particular candidates.

Labour

The government failed to promote any major items of legislation in the 1950–51 Parliament and gave the impression that its achievements between 1945 and 1950 had resulted in it running out of steam and that it was subsequently drifting along devoid of any purpose. Its impressive record in social reform was not advanced and the perception that nationalisation was unpopular (for reasons which included its failure to bring any tangible benefits to those employed in the affected industries) was one factor (apart from the difficulty of getting the legislation through the House of Commons) which resulted in proposals to nationalise the sugar and cement industries and to mutualise industrial insurance not being proceeded with. However, the 1949 Iron and Steel Act was implemented and the Iron and Steel Corporation took over the running of the industry on 15 February 1951. In July 1951, proposals were put forward to counter inflation by a policy of dividend limitation. The Conservatives viewed this suggestion as based on politics rather than economics, but the election intervened to prevent legislation to secure this purpose from being introduced.

The economic situation was good throughout 1950 and was evidenced by improvements in the balance of payments situation and increases in the nation's gold and dollar reserves which made it possible to suspend Marshall Aid in advance of its projected end in 1952. However, economic circumstances deteriorated rapidly in 1951. A dollar drain occurred, prices began to rise faster than wages, the price of raw materials rose in response to world stockpiling, and the defence programme hindered the export drive. Commodities remained in relatively short supply throughout the 1950–51 Parliament, although petrol rationing was ended in the summer of 1950.

Much of the government's attention after 1950 was directed at foreign affairs. War broke out in Korea in June 1950 and was prolonged by Chinese intervention. This conflict considerably intensified the Cold War and resulted in a major rearmament programme. In his April 1951 budget, Chancellor Gaitskell imposed tax rises to pay for this, including imposing charges on false teeth and spectacles which had previously been available free of charge under the National Health Service. Although the rearmament programme was not a subject of inter-party dispute, Gaitskell's budget caused acrimony within the Labour Party, especially in the constituencies. Additional problems took place in Persia (which are discussed below). In Europe, the launching of the Schuman Plan resulted in inter-party disputes as to whether the UK should participate in the arrangements.

After 1951 there emerged a division between those who wished to expand the Party's nationalisation proposals and those who wished to consolidate the developments which had occurred between 1945 and 1951. This essentially negative policy of resistance to further measures of nationalisation was supplemented by an attempt to redefine the ideology on which the future actions of the Labour Party would be based. Such 'new thinking' was articulated by organisations such as the Socialist Union, the Fabian Society and by journals such as *Socialist Commentary*. The decision of Chancellor Hugh Gaitskell in his 1951 budget to introduce charges into the hitherto free National Health sSrvice to pay for rearmament caused by the outbreak of war in Korea in 1950 provoked the resignations of Aneurin Bevan, Harold Wilson and John Freeman. The left of the Party viewed this as the inevitable consequence of the foreign policy pursued by Ernest Bevin whereby the government failed to pursue a distinctive 'socialist' approach and instead followed the lead of the United States. Bevan's resignation was of crucial importance to subsequent events in the Labour Party, since he possessed the stature and intellect to provide leadership to those on the left wing of the Party. In addition to the resignations of Bevan and Wilson, the personnel of the government was affected by the departures of Cripps and Bevin due to ill health. They were replaced by Gaitskell and Morrison.

Conservatives

The Conservative Party embarked upon a policy of opposition for opposition's sake in 1951. One of the tactics which was used was to present Prayers against Ministerial Orders which had to be debated at the end of the day's business, thus keeping Parliament in session all night. This tactic was initiated in March 1951 and aimed at wearing the government down since it was necessary to keep all Labour MPs on hand to avoid defeats in divisions while the Conservative Party was able to marshall all of its forces selectively on votes of its choosing. This particular problem was solved when the government avoided difficulties of this nature by using its majority to carry an adjournment motion, thus ensuring that Prayers could be presented only on occasions of the government's choosing. Of particular consequence for future domestic reform was the leadership's acceptance of an amendment moved at the October 1950 Conference which pledged the Party to build 300,000 houses a year.

Liberals

Liberal Parliamentarians were prominent in opposing the government's decision to prevent Seretse Khama, chief of the Bamangwato tribe, from returning to his homeland in the Bechuanaland Protectorate following his marriage to a white woman. The requirements of the nuclear armament programme prompted the government to pander to the racist views of the government in South Africa on this matter. However, Liberals (and some Labour backbenchers) were appalled at the implications of this decision for civil liberties and Clement Davies and Roderic Bowen initiated a debate in the House of Commons on this matter.

By-elections

Sixteen by-elections occurred in the 1950–51 Parliament. Labour held all eight seats it defended and the Conservatives similarly successfully defended six seats won in 1950. In Northern Ireland, the Ulster Unionists held two seats: one contest (in West Belfast) occurred when the 1950 Unionist victor, Rev. J. G. MacManaway, was disqualified. The other was an uncontested by-election in Londonderry after the 1950 victor, Sir Ronald Ross, was appointed Agent of the Northern Ireland government in London.

Conduct of the Election

Opinion polls suggested that Labour was holding on to its lead in 1950 but that the Conservative Party had moved decisively into the lead during 1951. At the outset of the campaign both Gallup and the *Daily Express* had the Conservative Party comfortably in the lead. This situation was borne out in by-election contests. Excluding the two in Northern Ireland, those held in the period until October 1950 provided an average swing from Labour to Conservative of 1.7 per cent. In those held after this date, the comparable swing between the two parties was 5.7 per cent.

Labour

The Labour Party election manifesto indicated that there were four major tasks for the nation – to secure peace, to maintain full employment and increase production, to bring down the cost of living and to build a just society.

It stated that Labour had worked hard since 1945 to bring all nations of the world together in worldwide cooperation through the United Nations. However, peace required not merely arms, but also securing freedom from poverty for lands where hunger and disease were prevalent. Labour's provision of economic assistance to such countries was contrasted with the Tory belief in imperialism and colonial exploitation. The maintenance of full employment for six years was asserted to be Labour's greatest achievement and it was argued that this situation had never occurred under the Conservatives when millions were without work. Under Labour, production had increased twice as fast each year as under the Conservatives and 20 per cent of national income was devoted to the provision of new capital equipment. Action was promised to attack monopolies and combines which restricted production and kept prices and profits too high and development councils would be set up, by compulsion if necessary, to aid industrial efficiency. It acknowledged that the shortage of raw materials had raised the cost of imports and reopened the dollar gap and promised to seek the development of new sources of raw materials, especially within the Commonwealth.

The manifesto acknowledged the rise in the cost of living, but asserted that this was lower than in other countries, as rising prices had been held back by Labour policies which included price control, rent control, food subsidies (which were worth twelve shillings a week to the average family), utility production and bulk purchase which kept down the cost of imports. Nationalisation had also ensured that the cost of coal was lower than in any country in Europe or in the United States. Labour had initiated discussions for a fairer distribution of raw materials and for lower and more stable prices which in particular had helped keep down the prices of textiles and clothing. It was hoped that this fall would extend soon to other areas and to achieve this it was proposed to extend and strengthen price controls and to set up new auction markets in provincial towns to reduce the price of fruit and vegetables to the housewife. Marketing in other trades would be overhauled with the same objective. It was argued that the Conservatives would cause a catastrophic rise in the cost of living as they favoured high profits, were opposed to controls, wished to abandon bulk purchase, to end the utility scheme and to allow landlords to raise rents.

Labour's attainment of full employment was contrasted with the mass unemployment, fear and misery of the inter-war years. Labour had provided social security for every man, woman and child and had instituted a National Health Service. The workhouse and Poor Law had been replaced by a National Insurance system which covered the entire population with greatly improved pensions and a humane scheme of National Assistance. It stated that much progress had been made, but that there was more to do in redistributing income and property to ensure that those who created the nation's wealth received their just reward. Half of Britain's wealth was owned by 1 per cent of the population. Labour would seek to extend social equality and the establishment of equal opportunities for all, and the policy of giving all young people equal opportunities in education would be extended. The taxation of wages, salaries, moderate incomes and moderate inheritance would be reduced when circumstances allowed this course of action but, on the other hand, dividends would be limited by law, taxation on the small minority who owned great fortunes, and large unearned incomes would be increased and large capital gains would be prevented. Labour had built 1,300,000 new dwellings since the war and pledged to maintain the present rate of 200,000 new houses a year and increase it as soon as raw materials and manpower could be spared. It was argued that the Conservatives opposed a more equal society and stood, instead, for privilege. In order to reduce the taxes of the well-to-do they would reduce the social services and had voted in Parliament against the creation of the National Health Service.

The manifesto argued that the nation's choice was to go forwards with Labour or backwards with the Tories. It asserted that after six years of Labour rule and in spite of post-war difficulties the standard of living for the majority of people was higher than it had ever been, old folk were better cared for and the young generation was happy and healthier than had ever been the case. By contrast, the Conservatives would take the nation backwards into poverty and insecurity at home and grave perils abroad.

At the outset of the campaign a Tribune pamphlet, *Going Our Way*, (whose authors included Bevan, Wilson and Freeman) put forward a left-wing manifesto which attacked the budget and some trade union members of the NEC for voting against the declared policies of the unions. However, internal divisions within the Party were played down during the contest, Bevan appearing on a Labour platform on the eve of the 1950 Scarborough Conference to state that the conflicts which he had with his former colleagues were negligible compared to the differences he had with the Conservatives.

The Labour campaign devoted much attention to the Conservatives. One television broadcast was used to counter the frequently made Conservative accusation that the cost of living had risen under Labour. Instead it was argued that the rise had began to flatten out until the outbreak of the Korean War caused it to rise. This broadcast also attempted to illustrate that a graph issued by the Conservatives regarding the cost of living was misleading. Attempts were made early in the campaign to assert that a Conservative government would reintroduce the 1927 Trade Disputes Act (which Conservatives vehemently denied) and desired a confrontation with the trade unions. Some of the attacks by Labour on the Conservative Party took the form of 'whispering campaigns' which entailed the circulation of defamatory rumours. Prominent among these was the charge of 'warmongering', in which the assertion that peace was more likely to be maintained under Labour than under the Conservatives became inverted to an accusation that war (particularly with the Soviet Union) was more likely to break under a Conservative government which could not be trusted to preserve the peace. Although the Labour campaign did not specifically present this case, individual candidates did make accusations of this nature and Labour asserted that the Conservative Party was dominated by obsolete imperialist ideals. Additionally, Conservative arguments regarding Persia could be associated with claims of this nature since it enabled Labour to allege that a Conservative government would have maintained the Oil Company presence in Abadan by the use of troops which would have made war with Persia a likely outcome.

The theme that peace was more likely to be preserved under Labour was developed by the *Daily Mirror* in its 'Whose Finger Is On The Trigger' series of articles. The Conservative Party was very uneasy concerning allegations of warmongering. This charge was specifically refuted in three of the Party's election broadcasts, including those given by Lord Woolton and Dr Hill, and induced Churchill to sue the *Daily Mirror* for libel (an action which was ultimately settled out of court in 1952). Other examples of perceived or actual whispering campaigns included accusations that the Conservatives were planning to repudiate the recent agricultural wages award, that they intended to increase the period of national service, that they would cut pensions, family allowances or the social services in general, and that Eden was a Catholic (Butler, 1952: 101).

Conservatives

The manifesto of the Conservative and Unionist Party argued the need for stable government to replace what it referred to as 'this evenly balanced party strife'. In contrast to the Conservative belief in serving all the people rather than merely a section of it, the Labour Party was accused of eroding national unity by their fomenting of class hatred and the imposition of doctrinaire socialism on the nation. In particular, Conservatives regarded nationalisation as a failure which had resulted in losses both for the taxpayer and consumer, and had failed to give satisfaction to those employed within the affected industries. The government was also accused of indulging in reckless spending, the consequence of which was devaluation which meant that we paid more for what we bought from abroad and got less for what was sold. This policy had also impaired the confidence of the rest of the world in Britain. The manifesto pledged that a Conservative government would cut out all unnecessary government expenditure and would increase national output. Increased output was presented as the surest way to maintain full employment, to halt the rising cost of living and to preserve the social services. The Party would also foster commerce within the Empire by maintaining imperial preference.

The manifesto expressed support for the ideal of a united Europe and for the socialist government's rearmament programme although it was argued that far better value could have been obtained for the manpower and money which this involved. A temporary Excess Profits Tax was proposed to counter the fortuitous rise in company profits attributable to rearmament. Restrictive practices on both sides of industry would be reduced, and a greatly strengthened Monopolies Commission would be empowered to correct any operations in restraint of trade.

The manifesto promised to stop all further nationalisation. The Iron and Steel Act would be repealed and the publicly owned rail and road haulage industry would be reorganised into regional groups. Coal would remain nationalised, but all of these concerns would come within the purview of the Monopolies Commission.

The manifesto stated that the Conservatives would give housing a priority second only to national defence, with a target of 300,000 homes per year. More freedom was proposed for the private builder to advance the concept of a property-owning democracy. Better value for money was promised in health and education, and the position of pensioners, including war pensioners, would be reviewed. Facilities in rural areas would also be improved as economic circumstances allowed.

On constitutional affairs, an all-party conference for the reform of the House of Lords was called for and the restoration of the university constituencies was promised. Effective Scottish control of Scottish affairs was proposed and a Cabinet Minister in charge of Welsh affairs would be appointed.

A second Conservative statement, *Britain Strong and Free*, discussed some of the key issues contained in the manifesto in greater detail. In particular it was argued that, although the Conservatives would do their best to make the United Nations an effective instrument by making the Soviet Union a fourth pillar, they believed that in a world threatened by Soviet imperialism the surest hope of peace lay in the close association of the British Empire and Commonwealth and the United States. The Party also put itself forward as a defender of traditional British values which it believed were undermined by the negative view held by socialism towards individual freedom. It was asserted that the true foundations of a free society were based on adequate rewards for skill and enterprise and for the creation of wealth, the belief that saving and investment were worthwhile, the diffusion of property, home ownership, the rule of law, the independence of the professions, the strength of the family, personal responsibility and the rights of the individual.

Conservative election broadcasts emphasised foreign affairs and peace and the cost of living. It was argued that increases in the cost of living were due to socialist extravagence and the devaluation of the Pound. A campaign mounted by the pro-Conservative newspaper, the *Daily Express*, against purchase tax was developed by its cartoonist, Cummings, to focus on this issue. He introduced the character entitled 'Mr Rising Price' whose long, thin form elongated each day of the campaign until he occupied two sheets of paper by its end. A Conservative leaflet further depicted a Pound note with one quarter torn away to illustrate their argument that the pound was now worth only 14s 9d. Divisions in the Labour Party between the moderates and the socialists were also discussed, for example in Dr Hill's broadcast on 16 October. Hill alleged that Bevan (whom he dubbed 'the Titan of Tonypandy') was biding his time in the wings to take over as Prime Minister should Labour win the election. References of this nature were sometimes developed into allegations of communist sympathies by a particular Labour candidate or party leader, particularly Bevan. Labour said little regarding this matter during the campaign: Bevan asserted that differences of opinion were a good thing in a democratic party and Attlee specifically denied in his broadcast on 20 October either that he intended to stand down should Labour win the election or that Bevan was a communist.

The main issue affecting foreign affairs was the crisis in Persia. In December 1950 the Persian government had refused to ratify an agreement with the Anglo-Iranian Oil company concerning the royalty payments for oil extraction. In March 1951 the situation was complicated by the assassination of the Persian Prime Minister, General Razmara, who was succeeded by Dr Mussadeq. He was an opponent of the Oil Company and initiated a Bill to nationalise it. The British government protested at the refusal of the Persian government to submit the matter to arbitration and in July obtained an injunction from the International Court to prevent interference with the company's operations. A deputation from the British government went to Persia but failed to ameliorate the problem. All Oil Company staff were withdrawn from Persia at the end of August, save for a small contingent at the main Abadan refinery. The Persian government ordered these to leave by early October. Britain referred the matter to the UN Security Council but, to avoid further escalating the dispute, evacuated these staff on 3 October. Although there had been no initial attempt by the Conservative Party to inject partisan politics into the dispute, the hasty evacuation turned the matter into an important political issue.

The Conservatives argued that the evacuation entailed the government breaking its undertaking to Parliament and they argued that the situation had arisen because of the indecisive manner in which the government had responded to the events which had occurred. Churchill alleged that the government had indicated to the world that Britain would offer no physical resistance to violence or aggression regardless of the circumstances, and that Egypt (whose government renounced the 1936 Treaty which defined British rights in the Suez Canal Zone and proclaimed King Farouk as King of Sudan on 8 October) would take advantage of this situation. Labour, however, sought to counter these arguments by asserting that foreign affairs were often affected by events which could not be anticipated in advance (such as Razmara's assassination) and (as has been argued above) by associating them with accusations of Conservative warmongering. Churchill played a low key role in the Conservative campaign, addressing few meetings outside his constituency. Eden, however, played a significant role in Conservative campaigning.

Liberals

On 26 September, the Liberal Party announced its decision to fight the election on a narrow front. Only 109 candidates were fielded and there were curious omissions in the seats left uncontested. These included Torrington, Caernarvon and Kinross and West Perthsire (where the Liberals had obtained second place in 1950). No Liberal candidate was fielded in Rochdale (where the Liberal candidates obtained 10,000 votes in 1950) for the first time since 1832.

Liberal headquarters prepared a questionnaire to be circulated by those constituencies without Liberal candidates. However, the central organisations of the Labour and Conservative parties prepared standardised answers and the questionnaire's use was further reduced by the failure of Liberal constituency associations either to advertise the answers given by the candidates from the major parties, or to advise their supporters how to vote on the basis of these responses (Butler, 1952: 172 and 198).

Liberal policies were contained in the manifesto, *The Nation's Task*. This referred to the urgency of the huge problems facing the nation which included the threat to peace, the rearmament programme which would affect the living standards of all, the widening of the dollar gap which, together with the shortage of all foreign currencies, posed the threat of the nation being unable to buy the raw materials needed to sustain full employment, and the rising cost of living. It argued that to combat these problems there was a need for national unity to replace the class divisions and party strife which characterised the previous Parliament. It thus argued that a strong Liberal Party was required in the next Parliament as it was the only party free from class or sectional interests and the existence of a strong, independent Liberal Party would strengthen the liberal forces in the other parties against their extremist wings. It asserted that Liberals would act as a brake on class bitterness and create a safeguard against the deadening power of the great party machines, being able to do this as they were radical without being socialist.

It was argued that the existence of a Liberal Party reminded individual MPs that the crack of the Party whip was not the be-all and end-all of a live democracy. Liberals were thus convinced that there needed to be more Liberal MPs and in a 'supreme effort' to bring this about the Party was contesting selected seats in areas of the country and concentrating its efforts on those. By doing this, the Liberal Party offered the nation an opportunity to send to Parliament first-class men and women who had a great contribution to make to the solution of the nation's problems and who would fight for the policies which they thought best for the nation, whether popular or not. It was argued that Liberals, with more MPs, could compel Parliament to face the problems and to ensure that measures taken to remedy them were based on common sense and social justice.

The specific policies which were emphasised in the manifesto included support for the principle of collective security and the United Nations Organisation. It was argued that the age of national self-sufficiency had come to an end and that Britain needed to act and think on an international plane. Support was thus expressed for the Council of Europe (which was depicted as a Liberal conception), for Britain's continued partnership with the United States and fresh groupings such as the North Atlantic Treaty Organisation. These were all depicted as the 'shape of things to come' which would guard against international anarchy and chaos. The Party also endorsed the present rearmament programme but demanded greater efficiency and value for money in military spending. The improvement of Commonwealth relations was also stated as a key objective and the colour bar which existed in certain parts of it was specifically condemned.

Domestic policies gave prominent attention to the need to keep wages up and prices down. This entailed making more and better things with the same amount of labour and selling at no more than a fair profit. Policies to enhance productivity included ensuring that producers had up-to-date plant and that all who made goods should do so in the most efficient ways. Bonus systems and profit-sharing were some of the ways to provide increased efficiency and production and it was argued that Parliament should strike at monopolies, price rings and other hindrances to trade. These were depicted as key aspects of the Party's national drive to bring down the cost of living. Lower taxes were also said to be dependent on the raising of the national income through hard work and increased efficiency but in the meantime the interests of pensioners and of all with small fixed incomes would be championed by the Party.

The housing shortage was depicted as the source of widespread misery and suffering and the Party advocated lowering building costs. The social services should be safeguarded and food subsidies should remain until increased productivity succeeded in bringing down the cost of living. The system of guaranteed prices and assured markets was advocated to support the agricultural industry. On constitutional issues, the Party declared its support for the establishment of separate Parliaments for Scotland and Wales.

The Party's stance during the campaign was to attack the Labour Party, especially exposing its alleged socialist extremism. Davies asserted on 2 October that if Labour won the election, Bevan would become Prime Minister and Attlee would be demoted to become Minister of Health.

Result of the Election

As in 1950, the period between the announcement of the election date and the dissolution of Parliament witnessed a lull in party politics. In 1951 this situation was partly caused by the serious illness of the King (who underwent an operation on 23 September) which made the expression of partisan sentiments seem inappropriate. During the election campaign the key issues emphasised by the parties were the maintenance of peace and the cost of living.

Opinion polls suggested a Conservative victory but its margin was far less than they predicted. One explanation for this was that Labour gained support during the latter stages of the campaign and succeeded in converting voters who were initially inclined to support the Conservative Party (Butler, 1952: 238–9).

A total of 1,376 candidates contested the 1951 general election. This reduction in number compared to 1950 meant that the number of straight fights substantially increased to 495. The result was:

Party	Votes	Vote %	MPs
Conservative*	13,443,271	47.0%	312
Labour	13,948,883	48.8%	295
Ulster Unionist	274,928	1.0% [59.4%]	9
Liberal	730,546	2.6%	6
Irish Nationalist**	125,961	0.4% [27.2%]	3
Scottish National Party	7,299	0.0% [0.3%]	0
Plaid Cymru	10,920	0.0% [0.7%]	0
Others	54,786	0.2%	0
Total	28,596,594		625

*   The Conservative total includes National Liberal and Conservative candidates.
** The Irish Nationalist total includes Irish Labour, Anti-Partition and Irish Republican candidates, all of whom were opposed to partition.

The turnout was 82.6 per cent. The swing from Labour to the Conservatives was 1.1 per cent.
Seventeen women MPs were elected, all of whom were members of the 1950–51 Parliament.

The Parties

The result of the election bore a close resemblance to the results obtained in the previous general election contest in 1950. Only 27 seats changed hands but Labour's net loss of 20 seats was sufficient to oust it from office even though Labour polled its highest ever vote at this election and obtained around 230,000 more votes nationally than did the Conservative Party and its Ulster Unionist allies. The average swing of 1.1 per cent from Labour to the Conservatives was relatively uniform across the country. The swing was least in the county of London, the Hampshire ports, Lincolnshire, Liverpool, Sheffield and Clydeside but greater in Sussex, Bristol, Nottingham and its adjacent constituencies, Manchester, Newcastle, rural South Wales, Edinburgh the smaller boroughs of North East England and the Scottish Highlands (Butler, 1952: 268–9).

The policies of the parties were put forward in a series of election broadcasts. Most of these were carried by BBC radio transmissions, and the allocation given to the parties in 1950 was maintained in 1951 (save that the reduction in the total number of Communist Party candidates lost them their broadcast). An important innovation was the use of televised election broadcasts, in which each of the three main parties was given one 15-minute broadcast. It was estimated that these reached less than 10 per cent of the electorate (Butler, 1952: 75). Apart from these broadcasts, as in 1950 the BBC studiously removed all reference to party politics from its news bulletins and current affairs programmes. The coverage which the press was able to give to the election was affected by the continued shortage of newsprint and the need to cover other events (especially those in Persia and Egypt).

Labour emerged from the election strong in East London, the Potteries, Durham and Industrial Wales. Trade unions sponsored 137 Labour candidates (of whom 104 were successful) and the Cooperative Party sponsored 38 candidates (of whom 16 were elected). Labour losses included two junior ministers, David Hardman (the Parliamentary Secretary at the Ministry of Education) and Aidan Crawley (Under Secretary of State for Air).The Conservatives were dominant in the business and residential areas of London, Surrey, Sussex and North Lancashire. Conservative victors included Lloyd George's son and former Liberal MP, Gwilym. His victory at Newcastle North (as a National Liberal and Conservative candidate) was secured despite the intervention of an Independent Conservative candidate.

Sixty-six of the 109 Liberal candidates forfeited their deposits and the Parliamentary Party was reduced to six MPs, only one of whom (Grimond) was opposed by the Conservatives. Losses included the 'radical Liberals' who consisted of Lady Megan Lloyd George at Anglesey (a seat she had represented since 1929), Emrys Roberts at Merioneth and Edgar Granville at Eye. The personal intervention of Churchill in support of a Liberal, Lady Violet Bonham Carter, failed to secure her election at Colne Valley despite being given a free run against Labour by the local Conservative Party. It was estimated that, although the vote obtained by the Liberals in 1950 did not divide between Conservatives and Labour in a totally uniform manner, the Conservative Party secured a greater proportion of it. A 60:40 split in this support would have been sufficient to account for eight of the 21 Conservative gains from Labour, and a 65:35 split would have provided the Conservatives with 16 of these gains (Butler, 1952: 242 and 270–2).

Scotland, Wales and Northern Ireland
The Conservatives and National Liberals won 35 of Scotland's 71 seats, achieving parity with Labour, and the Liberals won the remaining seat. The Conservatives secured their best results in the Scottish Highlands where the swing from Labour was 3.7 per cent. A major explanation for this was likely to have been the relatively high Liberal vote in 1950 and its disproportionate transfer to the Conservatives in 1951. In Wales, Labour won 27 of the 36 seats, the Conservatives and National Liberals won six and the Liberals three. Labour dominated industrial Wales, securing in excess of 60 per cent of the total vote. However, the Conservatives fared well in rural South Wales with an average swing of around 2 per cent, above the national average.

In Northern Ireland, three seats were won by candidates opposed to partition. John Beattie won West Belfast for the Irish Labour Party (an all-Ireland Party which affirmed its adherence to the national and social revolution ideals of James Connolly). Cahir Healey captured Fermanagh and South Tyrone as an Anti-Partition candidate, and M. O'Neill won Mid-Ulster as an Irish Republican. The Ulster Unionists won the remaining nine seats.

Consequence of the Election
The small size of the Conservative majority prompted the leader of the Conservative Party, Churchill, to seek to construct a deal with the Liberal Party which was compatible with previous Conservative attempts to cultivate the support of Liberal supporters. Following the election, meetings took place between Churchill and Clement Davies on 27 and 28 October. Churchill offered Davies a seat in the Cabinet with two other Liberals being appointed as Under Secretaries of State. Churchill's motive for this action was to bolster parliamentary support for his government by increasing its theoretical overall majority from 18 to the safer figure of 30. Davies consulted with senior colleagues before refusing the offer but pledged that his Party would support any measures put forward by the government which were in the interests of the country as a whole.

26 May 1955

Party Leaders
Sir Anthony Eden (Conservative)
Clement Attlee (Labour)
Clement Davies (Liberal)

Background to the Election
Timing of the Election
Sir Winston Churchill resigned as Prime Minister on 6 April 1955 and was replaced by Sir Anthony Eden who subsequently also became leader of the Conservative Party. Eden called an immediate election which was announced in a radio broadcast on 14 April in his first public speech as Prime Minister. There are several possible reasons to explain why he acted as he did. Perhaps he felt the need to obtain a personal vote of confidence from the country before any domestic or foreign policy issues could muddy the waters (which would also strengthen his hand in forthcoming diplomatic negotiations) or he may have feared (as the Labour Party argued during the campaign) that the economy would worsen later in 1955 and prejudice Conservative chances of re-election.

Electoral Procedures and Practices
The election took place following extensive changes to the boundaries of the parliamentary constituencies. This was the first general review of constituencies since the passage of the 1949 House of Commons (Redistribution of Seats) Act. Eleven new constituencies were created in England and six were abolished. It had initially been assumed that the changes proposed by the boundary commissions would benefit the Conservative Party to the extent of around 15 seats, but a later analysis of the result suggested that these changes exerted very little net effect on the strength of the major parties (Butler, 1955: 157), perhaps giving the Conservatives between five and 10 seats (*Times Guide*, 1955: 252).

Conservatives
The Conservatives entered office in 1951 facing a severe balance of payments crisis. The new Chancellor, Butler, responded to this with a series of import cuts and a raise in the bank rate. Although the country's economic condition remained difficult, subsequent budgets were not overly severe. The 1952 budget cut food subsidies and introduced charges for some NHS services, but pension and family allowances were also increased to provide aid to the most needy and, in December 1954, higher rates for old age pensions were announced. The 1952, 1953 and 1954 budgets introduced measures of taxation release, and although Labour asserted that the wealthy gained most from these actions, the government responded that their policies made several million people almost free from the payment of income tax. The Conservatives could also claim that after 1951 unemployment mainly remained low and that although prices rose in this period they were outstripped by increases in earnings and wages.

Other domestic policies included acts of denationalisation in the 1952–53 session of Parliament affecting the iron and steel industry and British Road Services. However, the government retained a considerable degree of control over the former industry and did not totally break up the latter. The house building target of 300,000 was achieved, food rationing was ended in July 1954 and many other direct controls (especially those affecting the building industry and commodities) were abandoned in place of fiscal and monetary constraints. Much of the attention of Conservative governments after 1951 was devoted to foreign affairs. The Korean War ended in 1953 and Stalin's death in 1953 seemed to offer the possibility of a thaw in the Cold War. Although Churchill's suggestion of a summit meeting of the world's leading powers did not take place immediately it had been agreed to hold a four-power summit when Eden became Prime Minister. In October 1954 an agreement was signed in Paris which led to the occupation of Germany being ended and her membership of NATO being approved, and in the same month an Anglo-Egyptian Agreement regarding the Suez Canal base was signed which served to defuse a potentially abrasive situation. Also in 1954, a conference was held in Geneva to discuss the Far East following the French defeat in northern Vietnam in that year which held out the hope of peace in that area. Colonial problems facing the Conservatives included the Mau Mau struggle in Kenya. A major development in defence policy was the announcement in February 1955 that Britain was manufacturing the hydrogen bomb. The Party was relatively united after 1951, although the decision to withdraw British troops from Egypt was resisted by 26 MPs who voted against the proposal.

Labour

The Labour Party obtained more votes than the Conservative Party in the 1951 general election, but was thrown out of office by the workings of the electoral system which gave the Conservatives more seats in Parliament. This defeat intensified the factionalism which had emerged within the Labour Party in the late 1940s, which was largely centred on the future direction which the Party should take. Nationalisation assumed the centre stage of this debate.

The resignation of Aneurin Bevan from the Cabinet in 1951 opened divisions within the Party. These were in the nature of a fissure between Labour's left and right wings, the former being associated with Bevan and the latter with those who were termed 'revisionists' who included Roy Jenkins and Tony Crosland. Revisionism was initially outlined in *New Fabian Essays* (1952) which was edited by the Bevanite, Richard Crossman. Bevan mounted unsuccessful challenges for the Party's deputy leadership in 1952 (when he was defeated by 194 votes to 82 by Morrison) and for party treasurer in 1954 (when he was soundly defeated by Gaitskell). Divisions in the Party were especially evident in foreign policy issues. In March 1952 Bevan and 56 Labour MPs defied a three-line whip to vote against the government's rearmament proposals and at the 1954 Party Conference divisions arose over the issue of German rearmament (in which the views of the constituency delegates were overruled by trade union block votes). On 2 March 1955 Bevan and Attlee clashed in the House of Commons concerning Britain's manufacture of the hydrogen bomb. This led to the Party whip being withdrawn from Bevan who narrowly avoided the NEC expelling him from the Party later that month.

Liberals

Following the 1951 election, attempts were made to improve Liberal organisation, especially at constituency level, by a plan referred to as 'Operation Basic'. Further defections to Labour occurred in this period, most notably that of Lady Megan Lloyd George. Overtures by the Conservative Party (which in 1951 had urged Liberal leaders to advise their supporters to vote Conservative in the absence of a Liberal candidate) continued to be rebuffed, the 1952 Liberal Assembly setting its face against fighting a future election on the 'one-point policy of anti-nationalisation'.

On the eve of the election, the Party took comfort from its good perfomance in the Inverness by-election in December 1954. The Liberal candidate, John Bannerman, secured 36 per cent of the vote and was within 1,300 votes of victory.

By-elections

Forty-eight by-elections took place in the 1951–55 Parliament. The results of these contests very closely followed the results obtained in 1951. The Conservative Party held all 24 seats which it was defending and the Ulster Unionists successfully contested four constituencies which they had won in 1951. Labour successfully defended 19 seats won in 1951 but lost one (Sunderland South) to the Conservative Party. This was the first occasion since 1924 when the party in power gained a seat from the opposition.

Conduct of the Election

No major issue separated the parties and the election was marked by the existence of considerable agreements between them on the maintenance of the welfare state and the mixed economy and also in connection with foreign affairs and Commonwealth policy. Although the Conservative Party had fared badly in the opinion polls and in local government contests in 1952, its fortunes subsequently improved and was especially apparent in by-elections (which included gaining a seat from Labour in March 1953 at Sunderland South). This suggested a Conservative victory which seemed confirmed by a Gallup Poll on 21 April which gave them a 4 per cent lead over Labour and whose supremacy was affirmed in most of the later polls.

The election campaign was dubbed a 'television election'. This referred not to the coverage of the contest by the BBC (since, apart from providing information of a technical nature in connection with issues such as the close of nominations, it adopted the policy of ignoring the election in order not to jeopardise its neutrality), but to the use made by the parties of election broadcasts to get their message across to the voters. Experiments regarding election broadcasts had been initiated in a limited way in 1951 but were built upon in 1955. By this date around one-third of homes of Britain had television sets (Butler, 1955: 52). Television had an adverse impact on the importance of sound broadcasts (which now seemed dull) and attendance at public meetings.

Conservatives

The Conservative manifesto, *United for Peace and Progress*, emphasised the achievements of the Party in office since 1951 which would form the basis of future improvements. It argued that the national standard of living could be doubled in 25 years through policies which included more investment at home or overseas and the development of foreign trade. During the campaign, the

Party emphasised the new national prosperity and Edith Pitt argued in an election broadcast that ordinary people had benefited since 1951 from Conservative policies which had secured high wages (outstripping the rise in prices), lower taxes and the end of rationing. The perception of prosperity was aided by their budget in April 1955 which lowered the standard rate of income tax, increased tax allowances and reduced the purchase tax on non-woollen household textiles (which were subsequently abolished before the election). Conservative election broadcasts referred to the Party's domestic achievements in building 300,000 houses a year and their foreign policy successes which included the end of the Korean War and the Geneva and Paris settlements. The manifesto pledged the Party to strive for world disarmament, but argued that this entailed continuing the the development and manufacture of the hydrogen bomb which they viewed as a key deterrent to aggression. Voters were thus urged to stick with the Party with the proven success record. The manifesto contained relatively few precise promises for future action. Support was expressed for free trade but with safeguards against unfair practices, especially in connection with the interests of the cotton textile industry. Inflation and excessive imports would be combated through the use of monetary and fiscal policies, and co-partnership and profit-sharing schemes would be encouraged as one means to improve human relations in industry. Further steps against monopolies and restrictive practices were promised, and the consumer would be safeguarded against rising prices. The Party was also committed to the maintenance of full employment and social services which would provide a basic standard of life for everyone but leaving persons free to rise above that standard through the use of their industry and talents. It was stated that in 1952 and 1953 the government had increased almost all social benefits and had restored the purchasing power of pensions to their original post-war level. Under the Conservative government a record number of new schools had been built and a record number of new teachers recruited and new hospital building had been restarted. The government had achieved the target of building 300,000 houses and year and intended to devote effort into eliminating the slums by rehousing at least 200,000 people a year from them. Support was also expressed for developing the concept of a property-owning democracy.

There were many negative aspects in the Conservative campaign. Its manifesto condemned the six years of Labour post-war government for its meddling and muddling which had injured the nation's strength and for fighting a campaign in 1951 which sought to project scares that the Conservatives were warmongers and would cut social services, both of which had been proven to be falsehoods. The pledges contained in Labour's manifesto were costed at £1,000 million a year, the money for which, Conservatives suggested, would be secured from increases on items such as income tax, purchase tax, alcohol, cigarettes and petrol. Divisions in the Labour Party between its left and right wings were also emphasised and proposals to nationalise the steel and chemical industries were condemned, the Conservative manifesto referring to Labour's continued faith in the 'broken reed of nationalisation'. Attempts were made to develop scares. It was alleged that Labour would reintroduce food rationing and a mock ration book was circulated to emphasise this intention. It was also suggested (in particular in the *Daily Sketch* newspaper) that should Labour win Attlee would be toppled and replaced by Aneurin Bevan. Eden played a prominent role in the Conservative campaign, embarking on a number of 'whistle-stop' tours when he addressed audiences who came to meet him. His name also featured prominently in the election addresses of individual Conservative candidates.

Labour

The 1953 Party Conference approved the statement, *Challenge to Britain*, which announced limited extensions of nationalisation and proposals to introduce comprehensive education for all children at the age of eleven. Its election policies were contained in the manifesto, *Forward with Labour,* which stated the Party's commitment to providing work for all, abolishing want, ensuring the fair distribution of income and property and ensuring a better system of education. The Party's commitment to the goal of world peace was emphasised and to achieve this it argued that Britain should propose the immediate cessation of further hydrogen bomb tests. It further advocated the reunification of Germany through free elections and the admission of China to the United Nations. Labour also pledged to continue the work of transforming the Empire into a Commonwealth of free and equal people. The period of National Service would be reviewed, although during the campaign some Labour candidates expressed themselves sympathetic to a cut in the length of national service.

The manifesto denied Conservative claims regarding prosperity by arguing that production had risen only half as fast as under Labour and the gold and dollar reserves were lower than they had been when Labour left office. The cost of living had risen since 1951 and, in contravention of Conservative election promises, prices had risen and food subsidies had been cut. Labour proposed to keep the cost of living steady by long-term purchasing agreements with the Commonwealth countries, by action against monopolies and price rings and by reforming the system of food distribution including the reimposition of controls where necessary. The return to food rationing was explicitly denied as a 'Tory lie'.

The Party was committed to security for all. It would continue to subsidise the building of houses by local authorities and would restore a free health service. The last taint of 'public assistance' would be removed by establishing a Ministry of Welfare to take over the work of the Ministry of Pensions and National Insurance and the National Assistance Board. An annual review of pensions, benefits and allowances would be instituted to maintain their real purchasing power and the Party promised to raise the rates of National Assistance. A 'radical reform' of education was promised which entailed increasing the number of teachers and improving the standard of schools. Comprehensive secondary schooling would be encouraged and all students admitted to universities would be entitled, in case of need, to a state scholarship. Labour promised to use the budget to remedy social inequality and increase production and accused the Conservatives of granting tax relief to those who least needed help. Investment and modernisation of industry would receive high priority and the manifesto pledged to renationalise the iron and steel industry and the road haulage industries on the grounds of them being essential to the nation's needs. Sections of the chemical and machine tool industries would be brought into public ownership.

During the campaign Labour emphasised that it had laid the foundation for economic recovery in the years following 1945. This argument was presented by Attlee in the Party's first television election broadcast. Much of the Labour campaign was directed at attacking the Conservative Party. It was argued that the timing of the election was influenced by their perception that the country was facing an economic crisis and that they wished to hold the election before this became obvious. This allegation was, however, undermined by the publication of figures in May which suggested that the nation's gold and dollar reserves were in a healthy state.

Labour justified their argument by referring to inflation, in particular the increased price of food: one of their posters stated 'Record High Prices – Toryism Doesn't Work'. It was argued that Conservative tax cuts were mainly to the benefit of the wealthy and would result in intensified inequality, and the plight of old age pensioners was especially highlighted, to whom Labour's pledge of conducting an annual review of pensions and other benefits was especially directed. Bevan attacked the Conservatives in a more combative style, alleging that they were 'morons' and that Toryism and Christianity were incompatible. Conservative allegations of Labour disunity further produced a riposte from Bevan who asserted that internal dissent was a good thing, and he likened Conservative unity to the biblical story of the Gadarene swine unitedly plunging headlong over a cliff to destruction. Many Conservatives were offended with this comparison but could perhaps take some comfort that the politician who had compared them with 'vermin' in 1948 had now upgraded them to 'swine'.

The Labour campaign suffered from a number of problems. The acceptance by the Conservatives of the welfare state and the goal of full employment coupled to its success in securing prosperity gave the Party fewer issues with which to base an attack on their main opponents who had become less feared in post-war Britain by many members of the working class. This difficulty was compounded by Eden's replacement of Churchill. Shinwell argued that whereas Churchill gave Labour something to get their teeth into, Labour now found itself confronting Snow White and the Seven Dwarfs. Attlee was at the forefront of projecting Labour's policies, speaking at a number of meetings. Unlike Eden, however, he was not prominently mentioned in the election addresses of individual Labour candidates.

Liberals

Clement Davies was ill and played little part in the Liberal campaign whose morale was adversely affected by the defection of Lady Megan Lloyd George to Labour on 26 April. The Party's one election broadcast emphasised that even with only 110 candidates the Liberals would make a difference and would fight excessive party discipline and centralisation. The Liberal manifesto, *Crisis Unresolved*, presented the Party as the nation's only defence against the two class parties, Conservative and Labour. It called for the abolition of protective tariffs, for a frontal attack to be mounted against monopolies and called for a Royal Commission to inquire into the role of trade unions. It argued that industrial peace required the general introduction of co-ownership in industry. The manifesto urged the establishment of separate parliamentary assemblies for Scotland and Wales and for a Royal Commission to inquire into the injustices of the electoral system.

Result of the Election

The contest aroused little interest and was dubbed 'an essentially dull, demure, routine affair' being 'the most apathetic yet seen in twentieth-century Britain' (Butler, 1955: 96 and 94). No great differences separated the parties and both Eden and Attlee projected themselves as safe politicians who could be trusted to run the country. A total of 1,409 candidates contested the election. This was the first time that every parliamentary constituency had been contested. The result was:

Party	Votes	Vote %	MPs
Conservative*	12,868,244	48.0%	335
Labour	12,405,254	46.4%	277
Ulster Unionist	442,647	1.7% [68.5%]	10
Liberal	722,402	2.7%	6
Sinn Fein	152,310	0.6% [23.6%]	2
Scottish National Party	12,112	0.0% [0.5%]	0
Plaid Cymru	45,119	0.2% [3.1%]	0
Others	111,641	0.4%	0
Total	26,759,729		630

*   Conservative candidates stood under a variety of labels which included, 'National Liberal', 'National Liberal and Conservative', 'Conservative and Liberal' and 'Conservative and National Liberal'.

The turnout was 76.8 per cent. The swing from Labour to the Conservative Party was 1.8 per cent. Twenty-four women MPs were elected.

The Parties

This swing to the Conservatives was relatively uniform across the country although there were more significant variations affecting individual constituencies than had been the case in 1951. In marginal seats the average swing to the Conservative Party was slightly less, which resulted in fewer Labour losses than arithmetically should have been the case on the national figure.

A number of prominent Conservatives were elevated to the peerage between 1951 and 1955. These included Sir David Maxwell Fyfe, Oliver Lyttleton, Brendan Bracken and Sir Arthur Salter. Conservative Parliamentarians who retired included Ralph Assheton and W. McNair Snadden, a joint Under Secretary at the Scottish Office. One Conservative who was elected in 1951 (Peter Baker for Norfolk South) was expelled from the House of Commons in December 1954 following his conviction for forgery for which he received seven years' imprisonment. The Conservatives were the first government since 1841 to improve their position in three successive general election contests. Swings considerably above the average were secured in the Midlands.

One hundred and twenty-nine Labour candidates were sponsored by trade unions, of whom 96 were successful. An additional 19 MPs were sponsored by the Cooperative Party. Labour fared better than average in rural areas, especially East Anglia, Wales and Northern Scotland, but performed worse in the industrial areas of the Midlands. Former MPs who failed to secure re-election included the former Minister of Food, Maurice Webb, and Michael Foot. The make-up of the Parliamentary Labour Party was also affected by the deaths of the former Minister of Education, George Tomlinson, in 1952 and Arthur Greenwood (who had been an MP for over 30 years and held several ministerial posts) in 1954. A further long-serving Labour Parliamentarian, Alfred Barnes, retired at the 1955 election.

The Liberal Party marginally improved its position, its candidates securing an average 15.1 per cent of the vote compared to 14.7 per cent in 1951. All six seats were retained (although only Grimond faced a three-cornered contest) and good results were secured in North Devon,

North Cornwall and Inverness, which helped to offset the decline in support in former Liberal-held seats in Eye, Merioneth, North Dorset and Anglesey.

Scotland, Wales and Northern Ireland
The situation in Scotland was broadly similar to that of 1951. The Conservative and National Liberal parties overtook Labour by winning 36 of the 71 seats and Labour won 34. Jo Grimond secured victory for the Liberals in the remaining one seat. In Wales, Labour remained the dominant party with 27 of the 36 seats. The Conservative and National Liberal parties won six seats and the Liberals three. In Northern Ireland, Sinn Fein (eight of whose candidates were serving prison sentences) contested all 12 constituencies and secured a very respectable 23.6 per cent of the vote. Two seats (Mid-Ulster and Fermanagh and South Tyrone) were narrowly gained by majorities of 260 and 261 respectively. Both Sinn Fein's successful candidates (Thomas Mitchell and Philip Clarke) were serving prison sentences for their part in a raid on the depot of the Royal Inniskilling Fusiliers at Omagh in County Tyrone in October 1954. The Ulster Unionists won the remaining 10 seats.

Consequence of the Election
Winston Churchill formed a Conservative government.

8 October 1959

Party Leaders
Harold Macmillan (Conservative)
Hugh Gaitskell (Labour)
Jo Grimond (Liberal)

Background to the Election
Timing of the Election
An election had to be held by early 1960 at the latest, but a date in autumn 1959 was widely predicted in the media. Macmillan's main justification for the timing of the election was that important international negotiations were imminent and it was important that the nation should first be able to determine which leaders should represent them at these events. An additional factor behind Macmillan's decision was that economic circumstances (measured by indicators such as increased productivity and stable prices) were good in 1959 and would be expected to aid Conservative prospects.

Electoral Procedures and Practices
Section 88 of the 1948 Representation of the People Act was repealed by the 1958 Representation of the People (Amendment) Act. This removed restrictions imposed by the 1948 measure on the use of motor cars to take voters to the polls and meant that henceforth the parties could use as many vehicles as they had available to them.

Conservatives
The initial performance of the Conservative Party in office was adversely affected by problems which were encountered at home and abroad. The 1955 pre-election budget (which included tax cuts amounting to £150 million) was followed in October by an emergency package designed to curb inflation. Abroad, successes were initially achieved in the summit meeting of the great powers which took place in 1955 and the visit of Khruschev and Bulgarin to Britain the following year. This thaw in the Cold War led the Chancellor, Harold Macmillan, to declare 'there ain't gonna be no war'. Self-government was also granted to the Federation of Malaysia and Ghana in 1957. However, problems emerged with the outbreak of violence in Cyprus and, most significantly, events which followed the announcement by Colonel Nasser of Egypt's nationalisation of the Suez Canal in July 1956. Initially, the British government sought to coordinate opposition to this action from other countries using the canal and from the United Nations. However, Israel's attack on Egypt encouraged military intervention by Britain and France which was then abruptly halted (due to American opposition). Eden found himself attacked on all sides (including by many of his own party) first for initiating military action and then for abandoning it before any of its objectives could be realised. Ill health forced his resignation on 10 January 1957. He was replaced by Harold Macmillan.

Conservative political fortunes suffered from events which took place after the 1955 general election and Macmillan failed to halt this trend initially. His announcement that British ships would recommence using the nationalised Suez Canal in May 1957 led to eight Conservative MPs resigning the party whip, and his belief that fighting inflation and over-expansion should take precedence over combating unemployment and industrial stagnation resulted in the bank rate being raised to 7 per cent in September 1957. His subsequent revision of these views resulted in the resignation of Chancellor Peter Thorneycroft and two other Treasury ministers in 1958 – an episode which the Premier dismissed as 'a little local difficulty'. Industrial unrest assumed major proportions in 1957 (especially in the engineering and transport industries) and in 1958 a seven-week strike hit London buses. In February 1959 unemployment stood at 620,000 which was a post-war record.

By-election gains by Labour and the Liberal Party after 1955 evidenced the fall in Conservative political fortunes, which were not offset by proposals to increase public spending in areas which included school building, road construction and old age pensions. However, the government's position began to improve in 1959. The cost of living had remained steady during the government's period of office and expansion occurred in a number of growth industries (such as electronics and motor car manufacture). Improvements in the economic situation prompted the government to reduce taxes in its April 1959 budget (which included taking 2d off the price of a pint of beer). Macmillan also gained prestige from his interventions in foreign affairs, most notably in the shuttle diplomacy which he undertook following Khruschev's reopening of the Berlin question which led to the Soviet Union suspending its ultimatum which was due to expire in May 1959. Macmillan's position as a key world statesman seemed evidenced when President Eisenhower visited Britain to discuss the coming summit meeting with Macmillan in August 1959 and appeared in a joint television broadcast with the British Prime Minister on 31 August.

Labour

The division between Labour's left and right wings had been muted after 1945. This was so for a number of reasons which included Attlee's conciliatory style of leadership (in which he refused to pursue any form of disciplinary action against the Bevanites), and the pre-eminence accorded by the trade unions to party unity (which induced them to follow the line endorsed by the leadership and not to support factionalism). However, internal disunity intensified following the 1955 general election defeat. Clement Attlee resigned as leader in that year and was replaced by Hugh Gaitskell. The arguments which surfaced after 1955 concerned ideology and how this should be implemented, and highlighted the diverse influences which had contributed to the creation and subsequent development of the Labour Party. Fundamentalists believed that public ownership was indispensable to socialism. Their goal of working-class supremacy depended for its success on basic changes to the country's economic structure. To them socialism was defined in terms of 'public ownership and an economic interpretation of all political and social phenomena' (Jones, 1996: 26).

Social democrats sought to move the Party away from fundamentalism by updating social democratic philosophy and policies. This approach was referred to as 'revisionism' (or revisionist social democracy) and was associated with Labour politicians who included Roy Jenkins and Tony Crosland. Revisionism was initially outlined in *New Fabian Essays*, published in 1952 and edited by the Bevanite, Richard Crossman. Crosland's *The Future of Socialism*, published in 1956, provided a full exposition of the revisionist case which 'sought to reformulate socialist principles and to revise Labour policies through a new analysis of the changed economic and social conditions of post-1945 British society' (Crosland, 1964: 69). This emphasised that capitalism was bringing a rising standard of living to many members of the working class, and that the hostility between the classes was being lessened by the impact of factors which included increased prosperity, social mobility and the welfare state. Although Hugh Gaitskell was not the driving force behind revisionism he had links with this wing of the Party. He had served as treasurer of the organisation Friends of Socialist Commentary between 1953 and 1955 and when he became leader he was identified with revisionist tendencies.

Social democrats believed it was now necessary for the Party to take into account the political significance of a number of social and economic changes which had occurred since 1900. In their view, these rendered fundamentalist socialism anachronistic. Perhaps the most significant factor was the manner in which former economic power relationships no longer applied in postwar Britain. Those who owned industry no longer controlled all aspects of its strategic operations or day-to-day management. Control was now dissipated with the state (which had assumed responsibility for full employment and economic growth) and trade unions (whose essential role in industry was recognised by Conservative governments) exercising major responsibilities. In particular, a new class of managers, technicians and experts had emerged. The latter, the product of a 'managerial revolution', was especially significant since it was asserted that their motives were not exclusively dominated by profit, but that factors such as social prestige also guided their conduct.

These changes suggested that ownership of the means of production was no longer relevant to the attainment of socialist goals and legitimised an attempt both to redefine socialism and the means through which its objectives could be attained. This differentiation between ends and means was a crucial feature of revisionist ideology. The former gave pre-eminence to the kind of society which Labour wished to create, thus placing emphasis on values. Tawney's conception of socialism being motivated by ethical concerns (as opposed to scientific or economic impulses) was endorsed by revisionists who put forward their own vision of society characterised by equality, social justice, classlessness, and freedom.

The most contentious aspect of revisionist thinking concerned the manner in which a society based upon such values could be created. Revisionism did not regard socialism as having to be intimately connected with public ownership of the means of production: 'state ownership of all industrial capital is not now a condition of creating a socialist society' (Jones, 1996: 128). This key objective of fundamentalism was downgraded to a tactic: it was one policy among many which could be pursued to secure control over the economy. But nationalisation was not viewed as the only mechanism through which the economy could be managed. Alternative methods of state intervention were endorsed by an approach which accepted a diverse range of ownership of industry which included placing state-owned industries alongside cooperatives and the privately owned sector.

The redistribution of wealth was crucial to the 'radical egalitarianism' of a society revisionists wished to create (Jones, 1996: 128). For revisionists, equality was 'primarily, if not

286 • Politico's Guide to UK General Elections 1832–2001

exclusively, material equality' (Desai, 1994: 88). However, they were sceptical of the potential of nationalisation to procure any substantial redistribution of wealth throughout society (in part as such industries had been bought from their owners rather than being expropriated), and thus examined other ways through which enhanced social justice could be achieved. Control of the economy was to be secured through Keynesian demand management, and the social reform which was required to achieve egalitarianism would be financed through a range of fiscal measures (including a gifts tax, capital gains and corporation taxes and stiffer death duties). The entire approach of revisionism was predicated on the continued buoyancy of capitalism to produce the wealth which could then be redistributed through the welfare state to the poorer and weaker members of society. Further policies to promote social equality in the sense of providing improved access to a range of services such as housing, education and health were advocated by some revisionsists, Crosland, for example, endorsing comprehensive education.

Initially the tensions which revisionism might have created were limited. The reasons for this included Bevan's accommodation with Gaitskell in the period which led up to the 1959 general election. Bevan had had the party whip withdrawn in 1955 in connection with the decision of the Parliamentary Party to abstain in the vote concerning British manufacture of the hydrogen bomb, but he subsequently cooperated with Gaitskell over Suez and re-entered the Shadow Cabinet, becoming Shadow Foreign Secretary. The government's announcement of their intention to end conscription in 1960 implied that Britain would henceforth rely on the deterrent effect of nuclear weapons. Many on the left were opposed to this position and became involved in the newly formed Campaign for Nuclear Disarmament. At the 1957 Party Conference Bevan appealed to delegates to endorse the position of the platform in connection with repudiating unilateral nuclear disarmament, thus making a public display of his loyalty to the Party and its leader. Labour's position in 1959 was to call for Britain and all other countries, save America and the Soviet Union, to form a club which would renounce the use of nuclear weapons.

Liberals
Clement Davies resigned at the Party's Assembly at Folkestone in 1956 and was replaced by Jo Grimond who initiated a period of discussion concerning the Party's role in the political system. Grimond rejected the exercise of political influence as a long-term aim, arguing that the Party would not survive if it was content to 'write in the margins of politics'. He set himself a 10-year target to 'get on or get out' and pitched his appeal to persons of a progressive non-socialist outlook. This suggested his desire to replace Labour as the dominant force on the left of British politics and resulted in attacks being directed at the Labour Party for its commitment to socialism and its defence of the vested interests of the trade unions. Younger, upwardly mobile members of the working class were a particular target of Liberal propaganda. Improved Liberal fortunes at by-elections (most notably at Rochdale in February 1958 and Torrington in March) also prompted attempts to fight the next election on a broader front which were complemented by organisation reform at constituency and federation levels.

By-elections
Fifty-two by-elections occurred during the 1955–59 Parliament. Labour held 18 seats which it had won in 1955 and gained three from the Conservatives and one (Carmarthen) from the

Liberal Party (where, to add insult to Liberal injury, the victor was the former Liberal MP Lady Megan Lloyd George). The Conservative Party held 26 of seats in which it secured victory in 1955, and lost three to Labour and one (Torrington) to the Liberal Party. This was the first Liberal Party by-election victory since 1929. The Ulster Unionists retained their seat in the East Belfast by-election in March 1959. Two further contests were held in Mid-Ulster which had been narrowly gained by Sinn Fein in 1955. In the first of these in 1955 (caused by the disqualification of the winning candidate, Thomas Mitchell), the same Sinn Fein candidate succeeded in holding the seat by an increased majority. As he was in prison when nominated, his Ulster Unionist opponent was declared elected on a petition, only to be disqualified himself for holding an office of profit under the Crown. A second by election took place in 1956 in which Mitchell was opposed by an Unofficial Unionist and also by an Anti-Partition candidate. This splitting of the Nationalist vote gave the Unofficial Unionists a comfortable victory.

The Sinn Fein victory in 1955 at Fermanagh and South Tyrone was also undone by the disqualification of the winning candidate in 1955. An election petition awarded the seat to the Ulster Unionists. No by-elections occurred in this seat. Television played a more prominent part in by-election contests, in particular at Rochdale in February 1958 when the local independent company, Granada, aired a series of programmes on the Rochdale by-election while it was in progress. This may have been to the advantage of the Liberal Party whose candidate, Ludovic Kennedy, was a well-known television presenter.

Conduct of the Election

The election was fought against the background of significant social changes which had been taking place during the 1950s. The net effect of these changes (which although not complete, were obvious by 1959) was to erode traditional class differences and to create a society which was increasingly middle class. This was brought about by a range of policies which included slum clearance. Between 1948 and 1958, one family in six moved into a newly built house or flat, many of which were located in new towns or in large, modern council estates. Home ownership also grew in this period so that by 1959 30 per cent of the population either owned or were buying their own homes (Butler and Rose, 1960: 12). These changes were complemented by significant alterations affecting working-class standards of living. The average real earnings of industrial workers increased by 20 per cent between 1951 and 1958 and this enhanced affluence, coupled with the easier availability of credit-enabled working-class people to acquire material possessions such as televisions, vacuum cleaners and cars which had traditionally been available only to the middle classes (Butler and Rose, 1960: 12–13).

Additionally, technological and scientific advances served to increase the availability of white-collar jobs (many being in the private sector), some of which went to the sons and daughters of working-class people who had been able to take advantage of educational reform inaugurated by the 1944 Education Act. Between 1951 and 1959 the number of white-collar occupations increased by around one million while the number of manual workers fell by around half a million (Butler and Rose, 1960: 14). Although these developments did not affect all parts of the United Kingdom equally (social change being most marked in the South East and the Midlands), where they occurred they provided the potential for political trends which seemed likely to benefit the Conservatives and harm Labour. Although this potential was not always realised, it was clear that the nation's political priorities were being redefined to emphasise the importance of prosperity and opportunity rather than the post-war goals of fair shares and social welfare.

By 1959 70 per cent of homes had access to televisions (Butler and Rose, 1960: 75) and television played an important role in the election. A major innovation in 1959 was the treatment accorded to the election by the television companies. The previous silence which the BBC had imposed upon itself previously was broken and news programmes of both the BBC and ITA companies discussed the election as part of its news coverage. Key innovations included Granada's *Marathon* programme which invited all candidates in the Granada area to appear on television (an invitation accepted by 294 of the area's 348 candidates). Opinion polls also played a more prominent role in the campaign, in that there were more of them and their predictions as to who would win the election were conspicuously aired by the media. The press, freed from newsprint restrictions, also devoted considerable attention to the election. Daily press conferences were also introduced by all main parties as a key source of information for the media to relay to voters. However, political activists noted an increased level of public interest in election meetings in 1959 compared to 1955.

Conservatives

The Conservative Party's preparations for the 1959 election were lengthy and entailed major innovations in the conduct of British politics. A campaign was initiated after 1957 which focused on the image of the Party rather than being concerned with specific policy issues, and was conducted by public relations professionals. The firm Colman, Prentis and Varley had been used to conduct short-term pre-election campaigns in 1949 and 1951 but the new campaign was sustained over a period of 27 months, costing the Party around half a million pounds (Butler and Rose, 1960: 20). The images which the campaign sought to identify the Conservative Party with were prosperity and opportunity. The aims of this campaign were to emphasise the differences between the Conservative and Labour parties, and to depict the Conservatives as the party of all social classes and not a party of the privileged minority. It was especially targeted at groups in the electorate which were perceived as containing large numbers of potential converts. These included housewives, the prosperous members of the working class and the young, the latter being an important consideration since by 1959 around 10 million voters (28 per cent of the total electorate) had spent all their adult lives under post-war governments (Butler and Rose, 1960: 11). The campaign encouraged electors to look forward to the future rather than to harp back on the past and during the election was best summarised in the slogan 'Life's Better Under the Conservatives – Don't Let Labour Ruin It'.

The Conservative manifesto, *The Next Five Years*, emphasised the themes of prosperity and peace, and stated that the main issues at the election were whether the nation wished, continue with the policies which had brought prosperity at home and whether they wished their current leaders to continue to represent them abroad.

The manifesto placed considerable emphasis on the record of Conservative governments since 1951. It was argued that, whereas the post-war Labour governments had failed to grapple with the problems facing the country, Conservative governments since 1951 had set the country on a path which was leading to prosperity and opportunity for all. It was alleged that the actions of

Conservative governments since 1951 demonstrated that Conservative freedom worked and that life was better under the Conservatives. It was argued that the economy was sounder in 1959 than at any time since the First World War, Sterling had been re-established as a strong and respected currency, exports had reached the highest peak ever and the balance of payments was heavily in Britain's favour. Capital investment at home was at a high level and people were saving more than ever before. Taxes had been cut in seven budgets but the social services had continued to be developed, over two million new homes and two million school places had been provided and a better health service and modern pensions plan had been introduced. The cost of living had been stabilised and full employment maintained. Additionally, controls had been swept away, national service was being abolished and, due to the initiative of the present Conservative government, the diplomatic deadlock between East and West had been broken.

The manifesto stated that the Party aimed to double the standard of living in this generation and ensure that all sections of society shared in the expansion of wealth. The Party's commitment to the creation of 'One Nation' extended beyond national frontiers and also embraced narrowing the gap between the industrialised and under-developed nations of the world. To achieve these goals required maintaining international confidence in Sterling as a sound and stable medium of exchange, further promoting the export trade through means which included the creation of an industrial free market embracing all Western Europe, and on maintaining national unity by government working closely with employers and trade unions.

Technical progress was applauded, but recognition was given to the problems which this sometimes caused, in particular the creation of local pockets of unemployment. Legislation was promised to remodel and strengthen the government's powers to deal with this issue which would be of particular help to Scotland and Wales. Government help was promised in relation to particular industries (such as fostering research and development in the aircraft industry), and retraining would be encouraged as part of the government's policy to provide for the mobility of labour.

The manifesto pledged the Party to sustain technological progress and translate this into productive capacity. Policies to achieve this included giving a Cabinet minister the task of promoting scientific and technological development and pressing ahead with the development of nuclear energy for peaceful purposes. The programme of modernising the railways through the introduction of diesel engines and track modernisation would be continued with, and the road-building programme would be expanded. The assurances to the agricultural industry contained in the 1957 Act would be continued throughout the life of the forthcoming Parliament, and legislation would be introduced to provide improvement grants for the horticultural industry and to help reform horticultural marketing. Amenities for those living in the countryside would be improved. The manifesto expressed its opposition to any extension of nationalisation. Industries already nationalised would be subject to less central control, and the situation regarding civil aviation would be reviewed and a new licensing authority would be created to bring a greater measure of freedom to nationally and privately owned airlines. The current finances of the Post Office would be separated from the Exchequer.

The manifesto stated the Conservative desire that everybody should have a fuller opportunity to earn more and to own more. Policies to achieve this included reducing the burden of taxation whenever possible, and enlarging educational opportunity at all levels. The grammar schools would be defended against doctrinaire socialist attack and be further developed. It was anticipated that by 1965 40 per cent of schoolchildren would stay on at school after the age of 15. Current housing policy would be vigorously proceeded with, key objectives being to clear the slums and relieve overcrowding. It was hoped that by 1965 another one million people would be rehoused from the slums. No further action to decontrol rents would be taken in the next Parliament. The process of home ownership (which had enabled 750,000 families to buy their own homes since 1951) would be developed through policies which included the government advancing £100 million to building societies for loans on older houses.

A big programme of hospital building would be embarked upon. It was argued that the purchasing power of retirement pensions was now higher than it had been in 1951 and that the new pensions scheme would put National Insurance on a sound financial footing, concentrate Exchequer help on those with lowest earnings and enable men and women with higher earnings to make increased provision for old age. The weekly amount which could be earned without deduction of pension by those who had retired or by widowed mothers would be further increased.

Conservative foreign policy emphasised the aim of peace with justice. It pledged to continue to build up the United Nations' strength and influence in the world and sought to improve relations with the Soviet Union. It expressed the desire to move forward by balanced stages towards the abolition of all nuclear weapons and reduction of armed forces to a level which would rule out the possibility of an aggressive war. The role of the British government in seeking to secure the suspension of the testing of nuclear weapons was referred to, and it was stated that the government's ultimate objectives included the end of all atmospheric tests and the establishment of a system of international control. The last Conservative election broadcast was delivered by Macmillan and focused on Britain's position in the world. Conservative policy also included the development of the Commonwealth by means which included making British capital available through loans and grants for Commonwealth development. The British contribution to the United Nations Special Fund for economic development would be substantially increased.

The manifesto concluded with an attack on Labour. It was argued that they were found wanting when last in office and that vital issues of defence and foreign policy divided that party. It was argued that a Labour government would extend nationalisation, reimpose controls, cause inflation and higher taxes, disrupt business at home and undermine confidence abroad. Labour policies were depicted as old-fashioned and irrelevant to the problems of the modern world.

Macmillan undertook a major speaking tour to put the Conservative case to the nation. The Conservative Party assumed at the outset that their cause would be best aided by a low-key campaign. However (as is argued below), the vigour shown by Labour in the early stages of the contest forced a revision of this approach. The format of the last two Conservative broadcasts (which had looked dated in comparison to Labour's) was hastily revamped, and more aggressive attacks on Labour were made, in particular with regard to the Party's taxation promises. Viscount Montgomery reinforced the Conservative onslaught by suggesting that anyone who voted Labour 'must be completely barmy, absolutely off his rocker ... and should be locked up in a lunatic asylum as a danger to the country'. Towards the end of the campaign, the Conservative theme of projecting Britain as a prosperous Britain was bolstered by statistics which showed that unemployment was falling, production was rising and that the gold and dollar reserves were increasing.

Labour

Labour mounted no equivalent campaign to that conducted by the Conservative Party after 1957. Many of its members felt that public relations firms and advertising techniques had no legitimate role to play in politics, and much Labour effort after 1955 was devoted to organisational reform (which was viewed as a key reason for defeat in 1955, Harold Wilson's report to the 1955 Party Conference famously describing the Labour machine as 'at the penny-farthing stage in a jet-propelled era') and to discussions on policy. Brief campaigns (such as Into Action in 1958) were mainly directed at galvanising the Party faithful rather than at public opinion in general although the pamphlet *The Future Labour Offers YOU* did enjoy a relatively wide circulation. The failure to project a positive image meant that the negative portrayals of Labour by its opponents went unanswered.

Labour's policies were contained in its manifesto, *Britain Belongs To You.* The contents of this were largely derived from existing policy statements and deliberately downplayed the Party's socialist ideology. The manifesto challenged the Conservative assertion that increased prosperity had eroded the historic division between the haves and have-nots and argued that the contrast between extremes of wealth and poverty was greater in 1959 than it had been in 1951. It was argued that those who had 'never had it so good' were the businessman with a tax-free expense account, the speculator with tax-free capital gains and the retiring company director with a tax-free redundancy payment due to a takeover bid. Their affluence was contrasted to the widowed mother with children, the chronically sick, the 400,000 unemployed and the millions of old age pensioners without adequate superannuation. Although the enhanced affluence of many workers was conceded, it was argued that the sick, disabled and old had continually seen the value of state benefits whittled away by rising prices. By contrast, Labour's aim was stated to be to expand production and simultaneously ensure that welfare was developed and prosperity was properly shared.

Labour argued that rising living standards depended on a steady expansion of production but that, under the Conservatives, Britain's productivity lagged behind most other industrial nations. Unemployment had been used as a weapon to counter inflation and remained heavy in some areas. It was argued that the living standards of more than half of Britain's old age pensioners was a disgrace which Labour would tackle by an emergency programme to raise the basic pension and other social security benefits by 10 shillings to £3 a week. Benefits would be reviewed each year and automatically increased to cover price rises. Considerable emphasis was placed on Labour's plan for National Superannuation which when fully operational would provide half-pay on retirement for the average wage earner and up to two-thirds for the lower paid workers. It was argued that the Conservative appproach, due to come into force in 1961, was mainly a device for shifting the burden of paying for pensions from the better-off taxpayers to workers earning between £9 and £15 a week. The manifesto also promised to review widows' pensions, paying particular attention to the earning's rule.

Educational policy entailed initiating a drive to abolish slum schools, to reduce the size of classes in primary and secondary schools to 30 and to expand facilities for technical and other higher education. The 11-plus examination would be abolished. Comprehensive education would be introduced, but would not be subject to any uniform model, thus leaving local authorities with the freedom to decide how best to apply this principle. Labour's housing policy was designed to help people buy their own homes and to ensure an adequate supply of decent homes at a fair rent. The Party pledged to repeal the 1957 Rent Act (which had decontrolled many rents) and to bring interest rates down. The Conservatives were accused of slashing the council building of rented houses and Labour promised to reverse this policy and encourage councils to press on with slum clearance. The Party proposed the municipalisation of rented houses whereby local councils would take over houses which were rent controlled before 1 January 1956 and which were still tenanted. These would then be repaired and remodernised and let at fair rents. However, these tenants would first be given the right to buy from the council house they lived in.

It was argued that the Conservative Party had opposed the creation of the National Health Service and in office had starved it of money. Labour promised to spend £50 million a year on hospital development and would restore the free health service by abolishing all charges, commencing with the prescription charge. Old people would also be provided with a free chiropody service. Labour further pledged to make provision for the pursuit of leisure activities by establishing and funding a Sports Council and an Arts Council and setting up a National Theatre. Support was also expressed for a third television programme when this was technically possible. Labour's policy for young people included re-equipping the Youth Service and creating a million new jobs through economic expansion.

The manifesto argued that a Labour government would not put up taxes in order to pay for improved social services. Instead, the money would be raised through planned expansion (which, it was argued, had not occurred under Conservative governments and industrial production had hardly risen for four years) and by changes to the tax system to deal with tax-dodgers and limiting tax-free benefits (including expense accounts, tax-free compensation paid to directors on loss of office, and capital gains made on the Stock Exchange and elsewhere).

The Conservative Party and big business were attacked for having sought to discredit public ownership. Steps undertaken by Conservative governments to undermine these industries (such as transfering work from publicly owned railway workshops to private firms) would be reversed and the Party pledged to restore the steel industry and commercial long-distance road haulage to public ownership. The manifesto stated that there were no other plans for further nationalisation, although, where an industry was shown after thorough enquiry to be failing the nation, Labour reserved the right to take all or part of it into public ownership. Labour would also ensure that the community enjoyed some of the profits and capital gains now going to private industry by arranging for the purchase of shares by public investment agencies such as Superannuation Fund Trustees.

The Conservatives were attacked for the rise in the cost of living to which they had responded by cutting production and deliberately creating unemployment. Labour advocated a policy of planned expansion and full employment without creating inflation by policies which included a high rate of investment in industry and the energetic application of science to all phases of economic life. Labour's tax policy would be directed towards helping private industry to mechanise, modernise and expand. Its alternative to using unemployment to halt rising prices was to use controls and secure trade union cooperation by measures which included a fair shares budget policy and the extension of the welfare state. A Code of Conduct (including a Workers' Charter) would also be introduced after consultations with unions and employers which would be designed to raise the status of wage-earners and extend privileges, such as sickness pay, already provided for most salaried employees. Measures were also promised to protect consumers.

Labour promised to help industries suffering depression and contraction, including shipbuilding and ship-repairing. The Distribution of Industry Act would be used to respond to local unemployment and unemployment pay would be raised to £3 a week. Labour also pledged to aid the agricultural industry by measures which included providing protection against unfair foreign competition and establishing a special credit organisaiton to provide loans at reasonable and stable rates of interest. Rural amenities would be improved and water supplies reorganised under public ownership. Labour would also take steps to increase and diversify industry and to stimulate agriculture in Scotland, Wales and Northern Ireland. A Secretary of State would be appointed for Wales.

The manifesto posed the question as to who should represent Britain at the forthcoming summit. It was argued that Britain needed to be represented by those who respected the rule of law in international relations. Suez displayed how the Conservatives paid lip service to this principle, but ignored it when it conflicted with their interests. Labour, however, upheld the decision of the United Nations on this issue. Additionally, Britain's representatives needed to have a track record in seeking a disarmament agreement. It was argued that Labour had set the pace in the field of disarmament, whereas the Conservatives had opposed a nuclear test agreement unless it was part of a general disarmament agreement and had opposed the suspension of nuclear testing when Russia offered to suspends hers. It was finally argued that Britain's representatives required to face up the the problems of a world divided into rich and poor nations and subjects and free people in order to gain the confidence of Asia and Africa. It was argued that episodes such as the beating to death of 11 African prisoners in Kenya and the Conservative insistence on pressing ahead with the federation to which most people in Nyasaland and Northern and Southern Rhodesia were opposed disqualified the Conservatives from ever gaining the trust of the peoples of Africa and Asia. It was also argued that the Conservatives had never faced up to the challenge posed by the poverty experienced by two-thirds of the world's population.

The manifesto said little about socialism, although it did conclude by arguing that Labour's social, economic and foreign policies were based upon the socialist belief in the equal value of every human being which inspired Labour's struggle for social justice and human rights.

Initially the Labour Party campaign progressed well, aided by the low-key approach adopted by the Conservatives. The Party's election broadcasts (which consisted of a series of election reports entitled *Britain Belongs to You*) were professionally prepared, being 'lively, smooth and technically polished' (Butler and Rose, 1960: 86). All were introduced by Tony Benn. The depiction of the Conservatives as a class party (which was a key theme of the pamphlet *The Tory Swindle*) and of Britain as a country in which considerable hardship existed (which was emphasised in Anthony Greenwood's political broadcast on 9 September and in many of Gaitskell's speeches) added to Labour's appeal. Their pledge to add 10 shillings a week to old age pensions (which was prominently aired in the early stages of the campaign) was popular and disconcerted the Conservatives. Labour was also aided at the outset when a City scandal occurred in connection with the Jasper group of property companies. This, argued Wilson, displayed the 'casino mentality of the City of London'.

However, Labour began to run into difficulties as the campaign progressed. In order to emphasise that Labour was not the party of high taxes, Hugh Gaitskell specifically declared in a speech at Newcastle on 28 September that the Party would not raise the standard or any other rate of income tax. This was soon followed by a press release which stated that Labour would remove the purchase tax from essential goods. Conservatives had consistently queried how Labour proposed to pay for the policies contained in their manifesto but now adopted a more vigorous stance and depicted Labour as a party which was making a number of cynical and rash promises regarding taxation in order to win votes – 'a bribe a day keeps the Tories away,' quipped Butler. This theme was taken up in the pro-Conservative press, the *Daily Sketch* suggesting on its front page that 'This is Spiv Stuff' and asking 'What Next – Free Fags?' Evidence suggested that these two promises (in addition to the pledge to raise old age pensions) were a key turning point against Labour (Butler and Rose, 1960: 61) as it brought into the open fears held by many concerning the Party's financial competence.

A further problem encountered by Labour was the major campaign waged against its nationalisation proposals by business groups. Campaigns of this nature had been waged in previous elections, but reached a new level of intensity in 1959. Although the manifesto's proposals in this area were modest, other policy documents implied more significant extensions of public ownership: *The Future Labour Offers YOU*, for example, referring to 600 giant privately owned firms which dominated production, investment, finance and trade of the private sector of Britain's economy and expressing Labour's belief that it was now appropriate that public control should be extended to ensure that the decisions of these companies were in line with the nation's interests. One innovation was a referendum on nationalisation in 1959 conducted by Colin Hurry which was designed to display the unpopularity of this policy and ensured that this issue received prominent attention. Opposition was also mounted by bodies which included the Iron and Steel Federation, the steel company Stewarts and Lloyds, the Economic League, the Institute of Directors, the Road Haulage Association and the National Union of Manufacturers.

Liberals
The Liberal manifesto was entitled *People Count*. In this, Grimond referred to the increase in support for the Liberal Party and stated the Liberal aim to consolidate and improve on this position as a first stage to the eventual formation of a Liberal government. The policies contained in the manifesto were directed at all progressively minded people. The Liberal task was stated to be the building-up of a progresssive alternative party which Labour could not achieve while it remained tied to nationalisation and was financed by the vested interests of the trade union establishment. It was further stated that a Liberal vote constituted a protest against the British political system being controlled by two powerful party machines, one largely financed by employers and the other by trade unions. It was argued that the young, the consumers, small business owners, professional men and technicians, craftsmen, farmers, fishermen, shopkeepers and pensioners had no interest in the Capital v. Labour struggle and were greatly harmed by it. At the conclusion of this document, voters were encouraged to desert the party they traditionally supported by being reminded that the vote did not belong to either of the main parties but to the people.

In order to counter the wasted vote arguments which had been made by the main parties at previous elections, the Liberal manifesto argued that the task of a general election was to choose a Parliament and not to elect a government. Thus, while it was accepted that the result of the contest would be either a Conservative or a Labour government, it was argued that the way in which either would act in office would depend on the strength of Liberalism in the House of Commons and the size of the Liberal vote. The manifesto argued that if another Conservative government was returned it was necessary to demonstrate that there was a large non-socialist block of opinion in the country which would not tolerate oppression in Africa, another Cyprus, or complacency over inflation, government expenditure and the set-up in the nationalised industries. Alternatively, a large Liberal vote would demonstrate that there were persons who shared Labour's concern regarding poverty but who were opposed to nationalisation. This would make it difficult for a Labour government to carry through the nationalisation of the steel and other industries. It was also argued that Liberals were required in Parliament and local government in order to raise distinct Liberal issues and to promote honest, above-board politics.

Specific Liberal policies were presented in the context of the Liberal belief that people counted. These included stopping Britain's programme of manufacturing and testing nuclear weapons and, instead, to offer to contribute to a general Western nuclear programme. This policy would also help to reduce taxes. Waste in the nationalised industries and government service would be eliminated. Prices would be cut by policies which included reducing tariffs, cutting distribution costs and banning price-fixing agreements. The Party expressed support for the principle of ownership for all. This included encouraging co-ownership and co-partnerhsip schemes in industry through tax reliefs. The Liberal Party was the only one to raise the issue of controlling the trade unions. Its policies included requiring unions to register with a Registrar of Friendly Societies which would guarantee fair elections and prevent victimisation.

Liberal social policy included raising the old age pension to £3 for a single person and £4 16s for a married couple. Private pension schemes should be transferable. The health service should become more human and less 'Whitehall'. More investment in education was proposed with priority given to secondary schools. A big expansion of university education was also advocated. Productivity should increase in order to provide jobs. More people should be encouraged to buy their own homes through policies which included the abolition of schedule A income tax and stamp duty. A land bank was proposed to provide cheap credit for farmers and rural industries. It was proposed that more money should be spent on roads.

On constitutional matters, Liberal support for self-government for Scotland and Wales was reaffirmed. The Party would establish separate Parliaments for these two nations, with the UK Parliament remaining responsible for foreign and defence policies. Fairer voting was also advocated for Parliament and local government. The Party's foreign policies included eradicating the domination of black people by white or white by black in Africa in favour of a system in which all races mixed freely with full respect for one another. It was also proposed to set up a Commonwealth Civil Service and a Commonwealth Development Fund to help the newer member states build up their economies.

The Liberals lacked resources to mount any major form of pre-election campaign. Their campaign was hindered by the lack of high-quality speakers to tour the country. Grimond devoted much of his time to his Orkney and Shetland constituency, although he did make an important innovation in electioneering when he embarked on a helicopter tour of Liberal marginal seats on 5 October.

Result of the Election

Opinion polls predicted a Conservative victory at the outset of the campaign. The size of this lead declined during the middle of the campaign and this, together with the large body of voters who described themselves as 'don't knows' in response to the pollsters' questions, gave Labour some grounds for optimism. However, a Conservative victory was widely anticipated.

The election was contested by 1,536 candidates (which included 216 Liberals, 20 Plaid Cymru and 12 Sinn Fein candidates). The result was:

Party	Votes	Vote %	MPs
Conservative	13,305,862	47.8%	353
Labour	12,216,172	43.8%	258
Ulster Unionist	445,013	1.6% [77.2%]	12
Liberal	1,640,760	5.9%	6
Others	92,121	0.3%	1
Sinn Fein	63,415	0.2% [11.0%]	0
Scottish National Party	21,738	0.1% [0.8%]	0
Plaid Cymru	77,571	0.3% [5.2%]	0
Total	27,862,652		630

The turnout was 78.7 per cent. The overall swing from Labour to the Conservatives was 1.2 per cent.

The successful Independent was Sir David Robertson. He initially represented his constituency, Caithness and Sutherland, as a Conservative but resigned the party whip in connection with Highland issues. He was not challenged by a Conservative candidate in 1959 and was returned as an Independent Conservative. Twenty-five women MPs were elected.

The Parties

The Conservatives gained 18 seats more than in 1955, although the overall swing in their favour was subject to considerable regional variation. The Conservatives fared especially well in the industrial central England (where they secured 11 gains, including three in Birmingham and Coventry South East) and in London and the Home Counties (where eight seats were won). Good performances were also secured in Lincolnshire, the North Eastern Coast (where Cleveland, Hartlepool and Newcastle-upon-Tyne East were wrested from Labour) and in the cities of Leicester and Stoke-on-Trent. Seven former Conservative Ministers retired. These included Dame Florence Horsbrugh (who was the first Conservative woman to be in the Cabinet), Sir James Stuart (a former Secretary of State for Scotland) and Sir Allan Noble. The main Conservative casualties in 1959 were J. Nixon Browne (joint Under Secretary at the Scottish Office) and Sir Ian Horobin (Parliamentary Secretary at the Ministry of Power).

There were overall swings to Labour in two regions, Clydeside and South East Lancashire, and the Party also performed well in Wales and the City of Manchester. The Parliamentary Labour Party lost a number of long-serving MPs, including seven former ministers who retired. The most prominent of these was Herbert Morrison (who accepted a life peerage), Hugh Dalton, George Isaacs and Tom Williams. Seven members of Labour's front beanch team in the 1955–59 Parliament were defeated. These included Arthur Blenkinsop (at Newcastle East) and

Frank Beswick (at Uxbridge), both of whom had represented their constituencies since 1945. The trade unions sponsored 129 Labour candidates, of whom 93 were elected. The Cooperative Party fielded 31 candidates, of whom 16 were successful.

An increased number of Liberal candidates, 216, contested the election, of whom 55 lost their deposits. The average poll obtained by Liberals in seats they contested was 14.2 per cent. Six Liberal MPs were returned and the Party was second in 27 seats (obtaining over one-third of the vote in North Cornwall, Bodmin, Torrington, Merioneth and Rochdale). Ironically, the Party fared worst in the seats where it had performed best in 1955, the Liberal vote falling in eight of the 13 in which over 30 per cent of the vote had been secured. The Party's biggest disappoinment was to lose Torrington which had been won at a by-election in 1958 but which reverted to the Conservatives in the general election. The Party did, however, succeed in gaining the neighbouring seat of North Devon, the victor being Jeremy Thorpe who overturned a Conservative majority of more than 5,000. His flamboyant style of campaigning was epitomised by the brown bowler hat which he wore throughout the contest.

Scotland, Wales and Northern Ireland
Labour performed well in Scotland, winning 38 of the 71 seats, and polled strongly in the industrial belt where it gained Lanark, Central Ayrshire and the two Glasgow seats of Craigton and Scotstoun from the Conservatives (although losing one seat, Glasgow–Kelvingrove). In one Glasgow constituency, Carthcart, there was a swing to Labour of around 13 per cent (mainly attributable to the influx of 20,000 council tenants). The Conservatives and National Liberals won 31 seats, the Liberals one and the remaining one was won by an Independent Conservative. The SNP mounted a relatively small challenge (consisting of five candidates) but secured over 20 per cent of the vote in Perth and East Perthshire and 15 per cent in the neighbouring constituency of Perth and Kinross.

The swing to the Conservative Party was about half the figure secured by this party in England, and Labour gained one seat from the Conservatives, Swansea West. Overall it won 27 of the 36 seats. The Conservatives and National Liberals won seven and and the Liberals two. Plaid Cymru fielded candidates in 20 of Wales's 36 seats but their total share of the vote rose by around 2 per cent in Wales compared to 1955. Good results were obtained in Merioneth and Caernarvon (where the Party secured over 20 per cent of the vote) and in Rhondda West (where it won 17 per cent).

All 12 seats in Northern Ireland were won by the Ulster Unionist Party. Sinn Fein again contested all 12 constituencies in Northern Ireland, but their overall poll markedly declined to around 11 per cent of the vote. The Party was, however, economic in its election spending: five of its candidates each spent below £10 on their campaigns.

Consequence of the Election
Harold Macmillan formed a Conservative government.

15 October 1964

Party Leaders
Harold Wilson (Labour)
Sir Alec Douglas-Home (Conservative)
Jo Grimond (Liberal)

Background to the Election
Timing of the Election
Speculation concerning the date of the election prompted the Prime Minister, Sir Alec Douglas-Home, to issue a statement in 9 April 1964 stating that it would not be held until the autumn of that year. The Parliament elected in 1959 thus ran its full term of five years (5 November being the last legal date when an election could be called), making it the longest serving Parliament in peacetime since the life of Parliament was reduced from seven years to five years in the 1911 Parliament Act.

Electoral Procedures and Practices
In 1963 Lord Home became the first peer to hold the office of prime minister since Lord Salisbury who finally resigned the office in 1902. He used the provisions of the 1963 Peerage Act to disclaim his hereditary title and, as Sir Alec Douglas-Home, entered the House of Commons as MP for Kinross and West Perthshire following a by-election on 12 November 1963.

Conservatives
Reforms undertaken after 1959 included the remodelling of local government by the creation of the Greater London Council by the 1961 London Government Act. Macmillan's Conservative government secured some successes on the international front. In 1960, Macmillan toured Africa and warned the South African Parliament of the 'wind of change' then sweeping through the Continent. Independence was granted to a number of African nations (including Nigeria, Tanganyika, Uganda, Kenya, Nyasaland, Northern Rhodesia), and the signing of a nuclear test ban treaty in July 1963 was widely regarded as a considerable success for the UK Prime Minister as the shooting down by Russia of an American U-2 reconnaissance plane in 1960 and the Cuban missile crisis in 1962 had suggested that a Soviet–Western detente was unlikely to be achieved. This success, however, was offset by the failure to achieve the entry of the UK into the EEC. Negotiations were initiated in 1961 but broke down in January 1963 when President de Gaulle of France announced that his country could not support the UK's entry.

Domestically, however, the government faced a number of difficulties. Although economic expansion occurred after the 1959 election, it became characterised by sluggish growth and problems in the form of a balance of payments deficit and speculation against Sterling arose. This prompted the Chancellor of the Exchequer to introduce a number of 'counter-infla-tionary' measures in 1961 which included taking powers to impose a 'payroll' tax and to vary purchase tax. He also raised the starting point of surtax from £2,000 to £5,000. These measures wee supplemented by others in July. The bank rate was raised from 5 per cent to 7 per cent, a surcharge on purchase tax was levied, and public expenditure cuts were announced. He also introduced a pay pause which was designed to enable productivity to catch up with wages and later set up the National Incomes Commission (with which the TUC refused to cooperate) and the National Economic Development Council (NEDDY) in 1962. The latter represented both sides of industry and the government and was designed to enable a common approach to be formulated concerning economic growth, rises in wages and increases in production. These measures did not enjoy success: the economy remained slack in 1962 and the pay pause encountered trade union resistance until it was ended in 1962. Additionally, towards the end of 1962 unemployment began to increase, especially in regions outside the South East, one response to which was to appoint Lord Hailsham with ministerial responsibility for the North East. These economic difficulties (compounded by the Vassall and Profumo scandals) resulted in government unpopularity, the main beneficiary being the Liberal Party. A by-election disaster at the marginal seat of North East Leicester in July 1962 (in which the Conservative candidate finished in third place) was the pretext for a major government reshuffle. Macmillan sacked the Chancellor of the Exchequer, Selwyn Lloyd, the Lord Chancellor and five other Cabinet ministers in the 'night of the long knives' which led the Liberal MP, Jeremy Thorpe, to remark, 'greater love hath no man than this, that he lay down his friends for his life'. Later that year Macmillan himself resigned on grounds of ill health.

The main contenders to replace Macmillan were R. A. Butler and Lord Hailsham. However, the eventual choice was the Foreign Secretary, Lord Home, who emerged through a secret process of 'soundings' not involving any election. Iain Macleod and Enoch Powell refused to serve in his government, thus accentuating the image of the Conservatives as a bickering party. Labour and Liberal politicians queried the credentials of the 'fourteenth earl' as a leader who would succeed in bringing Britain up to date. Initially, Home failed to dent Labour's lead in the polls and the 1964 local election results were bad for the government. However, by August and September, Labour's lead began to diminish. The main measures undertaken by Home's government were the abolition of resale price maintenance in 1964 (which upset small shop-keepers and caused dissent and rebellion among Conservative MPs) and an attempt to associate the government with modernisation which was the key theme advanced by the Party in the winter of 1963–64 and in the 1964 Queen's Speech. Concrete policies to achieve this aim included raising the house-building target to 400,000 houses a year (a proposal put forward by Home during his 1963 by-election campaign) and by accepting the recommendations contained in the Robbins report for the expansion of higher education (having earlier, in 1961, cut the university expansion programme). It was also proposed to abandon the stop-go economic cycles (in which periods of expansion were followed by balance of payments crises, deflation and investment cut-backs) with faster and steadier economic growth. Problems, however, arose in connection with the Ferranti affair (an allegation of excess profits being made in connection with a defence contract which resulted in the firm eventually repaying some of the money).

Labour

The defeat suffered by Labour at the 1959 general election prompted debate concerning party ideology and policies which led to internal disputes taking place between the fundamentalists and social democrats (an issue which is explained in the 1959 entry).

Revisionism had made some impact on party policy during the 1950s. However, the 1959 election manifesto largely failed to mirror these developments and continued to emphasise the traditional approach towards public ownership. Thus Labour's third election defeat in a row in 1959 (just three years after the Suez debacle) intensified the efforts of the revisionists to ensure that their views dominated the future direction of the Labour Party. Literature on the theme of 'must Labour lose?', emphasised social and economic changes affecting the working class in post-war Britain (especially the notion of enhanced working-class affluence, or embourgeoisement, which loosened the traditional ties between the Labour Party and sections of the working class) added fuel to the dispute on Labour ideology. Whereas fundamentalists believed that the correct way forward for Labour was to 'sell' the case for fundamentalism more vigorously (especially directing the argument to those members of the working class who did not support the Labour Party), revisionists did not believe that a Labour victory could be secured while the Party relied so heavily on working-class votes and instead wished to appeal to a wider political audience. They felt this would be achieved only when the Party was not associated in the public's eye with policies perceived to be unpopular (such as nationalisation), with the promotion of the interests of sectional groupings (particularly the trade unions) or with obsolescent attitudes (such as the class struggle).

The Labour leader, Hugh Gaitskell, attempted to assert unambiguously the pre-eminence of revisionism and a key aspect of his approach was the abandonment of Clause IV of the Party's constitution which committed it to nationalisation. At the 1959 Party Conference Gaitskell argued that Labour needed to adapt to the economic and social changes which had occurred in post-war Britain. He thus advocated that Labour objectives (which were then enshrined in Clause IV of the constitution) should be rewritten and he suggested a statement of basic principles of British democratic socialism. These emphasised moral values which embraced concern for the disadvantaged and oppressed, a belief in social justice involving the equitable distribution of wealth, the objective of a classless society, a belief in human relations based on fellowship and cooperation, the need for the public interest to override private interests, and a commitment to freedom and democratic self-government. This statement of socialist values constituted a rejection of socialism defined solely in terms of public ownership. The mixed economy was endorsed although support was expressed for the tactical use of public ownership as the means to attaining the objective of equality.

However, Clause IV was supported by wider sections of opinion within the Party for whom it possessed symbolic importance, indicating an ultimate commitment to transform society and establish a new social order. Particular opposition was encountered from the trade unions who were more concerned with bread and butter issues such as working conditions, pay and employment than abstract philosophical ideas projected by elitist intellectuals who lacked any substantial grass roots base in the Party. At the 1959 Conference, party unity was maintained by the intervention of Aneurin Bevan who upheld the principle of public ownership whilst rejecting wholesale nationalisation. Subsequently, Gaitskell devoted his energies in seeking to supplement Clause IV with a new statement of principles and aims. In March 1960, the National Executive Committee approved a statement of principles of British democratic socialism which would supplement the existing Clause IV: those sympathetic to his aims have argued that this decision did not constitute a defeat since he had never argued that Clause IV should be abandoned but had, rather, believed there was a need to add to it. In July 1960 (with the spectre of Gaitskell's potential defeat on defence policy looming on the horizon) the NEC revised its earlier decision to supplement Clause IV and resolved not to proceed with any amendment or alteration to it. It was agreed, however, to commend Gaitskell's statement of principles to the 1960 Conference which subsequently approved them.

Gaitskell's attempt to revise (or supplement) Clause IV later became intertwined with defence policy. The official stance of the party had been that of multilateralism. However, the cancellation by the Conservative government of the Blue Streak delivery system in 1960 added considerable strength to the unilateralists in the Party since Britain could only remain a nuclear power if America provided the means to deliver the weapon. This enhanced reliance on the United States gave credence to those on the left who argued the case for Labour to adopt a distinctive socialist defence policy. Although unilateralism and Britain's membership of NATO were the key policy issues of this debate, Gaitskell sought to project the underlying issue to be that of neutralism. For this reason he vowed to 'fight and fight and fight again' to reverse the unilateral nuclear disarmament motion which was endorsed at the 1960 Party Conference in Scarborough.

Gaitskell's attempts to redefine Clause IV and his determination to reverse the decision of the 1960 Party Conference concerning Britain's possession of an independent nuclear deterrent placed his leadership of the Party firmly on the agenda. However, the tide began to turn in his favour. In November 1960 he beat off a leadership challenge from Harold Wilson by 166 votes to 81. In February 1961 he succeeded in obtaining the support of the NEC for a multilateralist policy statement and the switch of two key trade unions (USDAW and the AEU) from unilateralism to multilateralism enabled him to succeed in reversing at the 1961 Party Conference the defence policy endorsed the previous year. The subsequent emergence of the issue of Britain's membership of the European Economic Community further aided the restoration of unity. Although revisionist opinion tended to support the case for Britain's entry, there was some opposition to this course of action on the grounds that membership might harm Britain's economy, that the system of taxation would become regressive, and that the institutions of the EEC were undemocratic. Gaitskell's 'five conditions' veered towards this position and his hostile speech towards membership delivered at the 1962 Party Conference (in which he argued that entry would presage the end of Britain as an independent state, thus terminating one thousand years of history) led him to break with his closest revisionist supporters. The breakdown of negotiations terminated the debate at this time. Finally, the retention of Clause IV (which implied that the transformation of society would be secured through public ownership), coupled with the endorsement of the mixed economy and the objective of economic growth which had been the key underpinning of the revisionists' goal of social equality, made possible a reconciliation between fundamentalists and revisionists. Party pronouncements such as *Labour in the Sixties* (1960), which launched the concept of the 'scientific revolution', and *Signposts for the Sixties* (1961) achieved this reconciliation, in particular by advocating an increased role for public ownership within the context of a national plan to provide for economic growth.

Gaitskell died in 1963. James Callaghan dropped out after the first ballot for the party leadership and in the second ballot Harold Wilson defeated deputy leader George Brown by 144 votes to 103. He subsequently attempted to heal divisions in the Party, especially by identifying the fundamentalist objective of socialism with the revisionist goal of economic growth and modernisation. This entailed the reform of British industry and other key institutions and the replacement of the stop-go economic cycles associated with Conservative governments with sustained economic growth based on advance economic planning. In particular, Wilson sought to identify Labour with the 'white heat of the technological revolution', to harness 'socialism to science and science to socialism' in order to pose it as a party which would bring Britain (and particularly its economic performance) up to date, enabling the benefits of economic rejuvenation to be spread widely throughout society.

Liberals
The improved fortunes of the Liberal Party which had been evidenced in 1959 continued after the election. Improvements were made to party organisation and, in particular, attempts were made by Grimond to develop party policy through attracting experts into the service of the Party. Grimond's aim of replacing the Labour Party as the main alternative to the Conservatives was now advanced through the advocacy of the electoral strategy of the realignment of the left. This sought to combine progressive forces consisting of Labour's social democrats, left-wing Conservatives and his own Liberal Party. The legitimacy of this tactic was enhanced by the divisions in the Labour Party concerning revisionism and was based on an acceptance that the Liberal Party could never by itself achieve a position of power. The role he ascribed to the Liberal Party was that of providing a rallying force for a new progressive grouping which, initially, entailed the Party demonstrating its own political strength in the hope that Liberal (rather than Labour) advance in a period of Conservative unpopularity would induce the social democrats to consider seriously Grimond's arguments for political realignment.

New sources of support were courted from those who viewed themselves as progressives (regardless of which party they currently supported) and this generalised message was refined in a specific appeal directed at what was referred to as the 'new man' (the upwardly mobile sons and daughters of traditional Labour supporters who had benefited from factors which included educational reform and the impact of technology on jobs previously performed by manual labour). The highwater mark of Liberal achievements in this period was to capture the safe Conservative seat of Orpington in 1962, increasing its share of the vote by 31.7 per cent. It was erroneously assumed that the 'new man' had made a significant contribution to the Party's success whereas, in reality, the additional support obtained by the Liberal Party after 1959 largely came from discontented Conservative (and in some cases, Labour) supporters who had no interest in the political realignment advocated by Grimond but merely wished to register a protest against their own party's performance in either government or opposition. Additionally, the Liberal Party improved its position in places where a tradition of Liberal support survived the Party's decline after 1945. By the end of 1962, however, Labour began to improve its position at by-elections and in the opinion polls, and the upsurge in Liberal support in 1961 and early 1962 began to trail off.

By-elections

There were 62 by-elections in the 1959–64 Parliament. Labour gained five seats and the Conservatives and Liberals one each. Two of these contests occurred in South East Bristol. In November 1960 the sitting Labour MP, Tony Benn, inherited his father's title and seat in the House of Lords. Benn attempted to renounce this peerage, but the Privileges Committee of the House of Commons refused to allow him to remain in that House and a by-election was called to fill the vacancy on 4 May 1961. Benn successfully fought this contest, but as he was deemed ineligible to be an MP, the candidate in second place (M. St Clair) was declared to be elected. The enactment of the 1963 Peerage Act gave Benn the opportunity to return to the House of Commons. St Clair immediately resigned his seat to allow this to happen and the Conservative Party did not oppose him in the by-election held on 20 August 1963.

Conduct of the Election

The election was fought against a background of pessimism concerning the perceived decline of Britain. Factors which included the failure to achieve the same economic growth rates as countries in the European Economic Community and the loss of Empire, without its replacement by a new role in the world, caused many commentators to suggest that Britain was rooted in the past and in danger of being overwhelmed by the tide of contemporary developments. Resistance to change and the amateur way in which affairs were conducted in Britain were highlighted as key explanations for the decline of Britain, and the theme of modernisation was avidly embraced by both Labour and Liberal parties who alleged that the Conservatives would never be able to bring Britain up to date because of the attachment of their elderly leadership to institutions such as the class system and their allegiance to the 'establishment'.

However, although the theme of modernisation seemed damaging to the Conservative Party which had been in office since 1951, during 1964 they generally fared better in by-elections and, although trailing Labour, the Party's standing in the opinion polls (Gallup being joined by National Opinion Polls in the early 1960s) also began to improve as the election approached. At the outset of the campaign, the polls showed an almost identical level of support for the two main parties.

Conservatives

The Conservatives made some use of survey research between 1962 and 1964, but less than Labour. Their policies were contained in their manifesto, *Prosperity with a Purpose*. Their appeal was based upon the achievements of Conservative governments in economic and foreign affairs, and voters were urged to support the Conservative Party in order to safeguard British prosperity and to maintain her role in world affairs. The manifesto argued that living standards had risen greatly since 1951 and pledged to give priority to a 4 per cent growth rate. It argued the virtues of an incomes policy and promised to foster the modernisation of British industry and job mobility. Total opposition to nationalisation was declared, and the manifesto promised to complete the denationalisation of the steel industry. Nationalisation was referred to in detail in the Party's second election broadcast. The manifesto pointed to the Conservative record in house building and promised to reach a target of 400,000 houses a year by 1965. It stated that all slums would be cleared by 1973 and house ownership would be stimulated by the Government Housing Corporation lowering mortgage deposits. Little was said concerning land prices other than the suggestion that these would be stabilised by releasing more land for building. A general review of all social security arrangements was promised and it was proposed to expand hospital building and community care services. The Party intended to raise the school leaving age to 16. The manifesto placed emphasis on the need to retain Britain's independent nuclear deterrent, and Home constantly referred to this policy in his campaign. Conservatives asserted that past history suggested that a Labour government would result in financial crisis and economic disaster, and electors were reminded that Labour was a socialist party led by a man associated with its left wing. In the Conservatives' last election broadcast, Home stated that Labour would discard Britain's nuclear weapons which, he maintained, were the key to Britain's authority in world affairs.

Immigration did not figure significantly in the national campaigns of any party, although Home defended the 1961 Commonwealth Immigration Act as being responsible for stopping a 'flood' of immigrants into the country, and Labour pledged in its manifesto to retain immigration contros until an agreement could be negotiated with the Commonwealth. However, it did assume considerable importance in the constituency of Smethwick where the Labour candidate, Patrick Gordon Walker, was defeated by a Conservative candidate, Peter Griffiths, who mounted an overtly racist campaign. The swing from Labour to the Conservatives was in excess of 7 per cent. Griffiths spoke out against a multiracial society, and called for a complete ban on immigration. Slogans such as 'if you want a nigger for your neighbour, vote Labour' were circulated during the contest. This event subsequently led the new Labour Prime Minister, Harold Wilson, to challenge the Conservative leadership to deny Griffiths the party whip so that he would spend his time in the House of Commons as a 'parliamentary leper'. Although this action was not forthcoming (perhaps on the basis that local election results since the early 1960s indicated that the seat would be lost by Labour in any case), Heath subsequently made it clear that the Conservative Party would not tolerate any candidate who sought to exploit the issue of immigration. Three other avowedly anti-immigrant candidates stood in London constituencies.

The Conservatives' emphasis on their defence policy of retaining an independent British nuclear deterrent was not viewed as a major issue by the electors (Butler and King, 1965: 129). Labour benefited by exploiting fears of an impending economic crisis. Additionally, some errors occurred in the Conservative campaign, especially Home's reference to the Party's proposed supplement for older pensioners as a 'donation', thus reinforcing the aristocratic image of a party which was aloof and condescending towards ordinary people. It is also doubtful whether interventions by Hogg aided the Conservative cause. In response to a reference made by a heckler at Plymouth to the Profumo affair debauching public life (an issue which Labour had avoided exploiting), Hogg asserted the presence of adulterers on Labour's front bench. Lord Attlee countered this by stating there was not a shred of evidence for this allegation and advised him to 'grow up'. However, not to be silenced, towards the end of the campaign, Hogg used a press conference on 12 October to attack the Liberals for being 'insignificant and meaningless' and to suggest that anyone who voted Labour was 'stark, staring bonkers'. The Conservatives also, with no 'hard evidence', accused Labour of hiring hecklers to disrupt their election meetings.

Home put the Conservative case across at a number of whistle stop tours and election rallies. Although this indicated a desire on his part to meet members of the electorate directly, he came face-to-face with relatively few and performed far less well in election rallies (especially when subjected to heckling as at Birmingham on 8 October which he had no effective means to deal with save soldiering on with his speech which no one was able to hear) and on television.

Labour

Labour made considerable use of survey research conducted by Dr Mark Abrams to shape its campaign. Target voters whose views on key issues were analysed in order to influence Labour's projection of issues and policies were identified.

Labour's election policies were contained in its manifesto, *The New Britain*, which placed an emphasis on growth, innovation and efficiency. It condemned the Conservatives' stop-go economic policies and the comparatively slow rate of economic growth, which (according to Brown in the Party's second election broadcast) would result in an impending economic crisis. It proposed to remedy the absence of planning with the creation of a Ministry of Economic Affairs to formulate a national plan and expressed the intention to create a Ministry of Technology to aid the application of technological processes to industry. Regional planning boards would be introduced to stop the drift to the South East, and the closing of the trade gap was stated to be a priority. Labour proposed to counter inflation (which, it was asserted, meant that the 1951 pound had fallen in value to only 13s 4d) with a national incomes policy (which included the reform of the tax system and the taxation of capital gains) and providing additional powers to the Monopolies Commission. It was argued that the public sector of industry made a vital contribution to the economy and pledged to expand the existing nationalised industries and to take over the steel industry and water supplies. Labour promised to set up a Land Commission to buy up land on which building or rebuilding was intended and to repeal the 1957 Rent Act. The aim of building 400,000 houses a year was expressed.

The Party pledged to raise National Insurance benefits which would be linked to average earnings with the eventual aim of providing half of the wages for the worker on average pay. The earnings rule for widows would be ended, the health service improved and prescription charges abolished. For education, it was proposed to end 11-plus selection, to reorganise secondary education along comprehensive lines and to transfer teachers' salaries from the rates to the Exchequer. The manifesto condemned the Conservatives for having sought to enter the European Economic Community on terms which would have harmed Britain's relationship with the Commonwealth and condemned the government's record for creating waste and inefficiency especially in connection with defence issues such as Blue Streak and Ferranti.

The Labour manifesto was dubbed 'a menu without prices' by Home which would allegedly cost £900 million to implement. Towards the end of the campaign (and probably too late to make any impact on the voters) Maudling argued that to pay for it would require nine pence on income tax, six pence on a gallon of petrol, four pence on 20 cigarettes, a penny on a pint of beer, three shillings on a bottle of spirits and six shillings on the weekly national insurance contribution (Butler and King, 1965: 124). Labour denied this, arguing its programme would be financed out of the growing expansion of British industry. Labour sought to undermine the Conservative claim of economic competence by pointing to the setbacks in 1961 and 1962 and to the large (£73 million) balance of payments deficit for the second quarter of 1964, and arguing that this was evidence of an impending financial crisis which the government had sought to stave off by borrowing from the European central banks. The need for modernisation was stressed by Wilson in Labour's last election broadcast.

The Labour campaign was dominated by Wilson, almost to the extent of making it appear that the Party was a one-man band. Relatively few problems were encountered in Labour's campaign. Brown suggested a possible cut in mortgage rates to 3 per cent (which was not official policy), and Wilson implied that the Conservatives fostered strikes (such as the unofficial one at the component firm Hardy Spicer at the beginning of the campaign) to harm Labour's electoral prospects.

Liberals
The Party's main aims in 1964 were to increase the size of its Parliamentary Party and to boost its total national vote (the figure of 3 million being widely cited within the Party). The Party's first election broadcast sought to convince electors of the worth of voting Liberal even though it had no chance of forming a government. It was emphasised that Liberal MPs were independent and would speak for the people rather than being beholden to the party machines. Seats deemed winnable were singled out for special assistance through a 'special seats' committee which was chaired by Jeremy Thorpe. A key argument to convert potential Liberals into actual supporters and thereby maximise the Party's vote (which was advanced after 1959) was the exhortation that 'if you think like a Liberal, vote like a Liberal'.

Liberal policies were contained in its manifesto, *Think for Yourself – Vote Liberal*. It welcomed the prospect of joining the European Economic Community and, like Labour, urged the strengthening of Britain's conventional forces. It sought to secure faster economic growth through the use of measures which included tax reform and retraining schemes to aid job mobility. Opposition was expressed to further acts of nationalisation, and support was expressed for co-ownership in industry. The manifesto committed the Party to a target of 500,000 houses a year together with an accelerated rate of slum clearance. Site value rating was advocated as a solution to rising land prices. It proposed raising the pension for married couples to eight pounds 10 shillings a week and to replace National Insurance stamps with a payroll tax. The 11-plus examination would be abolished. The Liberal campaign was primarily directed at the record of the Conservatives whose concern over losing support to the Liberals prompted Lord Blakenham to advise those considering voting Liberal to vote Labour instead if they would not support the Conservatives.

Result of the Election
The election was fought against a widespread belief that it was time for a change, although Labour speakers seldom referred to this explicitly. Press conferences remained a feature of the campaigns of all main parties, although unlike in 1959 each party largely ploughed its own furrow with little reference to the contents of those of their rivals, resulting in a 'decline in the extent of discourse' (Butler and King, 1965: 154).

A total of 1,757 candidates contested the election. The result was:

Party	Votes	Vote %	MPs
Labour	12,205,808	44.1%	317
Conservative	11,600,745	41.9%	292
Ulster Unionist	401,897	1.5% [63.0%]	12
Liberal	3,099,283	11.2%	9
Ulster Republican/Republican Labour	116,306	0.4% [18.2%]	0
Scottish National Party	64,044	0.2% [2.4%]	0
Plaid Cymru	69,507	0.3% [4.8%]	0
Others	99,558	0.4%	0
Total	27,657,148		630

The turnout was 77.1 per cent. The swing from the Conservatives to Labour was 3.1 per cent. Twenty-nine women MPs were elected.

The Parties

There were significant variations to the national swing which were principally of a regional nature. Bigger than average swings to Labour were obtained in North Western England, Clydeside, and Greater London while the swing to Labour in Liverpool was around 8 per cent. Alternatively, the Conservatives fared well in the West Midlands and East Anglia and the swing against them in the 27 constituencies dominated by the coal-mining industry was only around 1 per cent.

The Conservative share of the national vote declined by around 6 per cent from the figure achieved in 1959. Sir Winston Churchill retired from the House of Commons, two Cabinet ministers (Barber and Rippon) lost their seats and four other ministers (including Maurice Macmillan) were also defeated. The support obtained by the Labour Party rose in the top two social classes.

Wilson believed that the BBC made a crucial contribution to Labour's victory when, at his behest, the director general agreed to re-schedule *Steptoe and Son* which was due to be shown between 8.30 and 9 pm on the night of the election. Wilson feared that large numbers of Labour supporters would stay at home to watch the programme and would be unable to vote as the polls then closed at 9 pm. Wilson believed that the rescheduling decision could have enabled Labour to gain as many as 20 seats. Nineteen Labour MPs were sponsored by the Cooperative Party and 120 by trade unions.

The Liberal Party polled a national vote in excess of 3 million, its candidates securing an average share of 18.7 per cent of the vote in the constituencies they contested. Liberals finished second in 54 seats, double the number obtained in 1959. Overall the Party's votes were drawn more or less equally from the two major parties. There was some evidence of tactical voting by Liberal and Labour supporters, although this determined the outcome in only two or three seats (Steed, 1965: 348). Nine seats were won, all in three-cornered contests, the Party performing especially well in the Scottish Highlands.

Scotland, Wales and Northern Ireland
Labour reinforced its position as the largest party in Scotland by winning 43 of the 71 seats. The Conservatives won 24 and the Liberals the remaining four. The election in Wales was fought against the background of the creation in 1964 of the Welsh Office with a Secretary of State in the Cabinet. The outcome of the election in Wales was very similar to the 1959 result: Labour won 28 of the 36 seats, the Conservatives six and the Liberals two. Ulster Unionists won all 12 of Northern Ireland's seats, interventions by Labour (who polled 16 per cent of the total votes in the province and the Liberals, whose four candidates obtained 2.7 per cent of the Northern Irish vote) failing to yield any seats in the House of Commons.

Consequence of the Election
Although Labour possessed a very small overall majority, Harold Wilson did not consider the possibility of a coalition government and instead formed a Labour government.

31 March 1966

Party Leaders
Harold Wilson (Labour)
Edward Heath (Conservative)
Jo Grimond (Liberal)

Background to the Election
Timing of the Election
The 1964 Labour government had been elected with a narrow majority of five which subsequently declined to three. This made the task of sustaining a majority in the House of Commons a difficult one: some parliamentary defeats had occurred (most notably in July 1965) and the government was forced to sustain its majority by requiring sick MPs to vote.

Wilson was thus looking for an opportunity to increase his majority and the performance of the government at the Kingston-upon-Hull by election on 28 January 1966 (when it secured a favourable swing of around 4 per cent in what was a highly marginal seat) was a major factor inducing the Prime Minister to call a general election which, despite the narrowness of his majority, he was able to do at a time of his choosing.

Electoral Procedures and Practices
Eighty-one of the ministers appointed in 1964 were from the House of Commons. This required legislation (in the form of the 1964 Ministers of the Crown Act which amended the 1957 House of Commons Disqualification Act) to legalise their appointments. Two ministers (Patrick Gordon Walker and Frank Cousins) briefly held appoinments whilst being a member of neither House of Parliament. Both contested by-elections in January 1965. Cousins was elected as MP for Nuneaton but Gordon Walker's defeat in the previously safe Labour seat of Leyton led to his resignation from the office of Foreign Secretary and his replacement by Michael Stewart.

Conservatives
Sir Alec Douglas-Home resigned as Conservative Party leader in July 1965, having first devised a procedure to enable future Conservative leaders to be elected by the votes of MPs. The leadership contest took place on 27 July 1965: Edward Heath obtained 150 votes, Reginald Maudling 133 and Enoch Powell 15. Under the rules of the contest, the winner was required to obtain a 15 per cent winning margin over the nearest candidate. Heath failed to do this, but as both of the other candidates withdrew, a second ballot was not needed and Edward Heath became the new Conservative Party leader. He initiated a review of key policy areas (including the modernisation of the economy, social insurance, trade union reform and immigration) which was performed by a number of advisory groups whose work was based on the use of survey research.

Their work was the basis of the document, *Putting Britain Right Ahead*, which was commended to the 1965 Party Conference. Its proposals comprised taxation reform (including an increase in indirect taxation and the transfer of a proportion of the costs of social servcies from the Exchequer to the employer), a reiteration of the desirability of securing entry into the European Economic Community, an extension of productivity bargaining and the establishment of a variety of industrial courts to settle industrial disputes. In the area of social services, it proposed to concentrate aid to those most in need, to establish a Department of Health and Social Security, and to extend occupational pensions schemes to embrace the entire working population. Little was said about an incomes policy or national economic planning. Considerable use was also made of surveys to furnish information on matters which included the identification of target voters and on public attitudes towards issues and personalities.

Initially, Heath faced a number of difficulties. He found it hard to mount an effective challenge to Wilson's taunts that if Conservative policies were so good why had they not been introduced during the 13 years when they held office. Divisions also occurred over the attitude to be adopted towards the Rhodesian UDI. Initially, the Conservatives supported the government's policy of economic sanctions but then were split over the specific issue of an oil embargo. In a vote in the House of Commons on 21 December 1965, the leadership's policy to abstain was ignored by 50 MPs who voted against the government and a further 31 who voted with it. Eventually, Conservative unity was restored in February 1966, when the Party united behind the approach of holding talks with the Rhodesian prime minister, Ian Smith, with a view to a constitutional settlement. However, some successes were secured, in particular the opposition mounted to the complex Finance Bill in 1965 which included tabling 680 amendments and inflicting three defeats on the government on 6–7 July.

Labour

When he first became Prime Minister, Wilson promised the country 100 days of dynamic action and undertook some early steps to plan for the growth of the economy by setting up the Ministry for Economic Affairs, headed by George Brown whose role was to promote regional economic planning and to formulate a National Economic Plan. This was published in September 1965 and aimed to achieve 25 per cent growth between 1964 and 1970. A Ministry of Technology (headed by Frank Cousins) was also established with special responsibility for modernising industry. It was designed to associate the government with the 'white heat of the technological revolution'.

Progress in achieving economic expansion was, however, considerably hindered by the size of the balance of payments deficit (which was estimated to be around £800 million) and Wilson's desire to defend the value of Sterling. These problems dominated the early days of Wilson's government and a number of measures were put forward to tackle them, in particular to relieve the pressure on Sterling. A 15 per cent surcharge on all imports save foodstuffs and raw materials was introduced in 1964 and exporters were encouraged by being granted a tax rebate on the value of exports and through the provision of improved credit facilities. The November 1964 special budget raised National Insurance contributions and increased petrol duty. It further announced that income tax would increase in spring 1965 when a capital gains tax and corporation tax were introduced (the latter to replace the existing income and profits taxes levied on companies) and duties were raised on tobacco, spirits, beer and motor cars. The bank lending rate was raised in 1964, but the pressure on Sterling was not immediately relieved, which led the government in 1964 to seek aid from foreign central banks to prop it up. Further pressure on sterling in 1965 led to exchange controls being tightened, the cutting of hire purchase repayment periods and the introduction of public spending cuts. Further credits were obtained from foreign central banks in an attempt to alleviate the problem.

A major economic difficulty was that wages were leaping ahead of productivity and this was aggravating the balance of payments deficit. In addition to the import surcharge, the government considered a prices and incomes policy, a key problem being that the trade unions were hostile to such a proposal. Instead, a voluntary early warning system was introduced whereby industries and unions would give advance notice of proposed price and wage increases in order to try and keep wages in step with production. On 16 December 1964 a Declaration of Intent on Productivity, Prices and Incomes was concluded whereby management and unions undertook to remove obstacles which impeded productivity and to aid the operations of the new prices and incomes machinery. This initially took the form of the Secretary of State for Economic Affairs, George Brown, negotiating an annual norm for increases in pay and the creation of the National Board for Prices and Incomes in April 1965. However, although prices were successfully curbed, wages continued to rise rapidly without being linked to productivity and the balance of payments deficit grew. In foreign affairs, Wilson had to deal with the unilateral declaration of independence (UDI) in Rhodesia on 11 November 1965. He ruled out the use of force to impose a constitutional settlement, preferring instead the use of economic sanctions (in the form of an oil embargo and a trade ban) to bring this about.

A number of domestic reforms were introduced. A special budget in November 1964 announced an increase in old age pensions, sickness and unemployment benefits, the abolition of the earnings' rule for widows, and the ending of prescription charges from 1 February 1965. Crossman's 1965 Rent Act provided for the fixing of fair rents for private tenants. However, divisions in the Parliamentary Party occurred over the proposals published in a White Paper in April 1965 to renationalise the steel industry. Two MPs (Woodrow Wyatt and Desmond Donnelly) announced their intention to abstain, although they voted with the government after George Brown promised, in the debate in the House of Commons, that the government would consider alternative proposals if the industry brought these forward. Subsequently, the government dropped its commitment to implement this policy, no reference to it being made in the 1965 Queen's Speech. Additionally, Wilson faced problems with the left wing of his party which wished him to disassociate the government from American policy in Vietnam. The 1966 Defence Review refused to provide the navy with a replacement aircraft carrier which resulted in the resignation of the Minister of Defence for the Navy, Christopher Mayhew, in February 1966.

Liberals

The narrowness of the government's majority prompted Jo Grimond, the Liberal leader, to offer Wilson a pact in the form of concluding a long-range agreement with the government. This idea was first mooted in March 1965 (following Labour's loss of the Leyton by-election) but was revived in the summer of 1965 when Grimond proposed 'a joint programme' on which both parties would agree. This included issues such as action to tackle restrictive practices, the reform of government, regionalism and electoral reform. He subsequently advised the 1965

Liberal Assembly that his suggestion of a 'working arrangement' with the government would have involved a commitment from Labour to enact measures of which the Liberals approved. In the absence of such an agreement he pledged to compare the forthcoming Queen's Speech with Liberal policy as set out at the 1965 Assembly. In his speech at Scarborough on 22 September 1965, he stated that the Parliamentary Party would support the government in measures with which the two parties were in agreement, but would not shirk from voting against it, thus triggering a general election, when it was believed that the government was acting contrary to the national interest.

Although a small amount of interest was displayed in the Labour Party towards cooperating (in the form of concluding an electoral arrangement) with the Liberal Party during the early 1960s (most notably from MPs Woodrow Wyatt and Desmond Donnelly), nothing concrete came in response to Grimond's offer save some favourable noises being made regarding electoral reform, for example, in a speech delivered by the Chief Whip, Ted Short, in October 1965. The main reason for this was that the government did not lose its overall majority and thus the Parliamentary Liberal Party failed to hold the balance of power. This situation was aided when Roderic Bowen (the Liberal MP for Cardiganshire) accepted the post of Deputy Chairman of Ways and Means following the death of the Speaker, Sir Harry Hylton-Foster, in 1965. The government was required to fill this vacancy from its own ranks. Accordingly, Dr Horace King became Speaker, but Bowen's acceptance of this other official position enabled the government's precarious majority of three to be retained.

By-elections
Thirteen by-elections took place in the 1964–66 Parliament. The Conservative Party held seven and lost one (Roxburgh, Selkirk and Peebles) to the Liberal Party. The Labour Party held four and lost one (Leyton) to the Conservatives.

Conduct of the Election
Labour enjoyed a healthy lead in the opinion polls from around September 1965 onwards, and at the commencement of the campaign was 9 per cent ahead of the Conservatives in the Gallup Poll. This suggested a Labour landslide. Both main parties (and particularly their leaders) addressed rallies and meetings to put their case across in addition to press conferences which were a feature of the campaigns of all three main parties. Many of the meetings were subjected to heckling. On one occasion Wilson was hit in the eye by a stink bomb thrown from a crowd and Hogg used a walking stick to berate opponents who were waving Labour banners at him.

Conservatives
The Conservative campaign sought to direct attention away from its past record in office between 1951 and 1964 and instead to project new and radical policies for the future government of the country. The main issues which were initially focused upon were the economy (in which tax reform was emphasised), entry into the European Economic Community, the reform of trade unions, the reform of the health and social services to target help on the most needy, and housing. These formed the basis of the Party's election manifesto, *Action Not Words*, which supplemented earlier pronouncements by pledging to build 500,000 houses a year.

Additionally, it was promised to transfer £100 million from local rates to the Exchequer, to retain the Territorial Army and to maintain Britain's role East of Suez. References were also made to enhancing the cost-effectiveness of government. During the campaign, allegations of the intimidation of persons who did not wish to take unofficial industrial action at the British Motor Corporation's plants at Cowley (where a 'noose trial' was alleged to have taken place) and Reading were used to justify Conservative trade union reforms which were the main subject of the Party's second election broadcast.

The Conservative campaign also devoted attention to Labour's alleged failings. It was argued that Labour had failed to deliver on its 1964 promise to end stop-go and promote the steady expansion of the economy: in 1966 production was proceeding at a slower rate than under previous Conservative governments. In this sense it was suggested that electors were being asked to vote now and pay later. Towards the end of the campaign, Heath described Britain's economic situation as '9–5–1': this was a reference to economic indicators in 1965 which suggested a 9 per cent rise in wages, a 5 per cent increase in prices and a 1 per cent expansion in production. It was also argued that Labour had greatly increased the tax burden.

Labour

A key theme developed in Labour's campaign was put forward soon after the 1964 election. This was to assert that the country's economic problems were the doing of the Conservative Party which had provided Labour with a 'tarnished inheritance'. The 'Tory mess' was the key underpinning of Wilson's accusation of the existence of the 13 wasted years of Tory misrule and served to keep the Conservatives on the defensive. Labour's appeal was based on reassurance, being encapsulated in the slogan 'you know Labour government works', Wilson asserting that his government had accomplished more essential business in 500 days than the Conservatives had managed in 5,000. The Labour Party additionally entered the campaign following Callaghan's 'little budget' on 1 March 1966 which indicated that Britain's gold and dollar reserves were in a healthy state and announced a scheme of tax rebates for lower paid mortgage holders which would be funded by a 2.5 per cent tax on gambling stakes.

The effort devoted by Labour to survey research for the 1964 election was not repeated for the 1966 contest. In the last days of the 1964–66 Parliament, the government announced its intention to create a Ministry of Social Security, to proceed with leasehold enfranchisement and to step up the school-building programme. Its election policies were contained in the manifesto, *Time for Decision*. This defended Labour's record since 1964 and put forward proposals to develop the early warning system so that the Prices and Incomes Board could function effectively. Support for entering the European Economic Community was expressed, provided that British and Commonwealth interests were adequately safeguarded. The Labour stance which emphasised the prior need to negotiate items such as the Common Agricultural Policy was used by the Conservatives to support their allegations that Labour did not intend to join the organisation. The manifesto promised to reorganise and modernise Britain's ports through the creation of a strong National Ports Authority and publicly owned Regional Port Authorities, to create a National Freight Authority, to renationalise the aircraft industry on the basis of public participation and to curb the powers of the House of Lords.

Labour's campaign attacked Conservative proposals, and alleged that they intended to apply the means test to old age pensions and prescription charges and would be responsible for raising the price of food. Labour also asserted that the cost of the Conservative proposals contained in their manifesto was £850 million (as opposed to the figure of between £200 and 250 million to which the Conservatives referred). They thus queried how this would be raised.

Wilson was an effective television performer and had used his talents to good effect since 1964 where his appearances had been highly polished and professional. The tone of the campaign in 1966 emphasised his reputation as a reliable, statesmanlike figure who would provide the nation with stability.

Liberals
The Liberal campaign was based on the premise (which was explicitly articulated) that Labour would win the election and that an increased force of Liberal MPs, supported by a large national vote, was needed to restrain Labour's future excesses and provide a 'brake on socialism'. Their first election broadcast sought to justify this by targeting Wilson who was alleged to have previously been identified with the left wing of the Party and with the policy of nationalisation. The Party's election policies were contained in its manifesto, *For All the People*, and included site value taxation, a withdrawal from Britain's East of Suez role, the imposition of motorway tolls, an attack on restrictive practices, and the introduction of a non-discriminatory immigration policy. During the campaign the Party argued that the case for devaluation of the pound needed to be considered. Aid continued to be given to seats regarded as winnable by the Special Seats Committee, chaired by Thorpe. The death of Jo Grimond's son towards the end of the campaign forced him to downgrade his activities subsequently, resulting in Lord Byers assuming an enhanced role.

Result of the Election
A total of 1,707 candidates contested the election. The result was:

Party	Votes	Vote %	MPs
Labour	13,096,629	48.0%	364
Conservative	11,049,826	40.5%	242
Liberal	2,327,457	8.5%	12
Ulster Unionist	368,629	1.4% [61.8%]	11
Ulster Republican / Republican Labour	89,074	0.3% [14.9%]	1
Scottish National Party	128,474	0.5% [5.0%]	0
Plaid Cymru	61,071	0.2% [4.3%]	0
Others	143,587	0.6%	0
Total	27,264,747		630

The turnout was 75.8 per cent which was less than 1964. The extent of deliberate abstention was high since the electoral register on which the 1966 election was fought was a new one, coming into force on 15 February 1966. The overall swing from the Conservative Party to Labour was 2.8 per cent.

Twenty-six women MPs were elected.

The Parties

The main issues which dominated the election were the state of the economy, entry into the European Economic Community and trade union reform. Housing, immigration and nationalisation failed to emerge as key matters of political debate and neither did defence policy despite the resignation of Mayhew in 1966. Labour secured victory because of a widespread belief that the Conservatives were responsible for the country's economic problems and as it was accepted that Labour deserved a further period in office. The polls also suggested that Wilson was seen as having a stronger personality than Heath.

Unlike 1964, the swing was relatively uniform across the country, although it was greater in some larger cities (including Birmingham, Hull, Newcastle and Bradford). Labour obtained its largest vote, and the largest share of the vote since 1951. Although the national swing was relatively uniform, Labour did benefit from the minority ethnic vote, and in 23 seats in the London area with large minority communities the swing to Labour was 4.6 per cent. Smethwick in the West Midlands was regained with a swing in excess of 7 per cent to Labour. Eighteen Labour MPs were sponsored by the Cooperative Party and 132 by trade unions. The Conservative Parliamentary Party suffered a number of key losses. These included Henry Brooke, Peter Thorneycroft, Christopher Soames and Julian Amery.

The Liberal Party's share of the vote declined in comparison to 1964, primarily due to fielding a reduced number of candidates. The average vote obtained by Liberal candidates dropped by around 3 per cent compared to 1964. However, the number of Liberal MPs increased to 12, the best showing since 1945. This included gaining Cheadle from the Conservative Party which was outside of the Liberal Party's main area of electoral strength, and achieving success in Colne Valley, the only seat Labour lost in 1966. However, the Party's longest-serving MP, Roderic Bowen, was defeated at Cardigan, a seat he had represented for 21 years. The withdrawal of Liberal candidates in seats which were fought in 1964 tended to benefit the Conservative Party, whereas Liberal intervention in 1966 in seats not fought in 1964 tended to disadvantage the Conservative Party. This suggested that the second choice party for Liberal voters tended to be the Conservative Party, although the overall Liberal impact on the outcome of the election was estimated to have been minimal.

Scotland, Wales and Northern Ireland

Labour made modest gains in Scotland, winning 46 of the 71 seats. The Conservatives won 20 and the Liberals five, performing well in Northern Scotland. Labour also improved its position in Wales, winning 32 of the 36 seats. The Conservatives won three and the Liberals were reduced to one. In Northern Ireland, the dominance of the Ulster Unionist Party was continued in 1966, although one seat (West Belfast) was lost to a Republican Labour candidate, Gerry Fitt, who succeeded in a straight fight against the incumbent Unionist, James Kilfedder.

Consequence of the Election
Harold Wilson formed his second Labour administration.

18 June 1970

Party Leaders
Harold Wilson (Labour)
Edward Heath (Conservative)
Jeremy Thorpe (Liberal)

Background to the Election
Timing of the Election
The timing of the campaign was based upon a calculation by the incumbent Labour Prime Minister, Harold Wilson, that his party would be successfully re-elected. Although the Party had fared badly between 1966 and 1969, a dramatic improvement in the balance of payments situation towards the end of that year (which was sustained into the early part of 1970) improved the Party's standing in the polls and boosted the morale of ministers who could point to a dynamic Britain rather than one languishing in the doldrums. The improved economic situation (which Labour could say justified their pursuance of austerity policies after 1966) resulted in substantial pay rises (especially in the public sector), and an additional reason for holding an election towards the middle of June was that these wage settlements might fuel inflation which would be felt towards the end of 1970. In May 1970 a national opinion poll gave Labour a lead over the Conservatives (the first national poll to do so since March 1967) and the swing to Labour in the May 1967 municipal elections induced Wilson to call an immediate election.

Electoral Procedures and Practices
The government had enacted the 1969 Representation of the People Act whose main provision was to extend the vote to all persons aged 18 to 21. This measure additionally made it easier for people living in urban areas to vote by post, extended the hours of polling from 7am until 10pm and enabled candidates to attach their party label to the ballot paper. The key provisions of this measure were regarded as being beneficial to the Labour Party, although it was estimated that around one-quarter of the newly enfranchised electorate failed even to register to vote (Butler and Pinto-Duschinsky, 1971: 263). The Labour government's position was further perceived to have been helped by its decision not to implement the recommendations of the boundary commission in 1969. This would have sacrificed a number of small Labour-held constituencies and divided some large Conservative-held seats. Estimates suggested that these reforms would have produced a gain of between five and 20 seats for the Conservative Party (Butler and Pinto-Duschinsky, 1971: 46, n1). The Home Secretary, James Callaghan, brought forward a Bill to free himself from any legal obligation to present these proposals to Parliament, but when this was rejected by the House of Lords he used Labour's Parliamentary majority to vote them down.

Conservatives
The Conservative Party found the task of opposition arduous after 1966. The wide degree of consensus between the leadership of the two major parties made it difficult for the Conservative

Party to criticise key aspects of government domestic or foreign policy. Major Labour policies (such as an incomes policy, opposition to devaluation, entry into the European Economic Community and the maintenance of good relations with the United States of America) were endorsed by the Conservative leadership, although the introduction of Selective Employment Tax in 1966 did provide the basis of Conservative opposition to the government who declared their intention to abolish it. The hesitant progress of nationalisation after 1966 and the disinclination of the Labour government to pursue the policy of unilateral nuclear disarmament served to remove areas which would have been expected to have produced intense disagreement between the two parties. Additionally, recent memories of the performance of Conservative governments made it difficult to 'sell' the argument that they could manage the country more efficiently than Labour.

The effort expended in devising policy after 1964 was continued after the 1966 general election. The use of private polls was increased after 1966 and a number of policy groups, usually chaired by a shadow minister, were utilised in this process, one product of which was the publication *Make Life Better* which was presented to the 1968 Party Conference. The reform of industrial relations was considered in the 1968 publication, *Fair Deal at Work*, whose recommendations included making collective agreements legally enforceable setting up a new system of industrial courts and drawing up a code of good industrial relations practice. This was a key aspect of what was termed 'technocratic' economic policy (Butler and Pinto-Duschinsky, 1971: 70) which sought to lessen the impact made by government on the individual without significantly lowering the level of services which were provided. Other aspects of this policy included the intention to wage a 'war on waste' in Whitehall, and the proposal to shift the direction of taxation away from income tax. The main initiative to achieve this was the suggestion to introduce a value-added tax. However, the detailed nature of policy developed after 1966 failed to excite public opinion.

The lack of impact made by the Conservative Party in opposition, compounded by the lead that Wilson consistently enjoyed over Heath in the opinion polls, led to the development of factionalism in the Party. The Monday Club (formed in 1961) provided the focus for some right-wing opposition to the government, although its concern was mainly in foreign and colonial affairs. Voices in the Conservative Party calling for reduced government intervention in economic and social areas were then in their infancy, although they were articulated by Enoch Powell and other 'free marketeers' who argued that the country's economic problems were caused by the size of the public sector and government interference with market forces. Their proposed remedies entailed reduced taxation and denationalisation. The most publicised division within the Party surrounded the passage of the 1968 Race Relations Act. In April 1968 Enoch Powell made a speech at Birmingham in which he questioned the sanity of the current pattern of immigration, and likened its consequence to the Roman who saw 'the River Tiber foaming with much blood'. Heath dimisssed him from the Shadow Cabinet the next day. Although pro-Powell supporters exerted some influence on Conservative constituency parties, the importance of the issue (and Conservative factionalism in general) was reduced by the time of the 1970 election.

Labour

The period following 1966 witnessed some important measures which included the 1967 Shipbuilding Act, the 1968 Race Relations Act (which broadened the scope of the 1965 measure), the 1968 Transport Act (which set up national freight and bus companies), and the 1968 Industrial Expansion Act. The government announced plans to build 30 polytechnics and suggestions were put forward in 1969 to create the Open University. Additionally, important administrative reform was carried out which included the creation of the Civil Service Department in 1968. However, the period immediately following the 1966 general election witnessed severe economic troubles which were characterised by periodic runs on Sterling and adverse balance of payments problems and which were aggravated by ad hoc episodes such as the seamen's strike of May–July 1966. The government's failure to curb wage rises in the run-up to the 1966 general election aggravated the economic situation and made it inevitable that stern action would be taken soon after it. The Prime Minister's preference was to pursue defla-tionary policies as opposed to devaluation, and initial action was taken on 14 July (when the bank rate was raised) and on 20 July when a package of deflationary measures was announced. These included a surcharge on beer, alcohol and petrol, cuts in public investment and the impo-sition of restrictions on hire purchase. These cuts were viewed as inimical to the expansion sought by the National Plan and resulted in Brown's resignation (which was subsequently withdrawn). Additionally, a compulsory wages freeze was added to the Prices and Incomes Bill. This lasted for six months (July 1966 until January 1967) when it was replaced by a 'period of severe restraint'.

These measures enabled the position of Sterling to stablise temporarily, but did not cure the deep-seated causes of economic difficulties which required the restructuring and modernisation of industry. Accordingly, a further run on Sterling (against the background of the 1967 Arab–Israeli war which led to the closure of the Suez Canal) forced the government to devalue the pound (from $2.80 to $2.40) on 18 November 1967 and subsequently to introduce further deflationary measures including major cuts in public spending in January 1968 which mainly affected defence, health and education expenditure. Charges were imposed for doctors' prescriptions and the raising of the school leaving age was postponed. Additionally, the March 1968 budget (which followed an international currency crisis) imposed large tax increases which included a levy on high incomes, increased duties on cigarettes, spirits, petrol and car licences, and increases in purchase tax. In November 1968 an autumn budget which was designed to relieve pressures on Sterling was introduced which placed restrictions on imports and raised purchase taxes.

The government's incomes policy led to considerable disputes within the Parliamentary Party (34 Labour MPs abstaining on the second reading of the Bill to continue the Prices and Incomes Act and 23 voting against the measure at its third reading stage in 1968) and also resulted in a large number of industrial disputes (which were especially numerous in 1968) by workers whose livelihoods were threatened with unemployment arising from deflationary economic policies and from the increased cost of living following devaluation. Accordingly, the government altered its position, shying away from statutory wage controls in favour of controls over trade unions.

A Royal Commission on Trade Unions had been appointed in 1965 following the *Rookes v. Barnard* judgement which threatened the immunity given to unions in the 1906 Trade Disputes Act from actions for tort and arising from their activities in industrial disputes. Labour's reform proposals were contained in their 1969 White Paper, *In Place of Strife*, and the resultant Industrial Relations Bill. This proposed a series of restrictions and penal sanctions on trade unions (embracing strike ballots, fines and conciliation pauses) in order to combat industrial unrest, particularly unofficial strikes. This measure was greeted with considerable opposition within the Parliamentary Party (which included the possibility of a challenge being mounted to Wilson's leadership) (Butler and Pinto-Duschinsky, 1971: 42–3) from constituency parties and trade unions. This pressure led to the Bill's abandonment in return for a promise that the TUC would henceforth police unofficial actions more effectively.

Labour's foreign policy was underpinned by the objective of maintaining good relations with Washington. In May 1967 Labour formally applied to enter the EEC. This attempt (which when debated in the House of Commons in May 1967 led 35 Labour MPs to vote against the government and a further 50 to abstain) was rebuffed by de Gaulle's veto but a further application for membership was made in April 1969 following de Gaulle's resignation as president of France. At the time of the 1970 general election all major parties were broadly agreed on seeking membership, although there were opponents to this course of action in both the Conservative and Labour parties. In foreign affairs, the main issue was the attempt to find a settlement following Rhodesia's unilateral declaration of independence in November 1965. Direct negotiations between Wilson and the Rhodesian prime minister, Ian Smith, took place on HMS *Tiger* in December 1966 and on HMS *Fearless* in October 1968 but a settlement failed to be forthcoming. The government also announced its intention in 1968 to withdraw from its East of Suez role, thereby reversing its previous policy on this issue.

Measures which have been referred to above (including deflationary economic policies, the statutory control of wages, attempts to reform the trade unions and entry into the European Economic Community) witnessed considerable internal dissent within the Labour movement, especially in the Parliamentary Labour Party. The abstention of 42 Labour MPs on the 1967 Defence White Paper led Wilson to threaten not to renew the licence of those 'dogs' who continuously opposed the government. There were also divisions within the Cabinet. Although Wilson dominated his government, the spectre of disunity was raised when the Foreign Secretary, George Brown, resigned in 1968 over 'the way this government is run and the manner in which we reach our decisions': he was particularly unhappy about the outcome of Cabinet discussions on South African arms sales and used the pretext of his exclusion from a hastily convened Privy Council meeting to discuss the government's response to the international currency crisis in March 1968 as a pretext to quit the government.

Liberals

The main issue affecting the Liberal Party was the change of leadership. Wilson's refusal to enter into an agreement with the Liberal Party in 1965, followed by Labour's victory in 1966, substantially undermined Grimond's case for seeking a realignment of the left in British politics. Accordingly, he retired in 1967 and was replaced by Jeremy Thorpe, MP for North Devon. The method of election used (which involved only the votes of the 12 MPs) was one factor which led Thorpe to experience a number of problems with his party in the early years of his leadership culminating in a revolt against his leadership in 1968. The main failure of the Party after 1966 was its inability to tap into the mood of disillusionment with the two major parties which benefited the nationalist parties in Scotland and Wales after 1966. Liberal support in the polls was consistently around 7–11 per cent between 1966 and 1970 and despite the one by-election success in 1969 (when Wallace Lawler captured Birmingham Ladywood from Labour, becoming the first Liberal to represent the city in Parliament since 1886) the Party's overall performance in these contests was poor, with 12 deposits being lost in the 28 elections which were fought.

By-elections

Thirty-eight by-elections were held in the lifetime of the 1966–70 government. Labour held 11 of the seats it was defending, but lost 15 (12 to the Conservatives, and one each to the Liberal Party, the Scottish National Party and to Plaid Cymru). In the period from November 1967 to June 1968 it was beaten in eight consecutive contests by the Conservative Party. The Conservative Party held 11 of the seats it was defending, and the Ulster Unionists lost the seat of Mid-Ulster to an Independent Unity candidate (Ms Bernadette Devlin) in 1969.

Conduct of the Election

The government wanted a quiet election to form the background for their appeal for a continued mandate. It was a negative election in the sense that both major parties devoted a considerable amount of their campaigning to attacking the policies of their opponents. Attacks on the other party constituted 75 per cent of the content of Wilson's press releases and 70 per cent of Heath's (Robertson, 1971: 443).

The national campaigns of the Conservative and Labour parties were very focused on their leaders and in this sense the election was a presidential one. However, the campaigning style adopted by each was different. Wilson depicted himself as a leader who was in control of events, seeking to cultivate a sense of well-being amongst the electorate. He utilised a presidential style of campaigning, visiting party activists while shunning large public meetings. Heath, on the other hand, addressed a number of large meetings and also engaged in a number of walkabouts. Thorpe mainly confined his energies into defending his North Devon constituency, leaving a large burden of the national campaign to fall on the shoulders of Lord Frank Byers.

Conservatives

Conservative policies were contained in their manifesto, *A Better Tomorrow*. This was heavily based on prior policy statements and the January 1970 Selsdon conference. Although the section on VAT was ambivalent, suggesting it 'could' help to make our system of taxes on spending more broadly based, less discriminatory and fairer in its impact on different types of industry and service. The manifesto, however, did pledge that the Party would abolish the Selective Employment Tax. The trade union defeat of the government's proposals to restrict trade union practices by legislation was blamed for an increasing number of strikes, one of which (the national newspaper strike called by SOGAT) occurred during the campaign and helped to legitimise the Conservative Party's proposals for 'a fair deal at work' which would insist on a statutory cooling-off period before strike action could be undertaken.

Much of the Conservative manifesto was directed at the actions undertaken by the Labour government who were depicted as a party of more taxes which gave no new encouragement to earn and save. The main focus of the Conservative campaign was economic issues which also formed the cornerstone of the Party's offensive against the government. By the middle of 1970, price rises had heavily eroded wage increases made since the beginning of the year and it was asserted that, if current trends continued, the 1964 pound would be worth only 10 shillings (50 pence) by 1974. The 'ten bob pound' became a prominent feature of Conservative election broadcasts, and the Conservative appeal in what Heath referred to as a 'shopping basket election' was especially directed at housewives (the Party's fourth election broadcast appealing directly to them for support). Conservatives further pointed to Labour's record in raising taxes. Electors were warned that the government was not being totally open with the electorate regarding the state of the economy and that if Labour was re-elected bad times lay ahead. This theme was reiterated in the Conservative press. Conservatives raised the possibility of a new wage freeze and, following the publication of adverse trade figures in June, of further devaluation (which Labour vehemently denied, accusing the Conservatives of unpatriotic behaviour seeking to induce a run on the Pound). This attack was directed against Labour's 'sham sunshine'. The Conservatives also argued that Labour had broken its promises and could not be trusted whereas Heath was a man who would keep his word and could be trusted.

Labour

In office Wilson had sought to demonstrate his competence and responsibility, but this was undermined by the response of the government to economic difficulties which were encountered after 1966. Wilson had staked his reputation on avoiding devaluation but was forced to implement this measure in November 1967. He assured the British people that this action would not hurt the Pound in their pockets. He was also forced to abandon attempts to reform the trade unions. The balance of payments deficit rose during the first three years of the Parliament and Wilson's attempts to secure entry into the European Economic Community were rebuffed. Deflationary economic policies (whose consequences led to a rise in unemployment) also added to the unpopularity of the government which was evidenced in poor by-election results in 1967 and 1968, bad outcomes in local government contests in 1967 (when Labour was routed in the Greater London Council elections), 1968 and 1969, and extremely low opinion poll ratings (which fell to below 30 per cent approval in 1968). It was concluded that the government had 'an unenviable record of disaster' for much of the period after 1966 (Butler and Pinto-Duschinsky, 1971: 45).

However, as the election approached, the country's economic circumstances improved, as was seen in particular in the improved balance of payments situation. There was also little popular desire for the return of a Conservative government. Labour thus entered the campaign ahead in the opinion polls and Wilson sought to safeguard Labour's position by adopting a reassuring tone, seeking to convince the electorate that they had nothing to fear from the return of a Labour administration.

In October 1968 Labour's Research Department prepared a policy statement, *Britain: Progress and Change*, which they viewed as the basis of the Party election manifesto. It contained a number of radical proposals which included the justification of high taxation in order to spend more on social services and hinted at the introduction of a wealth tax. These proposals were built upon by subsequent Research Department policy statements, and resulted in an NEC statement, *Agenda for a Generation*, which was presented to the 1969 Party Conference. However, the left-wing nature of the ideas emanating from Transport House prompted the establishment of a Coordinating Committee in December 1968 whose role was to consider conflicts between the Labour organisation and government departments. The Labour manifesto, *Now Britain's Strong – Let's Make It Great to Live in*, directed the Party's appeal at those who had faith 'in the capacity and humanity of their fellow men'. The manifesto listed eight main tasks – a strong economy (which entailed steady expansion, to be achieved through investment in industry, industrial training, industrial reorganisation and planning and fighting inflation), prosperity in the regions, improved road, rail, sea and air communications, an improved system of education (which entailed the expansion of the comprehensive system) accompanied by measures to tackle social and economic inequalities elsewhere, the improvement of everyday living (which involved improvements in housing and the environment), a better system of health and social security, political reforms affecting the government of Scotland, Wales and Northern Ireland, and an adoption of a realistic approach to Britain's position in world affairs, which included Britain's membership of the European Economic Community, provided that British and essential Commonwealth interests could be safeguarded. It made no reference to a wealth tax.

The key issue around which the Labour campaign centred was the economy. Wilson emphasised how his government had turned around the debt inherited from the Conservatives in 1964 into a healthy surplus on the balance of payments by 1970. The Party's first election broadcast argued that Britain's economy was one of the strongest in the world and Labour intended to use this strength as a basis for the modernisation of the country; this theme was reiterated in its fourth broadcast. Labour thus used the defence of its record in this area as the main focus of its campaign, and dismissed the Conservative leadership as 'yesterday's men' who had failed the electorate before. Much of Labour's campaign was directed at attacking the Conservatives. Wilson adopted a mocking tone towards them and was especially critical of the policy pronouncements which emanated from a meeting of the Shadow Cabinet at the Selsdon Park Hotel, Surrey, in January 1970. He believed that their proposed reform of industrial relations and their intention to tighten the law regarding squatters and trespassers demonstrated outdated, backward-looking attitudes. He summed up their approach in the phrase 'Selsdon Man'.

Criticisms of the Conservative Party enabled Labour to keep relatively silent concerning the actions of a future Labour government. The cost of Conservative policies was also attacked (Labour costing them at between £750 and 1,050 million a year and arguing that this would add nine pence to income tax) and it was also asserted that Conservative agricultural policy would add 21 shillings to the cost of the average weekly food bill. They were thus branded by Labour as a party which would raise prices (a theme which was prominent in its fifth election broadcast). Other aspects of Conservative policy were also attacked. These included their support for selective secondary education and the allegation (which was denied) that they intended to reintroduce conscription.

Immigration also had little impact on the Conservative campaign. Powell called for a ban on immigration which led Tony Benn to equate his views on this subject with those of Nazism. However, this approach did not become a key theme of Labour electioneering. Towards the end of the campaign, Heath stated that he did not share Powell's pessimism on the future of race relations and that the Conservative aim was that all races should live in harmony.

Little was said during the campaign concerning the EEC, although there was a broad consensus displayed between the two main party leaders that, should they be elected, their government would make a decision concerning entry and present it to the House of Commons, applying the whips to get it through. Heath did, however, later in the campaign suggest that Conservative MPs who disapproved of entry would be allowed to abstain or vote against the recommendation. Powell opposed entry to the EEC but urged his sympathisers to vote Conservative.

Liberals

Liberal policies were contained in its manifesto, *What A Life!* This was particularly addressed to voters who were disillusioned with the record of post-war Labour and Conservative governments whose control over the country's affairs had resulted in the declined purchasing power of the pound, rising prices (which outstripped increased wages), mounting unemployment, paralysing strikes and an over-burdened health service. It was argued that 'the whole "system"conspires against the individual, the unrepresented and the weak, in favour of the well-organised big battalions'. The Liberal Party was depicted as 'the Party of power for the ordinary people' in contrast to the Conservative Party which was funded by big business and the Labour Party which was bankrolled by the trade unions. It concluded that 'Liberals care ! We care for those the big battalions forget. We care for the poor and oppressed ... We care for the citizen at the mercy of the bureaucratic machine ... We care for those who feel that government is remote and hostile ... We care for those struggling to make ends meet in the face of rising prices. We care for those who have no satisfactory place to live. We care for the old and the young who have no organisation to defend them ... We care because we are Liberals and because the basic principle of Liberalism is the supreme value of the individual human personality'.

During the campaign, the Liberal Party sought to emphasise its distinctive policies which included the reform of industrial relations through the establishment of works councils, the provision of tax incentives to encourage profit-sharing and plant productivity bargaining. They also advocated devolution in government and, in 1967, their MPs sponsored a Scottish Self-Government Bill. However, the distinctive character of this aspect of Liberal policy was partly undermined by the conversion of the Scottish Conservative Party to a form of devolution entailing the establishment of a Scottish 'Convention' (which was formally endorsed in May 1970) and was further complicated by the divisions within the Scottish Liberal Party on the wisdom of entering into a pact with the SNP for the 1970 general election (a course of action which was promoted by Grimond in a speaking tour of Scotland in 1969 but vehemently opposed by many Scottish Liberals including Russell Johnston MP).

The Liberal campaign was based on the assumption (which was explicitly stated in their second and third election broadcasts) that Labour would win the election, not because they deserved success but, rather, because the Conservatives deserved to lose. The Party's aims were to secure the election of an increased number of MPs. However, they faced considerable problems in getting their message across in the media.

Result of the Election

A Gallup poll published on May 12 gave Labour a 7 per cent lead over the Conservatives, and opinion polls during the campaign suggested the return of a Labour government. The main exception to this was an ORC poll published on the day of the election which gave the Conservatives a small, 1 per cent, lead. It was argued that a last minute swing to the Conservative Party was 'the most plausible explanation' for this situation (Butler and Pinto-Duschinsky, 1971: 185–6). There are several reasons why this belated swing might have occurred. These included the complacent and negative campaign waged by Labour, and economic indicators which might justify Conservative claims of an imminent economic crisis: unemployment rose and prices increased during 1970 and the June trade figures were poor. The elimination of the England football team from the 1970 World Cup following a 3–2 defeat by Germany may further have served to undermine the 'feel good' factor on which Labour was pinning its electoral hopes.

A total of 1,837 candidates contested the election. The result was:

Party	Votes	Vote %	MPs
Conservative	12,723,082	44.9%	322
Labour	12,208,758	43.1%	288
Ulster Unionist	422,041	1.5% [54.2%]	8
Liberal	2,117,035	7.5%	6
Unity (Northern Ireland)	140,930	0.5% [18.1%]	2
Other Ulster Loyalist Parties	45,652	0.1% [5.8%]	1
Republican Labour Party (Northern Ireland)	30,649	0.1% [3.9%]	1
Scottish National Party	306,802	1.1% [11.4%]	1
Others	174,833	0.6%	1
Plaid Cymru	175,016	0.6% [11.5%]	0
Total	28,344,798		630

The turnout was 72 per cent which was the lowest figure since 1935. The swing from Labour to the Conservatives was 4.9 per cent.

The 'other' was Stephen Davies, elected for Merthyr Tydfil. He had been deselected by the Labour Party on grounds of age (83) but comfortably held the seat which he had represented since 1934. Twenty-six women MPs were elected. No MPs from ethnic minority communities were elected, Dr David Pitt unsuccessfully defending the former Labour-held constituency of Clapham (Wandsworth).

The Parties

There were no significant variations to the national swing either in marginal seats or in the regions, although there were some sub-regional deviations: the Merseyside area and Hull provided lower than average swings to the Conservative Party whereas above average swings to Conservative candidates were recorded in 16 textile towns in Lancashire and in six seats wholly or partly in the boroughs of Dudley and Wolverhampton in the Black Country. Additionally, the election confirmed the support obtained by the two major parties being affected by the existence (albeit not a very pronounced one) of an urban–rural, North–South divide which had commenced at the 1955 general election (Steed, 1971: 397–8). Apart from the Wolverhampton constituencies, immigration failed to produce abnormal swings to Conservative candidates in the West Midlands.

Labour's share of the vote was down by 5 per cent compared to 1966, and was the lowest it had obtained since 1935. This was especially attributed to Labour supporters abstaining. Fifteen Labour MPs were sponsored by the Cooperative Party and 114 by trade unions. Labour retirements from the House of Commons in 1970 included Emmanuel Shinwell, and notable casualties who failed to get re-elected included the deputy leader of the Labour Party, George Brown, at Belper (whose excursions in support of other Labour candidates contributed to his own downfall), Jennie Lee at Cannock, and John Diamond at Gloucester.

The result was a severe disappointment to the Liberal Party which fielded more candidates than in 1966 but secured a lower vote and also lost six seats it had won in 1966 together with its by-election gain at Birmingham Ladywood in 1969. Jeremy Thorpe only narrowly secured re-election by a majority of 369 votes. The decline of the Liberal vote was especially significant in Scotland (where the SNP eroded Liberal support in the North East and the Highlands) and in Wales, although in comparison to 1966 the Party's fortunes improved in a handful of seats (including Rochdale, Southport, Birmingham Ladywood and Liverpool Wavertree).

Scotland, Wales and Northern Ireland
Labour remained the dominant party in Scotland, winning 44 of the 71 seats. The Conservatives won 23, the Liberals three and the SNP one. The swing from the Labour Party was less than in England (3.3 per cent) due to the rise in support for the Scottish National Party which capitalised on its by-election successes (which included gaining Hamilton from Labour in November 1967) and obtained 306,795 votes (11.4 per cent of the total Scottish vote), securing victory in one constituency (the Western Isles). However, 43 of its 65 candidates forfeited their deposits. This was considerably more support than that obtained by the Liberal Party which won three Scottish seats although obtaining only 5.5 per cent of the Scottish vote.

Labour won 27 of the 36 seats in Wales, the Conservatives seven, and the Liberals one. The remaining seat of Merthyr Tydfil was won by an Independent. The swing from the Labour Party was less than in England (2.8 per cent) due to the increased level of support obtained by Plaid Cymru which built upon its by-election successes (winning Carmarthen from Labour in July 1966 and polling 40 per cent of the vote in Rhondda West in March 1967 and Caerphilly in July 1968). It obtained 175,016 votes (11.5 per cent of the total Welsh vote). Although it won no seats (Carmarthen being regained by Labour), respectable second places were secured in Merioneth, Caernarvon, Rhondda East, Aberdare and Caerphilly.

The dominance exerted by the Ulster Unionist Party on Northern Irish politics was dented in 1970. Nationalists and republicans united behind 'unity' or 'national democratic' party labels and two victories were obtained. Bernadette Devlin (although opposed by two independent Catholic challengers) increased her majority obtained in a by-election in 1969 at Mid-Ulster and Frank McManus ousted the Unionist candidate at Fermanagh and South Tyrone. Gerry Fitt retained his West Belfast Seat for Republican Labour and, additionally, the Ulster Unionists lost North Antrim to Ian Paisley who was standing as a Protestant Unionist candidate. Ulster Unionists won the remaining eight seats.

Consequence of the Election
Edward Heath formed a Conservative administration.

28 February 1974

Party Leaders
Harold Wilson (Labour)
Edward Heath (Conservative)
Jeremy Thorpe (Liberal)

Background to the Election
Timing of the Election
The election occurred against the background of industrial action undertaken by the National Union of Miners who sought a pay increase in excess of that permitted under Stage Three of the government's incomes policy. An overtime ban in November 1973 resulted in the imposition of a three-day working week in December to conserve fuel stocks. Following a ballot in January, on 5 February 1974 the union announced a strike which resulted in a declaration of a State of Emergency. The incumbent Conservative government responded to the NUM's challenge to its incomes policy by calling an election which was effectively on the issue of who ran the country – the trade unions or an elected government. Industrial action by trade unions (which may be perceived as an attempt to place sectional interests above national considerations) often had an adverse impact on the Labour Party which is associated with these organisations, and the improved fortunes of the Conservative Party evidenced in opinion polls (one published by NOP in January 1974 giving the government its first lead over Labour for three years) was an added factor in persuading the Prime Minister to opt for an election in early 1974. One study suggested that the timing of the election was 'unprecedented' (Butler and Kavanagh, 1974: 44) in that it arose as the consequence of a challenge made from outside Parliament to a key aspect of government policy rather than as the result of a defeat suffered in the House of Commons.

Electoral Procedures and Practices
The election witnessed the first redistribution of seats since 1955. Changes proposed by the boundary commissioners which had been shelved by the Labour government in 1969 were implemented. Five additional constituencies were created and 429 constituencies were affected by boundary changes. Additionally, the election expenses of candidates were increased by legislation passed by the outgoing Parliament which had the effect of increasing them by around 30 per cent.

Conservatives
Ted Heath's government was responsible for a number of reforms affecting taxation arrangements, the social services (including the introduction of the Family Income Supplement), the structure of local government (which was embodied in the 1972 Local Government Act), the renting of property (which was governed by the 1972 Housing Finance Act), and the reform of industrial relations (the 1971 Industrial Relations Act laying down a new legal framework governing strike action which required trade unions to register and required a cooling-off period and a compulsory ballot before strike action could be undertaken). Some reforms

(including the curtailment of free school milk and the introduction of museum entry charges) were controversial, but none was as contentious as the government's successful negotiation of Britain's membership of the European Economic Community (EEC). Negotiations were concluded in July 1971 and, following approval of these terms by the House of Commons in October of that year, the United Kingdom entered the EEC on 1 January 1973.

The government's economic policy caused considerable political friction. The 1971 Industrial Relations Act sought to provide a legal framework within which industrial disputes would have to be conducted. It was assumed that this would bring order to wage bargaining and thus significantly contribute towards combating inflation. However, this approach was undermined when the TUC instructed unions not to register as was required by the 1971 Act, and by the actions of a number of trade unions which sought pay increases deemed by the government to be inflationary. Industrial unrest underpinned by trade unions seeking high wage increases included the 1972 and 1973–74 miners' disputes, the 1972 building workers' strike, and the 1972 docks strike.

In an attempt to attain its objective to control inflation, the government ultimately embraced an action it had expressly ruled out in its 1970 election manifesto and adopted a statutory incomes policy in November 1972 (which initially entailed a 90-day wages freeze) after attempts at securing voluntary restraints had failed. Key decisions concerning the counter-inflation policy were taken by the Pay Board and Prices Commission which was established in 1973. In addition, the Pound was floated in June 1972 in order to prevent the cyclical crises affecting the exchange rate and balance of payments. However, factors which included the decision by the Arab states to quadruple the price of oil in 1973 following the Middle East war and the increase in world commodity prices made the government's handling of the economy appear ineffective, and by the end of its period in office there was high inflation, a large balance of payments deficit, and rising interest rates (which were evidenced by increased mortgage payments). A particular problem was the absence of any consistent approach as to whether the prime concern was to control inflation or to secure economic growth.

Attempts to introduce a new ideological approach (which were embodied in the 'Selsdon Man' philosophy) were abandoned when the bankrupt Rolls Royce company was nationalised by the government in February 1971. Interventionist measures which were designed to combat inflation and reduce unemployment were subsequently introduced and public spending was not reduced after 1970. These factors made it appear that the government's approach to political affairs, especially its economic policy, was guided by pragmatism rather than ideology. The Conservative government also failed to halt the violence in Northern Ireland. The decision to introduce internment in 1970 heightened violence which was evidenced at events which included 'Bloody Sunday' in January 1972. The government's response to this situation was to suspend Stormont and introduce direct rule in 1972. Arrangements for the establishment of a power-sharing executive were hammered out in the 1973 Sunningdale Agreement and this took office in January 1974.

Labour

The Labour Party's inquest into the surprise victory of the Conservative Party in 1970 suggested that the 1964 to 1970 governments entered office with policies insufficiently worked out in advance and that, when in power, their socialist ideology had been sacrificed to pragmatism and the government had neglected its ties with the trade unions and the Party in the country. In order to counter these problems in the future, attempts were made to develop policies which would appeal to Labour's working-class support and much effort was expended after 1970 to develop up-to-date socialist policies. This culminated in an NEC document in May 1973 (*Labour's Programme*, 1973) which proposed to nationalise the top 25 companies (although in subsequent discussion this proposal was watered down to a commitment in principle to expand public ownership under the auspices of the National Enterprise Board). Additionally, attempts were made to secure improved relationships with the trade unions. This took the form of a social contract which emerged from a liaison committee established in 1972 to improve the relationship between the TUC and Labour's NEC. In February 1973 a document entitled *Economic Policy and the Cost of Living* outlined an agreement between the TUC and the Labour Party on issues which included food, prices, rents, transport, taxes and pensions, in return for which the unions promised to moderate wage demands. Attempts were also made to enhance the involvement in Labour Party affairs of grass roots activists: for example, Tony Benn's Participation '72 survey aimed to involve party members in the process of policy formulation.

The issue of entry into Europe caused dissension. Although the Wilson government had agreed to embark on negotiations to enter the EEC whilst in office, the actual terms negotiated by the government were rejected by the Labour Conference in October 1971. However, in the vote on these terms in the House of Commons, 63 Labour MPs defied a three-line whip and voted with the government. The deputy leader of the Party, Roy Jenkins, resigned from the Shadow Cabinet in 1972. Wilson subsequently persuaded the 1973 Party Conference not to commit the Party to total opposition to the NEC but, rather, to pledge to renegotiate the terms of entry agreed to by the Heath government. This was sufficient to persuade Jenkins to rejoin the Shadow Cabinet in November of that year.

Liberals

The result of the 1970 general election had a demoralising effect on the Liberal Party but its performance in parliamentary by-elections after the victory at Rochdale in October 1972 placed the Party in good heart for the general election when it seemed possible that the electorate's disillusionment with the inability of both Labour and Conservative governments to cure Britain's economic and financial problems would be to the Liberals' benefit. Further by-election victories were secured at Sutton and Cheam (1972), Ely, Ripon and Berwick-upon-Tweed (1973); in 1973 the Party won more votes in parliamentary by-elections than either of the two major parties and its rating in the opinion polls rose to 30 per cent. Good results were also secured in the 1973 local elections, including gaining control of Liverpool City Council.

By-elections

Thirty-one by-elections took place in the 1970 Parliament. Labour held 15 of the seats it had won in 1970 and gained one from the Conservatives at Bromsgrove in May 1971. The Conservative Party held eight seats where it had been successful in 1970, and lost four to the Liberal Party in addition to the one lost to Labour. The Liberals also gained one seat from

Labour (Rochdale in October 1972). The sitting Labour MP for Lincoln, Dick Taverne, resigned his seat and successfully defended it at a by-election as a Democratic Labour candidate. Labour also lost Glasgow Govan to the Scottish National candidate, Mrs Margo MacDonald.

Conduct of the Election

The election campaign was a very short one, stretching over a period of only three weeks. Some psephological studies suggested a decline in class-based voting after 1970. This attached particular importance to the campaign since an increased number of voters could be swayed by it. Opinion polls suggested that many voters did switch their allegiance during the campaign.

The election was fought against the background of the miners' strike which arose as the result of a direct challenge to the government's desire to impose a statutory incomes policy in order to counter inflation. All three parties identified inflation as the key issue of the campaign but there was a disagreement between the Labour Party and the Conservative and Liberal parties as to whether the prime necessity was to curb prices or wages. There were also considerable disagreements between the Conservative and Labour parties on other key policy areas – especially the EEC and public ownership which suggested that the post-war consensus was effectively ended.

Conservatives

The Conservative manifesto, *Firm Action for a Fair Britain*, referred to the dangers facing Britain from outside (caused by the dramatic increase in world prices of almost all raw materials and the huge increase in the price of oil) and within (derived from 'unrestrained inflation' which arose from excessive wage increases). The manifesto was especially concerned with the defence of the government's record since 1970 and asserted the importance of statutory controls over wages, prices and profits. A number of future reforms were suggested (including a twice-yearly review of pensions and welfare benefits, the introduction of a tax credit scheme, the initiation of schemes to enable tenants to buy council houses, and the amendment of the 1971 Industrial Relations Act to require conciliation procedures to take place before court action). Changes were also proposed to cut social security benefits to strikers' families. The stance of the manifesto was that of moderation, and the Labour Party was attacked for extremism. It was alleged that the Labour Party had been taken over by a combination of left wingers and power-hungry trade union leaders. However, the emphasis placed on Labour extremism in an election broadcast on 19 February was branded as a scare tactic by Labour and placed the Conservative Party on the defensive against accusations of 'mud-slinging'.

The Conservative campaign highlighted the need for strong government in the face of alleged exteremism and emphasised the importance of a statutory incomes policy to control inflation. However, Heath's first election broadcast indicated the abandonment of this position by stating that the miners' pay claim would be referred to the new relativities procedures of the Pay Board and that any recommended award would be backdated to 1 March 1974. The reliance placed by the Conservatives on the miners' dispute as a vote-winner was further eroded on 21 February when the Pay Board's relativities inquiry declared (on the basis of new statistics prepared by the Pay Board) that miners were underpaid in comparison to manual workers in manufacturing industry. This placed the Conservatives on the defensive which was especially evident in their inability to respond instantly to this situation and also resulted in increased levels of public and media support for the miners.

The Conservative campaign was based upon a strategy of rallying the moderates in the face of the crisis alleged to be facing the country. This was useful to distract the attention of the electors away from the unspectacular record of the government since 1970 which would scarcely warrant electors giving them a renewed vote of confidence. However, the relaxation of power restrictions, the absence of mass picketing by the miners as had occurred in 1972 and the relativities hearings which tended to defuse the miners' dispute all reduced the air of crisis. Nonetheless, the Conservatives did not effectively adapt to the changed circumstances in which issues raised by the Labour Party assumed an increased importance to the voters as the campaign progressed. The Party also became distracted in the later stages of the campaign with the resurgent Liberal Party. It responded to this situation by warning electors of the danger of weak minority government, which led to reduced attention being paid to Labour.

Labour
The Labour Party's proposals were contained in its manifesto, *Let Us Work Together – Labour's Way Out of the Crisis*. It accused the Conservatives of calling the election in a panic and proposed a social contract with the trade unions (although the precise details of this arrangement were left vague), the appointment of a Royal Commission on Income Distribution and the establishment of a non-governmental conciliation and arbitration service. The Conservatives' Pay Board and 1971 Industrial Relations Act would be scrapped. Substantial extensions in public ownership were proposed, including public ownership and control of North Sea oil and gas. The manifesto also proposed to take into public ownership development land, mineral rights, shipbuilding and repairing, marine engineering, ports, and the manufacture of airframes and aeroengines. The terms of the UK's entry into the EEC were to be renegotiated and the results of this would be placed before the electorate at either a future general election or in a consultative referendum. Inflation would be curbed by controlling prices, with wages being subject to voluntary constraints. Social reform included the expansion of the National Health Service and education, and the repeal of the Conservatives' Housing Finance Act. The manifesto was underpinned by an objective of securing a fundamental and irreversible shift in the balance of power and wealth in favour of working people and their families, although Wilson's election speeches deliberately downplayed socialism.

The Labour campaign aimed to divert attention away from the miners' dispute and instead sought to focus the nation on Conservative economic mismanagement in general and on their failure to adhere to their 1970 pledge to cut prices (in particular the cost of food). Labour's cause was aided by the publication of the retail price index on 15 February (which declared a record rise for a one-month period) and the monthly trade figures on 25 February (which indicated a large deficit which Wilson was able to compare unfavourably with the surplus Heath had inherited in 1970). Although the Conservatives attributed rising prices to external factors such as the rising cost of imports, Labour argued the situation arose from Conservative economic mismanagement which had led to a devaluation of the Pound by 25 per cent since it was floated. Heath was dubbed 'Mr Rising Price' by Wilson, and Labour offered to clear up the economic mess created by the Conservatives as they had done in 1964. The vote of housewives was especially targeted by this line of argument. Other issues emphasised by the Labour Party included higher mortgage rates, the collapse of the house-building programme and the terms of entry negotiated by the government for Britain's entry into the EEC. Europe, however, failed to become a major election issue (despite Enoch Powell's recommendation that Conservatives who were opposed to the EEC should vote Labour as he had done by postal ballot). The Labour campaign was less focused on Wilson than it had been in 1970. Considerable importance was attached to television to get the Party's message across since the Conservative bias of the press placed Labour at a disadvantage.

Liberals

The Liberal Party depicted itself as moderate and aloof from the image of confrontation which it sought to identify with the two major parties. Its manifesto, *Change the Face of Britain – Take Power and Vote Liberal,* asserted the need for a new approach to politics in which the general welfare of the nation would take precedence over the defence of sectional and partisan interests. It was argued that a Liberal vote constituted support for a new type of politics based upon a reform of 'the sterile class conflict of the two discredited parties'. The Party proposed a statutory policy to control wages, prices and profits. Additionally, it was suggested that workers and firms whose actions fuelled inflation by inflationary wage settlements or dividend increases would be subject to an anti-inflation surcharge. Other policies included greater popular participation in running affairs; this would be achieved by decentralisation and devolution of government and partnership in industry. The establishment of a minimum income and the fairer distribution of wealth were also proposed. It was emphasised that government should act on behalf of all people rather than being at the behest of a few sectional interests. Liberal arguments were especially directed at those voters who had become disillusioned with the previous records of both major parties and who were in the mood for a change underpinned by the spirit of reconciliation.

The Liberal Party's campaign was heavily centred on Thorpe who conducted the daily press conferences via a television link-up from his North Devon constituency headquarters in Barnstaple. The Party's opinion poll rating dipped in the first week of the campaign but rose thereafter, leading to debates as to Liberal actions in the event of neither major party obtaining an overall majority in the new House of Commons. Thorpe adhered to the position he had advanced at his 1973 speech to the Liberal Assembly at Southport where he had agreed to support a minority government on an agreed package of economic measures but insisted that both parties would have to change their policies radically before he would be willing to cooperate with them.

Result of the Election

For the second time running there was a last minute swing against the party which was leading in the opinion polls (all of which indicated a Conservative victory) and the party which was favourite to win the election at the outset of the campaign again ended up losing it.

A record number of 2,135 candidates contested the election. The result was:

Party	Votes	Vote %	MPs
Labour	11,645,616	37.2%	301
Conservative	11,872,180	37.9%	297
Liberal	6,059,519	19.3%	14
United Ulster Unionist Council	366,703	1.2% [51.1%]	11
Scottish National Party	633,180	2.0% [21.9%]	7
Plaid Cymru	171,374	0.5% [10.8%]	2
Others	431,153	1.4%	2
Social Democratic and Labour Party	160,437	0.5% [22.4%]	1
Total	31,340,162		635

The turnout was 78.8 per cent. This figure was aided by the newness of the electoral register. The overall swing from the Conservatives to the Labour Party was 0.8 per cent.

The 'others' were Eddie Milne (Blyth) and Dick Taverne (Lincoln), both of whom were Labour Party dissidents. Twenty-three women MPs were elected.

The Parties

The swing to Labour was relatively uniform across the regions with the exception of the North West (where the swing to Labour was 1.6 per cent) and the West Midlands (where it was 2.5 per cent). Labour's prospects in this region were aided by Powell's intervention who had refused to stand as a candidate and had urged electors to vote Labour. Twenty-eight Labour MPs did not stand in February 1974; they included Richard Crossman and Patrick Gordon Walker. Twelve Labour MPs who were elected in 1970 lost their seats. Sixteen Labour MPs were sponsored by the Cooperative Party and 127 by trade unions. In total, 39 Conservative MPs did not stand in February 1974, the most notable being Enoch Powell who viewed the election as 'essentially fraudulent' and decided not to recontest his seat of Wolverhampton South West which he had held since 1950. Additionally, Ernest Marples did not stand and Duncan Sandys left the House of Commons. Thirty-four Conservative MPs were defeated. The most senior Conservative to lose his seat was Gordon Campbell, who had served as Secretary of State for Scotland. He was defeated at Moray and Nairn by Mrs Winnifred Ewing of the SNP. Two junior ministers (Kenneth Speed and Nicholas Scott) also lost their seats and the vice-chairman of the Conservative Party, John Selwyn Gummer, lost Lewisham West to Labour.

The Liberal Party considerably increased its national vote in comparison to 1970, and its candidates secured 24 per cent of the vote in the constituencies in which the Party fielded candidates. It was estimated that the Liberal Party drew its additional votes more or less equally from both of the major parties. An outstanding success was achieved at the Isle of Wight where a 17,000 Conservative majority over Labour in 1970 was transformed into a Liberal majority of more than 7,000 votes.

Scotland, Wales and Northern Ireland

In Scotland and Wales, the election was fought against the background of the publication of the Kilbrandon Report in 1973. This report rejected independence but urged devolution for

Scotland and Wales. In both countries there was a net swing to the Conservative Party of around 1.6 per cent.

In Scotland, Labour won 40 of the 71 seats, the Conservatives 21 and the Liberals three. The Scottish National Party had performed well in by-elections after 1970, gaining over 30 per cent of the vote in the four contests it had fought. Its claims for independence were aided by the recommendation of the Kilbrandon Commission in 1973 for a Scottish Assembly, and the discovery of North Sea oil which countered criticisms that Scotland could not be economically independent. The Party suggested that the revenues obtained from North Sea oil and gas could finance the future budgets of a Scottish government and enable it to improve the living standards of the Scots. At the election it secured 21.9 per cent of the Scottish vote (compared to 11.4 per cent in 1970) and gained six seats in addition to its 1970 victory in the Western Isles which it retained.

Labour retained its grip on Welsh politics, winning 24 of the 36 seats. However, it lost two seats (Caernarvon and Merioneth) to Plaid Cymru and one (Cardigan) to the Liberals. The Conservatives won eight seats, and the Liberals and Plaid Cymru two each.

In Northern Ireland the election occurred against the defeat of the power-sharing executive by the Ulster Workers' Council strike and was regarded as a referendum on the Sunningdale Agreement. Supporters of power-sharing failed to coalesce behind a single candidate in the individual constituencies which meant that the pro-power sharing vote was divided amongst candidates reflecting the Province's traditional sectarian divide. However, opponents of the Sunningdale Agreement and of the power-sharing executive which took office at the beginning of 1974 (which comprised a section of the Ulster Unionist Party led by Harry West, Vanguard and the Democratic Unionist Party) did construct these arrangements and stood under the banner of the United Ulster Unionist Council (UUUC).

Eleven of Northern Ireland's 12 constituencies were won by the UUUC. Two Ulster Unionist pro-assembly candidates (Stanley McMaster and Rafton Pounder) were defeated at Belfast East and Belfast South respectively and two independent Northern Irish MPs (Bernadette McAliskey and Frank McManus) were defeated by UUUC candidates at Mid-Ulster and Fermanagh and South Tyrone. The remaining seat was won by Gerry Fitt, leader of the newly formed Social Democratic and Labour Party.

Consequence of the Election

Although Labour won more seats than the Conservative Party, the latter obtained more votes. This situation, together with the narrow margin between the two major parties, the large vote obtained by the Liberal Party, and the public opposition (expressed by those who voted Conservative and Liberal) to Labour's stance on an incomes policy and Europe encouraged Heath not to resign immediately but instead to discuss with the Liberal leader the possibility of his continuance in office, heading a Conservative–Liberal coalition government. This government would, however, have lacked an overall majority in the House of Commons. Heath also sought support from Harry West who led the seven dissident Ulster Unionist MPs by offering them the Conservative whip. A meeting of the 14 Liberal MPs on 4 March 1974 rejected a coalition government with the Conservatives. Although Thorpe had reaffirmed his willingness to support a Conservative government pledged to carry out an agreed and limited programme,

Heath rejected this and resigned from office the same day. Harold Wilson thus became Prime Minister, heading the first minority administration since 1929 which was 17 seats short of an overall majority in the House of Commons.

10 October 1974

Party Leaders
Harold Wilson (Labour)
Edward Heath (Conservative)
Jeremy Thorpe (Liberal)

Background to the Election
Timing of the Election
The election was triggered by Wilson's desire to secure an overall majority in the House of Commons, since a minority government was susceptible to parliamentary defeats, 18 occurring during this Parliament. The willingness of the government to hold a further general election in 1974 was strengthened by opinion polls which, for much of the life of this Parliament, indicated a healthy Labour lead.

Electoral Procedures and Practices
Harold Wilson headed a government with no overall majority in the House of Commons, a situation which prompted the Liberal Leader, Jeremy Thorpe, to declare on 6 March 1974 that 'we are all minorities now'. The life of the Parliament elected in February 1974 was the shortest since 1681 (Butler and Kavanagh, 1975: 18), lasting a mere six months and 11 days. This election was the first since 1924 when a minority government appealed for a mandate to the electorate (Butler and Kavanagh, 1975: 100). Wilson's tactic when he became Prime Minister in March 1974 was to act as if his party had an overall majority on the presumption that, should a defeat occur on a major issue, the monarch would not oppose a fresh election (Butler and Kavanagh, 1975: 19).

Conservatives
Attempts were made after the election to improve Conservative Party organisation through the appointment of Michael Wolff as director-general of the Party, whose role was to lead the next election campaign. The Conservative performance in the House of Commons was initially lacklustre. The Party was demoralised by its election defeat and the inability to construct a coalition with the Liberal Party, and was further weakened by the loss of a number of former ministers (including Sir Alec Douglas-Home, Anthony Barber and Christopher Chataway) from the front bench. Their performance did, however, improve during the lifetime of the Parliament, and on 19 June they succeeded in defeating the government's proposal to refund the £10 million in tax relief to those trade unions which had refused to register as had been required by the 1971 Industrial Relations Act.

Labour
Soon after taking office, the miners' strike was settled and the state of emergency was thus ended. Labour's first budget in March 1974 increased old age pensions and other welfare benefits, and

provided rent relief and food subsidies amounting to £500 million. Income and Corporation Tax was raised and VAT extended to petrol and sweets. A second budget in July cut the rate of VAT and announced relief for ratepayers. A number of Conservative policies were undone: the 1971 Industrial Relations Act was repealed, the Pay Board abolished and key aspects of the 1972 Housing Finance Act were dismantled by policies which encouraged local authorities to build more houses for rent and by the 1974 Rent Act which provided security of tenure to tenants in furnished property. The Channel Tunnel project was cancelled. However, Stage Three of the Conservatives' Prices and Incomes Policy was retained (a stance which ensured that the Conservatives did not vote against the Queen's Speech). Proposals were put forward in a White Paper in August in connection with the National Enterprise Board (in which voluntary planning with companies was proposed), and in September concerning devolution.

The government sought to create economic conditions which they felt would improve their chances of re-election. Measures which included imposing controls to halt price rises, the payment of subsidies to the nationalised industries, a reduction in VAT rates, the introduction of food subsidies, a large pension rise and pay increases under Stage Three of the Conservatives' Incomes Policy succeeded in reducing inflation to 8 per cent in the three months prior to the election and addressing public concerns about declining standards of living.

Liberals
The discussions which took place between Jeremy Thorpe and Ted Heath following the February 1974 general election caused dissent within the Liberal Party. During the Parliament, the Liberals reiterated their willingness to enter into a coalition government (or what Thorpe had initially referred to as a 'government of national unity') in order to combat the economic crisis facing the country. However, only the Conservatives showed any interest in this course of action, their draft election manifesto (issued in September 1974) indicating a willingness to bring in persons from outside the Party, even if the Conservatives secured an overall majority in the House of Commons.

By-elections
Only one by-election (at Newham South) occured in the lifetime of the Parliament elected in February 1974. This was caused by the elevation of Sir Elwyn Jones to the peerage on his appointment as Lord Chancellor. Labour held the constituency on a turnout of 25.9 per cent.

Conduct of the Election
The election took place against the background of an economic crisis which was characterised by a high balance of payments deficit (which was especially attributable to the rise in the cost of oil) and a high level of inflation. Although the rate of inflation was temporarily reduced immediately prior to the election, during the life of this Parliament, prices rose by 8 per cent, wages by 16 per cent and the real value of shares declined significantly (Butler and Kavanagh, 1975: 18). The economic crisis was the background to a more general public mood of pessimism that governments were unable to deliver on their promises and that the major parties seemed incapable of solving the nation's main difficulties. A key explanation of this situation was that politics were conducted around the politics of 'promising' whereby, at election times,

each party sought to outdo its opponents by promising improved standards of living to the electorate if it were returned to office. However, it was difficult to meet these promises because of factors which included the dependance on world trade patterns and the need to import raw materials, food and oil. Public disenchantment with the situation was especially directed at targets which were held responsible for, or which epitomised, a sense of national decline. These included the power of trade unions and the decline of law and order. Feelings of this nature, coupled with a sense of boredom with a second election being held only seven months after the February contest were key factors in explaining the reduced level of turnout in October.

Labour

The Labour Party's proposals were contained in its manifesto, *Britain Will Win With Labour,* which specifically ruled out the possibility of Labour participation in a coalition government. Labour's campaign emphasised teamwork rather than focusing on Wilson. It concentrated on the record of its tried and tested team of ministers to demonstrate that a Labour government had 'worked'. It was argued that minority government had been successsful and Labour had carried out many of its pledges contained in the February 1974 manifesto by passing some important pieces of legislation. Labour's campaign further asserted that the Party had the policies which would see the nation through the difficult years ahead. The Social Contract (as opposed to wage restraint) was a key aspect of Labour's appeal to the voters. It was depicted as a relationship with the unions which was unique to the Party, and the social harmony which it created was depicted to be in stark contrast to the confrontation between government and unions which had occurred during the previous Conservative government's period of office. It was observed that the Social Contract was 'an all-purpose phrase, meaning social justice, conciliation and cooperation, a style of government, an anti-inflation policy and, perhaps, some restraint on large wage settlements' (Butler and Kavanagh, 1975: 255). The theme of cooperation with the unions was developed into proposals to extend industrial democracy, and plans to extend nationalisation into areas which included development land and mineral rights were put forward. Labour stated its intention to provide for directly elected assemblies for Scotland and Wales as early as possible in the life of the new Parliament and to offer the electorate the final say on its renegotiated terms of membership of the EEC.

One difficulty facing Labour was how to maximise its vote. This might be done by appealing to the large number of working-class people who did not support the Party or alternatively to concentrate on middle-class and moderate voters. This dilemma was underpinned by the historic disputes within that party which are frequently depicted in terms of 'left' versus 'right' (Crewe and King, 1995: 15).

Conservatives

The Conservative Party's manifesto, *Putting Britain First*, sought to project a different image than that which had characterised its February campaign. It was based upon conciliation (a style which Heath adopted during his campaign appearances): the Party accepted Labour's repeal of its 1971 Industrial Relations Act, emphasised its commitment to consult with major interests and proposed to strengthen the National Economic Development Council. The Party thus sought to depict itself as a vehicle to provide national unity and promised to involve persons from outside the Party (the manifesto using the word 'consultation' as opposed to 'coalition') in government even if they obtained an overall majority of seats in the House of Commons. The emphasis which was placed on the Conservative Party as a vehicle to secure national unity was especially strong towards the end of the election campaign.

Significant attention was also devoted to the economic crisis facing the country and this was used as the justification for national unity. However, divisions within the Party concerning its anti-inflation policy were reflected in the diverse range of proposals which were put forward to combat this problem: these included restraint on the money supply, a prices and incomes policy (which would ideally be voluntary but with statutory powers held in reserve should agreement be impossible to reach), and the imposition of strict controls over public spending. There were, however, key differences between Conservative and Labour policies which were aired during the campaign. The Conservatives promised to withdraw Labour's proposals to extend comprehensive education, and intended to retain grammar and direct grant schools with enhanced rights for parents embodied in legislation. Labour's nationalisation plans were also attacked as providing evidence of the domination of the Party by its left wing. Aid to owner-occupiers was promised in order to attain the objective of the creation of a property-owning democracy, and during the campaign Margaret Thatcher promised to bring mortgage rates down to 9.5 per cent by Christmas 1974.

The Conservative Party faced a number of problems during its campaign. Many voters blamed it for its record in office between 1970 and 1974 (especially for the level of inflation) and for the confrontation between government and unions which occurred during that period. In September, Sir Keith Joseph publicly argued that inflation could be cured only by strict control over the money supply, even if this resulted in temporarily raising the level of unemployment. This enabled the Conservatives to be depicted as the party of unemployment. It has further been observed that Heath was not an electoral asset (Butler and Kavanagh, 1975: 88), a situation which prompted the Party to give a greater degree of prominence to other leading Conservatives than had been the case in the Party's February 1974 campaign.

Liberals

The Liberal Party's claim to be a national party was underpinned by fielding candidates in almost every constituency in Great Britain. It regarded the election as an unnecessary event which had been forced on the nation because of Wilson's refusal to accept the disciplines of minority government. The Party's Manifesto, *Why Britain Needs a Liberal Government*, emphasised the party's freedom from domination by the sectional interests of trade unions and business. Its anti-inflation policy was depicted as a contract with the nation (as opposed to one merely with the trade unions): it comprised statutory controls over prices and incomes and punitive taxes on workers and companies which broke the guidelines. The Party was pledged to scrap food subsidies (on the grounds that they were general in application, not reflecting need), and promised to overhaul the social security system in order to replace most of the means-tested benefits with a system of tax credits.

The Party's electoral strategy (encapsulated in the slogan 'one more heave') implied the desire to form a Liberal government. However, this objective was unlikely to be achieved and, instead, attention was shifted during the second half of the campaign to the desire to break the two-party system. Attaining the balance of power was conceivably a realisable electoral objective, but the main difficulty this posed to the Party was the stance it would adopt if no party secured an overall majority in the House of Commons. On 6 September 1974, Thorpe stated in a speech delivered at Morecambe that the decision to participate in a coalition government would be taken by the Parliamentary Party alone. The subsequent Liberal Assembly did not express outright opposition to involvement in a coalition government, but rejected any arrangement with the major parties under their present leaders and with their current policies. This non-committal stance meant that the electorate was uncertain about what the Party would do if it suceeded in securing the balance of power in the new Parliament.

Result of the Election

The campaign was a brief, three-week event, at the end of which the Labour Party was returned with a small overall majority of three seats. Most opinion polls had predicted a Labour victory, but had tended to overestimate its size. This was the first occasion since 1922 when a party had gained an overall majority in the House of Commons while securing below 40 per cent of the popular vote. A record number of 2,252 candidates contested the election. The result was:

Party	Votes	Vote %	MPs
Labour	11,457,079	39.3%	319
Conservative	10,462,565	35.8%	277
Liberal	5,346,704	18.3%	13
Scottish National Party	839,617	2.9% [30.4%]	11
United Ulster Unionist Council	407,778	1.4% [58.1%]	10
Plaid Cymru	166,321	0.6% [10.8%]	3
Social Democratic and Labour Party	154,193	0.5% [22.0%]	1
Others	354,847	1.2%	1
Total	31,221,362		635

The turnout was 72.8 per cent. The swing from the Conservative Party to Labour was 2.2 per cent. Twenty-seven women MPs were elected.

The Parties

Gwynoro Jones was the only Labour MP to lose his seat. He was defeated at Carmarthen by the President of Plaid Cymru, Gwynfor Evans. Overall, the Labour Party's performance was weaker than its opinion poll ratings had been suggesting since the February election. One reason for this may have been a last minute movement away from the Party, perhaps indicating that many electors feared the consequences of a large Labour majority. Sixteen MPs were sponsored by the Cooperative Party and 127 by trade unions. A number of senior Conservative stood down in October 1974. These included the former Prime Minister, Sir Alec Douglas-Home, and Anthony Barber (who served as Chancellor of the Exchequer between 1970 and 1974). Twenty-two Conservative MPs lost their seats, of whom the most senior was Lord Balniel who had served as Minister of State for Defence between 1970 and 1972 and Minister of State in the Foreign and Commonwealth Offfice between 1972 and 1974.

The outcome of the election was a disappointment for the Liberal Party which failed to improve upon the position it had obtained in February. The Party succeeded in raising its share of the vote in only 27 of the 145 constituencies in which it had achieved second place in February and in this election was runner-up in 105 constituencies. It lost two seats (Hazel Grove and Bodmin) and gained only one (Truro), notable failures including Christopher Mayhew's inability to gain Bath from the Conservatives. One hundred and thirty Liberal candidates lost their deposits and the average vote obtained by a Liberal candidate fell from 23.6 per cent in February to 18.9 per cent in October, and its total vote was reduced by around three-quarters of a million. These figures masked the key difficulty faced by the Party, which was to hang on to the vote obtained in one general election and use it as a springboard for the next: one estimate suggested that the Party lost around 2.5 million votes which it had polled in February, but gained around two million new votes, thus resulting in a more modest reduction in total Liberal support of around three-quarters of a million (Alt *et al.*, 1977: 348).

Both Independents elected in February (Dick Taverne [Social Democrat] and Eddie Milne [Independent Labour]) lost their seats to Labour, and the deselected Labour MP for Sheffield Brightside, Eddie Griffith, also failed in his attempt to secure re-election as an Independent Labour candidate.

Scotland, Wales and Northern Ireland

In Scotland, the Scottish National Party sought to establish itself as Scotland's second biggest party after Labour. It focused on the issues of Scottish oil and self-government, and argued that a large vote was a guarantee that the major parties would have to pay attention to Scotland's needs. The SNP succeeded in raising its poll in Scotland from 21.9 per cent in February to 30.4 per cent. This increase made it the second party to Labour in Scotland (which secured 36.3 per cent of the Scottish vote), the Conservatives trailing in third place with 24.7 per cent and the Liberals in fourth place with 8.3 per cent. In terms of seats, Labour won 41 of the 71 seats, the Conservatives 16, and the Liberals three. The size of the SNP's parliamentary representation increased from seven to 11 MPs, all four gains being at the expense of the Conservatives. The SNP success in obtaining more votes from Conservatives than from Labour was a key factor which explained the higher than average overall swing to Labour in that country.

Labour's domination of Welsh politics continued, the Party capturing 49.5 per cent of the Welsh vote and 23 of the 36 seats. The Conservatives won 23.9 per cent (eight seats), the Liberals 15.5 per cent (two seats) and Plaid Cymru 10.8 per cent. Their victory at Carmarthen gave them three seats. In Northern Ireland, the power-sharing executive was brought down by a strike organised by the Ulster Workers' Council in May 1974. The UUUC continued to control politics in Northern Ireland by winning 10 of the 12 seats (one of whose victors was Enoch Powell, elected for South Down). This situation effectively removed power-sharing from the Province's political agenda. However, the chairman of the United Ulster Unionist Parliamentary Coalition, Harry West, was defeated in Fermanagh and South Tyrone by an Independent, Frank Maguire. Gerry Fitt retained West Belfast for the SDLP.

Consequence of the Election

Harold Wilson formed a Labour administration.

3 May 1979

Party Leaders
Margaret Thatcher (Conservative)
James Callaghan (Labour)
David Steel (Liberal)

Background to the Election
Timing of the Election
The election was forced upon the government by its defeat on a Conservative motion of 'no confidence' moved by Margaret Thatcher which passed by one vote (311 : 310) on 28 March 1979. This was the first occasion a government had been defeated on a vote of confidence since the downfall of Ramsay MacDonald's Labour government in 1924.

Electoral Procedures and Practices
A number of decisions which had constitutional significance were taken between October 1974 and 1979. A national referendum was held on 5 June 1975 on the 'renegotiated' terms of entry for Britain's membership of the EEC (which had been completed at the Dublin summit in March 1975) when the electorate decided (by a vote of 2:1) to remain in this institution. Referendums were also held in connection with the government's 1978 devolution legislation for Scotland and Wales (which are discussed below). The conclusion by the government of an understanding with the Liberal Party in 1977 (which is discussed below) was the first occasion since 1931 that a government was dependent on an undertaking with a party not in government. The convention of collective ministerial responsibility was also waived during this period for the first time since 1932, initially in connection with the EEC referendum (when ministers were free to campaign against continued membership) and later in connection with the vote in the House of Commons in 1977 on the method of election for members of the European Assembly, a proposal which, in the spirit of the Lib–Lab Pact, the government recommended to the House of Commons but which was subject to a free vote.

The introduction of financial aid to opposition political parties in Parliament towards their research and administrative purposes was first given in 1975 (being termed 'Short money' after the minister, Ted Short, who introduced this initiative). Suggestions were also made during this period for the reform of the electoral system. In 1976 Lord Blake's report of the Hansard Society Committee recommended the adoption of the West German style of electoral system which was a mixture of the existing first-past-the-post system 'topped up' with additional members. An experiment with broadcasting proceedings of the House of Commons was first initiated in 1975. Permanent arrangements were introduced in April 1978.

Conservatives
The rumblings of discontent against Ted Heath's leadership of the Party which had surfaced after the February 1974 election arose again after the October defeat. In October the Executive

of the 1922 Committee determined that there should be a leadership election in the new Parliament. The rules initially drawn up in 1965 for the election of a Conservative leader were revised under a committee chaired by Lord Home. On the first vote on 4 February 1975, Heath trailed Margaret Thatcher by 119 votes to her 130 (with 16 being given to Hugh Fraser). Heath immediately resigned as leader and in the second ballot held on 11 February, Margaret Thatcher was elected leader by 146 votes to 79 for W. Whitelaw, 19 for G. Howe, 19 for J. Prior and 11 for J. Peyton.

The election of Margaret Thatcher as leader of the Conservative Party was viewed as a shift to the right, 'reflecting a reliance on market mechanisms rather than government intervention in the economy and on individual self-help rather than state-provided welfare benefits' (Butler and Kavanagh, 1980: 64). She depicted herself as a conviction politician (in the sense that she believed policies should derive from a coherent set of political principles) and was opposed to consensus politics. Sir Keith Joseph was given a prominent role in the development of party policy after 1975. He had set up the Centre for Policy Studies in 1974 which was favourable to monetarism, and new Conservative policies were articulated in *The Right Approach* (1976) and *The Right Approach to the Economy* (1977). The former document identified inflation as a key problem which it proposed to tackle using any feasible method save a statutory incomes policy. It emphasised the importance of enterprise, wider ownership, better education standards and the rule of law, and also proposed to repeal the 1975 Industry Act, the 1975 Community Land Act, the 1976 Education Act and to abolish the National Enterprise Board. The 1977 proposals highlighted the importance of the money supply and of responsible wage bargaining.

Labour

The key event which occurred after October 1974 was the resignation of Harold Wilson as Prime Minister. He announced his intention to resign on 16 March 1976 and in the first ballot of the Parliamentary Party, Michael Foot obtained 90 votes, James Callaghan 84, Roy Jenkins 56, Tony Benn 37, Denis Healey 30 and Tony Crosland 17. In the second ballot, Callaghan secured 141 votes, Foot 38 and Healey 38. In the final ballot on 5 April 1976, Callaghan became leader of the Party defeating Foot by 176 to 137 votes.

Although the government was returned with an overall majority of only three, its position was strengthened by the unlikely occurrence of all minor parties uniting against it, save perhaps on a vote of no confidence. This meant that many of the Party's October 1974 manifesto commitments were carried out. The National Enterprise Board was established and the 1975 Industry Act provided for planning agreements between the government and large companies (although the compulsory nature of the agreements provided for in the legislation was soon dropped). Changes in labour law beneficial to trade unions was provided for in the Trade Union and Labour Relations Acts of 1974 and 1976 and the 1975 Employment Protection Act which affected job security and redundancy rights.

Some progress was made in providing for devolution of government in Scotland and Wales. A measure to achieve this objective (the Scotland and Wales Bill) was introduced in 1976 but was withdrawn when it failed to secure a guillotine motion in February 1977. Further legislation (entailing separate Bills for Scotland and Wales) was introduced in the following parliamentary Session and passed in 1978 with the proviso that referendums in both countries would be held before it was enacted and, additionally, that to proceed the proposal had to have the support of 40 per cent of eligible voters. Referendums were held in March 1979 but failed to attain the 40 per cent hurdle and the legislation was thus not proceeded with. In Northern Ireland, however, direct rule (which had been re-established in May 1974 following the Ulster Workers' Council strike which brought down the power-sharing executive) was continued with when the Constituent Assembly (elected in 1975) was unable to agree on an internal political solution.

The main problem facing the Labour government was the economy. The key problems were unemployment (which hit the one million mark in July 1975), inflation (which rose from 8 per cent in October 1974 to 26 per cent in July 1975, being influenced by the rise in oil and commodity prices) and the falling value of the Pound. Initially, the government proceeded with a pay policy. Phase I was introduced in 1975, consisting of a voluntary agrement with the trade unions to limit pay increases in return for keeping prices down and placing limits on dividends. Phase II (in 1976) sought to impose a 5 per cent limit on pay increases up to a maximum of £4, and Phase III (in 1977) introduced a target of 10 per cent for wage increases. This was mainly applied to the public sector, although this phase provided for sanctions being applied to private sector firms (in the form of government aid or contracts being withheld) which ignored the guidelines.

Measures other than pay policy were introduced to deal with economic problems. In 1975 Chancellor Denis Healey introduced strict control of the money supply as a pragmatic way to combat inflation and in the same year imposed expenditure cuts and cash limits on government departments. This approach became increasingly important in 1976 when the Sterling crisis (which arose from a Treasury-managed devaluation that got out of hand and which led to a fall in the value of the Pound, accompanied by price increases and a falling standard of living) forced the government to seek loans from abroad. Initially short-term aid was acquired from American and Western European central banks, but longer-term aid had to be sought from the International Monetary Fund. This institution imposed strict conditions as a precondition of granting financial aid, in particular cutting the Public Sector Borrowing Requirement (which was achieved by measures that included reducing the level of public spending, selling the government's shares in British Petroleum and increasing excise duty).

However, by 1977 the economy began to improve. Revenue was secured from North Sea oil, the balance of payments moved into surplus in the third quarter of 1977, the Pound rose in value, gold and dollar reserves grew throughout 1977 and 1978 and living standards began to improve during 1978. Factors such as these suggested the wisdom of holding a general election towards the end of 1978. However, in a national broadcast delivered on 7 September 1978, Callaghan specifically ruled out this course of action. Although Labour's opinion poll ratings had improved during the early months of 1978, they revealed that the government lagged behind the Conservatives after the summer, in part due to the latter's use of the Saatchi & Saatchi whose campaign in August and September was on the theme of 'Labour Isn't Working'. It was also perceived that the lower tax rates and increased child benefits available in November 1978 and the new electoral register which became current in February 1979 would aid Labour fortunes in a later election.

Other problems faced by the government in this period included the rise of politically motivated violence. The politics of race caused violence when protaganists such as the National

Front and the Anti-Nazi League (which was established in 1977) clashed on the streets (as at Lewisham in August 1977). Violence associated with the politics of Northern Ireland resulted in the passage of the Prevention of Terrorism Act in November 1974 following the Birmingham public house bombings.

The Party also faced internal difficulties in the period after 1979 which can be depicted in terms of a left- versus right-wing battle for its control. After 1974, the Party's National Executive Committee (NEC) had a left-wing majority and was perceived as siding against right-wing MPs who were involved in reselection contests (such as that of Reg Prentice in North East Newham). Although attempts to make MPs and the leadership more accountable to the Party members made little headway in this period (Callaghan in particular ensuring that he kept control of the election manifesto in order to resist the inclusion of radical policies which were especially associated with the Home Policy Committee chaired by Tony Benn), left-wing proposals were put foward in a number of other policy documents. These included the NEC's *Labour's Programme* (1976) which proposed to nationalise the banks and insurance companies, introduce compulsory planning agreements and provide a wide range of welfare benefits, and the Research Department's *Keep Britain Labour* (1978) which put forward policies such as a wealth tax, the abolition of the House of Lords, greater public spending and the institution of compulsory planning agreements with the top 100 companies.

The ideas contained in the 1976 document were endorsed by that year's Party Conference and pressure within the Party also sought to pursue reflation and higher levels of state control. The right wing of the Party began to mobilise in this period, in particular with the formation of the Manifesto Group in 1976 (which was designed to counter the strength of the Tribune Group in the Parliamentary Labour Party). This became a component of the Campaign for Labour Victory when it was formed in 1977. Centre-right policies were stated in pronouncements which included *Priorities for Labour* which was issued by the Manifesto Group of Labour MPs in 1978. This rejected import controls, compulsory planning agreements, a massive reflation of the economy and expressed support for the mixed economy and a permanent incomes policy.

Liberals

Discontent with Thorpe's leadership of the Party had been made ever since he secured office in 1967, and problems between Thorpe and the chief whip, Cyril Smith, led to the latter's resignation in 1975. In 1976 a DTI report into the collapse of the London and Securities Bank (of which Thorpe had been a director) perhaps implied doubts over his judgement, but later that year a male model, Norman Scott, declared that he had had a homosexual affair with Thorpe, which subsequently developed into allegations that attempts to cover up this relationship had resulted in an attempt to murder of Scott. Thorpe and a number of alleged associates were tried in 1979 for conspiracy to murder but were acquitted. Jeremy Thorpe resigned the leadership of the Party on 10 May 1976 and was initially replaced on a caretaker basis by the former leader, Jo Grimond, until a permanent leader could be chosen. A special assembly in Manchester approved a new system for electing the leader whereby individual members would vote for candidates proposed by a least three MPs. On 7 July David Steel defeated his only rival, John Pardoe, by 12,546 votes to 7,032.

Steel had argued during the leadership campaign in favour of cooperating with one of the major parties in order to get desirable reforms. In 1977 he concluded an agreement to sustain the Labour government which was termed the 'Lib–Lab Pact'. The government's loss of its overall majority following defeats at by-elections at Workington and Walsall North, together with internal divisions caused by the spending cuts required as a condition of the IMF loan, placed the government's survival in doubt. Ministers believed they needed 18 to 24 months to restore Britain's ailing economy which made them susceptible to agreeing to an arrangement with one of the minor parties in order to provide them with this breathing space. The new Liberal leader, David Steel, was also eager to put into practice the sentiments he had articulated at the 1976 Llandudno Assembly and share power with another party. Both parties were thrown together by a Conservative no confidence motion in March 1977. Meetings took place between Steel and Callaghan which fashioned the 'Lib–Lab Pact', although Steel subsequently recorded that it was more in the nature of a 'Steel–Callaghan Pact, accepted by our respective colleagues with widely varying degrees of enthusiasm, or lack of it' (Steel, 1980: 153).

At the heart of the pact was joint consultation which took place between Steel and Callaghan and also between other government and Liberal parliamentary spokespersons. A government–Liberal consultative committee was also established. These arrangements gave the Liberal Party the ability to discuss measures which would be put before Parliament. The pact was negotiated in March 1977 and reaffirmed later that year. It was described as 'a public agreement on the terms on which the Liberals would guarantee to back the government on any confidence issue up to the end of the summer' (Butler and Kavanagh, 1980: 34). The pact was terminated in May 1978. It caused considerable unease in the Liberal Party, partly because many members felt that the government's unpopularity would damage Liberal prospects in the next general election and also because it failed to deliver any cherished Liberal policy such as proportional representation. In December 1977 a proposal to introduce this form of electoral system for the European elections was lost by 319 votes to 222. Although the pact failed to adjust the power relationship between the Labour and Liberal parties, it did provide the Liberals with access to government for the first time since 1945.

By-elections

Thirty by-elections took place in the life of the October 1974–79 Parliament. The Conservatives held all 10 of the seats they defended. Labour held 13, lost six to the Conservatives and one to the Liberals. The Liberal victory at Edge Hill occurred the day after the government was defeated on the Conservatives' motion of no confidence.

Conduct of the Election

The election was held against the background of the collapse of Labour's pay policy and widespread industrial unrest which was dubbed 'the winter of discontent'. Phase IV of Labour's pay policy (in 1978) sought to impose a limit of 5 per cent on pay increases but the agreement of the TUC could not be secured and the 1978 Labour Conference also rejected this policy. In December 1978, a strike at the Ford Motor Company was settled on terms far exceeding the government's pay norm, and its impotence to enforce its policy was further evidenced when the House of Commons rejected the imposition of sanctions on firms which broke the guidelines.

Industrial unrest spread to the public sector in 1979, culminating with a strike of around one million local government workers on 22 January. Industrial unrest on this scale inconvenienced the public and suggested the hollowness of the government's claim that only it could work with the trade unions. It also served to popularise Margaret Thatcher's proposals to regulate the unions by legislation.

The Conservative lead in the polls increased during January and February, and they entered the contest with the largest lead ever reported for a party by any opinion poll at this stage of an election (Butler and Kavanagh, 1980: 141). However, this lead ebbed away as the campaign progressed and on election eve, one poll, NOP, had Labour very marginally in the lead.

Conservatives

The advertising agency Saatchi and Saatchi was used to project the Conservative campaign. The Party's proposals were contained in *The Conservative Manifesto*. It harped back to some of the ideas which had been put forward in 1970, and a prime aim was to restore the balance in society which was asserted to have been tilted too much in favour of the state at the expense of the individual. Accordingly, the proposals contained in the manifesto were less interventionist than Labour's whose campaign defended the role of active central government. The Conservatives proposed to control inflation by exerting strict control over the money supply and by reducing the government's borrowing requirement and the state's share of national income. Spending cuts were proposed in most areas, a key exception being law and order where the Party promised to implement the full recommendations of the Edmund-Davies Committee on police pay. Reduced spending would pave the way for tax cuts, the reduction of which at all levels being a key aspect of the Party's campaign. Reforms to the operations of trade unions were put forward. It was proposed to place limitations on secondary picketing, to compensate workers who lost their jobs due to closed shop agreements and to provide public money for postal ballots. The Party announced its intention to repeal the 1976 Education Act which required local authorities to reorganise their secondary education on comprehensive lines, to provide for the sale of council houses, and to introduce a new Nationality Act to determine who had the right to settle in Great Britain. During the campaign, Thatcher emphasised the need for change and presented herself as a conviction politician. Considerable attention was drawn to the level of industrial strife experienced during the 'winter of discontent' and the government's inability to offer any effective solution to the problems it posed to the nation. The manifesto laid the groundwork for sacrifices required in the national interest.

Labour

Labour's policies were put forward in its manifesto, *The Labour Way is a Better Way*, which Callaghan depicted as proposals designed to strengthen national unity. The manifesto emphasised the achievements of the government since 1974 in controlling inflation, improving living standards and boosting welfare benefits and stated a key aim of reducing inflation to 5 per cent by 1982. This would be achieved by giving the Prices Commission greater powers to investigate and reduce prices, through discussions with both sides of industry designed to produce agreement on economic policy and through radical reform of the Common Market's Common Agricultural Policy. Labour promised to boost employment by an industrial and investment strategy designed to achieve a 3 per cent rate of growth, to give greater powers to the National Enterprise Board to make agreements with major firms, to increase old age pensions and welfare benefits, to introduce a wealth tax on those possessing in excess of £150,000, to initiate a substantial house-building programme, to extend industrial democracy and to embark upon talks to improve the devolution proposals put forward in the Scotland Act. Much attention was devoted in the Labour campaign to attacking Conservative proposals (Butler and Kavanagh, 1980: 87), a feature which was accentuated as the campaign progressed. Particular criticism was directed at the generality of Conservative proposals (such as the precise amount they intended to prune from public spending) and the perceived consequences of Conservative economic policies which, it was stated, would result in unemployment increasing to 1.2 million. The Conservative suggestion of legislation to regulate the trade unions was responded to by the announcement of a new Concordat which was designed to avoid the problems faced in the winter of 1978–79: Labour argued that the Conservative approach would worsen matters and lead to an enhanced level of confrontation and industrial unrest. Their main appeal was directed at those voters who did not wish for the radical change identified with Conservative proposals.

Liberals

The Liberal Party entered the election with a low standing in the opinion polls but a degree of optimism prompted by their victory at the Liverpool Edge Hill by-election in March 1979. This saw the return of David Alton with a 32 per cent swing to the Party, the largest recorded in any post-war by-election. The Party's manifesto was entitled *The Real Fight is for Britain* and considerable emphasis was placed on political and electoral reform, which was depicted as the mechanism for securing a cooperative style of politics and for achieving other social and economic changes. The Party's taxation proposals included a switch from direct to indirect taxes, the introduction of a tax credit scheme to replace the array of means tests, personal allowances and welfare benefits, and the introduction of a wealth tax. Profit-sharing and employee share ownership would be encouraged. It was suggested that a prices and incomes policy would become compulsory and that there should be no further nationalisation or de-nationalisation. The Party depicted a Liberal vote as an insurance against the follies which either of the two major parties might embark upon if unchecked by the Liberal Party and aimed to secure the election of around 20 MPs in a House of Commons in which neither major party possessed an overall majority – a situation which David Steel referred to as a 'People's Parliament'. One mechanism to achieve this modest increase in Liberal parliamentary representation was the overt advocacy of tactical voting. A key difficulty facing the Party was that although there was a mood in the country for change, it was coupled with the desire for a clear result (Butler and Kavanagh, 1980: 322).

Result of the Election

A new record total of 2,576 candidates contested the election. This number was boosted by third party candidates (including 303 National Front, 60 Workers' Revolutionary Party and 53 Ecology candidates) whose numbers were influenced by the decision to grant a televised party political broadcast to any party fielding above 50 candidates. The result was:

Party	Votes	Vote %	MPs
Conservative	13,697,923	43.9%	339
Labour	11,532,218	36.9%	269
Liberal	4,313,804	13.8%	11
Unionist Parties (Ulster)	410,419	1.4% [51.0%]	10
Scottish National Party	504,259	1.6% [17.3%]	2
Plaid Cymru	132,544	0.4% [8.1%]	2
Social Democratic and Labour Party	126,325	0.4% [18.2%]	1
Others	503,870	1.6%	1
Total	31,221,362		635

The turnout was 76.0 per cent. The swing from Labour to the Conservatives was 5.3 per cent.
The 'other' was Frank McGuire elected as an Independent Republican for Fermanagh and South Tyrone. Nineteen women MPs were elected.

The Parties

Conservative policies concerning taxes and law and order exerted an important influence on those who voted for them (Butler and Kavanagh, 1980: 334). However, the Party's claim to have secured a mandate to carry out its policies was tempered by its securing the smallest share of the national vote obtained by any Prime Minister in possession of a secure parliamentary majority since Bonar Law in 1922. Additionally, it was argued that factors such as industrial unrest during the 'winter of discontent' and the government's overall record since October 1974 in dealing with inflation and unemployment meant that Labour lost the election rather than the Conservatives won it (Butler and Kavanagh, 1980: 340). Seventeen of Labour's MPs were sponsored by the Cooperative Party and 133 by trade unions.

The national swing was subject to considerable regional variation. Although a North–South divide had been apparent in general elections since the 1950s, this was far more pronounced in 1979: if a line was drawn on the map of England just south of the Humber to the Mersey, the swing to the Conservatives south of this line was 7.7 per cent whereas to the north it was 4.2% per cent. Factors affecting voting behaviour which had occurred since 1970 (most notably class and partisan dealignment) had a significant impact on Labour fortunes in 1979 when the Party polled only 45 per cent of voters in the C2, D and E categories (Butler and Kavanagh, 1980: 8). A leading Labour figure who lost her seat was Shirley Williams in Hertford and Stevenage.

The Liberal Party's poor showing in the opinion polls was redressed as the campaign progressed, and the Party managed to retain the bulk of its parliamentary strength. However, three senior members were defeated, Thorpe (whose trial had been delayed in order to allow him to contest his North Devon seat), John Pardoe and Emlyn Hooson. The Liberal vote fell by 5.1 per cent in the seats contested by the Party in both the October 1974 and 1979 elections.

Scotland, Wales and Northern Ireland

Labour won 44 of the 71 seats in Scotland, the Conservative Party won 22 and the Liberals three. The key feature of the election in Scotland was the decline of the SNP, which lost nine of its 11 MPs and whose vote fell to 17.3 per cent of the total Scottish vote. A notable Conservative defeat occurred in Glasgow Cathcart where the Party's Scottish spokesman, Teddy Taylor, lost to Labour.

Although Labour retained its dominance in Welsh politics (winning 22 of the 36 seats), the Conservatives secured their best performance in the country since 1874, winning 11 seats, including gains at Montgomeryshire (from the Liberals) and Anglesey (from Labour). Plaid Cymru's share of the vote declined from 10.8 per cent in October 1874 to 8.1 per cent and the Party's leader, Gwynfor Evans, was defeated at Carmarthen, which meant that it returned two MPs to Westminster.

The politics of Northern Ireland made a dramatic impact on the early stages of the election campaign when the republican group, the Irish National Liberal Army, assassinated Airey Neave (who was then the Conservative spokesman on Northern Ireland) outside the House of Commons on 30 March 1979. The break-up of the United Ulster Unionist Coalition resulted in Loyalist parties fighting each other. The Ulster Unionists won five of the 12 seats, Ian Paisley's Democratic Unionist Party won three seats (two of which were gained in Belfast from the Official Unionists), and two further seats were won by Loyalist candidates. The SDLP won one seat and Frank Maguire won the remaining seat.

Consequence of the Election

A Conservative government was formed. Margaret Thatcher became Prime Minister, the first woman to hold this office.

9 June 1983

Party Leaders
Margaret Thatcher (Conservative)
Michael Foot (Labour)
David Steel (Liberal)
Roy Jenkins (Social Democratic)

Background to the Election
Timing of the Election
The incumbent Prime Minister, Margaret Thatcher, called a general election in the belief that her party would win a contest held relatively soon after the successful military operation to liberate the Falkland Islands from Argentinian occupation in 1982. Although opinions polls suggested that support for the government and Thatcher's leadership ebbed following the 1979 general election, Conservative fortunes had substantially improved by 1983 as the result of factors which included Michael Foot's unpopularity as Labour leader, success in curbing inflation, the popularity of the sale of council houses and the Falklands War. By May 1982 the government's support rose to 50 per cent popular approval and the Party henceforth maintained a lead of around 10 per cent in the opinion polls.

Elecoral Procedures and Practices
The main enactment affecting elections was the 1981 Representation of the People's Act. This prevented the nomination of felons and was designed to prevent any repetition of the action undertaken by Bobby Sands in 1981 who had stood for Parliament (and was elected for Fermanagh and South Tyrone) whilst in prison and on hunger strike. The measure also added time to the period between the close of nominations and the poll in order to enable the authorities to ensure that a candidate was not ineligible under this provision. The 1983 election used new parliamentary constituencies drawn up by the boundary commissions. It was estimated that the new arrangements were to the advantage of the Conservative Party to the extent of providing them with a 30-seat majority over Labour (Butler and Kavanagh, 1984: 27–8). The implementation of these recommendations was delayed until March 1983 as the result of an unsuccessful legal challenge which was mounted by the Labour Party.

Conservatives
Margaret Thatcher entered office pledging to abandon post-war collectivist and social democratic policies. Her approach was inspired by Friedrich Hayek and Milton Friedman and embraced two broad themes termed 'neoliberalism' and 'neoconservatism'. The former involved economic liberalism or 'rolling back the frontiers of the state'. This emphasised the importance of smaller government, private enterprise, the free market and individual responsibility. Neoconservatism entailed social authoritarianism, which argued that social malaise (evidenced by crime, disorder, hooliganism, indiscipline among young people, and moral decay) was

caused by the decline of 'traditional' values which were replaced by liberal and permissive attitudes and multicultural values. It demanded a return to traditional forms of authority such as the family.

Her key initial objective was to reverse Britain's economic decline which was to be achieved by policies which included monetarism (which entailed limiting the growth in the money supply in order to reduce wage settlements), cutting public expenditure (especially by pruning the civil service), reducing taxation and decreasing government intervention in industry (through policies which included privatisation and the selling of state enterprises to the public sector).

Initially, however, Conservative economic policies did not operate in the manner which had been intended. Monetarism proved hard to implement, and public spending rose as a proportion of the Gross National Product, especially because the heightened level of unemployment (which reached the symbolic figure of three million in January 1982) placed extra demands on the social security budget. Although tax cuts were introduced in the 1982 budget, most workers were paying more in taxation and National Insurance contributions in 1983 than had been the case in 1979, and inflation (which had stood at 10 per cent in May 1979) rose to 22 per cent in May 1980 as the result of factors which included the world recession and the rise in the price of oil. British manufacturing industry particularly suffered after 1979: industrial output fell by 11 per cent between 1979 and 1983 and exporters were adversely affected by high exchange rates. By 1983 Britain had become a net importer of manufactured goods for the first time since the industrial revolution (Butler and Kavanagh, 1984: 99). Trade union reform was pursued through the 1980 and 1982 Employment Acts, which narrowed the definition of a trade dispute to an action between an employer and his or her direct workforce. The 1980 Act made pickets liable to a range of civil actions if they attended any workplace other than their own to further industrial action, and the 1982 Act made the picketers' union responsible if it authorised action of this nature. Both measures also contained provisions which were designed to weaken the closed shop.

Opposition to Conservative policies was voiced through extra-parliamentary mechanisms which included the riots which were experienced in a number of urban areas in 1981 and industrial unrest (although this failed to develop into disputes on the scale experienced in 1978–79 since trade union militancy was tempered by the economic downturn). Lack of success was also evident in other policy areas. The death of 10 hunger strikers in Northern Ireland in 1981 (including Bobby Sands MP in May of that year) exacerbated existing tensions and helped to ensure that a political solution to the 'Troubles' (which was envisaged in the creation of a Northern Ireland Assembly in 1982) failed to materialise.

There were, however, some positive signs as the election approached. In the area of foreign affairs, a political settlement was finally reached in Rhodesia when that country received its independence (as Zimbabwe) in 1980. Also in that year a revision of the UK's contribution to the EEC budget was successfully negotiated. In the field of domestic policy, the transfer of resources from the public to the private sector which was provided for through the sale of council houses in the 1980 Housing Act proved a popular policy which further served to accentuate earlier trends of fragmenting the working class to the disadvantage of the Labour Party. By 1983 inflation had fallen to 5 per cent (its lowest level in 10 years) and in May had further fallen to 4 per cent, the lowest figure since 1968. These changes (which might be interpreted to suggest that Conservative economic policies were showing signs of working) were already occurring when the government secured a further boost to its fortunes. In April 1982 the Argentinians invaded the Falklands Islands. Despite recriminations as to who was responsible for encouraging that country to believe it could get away with a unilateral action of this nature, the government's response was uncompromising. A large task force was hastily despatched which succeeded in restoring British sovereignty on June 14. The government's actions in connection with the Falkland Islands served to rally public opinion behind it and in particular evidenced the resolute and uncompromising character of the Prime Minister whose dominance over the government was enhanced by her actions. The war also served to marginalise other news items which were detrimental to the government (including the progress of the Liberal–SDP Alliance).

Labour

The election defeat in 1979 intensified attempts by the left to dominate the affairs of the Labour party. They perceived that the actions undertaken by Labour governments between 1964 and 1970 and 1974 and 1979 had not made Britain a more socialist country. Particular criticism was directed at the actions of the Wilson/Callaghan governments in the 1970s for selectively abandoning the Party's election manifesto promises. Very little of the Alternative Economic Strategy had been implemented, the government had persisted with an incomes policy to which many of the left were opposed, the compact with the trade unions was perceived to have been needlessly thrown away and monetarist policies been pursued. Left-wing opinion concluded that the 1974–79 Labour government 'abandoned full employment, cut public services, and attacked the standards of living for working people. It refused to implement Labour's industrial policies, and carried through a foreign policy subservient to the USA and the EEC' (Labour Coordinating Committee, 1982: 6–7). The left were particuarly critical of the contents of the 1979 election manifesto, which had been formulated without any form of popular consultation. After 1979, the left sought to utilise the new balance of power within the Party to transform it in their own image by a series of constitutional reforms directed at its leadership, organisation and the policy-making processes which were advanced under the guise of enhancing internal democracy. These were designed to ensure that the Labour movement would exert a far greater degree of control over the actions of a future Labour government than had been the case under Wilson and Callaghan.

The 1979 Labour Conference accepted the mandatory reselection of Labour MPs, and endorsed the principle of ending the dominance exerted over the election manifesto by the party leader. Concrete proposals for achieving this objective would be debated in 1980 (but were finally rejected in 1981). Perhaps the most significant innovation was the removal of the exclusive power of Labour MPs to choose the leader and deputy leader. The introduction of an electoral college was debated at the Party Conferences in 1979 (when it was rejected) and 1980 (when it was approved in principle). A special Conference was subsequently held at Wembley in January 1981 to determine the mechanics of the new system. Henceforth the Labour leader would be elected by a process in which unions were allocated 40 per cent of the vote, while the MPs and constituency Labour parties each received 30 per cent. Callaghan's resignation in 1980 (before the Wembley Conference) meant that the new leader, Michael Foot, was elected under the old system involving MPs alone. He defeated Denis Healey by 139 : 129 votes. The college was first used in the election for Labour's deputy leader in 1981, when Denis Healey defeated Tony Benn by the margin of 0.8 per cent of the electoral college vote.

The strength of the left was also demonstrated at the 1979 Conference by policy resolutions which pledged the Party to reconsider the position of Britain's membership of the European Community, and which promised to take over without compensation all state assets subject to the government's privatisation policies. The 1980 Party Conference voted to withdraw Britain from the EEC, to initiate unilateral nuclear disarmament, to extend the programme of public ownership and to abolish the House of Lords. In 1981, party resolutions expressed support for unilateral nuclear disarmament, unconditional and immediate withdrawal from the EEC, a 35-hour week with no loss of earnings, total rejection of an incomes policy and measures to extend nationalisation to create 'a fully socialised economy'. In 1982 the Party Conference endorsed unilateralism by a two-thirds majority.

Increasingly, the right of the Party perceived itself to be a beleaguered minority in a party in which it had traditionally exercised a dominant position. Its ability to counter the campaign of the left suffered in particular from ideological weakness from which an attack on the left and the Alternative Economic Strategy could be based. A particular problem faced by revisionism was the absence of any strategy to secure economic growth. Events which preceded the 1970 general election indicated the fallibility of an ideology which assumed growth as an economic fact of life, and by the mid-1970s stagnation, industrial unrest and a sterling crisis further served to undermine the circumstances on which revisionism was reliant. The sterling crisis resulted in Britain seeking aid from the International Monetary Fund in 1976 and provided final and conclusive evidence of the impossibility of guaranteeing sustained economic growth which would enable an egalitarian distribution of the surplus thus produced to be spent on social welfare programmes. The main energies of the social democrats were expended on reaction and negativity, seeking to resist the policies put forward by the left. This defensive posture was especially marked in relation to the EEC. To revisionists, Europe became the means through which Britain would be modernised economically, institutionally, culturally and socially (Desai, 1994: 20). However, their advocacy of this approach resulted in their embarking up a collision course with the Party.

The Formation of the Social Democratic Party (SDP)

Following the 1979 election defeat, the Parliamentary Labour Party and Shadow Cabinet remained dominated by the left and the position of the right became increasingly marginalised.

For many social democrats, events came to a head between 1980 and 1981. The decisions of the 1980 Party Conference were regarded as the total rout of the right. It prompted the 'Gang of Three' (David Owen, Shirley Williams and Bill Rodgers) to write an open letter to members of the Labour Party in the *Guardian* and *Daily Mirror* on 1 August 1980 which expressed their opposition to the developments which had taken place. This letter attacked the doctrine of class war, condemned the creation of large public monopolies through nationalisation, rejected the emphasis placed by the Alternative Economic Strategy on import controls, and opposed the view that Labour lost votes because it had not been left wing enough. Instead the signatories espressed support for parliamentary democracy, the mixed economy, continued membership of the EEC and NATO, multilateral disarmament and an incomes policy to counter inflation.

The events at the 1980 Party Conference questioned the feasibility of the right remaining in the Labour Party. A number of subsequent developments further undermined the case for their remaining there. In October 1980 Callaghan resigned as leader. The leadership contest took place under the existing rules which ought to have favoured Denis Healey. However, Healey fought a poor campaign. He perceived that the right of the PLP would have no choice but to vote for him and thus failed to court their support. This eventually resulted in Michael Foot becoming party leader and hastened the decision of some social democrats to leave the Labour Party. Foot actively supported many of the policies which social democrats found abhorrent, and it was concluded that 'no single event did more to persuade right-wing MPs to quit the party than Foot's election' (Crewe and King, 1995: 30). The policies put forward by the Labour Party coupled with a perception that the right could not again dominate Labour Party proceedings were the chief causes of the defection of Labour MPs to the SDP. There were, however, other factors which suggested that a social democratic party divorced from Labour might possess considerable political appeal.

The swing of the Conservatives to the right of the political spectrum and Labour's lurch to the left during the course of the 1970s and early 1980s created space on the centre-left which a new political party might exploit to its advantage: 'the political seas had parted as if by magic, leaving the centre ground of British politics free for the first time in recent history' (Zentner, 1982: 35). A party of this nature might be expected to appeal to those voters associated with the Tory 'wets' and Labour social democrats. The formation of the SDP was further influenced by key changes affecting political behaviour after 1970. The first of these concerned the weakened popular appeal of both major political parties, particularly the Labour Party caused by partisan and class dealignment. This meant that a newly formed third party such as the SDP could secure a considerable degree of political support rather than being consigned to political oblivion.

The second of these was leadership which initially focused on the re-entry of Roy Jenkins into British political life. Jenkins became Britain's first President of the European Commission in 1977 and his term of office expired on 31 December 1980. Before he departed from Brussels he gave the Dimbleby lecture on BBC television in November 1979. His support for the Atlantic Alliance, Britain's position in Europe and Keynesian economic policies were at odds with contemporary developments in the Labour Party. He used this occasion as a platform to condemn the existing party system (which he claimed was responsible for Britain's economic decline), and to put forward arguments in favour of the strengthening of what he then termed the 'radical centre'. These were based upon the policies of radical social and constitutional reform, including support for proportional representation and the possibility of coalition government which, he claimed, worked well abroad. He endorsed a political approach in which state intervention and market forces played complementary roles. The media also played a significant role in the development of the Social Democratic Party. The intense treatment which it gave to divisions within the Labour Party after its 1979 election defeat (and especially to the rise of the left) encouraged leading social democrats to desert their party. A more balanced treatment might have put these divisions into perspective and persuaded the right to stay within the Party and fight the left.

The event which triggered the formation of the SDP came with the adoption by the Wembley Conference of the electoral college in 1981, according to a formula which gave the trade unions a dominant role in future election contests for the Labour leadership. Owen and other social democrats had two concerns about this innovation. The first was that the acceptance of it evidenced a perception that even bodies dominated by the Party's right wing were unwilling to stand up against the left. They also had a practical objection, being concerned about the undemocratic nature of the union block vote in Labour's leadership contests. They accepted that the election should be extended beyond the Parliamentary Party, but insisted on the principle of 'one member, one vote'. This event was sufficient to promote agreement between the four leading social democrats (Jenkins, Owen, Williams and Rodgers) which resulted in their establishing the Council for Social Democracy. Its formation was accompanied by the 'Limehouse Declaration' which referred to social democratic political objectives. These included the reversal of Britain's economic decline, the establishment of an open, classless and more equal society, and the need for Britain to be outward-looking rather than isolationist, xenophobic or neutralist. Its policies included the elimination of poverty and promotion of greater equality without stifling enterprise or imposing bureaucracy from the centre. The decentralisation of decision-making in industry and government was also advocated. The declaration asserted that the aim of the Council for Social Democracy was to rally all those committed to the values, principles and policies of social democracy, whether Labour Party members or not. Specific support was expressed for the principle of political realignment. The ideas embodied in the Limehouse Declaration were expanded upon in the writings of leading SDP members, especially Owen's *Face the Future* and Williams's *Politics is For People* (both published in 1981).

The formation of the Council for Social Democracy entailed a commitment to form a new party. This, the Social Democratic Party, was launched in March 1981. It was conceived not as a centre party but one on the left of the political spectrum, founded on the principle of one member, one vote. By the end of that year it had the support of 26 Labour MPs (and one Conservative), 18 peers, and 31 former Labour MPs. Its membership totalled 65,000 (Crewe and King, 1995: 45). Two more Labour MPs subsequently joined in 1982. The SDP depicted itself as a classless party, in the sense of a party that did not seek identity with the traditional classes whose support underpinned the Labour and Conservative parties. However, it has been observed that the membership of the SDP, and the support which it obtained, was overwhelmingly derived from the middle class. A key element of this support was derived from a particular social grouping, namely the 'well-educated, public service salariat' (Crewe and King, 1995: 64). In the period between the launch of the Party and the ratification of its constitution in June 1982, the affairs of the Party were conducted by a Steering Committee whose role included the handling of relations with the Liberal Party.

Liberal-SDP Alliance
The Liberal leader, David Steel, actively sought to secure the cooperation of both parties following the formation of the SDP in 1981. He believed that this would be necessary for a number of reasons. These included political expediency, since it made no sense for two parties seeking to occupy the centre-left of the British political spectrum to fight against each other. Even those in the SDP (such as David Owen) who held sceptical views of the Liberal Party

accepted the need for an electoral pact. A working arrangement between the two parties could further be justified by the political benefits which it was assumed would arise. It was believed that a party which emerged from Labour would be able to attract working-class support and succeed in urban and industrial areas where the Liberal Party's appeal had been generally weak after 1945. Two parties polling different electorates but working together would produce a strong challenge to the two major parties. Agreement between the two parties was given practical substance in the 1981 'Konigswinter Compact' which stemmed from a meeting of leading Liberals and members of the SDP at the Anglo-German Society's annual Konigswinter Conference in 1981. This committed both parties to broad agreement on principles, seat-sharing rather than fighting each other, and Joint Policy Commissions on major issues.

The performance of Roy Jenkins at the Warrington by-election in 1981 (which according to a BBC computer prediction would give the Alliance about 500 seats in a general election) transformed Jenkins into the dominant figure in the SDP. He had urged an alliance with the Liberal Party soon after the establishment of the SDP. He subsequently won the Glasgow Hillhead by-election in 1982 and became leader of the Party in that year. This ensured that a close alliance with the Liberals would be at the forefront of SDP tactics for the immediate future.

What was termed 'the Alliance' involved joint planning and activity in a number of areas. These entailed coordination at parliamentary level and the publication of a joint policy document in 1981 (*A Fresh Start for Britain – A Statement of Principles*) which set out some basic points on which both parties were agreed. This recognised that both parties stemmed from different political traditions and had different identities, but put forward areas of agreement on a number of policy areas concerned with Britain's economic and political future. These included electoral reform, an agreed strategy for incomes based upon a spirit of cooperation in industry, fairer distribution of the world's resources, multilateral disarmament, continued membership of NATO and the EEC, and economic recovery which involved the provision of more jobs, stable prices and a greater emphasis on conservation and ecology. Subsequently, commissions on major areas of policy were set up to prepare joint proposals. Initially these covered the Constitution, Employment and Industrial Recovery. The 1981 policy document further committed the parties to exploring ways which would make the electoral alliance effective.

The prime purpose of any form of arrangement between the two parties was to provide a single Alliance candidate for each parliamentary constituency. Initially the issue of by-elections was covered by a form of 'gentleman's agreement' whereby each would take it in turns to fight such contests. A more significant problem, however, rested with the allocation of parliamentary seats for the next general election. This constituted the heart of an arrangement between the two parties but was potentially the most difficult area over which to secure agreement. A Joint Negotiating Group (which consisted of six-strong Joint Negotiating Teams from each of the two parties) was set up in 1981 to manage (either by leading or observing) the process of the allocation of seats between the two parties at the next election. Guidelines governing the negotiations over seat allocation were published in October 1981. By 1 April 1982, agreement on a single Alliance candidate had been reached in around 500 seats. Latterly a system of arbitration was introduced when local agreement could not be secured. These procedures were ultimately able to produce a single Alliance candidate in all but three constituencies at the 1983 general election with both parties fielding more or less a similar number of candidates (Liberal 325 and SDP 311).

The Alliance experienced chequered fortunes between 1981 and the 1983 general election. Momentum was provided by by-election victories at Croydon North West, Crosby, Glasgow-Hillhead and Bermondsey, but other factors suggested that the Party was failing to live up to its earlier lofty expectations. Events which included the improvement of the economy (evidenced by the slowing down of the rise in unemployment and inflation) and the euphoria surrounding the successful liberation of the Falkland Islands by a British task force served to reduce the impact of the Alliance on the electorate. Additionally, internal wranglings in the Labour Party were reduced after Healey's victory in the election for deputy leader in 1981 and the right of the Party began to claw back some of the ground lost to the left, regaining control of the NEC in 1982, which subsequently initiated disciplinary action against the Militant Tendency. Other factors which included the failure of the media to concentrate attention on the Party (as it had done in its initial days) and Jenkins's style of leadership (particularly the problems he faced in the House of Commons) impeded the political fortunes of the Alliance. These difficulties resulted in an official relaunch of the Alliance in January 1983 in an attempt to regain momentum in time for the general election.

Conduct of the Election

The strength of the Conservative Party in the polls (which at the commencement of the campaign indicated a Conservative lead of between 12 and 18 per cent) meant that the outcome of the contest was certain at the outset. The main issue of genuine interest was whether the Liberal–SDP Alliance would claim second place at Labour's expense. Considerable acrimony between the Labour and Conservative parties occurred when some Labour politicians referred to the Falklands War as an episode which the Conservatives sought to exploit for their own political advantage. This included the infamous remark by Neil Kinnock (when responding to a heckler that Mrs Thatcher had guts) that 'it's a pity that people had to leave theirs on Goose Green in order to prove it'.

Conservatives

The Conservative Party's case to the electorate was presented in its statement, *The Conservative Manifesto 1983*. This defended the achievements of the Party since 1979 which were projected as the basis on which subsequent policies would be based. The further reduction of inflation was cited as the government's top priority, and a continuation of current economic policies was proposed including firm control of public spending and borrowing, the money supply and public sector pay. Lower rates of income tax were proposed and the denationalisation of state industries which included British Telecom and British Steel was advocated. Trade union reform would be accomplished through reforms which would give union members the right to elect their leaders in secret ballots, the removal of the legal immunities of unions to call strikes where there had been no prior approval in a secret ballot, and the TUC was to be invited to discuss ways in which members might decide if they wanted to pay the political levy. A future Conservative government would scrap the Greater London Council and take action to halt excessive rate rises by local authorities. The advertising agency Saatchi and Saatchi was again used to project the Party's case. Prominent attention was paid to the perceived failings of the Labour Party, especially the inability of any previous Labour government to reduce the number of unemployed.

Thatcher viewed the election as an opportunity to vanquish Marxist socialism. Much of the Conservative emphasis was of a negative nature, attacking the Labour manifesto as an extreme document (one Conservative leaflet highlighting the similarities between the Labour and Communist Party manifestos on 11 key policy areas) which would prove costly to implement (an assertion also made by the Liberal–SDP Alliance). Electors were warned that, by voting Labour, they were making 14 major commitments (which included abandoning their right to choose a school for their child and agreeing to place the police service under political control). The contradictions in Labour policies (most notably on defence) were also alluded to, particularly when differences of opinion in that party became apparent during the contest.

The Conservative campaign gave particular prominence to Thatcher and her qualities of leadership. Her main blemish during the campaign was scarcely concealed anger when a member of the public, questioning her on the television programme *Nationwide*, refused to accept the Premier's explanation regarding the sinking of the Argentinian cruiser, *General Belgrano*, during the Falklands conflict. A further defect in the Conservative campaign was evidenced in a Conservative-sponsored event when the comedian Kenny Everett received ecstatic applause from an audience of around 2,000 Young Conservatives after he had called for the bombing of Russia and suggested that Michael Foot's walking stick should be booted away. This suggested support within the Party for extreme right-wing political sentiment.

The Liberal–SDP Alliance posed the Conservative Party with considerable problems, since it was feared that if it performed well they might be harmed (including by the tactical voting of Labour supporters in Conservative-held constituencies). The Conservative problem, however, was that it was difficult to discern what arguments they could adopt against it. Many Alliance supporters were primarily opposed to the policies of the two major parties and it thus made little sense to concentrate on the policies of the Alliance which were not crucial to these voters' defections.

Labour

Morale in the Party was poor in the lead-up to the general election, and in particular there was widespread disillusionment with Foot's performance as leader. There would have been considerable pressure on him to resign if the Party had lost the Darlington by-election on 24 August 1983, but the 2 per cent swing to Labour that occurred at that contest ensured that he would remain in post.

Labour policies were contained in its manifesto, *The New Hope for Britain: Labour's Manifesto 1983*. It pledged a Labour government to leave the EEC within the lifetime of the next Parliament, and to pursue a non-nuclear defence policy (although Polaris would be included in future disarmament negotiations). Divisions on the the issue as to whether Polaris should be abandoned in any case (the unilateralist view) or only sacrificed in return for Soviet concessions in disarmament talks (the multilateralist position) were subsequently voiced during the election campaign. Labour economic policy would be founded on the National Economic Assessment which proposed that the two sides of industry and government would determine national economic priorities, including pay. A large rise in public spending was proposed and a new prices commission would be established with powers to order freezes and cuts. Labour was pledged to return assets which the Conservatives had privatised to public ownership, and the reduction of unemployment to one million within the next five years was advocated. Labour promised an immediate 50 per cent rise in local authority housing expenditure, a one-year freeze on council house rents, an end to compulsory council house sales and the right of local authorities to repurchase those that had been sold. The abolition of the House of Lords was also proposed. The manifesto was criticised for containing repetitions and lacking coherence and was dubbed by Peter Shore as 'the longest suicide note in history'.

The negative nature of much Conservative electioneering was also apparent in Labour's campaign. Attacks were made on the Conservative government's alleged 'broken promises' in areas which included the level of employment, the economy and taxation. All of the Party's party political broadcasts concentrated on the need to reduce unemployment and to save the social services from further Conservative attacks. Scare tactics sought to direct the electorate to the Conservatives' alleged 'undeclared intentions' of creating higher employment, abolishing employment protection measures and dismantling the welfare state, in particular the National Health Service. One Labour election leaflet depicted children in derelict schools and the unemployed being swept down a drain.

Labour's campaign was a poor one which failed to overcome popular reservations concerning the credibility of Labour promises and the wisdom of key aspects of policy, particularly defence. Labour's case was not helped by the negative stance of the press towards the Party in general (even the *Daily Mirror* expressing reservations about some aspects of Labour's manifesto) and towards Michael Foot in particular. He was depicted by Lord Hailsham as 'Worzel Gummidge' and the *Sun* newspaper posed the question 'do you really want this old man to run Britain?'

Liberal–SDP Alliance

A limited degree of integration of the two parties took place as the 1983 general election approached. The professional organisations of the parties were brought into a closer working relationship and a Joint Liberal-SDP Campaign Committee was set up when the election was called. A joint Alliance election manifesto, *Working Together for Britain: Programme For Government*, was produced for the campaign which offered the nation a new style of politics. This pledged to reduce unemployment by one million over two years without increasing inflation to be achieved by means of greater government borrowing, more public investment and new programmes of housing and environmental improvement. The manifesto proposed to halt the processes of nationalisation and privatisation, to implement reforms to enhance democracy in trade unions and industry (which involved secret ballots for the election of national executives and before strike action could be taken). An Alliance government would introduce a fair and effective prices and incomes policy by concluding agreements on annual pay rises with both sides of industry. An Assessment Board would deal with public sector pay disputes and a Pay and Prices Commission would be empowered to refuse price increases to companies which broke the guidelines and the Inland Revenue would enforce a counter-inflation penalty on companies which paid above the agreed range. The welfare state would be restructured by measures which included the integration of tax and welfare benefits. Measures directed at tackling poverty and extending education and training were also proposed.

The manifesto devoted considerable attention to constitutional changes. These included the incorporation of the European Convention of Human Rights into British law, a quasi-autonomous Parliament for Scotland with powers to tax, and devolution for Wales and the English regions if there was demonstrable support for such developments. The introduction of proportional representation was put forward as the 'lynchpin of our entire programme of radical reform' and was viewed as indispensable to the aim of the Alliance to cure the divisions in British society and to restore a sense of community in place of the politics of confrontation and polarisation.

The 1983 general election posed the Alliance with a number of dilemmas. The first concerned leadership. It was agreed that the two parties would retain their separate leaders but that the Alliance campaign would promote the position of a 'prime minister designate'. Steel believed that Jenkins, a former Home Secretary and Chancellor of the Exchequer, should occupy this role with himself as Alliance campaign leader. Thus Jenkins would effectively be the Alliance leader, who would become prime minister in the event of an Alliance election victory. The failure of the Alliance to 'take off', with continued evidence that Steel was more popular than Jenkins with the electorate, perceptions that Jenkins's performance (especially on television) had been poor, and that the electorate were confused with the concept of dual leadership resulted in a meeting of the Alliance Joint Campaign Committee at Steel's home at Ettrickbridge on 29 May. It has been alleged that a determined attempt was made at this meeting by the Liberals (headed by John Pardoe and Steel) to oust Jenkins as prime minister designate and replace him with the Liberal leader (Crewe and King, 1995: 17). The refusal by the SDP contingent to contemplate such a radical change during the campaign prevented this from occurring, but it was agreed that henceforth Steel would play a more prominent part in the Alliance campaign. The disunity between the Liberals and SDP at this meeting was not made public at the time and the increase in the standing of the Alliance in the polls (coupled with Labour's decline) defused the issue.

The second dilemma which faced the Alliance was its electoral objectives. Since the debacle of 1950 the Liberal Party had shied away from overtly suggesting it could form a government as the result of its involvement in one specific general election contest. However, the initial successes of the Alliance, and the level of public support evidenced in the polls, gave some political credibility to the objective of the formation of an Alliance government. This was broadly adhered to throughout the campaign although some of its leading members (particularly Owen) openly discussed the balance of power as an electoral objective. The Alliance did not, however, officially endorse this latter aim although the parties' reaction to this situation was considered in the event of it occurring. The desire to maintain equidistance from the two major parties was evident in their insistence that they were willing to work with either major party in the event of a hung Parliament, and would seek to bend their policies in the direction favoured by the Alliance. This would entail Labour having to adjust its public spending policies, abandon unilateral nuclear disarmament and agree to remain in Europe, while the Conservative Party would be required to bring down unemployment and initiate measures to procure the expansion of the economy.

The third dilemma concerned the image which the Alliance projected during the campaign. It emphasised the extremism of Thatcher's Conservative Party and Foot's Labour Party, and projected itself as a political vehicle which would recreate a sense of national unity. This emphasis exerted on the alleged extremism of the two major parties was essentially negative campaigning, possibly more suited to by-elections when electors are more willing to indulge in protest voting. Although this negative stance was associated with the positive desire to restore social harmony, it has been argued that the sense of national solidarity created by the Falklands War undercut the image of a divided Britain which the Alliance sought to project (Crewe and King, 1995: 18) but they failed to rethink their position in the light of this development.

Result of the Election

The 1983 election evidenced a vote against change and suggested that the expectations of the electorate were being reduced in line with the slowdown of economic growth. The contest reasserted the vitality of the two-party mould in the sense that 606 seats were won by candidates from the Conservative or Labour parties.

A total of 2,577 candidates contested the election. The result was:

Party	Votes	Vote %	MPs
Conservative	13,012,316	42.4	397
Labour	8,456,934	27.6	209
Liberal	4,210,115	13.7	17
SDP	3,570,834	11.7	6
(Total Alliance	7,780,949	25.4	23)
SNP	331,975	1.1 [11.8%]	2
Plaid Cymru	125,309	0.4 [7.8%]	2
All Unionist Parties (Ulster)	435,562	1.4 [57.1%]	15
SDLP (N. Ireland)	137,012	0.5 [17.9%]	1
Sinn Fein (N. Ireland)	102,701	0.3 [13.4%]	1
Others	288,379	0.9	0
Total	**30,671,137**		**650**

The turnout was 72.7 per cent. The swing from Labour to the Conservative Party was 4.1 per cent. Twenty-three women MPs were elected.

The Parties

The national swing from Labour to the Conservative Party was subject to widespread variation which reflected the socio-geographic features of particular areas. Of particular importance to the Conservative victory was the fact that the 'new working class' consisting of manual workers who lived in Southern England were home owners, employed in the private sector and not members of trade unions. The absence of uniform swing considerably undermined the remaining vitality of the 'cube law' which governed the exaggerative qualities of the electoral system whereby votes were translated into seats (Curtice and Steed, 1984: 360–1). Longer-term trends towards Labour in Scotland, Northern England and most urban areas accentuated the North–South divide which had been apparent in 1979. In the area south of a line drawn from the Wash to the River Severn (outside of London), Labour won only four seats, but performed much better in Northern England, securing net swings from the Conservative Party to itself in Manchester, Liverpool (and also in North Birmingham).

The Labour Party's support was heavily concentrated geographically. This resulted in winning 209 seats with a very similar national vote (27.6 per cent) to that polled by the Alliance. Three Labour former Cabinet ministers lost their seats – Tony Benn, David Ennals and Albert Booth.

Eight Labour MPs were sponsored by the Cooperative Party and 114 by trade unions. The Alliance polled 25.4 per cent of the vote in 1983, the strongest showing obtained for a third party for 60 years, yet secured only 23 seats. Under a system of proportional representation it would have won around 161. The Alliance suffered from a problem that had bedevilled the Liberal Party for many years – its ability to secure support more or less evenly across the social strata failed to provide it with sufficient votes to emerge as the victor in individual constituencies.

The profile of the Alliance vote bore close similarities to the characteristics of the Liberal vote. The balance between the two parties at parliamentary level changed to the Liberal Party's advantage. They had managed to retain 12 of the 13 seats they held at the dissolution (losing only Croydon North West) and they gained a further five seats. Of the 28 MP's who had defected to the SDP and stood in 1983, only five retained their seats (the victory of Ian Wrigglesworth in South Stockton being aided by revelations that his Conservative opponent had twice stood previously for the National Front). One further SDP gain was made by Charles Kennedy in the Highlands constituency of Ross, Cromarty and Skye.

Scotland, Wales and Northern Ireland
Labour won 41 of Scotland's 72 seats, the Conservatives 21, the Liberals five, and the SDP three. The SNP won two seats, obtaining 11.8 per cent of the total Scottish vote. In Wales, Labour won 20 of the 38 seats, the Conservatives 14 and the Liberals two. Plaid Cymru won two seats, obtaining 7.8 per cent of the Welsh vote. The number of constituencies in Northern Ireland increased to 17 for the election. The Ulster Unionist Party won 11 seats, the Democratic Unionist Party won three seats, and James Kilfedder representing the Independent Ulster Popular Unionist Party won North Down. The SDLP won one seat. A notable result occurred in West Belfast where the Sinn Fein candidate, Gerry Adams, ousted the incumbent Independent MP, Gerry Fitt. Overall Sinn Fein secured 40 per cent of the Nationalist vote, their one seat placing them on a par with the Social Democratic and Labour Party.

Consequence of the Election
Margaret Thatcher formed her second Conservative administration.

11 June 1987

Party Leaders
Margaret Thatcher (Conservative)
Neil Kinnock (Labour)
David Steel (Liberal)
David Owen (Social Democratic Party)

Background to the Election
Timing of the Election
The election was called because the government perceived that political circumstances were in their favour and that the Conservatives would thus be returned to office. Although the Labour Party had been ahead in the opinion polls at the time of their 1986 Conference, the Conservative Party's 1986 Conference marked the commencement of an improvement in their fortunes. Additionally, the upsurge in Alliance support (which was evidenced in the Greenwich by-election in February 1987) seemed to have stalled. The Conservatives obtained relatively good results in the May 1987 local government elections and on the eve of the general election their lead in the polls was between 11 and 13 per cent. This vast improvement in their position compared to one year previously (which was buttressed by the 1987 budget which offered both tax cuts and increased public spending especially directed at unemployment) prompted the Prime Minister to call an election.

Electoral Procedures and Practices
The provisions of the 1985 Representation of the People Act extended the franchise to British citizens who were living overseas provided that they had left the country in the past five years. This added around 11,000 voters to the electoral register. This legislation also extended provisions regarding absent voting to cater for those on holiday on the day of polling. The deposit of £150 was raised to £500 which became returnable for any candidate who polled one-twentieth of the votes cast.

Conservatives
The large majority possessed by the Conservative Party enabled it to exert a dominant position in the House of Commons between 1983 and 1987. One consequence of this was that opposition to the government's policies were frequently articulated through extra-parliamentary mechanisms including industrial action (such as the 1984–85 Miners' dispute), inner-city disturbances (especially the urban riots in 1985), protests at Greenham Common (commencing in 1983) in opposition to the housing of American Cruise missiles, and civil disobedience by Labour-controlled local authorities in Liverpool and Lambeth which refused to implement spending cuts and instead set deficit – hence illegal – budgets in the wake of the introduction of rate-capping in the 1984 Rates Act. To these were added acts of political violence associated with the politics of Northern Ireland, the most spectacular of which on the mainland occurred on 12 October 1984

when the Provisional IRA bombed the hotel used in Brighton by a number of leading Conservatives attending that year's Party Conference.

The economic policies pursued by the Conservative Party after 1983 enjoyed a degree of success and by 1987 the economy was in good shape. Monetarism was abandoned and the economy enjoyed growth (albeit it of a slow nature). North Sea oil contributed towards a favourable balance of payments, and although manufacturing industry continued to decline, the financial services sector expanded. Share prices boomed and the level of unemployment was slowly falling: although it remained in excess of three million throughout the life of the 1983 Parliament, the issue was viewed with reduced intensity by public opinion (Butler and Kavanagh, 1988: 43). Inflation stood at 4 per cent, but as wage settlements were averaging 7.5 per cent many people were enjoying improved living standards. On 8 May, the bank rate was cut for the fourth time in two months.

The Conservative Party used its parliamentary majority to implement a number of its key manifesto policies. Privatisation was vigorously pursued, and between 1983 and 1987 around one-third of state-owned industries were sold to the public: this list included British Telecom (1984), British Aerospace (1985), the Trustee Savings Bank, British Gas (1986) and British Airways (1987). The popularity of what was termed 'popular capitalism' was evidenced by the increase in the number of private shareholders whose numbers swelled from three million in 1979 to eight million in 1987 (Butler and Kavanagh, 1988: 20). Trade union reform was proceeded with by the enactment of the 1984 Trade Union Act which required ballots to be held before the commencement of strike action and major developments took place in the field of education including the introduction of a core national curriculum in schools, the introduction of city technology colleges and the abolition of the Burnham pay machinery for teachers.

Local government reform was also pursued. This included the abolition of the Greater London Council and the Metropolitan County Councils in 1985. Some innovations (particularly affecting education and local government) evidenced enhanced central government control which seemed at variance with other aspects of Conservative policy which sought to roll back the frontiers of the state. The signing of the Anglo-Irish Agreement in 1985 in the face of intense Unionist opposition (which included all 15 Unionist MPs resigning their seats at Westminster and thus initiating by-elections to serve as a referendum on the issue) indicated a new political approach to the political affairs of Northern Ireland in which Dublin would play some role.

In the field of foreign affairs, success was also achieved by the government renegotiating Britain's contribution to the EEC budget at the 1984 Fontainebleau Summit, and in 1986 it signed the Single European Act which sought to achieve a single market by 31 December 1992. A bilateral agreement between Thatcher and President Mitterrand of France over the construction of a Channel tunnel was also signed in 1986. The Prime Minister also derived considerable prestige from her visit to Moscow in April.

There were, however, difficulties experienced after 1983. The Conservatives were accused of under-funding key public services, most notably health and education. Although the government could point to increased funding of the health service, critics argued that this failed to keep up with the increased demand made upon it, in particular from a population with increased life expectancy. Internal problems also affected the government's standing. A scandal involving an extra-marital affair prompted the departure of Cecil Parkinson from the Cabinet in 1983, and in 1985 dissension in the Cabinet over the future of the Westland Helicopter Company resulted in the resignation of Michael Heseltine as Secretary of State for Defence and subsequently Leon Brittan as Trade Secretary. Allegations by Heseltine concerning the use of improper tactics by Brittan to advance his preference that Westland should be taken over by an American company (rather than a European consortium which was Heseltine's desire) implicated Downing Street and contributed to criticism that the margin between 'strong' leadership with which Thatcher was associated and 'bossy', 'high-handed' and 'authoritarian' behaviour could, on occasions, be a narrow one to draw.

Labour

Labour's initial reaction to defeat in 1979 witnessed the rise of the left whose demand for a more full-blooded socialist policy seemed legitimised by the nature of the economic crisis which resulted in high unemployment, high inflation and negative economic growth in the early 1980s. The perception that capitalism was on the verge of collapse, coupled with the unpopularity of the Conservative government, emboldened the left to advocate a clear socialist alternative. However, it has been argued that the Party's move to the left after 1979 was more apparent than real, and the key constitutional changes with which they were associated were approved through support accorded by the trade unions whom, it was alleged, wished to make a pointed gesture to Callaghan and his government at a time when a general election was a long way off (Thorpe, 1997: 204-6). The victories with which they were associated were narrowly won and some key objectives (particularly the desire to take the drafting of the party election manifesto out of the hands of the leadership) were not achieved. The weakening hold of the left on the Party was illustrated by Denis Healey's narrow defeat of Tony Benn in the election for the deputy leader in 1981 and the defeat of five left-wing candidates in the NEC elections in the same year which ended the control exercised by the left on that body. Thus, when Neil Kinnock became leader of the Party after the 1983 election, the tide was already swimming against the left. These negative feelings were accentuated by the scale of the Party's defeat which intensified feelings against the left.

Trade union leaders prompted Michael Foot's departure as Labour leader following the 1983 election defeat, and the resultant campaign for the party leadership was the first to use the electoral college. In this Kinnock was challenged by Peter Shore and Eric Heffer. Kinnock secured 73 per cent of the trade union vote, 91 per cent of the constituency vote and 47 per cent of the Parliamentary Labour Party vote. In the deputy leadership contest, Roy Hattersley beat Michael Meacher, securing votes of 88 per cent, 51 per cent and 56 per cent respectively in the electoral college. The size of Kinnock's victory indicated he had a clear mandate to initiate reforms to the Party and lead it in a new direction. The onslaught of the Conservative government against the trade unions made their leaders receptive to a leader and a policy which was sufficiently credible to win an election. Moves were initiated against the influence which the Trotskyite Militant Tendency possessed in some constituency parties whose entryist tactics sought to radicalise the Labour Party from within and use it as a means to foment revolution. This counter-attack meant that the parliamentary route for achieving socialism was reaffirmed. In 1983, the Party Conference expelled the paper's editorial board and at the 1985 conference Kinnock delivered a stinging attack on the actions of the Militant-dominated Liverpool City Council. The following year the Liverpool District Labour Party was suspended and expulsions of individual members of Militant took place.

Additionally, attempts were made to broaden Labour's electoral appeal by making its policy and underlying ideology more 'electable'. This entailed tackling Labour's electoral crisis. In 1983 the Party's share of the working-class vote had declined to below 50 per cent and it was concluded that Labour was the party of a segment of the working class – the traditional working class of the council estates, public sector, Scotland and the North. These were described as a 'slowly dwindling group' and it was argued that Labour had lost the support of the 'new' working class comprised of private sector workers, who were home owners and lived in Southern England (Crewe, 1983). Thus, following Labour's defeat in 1983, a series of reforms was embarked upon.

Labour's need to combat the influence of the 'hard' left, concern to distance itself from the Social Democratic Party and the desire to broaden the Party's electoral appeal beyond the downtrodden and the dispossessed suggested the importance of re-examining party ideology. In 1985, Kinnock delivered a Fabian lecture on the 'Future of Socialism' in which he sought to address all three of the above concerns. He differentiated what he referred to as 'democratic socialism' from both 'democratic centralism' and 'social democracy'. He associated democratic centralism with the 'ultra left' and particularly attacked their theory of 'vanguardism'. He was particularly critical of the tactic of entryism in which self-appointed elites 'opt for a parasitical life inside the mass labour movement'. However, he was equally critical of social democracy. He believed this version of reformism was insufficiently radical since it merely sought to ameliorate social disadvantage rather than to address the broader structural issues which impeded the pursuit of equality. By contrast, the values of democratic socialism were stated to be the interdependent ones of 'liberty, equality and democracy'. It sought to eradicate the social conditions which had initially called the Labour Party into being, and in particular to attain the objective of personal security. Liberty required action to reduce disadvantage and give individuals greater control over their own destiny, equality embraced both the elimination of those institutions which protected, rewarded and perpetuated inequalities which were both unnatural and unearned, and the promotion of the principle of equality of opportunity in all policy areas. Democracy rejected the centralisation of power in the hands of unaccountable bureaucrats in favour of participation in areas as diverse as the workplace, the housing estate or within the community, thus enhancing the goal of popular involvement in activities which affected the day-to-day life of the individual (Kinnock, 1986).

Kinnock's reappraisal of Labour ideology was accompanied by changes in the direction of Labour policy. The unpopularity of nationalisation and the level of deindustrialisation by the mid-1980s justified changes to the Alternative Economic Strategy. Thus in 1986 the policy of 'social ownership' indicated a movement away from old style nationalisation and constituted a halfway house towards the espousal of the market economy. These wider forms of social ownership included developments such as cooperative ventures and enterprise boards. Other policy shifts after 1983 included an acceptance of the sale of council houses, and agreement to remain in the EEC. Compromises on defence still remained, however, the Party wishing to remove all nuclear weapons from Britain's soil but promising to remain in NATO and to increase spending on conventional weapons.

Organisational reform was also initiated after 1983. These reforms were predicated on the belief that Labour could only win elections when it was perceived as a respectable, orderly and united party, which could tame the left and reduce the influence of the extra-parliamentary party, including the trade unions. They sought to create 'a more centralised, disciplined party, with power firmly located within its inner parliamentary circle' and inevitably resulted in the increased power of the party leadership at the expense of the National Executive Committee and the constituency Labour parties. Considerable emphasis was also placed on the packaging and presentation of the Party after 1983 which constituted key aspects of Labour's 'new strategic thinking'. These considerations exerted a dominant influence over other aspects of party affairs, principally the modernisation of organisation, programme and strategy. The new strategic thinking 'encouraged a steady drift to the right entailing not only the shredding of radical commitments inherited from the left but also the discarding of central elements of revisionist social democracy'. A key step taken after the 1983 election was the setting up of the Campaign Strategy Committee in 1983, chaired by Kinnock, which took decisions related to broadcasts, opinion polls and political campaigns. In 1985 Peter Mandelson was appointed Director of Campaigns and Communications. Thus, by 1987 Labour had been transformed into 'a more centrist, pragmatic, voter-orientated and disciplined party' (Shaw, 1994: 108, xii and 152), a key feature of which being the way in which Party Conferences became stage-managed.

However, although key developments in the areas discussed above occurred after 1983, progress was slow and internal problems often made the Party seem inward-looking. Issues which included the attitude the Party should adopt in key industrial disputes (such as the 1983 NGA dispute at Warrington, the 1984–85 miners' dispute, and the 1986–87 News International dispute), especially when extreme acts of violence occurred, the actions associated with the 'loony left' on local authorities and the wrangle over Black Sections detracted from the Party's ability to project the new aspects of its ideology and policy, especially when the media seized on these issues.

Liberal–SDP Alliance

The aftermath of the 1983 general election witnessed some press speculation about the possible merger of the Liberal and Social Democratic parties. In 1983 the voters were confused by the Alliance presenting them with two leaders, two sets of candidates yet only one policy (Crewe and King, 1995: 23); this resulted in support for a merger among many SDP activists, which was reinforced by their experiences of working with the Liberal Party especially in local government contests. There was also a belief by some Liberals that the problems which emerged in the 1983 general election indicated that it was impractical to continue with the Alliance in its present form, and that the future nature and direction of the Alliance should be resolved as soon as possible. The Liberal leader, David Steel, was, however, unable to give an early lead on this issue as he took a three-month sabbatical from politics following the 1983 election campaign.

Following the election, Roy Jenkins resigned as leader and was replaced by David Owen. His election as party leader in June 1983 led the SDP to consider officially the merits of the Alliance. Unlike Jenkins, who aspired to the eventual merger of the Liberal and Social Democratic parties, Owen viewed the Alliance as no more than an electoral pact which would operate until the SDP had sufficiently developed as a political force able to make its own independent contribution to British political affairs. This might mean, for example, that the SDP could enter into negotiations independently of the Liberal Party following a general election. Thus while he wished to retain working arrangements with the Liberal Party he was adamantly opposed to any consideration of a merger with them.

Owen's opposition to such a course of action was supported by the Council of Social Democracy which met following the 1983 election at Salford and was based on factors which included the assertion that the SDP possessed a distinct social democratic philosophy which was developed after 1983 to embrace the social market. This was designed to demonstrate political space between his party and both the revisionist socialists who remained in the Labour Party, and the Liberal Party. Owen's usage of the concept entailed an abandonment of the term 'mixed economy' and was based upon an acceptance of a new consensus based on the market economy, but which sought to instil social objectives into the operations of the market. This offered a solution to the inherent problems of social exclusion whose socially disharmonious repercussions had been particularly displayed in the riots of 1981. The social market was officially adopted as SDP policy at its 1984 conference in Buxton, and was articulated in works written by Owen, especially *A Future That Will Work* (1984).

Further antagonism towards the Liberal Party was based upon SDP hostility towards some Liberal policies (especially on defence and the environment) and on the manner in which Liberal Conferences asserted themselves in policy-making (which Owen judged to be anarchic). The latter view seemed justified in 1986 when a division of opinion emerged over the issue of defence policy, and in particular the future of Britain's nuclear deterrent. Owen wished to retain the latter to which many in the Liberal Party were opposed. A Joint Commission on Defence and Disarmament proposed a compromise position, that of a European nuclear deterrent. However, in 1986 the Liberal Assembly passed a motion to approve strengthening European defence on non-nuclear lines. This temporarily caused a rift both between the parties of the Alliance and also within them since the 1986 Assembly resolution was viewed as a rebuff to Steel. Although it proved possible to paper over these cracks in the 1987 election manifesto (which effectively committed the Alliance to a minimum British nuclear deterrent), the friction cost the Alliance support.

Other differences between the two parties were also discernible. The Liberal emphasis on community politics (underlaid by the objective of empowerment at a local level) was absent in SDP thinking and, to the minds of many in that party, provided the Liberals with a parochial outlook whereas the SDP wished to focus on the broader issues which were of overall concern to the nation. However, Owen became more willing to accept the long-term nature of the SDP's relationship with the Liberal Party as the 1987 general election approached, and relationships between Steel and Owen improved from the beginning of 1987. The negative views held by Owen towards the Liberal Party were replicated by many Liberals who were concerned about the elite nature of the SDP's policy-making process and the lack of clarity concerning the kind of society the Party's leadership wished to work towards.

Mechanics of Cooperation after 1983

Following the 1983 election, a Joint Leaders' Advisory Committee (which was renamed the Alliance Staretgy Committee in 1985) was set up to improve coordination between the Alliance parties. The 1984 elections to the European Parliament provided the first political event requiring cooperation. The allocation of seats was managed by regional coordinators whose remit was that each party should be given a fair share of all seats in the region, including an equitable division of those deemed to be the most winnable. The 1984 European elections were fought on a joint policy statement, *United for a Democratic Europe*, approved by the conferences of both parties in 1983. A Joint Campaign Committee was also established to manage the Alliance effort. The Alliance polled 19.1 per cent of the vote but failed to win any seats.

The division of parliamentary constituencies for the next general election, however, posed more severe problems. A key area of contention was the issue of joint selection of a single candidate to fight a specific constituency by activists of both parties. The Liberal Party favoured this process but the SDP leadership, Owen in particular, opposed it. His opposition was based on the political consideration that the Liberal Party, with more grass roots activists, would ensure that the bulk of seats would be fought by candidates from their party, and also by a perception that such a process effectively consituted a merger 'through the back door'. However, the opposition of the SDP towards joint selection of candidates eventually subsided when it was realised that this process was not the norm (being confined to 78 with some Liberal involvement in the selection of SDP candidates occurring in a further 60) and, further, that the SDP (whose performance in 1983 had been inferior to the Liberal Party's) remained roughly on even terms with regard to candidatures, including in the seats perceived to be the most winnable. For the 1987 general election, therefore, 78 seats changed hands between the parties and the SDP contested around 300 constituencies. The process of seat negotiation was mainly completed by the autumn of 1986, and in 1987 there were no instances of 'rebel' Liberal or SDP candidates fighting an Alliance nominee.

By-elections

Thirty-one by-elections took place between 1983 and 1987. The Liberals gained Brecon and Radnor from the Conservatives in July 1985 and Ryedale from the same party in May 1986. The SDP captured Portsmouth South from the Conservatives in June 1984 and Greenwich from Labour in February 1987. Labour gained Fulham from the Conservatives in April 1986 and in Northern Ireland the SDLP captured Newry and Armagh from the Ulster Unionists in January 1986.

Conduct of the Election

Conservatives

The Conservative Party entered the election in favourable economic circumstances: the May figure for unemployment (which was released in June) revealed that unemployment had fallen below the three million figure, the balance of payments figures for June were good, factory orders stood at a high level, and the Pound rose against both the dollar and Deutschmark. Although inflation rose marginally in March–April, the future prognosis in this area was healthy.

Conservative policies were contained in its lengthy manifesto, *The Next Moves Forward*. The conquering of inflation remained the government's top priority which would be achieved through strict control over the level of public spending and the reduction of government borrowing. The Party promised to continue the reform of local government which would lose most of their functions in education, housing and town planning and domestic rates would be replaced by a community charge. Council tenants would be enabled to choose their own landlords and parents and teachers would be provided with the right for their school to opt out of local authority control. The manifesto promised further privatisation, including electricity and water, additional trade union legislation and tax cuts.

Considerable attention was devoted in the Conservative campaign to the Party's achievements in office which were depicted as a springboard for even greater ones in the next Parliament. It was argued that the Conservatives had maintained Britain's defences and brought Russia to the negotiating table, had outlawed secondary picketing and its accompanying violence, had reduced income tax to its lowest level for 50 years, had sold one million council homes to their tenants, and that as a consequence of their economic policies the average wage earner's pay had risen over 20 per cent more than inflation. It was argued that Labour intended to undo many of these reforms (for example, by ending a tenant's automatic right to buy a council house and by restoring the right to secondary picketing). It was thus concluded that 'Britain is great again. Don't let Labour wreck it'.

Conservative attacks were also mounted on Labour's 'loony left' and especially on that party's economic competence. Reference was made to Labour's 'iceberg' manifesto in which only one-tenth of its socialism was visible but the other nine-tenths were lurking below the surface. It was claimed that Labour's policies would prove excessively expensive, the figure of £35 billion extra spending being referred to. It was argued that public spending of this level would result in either income tax or VAT massively rising so that all, and not merely the rich, would suffer from higher taxation under a Labour government. Labour defence policy was also attacked for constituting a policy of surrender. Electors were thus urged not to trust Labour.

The Conservative campaign was generally regarded as a poor one, perhaps reflecting tensions between Thatcher and Norman Tebbitt which gave rise to two campaign centres (No. 10 and Central Office) which were almost separate. The Conservative case was put across by the use of three advertising agencies but was aided by the very heavy use of advertising, especially in the press. The Conservatives also benefited from tabloid press support, which echoed some of the themes in the Conservative campaign. The alleged left-wing nature of that party was, for example, referred to in a headline in the *Sun* which carried a story 'Why I'm Backing Kinnock by Stalin'.

Labour

Labour entered the campaign against the reversal experienced at the Greenwich by-election in February 1987 when a left-wing candidate lost to the SDP and also to the failure of Kinnock's trip to Washington in March which (as with a similar visit in November 1986) failed to convince the Americans of the wisdom of Labour's defence policy. The latter stood in stark contrast to the success of Margaret Thatcher's visit to Moscow a week later. These events caused Labour's standing in the opinion polls to fall.

Labour's policies were contained in its manifesto, *Britain Will Win*. The Party pledged to create one million jobs in two years and to provide greater investment in industry. A minimum wage was promised and increases would be made to the old age pension. The manifesto promised a wealth tax and the social ownership of the privatised industries, British Gas and British Telecom. In the area of defence, the manifesto stated that Cruise missiles would be retained while the Gorbachev–Reagan disarmament talks were taking place, but Polaris would be decommissioned and Trident cancelled. A future Labour government would phase out private beds in the National Health Service but was not committed to close down private hospitals. During the campaign, Kinnock gave prominence to the contribution which good public services made to the quality of life.

Labour adopted a presidential-style campaign which focused on Kinnock. This was especially evident in the Party's first election broadcast which was written by Colin Welland and directed by Hugh Hudson (who had directed the film *Chariots of Fire*). The Party's election meetings were revivalist in nature and their election broadcasts concentrated on Kinnock's background and character. Considerable attention was devoted in Labour's campaign to the health service where Mrs Thatcher was depicted as uncaring. Key issues included the length of waiting lists which was personalised in a story in the *Daily Mirror* regarding a 10-year old boy, Mark Burgess, whose urgent operation for a hole in the heart had been cancelled several times. One aspect of the Conservative response to such accusations was to brand Labour's stance as hypocritical when it was revealed that Denis Healey's wife had paid for a private hip operations two years previously. Labour also focused on unemployment, accusing the Conservatives of doctoring the figures to make their record appear better than it was and pledging to reduce the figure by one million within two years. It was concluded that the Conservative view of freedom was designed to benefit the well-offs and not the have-nots.

Labour was supported by less of the popular press than the Conservative Party, although the *Daily Mirror* sought to resurrect the spirit of its 1945 'vote for them' campaign by urging readers to vote Labour in order to ensure that the concerns of the young, old and sick were addressed.

Liberal-SDP Alliance

The Alliance entered the election in good morale, and one Gallup poll on the eve of the election placed them ahead of Labour. The Alliance continued to secure some good results in by-elections and local government elections after 1983. By-election gains were secured at Portsmouth South (1984), Brecon and Radnor (1985), Ryedale (1986) and Greenwich (1987), and the Liberal Party further held its seat in Truro in 1987 following the death of the sitting MP, David Penhaligon. In the 16 by-elections which occurred during the Parliament elected in 1983, the Alliance polled 39 per cent of the vote, compared to the Conservatives' 30 per cent and Labour's 28 per cent, and in July 1985 the Alliance very briefly went ahead in the opinion polls. Successes were also achieved in local government contests. The Alliance gained 260 seats in the 1985 county council elections and 450 in the May 1987 council elections. Thus, by 1987 the Alliance either controlled or held the balance in 100 local authorities.

In order to plan for the election, an Alliance Planning Group was formed in November 1986 to prepare the Alliance campaign. A relaunch of the Alliance took place in January 1987 when a team of joint spokespersons was appointed and a joint policy statement, *The Time Has Come*, was issued. This formed the basis of the joint election manifesto *Britain United – The Time Has Come*. The policies promoted by the Alliance in 1987 emphasised the themes of a united Britain, constitutional reform and policies for unemployment and the public services. The details of constitutional reform were spelled out in a document launched at the outset of the campaign, *The Great Reform Charter*. The Alliance proposed the incorporation of the European Convention of Human Rights in British law through the enactment of a Bill of Rights, a Freedom of Information Act, electoral reform, fixed-term Parliaments, the election of the second Chamber, and an enhanced role for local government through decentralisation. Alliance economic policy included capital investment in the national infrastructure, an incomes strategy backed by a counter-inflation tax on companies, and membership of the European Exchange Rate Mechanism. During the campaign six Alliance themes were emphasised – reducing unemployment (by one million over three years), spending more on education, maintaining Conservative trade union legislation, upholding the rule of law, reducing hospital waiting lists and retaining a minimum nuclear deterrent. Much of the Alliance campaign was targeted at the record of the Conservative Party, reflecting the view that Labour stood no real chance of success.

During the election campaign the Alliance was concerned with issues other than policy. The leadership of the Alliance emerged as an issue as the 1987 election approached. Some Liberals sought one leader, but there was no possibility Owen would accept this since it was tantamount to the merger which he opposed. Thus the position adopted was that there would be no designated Alliance leader during the election campaign which would thus have dual leadership. In the event of an Alliance government being returned the leader of the largest of the two Alliance parties would become prime minister. However, Owen did not believe that it was possible for the Alliance to win power single-handedly and felt that the most realisable objective was participation in a coalition government in which power was shared with a major party. This stance was similar to that adopted by Steel towards Callaghan's Labour government in the 1970s and thus the Alliance moved towards a position of endorsing the balance of power (termed a 'balanced Parliament') as its electoral objective.

This objective required the Alliance to indicate how it would act in the event of such a situation occurring. It was thus announced that if the 1987 general election produced an indecisive outcome, the Alliance would negotiate as a unit. It would be willing to negotiate with either major party, but would commence discussions with whichever of them emerged as the largest. The Alliance would probably not join in a coalition government but would be prepared to support a minority government. Its conditions for cooperating with another major party were an agreement on a detailed programme of government which would run for two to three years. No details of this programme were, however, disclosed. It was agreed that any deal made with another party would have to be formally approved by both parties. It was also stated that in the event of either major party ignoring the Alliance and forming a government, the Alliance would immediately vote them out of office and force a second general election (Crewe and King, 1995: 44).

Pronouncements of this nature, however, masked differences between Steel and Owen concerning how to act in this situation. In turn this reflected a difference of opinion as to whether the real 'enemy' was Neil Kinnock or Margaret Thatcher. Divisions between Steel and Owen surfaced during the campaign, particularly with regard to whether the Alliance could negotiate with a Conservative Party led by Margaret Thatcher in the event of a hung Parliament: Owen believed that this course of action was feasible, whereas Steel favoured negotiations with the Labour Party. It remained possible, therefore, that in such a situation Owen might conceivably enter into unilateral negotiations with the Conservative Party (Crewe and King, 1995: 46). The high profile given to defence early in the campaign further suggested such a possibility based on SDP support for Conservative policies. Thatcher attacked Alliance policy as constituting 'one-sided disarmament' which was borne from a need to compromise diverse viewpoints in the Liberal Party and SDP. This produced an impassioned response from David Owen, who pointed out that he had broken with the Labour Party on this very issue and was not likely to suddenly embrace this position. In 1983 Alliance candidates had come second in 311 seats. This implied the relevance of tactical voting, particularly as a national campaign (TV

87) urged the mobilisation of the anti-Conservative vote. Relatively little success was achieved with this tactic, however. This was because the overt advocacy of tactical voting was not permitted in the Party's election broadcasts because the broadcasters felt this could be illegal, and also as advocating tactical voting would have resulted in large numbers of Alliance voters supporting the Labour Party as the best instrument to oust the Conservative government. Furthermore, surveys suggested that there were as many Alliance voters who were anti-Labour as there were those who were anti-Conservative (Butler and Kavanagh, 1988: 98). However, these considerations did not prevent individual Alliance candidates courting the support of Labour voters in their constituencies. The success of such appeals was, however, heavily influenced by the nature of the attacks mounted by the Alliance on the Conservative Party. Condemnation of Conservative policies towards unemployment and welfare might conceivably cultivate Labour support for Alliance candidates in constituencies in which the latter was the main challenger to the Conservatives. However, the issue of defence (which emerged as a prominent source of conflict between Owen and Thatcher in the early days of the campaign) was far less likely to advance this form of tactical voting.

Result of the Election

Presentation and packaging (in particular of party leaders) dominated the 1987 election campaign which was characterised by high levels of media management. Although the election result was not as foregone a conclusion as had been the case in 1983, a Conservative victory seemed the most likely result since the government had been ahead in the polls for 33 of the 47 months of the 1983 Parliament (Butler and Kavanagh, 1988: 37). The Alliance performance had been in the area of 20 per cent throughout that period, although its victory at the Greenwich by-election in February 1987 opened the possibility of it supplanting Labour for second place.

A total of 2,325 candidates contested the election. The result was:

Party	Votes	Vote %	MPs
Conservative	13,760,583	42.3%	376
Labour	10,029,807	30.8%	229
Liberal	4,173,450	12.8%	17
SDP	3,168,183	9.8%	5
(Total Alliance	7,341,633	22.6%	22)
All Ulster Unionist Parties	380,292	1.2% [54.8%]	13
SDLP	154,087	0.5% [21.1%]	3
SNP	416,473	1.3% [14.0%]	3
Plaid Cymru	123,599	0.4% [7.3%]	3
Sinn Fein	83,389	0.2% [11.4%]	1
Others	239,715	0.7%	0
Total	32,529,578		650

The turnout was 75.3 per cent. The swing from the Conservative Party to Labour was 1.7 per cent. Forty-one women MPs were returned. Four MPs from ethnic minority groups were elected.

The Parties

The overall swing from the Conservative to the Labour Party was subject to considerable regional variation so that in the South the swing was virtually non-existent, but it amounted to 3.6 per cent in Northern England and 5.8 per cent in Scotland. The election gave rise to a broad division in Britain consisting of the North–West (comprising Scotland, Wales and Northern England) where Labour advanced, and the South–East in which the Conservative Party improved on its 1983 performance, a key feature of which was to make inroads in the big cities, thus eroding the urban–rural divide which had been a feature of recent general elections. The North–South divide was also weakened by factors which included the good Alliance performance in the South West. There was evidence of tactical voting (especially in seats where Labour trailed the Alliance in third place) but it had a relatively limited impact on the outcome in individual constituencies. This factor did, however, help to account for the seven gains made by the Liberal–SDP Alliance and the Nationalist Parties and for Labour's gain at East Oxford (Butler and Kavanagh, 1988: 340).

The Conservative Party's election performance was aided by its successful Party Conference, the generous spending settlements announced in the autumn, the tax-cutting budget and by Labour's mistakes. Its success in 1979 and 1983 in securing support from the 'new working class' was continued in the 1987 contest whereby 36 per cent of the working-class vote was obtained compared to Labour's 48 per cent (Butler and Kavanagh, 1988: 275). The working class support obtained by the Party was aided by factors which included the depiction of Conservative economic successes by the tabloid newspapers. However, the Party performed especially badly in Scotland and Wales.

Labour fought the election as a united party and conducted a very professional campaign, but its outcome was a disappointment. It increased its poll to 30.8 per cent and gained a small number of seats. The Party's total vote was over 11 per cent adrift of the Conservatives and they would require a large swing of around 8 per cent to win a future general election. This result reflected the Party's shrinking core vote in a society which was becoming increasingly middle class (measured by indicators which included home ownership, share ownership and the decline in trade union membership). Presentation dominated the Party's 1987 election campaign at the expense of policy, much of which remained either vague or non-committal (such as the Party's tax and benefits plans) or was absent entirely (such as proposals to extend the right to buy to private tenants and the relegalisation of secondary picketing). This situation was borne out of the need to reconcile divergent views within the Party and indicated the relatively slow progress of reforms to ideology and policy. It was suggested that while Labour policies on health and social services, unemployment and jobs and education had appealed to voters, they lagged behind the Conservatives on defence, law and order and taxation. In particular, electors distrusted Labour's ability to manage the economy and were concerned that a Labour government would result in higher taxes, rapidly rising inflation and the fulfilment of promises which the country could not afford (Butler and Kavanagh: 1988: 245 and 275). Nine Labour MPs were sponsored by the Cooperative Party and 134 by trade unions.

The Alliance campaign was initially jolted when David Steel was falsely accused of an extra-marital affair. This libel eventually cost the *Daily Star* a large financial penalty. The Alliance polled 7.3 million votes (23.1 per cent of the national vote) but secured the return of only 22

MPs (17 Liberal and five SDP). An arithmetical share of the seats would have given them 149. It performed best in Devon and Cornwall and in Southern England but lost support in Northern England, and (measured in terms of votes) in Scotland and Wales, thereby weakening the pattern of an even spread of support which had previously been a feature of Liberal general election campaigns. The result was a disappointment since at the outset of the campaign it had been assumed that the figure of 50 to 100 seats was a realisable objective.

The chief Liberal casualty was Clement Freud who was defeated in Ely, but the result was a total disaster for the SDP. This party was reduced from eight MPs to five (which included the defeat of Roy Jenkins in Glasgow Hillhead), and it failed to gain a single seat. Fourteen of the Alliance MPs represented rural constituencies which had thus become predominantly the political vehicle of the Celtic Fringe. The failure of the Alliance performance to live up to its earlier loftier expectations was attributed to a number of factors. These included the relatively poor quality of the Alliance campaign (especially compared to the improved Labour campaign which concentrated on Kinnock), the way in which dual leadership confused the electorate, the lack of public sympathy for an election outcome which produced a minority or coalition government, and the tactics utilised in the early stages to attack the Conservative Party rather than Labour (the reverse having been the case in 1983). It was assumed that the Conservative Party would win the election and thus Conservative-inclined floating voters were initially targeted.

Scotland, Wales and Northern Ireland

Labour won 50 of Scotland's 72 seats, the Conservatives 10, the Liberals seven and the SDP two. The SNP picked up one seat to return three MPs to Westminster. In Wales, Labour won 24 of the 38 seats. The Conservatives won eight and the Liberals three. The result achieved by Plaid Cymru reflected a trend which had been noticeable in general elections since 1970 whereby its support was increasingly concentrated in rural, Welsh-speaking areas of the country. It won three seats, a net gain of one.

In Northern Ireland, the various Unionist parties had concluded an agreement in 1987 not to stand candidates against each other's sitting MPs. There was only one exception to this, in North Down, where the incumbent James Kilfedder of the Ulster Popular Unionist Party was challenged by an candidate from the OUP (although both he and the constituency party were expelled from the Party for this action). Overall, Unionists won 13 of the 17 seats (Ulster Unionists nine, Democratic Unionists three and the Ulster Popular Unionist Party one). No pact was concluded between the SDLP and Sinn Fein which meant that Nationalist candidates fought against each other in 13 constituencies. The trend evidenced in the 1986 by-elections of Sinn Fein losing ground to the SDLP was continued in 1987. The SDLP held on to its by-election gain of Newry and Armagh and also wrested South Down from Enoch Powell. It thus returned three MPs to Sinn Fein's one. The Alliance Party's vote of 9.9 per cent was the Party's best performance in any election since 1979.

Consequence of the Election

Mrs Thatcher formed her third Conservative administration. She was the first Prime Minister since Lord Liverpool in the 1820s to win three consecutive general elections.

9 April 1992

Party Leaders
John Major (Conservative)
Neil Kinnock (Labour)
Paddy Ashdown (Liberal Democrat)

Background to the Election
Timing of the Election
The 1987–1992 Parliament was the second longest Parliament (after the one held between 1959 and 1964) since the enactment of the 1911 Parliament Act. The Prime Minister, John Major, had declined the option of holding an election in 1991 in the hope that economic improvement would aid his party's fortunes in the following year. However, by the end of 1991, problems which included a record trade deficit, increased unemployment, poor retail sales and mortgage repossessions suggested that these had failed to materialise. Major's only justification for calling an election in April 1992 was that the economy could get even worse during that year and that further delay would push him into a position in which he lost any choice over its timing.

Electoral Procedures and Practices
The 1985 legislation which permitted British citizens residing abroad to vote was amended by the 1989 Representation of the People Act whereby persons who had left Britain for a period of up to 20 years had the right to vote. This constituted around 30,000 voters in 1992. An extra constituency was created in Buckinghamshire. On 21 November 1990 the televising of the House of Commons was introduced on a permanent basis.

Conservatives
A number of existing policies were continued with after 1987. Administrative reform (based on the approach outlined in *Next Steps*, 1988) resulted in the hiving off to executive agencies of a number of executive functions currently being carried out by government departments. Further measures of privatisation (which raised £22 billion between 1987 and 1992) were pursued, although the application of this policy to the water industry in 1989 and electricity in 1990 was controversial. The introduction of market principles into public services was pursued through approaches which included the compulsory competitive tendering of local authority services, and the granting to hospitals of a degree of autonomy through the award of trust status. Some family doctors were also given fund-holding status in the 1990 National Health Service and Community Care Act. A significant measure, the 1988 Education Reform Act, introduced the testing of children at the age of seven, initiated a system of student loans and provided mechanisms for schools to opt out of local authority control.

Despit the stock market collapse in October 1987, the economic climate remained relatively favourable following the 1987 election, and in the 1988 budget the top rate of income tax was reduced from 60 per cent to 40 per cent and the standard rate from 27 per cent to 25 per cent.

In May 1988, the interest rate of 8.5 per cent was the lowest figure for 10 years. Subsequently, however, severe economic problems surfaced and cost the Party support. Worldwide economic recession especially affected Britain, driving up unemployment: the 40,000 increase which was announced during the campaign being the twenty-second consecutive month to show an increase. The balance of trade deficit widened and between 1988 and 1991 the annual growth rate fell from 3 per cent to zero. In the same period inflation (which was fuelled by a credit surge) increased from 3 per cent to 10 per cent, and by the end of 1989 mortgage and interest rates were rising. Chancellor Nigel Lawson's policy to counter inflation was to manage exchange and interest rates (rather than exerting strict control over the money supply). His personal preference was to join the European Exchange Rate Mechanism (ERM) in order to secure stable exchange rates, but as Thatcher was opposed to this course of action he alternatively shadowed the Deutschmark until the United Kingdom finally entered the ERM in October 1990.

The standing of the Conservative Party was weakened by difficulties other than their handling of the economy in time of recession. Official crime statistics evidenced a large rise in crime rates and well-publicised miscarriages of justices (which included the Guildford 4 who were freed by the Court of Appeal in October 1989) questioned the fairness of the judicial system. Prison riots (including that in Strangeways Prison, Manchester, in January 1990) further cast doubt on the effectiveness of Conservative policies to combat crime and disorder. Perhaps most contentious of all was the implementation of the 1987 manifesto commitment to replace domestic rates by the Community Charge (popularly referred to as 'Poll Tax'). This produced widespread opposition (including civil disobedience by those who refused to pay their bills) when it was implemented in Scotland in 1989 and England and Wales in 1990, on the grounds that all were required to make a contribution regardless of their personal circumstances.

Concern regarding the economy and other aspects of Conservative Party policy resulted in disquiet directed against the leadership of Margaret Thatcher, which were fuelled by poor electoral performances such as the May 1989 European elections when Labour gained 13 seats. The resignation of Chancellor Nigel Lawson on 31 October 1989 (who objected to the influence wielded by Thatcher's adviser, Sir Alan Walters, over government economic policy) formed the backdrop to the first leadership challenge, which was mounted by the relatively unknown (outside Westminster) backbench MP, Sir Anthony Meyer. In the ballot held on 5 December 1989 he was defeated by Thatcher by the large margin of 314 to 24. However, the abstention of 31 additional MPs suggested that Thatcher's position was not impregnable.

A further challenge was inevitable following the resignation of Sir Geoffrey Howe in 1990. This was prompted by Thatcher's negative feelings towards the loss of sovereignty to institutions of the European Community which were expressed following the meeting in Rome of the European Council in October 1990 (when European Monetary Union had been discussed) and seemed to echo the hard line she had announced in her Bruges speech delivered on 20 September 1988 when she firmly opposed the creation of a European superstate. Howe's resignation speech on 13 November 1990 amounted to a call to arms for those disquieted with her leadership. On the first ballot held on 20 November, Thatcher defeated Michael Heseltine by 204 votes to 152. However, this was two votes below the required 15 per cent margin of victory. Although Thatcher's instinct was to stand in the second ballot, advisers secured her withdrawal on the grounds that her position was irretrievably weakened by the result. Thus, on 22 November 1990, John Major (with 185 votes) defeated his two rivals, Michael Heseltine (131 votes) and Douglas Hurd (56 votes), and was sworn in as Prime Minister the following day.

Under John Major, many of the policies associated with (or initiated by) Thatcher were continued, although the Poll Tax was abandoned in favour of a new Council Tax. Major also attempted to commence mapping out a new agenda for the 1990s, a key aspect of which was the introduction of the Citizens' Charter on 22 July 1991 which aimed to give enhanced rights to users of public services, including greater choice, more information and improved opportunities to make complaints. Unsuccessful attempts (through the abortive all-party talks initiated in 1992 by Northern Ireland Secretary Peter Brooke) were made to secure a political settlement to the 'Troubles' in Northern Ireland but divisions in the Conservative Party over Europe were temporarily masked when the Maastricht Summit in 1991 (which was concerned with providing a legal basis for European economic and political union) agreed that the United Kingdom could be exempted from the provisions of the Social Chapter and could join a common currency at a later date when Parliament had approved this course of action. War was successfully prosecuted against Saddam Hussein, resulting in the liberation of Kuwait (which had been invaded by Iraq in August 1990). The political standing of the Conservative Party did not significantly improve with the change of its leader. Although the Party moved ahead in the opinion polls following Major's victory in the Conservative leadership ballot, it performed weakly in the May 1991 local elections, losing 900 seats.

Labour

The result secured by Labour in 1987 underlined the need for the Party to appeal to a wider political audience: it would require an 8 per cent swing in order for Labour to win the next election. Two hundred and twenty-nine of its MPs represented constituencies in Northern England, Scotland and Wales. There were few further advances that Labour could make in these areas and in order to stand a realistic prospect of winning a general election it needed to secure support, and seats, elsewhere, especially in southern England and the Midlands. This enhanced the need for a comprehensive review of ideology and policy, which was referred to as 'modernisation'.

Modernisation involved two main elements. The first was a restatement of Labour ideology, contained in the 1988 publication *Democratic Socialist Aims and Values*. This document was designed to provide the underpinning for a detailed review of policy which was undertaken by seven Policy Reviews initiated by Kinnock in 1987 which were due to report to the Party Conference in 1989 and whose aim was to sell Labour to a wider political audience. An interim document, *Social Justice, Economic Efficiency*, was presented to the Party Conference in 1988, designed to provide the framework for the more detailed process of policy review whose proposals were embodied in the statements, *Meet the Challenge, Make the Change* (1989), and *Looking to the Future: A Dynamic Economy, a Decent Society, Strong in Europe* (1990). These resulted in public ownership being abandoned as a major item of Labour policy, and the Party's anti-EEC stance being replaced by a pro-European one (to the extent that Kinnock attacked the opt-out clause on monetary union which had been negotiated by Major and Douglas Hurd at Maastricht in 1991). Labour's commitment to initiate unilateral nuclear disarmament was also dropped. The Party adopted a more flexible attitude towards taxation policies and its response to Conservative trade union reforms.

The Policy Review reflected the need for Labour to adjust to the beliefs, values and aspirations advocated by Conservatism, a key aspect of which was that personal betterment resided not in the operations of the state but in the hands of individuals, particularly in the sense of their ability to acquire goods in the mass consumption economy. The developments which took place after 1983, and particularly between 1987 and 1989, transformed Labour into a party which explicitly accepted the market-orientated mixed economy, although the need for intervention by the state to provide services (such as health care and education) that would not otherwise be supplied, or to mitigate the operations of the market, was accepted. Terms such as 'new realism' or 'market socialism' were applied to the outlook and policies adopted by the Labour Party during the 1980s.

The Policy Review was influenced by a desire not to increase taxation and its objectives were more modest than those of the revisionists, shying away from Crosland's radical egalitarianism. The limited nature of Labour's intentions was publicised in statements which included 'we will not spend, nor will we promise to spend, more than Britain can afford' and the promise that welfare benefits would be improved 'as rapidly as resources allow' (Labour Party, 1990: 8, 35). Labour's new approach, therefore, was to endorse the market economy but to intervene selectively in its operations in pursuit of collective purposes serving social needs. This was latterly endorsed in Part Two of the new Clause IV of Labour's constitution in which the Party endorsed the goal of 'a dynamic economy ... in which the enterprise of the market and the rigour of competition are joined with the forces of partnership and cooperation'.

A number of organisational reforms were also introduced after 1987. Limited moves were made towards the implementation of the 'one member, one vote' principle. This was viewed as an indispensable reform to mobilise the moderate rank-and-file members, (thus marginalising the 'hard left') as well as reducing the hold exerted by the trade unions on Labour affairs. Other reforms included the introduction of localised electoral colleges for the selection – and deselection – of parliamentary candidates and changes to the voting procedures for the constituency sections of the leadership electoral college and the National Executive Committee. A number of moves were taken to end the influence exerted by the Militant Tendency in Labour politics. The impotence of the left was revealed in Tony Benn's unsuccessful challenge for the leadership of the Party in 1988, in which Kinnock secured almost 90 per cent of the votes. It was left to Kinnock's successor, John Smith, to conclude this process of organisational reform with the implementation of a form of 'one member, one vote' in 1993.

Liberal Democrats

Steel pre-empted a consideration of the Liberal–SDP Alliance's future direction following the 1987 general election by calling for a merger (which he termed a 'democratic fusion') of the two parties. There were several factors which prompted him to act as he did. The consolidation of the Labour Party behind Kinnock and subsequent developments in policy led to the reduction of the differences between the two major parties and the establishment of the basis for a new political consensus. This meant that the middle ground was eroding and could not accommodate two political parties whose periodic airing of differences tended to reduce the appeal of progresssive politics. It was also perceived that the dual leadership cost the Alliance electoral support, amounting to 1 per cent of electoral support in 1983 and 6 per cent in 1987, which might have amounted to around 10 seats in the latter campaign, still far behind the total achieved by Labour (Crewe and King, 1995: 458). Reasons to justify the need for two independent parties were also less valid by 1987. The SDP largely failed to attract Labour working-class voters to the Alliance, which emerged from the 1987 election heavily dependent on sources of electoral support which the Liberal Party was largely capable of attracting for itself. There were also practical considerations in favour of a merger, especially the demoralisation felt by many SDP activists concerning their party's performance in 1987 who were thus likely to be more receptive to this course of action than had been the case following the 1983 election.

A merger was not, however, on the agenda of the SDP leadership. Owen was firmly opposed to any such move, believing that a merged party would effectively constitute a takeover of his own party by the Liberals who might subsequently endorse working with the Labour Party. Owen accordingly put forward the notion of a federation as an alternative to a merger. This envisaged even closer ties with the Liberal Party but enabled the SDP to retain its independent identity.

The first meeting of the SDP National Committee held after the election agreed to defer a decision until a future meeting on 29 June. This latter meeting proposed to ballot members of the SDP regarding a merger. This course of action was favoured by the Owenites as they felt their views would prevail. Owen had declared that he would not have any involvement with a merged party should one be formed, which meant that the vote was effectively transformed into a vote of confidence in him. The SDP's 58,000 members were asked to choose between two propositions – that the National Committee should negotiate a closer constitutional relationship for the Alliance short of merger which preserved the SDP's identity, or that the National Committee should negotiate a merger with the Liberal Party to form one party. The SDP's National Committee endorsed option one, the Owenites taking the view that this effectively ruled out a merger for ever. However, the SDP's members voted (in a 77 per cent turnout) for option two by 25, 987 votes (57.4 per cent) to 19,228 (42.6 per cent). Owen immediately resigned as leader of the SDP. He was replaced by Robert Maclennan, SDP MP for Caithness and Sutherland. The desire to merge was affirmed at the SDP Conference at the end of August, and in September the Liberal Assembly also voted to proceed with discussions of this nature. The Alliance was formally ended on 26 August 1997 when Owen and Steel agreed to go their separate political ways. Both parties then entered into protracted negotiations (a key concern of which was to draw up a constitution) which lasted from September 1987 until January 1988.

A number of difficulties arose during the discussions on the merger of the two parties. These included which name the party should adopt and its constitution. Liberal concerns regarding the latter included the distribution of power within the Party, and also whether Britain's membership of NATO should be viewed as a policy or was of sufficient importance to be included in the new Party's constitution. The most publicised difficulty, however, concerned policy. The drafting of a policy document, which would be put to a ballot of members of both parties alongside the proposed constitution, was largely left to Robert Maclennan. The Liberal leadership, particularly Steel, gave him a free hand in this task, which was eventually completed under the title *Voices and Choices For All*. The contents of this reflected Maclennan's desire to ensure that the new party reflected SDP policy concerns and thus sought to commit the new party to the retention of a British nuclear deterrent (which meant the retention of Trident), taxation reforms (including the abolition of the married man's tax allowance), the funding of an anti-poverty programme (financed from the imposition of VAT on food, children's clothing and domestic fuel), and the establishment of a single European market.

Liberal opposition to this policy statement (which was dubbed a 'dead parrot') was considerable. The Party's National Executive voted against it, which prompted the Liberal Parliamentary Party to suggest that an alternative policy statement, based upon the 1987 Alliance manifesto, should be substituted for Maclennan's document, and the National Executive approved this course of action. A new policy document was hastily drawn up in which the most contentious aspects of the original policy document were abandoned. On 23 January 1988 a special Liberal Assembly approved the merger on the basis of the new constitution and amended policy document by 2,099 : 385. The SDP Council for Social Democracy subsequently approved it by 273 : 28, and it was endorsed by a postal ballot of SDP Party members by 18,722 : 9,929. On 3 March 1988, the Social and Liberal Democrats were officially launched, temporarily under the interim leadership of Steel and Maclennan. A leadership contest was held later in 1988 which resulted in victory for Paddy Ashdown over Alan Beith by the margin of 41,000 votes to 16,000. The Party subsequently changed its name to the Liberal Democrats following a ballot in October 1989.

Ashdown sought to move the Party in a new direction. He discarded the aim of replacing Labour and sought to establish radical credentials for the Party. Support for an incomes policy and quasi-corporatist management of the economy was abandoned in favour of the free market and enhanced competition. The 1991 Party Conference approved the imposition of 1p on the standard rate of income tax in order to specifically finance improvements in education. However, the new party did not get off to a good start. Losses were suffered in the local elections in 1988, 1989 and 1990. Additionally, the 1989 elections to the European Parliament evidenced widespread support for the Greens whose total vote surpassed that obtained by the Liberal Democrats. The early 1990s, however, produced encouraging signs with by-election victories at Eastbourne (1990) and Kincardine and Ribble Valley (1991). The most significant factor, however, was the Party's showing in the 1991 district council elections. To the surprise of many political commentators, over 500 seats were gained. The level of media exposure given to Paddy Ashdown during the Gulf War also aided the Party whose popular support (which had once been as low as 4 per cent in the polls) stood at 16 per cent by March 1991.

By-elections
Twenty-four by-elections occurred in the 1987–92 Parliament. The Conservatives lost seven seats, Labour gained four, the Liberals Democrats gained three, and the SNP gained one seat (Glasgow–Govan) from Labour.

Conduct of the Election
The election campaign of the two main parties was divided into two stages. These were in the winter of 1991–92 (which in Conservative circles was referred to as the 'near campaign',

modelled on President Reagan's successful 1984 campaign when success was achieved against the background of economic recession) and in the weeks preceding the actual election in April.

Conservatives

The aim of the initial ('near') campaign was to gain control of the political agenda and to make clear the Conservative Party's differences with Labour. It lasted for a period of 11 weeks in which different themes were focused upon. It included attacks on the costs of Labour's spending plans which, according to the 'tax bombshell' poster of January 1992, would cost the average family around £1,250 per year. Electors were further warned that they would suffer a 'double whammy' under Labour whereby both taxes and prices would rise. Other issues which were raised in this campaign included defence, education, foreign affairs, and law and order. The focus on taxation contributed significantly to overturning Labour's lead in the opinion polls to the benefit of the Conservative Party and set the scene for the subsequent campaign against Labour when the election was called. The public were also courted by public expenditure settlements which provided for pay rises in excess of inflation to teachers and health service employees and by Norman Lamont's March budget which introduced a new 20p tax band for the first £2,000 of taxable income in order to aid the low paid.

Conservative policies for the election were contained in its manifesto, *The Best Future for Britain*. The main themes which were advanced were those of choice, ownership, responsibility, greater opportunity, low taxes and decent public services. Much of their electioneering entailed negative attacks on Labour. In addition to the continuance of existing policies in the areas of health, education and housing, proposals were put forward to sell off British Coal and some British Rail services, to set up an Urban Regeneration Agency to provide for the rejuvenation of cities, and to establish a rents-to-mortgage scheme for council tenants. More resources were pledged for the health service which, the manifesto stated, would not be privatised nor subjected to any further structural changes. It was alleged that neither Labour nor Kinnock could be trusted and the alleged cost of Labour's proposals was emphasised. Arguments advanced during the 'near' campaign regarding the 'double whammy' (to which allegations that mortgage rates would increase under a Labour government were added) claimed that Labour's proposals would cost £38 billion and were reiterated during the campaign which spoke of 'five years' hard Labour'. Major also spoke out against constitutional reform, urging the preservation of the United Kingdom and its electoral system. A reference by Major predicting a 'nightmare on Kinnock Street' if Labour won the election was developed by the *Sun* newspaper which mounted a series of attacks on Kinnock, culminating on polling day with the plea 'if Kinnock wins today will the last person in Britain please turn out the lights'. Subsequently this tabloid asserted that 'it's the *Sun* wot won it'.

The Conservative case was vigorously presented by Major who used a soapbox to address the public directly during the latter stages of the campaign. Additionally, Conservative election broadcasts were carefully crafted, the first (entitled *The Journey*) aping Labour's 1987 broadcast concerning Kinnock's background. This was directed by John Schlesinger and plotted Major's career from boy to Prime Minister. The tone of these broadcasts was, however, primarily negative, attacking the cost of Labour proposals and depicting Kinnock as a desparate man who would do anything to obtain power.

Labour

Social issues were at the forefront of the campaign mounted by the Labour Party in the winter of 1991–92. The specific themes which were projected included the modernisation of industry through increased investment, and the improvement of public services, particularly the health service. Electors were advised that the Party's taxation and benefits proposals meant that they would be 'better off with Labour'. Emphasis was also placed on areas where it was perceived the Conservatives were vulnerable, in particular in connection with increased hospital waiting lists, the greater number of bankruptcies and increased rates of unemployment. Problems, however, emerged in this campaign especially in connection with the stance the Party should adopt towards proportional representation, whether higher National Insurance contributions should be phased in and the relative unpopularity of Kinnock compared to Major.

Labour election promises were contained in its manifesto, *It's Time to Get Britain Working Again*. It expressed the Party's support for the European Community and for membership of the Exchange Rate Mechanism, and confirmed that unilateralism had been abandoned and that nuclear weapons would be retained as long as others had them. It promised to invest in education and training and to aid industrial recovery. The renationalisation of corporations and firms which had been privatised under Conservative governments was ruled out, although these would be subjected to an enhanced degree of regulation and competition. Labour proposed the introduction of a minimum wage, a national investment bank and regional development agencies. Conservative reforms which included the need for ballots before strike action and for the election of trade union officials would be retained, although compulsory competitive tendering would be ended. A Scottish Parliament with tax-raising powers, a Bill of Rights and a Freedom of Information Act were proposed, and during the campaign Kinnock expressed support for the introduction of proportional representation. Labour focused on the economic recession (characterised by the three Rs of recession, redundancy and repossession) as the context which justified a change of government, and advanced themes which included the need to save the health service (which they proposed to aid by an investment of £1.6 billion), and their plans to increase pension and child benefits.

It was emphasised that the Party had changed under Kinnock's leadership. During the campaign Shadow Chancellor John Smith published a budget in an attempt to counter Conservative arguments regarding the costing of its proposals. The manifesto failed to contain the earlier pronouncement that 'we will not spend, nor will we promise to spend, more than Britain can afford'. Smith's budget proposals promised to raise the top rate of taxation from 40 per cent to 50 per cent and to remove the exemption of top incomes from the 9 per cent National Insurance contribution. It was argued that most people earning below £21,000 a year would be better off since the rich would be paying more. Attacks were also mounted on the Poll Tax. One issue which caused considerable acrimony between the two main parties was the so-called 'war of Jennifer's ear'. In their second election broadcast, Labour highligted the case of two young girls suffering from 'glue ear'. One had her NHS operation cancelled on a number of occasions whereas the other paid for it privately and suffered no delay. This was compatible with the Labour accusation that the Conservatives had a secret agenda to privatise the social services, but led to a slanging match between Labour and the Conservatives over issues which included whether all the details claimed by Labour were accurate. A Conservative spokesman, William Waldegrave, likened Labour's behaviour on this matter to that of the Nazi propaganda machine, and the *Sun* asked its readers to consider 'are liars fit to govern ?'

The Labour case was presented in a number of carefully orchestrated meetings. The final one of these, held in Sheffield seven days before polling, was widely regarded as counter-productive. This rally was effectively designed to celebrate a Labour victory before the voters had delivered their verdict. Razzmatazz and triumphalism were emphasised at this event which William Waldegrave likened to a Nuremberg rally.

Liberal Democrats

Paddy Ashdown received a prominent focus in the Party's campaign. Liberal Democrat election policies were contained in the manifesto, *Changing Britain for Good*. Considerable emphasis was given to the proposal to fund educational improvements by the imposition of 1p on the standard rate of income tax. It advocated the repeal of a number of policies pursued by the Conservative government, including City Technology Colleges, the general practitioners' fund-holding scheme and hospital trusts. The Party promised to play a more active role in the European Community, and the Liberal Democrat commitment to Europe was emphasised when Paddy Ashdown addressed a meeting in Boulogne. The Party's fourth election broadcast called for a coalition government, and the possibility of the election producing a hung Parliament prompted Ashdown to assert the position which his party would adopt in this situation. He adopted a stance of equidistance between the two major parties, stating that he would cooperate with any party that would offer a deal which lasted for the lifetime of the Parliament, provided that proportional representation was part of that deal. He threatened to vote down a Queen's Speech which failed to deliver this reform.

Result of the Election

The campaigns of all parties displayed a considerable degree of central contral and coordination in 1992. Opinion polls attested to the fact that the outcome of the election was not inevitable. Fifty reputable nationwide polls were published during the campaign: 10 placed the Conservatives ahead, 38 put Labour in front and two recorded a dead heat (Butler and Kavanagh, 1992: 135). Ultimately the opinion polls predicted the result incorrectly. The final 'poll of polls' issued on polling day suggested a narrow Labour lead of 0.9 per cent which compared to the actual result of the Conservatives securing a 7.6 per cent lead over Labour in terms of popular vote. Additionally, the exit polls used by the BBC and ITV organisations suggested that the maximum number of seats which the Conservative Party would win was 305, which was likely to produce a minority Labour government. However, the Conservative Party actually won 336 seats and, thus, a small overall majority in the House of Commons.

These findings suggested the possibility of a 'last minute swing' to the Conservative Party. One factor accounting for this may have been Kinnock's move towards supporting proportional representation towards the end of the campaign which motivated lukewarm Conservative voters to turn out to avoid either a Labour government or a hung Parliament and possibly led some anti-Labour former Alliance voters also to vote Conservative. Other factors which were said to contribute to Labour's failings included the over-exuberant behaviour of Kinnock at the Sheffield rally and a failure to convince voters that eight out of 10 families would be better off under a Labour government. The belief that fear of Labour and distrust of Kinnock caused Labour's defeat led to the conclusion that the result was more a rejection of Labour than an endorsement of the Conservatives (Butler and Kavanagh, 1992: 275).

A total of 2,949 candidates contested the election (a total boosted by 309 candidates from the Natural Law Party, which argued that Vedic science was the source of all order and harmony and whose case was especially presented through a nation-wide poster campaign). Additionally, the Greens fielded 256 candidates. The result was:

Party	Votes	Vote %	MPs
Conservative	14,093,007	41.9%	336
Labour	11,560,484	34.4%	271
Liberal Democrat	5,999,606	17.8%	20
Ulster Unionist Parties	393,393	1.2% [50.1%]	13
Plaid Cymru	154,947	0.5% [8.9%]	4
SDLP	184,445	0.5% [23.5%]	4
Scottish National Party	629,564	1.9% [21.5%]	3
Sinn Fein	78,291	0.2% [10.0%]	0
Others	520,337	1.6%	0
Total	33,614,074		651

The turnout was 77.7 per cent. The swing from the Conservative Party to Labour was 2.1 per cent.

Sixty women MPs were elected. Six MPs were from ethnic minority communities, five of whom were Labour and one, Nirj Deva, was elected as the Conservative member for Brentford and Isleworth. He was the first Asian to sit on the Conservative benches since Sir Mancherjee Bhownaggree who represented NE Bethnal Green from 1895 to 1906.

The Parties

The national swing of 2.1 per cent from the Conservatives to Labour ought to have given the Conservatives more seats, but factors which included a better than average performance by Labour in marginal seats and tactical voting (which, it is estimated, may have cost the Conservative Party 10 seats) (Curtice and Steed, 1992: 336) served to narrow the size of the Conservatives' parliamentary majority. As in previous post-war elections, there were considerable regional differences in the swing, in particular a North–South divide. However, this was the reverse of the pattern which had been emerging since 1959 so that Labour performed well in Southern Britain, London and much of the Midlands but less well in the North with Scotland producing a swing to the Conservative Party. The impact of recession on Southern Britain (resulting in unemployment and a decline in house prices) was an important reason for the Labour Party's good performance there.

Margaret Thatcher retired from Parliament and nine Conservative ministers were defeated. The main Conservative casualty was Party Chairman Chris Patten who lost his constituency of Bath to the Liberal Democrats. Additionally, the black barrister, John Taylor (who had been the victim of racial abuse from members of his own party when selected for the seat of Cheltenham), failed to secure election, also being beaten by the Liberal Democrats.

A number of prominent Labour politicians, including Denis Healey and Merlyn Rees, retired from Parliament. Labour viewed its defeat as the result of the pro-Conservative stance of much of the media. The *Sun* was particularly singled out since many of its readers were either Labour supporters or uncommitted voters, suggesting the potential of this tabloid to convert voters to the Conservative cause (Butler and Kavanagh, 1992: 207–8).

The Liberal Democrats won 20 seats. The Party polled very well in the South West and well on the South Coast, in the South Metropolitan region and the Thames Valley. But it fared less well elsewhere, and the number of its candidates in second place fell from the 261 achieved in 1987 to 154 (Butler and Kavanagh, 1992: 334). One of its victors was Paul Tyler at North Cornwall, who had briefly represented Bodmin in the February–October 1974 Parliament. Russell Johnston also set a record for obtaining the lowest percentage of the vote to achieve election when he retained Inverness, Nairn and Lochaber with only 26 per cent of the poll.

Scotland, Wales and Northern Ireland
In July 1998 the opposition parties in Scotland established a campaign for a Scottish Parliament and a constitutional convention was subsequently set up to devise plans to achieve this. Although the SNP subsequently withdrew, the other parties continued with the venture whose subsequent recommendations included the introduction of electoral reform for elections to this body. At the election, Labour won 49 of Scotland's 72 seats and the Conservatives 11. The Liberal Democrats won nine (obtaining 13.1 per cent of the Scottish vote) compared to the three won by the SNP which secured 21.5 per cent of the vote. In Wales, Labour won 27 of the 36 seats, the Conservatives six, Plaid Cymru four and the Liberal Democrats one.

In Northern Ireland, Conservative candidates contested 11 seats in an attempt to erode its 'tribal politics'. They failed, however, to make any impact on the election results, securing 5.7 per cent of the vote and winning no seats. Unionist factions clashed in only three constituencies whereas the Nationalist parties (Sinn Fein and the SDLP) fought each other in 13. A notable result was secured by the SDLP in West Belfast where sufficient Unionists voted for its candidate, Dr Joe Hendron, to secure the defeat of Sinn Fein's Gerry Adams. Overall, the Ulster Unionists won nine of the 17 seats, the Democratic Unionists three and the Ulster Popular Unionist Party one. The SDLP won the remaining four seats.

Consequence of the Election
John Major formed a Conservative administration.

1 May 1997

Party Leaders
John Major (Conservative)
Tony Blair (Labour)
Paddy Ashdown (Liberal Democrat)

Background to the Election
Timing of the Election
By-election defeats, poor performances in European and local government elections and opinion poll rating evidenced the government's steadily declining political fortunes after the 1992 general election. The Party lost all eight by-elections caused by the deaths of Conservative MPs, was reduced to 18 (out of 87) seats in the 1994 European elections, and performed so badly in local government elections that it had fewer councillors than the Liberal Democrats by 1996. It lost its overall majority in the House of Commons on 3 November 1996 following the death of Barry Porter MP but was able to limp on through support given by the Ulster Unionists and the difficulty of finding an issue which would succeed in getting all of its opponents in the same lobby in the House of Commons. Defeat in the next general election was virtually a foregone conclusion (Butler and Kavanagh, 1997: 24). In these circumstances it was inevitable that the government would remain in office as long as it could in the (as it proved, vain) hope that a political miracle would provide salvation. The last legal date for a general election would have been 22 May, but 1 May was the last practicable date for this contest to take place, making the Parliament elected in 1992 the longest since the passage of the 1911 Parliament Act.

Electoral Procedures and Practices
The 1993 Redistribution of Seats Act required the redrawing of constituency boundaries to be completed by December 1995. Only 165 constituency boundaries were totally unchanged as a consequence of this review. Although it had initially been assumed that this process would substantially aid the Conservative Party (Butler and Kavanagh, 1992: 278) representations made by the Labour Party to the boundary commissions prevented this from happening.

Conservatives
A number of existing policies were developed following the 1992 election. These included privatisation (which was extended to the railway industry), the application of the Private Finance Initiative to services which included the prisons, and the internal market in the National Health Service (permitting fund-holding general practitioners to buy hospital treatment for their patients on a competitive basis). New policies included the resurrection of one-tier (or unitary) local authorities under the provisions of the 1992 Local Government Act, the introduction of the National Lottery in November 1994, and attempts (albeit, abortive) to find a political settlement in Northern Ireland following the Downing Street declaration signed by Major and the Irish Taoiseach, Albert Reynolds, on 15 December 1993 which resulted in an

IRA ceasefire from 31 August 1994 until 9 February 1996. Nationalists believed that the government's inability to utilise the ceasefire to greater effect derived from their reliance on the votes of the Ulster Unionist MPs in the House of Commons who were opposed to the involvement of Sinn Fein in all-party talks unless the IRA first disarmed.

The 1992–97 Conservative government was beset by numerous difficulties which had a telling effect on its standing with the electorate. The basis of its economic policy was to seek competitiveness and defeat inflation by the use of strict fiscal and monetary policies. Membership of the Exchange Rate Mechanism (ERM) was a key aspect of this policy. However, Britain had entered the ERM in October 1990 at what turned out to be too high a level, and after the 1992 general election pressures derived from factors which included currency speculation and demands for currency realignment resulted in the pound falling to its permitted floor of DM 2.87. The Chancellor, Norman Lamont, expended in excess of £10 billion of reserves to prop up Sterling and on 'Black Wednesday' (19 September 1992) adopted a number of further measures to achieve this objective, which included raising the bank rate twice (first to 10 per cent and later that day to 15 per cent), before conceding defeat and unilaterally withdrawing the UK from the ERM. Lamont's standing was severely affected by this episode and further problems made his position untenable. Following the 1992 election, the Public Sector Borrowing Requirement rose because of factors which included the loss of tax revenues and increased spending on welfare benefits during the 1990–92 economic recession. Accordingly, Lamont broke the 1992 pledge not to raise taxes. Initially, increases on National Insurance contributions were levied and, in his March 1993 budget, the imposition of VAT on domestic fuel was announced. The unpopularity of the latter policy was emphasised at the Newbury by-election on 6 May 1993 when the Liberal Democrats gained what had previously been a safe Conservative seat with a majority of over 22,000. Lamont was offered a move to the Department of the Environment, which he rejected in favour of resignation.

Lamont's successor, Kenneth Clarke, subsequently presided over economic recovery in which unemployment fell to a figure of below two million by the end of 1996, inflation levelled out to a figure of around 3 per cent for much of the remainder of the Parliament, and the rate of economic growth increased, reaching 4 per cent towards the end of 1994. House prices increased, and problems related to negative equity became of lesser importance. Income tax was cut by 1p in the pound in both the 1995 and 1996 budgets. However, although withdrawal from the ERM aided subsequent economic recovery (since the devaluation of the Pound was beneficial to British exports and the Chancellor had freedom to adjust interest rates to aid economic revival), the government failed to benefit from this situation as public confidence in its reputation for economic competence was severely shaken since success was based on the abandonment of a major pillar of its policy. Recovery also proceeded at a sustained rather than accelerated pace, which failed to create a sense of security among voters, many of whom did not feel themselves to be better off. The Conservative advantage over Labour at the 1992 election evaporated after 'Black Wednesday' and, by the end of 1993, Labour enjoyed a 20 per cent advantage which it more or less retained up until the 1997 election. Additionally, public satisfaction with Major's performance as Prime Minister was also low.

Public dissatisfaction with the government was based on factors other than its handling of the economy. Considerable internal disunity was displayed in connection with the UK's relationship with the European Community when the government's line was challenged by Conservative Eurosceptics whose actions seemed legitimised following the debacle over the ERM. The government suffered two defeats on issues related to Maastricht on 8 March and 22 July 1993, and although the treaty was ratified in August of that year, attacks continued to be made on it by Eurosceptics. Fearing defeat on the second reading of the European Communities (Finance) Bill in 1994, the government decided to make the matter an issue of confidence. However, on 28 November 1994, eight Euro-rebels abstained and immediately had the whip withdrawn from them. A further MP voluntarily quit the Parliamentary Party alongside them. The whip was subsequently restored on 25 April 1995 without any conditions regarding the MPs' future behaviour being imposed. The European Single Currency then emerged as a key issue, the government promising in April 1996 that this issue would be put to a referendum if a future Conservative government decided to join. Internal difficulties over Europe had an adverse impact on Major's authority as leader. In June 1995, to pre-empt a challenge being mounted against him, he urged his opponents to 'put up or shut up' by resigning the leadership and seeking re-election. In the contest which was held on 4 July 1995 he beat John Redwood by 219 votes to 89 (with 22 MPs abstaining).

Contentious policy issues caused further problems for the government's standing. A decision by Michael Heseltine to close 30 coal mines hastily as a prelude to the privatisation of the industry seemed to justify the arguments presented by Arthur Scargill during the 1984–85 miners' dispute concerning government intentions for the industry. This was subsequently declared to be 'unlawful and irrational' by the High Court. The establishment of the Child Support Agency resulted in well-publicised accusations of injustice, and the government suffered recriminations for not speedily banning the cattlefeed which was held responsible for causing 'mad cow' disease in cattle when it was acknowledged in 1996 that this disease was capable of being transferred to humans. To these problems were added accusations of 'sleaze'.

'Sleaze' refers to the abuse of power by elected public officials who improperly exploit their office for material or sexual gain or party advantage. Accusations were made of Conservative MPs obtaining cash for tabling questions in the House of Commons, and allegations regarding the acceptance of hospitality from Mohamed al-Fayed at the Ritz Hotel in Paris led to the resignation of two junior ministers and the withdrawal of a Cabinet minister, Jonathan Aitken, to fight a libel action in connection with this matter. These events resulted in the establishment of a new House of Commons Standards and Privileges Committee which would receive reports from an independent Parliamentary Commissioner. The payment of large salaries to senior executive and directors of the privatised industries (who were termed 'fat cats') further reinforced the perception that Conservative policies could result in excessive benefits for a privileged few. Complaints of improper conduct were not, however, confined to central government but also extended to local government, one example of which was accusations of gerrymandering being practised by the Conservative leadership at Westminster City Council in the 'homes for votes' row.

Charges of hypocrisy and dishonesty were also made concerning the conduct of government after 1992. Major's 1993 'back to basics' policy was designed to concentrate on issues such as law and order and education. However, it was given a moral stance by the media and undone by accusations of marital infidelity by some ministers. It seemed, therefore, that the government was instructing others to live by moral standards to which some of its own members (including, it subsequently emerged, Major himself) were not adhering to. The collapse of the trial of three businessmen accused of selling arms to Iraq in October 1992 (the Matrix-Churchill case) following revelations by a former Trade Minister, Alan Clark, that these actions had received tacit official approval led to an inquiry headed by Lord Justice Scott. In February 1996 his report criticised the conduct of some civil servants and ministers. He stated that William Waldegrave had inadvertently misled the House of Commons when answering questions regarding this issue and found fault with the manner in which the Attorney General, Sir Nicholas Lyell, had handled the subject of Public Interest Immunity Certificates. On 22 February 1996 the government secured a majority of one vote following the debate in the House of Commons on the Scott Report.

Labour

Labour's failure to secure victory in 1992 might be explained by a number of factors. Radicals perceived an absence of an ideology which would offer the electorate a clear alternative to Thatcherism on which the future actions of a Labour government would be based. Consequently, Labour's appeal in 1992 was that it could manage the economy 'with its current set of priorities and concerns' better than the Conservatives, and the Party's economic proposals were seen as 'fundamentally cautious, conservative and unambitious' (Taylor, 1997: 97–8). A further criticism from this perspective pointed to Labour's failure in 1992 being explained by the preoccupation with image and presentation to the detriment of policy and philosophy. However, alternative views suggested that Labour's failure in 1992 derived from its taxation policies which failed to convince middle-income voters that they would not be worse off under a Labour government. This perception, coupled with the belief that the Conservative Party was more competent to handle the economy, secured the narrow Conservative victory. In order to win a future election, therefore, it was necessary for the Party to extend its appeal beyond its core voters by pursuing policies and espousing values which would find support from the more individualistic and middle-class society which was the key inheritance of Thatcherism.

Neil Kinnock resigned soon after the election and was replaced by John Smith who easily defeated the challenge of Brian Gould by the margin of 9:1. The pace of reforms to ideology and policy initiated by Kinnock was slowed down under Smith, whose main contribution as party leader was to reconcile the differences between the traditionalists and modernisers, thus helping to create a unified party. However, he also advanced the process of modernisation through further organisational reform. This culminated in the adoption by the 1993 Party Conference of the 'one man, one vote' principle. This ended the trade union block vote at the Party Conference, in the electoral college for leadership elections and in the ballots by constituency Labour parties for candidate selection. Henceforth, only individual trade union members who paid the political levy and declared themselves to be Labour supporters could vote. The diminished role of trade unions over Labour affairs was further underlined by reducing their vote in the electoral college for choosing the Party's leader and deputy leader from 40 per cent to 33 per cent.

Smith also appointed the Commission on Social Justice whose remit was to consider the relationship between social justice and the goals of economic competitiveness and prosperity. The final report, *Social Justice: Strategies for National Renewal* (published in 1994), gave considerable prominence to five broad policy areas – education, employment, welfare, social policy and taxation. Ideas acceptable to progressive opinion were embodied in proposals to improve nursery education, cut long-term unemployment and tackle pension provision. Economic success was perceived as the crucial underpinning of social justice. Priority was also given to political and civil rights. The commission spoke of the need for a reorientation between those who governed and those who were governed.

Attempts by Labour leaders to bring Labour ideology up to date were accompanied by suggestions of the need to abandon or rewrite Clause IV of the Party's constitution. John Smith commenced work on preparing a statement of values which would have been debated at the Party Conference in 1995, but his initiatives were terminated by his premature death in May 1994. The new Labour leader was Tony Blair who defeated John Prescott and Margaret Beckett, securing around 58 per cent of the total vote cast. Initially, he concentrated on an ideology which he described as 'democratic socialism' embracing 'social justice, the equal worth of each citizen, equality of opportunity, community' (Blair, 1994: 4). At the 1994 Labour Conference he proposed to rewrite Clause IV. A number of changes affecting the post-war world could be cited to justify a move away from old-style, Clause IV socialism. These included the collapse of communism, globalisation (which made economic isolation neither desirable nor feasible and which additionally made it problematic to seek egalitarianism through the use of taxation and social welfare policies since capital would go elsewhere), the massive growth in service industries coupled with the development of a consumer culture, and changes to the composition of the workforce (particularly the number of women who were employed, many on a part-time basis) (Blair, 1994: 5). Additionally, this reform would prevent the Party being misunderstood or misrepresented in future elections (especially in connection with being associated with high taxation and state socialism), and would further provide a symbol of the Party's modernisation.

In December 1994, the NEC voted to hold a special Conference the following April to vote on the proposed constitutional change. The new Clause IV was approved by the NEC on 13 March 1995. It emphasised the value of community, social justice and democracy, and Part Two redefined the Party's economic aims as accepting the competitive market economy operating in the public interest, and espousing a partnership between private and public ownership. It thus rejected the belief that centralised planning and state control were the only routes to economic success. The special Conference approved this new statement on 29 April 1995 by a 3:1 majority. These changes amounted to Labour's acquiescence to a capitalist society which they would seek to improve and reform. This new stance of the Labour Party led it to being henceforth christened 'New' Labour.

Subsequently, a number of key ideas were promoted. These included the promotion of individual liberty by the state performing an enabling role, and a belief in strong communities as a key characteristic of Labour's 'Third Way' between between statism and untrammelled individualism (Cook, 1998). This was inextricably linked to the stakeholder economy which Labour wished to create. In contrast to a market economy which created social divisions between the 'haves' and 'have-nots', Labour wished to ensure that society as a whole benefited from the operations of a market economy. Stakeholding was directed towards the pursuit of social justice and the provision of wider opportunities for all within a market economy, but could also be depicted as a reform which was essential to its smooth operations since a permanently excluded underclass jeopardised the flexibility which a dynamic market economy required.

Further organisational reform was pursued under Blair, who wished to impose strong central control over the Party to prevent internal dissent from weakening its electoral appeal. One aspect of this was the approval given by the NEC in January 1997 to adjusting the role of the Party Conference to neuter the challenge it could pose to the actions of a future Labour government.

Liberal Democrats

The position obtained by the Party in 1992 improved during 1993. In May, David Rendel overturned a Conservative majority of around 12,500 in a by-election at Newbury. On the same day the Party gained in excess of 300 seats in the county council elections, obtaining 24 per cent of the vote. Labour gained a more modest 92 seats in these elections and this left the Conservative Party in control of only one county council. Paddy Ashdown concluded that 5 May 1993 was 'the most successful day to date in the electoral history of our party', which confirmed the Liberal Democrats as the growing third force in British politics. The Party's next test was provided at the Christchurch by-election. This was the fifteenth safest Conservative seat in Britain, having been held by a majority of 23,000 in 1992. This too fell to the Liberal Democrats with a majority of over 16,000. As at Newbury, the Labour candidate lost his deposit, suggesting tactical voting by Labour sympathisers. By 1995, the Party had over 5,000 councillors and controlled 51 councils. However, the most important issue which faced the Party after 1992 was the attitude it should adopt towards Labour.

The Liberal Party/Liberal Democrats had traditionally viewed their role as being that of offering the electorate an alternative to the Conservative Party. Their historic opposition to Labour, whose constitution embraced fundamentalist ideals, justified a negative view of that party and a desire to replace it (either independently or in conjunction with other progressive non-socialists through a process of realignment) as the main political vehicle on the left of the political spectrum. However, changes associated with Kinnock, Smith and Blair made it easier for the Liberal Democrats to consider working closely with Labour. Additionally, Liberal Democrat gains in that period (particularly at parliamentary level) were primarily at the expense of the Conservative Party which suggested that opposition to Labour was unlikely to produce any significant political dividends at the level of national politics. By the mid-1990s, the Conservative government was unpopular and it seemed conceivable that the Liberal Democrats might deny Labour an overall majority by securing significant gains from the Conservatives in the South East. This highlighted the need to consider how the Liberal Democrats might utilise this position should it occur. Accordingly, on 26 May 1995, Ashdown formally abandoned the stance of equidistance and placed the Liberal Democrat Party as an ally of Labour in joint opposition to the Conservative government. His pretext for doing this was to give a commitment that, should his party hold the balance of power after the next general election, they would not prop up a 'sleazy, rotten' Conservative government. He argued that 'people must know if they kick the Tories out through the front door, we Liberal Democrats will not allow them to sneak in through the back door'. He insisted, however, that this stance did not entail 'cozying up' to Labour and that his party would continue to campaign on the principles and policies they believed in (Ashdown, 1995). This stance was also based on the cooperation which had taken place between both parties after 1992.

The Scottish Constitutional Convention (whose inaugural meeting had been held in 1989) provided a forum within which both parties were able to agree upon a joint programme of constitutional change for Scotland which centred on the creation of a Scottish Parliament. In 1996 the Liberal Democrat and Labour Party leaders asked two of their senior parliamentarians

(Robin Cook and Robert Maclennan) to explore the possibility of cooperation between the parties on constitutional reform. A Joint Consultative Committee was subsequently established whose *Report of the Joint Consultative Committee on Constitutional Reform* (1997) put forward an agreed programme underlaid by a mutual commitment to seek the empowerment of the people. Cooperation between the two parties had also become a regular feature of the operations of 'hung' councils, 21 joint Liberal Democrat–Labour administrations (in three cases with Independent support) being identified in 1995. Closer ties were sought by the Labour organisation LINC (Labour Initiative on Cooperation), whose aims included the promotion of a continuing dialogue of ideas either formally through the official party structures or informally through cross-party campaigns and organisations.

By-elections

A total of 18 by-elections took place in the 1992–97 Parliament. Labour held nine, the Conservatives lost eight (three to Labour, four to the Liberal Democrats and one to the Scottish National Party). A further contest occurred at North Down in Northern Ireland. A candidate from the UK Unionist Party made a technical gain from the Popular Unionist Party which was not defending the seat.

Conduct of the Election

The Wirrall South by-election on 28 February 1997 (in which there was a 17 per cent swing to Labour on a 70 per cent turnout) provided stark evidence of the slump in Conservative fortunes since 1992.

Conservatives

In preparation for the election, the Conservatives sought to give prominence to their achievements in government, in particular the favourable economic circumstances in which the election would be fought. New policies (including the privatisation of the old age pension but with a state guarantee in cases of hardship) were also announced in early 1997. Much attention was paid to the Labour Party. Electors were courted with the slogan 'Britain is Booming, Don't Let Labour Blow It', and it was alleged that sinister forces inside the Labour Party would manipulate Tony Blair, were he elected, into pursuing policies from which 'New' Labour was seeking to distance itself (such as the resurrection of trade union power). In 1996 a 'New Labour, New Danger' campaign was initiated, one aspect of which was the an infamous 'demon eyes' poster which sought to create public suspicion and unease regarding Labour. This featured a close-up of Blair with a hideously grinning mouth and the slogan 'what lies below the smile?' It was also alleged that a tax rise of £2,300 would be the consequence of electing Labour to office.

The Conservative election manifesto, *You Can Only Be Sure with the Conservatives*, included proposals to tax benefits to married couples and others with dependants. It stated the goal of a 20p in the pound standard rate of income tax, pledged to keep public spending below 40 per cent of GDP and proposed the phasing out of State Earnings-Related Pension Schemes. The privatisation of Parcelforce and the London Underground were referred to and opposition was expressed to the creation of a European federal state. The manifesto put forward a 'negotiate and then decide'/'wait and see' approach towards joining a single European currency. It asserted that, as it was unlikely that there would be sufficient convergence of economic conditions across Europe for a single currency to proceed safely on the target date of 1 January 1999, legislation related to a single currency would not be included in the first Queen's Speech. If during the course of the next Parliament a Conservative government concluded that it was in the national interest to join such a currency, the British people would be required to give their express approval to this decision in a referendum before it was implemented. However, many Conservative candidates disapproved of this course of action and over 300 of them (including some junior ministers) explicitly declared their opposition to a European single currency. The presence of the Referendum Party was partly responsible for emboldening them in their opposition to the official party line, but the existence of divisions on this key issue was prominently aired in the media and detracted from the positive issues (in particular economic recovery) which the Party sought to project during its campaign. At the end of the campaign, Major emphasised his opposition to constitutional reform (especially devolution) by embarking upon a 72 hour crusade to 'save the Union'.

During the campaign, attention was drawn to Labour's perceived weaknesses which included their need to agree to the Conservative suggestion to privatise the National Air Traffic Control System (a proposal which had been initially opposed by Labour) in order to plug the 'black hole' in their spending plans and the Party's past opposition to the Prevention of Terrorism legislation. Personal attacks on Blair were made, in particular in a political broadcast which depicted him as a Faust-like figure who had sold his principles in order to get elected. Attempts to attack Labour's new pro-European stance (which included a poster depicting Blair as a ventriloquist's dummy sitting on Chancellor Kohl's knee) tended, additionally (or perhaps instead) to create dissent within the Conservative Party whose pro-Europeans were antagonised by this statement. Conservative election broadcasts were especially centred on Major. Initially, in his election tours he put his case across by the use of his soapbox which had been put to good effect in 1992. However, this was abandoned in favour of impromptu speeches delivered from his battlebus.

Labour

The key theme of Labour's campaign in 1997 was that of reassurance – seeking to insist (in particular to middle-England voters) that there was nothing to fear from a Labour government (in particular in terms of policies such as tax rises). Labour's main effort would be expended in managing the economy more efficiently than the Conservatives (whose competence to achieve this had been dented by the events of 'Black Wednesday') and they would re-establish honesty in the conduct of politics.

The press began to turn against Major after 1992, and Blair seized the opportunity this offered to court the tabloid proprietors. One important aspect of this was his visit to Australia in July 1995 when he informed an audience of News International executives that Labour had irrevocably changed. At the outset of the campaign the *Sun* endorsed Labour (arguing that the Conservatives were 'tired, divided and rudderless') and the *News of the World* followed suit. This was the first election campaign in which Labour secured the support of the majority of the national daily press.

Policy was refined through the use of focus groups, and key stakeholders were also consulted (including business leaders regarding economic policy). A draft manifesto was issued in July 1996 in which a rise in income tax rates was specifically ruled out and it was further promised to reduce the rate of VAT on heating to 5 per cent. Subsequently, in January 1997, the Party unequivocally stated that it would freeze existing public spending levels for two years, would not increase the standard rate of income tax and would not impose a top income tax rate of 50p in the pound. Pledges were also made not to abolish selection in education nor to remove charitable status from independent schools, a more sceptical stance on Europe was put forward (especially regarding membership of the single currency), and a tough stance on law and order was promoted. In the build-up to the campaign, Labour also attacked the Conservatives for breaking their 1992 election promises (pointing to 22 tax rises in that period and referring to a threat to impose VAT on food) and sought to question Major's trustworthiness.

Labour's manifesto was entitled *New Labour Because Britain Deserves Better*. It put forward a ten-point 'contract with the people' which entailed increasing the share of national income spent on education, providing stable economic growth with low inflation, promoting dynamic and competitive business at home and abroad, and pledging to move 250,000 young people from benefit into work. Labour promised to rebuild the NHS by reducing spending on administration and increasing spending on patient care, to be tough on crime and on the causes of crime and to halve the time it took for persistent juvenile offenders to be taken to court, and to build strong families and strong communities and lay the foundations of a modern welfare state in pensions and community care. The Party pledged to safeguard the environment and develop an integrated transport policy to fight congestion and pollution, to clean up politics, to decentralise political power throughout the UK and to place the funding of political parties on a proper and accountable basis. The manifesto gave an undertaking to provide the leadership in Europe which Britain and Europe required. Increases in basic or top rates of income tax were explicitly ruled out, although during the campaign much prominence was given to the proposal to impose a windfall tax on utilities which were regulated and licensed by the state. Additionally, further privatisation was not ruled out on principle.

The Party sought to capitalise on a perceived mood for change in the country by pointing to alleged Conservative failures and asserting that 'Britain Deserves Better'. This was articulated in Blair's response on the election eve to Major's 'save the union' campaign which stated that there were 'just 24 hours to save the NHS', give children the education they needed and provide security for the elderly. Crucially, the entire Labour campaign aimed to provide the electorate (and middle-England voters in particular) with reassurance that the reforms which they favoured would not require any radical measures such as income tax rises. Scare tactics (which included allegations that a future Conservative government would impose VAT on food and would abolish the old age pension) were also used to undermine Conservative credibility.

'New' Labour was especially keen to secure the support of business. A specific business manifesto, *Equipping Britain for the Future*, was launched, which included commitments to secure a 2.5 per cent or less rate of inflation, pursuing the modernisation of services such as transport through public–private sector cooperation and to make improvements in the education system in order to secure a skilled workforce. Entrepreneurs who included Anita Roddick (of Bodyshop) and Alan Sugar (of Amstrad) declared support for a Labour government, and Richard Branson was willing to be seen publicly travelling on Blair's train (although he did not say for whom he would be voting).

The Labour campaign was highly centralised through the Campaign and Media Centre which operated from Millbank Tower, in London, under the charge of Peter Mandelson and

Gordon Brown. Blair was followed around during the campaign by an actor dressed as a chicken who on one occasion had to be taken into police protection for his own safety following threats by Labour sympathisers to dump him into a harbour.

Liberal Democrats
The Liberal Democrat proposals were contained in their manifesto, *Make the Difference*. The Party proposed to boost spending on education by £2 billion a year, to recruit more doctors and nurses and reintroduce free eye and dental checks. The manifesto argued that all spending proposals put forward by the Party could be funded by a 1p increase in the standard rate of income tax and placing an additional 5p on the cost of cigarettes. Labour's move to the right of the political spectrum after 1992 created political space which the Liberal Democrats sought to exploit by pointing to the similarities which existed between the Labour and Conservative taxation policies and spending proposals. Their pledge to increase income tax to fund improvements to education and health thus featured prominently in their campaign and was put forward as a radical proposal in contrast to the stated intention of Gordon Brown to adhere to the Conservative government's spending and tax commitments. The Liberal campaign gave considerable prominence to Ashdown who travelled over 17,000 miles and visited 64 constituencies. The second of their election broadcasts was devoted to 'Ashdown the Man'. He attempted to highlight the positive aspects of his party's campaign by comparing these to the slanging match embarked upon by the 'Punch and Judy' two main parties.

Result of the Election
At the outset of the campaign, Labour enjoyed an average lead of 22 per cent in the opinion polls and only one isolated poll indicated a lead of below 10 per cent throughout its duration.

A total of 3,724 candidates contested the election. (This number was bosted by 547 from Sir James Goldsmith's Referendum Party, which sought a referendum on Britain's future in Europe, 194 from the UK Independence Party, which desired UK withdrawal from Europe, and 196 from the Natural Law Party and 95 by the Greens.) The result was:

Party	Votes	Vote %	MPs
Labour	13,541,826	43.3%	419
Conservative	9,600,943	30.7%	165
Liberal Democrat	5,242,947	16.8%	46
Ulster Unionist Parties	389,442	1.2% [49.3%]	13
Scottish National Party	621,550	2.0% [22.1%]	6
Plaid Cymru	161,030	0.5% [9.9%]	4
SDLP (Ulster)	190,814	0.6% [24.1%]	3
Sinn Fein (Ulster)	126,941	0.4% [16.1%	2
Others	1,410,891	4.5%	1
Total	31,286,284		659

The turnout was 71.4 per cent, the lowest since 1945. The overall swing from the Conservative Party to Labour was 10.2

per cent. The 'other' was Martin Bell (Tatton, Independent). Women MPs numbered 120, 101 of whom were Labour.
Following the 1993 Party Conference, all-women shortlists had been introduced in an attempt to provide a fairer gender
balance in the Parliamentary Party. Although this procedure was declared illegal by an industrial tribunal in January
1996, it did succeed in boosting the number of successful women candidates in 1997. Nine MPs were drawn from ethnic
minority communities, one of whom (Mohammed Sarwar in Glasgow Govan) was the first Muslim MP to be elected.
Nirj Deva, the Conservatives' only MP from an ethnic minority community was defeated by Labour.

The Parties

The national swing was subject to no significant regional variation, indicating that disenchantment with the Conservatives was nation-wide and not dependent on factors such as regional
variations in economic circumstances. Accordingly, the 1997 election bucked the long-term
trend which had evidenced a North–South electoral divide.

There was evidence of heightened levels of tactical voting in 1997. This was cultivated by
campaigns such as that mounted by the *Observer* on the Sunday prior to the election which
advised its readers 'What You Can Do to Secure a Total Tory Defeat'. It was subsequently
estimated that tactical voting by Labour and Liberal Democrat supporters contributed to
Labour victories in 15 to 21 seats and enabled the Liberal Democrats to gain between 10 and
14 seats (Curtice and Steed, 1997: 313).

Highly centralised campaigns in which spin doctors performed major roles were mounted by
both major parties. The campaign was a very long one (six weeks). It had been hoped by the
Conservatives that this would enable 'New' Labour to be subject to prolonged scrutiny,
although in practice they suffered the adverse consequences of elongated examination particularly with regard to accusations of sleaze. The prorogation of Parliament meant that the report
of Sir George Downey to the House of Commons's Standards and Privileges Committee would
not be considered before the election. One of those whose conduct had been examined by
Downey was Neil Hamilton. His constituency of Tatton endorsed his candidature and formally
re-nominated him. Major's failure to step in and repudiate his candidacy was used by Blair as
examples both of Conservative standards and Major's weakness, and ensured that the issue of
sleaze would dominate the early days of the campaign. Labour and Liberal Democrats withdrew
their candidates to give an 'anti-sleaze' candidate a free run against Hamilton. This person, the
BBC war correspondent Martin Bell, was comfortably elected in what had been the fifth safest
Conservative seat in Britain, polling 29,354 votes to Hamilton's 18,277.

A number of prominent Conservatives, including Kenneth Baker, Douglas Hurd and Sir
Patrick Mayhew, retired from the House of Commons, and deselections included Sir Nicholas
Scott and Sir George Gardiner (who subsequently joined the Referendum Party). The swing to
Labour eliminated all Conservative MPs from both Scotland and Wales and most from urban
Britain, where the Party won only 17 of the 172 seats in Greater London and the other major
urban conurbations. This meant that the Conservatives had become 'almost exclusively a rural
and suburban party' (King *et al.*, 1997: 8).

Seven cabinet ministers (Ian Lang, Malcolm Rifkind, Michael Forsyth, Michael Portillo,
William Waldegrave, Tony Newton and Roger Freeman) failed to secure re-election. Former
Chancellor Norman Lamont was also unsuccessful in his new constituency of Harrogate and
Knaresborough which was won by the Liberal Democrats. A particular problem faced by the

Conservatives in 1997 was that the relatively even geographic spread of their vote which (as had once been the case with the Liberal Party) made victory in individual constituencies less easy to achieve and contributed to the scale of Labour's victory.

Trade union sponsorship of Labour MPs was discontinued in 1995 in order to distance individual MPs from money provided by trade unions since this might be viewed as improper or depicted as corrupt. Sponsorship was replaced by 'constituency plan agreements' which were concluded between unions and constituency Labour parties (CLPs) whereby a union donated some money to the local party in return for which it was allocated representation on the CLP's general committee. Sponsorship of Labour candidates by the Cooperative Party was also discontinued in favour of a process whereby the Cooperative Party assumed equal status with Labour whose candidates became joint nominees of both parties.

A number of leading Labour parliamentarians including Roy Hattersley and Peter Shore retired from the House of Commons. Labour secured a victory of landslide proportions, polling especially well among the lower-middle-class electorate. Its success was founded on its appeal to all social classes whereas the Conservatives were viewed as a party which represented the interests of only one class (Butler and Kavanagh, 1997: 230–1). Labour made significant inroads in the South East and secured support among the middle class and former Conservative voters: around one-third of Labour's support was obtained from electors who had not voted Labour in 1992 (Butler and Kavanagh, 2002: 23). It won 418 seats which provided it with an overall majority of 179.

The former Liberal leader Sir David Steel and the senior Liberal parliamentarian, Sir Russell Johnston, retired from the House of Commons. Although the Party's share of the national vote amounted to only 17 per cent, its strategy of targeting a relatively small number of seats enabled it to win 46 seats (28 of which were gained from the Conservatives). Although the Party's poll was relatively uniform across the country, it managed to concentrate support in key areas (in particular the South West) and in other places where it had a good track record in local government contests.

Minor parties made relatively little impact, the Referendum Party succeeding in polling 5 per cent or more of the vote in only 39 constituencies.

Scotland, Wales and Northern Ireland
Labour won 56 of Scotland's 72 seats, and the Liberal Democrats 10. The SNP's poll of 22.1 per cent only yielded six MPs. Although the Conservatives obtained 17.5 per cent of the vote (which was 4.5 per cent more than the total won by the Liberal Democrats), they failed to win a single seat. In Wales, Labour won 34 of the 40 seats, Plaid Cymru became the second party with four seats and the Liberal Democrats won two. As in Scotland, the Conservatives were wiped out, winning no seats despite obtaining 19.6 per cent of the vote. In Northern Ireland, the Ulster Unionists won 10 of the 18 seats, the Democratic Unionists two and the UKUP one. On the nationalist side, the SDLP won three seats and Sinn Fein two, the failure of the IRA to call a ceasefire over the election period failing to dent the electoral challenge of their political wing. Gerry Adams recaptured his former seat of West Belfast from the SDLP and Martin McGuinness was successful in Mid-Ulster, where he defeated the DUP candidate, William McCrea.

Consequence of the Election
Tony Blair formed a Labour administration.

7 June 2001

Party Leaders
Tony Blair (Labour)
William Hague (Conservative)
Charles Kennedy (Liberal Democrat)

Background to the Election
Timing of the Election
The contest was prompted by Labour perceptions that economic and political circumstances (the latter attested by large leads in the opinion polls on the key electoral issues) were favourable to Labour's chances of re-election but these could not be guaranteed to last indefinitely. The April 2001 budget was designed to be a curtain-raiser for the election, but it (and the local elections) had to be briefly postponed due to the outbreak of foot-and-mouth disease in February 2001.

Electoral Practices and Procedures
The 1998 Registration of Political Parties Act required political parties to register their names in an attempt to prevent candidates deliberately seeking to confuse electors. In October 1998 the Neill Committee on Standards in Public Life published a report on party fundraising and election expenses. Proposals put forward in this report were embodied in the 2000 Political Parties, Elections and Referendums Act which set up a statutory Electoral Commission whose role was to register party names, oversee public reporting of donations and campaign expenditure, to report on the conduct of elections and to suggest further reforms. This legislation further capped party expenditure in general election years. The Act also made postal voting easier by the creation of a rolling register.

Labour
In office, Labour's key problem was how to keep on board those middle-class (or 'middle England') electors who had voted for the Party in 1992, but without totally alienating Labour's core supporters. This gave rise to an approach which was referred to as the 'Third Way' which attempted to marry policies to promote economic dynamism with others seeking to secure social justice.

Labour inherited a sound economy which remained in good health throughout the 1997–2001 Parliament. Unemployment steadily dipped, falling below one million in 2001. Inflation stayed below 3 per cent and the GDP grew by about 2.5 per cent between 1997 and 2001. The size of the national debt was considerably reduced. The only main difficulty concerned the strength of the Pound which caused problems for the export of manufactured goods. Other departures in economic policy included handing control over interest rates to the Monetary Committee of the Bank of England.

The new Chancellor of the Exchequer, Gordon Brown, entered office on the back of a pledge not to increase marginal rates of income tax for the lifetime of the next Parliament. He accepted the spending plans of his Conservative predecessors for the future two years (although in 2000 promised an extra £63 billion for spending on the public services over the next three years).

This entailed rejecting any significant increases in spending on social reform although limited schemes to redistribute wealth were pursued. A national minimum wage was introduced in April 1999, and the budget of that year initiated a 10 per cent bottom rate of income tax which was of particular benefit to the low-wage earners.

In addition, a range of schemes which were designed to help the poorer members of society were put forward. These included 'welfare to work' (funded from a 'windfall' tax on public utilities) which was focused at the young long-term unemployed, the provision of financial aid to poorer families through innovations such as the Working Families Family Tax Credit which was introduced in 1999, attempts to raise standards in education by initiatives such as the Sure Start Programme, intensive nursery schemes, the Fresh Start Scheme and action against truancy, and neighbourhood regeneration which included policies designed to tackle poverty in urban areas under the auspices of the New Deal For Communities which was launched in 1998. These schemes were, however, sold to middle England not in connection with the socialist objective of securing greater equality and fighting injustice, but, instead, by the beneficial impact these schemes would have on the level of crime, especially juvenile crime. These were reinforced with attempts to tackle drug use (on the grounds that much crime was driven by the need to feed drug habits) and the rhetoric of the need to remoralise society.

Labour largely pursued the penal populist approach towards crime and lawlessness associated with its Conservative predecessor. A significant reform was provided in the 1998 Crime and Disorder Act which provided a wide range of options for a community to deal with juvenile crime. This was followed up in 1999 with the Youth Justice and Criminal Evidence Act which sought to enhance the level of community involvement in responses to youth offending.

The government exploited the political situation in Ireland to mount a new peace initiative. This took the form of the April 1998 Good Friday Agreement which resulted in the creation of a devolved power-sharing Assembly in Northern Ireland which took office later that year. The path to peace was, however, subject to subsequent difficulties. Paramilitary groups (most notably the 'Real IRA') continued with their campaign of violence. A particular problem, however, was that the aspirations of the Loyalist and Nationalist communities regarding the new Assembly were different: Loyalists saw this as the final stage in a constitutional process whereas Nationalists viewed it as the start, with Irish unity as the eventual goal. Devolved government was also provided in the form of the establishment of a Scottish Parliament, a Welsh Assembly (both of which were elected in 1999) and a new system of local government for London which was headed by an American-style mayor in 2000. These bodies were elected by systems other than the first-past-the-post electoral system (namely the additional member 'top-up' system for Scotland and Wales and the supplementary vote system for the Mayor of London). Additionally, the November 1999 House of Lords Act ended the right of hereditary peers to sit in the House of Lords, although as a temporary measure 92 of these were elected to remain in the Upper Chamber together with the bishops and the Law Lords. The European Convention of Human Rights was incorporated in UK domestic law by the 1998 Human Rights Act which made it possible for UK citizens to pursue cases which alleged that their human rights had been breached in UK domestic courts rather than in the European Court of Human Rights at Strasbourg.

Hesitancy was the hallmark of the government's European policy, underpinned by opinion polls which indicated popular hostility towards Britain joining a single currency and scepticism towards Europe itself. The government accordingly ruled out entry into the single currency before the next general election. Other difficulties faced by the government included accusations of 'sleaze' (especially in connection with the Ecclestone donation to the Party and the government's subsequent decision to delay the introduction of new rules against the advertising of tobacco products in Formula 1 racing). Further problems arose from the government's desire not to increase drastically public spending. This meant that its performance in improving education and the NHS (issues which had been prominently featured in the Party's 1997 campaign) was increasingly subject to criticism.

However, the major problems which the Labour Party faced during its term of office was the BSE crisis and the protests of rural Britain to its perceived neglect by a 'towny'-led Labour government. Outrage was especially voiced against proposals to outlaw fox hunting, which resulted in a huge demonstration organised by the Countryside Alliance in March 1998 following the overwhelming endorsement in the House of Commons of a Private Members' Bill in the House of Commons to outlaw this pursuit in 1997. However, realising that opposition to fox hunting was unlikely to attract support amongst a nation of supposed animal lovers, rural Britain required a broader issue with which to confront the Labour government. This was provided in the high cost of duty placed on fuel, which was aggravated by increases in the price of fuel in August 2000 caused by a decision of OPEC to cut oil production. Labour's promise not to increase income tax had made it particularly reliable on indirect (or 'stealth' taxes) and fuel was particularly affected since around 77 per cent of the cost of a litre of fuel derived from fuel duty and VAT. Protests by French farmers in August 2000 prompted persons associated with the agricultural industry to blockade oil refineries to make the government aware of public concerns and to depict them as out of touch with public feeling on this issue. This action resulted in Britain virtually running out of fuel and the inability of the government to control the crisis resulted in a considerable, albeit temporary, loss of public support. The crisis was eventually ended when the government insisted that this protest would cost lives because the NHS could not function effectively and from the actions of the Transport and General Workers' Union whose officials persuaded tanker drivers in Grangemouth to return to work.

The key innovation associated with the Labour government was in the field of presentation. Its relationship with the public via the media was mediated by what were referred to as 'spin doctors' whose role was to ensure (by fair means or foul) that government policies received favourable coverage in the media. Chief among the spin doctors was the Number 10 Press Secretary, Alastair Campbell, whose desire to promote Labour policies resulted in clashes with Labour politicians who seemed to be in a position of subservience to Campbell's public relations exercises. These rebounded on the Prime Minister himself who was viewed as a 'control freak'. Perceived failures in the government's ability to improve key public services also led to charges that this was a government of 'spin, but no substance'.

The government's main involvement in foreign affairs was to participate in military action against the Serbian President, Slobodan Milosevic, when his forces embarked upon a policy of ethnic cleansing to drive ethnic Albanians out of Kosovo. This succeeded in driving Serbian forces back and ousting Milosevic from office.

Internal party reforms which were pursued after 1997 included the Partnership in Power arrangements which were approved at the 1997 Conference. This reconstructed the NEC and altered the role of the Party Conference. Members of Parliament were given their own section in the NEC elections but at the same time were disqualified from standing in either the constituency or trade union sections. The Women's Section was also abolished and the unions lost their majority on this body. The role of the annual conference was also altered in 1997. Its proceedings were henceforth subjected to a high degree of stage management, and its influence on policy was reduced by the introduction of the Joint Policy Committee and the National Policy Forum whose roles were to review party policy through the mechanism of policy commissions which operated on a two-year cycle. These changes were designed to reduce the role of the established internal bodies over Labour policy.

Conservatives

John Major resigned after the election. Five candidates stood in the first ballot held on 10 June (Kenneth Clarke, William Hague, John Redwood, Peter Lilley and Michael Howard) and on 17 June a second ballot took place involving the first three names who scored 64, 62 and 38 votes respectively. On the third ballot held on 19 June, William Hague defeated Kenneth Clarke by the margin of 92 : 70 votes and thus became the new leader, aged 36. In 1998, Hague embarked upon a series of organisational reforms under the heading of 'fresh future' which supplemented the functions of the annual conference and spring assembly by the creation of the National Conservative Convention and the Conservative Party Forum whose role was to advise on party policy. The National Union of Conservative and Unionist Associations and Central Office were merged and placed under the control of a 15-member board which would determine all party organisational issues. Changes were also made to the proceedure for electing the party leader. Under the new proposals, MPs alone could trigger a contest. Fifteen per cent of MPs could propose a vote of no confidence in the leader. If this were carried, the leader could not enter the ensuing leadership contest which proceeded in two stages. Stage one involved a ballot of all MPs. A candidate was required to get the support of 10 per cent of MPs to stand in this ballot, and any candidate who secured 25 per cent of the vote of MPs could participate in the second round. Stage two enabled party members to chose the leader from those MPs who were eligible to stand in the second round. The victor was determined by a simple majority, with each member having one vote. Hague submitted these reforms and his leadership to a vote of party members which approved them by 143,299 to 30,092. Attempts were also made to cast off the party image as remote by transforming it into a 'listening party' through the launching of the 'Listening to Britain' initiative by the new deputy leader, Peter Lilley, in July 1998.

In opposition, the Party's performance in Parliament was hampered by a number of factors. Although Hague generally performed well in Prime Minister's Question Time, a large number of former ministers had been defeated and the initial Queen's Speech debate in 1997 was marred when some of those who survived attacked each other rather than focusing their attention on the new government. Subsequently, problems arose with the proposals to reform the House of Lords (when a deal struck with the government by Lord Cranborne regarding letting 92 hereditary peers remain in the Upper Chamber pending comprehensive reform was concluded behind Hague's back to which Hague responded by sacking Cranborne as party leader in the Lords), and the disaffection of Europhile MPs (especially Michael Heseltine and Kenneth Clarke) to the increasingly Euroscpetic line of the Party on issues such as entry to the

Euro, in which Major's 'wait and see' attitude was replaced by ruling out entry in both the current Parliament and the next, and the impact of Europe on British sovereignty.

The key problem faced by the Conservative Party after 1997 was that Labour's move to the centre/centre-right of the political spectrum (on issues which included law and order, public spending and taxation) made it hard for them to find issues with which to challenge the Labour government and in some cases (such as Shadow Chancellor Michael Portillo's endorsement of the minimum wage in 2000) they were forced to embrace Labour policies. A particular difficulty was Labour's rhetoric after 2000 on the need to 'invest' in public services and to propose increased spending on them. Although this invited a response from the Conservatives to advocate tax cuts, this was deficient as it would damage public services which many members of the general public perceived as being under-funded. Accordingly, they had to tread carefully and particularly focused their concern on indirect taxes. In 2000 Portillo proposed to reduce petrol duty together with the tax on unearned income for those earning below £32,785 a year. However, at the same time he endorsed Labour's proposals for increased spending on health, education and law and order for the period 2000–03, arguing that the apparent contradiction between tax cuts and increased spending could be met by economies elsewhere in government.

The similarities between Labour and the Conservatives in many key areas prompted them to embrace right-wing policies which included 'save the Pound', and the need to take a hard line against drug users, criminals and asylum seekers. However, the stance which was either considered or adopted on some of these issues was not regarded as being of crucial importance by voters and also resulted in the Conservatives being seen as extreme by many of its centrist, One-Nation supporters.

Liberal Democrats

The Party followed up its performance in 1997 by faring well in the June 1999 Euro elections when, following the introduction of proportional representation, 10 of its candidates were returned. The involvement of the Party in a Cabinet Sub-Committee examining constitutional issues together with Archie Kirkwood's chairmanship of the Social Security Select Committee indicated its increased importance in UK politics which was enhanced by the formation of a Labour–Liberal Democrat Coalition government in Scotland in May 1999 and (although not immediately) also in Wales. Party spirits were kept up when a successful challenge to the Liberal victory in Winchester was upheld and a by-election was held. In this, the Liberal victor in June, Richard Oaten, increased his tiny majority of two votes to one in excess of 20,000. This success was followed up in May 2000 when the Party captured the Conservative seat of Romsey in a by-election. Successes were also achieved in local government, including taking control of Liverpool in May 1998 and Sheffield in May 1999. However, a key problem faced by the Party was which of the two major parties were regarded as the key enemy. Although Ashdown sought to cultivate close links with Labour (perhaps implying the eventual realignment of these two parties) many local government activists (particularly in Northern England) viewed Labour as their principal enemy. Further, any attempt by the Party to secure support by seeking to outflank Labour on the left would alienate many of its voters who were drawn from the right wing of the political spectrum.

The Liberal Democrats experienced a change of leadership when Paddy Ashdown announced his decision to retire in January 1999. He was replaced in August 1999 by Charles Kennedy who defeated Simon Hughes, Malcolm Bruce and Jackie Ballard by the margins of

22,724 : 16,233, 4,643, 3,978. After the reallocation of the votes of the two latter candidates, Kennedy was declared the winner by 28,425 : 21,833.

By-elections

A total number of 17 by-elections occurred in the 1997–2001 Parliament. The Conservatives held four seats, Labour held eight and gained one (which was the 'technical' gain of the seat held by the former Speaker at West Bromich West), and the Liberals Democrats held one (when a rerun was ordered at Winchester) and won one (the former Conservative seat of Romsey). Plaid Cymru held its seat of Ceredigion and in Northern Ireland the Democratic Unionist Party gained South Antrim from the Ulster Unionist Party.

Conduct of the Election

The main feature of the election was the extreme degree of central control exerted over the campaigns of the main parties, both of whom seemed obsessed with presentation. The two enduring episodes of the election arose when this control broke down. Both occurred on 16 May. This happened firstly when a protester managed to confront Blair (to his obvious discomfort) in full view of the media about the inadequacy of Labour's reforms to the NHS, and secondly when John Prescott lost his temper with a protester who had thrown an egg at him and waded into the crowd to 'sort him out'.

A further novel feature of the election was the extent which all main parties made use of the internet to put their own case across and denigrate that of their opponents. There were, however, key problems associated with this form of communication. It was necessary to devote efforts to obtain email addresses and it was not clear whether this form of electioneering won new votes or merely reinforced a voter's established political habits. Tactical voting was also advanced in this way when the pop singer, Billy Bragg, set up a website so that Labour and Liberal Democrats could enter into arrangements to exchange votes with a view to ousting the four incumbent Conservative MPs in Dorset.

The outcome of the election was certain at its outset and the fact that it would serve no purpose other than to reaffirm Labour's political supremacy was one factor which had a detrimental impact on the turnout. This problem had been signposted in June 1999 when the turnout for the Euro elections had been 24 per cent, a record low for the UK, and was attributed to a number of other factors which included a disinclination by core Labour supporters to vote because of their perception that policies designed to be attractive to middle England entailed a 'sell-out' to those whose needs were failing to be addressed adequately. In addition, public anxiety regarding both the operations of the parties (caused by issues such as 'sleaze' and ideological convergence) and the effectiveness of conventional politics to remedy pressing problems (because of factors which included the control exerted by business and multinational corporations over public policy, globalisation, and the control over domestic policy by supranational institutions such as the EU) tended to reduce the level of public interest in the contest.

Conservatives

The key problem facing the Conservative campaign was its inability to oppose the Labour government in areas which the electors identified as key issues and the lack of any central theme which could underpin their campaign. This problem arose in part from the extent of ideological convergence between the two parties (in particular on the key issue of the acceptance of the market economy) and also because Labour enjoyed large leads in the opinion polls on other major policy areas such as the economy, health and education. This meant that the Conservatives were forced to campaign on other issues where polls indicated that the standing of the two parties was similar, the most important of which were crime, Europe and the issue of asylum seekers. This gave rise to Hague's use of xenophobic language at the Party's spring Conference in March 2002 which was especially directed at asylum seekers but which made the Party appear extreme and racist.

Racism surfaced as a problem for the Party in the lead-up to the election. One retiring MP, John Townend, attacked multiculturalism and asserted his belief that immigration was undermining Britain's homogenous, Anglo-Saxon society. He criticised a speech by the Foreign Secretary, Robin Cook, asserting that the government sought to transform Britons into a 'mongrel race'. His views were echoed by another retiring Conservative MP, Christopher Gill, who alleged that the rising number of asylum seekers was responsible for diluting Britain's 'national character'. The black barrister and Conservative peer, Lord Taylor, insisted that Townend should be thrown out of the Conservative Party, but William Hague refused to follow this advice and at one stage it seemed that Taylor himself might be disciplined for voicing views which were critical of the Conservative leadership. Eventually, Townend was prevailed upon to apologise for his 'ill-chosen words', to withdraw them, to undertake not to repeat them and to accept that racism had no place in the Conservative Party.

A key issue in the Conservative campaign was the allegation that Labour had failed to make tangible improvements in the public services. In March, the Party launched a poster campaign with the theme 'can you really wait another four years for improvements to public services ?'

One difficulty with a campaign of this nature, however, was that electors might still place most of the blame for underfunding on the shoulders of the Conservative Party which had been in power for 18 years compared to Labour's four. The Party's manifesto, *Time for Common Sense*, proposed to cut taxes by £8 billion whilst matching Labour's spending plans on health, education and the police. A cut of 6p per litre in the cost of fuel was proposed and taxation reforms were put forward which included a tax cut of £1,000 per couple and a tax credit of £200 for children below five. An increased state pension was also advocated. The manifesto opposed any further transfer power to the institutions of the EU, attacked the creation of a European defence force outside NATO and promised to 'keep the Pound'. The latter commitment was a constant theme of Conservative electioneering. It also argued in favour of the introduction of a tougher policy on asylum seekers and promised to end the policy of the early release of convicted prisoners. These policies were elaborated (and in some cases expanded) upon by Conservative spokesmen during the campaign: Oliver Letwin promising that a Conservative government would cut public spending by £20 billion during the lifetime of the next Parliament. This gaffe (which he later withdrew in favour of the official policy to make cuts of £8 billion) led to his temporary disappearance from the campaign to which Labour responded by publishing 'wanted' posters of him and despatching Andrew Smith to his Dorset constituency to look for him. However, remarks of this nature made it possible for Labour's campaign to argue that the Conservatives would harm public services such as the hospitals.

A number of difficulties arose during the campaign. The emphasis placed on Europe failed to captivate the public who were more interested in policies on health and education.

Internal dissent surfaced during the campaign. A significant number of Conservative candidates expressed irrevocable opposition to Britain joining the Euro (as opposed to the official line that this would not occur during the next Parliament), and one candidate, Sir Peter Tapsell, compared the single currency with Hitler's plans to unify Europe. The 'never' line was articulated by Margaret Thatcher in her 'Mummy Returns' speech at Plymouth on 22 May.

Considerable negativity was displayed by Conservative political broadcasts towards Labour's record in office. It was accused of having been 'soft' on crime, and lenient towards truancy.

The Conservatives seemed prepared for defeat before the campaign had ended and sought to limit the scale of Labour's victory by arguing that a Blair landslide would give rise to what Thatcher now referred to as an 'elective dictatorship'.

Labour

The claim to have successfully managed the economy and to have reduced unemployment were the main underpinnings of Labour's attempt to secure re-election. Brown's final budget provided the launching ground for Labour's campaign in which he was able to utilise the economic stability secured since 1997 in order to boost spending on public services, in particular on schools and hospitals. The Chancellor did not initiate tax cuts, although he did widen the 10p starting rate of income tax. The budget statement was probably designed as the prelude to a general election in April or early May 2001, but the outbreak of foot-and-mouth disease (which commenced in late February 2001) forced a postponement.

Labour's manifesto, *Ambitions for Britain*, was drafted by leading members of the No. 10 Policy Unit. The 1997 pledge that Labour would not raise income tax rates was reaffirmed which indicated that the Party's campaign was particularly directed at those who had switched to Labour in 1997. During the campaign, however, Gordon Brown refused to rule out the possibility of securing extra revenue from increased National Insurance contributions. In 2001, the overall theme of reassurance which had dominated Labour's 1997 campaign was abandoned in favour of a more vigorous statement of future ambitions which included the reform of public services (in particular concerning an enhanced role for the private sector in managing them), the taking of a more positive stance towards Europe and an assertion of the importance of community (a theme which had especially underpinned Labour's law and order policies). These policies were designed to illustrate how Labour's 'Third Way' differed from both old-style Labour and Thatcherism. The manifesto's specific commitments included adhering to a 2.5 per cent inflation target, promising further spending on transport and urban renewal, indicating the provision of a £4.20 minimum wage, and promising to continue winter fuel payments. Gordon Brown's five conditions were emphasised by Labour spokespersons in regard to Britain joining the single European currency. During the campaign, Blair made a number of speeches in which he focused on the views, convictions and beliefs of New Labour, and insisted that Britain's isolation and marginalisation within Europe was not a patriotic course of action.

Liberal Democrats

The manifesto, *Freedom, Justice, Honesty*, was initially presented to the September 2000 Party

Conference and subsequently redrafted. Freedom was depicted as the Party's core value, and the manifesto also put forward a fully costed programme. The manifesto proposed a 1p rise in the basic rate of income tax and a 50 per cent top rate for incomes in excess of £100,000. This extra revenue was earmarked for the recuitment of increased numbers of doctors, nurses, teachers and policemen and to enable university tuition fees to be abolished. An attempt was also made to distance the Party from the tough line taken by both Jack Straw and Ann Widdecombe against asylum seekers, and the manifesto also emphasised the Party's commitment to environmental issues. Little was said during the campaign concerning proportional representation.

The Liberal Democrat campaign benefited from the relative lack of attention which the two main parties paid to it. This enabled Charles Kennedy to 'do his own thing' and come across as an affable but formidable leader. The main themes in his speeches were that Labour was too timid on increasing public spending and the the Conservatives were a party of extremists.

Result of the Election

Overall the result of the election was similar to the outcome obtained in 1997: only 21 seats in mainland Britain changed hands.

A total of 3,133 candidates contested the election, a total which was swollen by the 428 candidates fielded by the UK Independence Party and the 145 of the Greens. The result was:

Party	Votes	Vote %	MPs
Labour	10,756,701	40.8%	413
Conservative	8,357,292	31.7%	166
Liberal Democrat	4,816,137	18.3%	52
Ulster Unionist	216,839	0.8% [26.8%]	6
Scotish National Party	464,314	1.8% [20.1%]	5
Democratic Unionist Party	181,999	0.7% [22.5%]	5
Sinn Fein	175,933	0.7% [21.7%]	4
Plaid Cymru	195,893	0.7% [14.3%]	4
SDLP	169,865	0.6% [21.0%]	3
Others	1,033,557	3.9%	1
Total	26,368,530		659

The turnout was 59.4 per cent. The overall swing from Labour to the Conservative Party was 1.8 per cent. The 'other' was R. Taylor (Independent, Wyre Forest). One hundred and eighteen women MPs were elected (95 Labour, 14 Conservative, five Liberal Democrat, one SNP, one Sinn Fein, one Democratic Unionist Party, one Ulster Unionist). Twelve MPs were drawn from ethnic minority communities.

The Parties

The election confirmed Labour's ability to hold on to the support it captured from the Conservatives in 1997 from middle-England, middle-class voters, and also to develop further its strength in South Eastern England. As in 1997, the concentration of Labour's vote in seats with declining populations and lower turnouts disproportionately benefited the Party in terms of seats won. Thus, the relatively small swing to the Conservative produced a net gain of only one seat.

The Liberal Democrats managed to distribute their vote efficiently in terms of gaining seats (Butler and Kavanagh, 2002: 255) and won more than at any time since 1929, with a net gain of six seats. They benefited both from antagonism towards the Conservatives' social liberalism and also from New Labour's loss of support amongst its traditional core voters, thus fulfilling the role of a party of protest for those Conservative and Labour voters who were unhappy with the stance of their party (Curtice and Steed, 2002: 313).

A significant number of senior parliamentarians retired before at the election. Conservative retirals included former prime ministers Ted Heath and John Major. They were joined by others who included Michael Heseltine, Peter Brooke and Tom King. Tony Benn and Mo Mowlam retired from the Labour benches and Paddy Ashdown, Robert McLennan and Jim Wallace from the Liberal Democrat ranks.

Scotland, Wales and Northern Ireland

One difficulty experienced during the campaign was the way in which insufficient acknowledgement was paid in national policy statements to the new devolved arrangements for government in Scotland, Wales and Northern Ireland.

The SNP secured 29 per cent of the vote in the elections to the Scottish Parliament in May 1999, thus affirming its position as Scotland's second party. In September 2001, Alex Salmond resigned as leader and was replaced by John Swinney. Labour remained Scotland's main political party winning 55 of the 72 seats. The SNP won five seats, losing one (Galloway and Upper Nithsdale) to the Conservatives. However, although polling 15.6 per cent of the vote, no other Conservative candidate was successful, Malcolm Rifkind failing in his attempt to win back his former seat of Edinburgh Pentlands. The Liberal Democrats remained the second party in terms of seats, winning 10 with 16.4 per cent of the vote.

Plaid Cymru performed well in elections to the Welsh Assembly in May 1999 when it secured 31 per cent of the vote. In August 2001 Dafydd Wigley retired from the leadership and was replaced by Ieuan Wyn Jones. Labour remained the dominant party in Welsh politics winning 34 of the 40 seats and, as in 1997, the Conservatives failed to win a single seat despite polling 21 per cent of the vote and securing an overall swing from Labour of around 3.75 per cent. Plaid Cymru won four seats (losing Ynys Mon to Labour but capturing Carmarthen East and Dinefwr from Labour), and the Liberal Democrats retained the two seats which were won in 1997.

The turnout in Northern Ireland (68 per cent) was far higher than that achieved on the mainland and the main beneficiaries of this were the Democratic Unionist Party and Sinn Fein (which overtook the SDLP in terms of both votes and seats). Seven of the 18 seats changed hands: the Ulster Unionists won six, the Democratic Unionists five, Sinn Fein four and the SDLP three. The increased polarisation of Northern Irish politics was likely to have significant consequences for the peace process by heightening the tensions between Nationalist and Loyalist politicians and making it harder for them to work together.

Consequence of the Election

Tony Blair formed his second Labour government. Conservative leader, William Hague, resigned almost as soon as the result of the contest was known.

References and Key Texts

J. Alt *et al.* (1977) 'Angels in Plastic: The Liberal Surge in 1974', *Political Studies*, Volume 25

P. Ashdown (1995) statement on 26 May, quoted in the *Guardian*, 27 May

T. Blair (1994) *Socialism* (London: Fabian Society, Fabian Tract 565)

N. Blewett (1972) *The Peers, The Parties and The People: The General Elections of 1910* (London, Macmillan)

D. Butler (1952) *The British General Election of 1951* (London, Macmillan)

D. Butler (1955) *The British General Election of 1955* (London, Macmillan)

D. Butler and R. Rose (1960) *The British General Election of 1959* (London, Macmillan)

D. Butler and A. King (1965) *The British General Election of 1964* (London, Macmillan)

D. Butler and A. King (1966) *The British General Election of 1966* (London, Macmillan)

D. Butler and M. Pinto-Duschinsky (1971) *The British General Election of 1970* (London Macmillan)

D. Butler and D. Kavanagh (1974) *The British General Election of February 1974* (London, Macmillan)

D. Butler and D. Kavanagh (1975) *The British General Election of October 1974* (London, Macmillan)

D. Butler and D. Kavanagh (1980) *The British General Election of 1979* (London, Macmillan)

D. Butler and D. Kavanagh (1984) *The British General Election of 1983* (Basingstoke, Macmillan)

D. Butler and D. Kavanagh (1988) *The British General Election of 1987* (Basingstoke, Macmillan)

D. Butler and D. Kavanagh (1992) *The British General Election of 1992* (Basingstoke, Macmillan)

D. Butler and D. Kavanagh (1997), *The British General Election of 1997* (Basingstoke, Macmillan)

D. Butler and D. Kavanagh (2002) *The British General Election of 2001* (Basingstoke, Palgrave)

P. Clarke (1981) *Liberals and Social Democrats* (Cambridge, Cambridge University Press, first published 1978)

J. Conacher (1958) 'Peel and the Peelites, 1846–1850', *English Historcial Review*, Volume LXXIII

C. Cook (1975) *The Age of Realignment: Electoral Politics in Britain 1922–1929* (London, Macmillan)

R. Cook (1998) speech to the Social Market Foundation, London, 22 April, quoted in the *Guardian*, 23 April

F. Craig (1987) *Chronology of British Parliamentary Elections, 1833–1987* (Chichester, Dartmouth)

F. Craig (1989) *British Electoral Facts 1832–1987* (Chichester, Dartmouth, fifth edition)

I. Crewe (1983) 'The Disturbing Truth Behind Labour's Rout', *Guardian*, 13 June

I. Crewe and A. King (1995) *The Birth, Life and Death of the Social Democratic Party* (Oxford, Oxford University Press)

T. Crosby (1976), *Sir Robert Peel's Administration 1841–1846* (Newton Abbot, David and Charles)

T. Crosland (1956) *The Future of Socialism* (London, Jonathan Cape, 1964, 2nd edition, first published in 1956)

J. Curtice and M. Steed (1984) 'Analysis' in D. Butler and D. Kavanagh, *The British General Election of 1983* (Basingstoke, Macmillan)

J. Curtice and M. Steed (1992) 'The Results Analysed', in Butler and Kavanagh *The British General Election of 1992* (Basingstoke, Macmillan)

J. Curtice and M. Steed (1997) 'The Results Analysed' in Butler and Kavanagh, *The British General Election of 1997* (Basingstoke, Macmillan)

J. Curtice and M. Steed (2002) 'The Results Analysed' in Butler and Kavanagh, *The British General Election of 2001,* (Basingstoke, Palgrave)

S. Dangerfield (1980) *The Strange Death of Liberal England* (New York, Perigree, first published 1935)

R Desai (1994) *Intellectuals and Socialism: 'Social Democrats and the Labour Party'* (London, Lawrence and Wishart)

J. Dunbabin (1966) 'Parliamentary Elections in Britain: A Psephological Note, *English Historical Review*, Volume LXXXI

N. Gash (1979) *Aristocracy and People, 1815–1865* (London, Edward Arnold)

H. Hanham (1959) *Elections and Party Management: Politics in the Time of Gladstone and Disraeli* (London, Longman)

A. Hudson (2003) 'The History of the Lib–Labs', *Journal of Liberal History*, Issue 41 Winter

T. Jenkins (1994) *The Liberal Ascendancy 1830–1886* (Basingstoke, Macmillan)

T. Jones (1996) *Remaking the Labour Party from Gaitskell to Blair* (London, Routledge)

A. King *et al.* (1997) *New Labour Triumphs at the Polls* (New Jersey, Chatham House)

N. Kinnock (1986) *The Future of Socialism* (London, The Fabian Society, Fabian Tract 509)

S. Koss (1975) *Nonconformity in Modern British Politics* (Hampden, Connecticut, Archon Books)

Labour Coordinating Committee (1982) *The Realignment of the Right: The Real Face of the SDP* (London, Labour Coordinating Committee)

Labour Party (1990) Policy Review *Looking to the Future: A Dynamic Economy, A Decent Society, Strong in Europe* (London, Labour Party)

K. Laybourn (1988) *The Rise of Labour* (London, Edward Arnold)

T. Lloyd (1968) *The General Election of 1880* (Oxford, Oxford University Press)

P. Mandler (1990) *Aristocratic Government in the Age of Reform: Whigs and Liberals 1830–1852* (Oxford, Clarendon)

J. Martin (1874) 'The Elections of 1868 and 1874', *Journal of the Statistical Society*, XXXVII

R. McCallum and A. Readman (1947) *The British General Election of 1945* (Oxford, Oxford University Press)

R. McKenzie (1963) *British Political Parties* (London, Heinemann, 2nd edition)

H. Nicholas (1951) *The British General Election of 1950* (London, Macmillan)

C. O'Leary (1962) *The Elimination of Corrupt Practices in Elections, 1868–1911* (Oxford, Oxford University Press)

C. Rallings and M. Thrasher (eds) (2000) *British Electoral Facts 1832– 1999* (Aldershot, Ashgate)

Robertson (1971) 'The Content of Election Addresses and Leaders' Speeches in Butler and Pinto-Duschinsky, *The British General Election of 1970* (London, Macmillan)

A. K. Russell (1973) *Liberal Landslide: The General Election of 1906* (Newton Abbot, Devon, David & Charles (Holdings) Limited)

G. Searle (1992) *The Liberal Party: Triumph and Disintegration, 1886–1929* (Basingstoke, Macmillan)

B. Semmel (1960) *Imperialism and Social Reform: English Social Imperial Thought 1895–1914* (London, Allen and Unwin)

E. Shaw (1994) *The Labour Party since 1979: Crisis and Transformation,*(London, Routledge)

T. Stannage (1980) *Baldwin Thwarts the Opposition* (London, Croom Helm)

M. Steed (1965) 'An Analysis of the Results' in Butler and King, *The British General Election of 1964* (London, Macmillan)

M. Steed(1971) 'An Analysis of the Results' in Butler and Pinto-Duschinsky, *The British General Election of 1970* (London: Macmillan)

D. Steel (1980) *A House Divided* (London, Weidenfeld and Nicolson)

D. Tanner (1997) 'Class Voting and Radical Politics: The Liberal and Labour Parties 1910–1931' in J. Lawrence and M. Taylor (eds) *Party, State and Society: Electoral Behaviour in Britain since 1821* (Aldershot, Scolar Press)

G. Taylor (1997) *Labour's Renewal ? The Policy Review and Beyond* (Basingstoke,Macmillan)

A. Thorpe (1991) *The British General Election of 1931* (Oxford, Clarendon Press)

A. Thorpe (1997) *A History of the British Labour Party* (Basingstoke, Macmillan)

The Times (1950) *Times Guide to the House of Commons 1950* (London, Times Publishing)

The Times (1951) *Times Guide to the House of Commons 1951* (London, Times Publishing)

The Times (1955) *Times Guide to the House of Commons 1955* (London, Times Publishing)

The Times (2001) *Times Guide to the House of Commons 2001* (London, Times Publishing)

T. Wilson (1968) *The Downfall of the Liberal Party* (London, Fontana, first published 1966)

Sir L. Woodward (1962) *The Age of Reform* (Oxford, Oxford University Press)

P. Zentner (1982) *Social Democracy in Britain: Must Labour Lose ?* (London, John Martin)